Legal Compliance Guide
to
Personnnel Management

Roger B. Jacobs, Esq.
with Cora S. Koch

PRENTICE HALL

Prentice-Hall International (UK) Limited, *London*
Prentice-Hall of Australia Pty. Limited, *Sydney*
Prentice-Hall Canada, Inc., *Toronto*
Prentice-Hall Hispanoamericana, S.A., *Mexico*
Prentice-Hall of India Private Limited, *New Delhi*
Prentice-Hall of Japan, Inc., *Tokyo*
Simon & Schuster Asia Pte. Ltd., *Singapore*
Editora Prentice-Hall do Brasil, Ltda., *Rio de Janeiro*

© 1993 *by*

Roger B. Jacobs

This publication is designed to provide accurate and authoritative information in regard to the subject matter covered. It is sold with the understanding that the publisher is not engaged in rendering legal, accounting, or other professional service. If legal advice or other expert assistance is required, the services of a competent professional person should be sought.

. . . From the Declaration of Principles jointly adopted by a Committee of the American Bar Association and a Committee of Publishers and Associations.

10 9 8 7 6 5 4 3 2 1

Library of Congress Cataloging-in-Publication Data

Jacobs, Roger B.,
    Legal compliance guide to personnel management / Roger B.
Jacobs with Cora S. Koch.
        p.   cm.
    Includes index.
    ISBN 0-13-720566-X
    1. Labor laws and legislation—United States. 2. Personnel
management—United States. I. Koch, Cora S. II. Title.
KF3457.J33 1993
344.73'01— dc20
[347.3041]   92-39439
                                                                  CIP

ISBN 0-13-720566-X

PRENTICE HALL
Career & Personal Development
Englewood Cliffs, NJ 07632
Simon & Schuster, A Paramount Communications Company

Printed in the United States of America

DEDICATION

To my lovely, thoughtful wife, Robin Hodes Jacobs, who supported me in writing this book and always encourages me in whatever I do; and to my children, Joshua and Rachel, who are a continuing inspiration to my growth and vitality.

ACKNOWLEDGMENTS

I would like first to acknowledge the assistance of my partner, Cora S. Koch, who has worked with me to draft this book. Her tireless devotion has made this book possible. Additionally, we have been very fortunate to have the professional support of our assistant, Jacquelyn Onufer, who diligently worked over many revisions of the manuscript for the last year. Her patience, devotion, and dedication have made this work possible. Thanks also to Caroline Marchitto, a new lawyer and recent graduate of Seton Hall Law School, who provided editorial and other assistance, and Andrew Stein, a law student at New York Law School. Sandra Jankola, our paralegal, also assisted in cite checking and offered general inspiration. Finally, we would like to acknowledge our editor, Gerry Galbo, who worked with us from the outset to get this book off the ground, on track, and through to completion. Without Gerry's devotion, assistance, and editing skills, we never would have made it to the final stage. We are also grateful for the assistance we received from the Prentice Hall staff.

ABOUT THE AUTHORS

Roger B. Jacobs

Roger B. Jacobs is a senior partner at Jacobs and Koch, a law firm specializing in Labor and Employment Law, located in New York City and Newark, New Jersey. He is also an Adjunct Professor at Fordham Law School and teaches at the Institute of Management and Labor Relations at Rutgers University. He received the Walter M. Jeffords Distinguished Writing Award from New York Law School in 1974, where he was also an Adjunct Professor.

Jacobs is an active member of the American, New York & New Jersey bar associations and recently served as Chair of the Committee on Labor Relations of the New York County Lawyer's Association. He is on the Editorial Board of the *New Jersey Lawyer* newspaper, published by the New Jersey State Bar Association, as well as *New Jersey Lawyer* magazine. Jacobs has had many articles published in law review and labor law publications and has also served on the faculty of the Annual Conference on Labor Law held by New York University.

He is an honors graduate of Cornell University, where he was a member of Phi Kappa Phi national honor society. He is a graduate of New York University School of Law, where he received his J.D. and LLM in Labor Law, and where he was the Elias Lieberman Fellow in Labor Law.

Cora S. Koch

Cora S. Koch is currently a partner in Jacobs and Koch, located in New York City and Newark, New Jersey, handling all aspects of labor and employment law. Ms. Koch has had numerous articles published in various journals, including the *National Law Journal, Labor Law Journal,* and the *Employee Relations Law Journal.*

Koch is a graduate of Georgetown University and Boston University School of Law. She is a member of the Bars of the States of New York and New Jersey and has received an LLM in Labor Law from New York University School of Law.

WHAT THIS BOOK WILL DO FOR YOU

In recent years, the field of employment law has experienced rapid and significant change. Employers are constantly being challenged with new and different theories of liability. A need has arisen for personnel specialists who are well versed in employment-related law as well as personnel administration practices. Those responsible for advising employers or for making complex employment-related decisions require resource materials that provide up-to-date information on the law as it impacts on personnel administration.

The relationship between employer and employee has evolved from the simple common law concept of employment-at-will to one governed by complex rules and regulations. The field of personnel administration requires familiarity with and an understanding of the laws, issues, and realities that dominate and control the employment relationship and the workplace. You who advise, decide, implement, and enforce personnel policies need to know the scope, application, and consequences of federal, state, and local regulations that impact on every employment-related decision.

Legal Compliance Guide to Personnel Management is designed to guide you through all aspects of the employment relationship, from recruitment, selection, hiring, employment, and promotions, to layoffs, retirement, and termination. It will provide you with concise explanations of the laws governing various employment-related situations, illustrative examples and case histories, step-by-step guidance of how to avoid claims and liability, and recommendations for how to handle claims if they occur. The book also contains valuable sample forms of policy statements and typical governmental forms you may encounter in various employment scenarios, as well as forms that are designed to avoid or minimize liability. These forms can be adapted to accommodate the needs of an individual organization.

Legal Compliance Guide to Personnel Management provides fascinating insights into how the courts and legislation are changing the status of at-will employment; new theories such as negligent hiring, negligent supervision, and self-publication in a defamation claim; the recent changes in polygraph testing; the successful use of employee committees; how to operate during a strike; and much more.

ix

Specifically, *Legal Compliance Guide to Personnel Management* will lead you through the many anti-discrimination statutes, including the employer's equal employment opportunity obligations under Title VII of the Civil Rights Act of 1964 (Title VII); the Age Discrimination in Employment Act (ADEA); the Americans with Disabilities Act (ADA); the Vocational Rehabilitation Act of 1973 (VRA); and state and local laws that protect against discrimination on the basis of one's race, color, religion, sex, national origin, age, mental or physical handicap, sexual orientation, marital status, pregnancy, and military status, among other characteristics. You will see numerous examples and case histories, typical forms used by the government in processing anti-discrimination claims, tips to help protect against liability or to help you respond to a claim, and sample policy statements. You will also learn what the employer's obligations are in various employment situations, such as investigating a sexual harassment claim or accommodating the special needs of a disabled worker.

Legal Compliance Guide to Personnel Management will inform you and assist you in handling claims and avoiding claims under other significant laws that regulate the employment relationship. For example, there are informative discussions in the following areas:

♦ Affirmative action requirements and plans are discussed with suggestions as to how to comply best with the law. If you elect to adopt an affirmative action plan voluntarily, what you need to know is included in Chapter 10.

♦ The Immigration Reform and Control Act (IRCA), which requires a new hire to prove, and an employer to verify, the new hire's eligibility to work in the United States, is covered.

♦ Preemployment and postemployment testing and inquiries of employees for skill or ability are addressed in the GUIDE. You will learn what you may and may not do when testing applicants or employees for a new position with regard to their skills or level of ability as well as background checks. Issues such as employee monitoring and employee privacy rights and how to respond to these new and increasing types of claims are discussed as well.

♦ The Employee Polygraph Protection Act and other tests for honesty or truth deception have extremely limited use in the workplace. You will learn what those restrictions are, when it is appropriate to do such testing, and how such tests should be conducted.

♦ The Drug-Free Workplace Act of 1988 and substance abuse policies (i.e., drug and alcohol testing) and the difference between restrictions in private and public employment are explained. You will learn what the restrictions are and if they apply to your company and how to comply with the restrictions if you are a government contractor; suggestions are also made on whether a substance abuse policy is appropriate.

◆ The changes the at-will employment doctrine has undergone and the theories that will continue to alter this basic relationship are discussed. Also, the discussion on the advantages and disadvantages of employment manuals will aid you in the decision to implement, continue, or modify such a manual.

◆ Defamation has emerged as one of the newest weapons of a disgruntled former employee against his former employer, and this informative discussion will aid you in understanding the risks of providing negative information both in and outside of the company, and how to avoid liability.

◆ Other new theories of employer liability for terminating or disciplining an employee are also discussed, including negligent hiring and negligent supervision— employers are now being sued because they should have known that employee X was dangerous and likely to cause harm or that no one told employee Y that her work was poor and that she was at risk of being terminated. This chapter explores these new theories and suggests how to avoid such claims.

◆ The Equal Pay Act of 1973 and the Fair Labor Standards Act (FLSA) are described. These laws govern the compensation aspect of employment. You will learn what the employer's obligations are regarding minimum wage, overtime, equal pay for equal work, child labor, and exceptions to these basic rules.

◆ The Employee Retirement Income Security Act (ERISA), the federal law that preempts almost the entire area of employee welfare and pension benefit plans, is discussed, including examples of various forms of pension plans and deferred compensation plans as well as the employer's responsibilities under this Act.

◆ Employee benefits are also discussed, including medical benefits and the obligation to continue certain medical benefits upon termination of employment, as governed by the Consolidated Omnibus Reconciliation Act (COBRA).

◆ The Occupational Safety and Health Act (OSHA) is discussed. State laws are reviewed, with explanations of the reporting and record-keeping processes under the Act and examples of problems an employer faces with suggestions as to how to handle or avoid safety-related issues in the workplace.

◆ The National Labor Relations Act (NLRA) is described. This law protects all employees' rights to engage in concerted activity and governs management-union matters; it is of special concern to employers with a unionized workforce. This material covers the basic rights of employees, unfair labor practices, union organizing tactics, collective bargaining, and how to handle a strike situation.

♦ Workers' compensation and unemployment compensation laws are discussed, including examples, forms, and strategies for handling these claims. See our extensive guidelines for each of these concerns.

♦ The Workers Adjustment and Retraining Notification Act (WARN) requires employers of a certain size to provide notice to employees in the event of a mass layoff or plant closing. The book provides a detailed explanation of who is obligated and what you must do to comply with the law.

♦ Whistle-blower protection laws, both on the federal and state levels, are included because of increasing concerns that employees who know of wrongdoing that endangers the public welfare should be encouraged to come forward. This is currently one of the most rapidly changing areas in the employment field as more and more legislative protection is enacted. However, it varies greatly from state to state and industry to industry; these differences are highlighted and discussed.

Here are just a few reasons that you will find *Legal Compliance Guide to Personnel Management* a necessary tool for the successful administration of personnel issues:

♦ It provides a review of an employer's equal opportunity obligations with brief explanations of the underlying theories that are essential to avoiding legal liability.

♦ It highlights areas of potential liability and recent changes and developments in the field of personnel administration.

♦ It gives comprehensive treatment to the employment process from recruitment through termination with special attention to preventive measures that aid in limiting liability.

♦ It offers guidance through the many federal and state statutes and regulations, including procedures that govern a wide spectrum of employment-related claims.

♦ It provides practical help with regard to how to cope when a union seeks to represent your employees and what to do if the union is already on the scene.

♦ It provides the legal perspective necessary in every employment-related decision.

♦ It complements other personnel handbooks that focus only on administration and personnel practices because it supplies the basic legal background that aids in understanding general employment law.

♦ It is of special interest to human resource managers because it discusses not only recent developments in the well-established theories of employment law but also gives in-depth treatment to emerging theories of liability.

♦ It gives detailed guidelines and preventive steps to aid you in making the right decision for the employee and employer.

♦ It contains tested forms that are adaptable to fit different situations and the needs of your organization.

♦ It has a detailed table of contents and an index cross-referenced for ease of use that allows you to locate quickly practical answers to complex employment-related issues.

The informative discussions and practical techniques found in each chapter are the result of the authors' years of experience practicing in the labor and employment law field. The information contained in each chapter was gleaned from exhaustive research and utilized in representing management in employment-related disputes. *Legal Compliance Guide to Personnel Management* will greatly enhance your ability to reach the best decision possible in all your employment-related matters. No personnel professional or employment law practitioner should be without this thorough yet easy-to-use guide on his or her desk.

Condensed
Table of Contents

CONTENTS

1

AN OVERVIEW OF MAJOR LAWS GOVERNING CRITICAL PERSONNEL ISSUES

The employment relationship between employer and employee has evolved from the simple common law concept of employment-at-will to one governed by complex rules and regulations. The field of personnel administration requires familiarity with and an understanding of the laws, issues, and realities that dominate and control the employment relationship and the workplace. You who advise, decide, implement, and enforce personnel policies need to know the scope, application, and consequences of federal, state, and local regulations that impact on every employment-related decision.

Before turning to a discussion of these laws, we would like to illustrate some of these workplace issues with case studies.

CASE STUDIES ILLUSTRATING COMMON PROBLEMS IN THE WORKPLACE

In these case study examples we hope to call your attention to a few fairly typical problems that you may have dealt with and wondered what consequences, if any, there were as a matter of law and where could you turn for a simple, concise, easy-to-understand answer.

1

Case Study No. 1: EEOC Complaints and Lawsuits

Corporation ABC is a large multiple-plant facility with locations throughout the United States and the world. A short time ago it received a complaint of employment discrimination from a federal enforcement agency (Equal Employment Opportunity Commission). We handled the investigation for the firm, and the company thought the matter had been resolved satisfactorily. The former employee had brought allegations of sex and handicap discrimination among other things. Despite my cautionary comments, the company essentially closed the file and assumed it would never hear from this employee or his attorney again.

About a year later, lo and behold, a complaint filed in state court appeared. Much to the company's surprise and my disappointment, we were now faced with defending a lawsuit that nearly identically tracked the EEOC complaint of a year earlier.

Here is a question to consider: Can an employee pursue remedies for employment discrimination in both state court and the Equal Employment Opportunity Commission?

The answer is probably yes in most jurisdictions, although a specific answer depends upon the circumstances and facts of each and every case.

For further insight into this question, we have presented material regarding various provisions of Title VII, the laws regarding handicap discrimination including the Rehabilitation Act and the new Americans with Disabilities Act, and the procedural requirements both administrative and otherwise for a discrimination complaint. This information can be found in Chapters 5, 8, and 9.

Case Study No. 2: The AIDS Dilemma

Many employers have been faced with problems regarding AIDS-related complaints from current employees, former employees, or customers. In a recent situation, a company terminated an employee who had Acquired Immune Deficiency Syndrome, commonly known as AIDS. Several agencies process complaints of AIDS/handicap discrimination. For example, such a complaint can be filed under the Rehabilitation Act or the new Americans with Disabilities Act (effective in June 1992). Similarly, most state anti-discrimination agencies provide jurisdiction as do certain city agencies such as the New York City Commission on Human Rights. When Company A received a complaint and forwarded it to us, there were several questions that occurred to me, and perhaps if I had been involved earlier or if they had consulted this book, a complaint or hearing might have been avoided.

For example, one of the key inquiries in such a situation is to determine whether or not the individual is able to do his or her job in the workplace. If the individual is "disabled" and seeks to go on disability, then he is not a handicapped individual who is otherwise able to continue to work. Thus the first and simplest inquiry is one of job ability and disability. Additionally, keeping the lines of communication open is a key problem-solver and problem-avoider. Sometimes, if the lines of communication are working properly, an employee who is unable to continue in his current position may work out a modified schedule or go on disability after a reasonable, rational discussion with you.

Case Study No. 3: What to Do When the Union Calls

Recently, a medium-sized company called to say that union authorization cards were being handed out at the firm's bilingual facility at a suburban location. After some inquiry I learned that the firm had several facilities in addition to that plant and that it had recently acquired the suburban facility. Unfortunately, due to a declining economic environment and the increasing cost of health care, costly changes in health insurance had been implemented by the new owners, but clear explanations had not been given to the employees, many of whom did not understand English. This resulted in obvious confusion, disappointment, and even anger in some cases.

There are certain steps that can be taken in a nonunion environment when the union organizer appears at your door. We will walk you through in basic steps the kinds of responses that are possible, and you and your company can decide based upon economics and other business considerations how you wish to respond to a union organizing attempt. *However, it is imperative that you understand the law and not make mistakes or mis-statements that may later hurt you and your company and your employees.*

Case Study No. 4: Defamation—What Can You Say and How Can You Say It?

Recently, an employee of a large company with an extensive employment manual and doing business all over the United States was terminated, purportedly for job performance and other reasons. This individual had earned commissions based upon sales. The salespeople reporting to him were advised that he was terminated because of serious personal problems and for the way in which he dealt with higher management. Additionally, when a request for information was received from the local unemployment office, a lower-echelon employee replied on behalf of the company that the dismissed person had spoken inappropriately to the president and was fired as a consequence of that conduct.

After working for the company for 20 years and being summarily terminated, this individual filed a lawsuit in federal court alleging wrongful discharge, employment discrimination, and several counts of defamation and other tort theories.

Situations like this are not uncommon. Tort-based or negligence-based theories are common today in the workplace. Almost every discharge seems to result in some form of adversarial proceeding. However, these can be avoided and minimized if you are aware of some of the common mistakes. For example, while most communications like those to an unemployment agency are privileged, you may misspeak, and those communications may no longer be privileged. Similarly, after an employee is terminated, his colleagues should be advised in a neutral manner of his termination and not given a personalized characterization for the dismissal, including the reasons. By using these techniques, you will minimize or avoid claims of defamation, which are becoming one of the most prevalent claims in the workplace. Likewise, when you are asked for a reference about that individual, you are in a dilemma. However, we give you some insights into that dilemma in Chapter 13, which will guide you through the shoals of modern personnel law for the human resources professional.

FEDERAL REGULATION OF THE EMPLOYMENT RELATIONSHIP

There are a variety of laws that govern the employment relationship today. You should become familiar with them and when they apply.

Title VII of the Civil Rights Act

In 1964 Congress passed a civil rights act that included significant prohibitions against specific types of discrimination in employment. These provisions are known collectively as Title VII,[1] and they prohibit employers, labor organizations, and employment agencies that supply employees to such employers from discriminating against employees with respect to all terms and conditions of employment because of race, color, sex, religion, or national origin. Claims relating to pregnancy discrimination or sexual harassment are also included within the scope of Title VII.

You don't have to hire an individual just because he or she is a member of a minority group; you should look at the hiring guidelines in Chapter 2.

There are certain exceptions to these general provisions; Title VII is discussed in detail in Chapter 2.

Title VII is administered by the Equal Employment Opportunity Commission (EEOC).

The following questions (here provided with answers) are often asked about Title VII.

Question: Who is covered?

Answer: Employers with 15 or more employees.

Question: Why are these laws important to me?

Answer: You must be aware of the implications of every decision you make to hire—or not to hire or fire or discipline or set wage rates—the list goes on and on. For example, when hiring you may wish to give a preference to an American citizen.

Question: Is that lawful? What laws are involved?

Answer: You have reached the right conclusion if you stopped to think about the implications of such a hiring philosophy. Title VII prohibits discriminating based upon national origin. But IRCA (Immigration Reform and Control Act) permits a preference to American citizens as long as other qualifications are equal.

Civil Rights Acts of 1866 and 1871 (Sections 1981, 1983, and 1988)

Several laws passed after the Civil War called the Reconstruction Acts have been used to enforce discrimination claims primarily based upon race or "color."[2]

Age Discrimination in Employment Act of 1967

ADEA prohibits discrimination in employment because of age.[3] The protected age group begins at age 40. Employers of 20 or more employees must comply with ADEA. An adverse employment decision may not be based solely or in substantial part upon the employee's age. Similarly, an employer must avoid indicating or specifying a maximum age in solicitations or during the recruitment process. Discrimination may be found where the employee is discriminated against in favor of another person who is in the same protected age group. Many aspects of ADEA parallel Title VII.

Employers may use age as a bona fide occupational qualification under extremely limited circumstances. An employer may also differentiate between employees on the basis of reasonable nondiscriminatory factors other than age. Actions taken in accordance with a bona fide seniority system are also exempted from the terms.

Key ADEA Concerns.

- Age-related questions during interview
- Comments about changing the "old guard"
- Layoff scenarios when primarily older workers are affected

ADEA Remedies.   The remedies available under ADEA include back pay and fringe benefits, front pay, reinstatement, hiring, liquidated damages for willful violation, prejudgment interest, injunctive relief, and attorneys' fees.

Americans with Disabilities Act, Handicap Discrimination and the Vocational Rehabilitation Act of 1973

"Handicapped" or "disabled" employees will continue to play an increasingly important role in the work force. There are now two primary federal laws that apply in this area. You need to become familiar with them to determine if you are covered and what you must do.

The Americans with Disabilities Act. The ADA was signed into law in 1990 but did not become effective until July 1992. Employers with 25 or more employees are covered initially, but this number is reduced to 15 a year later. Enforcement for the ADA has been assigned to the EEOC.

The ADA will permit disabled individuals to file discrimination complaints and lawsuits.

The human resources staff must determine the following:

– Can the employee do the job?

– Is reasonable accommodation necessary?

– What is reasonable accommodation?

ADA is different from the Vocational Rehabilitation Act of 1973 (VRA); these two statutes are discussed in detail in Chapters 8 and 9.

The Rehabilitation Act. The VRA has two main provisions:

§503   Requires government contractors to take affirmative measures regarding employment of handicapped individuals

§504   Prohibits discrimination when employer receives "federal financial assistance"

Summary of Statute. Discrimination against individuals with physical or mental disabilities is prohibited by the Vocational Rehabilitation Act of 1973 (VRA), 29 U.S.C. §701, et seq. Specifically of interest to employers are Sections 703 and 704 (often referred to as Sections 503 and 504 because of the statute's original numbering system). A handicap or disability protected under this statute is defined as "a physical or mental impairment which substantially limits one or more of such person's major life activities." The Act also protects any individual *perceived* as having such an impairment.

The VRA applies to government contractors and recipients of federal financial assistance. A handicapped individual must be "otherwise qualified" to perform the job. Employers are obligated to make reasonable attempts to accommodate a handicapped employee.

NOTE: There are different standards under the ADA for reasonable accommodation. This is discussed in Chapter 8.

This Act also requires employment and promotion of handicapped employees by way of affirmative action.

Possible remedies for successful legal action include:

- Back pay
- Front pay
- Reinstatement
- Hiring
- Injunctive relief
- Attorneys' fees

National Labor Relations Act

This law protects the right of an employer to organize or to decline organization. Collective bargaining, strikes, union-management relations, and union-employee relations are all governed by the National Labor Relations Act (NLRA), 29 U.S.C. §151, *et seq.*

The National Labor Relations Board (NLRB) operates as the overseer of the Act and its enforcement. The extensive administrative scheme of the NLRA is discussed in Chapters 19–21.

NOTE: Employers should exercise great care when a union arrives upon the scene or is already in place.

Immigration Reform and Control Act of 1986

Determination of employment eligibility is an important aspect of any hiring process. The Immigration Reform and Control Act (IRCA), 8 U.S.C. §1324a, imposes a duty upon employers to verify the employment eligibility of every new hire.

NOTE: Only U. S. citizens, nationals, resident aliens, and others authorized by the Immigration and Naturalization Service (INS) are eligible for employment.

WARN—Workers Adjustment and Retraining Notification Act (Plant Closings)

Any decision to close, relocate, or reduce operations at a facility must include an analysis of the employer's duty to warn employees of such action. The Workers Adjustment and Retraining Notification Act (WARN), 29 U.S.C. §2107(a), et seq., requires employers who meet the threshold coverage requirements to provide 60 days' written notice of a plant closing or layoffs that are to exceed 6 months or a reduction of work of more than 50 percent within a 6-month period.

The Act covers employers of more than 100 full-time employees or of 100 or more (including part-time) employees who in aggregate work at least 4,000 hours per week (exclusive of overtime hours). If you have contemplated layoffs, this information is essential prior to implementing your plans. There is a more complete discussion in Chapter 25.

Fair Labor Standards Act (Wages, Overtime)

The Fair Labor Standards Act (FLSA) enacted in 1938, is a comprehensive wage and hour law, regulating minimum wage, hours, child labor, and overtime, in a uniform manner. This law sets the minimum standards and states may enact more restrictive standards. The Act is administered and enforced by the U.S. Department of Labor—Wage and Hour Division.

Wages can be salary or other forms of compensation *including vacation pay*.

The *minimum wage* standard is fixed by Congress. The FLSA basically provides that *a workweek consists of 40 hours*. Hours worked beyond 40 are considered overtime.

There are many exceptions to FLSA provisions; see Chapter 17 for details.

NOTE: Pay plans need to consider carefully all these factors.

Equal Pay Act of 1963

The Equal Pay Act, 29 U.S.C. §206(d), although under the purview of the Fair Labor Standards Act, is an anti-discrimination statute. The Act requires that men and women receive equal pay for equal work for jobs that require equal skill and effort and are performed under similar working conditions.[4]

NOTE: This is a sex-based statute. It applies only to male-female pay comparisons.

All employers covered by the FLSA must comply with the Equal Pay Act. The Act applies to all employees to whom the FLSA applies as well as to executives, administrators, professional employees, and outside sales people.

There are basically four exceptions:

1.   A seniority system

2.   A merit-based system

3.   A system that measures earnings by quantity or quality of production

4.   A differential based on any factor other than sex

Occupational Safety and Health Act of 1970

The purpose of the Occupational Safety and Health Act of 1970, 29 U.S.C. §651, *et seq.*, is to assure safety and healthful working conditions for all employees.

The Act was enacted in response to the staggering costs in lives and production due to industrial-related deaths and disabilities.

Who Is Covered? It applies to all places of employment, throughout the United States and its territories and possessions. But the Act does *not* apply to working conditions of employees over whom other state and federal agencies exercise statutory authority with respect to standards or regulations affecting safety and health.

What Does the Act Do? Employers, under the Act, are required to keep their places of employment free from recognized hazards that are causing or are likely to cause death or serious physical injury to its employees. The Act also requires that employers comply with standards and regulations promulgated under the terms of the Act.

OSHA provides rules and regulations that govern workplace safety. The Act also permits searches by inspectors and investigators.

Some questions you might think about are

- Can my premises be searched?
- Does the OSHA inspector need a warrant?
- What if I refuse to let him in?
- Are there fines and penalties for OSHA violations?

Answers to these questions can be found in Chapter 15.

Employee Retirement Income Security Act of 1974

ERISA links personnel/compensation issues such as pension, profit-sharing, health, and welfare with certain tax advantages. The Act is remedial in nature and establishes minimum standards for pension plans. ERISA also covers a broad range of "welfare" plans including health/medical, vacation, sick pay, day care, prepaid legal services, severance pay, and death benefits.[5]

Who Is Covered? Any employer who has pension, health, severance, or other welfare-related benefits must comply with the provisions of the Employee Retirement Income Security Act, 29 U.S.C. §1001, *et seq.*

ERISA's coverage extends to all employee benefit plans established and maintained by an employer engaged in commerce or employee organization representing employees engaged in commerce including any plan of an employer or employee organization engaged in any industry or activity affecting commerce.

ERISA is a relatively complex statute similar to the Tax Code. There are many exceptions. For a full discussion, go to Chapter 18.

Employee Polygraph Protection Act of 1988

Lie detector tests and employment-related truth deception tests of all kinds are regulated by several statutes. You may or may not have a right to test.

NOTE: Before you test, know the law!

In Chapter 4, we discuss the Polygraph Protection Act and a variety of other regulations concerning job testing. If you engage in such testing, you may be violating the law.

Whistle-blower Protection

Numerous federal statutes contain so-called "whistle-blower" protection.[6]

NOTE: Each instance of "whistle-blowing" must be examined carefully to determine whether an employee is protected from any adverse employment decision.

STATE REGULATION
OF THE EMPLOYMENT RELATIONSHIP

State regulation of the employment relationship varies significantly from state to state and usually involves discrete rights or restrictions. In general, these areas are summarized on a state-by-state review and analysis in Chapter 22.

ENDNOTES

1.   42 U.S.C. §2000e, *et seq.*

2.   These early anti-discrimination statutes were initially enacted to aid minorities, specifically freed slaves. These provisions are based on the Thirteenth and Fourteenth Amendments to the U. S. Constitution. They provide a contractual remedy with respect to hiring, placement, and continuation of employment and apply to all employers.

Sections 1981 and 1983 provide separate and distinct bases for race or "color" discrimination claims. However, they do not prohibit discrimination on the basis of sex or religion. These provisions are not subject to the procedural requirements of Title VII.

The remedies available under section 1981 vary slightly from those available under section 1983. In general, both provide compensatory, punitive, and nominal damages, including awards for emotional distress, back pay, reinstatement, hiring, injunctive relief, and attorneys' fees. Also under section 1981, an individual may receive retroactive or constructive seniority.

3. Prior to the enactment of ADEA, the federal government adopted an age discrimination policy embodied in Executive Order 11141 and applied to all government contractors and subcontractors.

4. The Equal Pay Act differs from the concept of comparable worth that dictates equal pay for "comparable" jobs and is much more difficult to quantify. See a complete discussion of comparable worth in Chapter 17.

5. Pension and welfare plans are subjected to different standards and regulation under ERISA. For example, there are practically no minimum requirements with regard to welfare plans other than basic disclosure requirements, fiduciary standards, federal common law, and certain enforcement provisions.

6. Whistle-blowing generally refers to instances of individuals reporting conduct or behavior that violates a statute or law. These laws protect against employer retaliation when employees come forward and report this conduct, and include NLRA, 29 U.S.C. §158(a)(4); OSHA; 29 U.S.C. §660(c)(1); Civil Rights Act of 1964 (Title VII), 29 U.S.C. §2000e-3a; FLSA, 29 U.S.C. §215(a)(3); Equal Employment Opportunity Act, 42 U.S.C. §2000e-16(d); Age Discrimination in Employment Act, 29 U.S.C. §623(d); Clean Air Act, 42 U.S.C. §7622; Energy Reorganization Act, 42 U.S.C. §5851; Safe Drinking Water Act, 42 U.S.C. §300j-9(i); Solid Waste Disposal Act, 42 U.S.C. §697; Toxic Substances Control Act, 15 U.S.C. §2622; Water Pollution Control Act, 33 U.S.C. §1367; Asbestos School Hazard Detection and Control Act, 20 U.S.C. §3608; Civil Service Reform Act, 5 U.S.C. §2302(b)(8); Comprehensive Environmental Response, Compensation and Liability Act, 42 U.S.C. §9610; and Federal Mine Safety and Health Act of 1977, 30 U.S.C. §815(c)(1).

2

RECRUITMENT
AND APPLICATIONS

The place to begin with preventing potential discrimination conflicts in the employment setting is at the beginning—when the need for new employees arises. The recruitment and hiring processes are subject to all the prohibitions that other employment practices are subject to under federal and state anti-discrimination laws. Thus the search or recruitment process must be carefully planned, implemented, and consistently complied with from the moment it starts.

The recruiting officer must be knowledgeable regarding applicable federal and state laws and regulations that apply to recruiting and hiring, including Title VII, ADEA, IRCA, ADA, and state and local anti-discrimination laws. This chapter explores the recruitment and application process and ways to conduct a hiring search with a minimum of risk of running afoul of anti-discrimination laws.

IDENTIFYING RECRUITMENT SOURCES

Recruiting practices vary widely among employers. Recruitment sources include:

Promotion from within

Employee referrals

Walk-in applicants

Advertising through newspaper, magazines, direct mail, and radio or television

Colleges

Vocational institutions

High schools/trade schools

Professional societies

Unions

Government and private employment agencies

Search firms

Employee leasing firms

Career conferences/job fairs

Whatever recruiting sources you may use there are basic guidelines you should follow whenever conducting a search for employees.

GUIDELINES FOR RECRUITING

When applicants begin to respond to the recruitment efforts, you must then conduct a fair application process. As with recruitment practices, the application process may vary widely. Some employers use none or only very simple job applications, while others utilize an exhaustive form.

NOTE: A fundamental rule is not to ask more than you need to know for any particular position.

Some frequently encountered dilemmas for employers include:

- How to word your advertisement to attract only those qualified for a particular position
- A referral only policy
- An applicant with a foreign accent
- An applicant with good skills but poor personal habits
- A pregnant applicant
- An applicant with young children
- An older, overqualified applicant
- An applicant with an arrest record
- Reliance on an employment placement agency to screen eligible applicants
- An applicant that observes certain religious holidays
- An overweight applicant
- An applicant that does not "fit" with the work force

These and other problems will be addressed in this chapter.

HOW TO AVOID LIABILITY IN RECRUITING

Be sure you are in compliance with all pertinent laws when you recruit.

Advertising the Position

Federal law specifically prohibits employers, unions, or employment agencies from using any notice or advertisement for employment indicating any preference, limitation, specification, or discrimination based on race, color, religion, sex, age, or national origin, physical or mental disability except in cases where a bona fide occupational qualification requires such specification.[1] State and local laws extend these prohibitions to characteristics including marital status, sexual preference, or age before 40 years. For this reason, it is very important to check your state and local laws prior to placing an advertisement.

Example:

> HELP WANTED - FEMALE - WOMEN'S STATE PENITENTIARY SEEKS COOK; ENGLISH SPEAKING ONLY; 1–2 YEARS EXPERIENCE REQUIRED; APPLY IN PERSON TO JANE DOE.

This advertisement violates the law because it designates females. It is unlikely that a cook at a women's prison must be female. The English-speaking-only requirement may also violate the law, and the employer will have to be prepared to defend this requirement. It could be viewed as a way to screen out applicants on the basis of ethnicity or citizenship. Also the "apply in person" requirement may be construed as an unlawful screening device to eliminate certain types of applicants, again on the basis of ethnicity, age (cf. minimum experience requirement), or even race.

Example:

> LARGE CORPORATION SEEKS QUALIFIED ELECTRICAL ENGINEER IN GOOD HEALTH; HEAVY PHYSICAL DEMANDS; U.S. CITIZEN; 5 YEARS' EXPERIENCE.

This advertisement emphasizes it is seeking youths and/or nonhandicapped individuals. The employer must be prepared to back up the good health and heavy physical demand statements. Moreover, the U.S. citizenship requirement is applicable only if the employer is a defense contractor and the position entails national security interests. In other words, the employer will have to show that this requirement is a bona fide occupational qualification.

Using a Word-of-Mouth/Employee Referral Policy

Subjective recruitment procedures such as "word of mouth" or employee referrals can lead to racial discrimination because important information may be available only to whites and because such practices place no check on individual biases. Where an employer's work force is predominantly Caucasian, the foreseeable and certain result of such practices is that potential minority group applicants as a class are denied knowledge of available vacancies. The most significant problem with this type of recruiting tool is that it is very limiting if it is the only recruiting tool.

NOTE: The lack of fixed or reasonably objective standards and procedures for hiring may be a basis for finding a discriminatory practice.

A company that relies on word of mouth for hiring, conducts only informal review for promotions, and/or does not advertise its job openings risks liability to a nonapplicant since there was no way for the nonapplicant to have had knowledge of the vacancy or knew that it would be futile to apply since he or she did not come from any of the resources used by the employer.

Handling Walk-in Applicants

Walk-in applicants are entitled to the same treatment as any other applicant absent an employer policy to the contrary. However, an employer's policy of not hiring walk-in applicants is an invitation for EEOC scrutiny. Such a policy should be grounded in a legitimate business reason.

Case Study No. 1: No On-Site Hiring

Several minority individuals apply directly to a construction site for bricklayer positions. They are refused employment because they were not known to the job superintendent who hires only bricklayers with whom he had previously worked or who came recommended as skilled in such work. The company policy is not to hire at the gate, in part, because the company needed experienced and highly qualified bricklayers. At least one black applicant had previously worked for the superintendent and was eventually hired.

Will the employer be held liable for race discrimination for the superintendent's refusal to hire qualified minority individuals who applied at the gate and can the court require a method of hiring that permits consideration of the largest number of minority applicants?

The employer is likely to be liable for discrimination as to the individual who minimally fit the superintendent's hiring policy. However, the court is not empowered to require a recruitment method which allows the employer to consider the qualifications of the largest number of minority applicants.

ESTABLISHING A POLICY REGARDING
VERBAL RECRUITING STATEMENTS

The temptation to induce a hot prospect to join your organization sometimes leads an unwary recruiting officer into making promises the company cannot or will not honor at some future date. Verbal representations made during the recruitment and application process may be construed as an enforceable promise in some jurisdictions or may be just puffing. It is important to have a standard and consistent policy or guidelines for what verbal statements may be used to attract and keep employees. There are a whole host of situations that may arise from reliance on verbal inducements.

Some common mistakes to be wary of include

- "As long as you do your job, you will have a job with us."

- "Good workers don't get fired here."

- "We are like one family."

- "We let people go only if they are involved in serious misconduct."

Other promises that should not be made if there is a possibility that they will not be delivered or generally are outside standard operating procedure include

- "Take the job and in six months you'll be a manager."

- "We will pay certain benefits and/or moving expenses."

These kinds of statements may subject you to unnecessary contract litigation.

Case Study No. 2: Verbal Assurances

You have an exciting candidate for a position that has proven difficult to fill with just the right person. Max, a sound engineer with a rival company located on the other coast, has responded to your recruitment efforts. However, he has a number of concerns that you try to allay with reassurances. You indicate that of course all expenses associated with relocating his family will be covered by the company, that within six months he will be supervising his own team along with a substantial raise, that as long as he does a good job he will have job security, and that the company policy of not providing insurance coverage for the family for the first six months of employment will not apply in his case. None of these representations is made in writing.

Max, satisfied that the switch to your company is now worthwhile, leaves his job of ten years, packs up his family of five, and moves across the country. He is unable to sell his house and must leave it unrented because the company needs him right away. He reports for work and is told that the insurance company will not cover his family for the first six months pursuant to the written policy. He also finds out that the company has instituted new performance review policies that will make it substantially more difficult for him to advance as rapidly as he had been promised. He submits his expenses for his move including his carrying costs for the unrented home he left behind. He is advised that the company is prepared to cover only actual moving expenses and not costs such as the mortgage or other expenses associated with his home.

Max feels that he has been lied to and he relied on the representations made to him. He files a breach of contract and fraud suit against the company to recover all the expenses he incurred due to moving, the additional expense of procuring medical coverage for his family, damages for losing his "secure" job, and pain and suffering for the company's misrepresentations.

Is the company liable to Max for these promises? Did he reasonably rely upon such promises? Can he recover for all the promises made?

The company may have to pay Max some or all of the claims that he makes if he shows that he acted with reasonable reliance upon the oral representations made to him which induced him to leave a long-term job and move a great distance.

Some jurisdictions have begun to recognize that *oral representations may constitute an implied contract* and provide a basis for a lawsuit for breach of contract, malicious interference, fraud, and other causes of action.[2]

Most of these types of promises are made during the recruitment and application process. Personnel administrators and those responsible for hiring must be circumspect in the oral representations that they make when trying to attract highly desirable employees.

ESTABLISHING AN APPLICATION PROCESS

Once you have attracted a number of candidates through your recruitment efforts, you must begin the application process. Many employers generally have an application form to be completed by the applicant. This form may range from a simple series of questions about the applicant's past employment and educational background to a more complex form that seeks detailed information about the applicant.

NOTE: The application form should be appropriate to the position and ask only for information necessary to determine if the person is at least minimally qualified for the position.

Everyone who inquires about a position with your organization should be given the opportunity to complete an application form. The application form should limit questions to those that relate to the individual's ability to perform the job. The underlying principle for the entire recruiting and hiring process is that *all hiring standards should relate to the job.*

Preemployment inquiries regarding race, color, sex, age, religion, national origin, or handicap are not, by themselves, a violation of Title VII or other anti-discrimination laws. However, such inquiries are generally irrelevant with regard to an applicant's ability or qualifications and should be avoided.

> NOTE: In limited circumstances the position may require inquiry into special characteristics that are generally precluded from the employer's employment decision-making process. An exception is made where religion, sex, national origin, or handicap constitutes a Bona Fide Occupational Qualification (BFOQ). Note that *race never constitutes a BFOQ.*[3]

Guidelines for Drafting Application Forms

Application forms should be drafted with the following guidelines in mind. Obvious taboo topics such as race, age, sex, national origin, and religion should not appear on the application form. Other areas that should also be avoided include the following:

Marital Status. In the past some employees have refused to hire a married woman for certain jobs. Most airlines, for example, refused for many years to permit a married woman to be a flight attendant, though other employees could be married. This practice was found to violate Title VII. The marital or family status of an individual violates the law when it discriminates on the basis of sex. For example, it is discriminatory for an employer to hire married men but not married women or men with young children but not women with young children. Many states have specifically identified marital status as a protected category under its anti-discrimination statutes.

Thus inquiries with regard to maiden name; spouse's name; spouse's work; widowed, divorced, or separated status; and prior married name are not relevant to a person's ability to perform a job and may be used for or indicative of a discriminatory purpose, that is, an indication of religion, national origin, or marital status. However, an employer may inquire into some of these areas after an offer of employment has been made if there is a legitimate purpose for the information, such as insurance forms or next-of-kin information.

Age or Date of Birth. A request for age-related information is not, in itself, a violation of the law. However, such a request may tend to deter older applicants or otherwise indicate discrimination based on age. If such a request is used, it should be accompanied by a statement to the following effect:

> The Age Discrimination in Employment Act of 1967 prohibits discrimination on the basis of age with respect to individuals who are at least 40 years of age.

Keep in mind that some states protect applicants and employees who are as young as 18 years of age. Thus age-related information should be requested only at the time it is necessary for a legitimate business purpose, such as insurance information.

National Origin. National origin discrimination is broadly defined as including the denial of equal opportunity because of an individual's or his or her ancestor's place of origin or because the individual has the physical, cultural, or linguistic characteristics of a particular ethnic group. Certain inquiries may become suspect if they are unrelated to job performance and/or if combined with other evidence of a discriminatory intent.

A related issue concerns the citizenship status of the applicant. Citizenship requirements may also adversely impact against an individual on the basis of his or her national origin. Certain government-related positions may legitimately require U. S. citizenship. However, *an employer may prefer to hire a U. S. citizen over an equally qualified non-citizen.*[4]

Language. Questions relating to language ability should be asked only when a particular language or languages are necessary or helpful in performing the job.

Religion. An individual's religious beliefs are not relevant to his or her ability to perform a job except in extremely limited cases, which generally involve a religious institution. Thus inquiries into this area should be strictly limited to where there exists a specific need to know or hire someone with particular religious beliefs.

The duty to accommodate an employee's religious beliefs or practices pertains to prospective employees as well as current employees. Thus the employer may not permit an applicant's need for a religious accommodation to affect in anyway its decision unless it can demonstrate that it cannot reasonably accommodate the applicant's religious practices without undue hardship. Inquiries which determine an applicant's availability to work during an employer's scheduled hours may have an unlawful exclusionary effect and will be examined closely. The employer must show that its availability inquiries do not exclude applicants needing an accommodation or that such inquiries are otherwise justified by business necessity.[5]

It is recommended that employers state the normal work hours for the position and communicate that the applicant should indicate the need for any absences for religious practices during scheduled hours. Employer may ask whether applicant is otherwise available to work those hours. After the position is offered, but before the applicant is hired, employer may inquire into the need for religious accommodation and determine whether an accommodation is possible pursuant to the EEOC guidelines.

Sex. On an application form, an employer may ask the sex of an applicant or "Mr.," "Mrs," "Miss," provided that the inquiry is made in good faith for a nondiscriminatory purpose. Any preemployment inquiry which expresses directly or indirectly any limitation, specification, preference, or discrimination as to sex is unlawful unless based upon a bona fide occupational qualification.

> NOTE: It cannot be emphasized often enough: the employer should avoid such inquiries unless the information is related to the job.

Pregnancy. An employer may not exclude any applicant because of pregnancy, childbirth, or related medical conditions. The employer may not refuse to hire a woman because of her pregnancy-related condition so long as she is able to perform the major functions necessary to the job. Nor can an employer refuse to hire her because of its preference against pregnant workers or the preferences of coworkers, clients, or customers.[6]

The Supreme Court has recently stated that many employers' fetal protection policies are unlawful.[7]

> NOTE: Employers may not bar women from jobs that may be hazardous to unborn children.

Recent studies have indicated that the risk to a fetus in certain jobs was not nearly as great as was initially reported in earlier studies. These two factors have caused companies to revise their fetal protection policies and eliminates a major reason for prohibiting pregnant workers from working in certain jobs.

Children. In a related area of inquiry, questions regarding the number or age of the applicant's children and child care arrangements are troublesome and may be discriminatory in effect. Generally, the purpose of these questions is to explore an area that employers believe to be a source of absenteeism and tardiness. However, such questions tend to impact on women in a disproportionate manner. The Supreme Court ruled that in the absence of proof of business necessity, Title VII prohibits an employer from having one hiring policy for women and another for men—each having pre-school age children.[8]

Physical Characteristics: Height and Weight. Inquiries with respect to height and weight should be avoided unless such information is job-related. Height and weight requirements may tend to exclude individuals on the basis of sex or national origin and constitute discrimination due to an adverse impact on a particular group.[9]

Handicap. You may not ask an applicant if he or she is disabled! Applicants may be asked voluntarily to reveal their handicaps, and an employer may ask if there is any limitation on an applicant's ability to perform essential job-related functions. But as with religious practices, the fact that an accommodation may have to be made is not grounds for refusing to hire a disabled individual.

A preemployment medical examination may be required of an applicant but only after an offer of employment has been extended and all entering employees are subjected to the same requirement regardless of an existing or perceived disability. The offer may be conditional upon results of the medical examination. However, at all times the employer is required to make accommodations if it is reasonable to do so and it does not cause undue hardship.

Arrest and Conviction Records. Statistics show that minorities are disproportionately arrested for "suspicion." Thus inquiries into applicant's arrest records are almost never permitted unless there is a compelling business reason with regard to the particular position. Many states prohibit consideration of an individual's arrest record. An arrest is not an indication of guilt. You must refer to particular state law to determine whether you may make any inquiries into this area.

On the other hand, inquiries into an applicant's conviction record are generally lawful.

NOTE: A conviction record may be used in evaluating the qualifications and character of an employee or prospective employee.

If the conviction is very old or for an offense unrelated to the position, the conviction cannot be used as the basis of an employment decision.[10]

Several state statutes prohibit inquiries into record of arrests for applicants while permitting inquiries into record of convictions. A typical state restriction on such inquiries provides that an employer, public or private, may not ask an applicant to disclose information concerning an arrest or detention which did not result in a conviction. However, the employer may ask about an arrest for which an employee or applicant is out on bail or on his or her own recognizance pending trial. Exceptions to this prohibition include applicants for criminal justice positions; jobs with access to patients, drugs, and medication; certain government positions; and school positions.[11]

In addition, some jurisdictions require that arrest and/or conviction records be affirmatively examined for certain positions. Typically, these positions involve working with or care of children or patients or handling or production of certain pharmaceutical drugs or are sensitive government positions.

Military Experience. This is another sensitive area due to the fact that minority group members have often received less than honorable discharges for an activity that may have no effect on their ability to perform the jobs for which they apply. Thus the employer should ask for the circumstances of a less than honorable discharge.

Another consideration for employers regarding military experience is that the Vietnam Era Veterans Readjustment Act provides that such veterans may be given preference for employment under certain circumstances.

Credit History/Garnishment Record. An individual's credit history or garnishment record generally has no relevance to his or her ability to perform a job. Credit ratings may discriminate against women and minorities who have in the past been denied equal credit opportunity.

An employer should inquire into these areas *only* if it has a legitimate business necessity for such information. Federal and state laws generally prohibit discrimination based upon a garnishment record where the individual has only one outstanding garnishment.

References. This inquiry is proper if the employer actually checks the references for employment suitability. The listing of references which may indicate an ethnic grouping, without intent to check, is not appropriate. When checking references, care should be taken not to solicit information that could not properly be asked on an application.

Experience or Education. Experience and education requirements should reasonably be related to predicting job performance. Avoid inflated requirements as this practice could be interpreted as a mechanism for screening out minorities.

Organizational Membership. Only job-related and/or professional, service, or trade organizations are relevant and proper areas of inquiry. Avoid requests for list of memberships which could reveal sex, race, religion, national origin, age, ancestry, or handicap status of the members and hence of the applicant.

Summary: Tips for Assuring That Your Recruitment and Application Procedures Are Lawful

Although the employer is ultimately responsible for determining what a particular job requires and the information it needs to select a qualified employee for a particular position, the foregoing constraints on that responsibility govern the recruitment and application process. Thus the employer must at all times be able to justify its hiring criteria and methods of collecting the necessary information as being reasonably related to the position and the existence of a legitimate business reason for its methods and practices.

Recruitment and application practices of an employer provide the first contact an employer has with a prospective applicant or employee. It is here that solid equal employment practices are invaluable in preventing embarrassing and costly disputes. We have outlined several preventive steps a personnel manager should follow to ensure compliance with the myriad anti-discrimination and other employment-related laws that govern recruitment and application procedures.

♦ Periodically review recruitment practices and application forms for compliance with federal and state laws and that they comply with established company policy.

♦ Review all advertisements for compliance with the law. Avoid the use of "red flag" terms such as "citizens only"; "English only;" "female" or "male" specific designations.

♦ Structure all advertisements and application forms so that they are easily understood and refer only to valid job-related criteria.

♦ Draft job descriptions that accurately state the essential functions of each position in the company.

♦ Draft a written policy for recruiting and accommodating disabled workers or those with religious practices.

♦ Include in the application form a statement setting forth the age discrimination disclaimer, that the company is an equal opportunity employer, and that applicants may indicate a disability voluntarily.

♦ Train all personnel who are involved in recruitment or the application process to be conversant with the anti-discrimination laws. Instruct them to be courteous to all applicants.

♦ Do not refuse to give an application form to anyone who wants one.

♦ Maintain a consistent policy in recruiting and processing applicants. Deviation from established or written policy may be used as indicia of discrimination.

ENDNOTES

1. Bona fide occupational qualification may exist regarding sex, religion, disability, or national origin. A detailed discussion of the appropriate use of a BFOQ appears in Chapter 5. See *Capaci v. Katz & Besthoff*, 711 F.2d 647 (5th Cir. 1983), *reh. denied* 720 F.2d 1291, *cert. denied* 466 U.S. 927 (1984).

2. See *Shebar v. Sanyo Business Systems Corp.*, 111 N.J. 276 (1988), where employer orally promised to discharge employee only for cause based on supervisor's representation that he would have continued employment at the company and employee relied upon these representations in declining a position with another employer. Employee was terminated four months after these representations were made to him.

3. The BFOQ exception can be found in Title VII, 42 U.S.C. §2000e-2(e). The Americans with Disabilities Act contains a similar exception, 42 U.S.C. §12112(b)(6). The BFOQ defense is read narrowly and is difficult to establish.

4. See discussion on the Immigration Reform and Control Act of 1986, 8 U.S.C. §1324a, in Chapter 3.

5. For a complete discussion on religious accommodation, see EEOC Guidelines on Religious Discrimination, 29 C.F.R. Part 1605, and Chapter 5.

6. See Pregnancy Discrimination Act, 42 U.S.C. §2000e(k), and EEOC Guidelines, 29 C.F.R. Part 1604.10.

7. *United Auto Workers v. Johnson Controls, Inc.*, 111 S.Ct. 1196 (1991). In *Johnson Controls*, employer's policy that banned women who could not prove they were infertile from working in areas of the plant where they would be exposed to lead was found to discriminate on the basis of gender. The Supreme Court rejected the employer's BFOQ defense and held that a safety exception is limited to instances in which sex or pregnancy actually interfere with the employee's ability to perform the job.

8. *Phillips v. Martin Marietta Corp.*, 400 U.S. 542 (1971).

9. See EEOC National Origin Discrimination Guidelines, 29 C.F.R. Part 1606, and *Dothard v. Rawlinson*, 443 U.S. 323 (1977).

10. For example, New York Corrections Law, Article 23-A, §754, provides that an applicant may not be denied employment on the basis of a conviction record unless there is a direct relationship between the offense and the job or unless hiring the applicant would constitute an unreasonable risk to property or the safety and welfare of certain individuals or the general public. An ex-offender denied employment in New York is entitled to a statement of the reasons for such denial.

11. See California Labor Code §432.7 and Illinois Human Rights Act, Ill. Rev. Stat. Ch. 68, §2-1-3.

3

INTERVIEW, SELECTION AND HIRING

The recruitment and application process has paid off—you have a number of candidates from which to select, and you are ready for a face-to-face encounter. You interview the candidates that you have selected from the applicants. The job interview is a valuable selection tool that should be used to its full advantage but also presents an opportunity for potential, yet generally avoidable, problems.

After the interviews are completed, you are ready to select the candidate you feel is the most suited for the position. The selection of the candidate must be done with careful consideration given to the terms of the offer of the position, including any conditions that must be met before the person becomes an employee. Misstatements or representations may create either a discrimination issue or alter the "at-will employment" relationship by creating an employment contract where none was intended. We will examine these two functions separately. Keep in mind that

- Anti-discrimination laws must be adhered to throughout the entire hiring process.

- Representations or policies may create a binding employment contract.

Once the offer of employment has been extended, the employer must determine whether the candidate is eligible for employment. This determination of employment eligibility has become an important aspect of the hiring process. The ways to determine employment eligibility are discussed in this chapter.

CONDUCTING THE INTERVIEW

The concerns raised during the recruitment and application procedure remain throughout the interview and selection processes. Therefore, the interviewer should be mindful of the issues we discussed in Chapter 2 with regard to the application process.

Do not inquire orally, or by written means, into areas concerning age, race, color, religion or sex, ethnic origin, marital status, handicap (except where job-related), arrest record, child care, and the like, unless you have a genuine job-related need to know such information.

Verbal statements are discussed at length in Chapter 2. However, since interviews generally involve only verbal communication, it is necessary to discuss the impact of inappropriate statements, promises, and misrepresentations that may occur during the interview process.

> NOTE: Statements made to the candidate may provide a basis for a claim of discrimination or an employment contract, both results which may have been unintended by the speaker.

However, an employer may be held responsible for unlawful discrimination based on comments or for any promises that an employee relied upon made during an interview.

Basic Interview Guidelines

1. Avoid making statements that may be construed as a promise or commitment. For example,

   – "As long as you do your job, you will have a job here."
   – "You will have a job here so long as you want it."

   These types of statements may be construed as establishing a "just cause" type of standard for dismissal. This would alter the status of an "at-will" employee who may be discharged for any or no reason (except for a discriminatory reason).

2. Avoid questions or statements regarding child care arrangements, intention of starting a family, ethnic background (unless relevant), religious practices (unless relevant), physical or mental problems, age, and other areas of inquiry that may indicate a discriminatory bias of the employer or the interviewer.

NOTE: Nothing prohibits the individual candidate from raising some or all of these issues voluntarily. However, discretion should be exercised whenever these areas are discussed.

3. Limit statements to job-related issues such as qualifications, experience, job description and duties, and expectation of performance.

4. Avoid statements indicating that an employee may be entitled to certain career enhancement opportunities such as training or promotions. You may indicate that the burden of an individual's advancement is on the employee.

5. Educate all interviewers to the fact that oral promises and/or commitments may be enforced as contracts.

The concerns become more serious where the applicant is an internal candidate transferring or seeking promotion. Familiarity may cause interviewers to be less cautious in what they *say* (read promise) to the candidate. Therefore, steps should be taken to educate the interviewers that all potential candidates should be interviewed in compliance with an established format and these policies be consistently followed.

Recent developments in case law have brought verbal representations to the forefront of employment relations. Please refer to Case Study No. 2 in Chapter 2, which examines the problem of representations being construed as an enforceable promise.[1]

The use of a standardized interview form that has specific categories regarding experience and job requirements will aid interviewers in keeping the discussion focused on the interviewee's qualifications and experience.

Although the interview process involves subjective evaluations of an individual's demeanor, personality, and appearance, the evaluation form will provide some objective overall perspective of an individual's suitability for a particular position. As with all employment-related decisions, consistency and uniformity of practices is one of an employer's best defenses against a charge of discrimination.

Case Study No. 1: A Question of Discrimination?

An applicant has been called in for an interview, based on his excellent written credentials, for a position as a product representative with an American manufacturer of automobile accessories. The employer is heavily unionized. The applicant was born in Japan but has an anglicized name. He reads and writes excellent English. However, he speaks with a moderate accent, but is understood with little problem. The position requires contact with clients and the public. He has the appropriate credentials and is qualified for the position. The interviewer is a veteran of World War II. Many things are discussed, including his background and education in Japan, his experience here, his goals, the duties of the job, the effect of World War II on Japan's economy, and other job- and nonjob-related topics.

There are no other employees of Japanese or Asian descent employed at this or higher-level executive positions at this company. The company also lacks any specific hiring guidelines or policies, and the decision to hire relies heavily on the results of the interview. He is personable yet he is not hired for the position.

The candidate alleges discrimination for the employer's failure to hire him due to the interviewer's or employer's bias against the Japanese, the current buy-American campaign by the unions aimed at Japanese-made products, and the fact that there are no other Asian employees who hold significant positions.

Did the interviewer act improperly in discussing nonjob-related issues? Is the concern about the union's potential negative reaction to a Japanese representative selling the products a legitimate one? Was it proper for the company to rely on the subjective and possibly biased judgment of the interviewer?

The interviewer, by not keeping to job-related issues, may have revealed an actual or subconscious bias that improperly influenced his decision. It is important to stay with an objective evaluation and selection process, to avoid this problem. The courts have found that hiring decisions based more on the exercise of personal judgment or the application of subjective criteria rather than on precise or formal objective criteria may expose the employer to liability for discrimination.[2] The employer is not entitled to rely on its concern of problems with its unions because of the unions' campaign against Japanese products. The preference or bias of a customer or other business entity is not a valid basis for discriminating against an applicant or employee.

It is helpful to the interviewer to use an interview decision-making guide, such as the one shown in Exhibit 3.1, or some similar form that is completed after the interview is over. The use of such a form aids in conducting an organized and informative interview as well as creating a well-balanced report that may be relied upon in making a hiring decision.

HOW TO SELECT THE BEST CANDIDATE

Once you have interviewed and tested the candidates for a position, you must then make your selection. The hiring decision should be based on selecting the candidate with the best qualifications for the position, including skills, experience, personality, and other intangible characteristics. However, these characteristics must be directly related to how you anticipate the person will perform the functions of the position.

– EXHIBIT 3.1 –
Interview Decision-Making Guide

POSITION _____

CANDIDATE NAME _____

INTERVIEWER _____ DATE _____

INTERVIEW DECISION-MAKING GUIDE

INSTRUCTIONS: Use this guide to review your impression of the candidate. Below each main category are several illustrative behaviors which further describe the category. Evaluate each category separately from the others, enter the nine ratings, and then complete the back of the form including your hiring recommendation.

Remember that the importance of a category or behavior will vary from job to job. This requires you to weigh your final hiring recommendations accordingly. Also, some behaviors are more easily "trained" than others. Please submit this completed guide to your human resources manager.

1	2	3	4	5
UNSATISFACTORY	MARGINAL	ADEQUATE FOR THE JOB	ABOVE AVERAGE	EXCEPTIONAL

1. IMPACT
- Dresses appropriately
- Comfortable around people
- Tactful
- Establishes rapport well
- Posture and mannerisms don't get "in the way"

2. BUSINESS/TECHNICAL KNOWLEDGE
- Well versed in specialty
- Understands function
- Appropriate education
- Keeps abreast of industry
- Listens well
- Continually improves knowledge
- Aware of business trends

3. PLANNING
- Anticipates events
- Sets clear goals
- Has realistic objectives
- Coordinates plans with others
- Involves subordinates in plans (if applicable)
- Uses time effectively

4. DIRECTING AND CONTROLLING
- Meets deadlines
- Delegates well
- Stays within budgets
- Follows up
- Results oriented
- Works Independently

5. PROBLEM SOLVING
- Shows good judgment
- Evaluates solutions
- Makes timely, fact-based decisions
- Remains calm under pressure
- Takes risks

6. WORKING WITH OTHERS
- Relates well to others
- Team player
- Shows maturity
- Faces and resolves conflict
- Can deal with company "culture"
- Displays integrity
- Aware of strengths/weaknesses

7. COMMUNICATIONS
- Oral communications
- Written communications
- Personal impact
- Self-confidence
- Keeps others informed
- Makes effective presentations

8. INITIATIVE
- Innovates
- Creates, thinks imaginatively
- Exploits opportunities
- Seeks/accepts responsibilities
- Has ambition to grow

9. INTEREST IN THE JOB
- Knowledgeable about company
- Prepared for interview
- Knowledgeable about position
- Shows genuine interest
- High energy level

CANDIDATE STRENGTHS:

- _____
- _____
- _____
- _____

CANDIDATE WEAKNESSES:

- _____
- _____
- _____
- _____

ADDITIONAL COMMENTS:

- RELOCATABILITY_____

- FIT WITHIN COMPANY_____

- CAREER ASPIRATIONS_____

- REFERENCES THAT CAN BE CHECKED_____

  _____

  _____

- OTHER_____

HIRING RECOMMENDATIONS:

HIRE _____   REJECT_____   UNDECIDED _____

ISSUES: 1. _____

2. _____

3. _____

4. _____

SEND TO HUMAN RESOURCES MANAGER: _____

Generally, the employer, in selecting employees, must not intentionally or inadvertently screen out minority group applicants. During the interview or separately, the employer may conduct certain preemployment tests to aid in the selection process. Preemployment testing standards and uses are discussed in the next chapter. However, testing as selection criteria will be briefly addressed here. The company may be called upon to show that it uses nondiscriminatory standards in selecting employees for hire or promotion. In any event, hiring standards must be job-related and reasonable.

Selection Procedures

An employer who uses employment tests or other job screening standards, such as a high school diploma, must be able to show that they are "demonstrably a reasonable measure of job performance."[3] We turn now to the elements with which a personnel professional must be familiar when utilizing selection procedures.

Adverse Impact. Selection criteria, such as written tests or educational requirements, may appear to be neutral or nondiscriminatory on its face, but may, in practice, screen out most or all minority applicants. Such a procedure is said to have an "adverse impact" on employment opportunities of a particular race, sex, or ethnic group and are illegal under Title VII. If adverse impact exists, it must be justified on grounds of business necessity. A finding of adverse impact does not require discriminatory intent.

NOTE: Adverse impact analysis is applied to objective and subjective selection criteria.

The following concepts are typical methods of preliminarily determining whether adverse impact exists.

The "Four-fifths" Rule. The EEOC Uniform Guidelines adopt a rule of thumb as a means of determining "adverse impact" known as the "Four-fifths" or "80 percent" rule, which says that

A selection rate for any racial, ethnic, or sex group which is less than four-fifths of the rate for the group with the highest rate will generally be regarded as evidence of adverse impact.

This rule is discussed in detail in Chapter 4, which covers testing in the workplace.

"Bottom-Line" approach. The government, in deciding whether to take enforcement action, favors a "bottom-line" approach, that is, the employer's total selection process and its overall impact, rather than the individual impact of each component of the selection procedure, is evaluated by the enforcing agency.

NOTE: A "bottom line" that shows an appropriate minority balance does not preclude an employee from making a *prima facie* case of discrimination nor does it provide an employer with a defense.

Employee Testing. Any professionally developed ability test may be used provided that such test, its administration, or action upon results is not designed, intended, or used to discriminate because of race, color, religion, sex, or national origin. The courts have expanded the scope of this rule to prohibit any test which has an adverse impact on minority applicants regardless of whether the employer intended to discriminate. Testing of applicants and employees is discussed in detail in Chapter 4.

Validation. An employer using an ability test which has a discriminatory impact may modify or eliminate the testing procedure or validate the test by showing that it is job-related. As discussed in Chapter 4, the EEOC Uniform Guidelines on Employee Selection Procedures provide certain technical standards and documentation requirements for various validation techniques.[4] However, it is important to note that three concepts are used to validate a selection procedure:

1. *Content validity.* The procedure is justified by showing that it representatively samples significant parts of the job, such as a typing test for a typist.
2. *Construct validity.* This requires identification of the psychological trait which underlies successful performance of the job and a demonstration that the procedure measures the presence and degree of the trait, for example, test of "leadership ability."
3. *Criterion-related validity.* The procedure is justified by a statistical relationship between scores on the test or other selection procedures and job performance of a sample of workers.

Validation must be established through professionally accepted methods.

"Business Necessity" Versus "Job-relatedness." These terms are not synonymous and constitute different standards of evidence in defending a discriminatory selection procedure.

"Business Necessity" Standard. Employer must show that the selection procedure or criteria is necessary to the business and that there are no alternative selection procedures with a less adverse impact.

"Job-Related" Standard. Employer need only validate the selection procedure, thus requiring the plaintiff to show that there are alternative procedures available. The employer must demonstrate job-relatedness after a complainant has established a prima facie case of discriminatory impact.

Making an Offer of Employment

Once you have interviewed and tested the applicant and determined that he or she is the right person for the job, you prepare an offer of employment. The offer of employment should be straightforward, setting out only terms and conditions of employment of the employer's choosing, including

- The title or duties of the position
- Starting salary
- Starting date
- Any conditions that must be met before employment begins
- Other necessary information that reflects any agreement between the parties, such as arrangements for relocating or other accommodations agreed upon

The offer of employment may be verbal or in writing. The employer may have a policy that all offers of employment are written, others may give only verbal offers, and still others may give some verbal offers and others in writing. There are advantages and disadvantages to either form.

A verbal offer may be interpreted differently by the employer and the employee. The employer says one thing, the employee hears something else. If a dispute occurs, you must rely on the parties' memories of what was said sometimes years earlier. However, it is more difficult to establish that a contract has been formed when the offer was verbal.

A written offer provides a record of what was offered and at least some of the terms and conditions of employment. It reduces the risk of misunderstanding and sets out what is expected of the employer and employee at the beginning of the employment relationship. However, the more formally presented an offer is, the greater the risk that the offer will be construed as a contract binding the employer to terms that it may not have originally contemplated.

NOTE: The employer will be held to the terms of the offer of employment, so it should be drafted clearly and with care.

The offer of employment should be constructed in such a way as not to be an employment contract. An employment contract is a formal agreement between the parties specifying such things as the actual term of employment (one year, five years, etc.), expectations of the parties, relocating details, termination provision, noncompetition clause, and more. An offer allows that some boundaries are set while permitting a flexible employment relationship. You want to avoid the appearance of a contract if one is not intended, because the employer will be bound to terms it may not have intended but have been implied by a court.

NOTE: It is helpful to state in the offer that employment is "at-will," which means that the employer may terminate the employment relationship for any reason or no reason, so long as it is not for an unlawful discriminatory reason. On the other hand, the employee may terminate the employment for any reason at any time.

An offer of employment may be conditioned upon several factors, including completion of a preemployment physical, proof of eligibility to work in the United States, successful completion of training, or other reasonably job-related factors. A sample is shown in Exhibit 3-2.

– EXHIBIT 3.2 –
Sample Offer of Employment

The ABC, Inc., is pleased to offer you the position of Manager of Sales for the Southeast Region. Your base salary will be $30,000 per annum with a commission rate of 5 percent (5%) of any direct sales by you and 2.5 percent (2.5%) of sales made by your department. Your territory will include all of the Southeastern States of the United States of America. You will be responsible for the successful sale of our products throughout this region and the proper functioning of the southeast regional office.

We will expect you to commence employment within the next thirty (30) days.

This offer and its terms are conditional upon your successful completion of a medical physical examination to be conducted by a company-appointed physician. Kindly make yourself available for said examination within the next two weeks. Please see the enclosed notice that provides information regarding the physical examination.

Please be advised that your employment is terminable at the will of the company or yourself at any time, with or without notice, and for any lawful reason or no reason.

We look forward to you joining our ABC team and hope that together we will be successful in bringing our products into every American home.

HOW TO DETERMINE EMPLOYMENT ELIGIBILITY

Once the offer has been extended and accepted, the hiring process is not complete until the employee has been verified as eligible for employment. As a result of legislation, employers must ascertain whether a new employee is eligible to work in the United Sates. The Immigration Reform and Control Act of 1986 (IRCA), 8 U.S.C. §1324a, imposes a duty upon employers to verify the employment eligibility of every new hire.

NOTE: Only U. S. citizens, nationals, resident aliens, and others authorized by the Immigration and Naturalization Service (INS) are eligible for employment.

Since this law applies at the time of hire, we will examine its requirements and methods for compliance in this chapter.

Case Study No. 2: Eligibility Documentation

The APEX Company, located in Chicago, has three applicants who are all at least minimally qualified for a position as shift manager in its manufacturing plant. During the interview process but prior to making an offer, APEX insisted that all applicants show at least one of three documents: a driver's license, U. S. passport, or green card.

The most qualified candidate, Manuel, is not a citizen but has legitimate eligibility to work papers. However, he has none of the three documents requested and is rejected for the position. Another well qualified applicant, Yuri, speaks with a heavy Eastern European accent but is never asked for any eligibility papers and is rejected. He is told that they cannot hire him because he was not born here. In fact, he has a green card and is a resident alien. The applicant hired is Tom, a citizen. He was the least qualified of the three, and he produced only a driver's license.

Consider the following questions:

♦ May the employer insist that an applicant produce only certain types of identity and eligibility to work documents?

♦ May the employer reject someone because he or she is not a citizen or has a foreign appearance or accent?

♦ May the employer prefer to hire a citizen rather than an eligible alien?

Under the law, the employer is required to review certain identity *and* eligibility to work documents. As you will see, there are a number of different types of acceptable documents. APEX may not determine what documents it will or will not accept with regard to these requirements. The documents need not be produced until after the offer of employment has been made. All offers of employment are contingent upon the individual producing the proper documentation within three days of hire. Thus APEX's demand for documents prior to hire may violate the law. Also, a driver's license alone is insufficient since it is only a document of identity and not of eligibility. (Proper documentation is discussed in detail in this chapter.)

Furthermore, APEX discriminated against Yuri when it rejected him because he was not a citizen and because of his foreign accent. Under IRCA the employer may not discriminate against anyone because of ethnic background or citizenship status so long as the person is eligible to work.

APEX also violated IRCA when it preferred Tom over more qualified and eligible aliens. The employer may prefer a citizen only under two circumstances: (1) when citizenship is a requirement of the job and (2) when the citizen is at least as qualified as the eligible alien.

Complying with IRCA—The Immigration Reform and Control Act

We will briefly review the provisions of IRCA to aid in your understanding of the law. Step-by-step guidelines are provided in Exhibit 3.3 to aid you in complying with the requirements of the law. We will discuss some of these items following the exhibit.

IRCA prohibits all employers from recruiting, hiring, or continuing to employ illegal immigrants. The law also prohibits discrimination by employers on the basis of national origin or citizenship status. The law applies to all private and public sector employers regardless of size.

– EXHIBIT 3.3 –
Compliance Guidelines for Employment Eligibility

---

1. Interview all applicants to determine the qualifications for the job in question.

2. Do not reject any applicant because he or she speaks a foreign language or appears to not be a native of the United States.

3. You are not required to hire anyone specifically because of alienage or national origin.

4. Confine your questions about work eligibility to work-related areas only.

5. Do not ask individuals about their country of birth or citizenship status because that may violate Title VII.

6. Upon being hired, employees must complete Section 1 of the Employment Eligibility Verification Form, I-9. This form must be signed and dated by all new employees. Supporting documentation must be presented as soon as the employee is hired or no later than within 72 hours of commencing employment. (If the employer hires an employee for fewer than three business days, the employer must complete the certification form before the end of the employee's first working day.)

7. Examine all documents presented by the employee. You should make sure that they reasonably appear to be genuine.

8. Do not accept verification documents that appear to be or that you know to be false. Review the certification form to ensure that it is legible, properly completed, and dated.

9. Request verification documentation from all employees hired after November 6, 1987. You may ask these employees to present appropriate documents verifying their status under IRCA.

10. Illegal aliens who do not have the necessary documentation may legally work until September 1, 1987, provided they attest that they intend to apply or have applied for legalization. Such attestation should be noted by the employer on the I-9 form. Alternatively, the Attestation Form may be used and attached to the I-9 form.

11. Newly hired employees unable to complete and sign the certification form due to physical or mental disability or inability to read or write English may be assisted. The person providing such assistance must complete and sign the Preparer Translator Certification located above Section 2 on the I-9 form.

12. Section 2 of the verification form may be completed by recording the required information from the documents presented by the newly hired employees.

13. After you have reviewed the documents presented by the employee, verify and attest that this employee is eligible for employment by signing the certification on the I-9 form.

14. Retain photocopy of the documents presented by the newly hired employee and place them in your files. These documents may not be used for *any* purpose other than compliance with the immigration and naturalization laws.

15. Keep all verification documents and forms in a central file. Remember, you are subject to "spot" visits by the Immigration and Naturalization Service to monitor your compliance. These records must be kept for three years from date of hire or one year after termination of an employee, whichever is later.

16. Do not discharge employees simply because they speak a foreign language or have a foreign appearance.

Under IRCA, the new employee must produce documentation that establishes his or her identity and eligibility for employment within *three* days of commencing employment. The employer must complete and keep on record an I-9 form for three years. A copy of an I-9 form, which must be completed for every new hire, is shown in Exhibit 3.4. The Immigration and Naturalization Service may audit an employer upon notice.

Employers of four or more employees are specifically prohibited from discriminating on the basis of citizenship or national origin.

NOTE: The anti-discrimination provision does not apply to unauthorized (illegal) aliens or where citizenship is required by law. Also, if you have a choice between equally qualified applicants, one a U. S. citizen and the other an otherwise eligible applicant, the employer may choose the citizen without violating the law.

Verifying Employment Eligibility

The employer's representative must see proof of identity and eligibility provided by the new employee. Such proof may consist of various documents either alone or in combinations, so long as the identity of the person is established and his or her eligibility to work here is established. This proof may include any of the following:

- Birth certificate or social security card *and* driver's license with photograph
- U. S. passport or foreign passport with employment authorization stamp
- Certificate of U. S. citizenship
- Certificate of naturalization
- Resident alien card with photograph

– EXHIBIT 3.4 –
Employment Eligibility Verification (Form I-9)

EMPLOYMENT ELIGIBILITY VERIFICATION (Form I-9)

1 **EMPLOYEE INFORMATION AND VERIFICATION:** (To be completed and signed by employee.)

Name: (Print or Type) Last	First	Middle	Birth Name
Address: Street Name and Number	City	State	ZIP Code
Date of Birth (Month/Day/Year)		Social Security Number	

I attest, under penalty of perjury, that I am (check a box):

☐ 1. A citizen or national of the United States.
☐ 2. An alien lawfully admitted for permanent residence (Alien Number A _____).
☐ 3. An alien authorized by the Immigration and Naturalization Service to work in the United States (Alien Number A _____ .
or Admission Number _____ , expiration of employment authorization, if any _____) .

I attest, under penalty of perjury, the documents that I have presented as evidence of identity and employment eligibility are genuine and relate to me. I am aware that federal law provides for imprisonment and/or fine for any false statements or use of false documents in connection with this certificate.

Signature	Date (Month/Day/Year)

PREPARER/TRANSLATOR CERTIFICATION (To be completed if prepared by person other than the employee). I attest, under penalty of perjury, that the above was prepared by me at the request of the named individual and is based on all information of which I have any knowledge.

Signature	Name (Print or Type)	
Address (Street Name and Number)	City	State	Zip Code

2 **EMPLOYER REVIEW AND VERIFICATION:** (To be completed and signed by employer.)

Instructions:
Examine one document from List A and check the appropriate box, **OR** examine one document from List B **and** one from List C and check the appropriate boxes. Provide the **Document Identification Number** and **Expiration Date** for the document checked.

List A Documents that Establish Identity and Employment Eligibility	List B Documents that Establish Identity	**and**	List C Documents that Establish Employment Eligibility
☐ 1. United States Passport ☐ 2. Certificate of United States Citizenship ☐ 3. Certificate of Naturalization ☐ 4. Unexpired foreign passport with attached Employment Authorization ☐ 5. Alien Registration Card with photograph	☐ 1. A State-issued driver's license or a State-issued I.D. card with a photograph, or information, including name, sex, date of birth, height, weight, and color of eyes. (Specify State)_____) ☐ 2. U.S. Military Card ☐ 3. Other (Specify document and issuing authority)		☐ 1. Original Social Security Number Card (other than a card stating it is not valid for employment) ☐ 2. A birth certificate issued by State, county, or municipal authority bearing a seal or other certification ☐ 3. Unexpired INS Employment Authorization Specify form # _____
Document Identification # _____	**Document Identification** # _____		**Document Identification** # _____
Expiration Date (if any) _____	**Expiration Date (if any)** _____		**Expiration Date (if any)** _____

CERTIFICATION: I attest, under penalty of perjury, that I have examined the documents presented by the above individual, that they appear to be genuine and to relate to the individual named, and that the individual, to the best of my knowledge, is eligible to work in the United States.

Signature	Name (Print or Type)	Title
Employer Name	Address	Date

Form I-9 (05/07/87)
OMB No. 1115-0136

U.S. Department of Justice
Immigration and Naturalization Service

Employment Eligibility Verification

NOTICE: Authority for collecting the information on this form is in Title 8, United States Code, Section 1324A, which requires employers to verify employment eligibility of individuals on a form approved by the Attorney General. This form will be used to verify the individual's eligibility for employment in the United States. Failure to present this form for inspection to officers of the Immigration and Naturalization Service or Department of Labor within the time period specified by regulation, or improper completion or retention of this form, may be a violation of the above law and may result in a civil money penalty.

Section 1. Instructions to Employee/Preparer for completing this form

Instructions for the employee.

All employees, upon being hired, must complete Section 1 of this form. Any person hired after November 6, 1986 must complete this form. (For the purpose of completion of this form the term "hired" applies to those employed, recruited or referred for a fee.)

All employees must print or type their complete name, address, date of birth, and Social Security Number. The block which correctly indicates the employee's immigration status must be checked. If the second block is checked, the employee's Alien Registration Number must be provided. If the third block is checked, the employee's Alien Registration Number *or* Admission Number must be provided, as well as the date of expiration of that status, if it expires.

All employees whose present names differ from birth names, because of marriage or other reasons, must print or type their birth names in the appropriate space of Section 1. Also, employees whose names change after employment verification should report these changes to their employer.

All employees must sign and date the form.

Instructions for the preparer of the form, if not the employee.

If a person assists the employee with completing this form, the preparer must certify the form by signing it and printing or typing his or her complete name and address.

Section 2. Instructions to Employer for completing this form

(For the purpose of completion of this form, the term "employer" applies to employers and those who recruit or refer for a fee.)

Employers must complete this section by examining evidence of identity and employment eligibility, and:
- checking the appropriate box in List A *or* boxes in both Lists B and C;
- recording the document identification number and expiration date (if any);
- recording the type of form if not specifically identified in the list;
- signing the certification section.

NOTE: Employers are responsible for reverifying employment eligibility of employees whose employment eligibility documents carry an expiration date.

Copies of documentation presented by an individual for the purpose of establishing identity and employment eligibility may be copied and retained for the purpose of complying with the requirements of this form and no other purpose. Any copies of documentation made for this purpose should be maintained with this form.

Name changes of employees which occur after preparation of this form should be recorded on the form by lining through the old name, printing the new name and the reason (such as marriage), and dating and initialing the changes. Employers should not attempt to delete or erase the old name in any fashion.

RETENTION OF RECORDS.

The completed form must be retained by the employer for:
- three years after the date of hiring; or
- one year after the date the employment is terminated, whichever is later.

Employers may photocopy or reprint this form as necessary.

U.S. Department of Justice
Immigration and Naturalization Service

OMB #1115-0136
Form I-9 (05/07/87)

However, the employer may not require that the employee show only certain types of identification and proof of eligibility. Any of the documents identified by IRCA are to be accepted. See our discussion under Case Study No. 2.

Employers are subject to penalties for failure to comply with the verification procedures and/or for the violation of the anti-discrimination provision.

Violations of the verification requirements include

– Fines for knowingly recruiting, hiring, or continuing to employ an illegal immigrant

– Fines for failure to comply with verification procedure

– If a pattern or practice of intentional violations are found, fines or imprisonment

The remedies against an employer for violation of the anti-discrimination provisions include

– A cease-and-desist order

– Compliance with administrative order

– Reinstatement or hiring

– Back pay

– Civil penalties

– Attorneys' fees

Employees hired prior to November 7, 1986, who remained continuously employed retain employment eligibility under a "grandfather clause" and need not be verified. However, if there is a significant break in their employment and they are rehired or recalled, they become subject to the verification requirement.[5]

Employers who make a reasonable attempt to comply with the provisions of IRCA or who have a reasonable basis to believe the eligibility documents presented by the new employee are legitimate may assert what is called a "good faith" defense if they are charged with violations. However, this defense will not generally be accepted in cases of alleged discrimination. It usually has force when the documents of identity or eligibility relied upon by the employer turn out to be invalid or forged. The employer is not expected to be an authority on the authenticity of such documents. However, there is no defense if the documents are obviously faked or the employer knew that they were not genuine.

NOTE: Ignorance of the requirements of IRCA is not a defense.[6]

A handy reference list of acceptable employment eligibility documents together with a telephone number for questions about IRCA can be found in Government Notice to Employers shown in Exhibit 3.5.

HOW TO AVOID NEGLIGENT HIRING LIABILITY

Recently, concerns have been raised by many employers with respect to potential liabilities under a theory of negligent hiring.

NOTE: The employer may be held liable for negligently hiring or retaining in its employment an employee it knew or should have known was unfit for a particular position so as to create an unreasonable risk of harm to third parties.[7]

Under the negligent hiring doctrine, the employer has a duty to exercise reasonable care in view of all the circumstances in hiring individuals who, because of the employment, may pose a threat of injury to members of the public.

The issue of negligent hiring is discussed in detail in Chapter 14, which reviews the various negligence theories that an employer should be aware of and how to avoid such problems. However, the negligent hiring theory is raised here so that the individuals who are responsible for hiring new employees are aware of this potential claim and can act accordingly.

Although preventive steps are discussed more fully in Chapter 14, here are a few to keep in mind:

– Conduct thorough background investigations in appropriate cases.

– Always check references and previous places of employment.

– Conduct appropriate skill testing.

These simple steps taken at the beginning of the employment relationship will aid in avoiding potential liability in the future. Background checks and other preemployment inquiries and tests are discussed in the next chapter.

– EXHIBIT 3.5 –
Government Notice to Employers

The American Policy Is Our Policy

To comply with the Immigration Reform and Control Act, it is necessary to establish both your identity and your employment eligibility. In order to do this, you are required to present either one document from Section A, or one document each from Section B and Section C.

The following is a partial list of acceptable documents. For a complete list, see the INS Handbook for Employers available at your neighborhood library.

Identity and Employment Eligibility

You must submit one document to verify your identity and employment eligibility.

- **U.S. Passport**
- **Certificate of U.S. Citizenship** (INS Form N-560 or N-561)
- **Certificate of Naturalization** (INS Form N-550 or N-570)
- **Unexpired Foreign Passport with Employment Authorization**
- **Alien Registration Card** (with photo). (INS Form I-151 or I-551)
- **Temporary Resident Card** (INS Form I-688)
- **Employment Authorization Card** (INS Form I-688A)

OR

Identity

You must submit one document to verify your identity and a second document from Section C to verify your employment eligibility.

- **State Issued Driver's License** (with photo or name, sex, date of birth, height, weight and color of eyes). Or, one issued by a Canadian Province.
- **Federal, State or Local Government Issued I.D. Card** (with photo or name, sex, date of birth, height, weight and color of eyes).
- **U.S. Military Card, Draft Record of Military Dependent's I.D. Card**
- **School I.D. Card** (with photo).
- **Voter's Registration Card**

AND

Employment Eligibility

- **Original Social Security Card** (other than one stating that it is not valid for employment).
- **Birth Certificate** issued by state, county or municipal authority in the U.S. bearing their seal or other certification, or by the U.S. State Department. (Form FS-545 or DS-1350).
- **Unexpired INS Employment Authorization**
- **Unexpired Re-entry Permit** (INS Form I-327).
- **Unexpired Refugee Travel Document** (INS Form I-571).
- **U.S. Citizen Identification Card** (INS Form I-197 or I-179).

Working For A Better America.
Immigration and Naturalization Service

Questions?
Call the Immigration and Naturalization Service (INS), toll-free:
1-800-777-7700

We hire only U.S. Citizens and Lawfully Authorized Alien Workers.

ENDNOTES

1. A New Jersey case, *Shebar v. Sanyo Business Systems Corp.*, 111 N.J. 276 (1988), put employers on notice that oral representations may now form the basis for an implied contract and a lawsuit alleging breach of contract, malicious interference, fraud, and other causes of actions. See Roger B. Jacobs, "Oral Representations: An Employment Law Primer," *New Jersey Law Journal*, March 24, 1988.

2. See U.S. Supreme Court case, Watson v. Fort Worth Bank & Trust, 108 S.Ct. 2777 (1988), where a black employee was rejected for four promotions to supervisory positions in favor of white applicants. The Bank had not developed a precise and formal criteria for the position, but instead, relied on the subjective judgment of white supervisors who were acquainted with the candidates and the jobs. Disparate impact analysis applied for the first time to hiring/promotions decisions based on the exercise of personal judgment or the application of subjective criteria.

3. EEOC Uniform Guidelines on Employee Selection Procedures (1978), 29 C.F.R. Part 1607. See *Griggs v. Duke Power Co.*, 401 U.S. 424, 91 S.Ct. 849 (1971).

4. EEOC Uniform Guidelines on Employee Selection Procedures, 29 C.F.R. Part 1607.

5. See *League of United Latin American Citizens v. Pasadena Independent School District*, 662 F. Supp. 443 (S.D.Tex. 1987) (unfair immigration practice to terminate undocumented aliens for giving false social security number when aliens were eligible for legalization under new Act), and *U.S. v. Mester Manufacturing*, E.O.I.R., No. 8700001 (June 17, 1988), is the first reported case that deals with the appeals process under IRCA. Mester is the first company to go through the appeals process available to employers charged with violating IRCA. The company appealed the notice of intent to fine it $500.00 for each of seven workers and $250.00 for each paperwork violation. The administrative law judge found that Mester had knowingly employed six illegal aliens and dismissed all ten paperwork violations.

6. In the matter of *In re Charge of Martinez, U.S. v. Marcel Watch Corp.*, OCAHO, No. 8920085 (March 22, 1990), the company refused to hire a citizen (from Puerto Rico) who could not produce a green card. The administrative law judge ruled that the company's alleged ignorance of IRCA requirements and of U.S. geography was not a good faith defense to the anti-discrimination provision of the law. There was no evidence that the company imposed this requirement on all job applicants, citizens, or otherwise.

7. See *Ponticas v. KMS Investments*, 331 N.W.2d 907, 910–11, note 4 (Minn. 1983) (and cases cited therein).

4

INVESTIGATION OF EMPLOYEE BACKGROUND AND CONDUCT: TESTING IN THE WORKPLACE

Investigation of an employee —whether it is an applicant's or new hire's background, an accident, misconduct, or some other incident—requires knowledge of permissible investigation and testing techniques. For example, an employer hiring a security guard naturally wants to know how trustworthy an applicant is; can the employer require the applicant to take a lie detector test? The response to this situation and many others are discussed in this chapter. Also, an important issue is the intrusion on an employee's right to privacy through the use of particular investigation or testing techniques.

The employment relationship is governed by industry practices, statutory rules and regulations, and the common law. Increasingly, employers are subject to rules restricting the use of certain testing or investigation procedures. This chapter will address such areas as drug and alcohol testing, medical screening, polygraphs and other truth deception techniques, psychological testing, skill tests, as well as other means of investigations such as credit checks and arrest/conviction records. The rules may vary according to whether the individual being investigated or tested is an applicant or an employee. For that reason we will address the type of testing or investigation technique generally and what effect, if any, an individual's employment status has on the use of a particular technique.

TYPICAL PRE-EMPLOYMENT INQUIRIES AND TESTS

The employer, when it hires a new employee or seeks to promote an employee into a new position, wants to be able to judge whether that individual has the background and skills necessary to perform successfully in the position. Different types of positions require different levels of skill and certain intangible attributes not easily subject to testing. This section will address the types of tests utilized to determine skill level and capability, statutory guidelines governing such tests, and other investigative techniques that aid an employer in assessing the overall qualifications of a candidate for a particular position.

An area in which the personnel professional should be conversant is in the determination of an appropriate test for evaluating the ability of a person to do a particular job. This may include specific skills tests (such as typing), intelligence tests, honesty or truth deception tests (such as a polygraph), psychological testing, as well as others. Many of these tests are subject to the EEOC's guidelines of testing or other federal and state laws as well as the privacy rights of an individual.

NOTE: An employee selection procedure must be lawful and be job-related.

Complying with EEOC Guidelines

Objective tests and criteria, generally those related to skill or endurance, are regulated by the EEOC validation requirements. If the use of any such test is challenged, the employer must be prepared to show, usually through complex statistical evidence, that the test demonstrates a relevant relationship to the job or is a predictor of job performance.

The Uniform Guidelines on Employee Selection Procedures promulgated by the EEOC are not binding but indicate what that agency will consider as acceptable practices.[1] The guidelines are intended to provide a means of determining if an employment selection procedure has an adverse impact on a protected group and, if so, methods an employer may use to validate the procedures as job-related.

Four-fifths Rule. The adverse impact of an employee selection procedure is measured by a rule of thumb known as the *four-fifths rule* or the *80 percent rule.*[2] This rule involves the following analysis:

1. Determine the rate of selection for each group (divide the number of persons selected from a group by the number of applicants from the group).

2. Observe which group has the highest selection rate.

3. Calculate the impact ratios by comparing the selection rate for each group with that of the highest group (divide the selection rate for a group by the selection rate for the highest group).

4. Observe whether the selection rate of any group is substantially less (i.e., usually less than four-fifths or 80 percent) than the selection rate for the highest group. If it is, adverse impact is indicated in most circumstances.

EXAMPLE

Applicants	Hires	Selection Rate (% hired)
90 white	55	55/90 or 61%
40 black	13	13/40 or 32.5%

A comparison of the black selection rate (32.5%) with the white selection rate (61%) shows that the black rate is 32.5/61 or 53%, just over one-half of the white rate. Since 53% is less than four-fifths (80%), adverse impact is indicated.

NOTE: The four-fifths rule is merely a numerical indicator for an initial inference of discrimination. Additional information will be required to establish whether discrimination was in fact the reason for the disparity in employee selection results found under this rule.

Validation. In the event that there appears to be a substantially different rate of selection in hiring, promoting or other employment decisions to the disadvantage of protected groups, there is the appearance of adverse impact. However, that does not necessarily mean that the employer's selection procedures are unlawful. The guidelines provide several theories under which a selection procedure may be validated.

Validation means that there can be established a relationship between the testing procedure or instrument and performance on the job. The validation process may be highly technical and involve complex statistical analyses. In the course of the validation process, it is necessary for the employer to consider alternative methods that will achieve its legitimate business purpose with a lesser adverse impact on protected groups.

Validation involves a two-part analysis in that

1. There must exist a legitimate business purpose for the challenged practice sufficient to override the adverse impact to the protected group.

2. There must not be any acceptable alternative policies or procedures that would accomplish the same purpose equally well with lesser adverse impact.[3]

Validation Concepts. The guidelines suggest three distinct concepts under which an employment selection procedure may be validated:

1. *Content validity.* Where the data demonstrate that the content of a selection procedure is representative of an important aspect of performance of the particular job, the test is valid. For example, a test consisting of basic math

(addition, subtraction, multiplication, and division) for an entry-level bookkeeping position or typing for a secretarial assistant would satisfy the content validity standard.

2. *Construct validity.* In other cases the data may show that the selection procedure measures the degree to which applicants have identifiable characteristics that have been determined to be important for successful job performance. For example, a psychological test that has been shown to test reliably for leadership qualities necessary for a manager's position would be acceptable under this standard.

3. *Criterion-related validity.* Where the data demonstrate that the selection procedure results are predictive of or significantly correlate with measures of job performance, then the procedure is valid. Again, an example of a psychological test revealing cognitive skills that enable a person to do certain problem solving may be valid for a computer programmer or analyst.

NOTE: The key with regard to validation is that the test must measure a skill or characteristic that relates to the performance of the job in a significant way.

Documentation. The adverse impact of a challenged selection procedure must be documented. Where such adverse impact is found with regard to a selection procedure, documentation of the procedure's validity will be required. Employers of fewer than 100 employees may satisfy the documentation requirement by maintaining records that show, for each year

– The number of persons hired, promoted, and terminated for each job, by sex, or where appropriate, by race and national origin
– The number of applicants for hire and promotion by sex, race, and national origin
– The selection procedures utilized

It is suggested that such records be kept for each race and national origin group constituting more than 2 percent of the labor force in the relevant labor area. If there is an indication that the selection procedure has an adverse impact, evidence of validity of the procedure should be compiled and maintained. For certain larger employers, many of these records are already maintained under their affirmative action program.

Testing for Skills

Testing for skills or level of ability may encompass a wide range of tests. Depending upon the job requirements you may be testing for such things as typing; knowledge of computer programming and use; reading comprehension;

strength; welding; crane, truck, or machinery operation; and myriad other skills necessary to a specialized function, whether it is in clerical, manufacturing, or research and development areas.

> NOTE: All tests measuring a particular skill or level of ability must be able to demonstrate a significant relationship between what is being tested and the essential functions of the position.

These tests must be fairly administered and scored. The less objective the test, the more subject it will be to a challenge where there is evidence of discriminatory adverse impact.

Administering Honesty Tests

The use of so-called "honesty" tests, also referred to as personality-based integrity tests, is on the rise due to the restrictions placed on the use of more traditional truth deception tests such as polygraphs. Polygraphs and other traditional truth deception techniques are discussed in detail in the following sections.

Employers considering the use of such tests should observe the following precautions:

1. Research the test and see if it has been involved in any litigation.

2. Request from the vendor of the test independent validation results that indicate the usefulness of the test as a predictor of workplace behavior.

3. Ask the vendor if it will back up the test with expert testimony in the event of litigation.

4. Have the applicants taking the test sign a consent form.

5. Keep the results confidential and reveal only to those persons who have a need to know such information.

6. Track test results with regard to work force and applicant demographics.

7. Use the test as only one tool in the selection process, not as the only tool.

Administering Psychological Tests

Employers are using ever-more- sophisticated testing measures in screening applicants for certain sensitive positions such as air traffic controllers, police officers, nuclear power plant operators, and security-related jobs. Some tests are designed to screen out emotionally unfit applicants and can have hundreds of questions. An example of a psychological test often used is the Minnesota Multiphasic Personality Inventory (MMPI). However, such tests must be administered and used properly—the results, if not applied or analyzed in an appropriate manner, may result in liability to the employer or costly retesting of the subject.[4]

These tests should be used with extreme caution, as the following case example illustrates.

Case Example

Bull's-eye Department Store required applicants for a security guard position to take a psychological screening case, known as "Psychscreen." Three people took the test which had 704 questions. One was hired and two were not. Some of the questions inquired into a person's religious beliefs and sexual orientation. One question stated "I am very strongly attracted by members of my own sex." There were also questions regarding whether one "feels sure that there is only one true religion." All three persons complained later that they were deeply offended by such questions. They sued to prevent the company from using that test on the basis that it violated an individual's right to privacy and the state's anti-discrimination laws.

Result: The court, on appeal, agreed with the plaintiffs and ordered that the company cease use of the test. The court ruled that the company had failed to show the required relationship between the test and the duties of security guards. The company, it was acknowledged, has an interest in employing emotionally stable people, but testing people about their religious or sexual orientation does not further this interest.

The rule established in this case is that the intrusion by the employer into the private life of a person must be justified by a "compelling" interest rather than merely a reasonable need for disclosure of such personal information.[5]

HOW TO USE POLYGRAPHS
AND OTHER TRUTH DECEPTION TECHNIQUES

Polygraph and lie detector tests have traditionally been regulated by the states. The majority of states have enacted some form of statutory limitation on the administration of lie detector tests in the workplace. However, such regulation is no longer limited to the states alone. A federal law enacted in 1988, The Employees Polygraph Protection Act, bans the use of any type of lie detector test by most private sector employers.[6] This section examines the federal legislation and representative state laws regulating the use of lie detector tests in the workplace.

Provisions of the Federal Employees Polygraph Protection Act

Employers cannot require current or prospective employees to take such tests, nor can they request that the test be taken. Employers are prohibited from refusing employment or firing or disciplining employees on the basis of test results or because of refusal to take a test. Employers cannot use, accept, refer to, or inquire about any lie detection test taken by current or prospective employees. Violations of the law may bring substantial penalties.[7]

Exemptions from Coverage. The Act provides for exemptions from its coverage. For example, government employers are exempted. In addition, the national defense and security exemption covers certain private employers working with the Department of Defense, Federal Bureau of Investigation, Central Intelligence Agency, National Security Agency, Defense Intelligence Agency, or Department of Energy.[8]

Exceptions to Prohibition Against Polygraph Use. The federal Act also provides the following limited exceptions to the general prohibition against private sector polygraph use:

- ♦ When the employer's primary business purpose consists of providing security services, which includes the protection of currency,[9] precious commodities or instruments, negotiable securities or proprietary information; electric or nuclear power production and transmission; public water supplies; toxic waste shipments; and other facilities, materials, or operations having a significant impact on health or safety of the public.

- ♦ Where the employer is authorized to manufacture, distribute, or dispense controlled substances; if the test is given in connection to an ongoing criminal investigation and the employee tested had access or would have had access to the subject of the investigation.

- ♦ Employers may test employees in connection with ongoing investigations involving economic loss or injury to the employer, such as theft, embezzlement, misappropriation, unlawful industrial espionage, or sabotage, if certain requirements are met.[10]

Defining the Reasonable Suspicion Requirement. Under the exceptions to the law, the employer may test only those employees who had access to the property that is the subject of the investigation. The employer must have a "reasonable suspicion" that the employee was involved in the incident or activity under investigation. The regulations define "reasonable suspicion" as an observable articulable basis in fact which indicates that a particular employee was involved in, or responsible for, an economic loss. Access in the meaning of possible or potential opportunity, standing alone, does not constitute a basis for reasonable suspicion under the Act.[11]

Case Example Study

Gem Rings, a fine jewelry store, employs ten employees, but only four have authority to open the safe. Gem is conducting an investigation of the theft of two expensive pieces of jewelry, a matching diamond ring and bracelet. Martin was seen in the vicinity of the opened safe one hour before the opening time of the store on the day the theft was discovered. Martin has the safe's combination and is responsible for opening the safe just prior to the daily opening of the store to arrange displays. However, he usually reports to work 15 minutes before opening.

Does reasonable suspicion exist for testing Martin on a polygraph? Maybe. If Martin has no business being near or opening the safe one hour before the store opening and this is an unusual occurrence, the circumstances combined with his access to the safe may constitute sufficient reasonable suspicion under the law. However, if Martin was requested to report to work one hour early that day and had a reason to be near the opened safe, his access, alone, is not sufficient to find reasonable suspicion.

> NOTE: It is the employer's responsibility (burden) to establish that the specific individual to be tested is "reasonably suspected" of involvement in the economic loss or injury under investigation.

How to Conduct Polygraph Testing.   In cases where polygraph testing is permitted, the employer must follow certain procedures set out in the Act and regulations. These procedures are designed to safeguard the rights of the employees being tested and to regulate the proper use of the test results.

The procedure for conducting truth deception tests in connection with an ongoing investigation requires the following:

♦ The employer must file a report with a law enforcement agency, government regulatory agency, or a claim with its insurer or execute a statement detailing the specifics of the incident and basis for testing the employee. Such a statement must be retained for three years.

♦ The employee is provided with reasonable written notice of date, time, and location of the test; of the nature and characteristics of the tests and instruments involved; and of the right to obtain and consult with legal counsel or an employee representative before each phase of the test.

♦ The employee must be allowed to review the questions in advance.

♦ The employer may not ask any questions concerning employees' beliefs or practices with respect to religion, politics, labor unions, racial matters, or sexual behavior or questions designed to degrade or needlessly intrude on the examinee.

♦ The employee may stop the examination at anytime.

♦ The employee may not be fired or disciplined on basis of test results or refusal to take test "without additional supporting evidence" that he or she was involved in the incident under investigation.

♦ The employer must not conduct a test if there is sufficient evidence by a physician that examinee is suffering from a medical or psychological condition or undergoing treatment that may cause abnormal responses during the actual test.

NOTE: Polygraph examiners may not ask employees or job applicants about matters of race, color, religion, sex, or national origin or ask questions concerning membership in or opinion regarding a labor organization.

Avoiding Negligent Administration of Polygraph Test. Although many courts have declined to recognize an action for negligent administration of a lie detector test, it remains an area of potential liability.[12] Liability for such negligent administration may run to the entity actually administering the test.[13] However, the issue remains open in the case where the employer, itself, administers the lie detector test in such a way as to violate a duty of care not to harm the employee.

Employers should consider having all polygraph-type testing conducted by a reliable outside investigative agency so as to remove the direct relationship which may lead to liability in the event of a reckless or negligent administration of such tests.

State Regulations Regarding the Use of Polygraph Tests

Each state has taken its own approach to regulating the use of the lie detector tests in the workplace.[14] Some states have restricted or regulated the use of all forms of lie detection. Other states may restrict only one particular method of lie detection. The degree of regulation varies, that is, it may apply only to those who administer the tests who must meet licensing requirements. Another common form of regulation occurs by limiting the scope of inquiry.

Among the most restrictive laws regulating the use of lie detector tests are those of Massachusetts and New Jersey. Massachusetts absolutely prohibits any employer from subjecting or requesting any employee or prospective employee to take any test that purports to detect deception.[15] The New Jersey statute prohibits an employer from requesting, requiring, or influencing an employee or prospective employee to take or submit to any type of lie detector test.[16] Several other states also forbid employers to require, request or suggest that an employee take or submit to a lie detector test.[17]

Provisions of the New Jersey Statute. New Jersey statutory and case law illustrates one of the most restrictive bans on the use of lie detector tests in employment. The New Jersey statute provides that

[a]ny person who as an employer shall *influence, request* or *require* an employee or prospective employee to take or submit to a lie detector test as a condition of employment or continued employ, commits a disorderly persons offense.[18] [emphasis added]

Under the New Jersey statute, an employer is prohibited from exerting even the slightest pressure on an employee to take a lie detector test. The statute allows only the following exceptions:

1. An employer authorized to manufacture, distribute, or dispense controlled dangerous substances pursuant to the provisions of the New Jersey Controlled Dangerous Substance Act (N.J.A.C. 2C:24.1)

2. An employee or prospective employee who is or will be directly involved in the manufacture, distribution, or dispensing of, or has access to, legally distributed controlled dangerous substances

Where an employer is permitted to test employees, the New Jersey statute imposes limitations on the administration of lie detector tests. The test may not cover a period of time greater than the five years preceding the test. In general, the test is limited to the work of the employee or prospective employee and the individual's improper handling, use, or illegal sale of controlled dangerous substances. Any employee or prospective employee is entitled to be represented by legal counsel.

The information obtained from the test must be provided in writing to the employee upon his or her request and maintained in a confidential manner. The results cannot be released to any other person or employer. The individual tested must be informed of his or her right to present the employer with the results of an independently administered second lie detector test prior to the rendering of any personnel decision based on the original test.

Case Example

Evidence of a theft was discovered implicating the security personnel of Milky Way, a large department store. Certain employees approached the assistant manager and offered to take polygraph tests. Several employees were questioned, and a polygraph machine was brought to the store. One employee, Carla Cane, was asked by her supervisor why she had balked at taking the test. The supervisor also had expressed her desire that all security personnel take the test. Carla did not take the test and was transferred to another store to remove the "cloud" from the department. Carla did not report to her new assignment and, as a result, was discharged.

Did the supervisor's expressed desire that all employees in her department take the test violate a strict statute against administration of lie detectors in the workplace? In this case example, the supervisor's conduct violated New Jersey's polygraph law.[19] A court found that the employer had exerted "psychological influence" upon the employee to take a polygraph test as a condition of continued employment. Such conduct is a violation of the statute. Here a violation of the polygraph ban occurred even though the employee had not actually submitted to a lie detector test.

Determining Liability for Wrongful Discharge. Since statutory proscriptions such as those found in New Jersey and Massachusetts are so broad and consistently applied, the most significant area of concern for employers in these and other states with similar prohibitions (with respect to administering polygraph tests to their employees) is potential liability for wrongful discharge. The termination of an employee because he or she refuses to submit to or "fails" a lie detector test will expose the employer not only to criminal liability under the statute but also to civil liability for the tort of wrongful discharge. This is because the statutory ban on the use of polygraphs in the workplace modifies the employment-at-will relationship.[20]

> NOTE: An employee may be protected from termination in retaliation for the exercise of his or her statutory right to refuse to take a lie detector test, and such conduct should permit the invocation of tort liability for wrongful discharge in breach of clear public policy.[21] Therefore, employers should be mindful that much more than a minor criminal penalty may be incurred if an employer influences, requests, or requires that its employees submit to a lie detector test. It may be subject to significant liability in a wrongful discharge suit as well.

Psychological Stress Evaluators Versus Polygraphs

Psychological stress evaluations (PSEs) and polygraphs differ significantly in administration and operation.[22] The major differences between them are discussed in the paragraphs that follow.

Generally, PSEs consist of techniques designed to detect deception through vocal changes. In other words, a psychological stress evaluator is a mechanical device which purports to determine the truth or falsity of statements on the basis of vocal fluctuation or vocal stress. No physiological contact with the subject's body is necessary. The subject can be tested unknowingly merely by engaging in conversation.

On the other hand, the polygraph is a device that measures three physiological responses simultaneously, that is, breathing pattern, blood pressure and pulse, and skin resistance to external current. These responses are measured by direct contacts with certain portions of the subject's body.

> NOTE: PSEs have been viewed as a gross invasion of an employee's privacy, in part, because such devices can be and are often utilized without the individual's knowledge or consent.

A handful of states specifically regulate or prohibit the use of psychological stress evaluators in the workplace.[23]

In contrast to New Jersey's restrictions, some states have little if any restriction on the use of polygraph tests in the workplace. New York is one such example. New York does not prohibit the use of lie detector or polygraph tests in the employment situation.[24] In such cases, the employer is bound only by the federal law.

Provisions of the New York Statute. New York has made it unlawful for an employer to require, request, suggest, or knowingly permit any employee or prospective employee to submit to a psychological stress evaluator (PSE) examination. "Psychological stress evaluator" is defined, at least in New York, to be "any mechanical device or instrument which purports to determine the truth or falsity of statements made by an employee or prospective employee on the basis of vocal fluctuations or vocal stress."[25] The statute is specifically directed at the employer-employee relationship. An employer faces a misdemeanor criminal charge for violating the statute.

Under the statute, an employee or prospective employee (hereinafter referred to collectively as "employee") is protected against retaliatory discharge or discipline for filing a complaint or testifying in any proceeding involving violation of the statute. An employee damaged as a result of a violation of this statute may file a civil action against the employer. The statute also prohibits the administration of a PSE examination within New York to any individual seeking employment or for the purpose of continuing employment outside the state.

Provisions of Other States' Statutes. States may choose to regulate only a specific test such as the polygraph or voice stress analysis. For example, Maine's statute specifies only "polygraph examination."[26] Moreover, the term "polygraph" is given a broader meaning in some states than in others. For example, Michigan broadly defines "polygraph examination" to include any "procedure which involves the use of instrumentation or a mechanical device to enable or assist the detection of deception."[27]

Contrast Michigan's definition of polygraph to the more common definition of polygraph as a device that measures the physiological responses simultaneously, that is, breathing pattern, blood pressure and pulse, and skin resistance to external current. These responses are measured by direct contacts with certain portions of the subject's body.[28]

Several states permit the use of lie detector tests in the workplace only if an employee knowingly and voluntarily consents.[29] But keep in mind the New Jersey example presented earlier.

Provisions of the Michigan Statute. The Michigan statute provides that an employer may not request or require that an employee or applicant take or submit to a polygraph examination. However, the employee or applicant may voluntarily request to take a polygraph test.[30] The statute sets out the procedure for administering the test to such an employee. The employee must be informed of his or her rights under the statute. The examiner must inform the employee of all specific question areas prior to the examination. The employee may halt the examination at any time. He or she is not required to answer any questions or give any information. Any information volunteered by the employee could be used against the employee or made available to the employer. The examiner must provide the employee with a copy of the test results and all reports done by the examiner that are shared with the employer.

Also, the employer may not take any action against the employee based upon an alleged or actual opinion that the employee did not tell the truth during the polygraph test. The employer must keep information about the results or analysis of an employee's polygraph test strictly confidential. The employer also may not communicate the fact that the employee refused to submit to a polygraph test. Any information obtained from an employee during a polygraph test is not admissible in a criminal proceeding.[31]

Guidelines for Using Polygraph Tests

The federal Act provides a minimum basis for regulation for the use of lie detector tests in the workplace. The individual state statutes are not displaced by the federal law if they impose stricter standards. The state statute remains in force and must be complied with by the employer. Therefore, an employer should become familiar with both the federal law and the applicable state statute regarding truth deception tests. The following is a set of general guidelines that highlight the most common restrictions on the use of lie detector tests in the workplace.

In general, where lie detector tests are permitted in the workplace, it is likely that the state has specific procedures in place. The employer should adopt policies that comply with the statutory requirements and restrict the scope of the inquiry to avoid potential liability.

Where an employer is permitted to administer lie detector tests to its employees, it should

1. Determine the applicable state and federal law.

2. Develop a checklist of the proper state and federal procedures to ensure compliance.

3. Test only where there is a specific need or reason warranting such testing.

4. Restrict the scope of the inquiry to the incident or activity under investigation and where reasonable suspicion supports such testing.

5. Use only reliable and licensed polygraph examiners.

6. Avoid any questions with regard to the individual's opinions or affiliations regarding religion, race, politics, sexual behavior, marital status, and labor organizations (unless such questions are relevant to the investigation).

7. Test all the individuals who have access to or involvement with the incident or activity under investigation and where reasonable suspicion supports such testing.

8. Avoid random testing of employees or prospective employees.

9. Provide written notice of the rights the subjects may have prior to testing.

10. Obtain a voluntary and knowing waiver whenever possible and permissible.

11. If the test result is inconclusive or indicates deception, retest the employee.

12. Always maintain all information obtained during testing including the results with strict confidentiality.

13. Avoid relying solely on the lie detector test result and support any adverse employment decision with other evidence.

DRUG AND ALCOHOL TESTING IN THE WORKPLACE

Employers have increased the use of testing and screening for drug and alcohol use in the workplace. Substance abuse by employees causes significant losses in terms of lower productivity and quality, lost work hours, higher rate of accidents and injuries, increased health costs, and property loss through damage or theft.

This section will address an overall view of the restrictions placed on employers who wish to test their employees for drugs and alcohol use. A number of factors impact on the employer's ability to insist on such tests, including private or public status of the employer, method of testing, random or suspicion-based testing, public safety interest, as well as many others. Employers are subject to federal and state regulations governing such testing. This area of the employment relationship is far from settled, with ever-increasing legislation anticipated on both the state and federal levels.

Drug and alcohol testing procedures may be conducted in a variety of ways. The policy may call for

- Random (without notice) testing, also referred to as "suspicionless" testing

- Mandatory testing for all employees with or without notice

- Postaccident testing (testing only employees involved in an accident or injury on the job)
- Reasonable suspicion testing

Reasonable suspicion testing may be based upon, among other things,

- Observable phenomena, such as direct observation of drug use or possession and/or other physical symptoms of being under the influence of a drug
- A pattern of abnormal conduct or erratic behavior
- Arrest or conviction for a drug-related offense or the identification of an employee as the focus of a criminal investigation into illegal drug possession, use, or trafficking
- Information provided either by reliable and credible sources or independently corroborated
- Newly discovered evidence that the employee has tampered with a previous drug test

Although reasonable suspicion testing does not require certainty, mere "hunches" are not sufficient to meet this standard.

The type of test used to determine the presence and/or level of drug or alcohol also varies. Tests may range from the well-publicized urinalysis, blood tests, breathalyzer (for alcohol), or hair samples. The different tests have varying levels of reliability and accuracy, especially if carelessly conducted and a proper history of the subject is not recorded. Some of these methods are more prone to tampering (especially urinalysis) than others, and the costs associated with these tests vary significantly. Thus many difficult choices are presented when an employer seeks to institute such testing programs in the workplace.

> NOTE: Certain drugs remain in the body for long periods of time and may result in a positive test despite absence of recent use. Presence of a prohibited drug does not always equate with impairment. Presence-only testing opens up issues of the employer's right to regulate off-duty conduct, and if no impairment is shown, what is the basis for disciplinary action?

Requirements for Testing in the Public Sector

The government and its various subdivisions and agencies have significant restrictions placed upon them with regard to testing their employees for drug use. Public employers are subject to the Fourth and Fourteenth Amendments to the U.S. Constitution that prohibit unreasonable search and seizure.[32] The administration of a drug test to government employees constitutes a search under the Constitution. Such a search must be reasonable. As a consequence of this requirement, the most frequent reported cases challenging the legality of drug testing involve government employees.

Defining the Constitutional Standard. What constitutes a reasonable search in a governmental workplace? The U.S. Supreme Court introduced a two-part analysis in responding to this question. First, it is determined what a government employee's reasonable expectation of privacy is in the particular context of the search (i.e., drug or alcohol testing). Then a balancing of interests is applied to determine the appropriate standard of reasonableness applicable to the search. The Court stated that the standard of reasonableness requires "balancing the nature and quality of the intrusion on the individual's Fourth Amendment interests against the importance of the governmental interests alleged to justify the intrusion."[33]

> NOTE: In the case of a public employer search, the invasion of the employees' legitimate expectations of privacy must be balanced against the government's need for supervision, control, and the efficient operation of the workplace.[34] Thus the search or drug test must be reasonable in its inception and scope.

In addition, the manner of testing must provide guarantee of accuracy and reliability to meet the reasonableness standard required under the Fourth Amendment. The testing procedures must also have safeguards to ensure, among other things, nonadulteration of specimen, protection of chain of custody, and provisions for a confirmatory test.

Recognizing Legitimate Governmental Interests. Government interests are recognized as legitimate bases for requiring mandatory drug testing, in appropriate circumstances. The following concerns are sometimes sufficiently compelling to justify mandatory drug testing in the absence of individualized suspicion:

– Government's interest in maintaining the integrity of its work force

– Public safety

– Protection of "truly sensitive information"[35]

These concerns have been the basis for upholding testing of employees in specific industries or areas of government-related work.

Specific Employment Categories for Drug Testing. Public employees fall into different categories for purposes of drug testing restrictions. The level of reasonableness varies with the type of work performed by particular employees.

Categories where random drug testing has been upheld are those that directly impact on safety-sensitive positions and include

- Railroad officials
- Customs operators
- Bridge operators [36]
- Power plant employees
- Police and fire
- Corrections officers[37]
- Department of Transportation
- Army Department civilians or employees in aviation jobs
- Justice Department employees with top-secret security clearances

With regard to employees who are not in direct public safety positions, the public employer must negotiate policy and procedures for testing clerical workers, teachers, and those employees who perform other nonsafety-related tasks. Such testing programs may be pursuant to an incident-based and/or reasonable suspicion–based policy rather than on a random basis or mandatory basis. Across-the-board mandatory testing of employees not suspected of illicit drug use or who are not in safety sensitive jobs has been invalidated.[38]

Provisions of the Omnibus Transportation Employee Testing Act.

In 1991, Congress enacted the Omnibus Transportation Employee Testing Act, which provides for drug and alcohol testing of persons who operate aircraft, trains, and commercial motor vehicles, including trucks and buses.[39] The Act not only requires testing, it requires that rehabilitation programs be implemented.

The Act provides minimum testing requirements for pre-employment, reasonable suspicion, and random and postaccident testing of airmen, crew members, airport security screening personnel, and other air carrier employees responsible for safety-sensitive functions. Employees of the Federal Aviation Administration responsible for safety-sensitive functions are subject to similar testing. Similar requirements are established for all railroad, motor carriers, commercial motor vehicles, and mass transportation employees responsible for safety-sensitive functions.

The Department of Transportation (DOT) has instituted extensive regulations regarding drug testing of certain employees and when, where, and how such testing is to be done.[40] These rules govern workplace drug testing programs in six transportation industries: U.S. Coast Guard, Federal Aviation Administration, Federal Railroad Administration, Federal Highway Administration, the Urban Mass Transportation Administration, and the Research and Special Programs Administration. The DOT drug testing rules apply to any entity employing one or more employees subject to the DOT regulations. The drugs tested for include marijuana, cocaine, opiates, amphetamines and phencyclidine. The regulations provide detailed requirements for all aspects of the testing procedure, from preparation for testing, chain of custody, specimen collection, laboratory personnel and analysis, confirmatory testing, quality assurance and control, reporting and reviewing results, and confidentiality of employee test records to access by the individual to his or her own test records.[41]

How to Handle Off-Duty Drug Use. An issue that frequently surfaces when drug testing reveals it, is off-duty use of illicit drugs. Since traces of drugs remain in the body for some time after use, a weekend indulgence will show up on a test conducted the following week. Thus an employee who tests positive is subject to discipline for using drugs even though there is no evidence that the drug use took place in the workplace. Government employers may test for such off-duty use where the employee occupies a safety- or security-sensitive position. However, such testing of employees who do not hold safety- or security-related jobs even when testing is based upon reasonable suspicion is unconstitutional where the government cannot establish a relationship between off-duty drug use and government efficiency or general integrity or deterrence rationales.[42]

> NOTE: The government cannot intrude upon constitutionally protected privacy interests of ordinary employees with speculation about possible future job impairment or rules violations.

A government employer may test workers who do not hold safety or security-sensitive positions only where reasonable suspicion exists of on-duty drug use or drug-impaired performance.

Complying with the Drug-Free Federal Workplace Mandate

President Reagan issued Executive Order 12564 (Order) in 1986 ordering random urinalysis drug testing for federal employees in sensitive positions and for reasonable suspicion testing for other federal employees. E.O. 12564 subjects more than 1 million federal employees to random drug testing for illegal drug use.[43] This Order has the force of law, and federal agencies must comply with its provisions.

The purpose of the Order is to improve the efficiency of the federal service and establish standards and procedures to ensure fairness in achieving a drug-free workplace and to protect the privacy of federal employees. The Order applies to all agencies of the Executive Branch of the federal government.[44] The head of each executive agency must develop a plan for achieving the objective of a drug free workplace. Each agency plan must include

- Statement of policy
- Employee assistance programs with provisions for education, counseling, referral to rehabilitation, and coordination with community resources

- Supervisory training to assist in identifying and addressing illegal drug use

- Provision for self-referrals as well as supervisory referrals to treatment with respect for individual confidentiality consistent with safety and security issues

- Provision for identifying illegal drug users, including testing in a controlled and carefully monitored manner

Drug Testing Under E.O. 12564. The Order mandates testing for the use of illegal drugs by employees in sensitive positions. The extent to which employees are tested and the criteria for such testing are determined by the agency head, based upon the following factors:

- Nature of the agency's mission and its employees' duties

- Efficient use of agency resources

- Danger to public health and safety or national security that could result from the failure of an employee adequately to perform his or her duty

Other bases for testing employees for illegal drug use may be

- Voluntary employee drug testing

- A reasonable suspicion that an employee uses illegal drugs

- An examination authorized by the agency regarding an accident or unsafe practice

- As part of or as a follow-up to counseling or rehabilitation for illegal drug use through an employer assistance program

In general, the agency head is authorized under the Order to test any applicant for illegal drug use.

Testing Procedures Under E.O. 12564. The Order sets forth the basic notice and procedural requirements for drug testing in the federal workplace. These procedures include

- Providing 60 days' advance notice to employees of the agency's implementation of a drug testing program and permitting employees to seek counseling and rehabilitation

- Prior to conducting the drug test, permitting employees to submit medical documentation supporting the legitimate use of a specific drug

- Testing programs that have procedures for the timely requests for retention of records and specimens, retesting, and confidentiality of results and related medical and rehabilitation records

– Developing procedures for collecting urine specimens that allow individual privacy unless the agency has reason to believe that a particular individual may alter or substitute the specimen to be provided

– Testing in accordance with appropriate scientific and technical guidelines promulgated by the Secretary of Health and Human Services

Personnel Actions That May Be Taken. The agency, in addition to taking appropriate personnel actions, is to refer any employee found to be using illegal drugs to an employee assistance program (EAP)[45] for assessment and counseling. Disciplinary action is initiated against any employee found to be using illegal drugs. However, no disciplinary action should be taken in the following circumstances:

◆ Employee has identified himself or herself as a user of illegal drugs or who volunteers for drug testing, prior to being identified through other means

◆ Employee obtains counseling or rehabilitation through an EAP

◆ Employee thereafter refrains from using illegal drugs.

An employee who is found to use illegal drugs is not permitted to remain on duty in a sensitive position. An employee may be returned to active status, upon successful completion of rehabilitation, or as part of a rehabilitation or counseling program, if it is determined that this action would not pose a danger to public health, safety, or national security.

Removal from service occurs when an employee who is found to use illegal drugs

– Refuses to obtain counseling or rehabilitation through an EAP, or

– Does not thereafter refrain from using illegal drugs.

NOTE: Any action to discipline an employee who is using illegal drugs, including removal, must be taken in compliance with otherwise applicable procedures, including the Civil Service Reform Act.

Testing is not the only method of determining whether an employee is using illegal drugs under the Order. Other appropriate evidence includes direct observation, a criminal conviction, or administrative inquiry. A positive drug test result may be rebutted by other evidence that an employee has not used illegal drugs. Moreover, confirmed positive test results may be considered in the processing of any adverse action against the employee or for other administrative purposes. Finally, the Order provides that drug testing may not be conducted for the purposes of gathering evidence for use in criminal proceedings.

E.O. 12564 represents significant restrictions in the federal workplace. Federal agencies are bound to develop and implement antidrug policy and testing procedures.

Meeting the Requirements of the Drug-Free Workplace Act of 1988

Federal contractors and recipients of federal grants are required to maintain drug-free workplaces under the Drug-Free Workplace Act of 1988.[46] The Act is a natural outgrowth of E.O. 12564 but differs from the Order in several respects. For example, drug testing is not required under the Act but has similar provisions favoring rehabilitation through an employee assistance program.

> NOTE: A "drug-free workplace" means a site for the performance of work done in connection with a federal contract at which the employees of the contractor are prohibited from engaging in the unlawful manufacture, distribution, dispensation, possession, or use of controlled substances.[47]

The Act imposes several obligations upon a federal contractor for that contractor to be eligible to receive government contracts. The requirements imposed upon contractors under the Act are discussed in paragraphs that follow.

Elements of the Act. The Act applies to contractors awarded a federal contract for procurement of property or services in the amount of $25,000 or more. Such contractors must certify that they will provide a drug-free workplace.

If a single contractor has several contracts that when added together total $25,000 or more, the contractor is not subject to the Act. The contractor is subject to the provisions of the Act only if the value of a single contract is $25,000 or more.

The certification must provide that the contractor has done the following:

♦ Published a statement notifying employees that the unlawful manufacture, distribution, dispensation, possession, or use of a controlled substance is prohibited in the person's workplace and specifying the actions that will be taken against employees for violations of such prohibition.

♦ Established a drug-free awareness program informing employees about
- The dangers of drug abuse in the workplace
- The policy for maintaining a drug-free workplace
- Any available drug counseling rehabilitation and employee assistance programs
- The penalties that may be imposed upon employees for drug abuse violation.

♦ Given to each employee working under the contract a copy of the drug-free policy statement required.

♦ Notified employees that as a condition of employment under the contract, the employee will
  – Abide by the terms of the drug-free policy statement
  – Notify the employer of any criminal drug statute conviction for a violation occurring in the workplace no later than 5 days after such conviction.

♦ Agreed to notify the contracting agency within 10 days after receiving notice of a drug-related criminal conviction from an employee or otherwise receiving actual notice of such conviction.

♦ Agreed to impose a sanction on an employee who has such a conviction or requiring the satisfactory participation in a drug abuse assistance or rehabilitation program by the employee.

♦ Agreed to make a good faith effort to continue a drug-free workplace through the implementation of a policy outlined in these provisions.

Contracts performed partly inside the United States and partly outside the country are covered by the Act, but the Act applies to only those portions of the contract to be performed inside the United States.

Imposing Employee Sanctions and Implementing Remedies.
The Act makes the contractor the enforcer in the workplace regarding illegal drug use. The contractor, within 30 days of receiving notice of an employee's criminal conviction for drug-related violations in the workplace, must take the following action (in addition to notifying the agency promptly of such conviction):

♦ Take appropriate personnel action against the employee up to and including termination.

♦ Require such employee to satisfactorily participate in an approved drug abuse assistance or rehabilitation program.

Penalties for Noncompliance.
The Act provides certain penalties in the event that the head of the contracting federal agency determines that the contractor has violated the provisions of the Act or has failed in its obligations under the Act. The following events will trigger penalties:

♦ The contractor has made a false certification.

♦ The contractor violates the certification by failing to carry out the requirements of the law.

♦ Such a number of the contractor's employees have been convicted of criminal drug statutes for violations occurring in the workplace as to indicate that the contractor has failed to make a good faith effort to provide a drug-free workplace as required under the law.

The penalties for the violations include

- Suspension of payments under the contract
- Termination of the contract
- Or both
- Suspension or debarment

Suspension or debarment under the Act is extremely serious for a government contractor. The effect of a suspension or debarment is to render the contractor ineligible to compete for or acquire any government contracts from that agency for a set period of time (but less than five years) in the case of suspension and a complete ban on any government contract from any agency in the case of debarment (but not to exceed 5 years). Generally, a contractor is permitted to rehabilitate its conduct or procedures, in which case the agency may reinstate the contractor's bidding privileges. Also, the Act provides that the head of the agency may waive any or all of these penalties if it would result in serious disruption to the operation of the agency to the detriment of the federal government or general public.

The contracting agency, prior to imposing these penalties on a contractor, must notify the contractor in writing of the violation(s). The agency takes appropriate action pursuant to the Federal Acquisition Regulation and its own agency procedures. The contractor must be provided with notice, opportunity to respond in writing or in person, and such other procedures as may be necessary to provide a full and fair proceeding to the contractor.

For more information on drug-free government workplace requirements, the Office of Management and Budget has issued final rules implementing the requirements of the Drug-Free Workplace Act.[48]

Requirements for Testing in the Private Sector

In contrast to government or public sector employers, private sector employers are not subject to the same restrictions regarding drug or alcohol testing of their employees. The prohibition of the Fourth Amendment against unreasonable search and seizure does not apply in the private sector. Private sector employers have been utilizing drug testing procedures more and more, spurred on, in part, by the Drug-Free Workplace Act of 1988.

Substance abuse by employees in the workplace takes a high toll in terms of productivity, performance, absenteeism, and health care costs, as well as liability to third parties. Employers seeking to reduce the damage caused by substance abuse–related problems in the workplace may consider implementing a drug testing program. Such programs should set up objective screening criteria as the bases for personnel actions.

Drug testing in the private sector has been upheld in the following situations:

♦ A preemployment drug test policy did not violate the privacy clause in the California constitution by requiring job applicants to provide urine samples for drug screening.[49]

♦ Random drug testing of employees by private employer did not violate the New Jersey or federal constitutions with regard to unreasonable searches or privacy rights.[50]

Heavily Regulated Industries. This does not mean, however, that the private sector employers may test any or all of their employees with impunity. Certain heavily regulated industries may have specific drug testing regulations.

For example, random drug testing of jockeys and others in the horseracing industry has been upheld. In support of this result, the courts found that the horseracing industry is subject to extensive governmental regulation, legitimate concern for safety and health of participants in racing, and financial concern in the tax dollars collected from parimutuel betting.[51]

How to Avoid Liability in States with Constitutional Right of Privacy. In states where a constitutional right of privacy may restrict an employer's right to conduct drug testing, the following criteria generally will avoid liability:

♦ The drug testing policy provides notice in advance to applicants and employees that testing will occur

♦ The sample is collected during regular preemployment physical examination conducted by medical personnel under conditions designed to minimize intrusiveness of the procedure

♦ Procedural safeguards exist to restrict access to test results.[52]

Random Testing and Public Policy. Many employees have brought challenges to random drug testing in the private sector as a wrongful discharge in violation of public policy. However, random testing has been found not to violate public policy and that neither individualized suspicion nor a special need for such testing is required.[53] Thus an employee discharged on the grounds of a positive test result may not maintain an action for wrongful discharge in violation of public policy in such jurisdictions.

This is not an established rule and may vary from state to state, depending upon how broad or narrow the public policy exception is interpreted. Check with counsel as to your state's position in this matter.

Unions and Drug/Alcohol Testing

Drug and alcohol testing by employers with a work force represented by a union involves additional concerns. The decision to implement or modify an existing testing program is a mandatory subject of bargaining; that is, the employer must bargain with the union regarding such plans.[54] Under the position enunciated by the National Labor Relations Board, the employer who seeks to implement or modify a drug/alcohol testing program must

- Notify the union in advance of institution of or change in the program

- Upon request, bargain with the union about the matter

NOTE: Employers must bargain in good faith with the union about a decision to institute drug or alcohol testing and the content, procedures, and effects of such a program.

The union must be given a meaningful opportunity for bargaining about such testing. A drug/alcohol testing plan may be implemented only after the parties reach an agreement *or* their negotiations deadlock in a good faith impasse.[55] See our discussion on mandatory issues of bargaining and impasse in Chapter 21 on collective bargaining.

The Americans with Disabilities Act and Drug Testing

The Americans with Disabilities Act (ADA), discussed extensively in Chapter 8, provides that employers may conduct drug tests in the workplace. It especially sanctions the use of preemployment drug testing. However, the Act specifically provides that "rehabilitated drug users" and "recovered alcoholics" are disabled under the Act and are protected from employment discrimination on the basis of past drug use or alcoholism. To avoid possible liability and minimize challenges under the ADA, the employer should offer rehabilitation to employees who test positive. The offer of an assistance program shows that the employer tried to accommodate an employee's drug or alcohol problem. However, the employer should limit the number of times treatment is offered before discipline is imposed, and the employee should be held strictly accountable for staying off drugs or alcohol.

Thirteen Guidelines for Establishing a Drug/Alcohol Testing Program

The decision to implement and maintain a drug/alcohol testing policy is a complex matter. Many issues must be carefully weighed and balanced. The employer must be committed to conducting its testing program in a proper and considerate manner. The restrictions on such testing vary: the following are general guidelines to assist any employer who is considering instituting a testing program or already has one in place.

1. Develop and publicize your organization's commitment to a drug- and alcohol-free workplace. Institute, with notice and explanation to employees, straightforward and consistent policies and procedures for drug and alcohol testing.

2. Educate employees about the dangers that substance abuse poses to their lives both at work and at home with regard to marital, financial, health, safety, career, and other such matters.

3. Advise employees what substances will be tested for, the method(s) of testing, procedures, and the fact that results and other information obtained (such as a medical condition or pregnancy) will remain confidential.

4. Maintain strict confidentiality of the fact of the test, the results, and other information, and limit access to such information to only those management officials who have a need to know. For example, designate a single individual to receive the laboratory reports, preferably a medical or human resources official.

5. Use only a reputable testing service and laboratory that use appropriate confirmation tests. Run periodic audits and establish built-in checks to assure the integrity of the results.

NOTE: An employer's greatest liability exposure lies in the manner in which a test is conducted and how the results are communicated.

6. Institute an employee assistance program offering assistance to employees who need help. Such a program reinforces the employer's commitment to a drug/alcohol-free workplace.

7. Consider "preventive" drug and alcohol tests for applicants and annual physical examinations for employees, but only if you are prepared to commit the resources necessary to test and follow up properly.

8. Do not institute a drug/alcohol testing program unless you determine after careful investigation and research that such testing would be appropriate for your organization. It is costly to maintain and could be a source of costly litigation as well.

9. Keep in mind that testing is not a substitute for effective supervision; whenever possible, testing should be used to confirm, not replace, the informed judgments of experienced supervisors.

10. Train your supervisors to recognize the symptoms of impairment or chronic abuse of drugs or alcohol. Effective supervision, observation, and investigation will aid either in eliminating the substance abuse as a cause of the problem or in providing "cause" to conduct a test.

11. Remember that even if the individual should test negative, there may exist a serious problem unrelated to drug or alcohol that poses a potential danger in the workplace and for which the employee may need assistance.

12. Do not rely only on proof of "presence" of a prohibited substance—if you can prove impairment do so.

13. Avoid random testing without notice, except in safety-sensitive positions. However, it may be used as follow-up in a dependency treatment situation to monitor the employee after treatment for a period of time.

HANDLING THE EMPLOYEE'S RIGHT TO PRIVACY

Employers are increasingly using various methods to observe and monitor employee performance, productivity, honesty, and employee theft of company materials and goods and for other investigatory purposes in the workplace. The increased use of drug testing, electronic monitoring, and other methods of investigation has spurred increased sensitivity of employees about their right to privacy both in and outside of the workplace. As employment claims broaden and lawsuits increase, allegations of breach of privacy will become more common. Various methods of investigation and monitoring of employee's performance and the like require a balance between the needs of the employer to know what is going on and the personal privacy rights of employees.

Studies have revealed that as many as 6 million workers in 1987 were being monitored. Also as many as 66 percent of all computer operators are monitored. Legislation has been proposed, but not yet passed, that would require surveillance to be relevant to an employee's job performance and would give employees the right to see the information gathered.[56]

Many concerns are raised by monitoring techniques, searches, and surveillance in the workplace. This section addresses the privacy concerns of employees as it conflicts with the employer's right and/or desire to a safe, productive, and profitable workplace.

Identifying Sources of Privacy Rights

An employee's privacy interest is protected in many jurisdictions by federal and state statute, common law or public policy, and, in particular for public employees, the U.S. Constitution. The right to privacy is purely a personal one. The right goes to the individual alone who must show an invasion of his or her own right of privacy before he or she can recover.

NOTE: The standard by which the alleged invasion of privacy is measured is the "ordinary person." However, ordinary inconveniences and annoyances which commonly face employees and people in general are not actionable; it is only where the intrusion has gone beyond the limits of decency that liability will accrue.

In workplace privacy actions, the most significant factual issue determining liability is whether the person who allegedly committed the invasion of privacy had legitimate reasons to take the actions that are the subject of the lawsuit. Also extremely significant is the individual employee's expectation of privacy with regard to the intrusion. Where a legitimate purpose is not served, an employer may become liable for an invasion of privacy, as for example, a supervisor's unnecessary inquiry into an employee's home life or a manager's disclosure of an employee's psychiatric history to the employee's coworkers may lead to employer liability for such conduct.

Monitoring in the Workplace

A number of claims have arisen with regard to various monitoring techniques and procedures utilized in the workplace. Generally, it is some form of electronic monitoring that occurs using computers, telephones, video cameras, and/or internal company communication systems. The advent of electronic mail (interoffice communications via computer terminals) has raised issues regarding employee's privacy rights clashing with employer's monitoring the use of its own equipment. The purpose of workplace monitoring may range from a desire to improve productivity to controlling spiraling costs attributable to employee theft or misconduct or as a way of measuring or evaluating employee performance. All types of electronic monitoring involve issues of prior notice to employees, employees' expectation of privacy, and employees' consent to the monitoring.

NOTE: Any employer considering electronic monitoring of its workplace must be aware that in implementing such monitoring, it may be violating federal and/or state antieavesdropping statutes, implicating employee privacy concerns or straying into union-related issues.

Provisions of the Federal Antieavesdropping Statute. Federal law prohibits public and private employers from surreptitiously intercepting any employee's wire, oral, or electronic communications. The Federal Omnibus Crime Control and Safe Streets Act of 1968 [57] provides for the imposition of criminal and civil penalties, including the award of actual and punitive damages, equitable relief, attorney's fees, and litigation costs to individuals whose wire, oral, or electronic communications are illegally monitored.

The federal Act contains an exception that permits an employer "in the ordinary course of its business" to monitor employees' telephone calls. [58] This is the so-called "telephone exception." The following example illustrates this exception. An additional exemption contained in the Act legitimatizes the interception of oral communications if any one of the parties to the communication gives prior consent to the interception.

Case Example

News, Inc., instituted a monitoring system on the employees' telephone lines. It provided advanced notice of the monitoring, and the system was installed by the telephone company. The purpose of the company's monitoring was to improve employee training, supervision to those employees dealing with the public by telephone, and to help thwart abusive telephone calls from irate customers. The telephone calls were monitored during business hours only.

Did News, Inc., violate the Federal Omnibus Act? No. The company gave advance notice to its employees that it was instituting this monitoring system, and there was a legitimate purpose expressed for such system. In addition, the monitoring was limited to telephone calls during business hours. This qualified under the federal Act as coming within the telephone exception rule.[59]

NOTE: An employer's continued monitoring of an employee's telephone call after the employer could reasonably conclude that an employee was not on a business call, but was personal, may violate the federal law.[60]

Provisions of the State Antieavesdropping Laws. Some   states have enacted antieavesdropping, wiretapping, or electronic surveillance statutes which provide for the imposition of criminal penalties for violations. The statutes vary from jurisdiction to jurisdiction; however, many mirror the federal law and contain a similar "telephone exception" and a prior consent exception.

Personnel professionals must analyze both the federal and state law relevant to their location when investigating the implementation of electronic surveillance in the workplace. The state laws may differ from the federal law in significant areas that affect an employee's individual right. For example, Maryland's prior consent exception requires consent from all parties to the communication, whereas federal law requires consent from only one party.[61] In addition, other states restrict employer surveillance of employee activity in certain locations within the workplace, typically private places such as rest rooms.[62]

NOTE: Virtually in all cases of electronic surveillance under federal or state statutes, the courts will evaluate the legitimacy of an employer's right to conduct such surveillance where no legitimate reason exists for it.[63]

Conducting Searches in the Workplace

Workplace searches often occur during an investigation of criminal activity or loss of products or goods. The courts have drawn a distinction between permissible searches by public employers versus private employers. In the public sector, the expectation of privacy is deemed stronger than in the private sector. Public employers must be concerned that their actions may violate the Fourth Amendment prohibition against unlawful searches and seizures. On the other hand, searches conducted by private employers may be subject to legal challenge on a number of grounds; however, such challenges are rarely successful.

For example, a reasonably conducted search of employees as part of a legitimate workplace investigation or as part of an announced policy is likely to be held lawful in the face of invasion of privacy or other legal challenges. Employees who are likely to succeed on these claims are those who can show that a reasonable expectation of privacy has been violated by the employer's behavior.

Case Example

Eddie Lane, an employee of the Big Mart Store, put his own personal lock on his company locker. The employer removed the lock.

The court found that the employer was found to have unreasonably intruded into the employee's privacy by removing the personal lock on the company locker.[64] The personal lock exhibited an expectation of privacy on the part of the employee.

NOTE: Employees who refuse to submit to a search even when it would otherwise be illegal, may not bring a cause of action for invasion of privacy based on alleged unlawful behavior that never occurred. Also, the taking of photographs at work in common areas does not constitute a search or invasion of an employee's privacy. Similarly, the use of a metal detector to detect weapons or stolen goods has been found to be lawful.[65]

Employer searches may survive a challenge and found to be lawful if

- A policy exists and has been disseminated to employees authorizing searches and stating under what circumstances and in what manner searches will be conducted
- Consent from the employee has been obtained
- The search has been conducted in a responsible, nondiscriminatory manner

Thus a reasonably conducted search of employees and the workplace as part of a legitimate investigation or as part of an announced policy is likely to be found lawful in the face of an invasion of privacy claim.

Union or Collective Bargaining Concerns

In a unionized workplace, the employer's unilateral implementation of electronic monitoring of employees or a change in an existing surveillance or search policy may violate a duty to bargain over such changes. This issue remains open. For example, the National Labor Relations Board found that the employer's unilateral decision to produce videotape of employees for dissemination to employees to demonstrate company policies did not violate employer's duty to bargain where employee participation was voluntary.[66] See our discussion on the employer's duty to bargain regarding drug and alcohol testing in Chapter 21 on collective bargaining.

However, arbitrators in grievance proceedings seem willing to admit evidence obtained through monitoring and validate employer use of electronic monitoring if the employer has a reasonable basis for such monitoring or where employees were informed in advance of the monitoring. Thus the use of a closed-circuit television to observe employees for the purpose of detecting and preventing loss of material and equipment from the receiving department has been ruled legal.[67] So has the installation of a videotape camera system scanning the employee entrance to the plant to monitor the time clock area to confirm suspected violations.[68]

For non-union employers, a concern raised by the implementation of monitoring procedures where the employer surveillance of employees which is surreptitious lacks justification, or which is inherently unreasonable, may be the impetus to union organizing. Thus it is critical that the decision to implement electronic monitoring in the workplace is carefully investigated, researched, and analyzed with regard to the particular needs of the employer and the ramifications of such a decision.

ENDNOTES

1. The EEOC Guidelines are codified in 29 C.F.R. Part 1607. These Guidelines apply only to those entities subject to Title VII and in no way apply to responsibilities under the Age Discrimination in Employment Act, the Vocational Rehabilitation Act, or Americans with Disability Act regarding age and handicap discrimination, respectively.

2. See our discussion on adverse impact in Chapter 5 regarding discrimination theories under Title VII.

3. See *Albermarle Paper Co. v. Moody*, 422 U.S. 405 (1975), and *Robinson v. Lorillard Corp.*, 444 F.2d 405 (4th Cir. 1971).

4. See *Newsome v. Ward*, a New York City case reported in the *New York Law Journal*, October 10, 1991, wherein a police officer candidate's results on an MMPI test were incorrectly relied upon for rejection.

5. See *Soroka v. Dayton Hudson Corp.*, 6 I.E.R. Cases (BNA) 1491 (Cal. Ct. App. 1991), rejecting the rule that private employers need show only a reasonable need for requiring job applicants to take urinalysis tests as stated in *Wilkinson v. Times-Mirror Corp.*, 4 I.E.R. Cases (BNA) 1579 (Cal. Ct. App. 1988).

6. 29 U.S.C. §2001, *et seq.*

7. Wendy's Restaurants was found by the Department of Labor (DOL) to have unlawfully forced employees to take lie detector tests, and the DOL proposed a fine of $315,000 for the 152 individual testing violations. An additional fine of $10,000 may be imposed due to the firing of an employee based upon results of an illegal test. The company will likely seek an administrative hearing to challenge the proposed penalties. See I.E.R. *BNA Labor Relations Reporter*, Vol. 6, no. 8, April 23, 1991.

8. 29 U.S.C. §§2006(a) and (b).

9. Employers who are in the business of providing security services to institutions such as casinos, racetracks, lotteries, and "other business" activities where large amounts of cash are acquired from or dispensed to customers. 29 C.F.R. §801.24(e) (1991).

10. 29 U.S.C. §§2006(d–f).

11. 29 C.F.R. §801.12(f).

12. See *Burwell v. Dean Witter Reynolds, Inc.*, a pre-Act case, (New York Supreme Court, New York County, 1A of Part 4), in which the court dismissed such a claim in a wrongful termination action. *New York Law Journal*, June 5, 1990, p. 1; and *Hall v. United Parcel Service*, 544 N.Y.S.2d 250 (4th Dept. 1990).

13. *Zampatori v. United Parcel Service*, 125 Misc.2d 405 (N.Y. Sup. Ct. 1984). The claim against the employer, UPS, was dismissed on summary judgment but remained against the investigative agency that conducted the test.

14. The following states have *not* regulated the administration of lie detector tests in the workplace: Colorado, Indiana, Missouri, New Hampshire, Ohio, South Dakota, and Wyoming.

15. Mass. Gen. Laws Ann., Ch. 149, §§19B(1) and (2). The single exception is a test administered by law enforcement agencies in aid of a criminal investigation. The District of Columbia similarly prohibits *any* use of lie detection tests in employment. D.C. Law 2-154.

16. N.J.S.A. 2C:40A-1. This statute permits an exception for drug use manufacturers or distributors whose employees have or would have access to controlled dangerous substances.

17. See for Alaska, Alaska Stat., §23.10.037; for Delaware, Del. Code, Title 19, §704; for Iowa, Iowa Code §321-5-56; for Maine, Me. Rev. Stat. Ann., Ch. 87, L. 17.79, §§7151, 7167; for Minnesota, Minn. Stat. Ann., §181.75; for Washington, Wash. Rev. Code Ann., §49.44.120; for Wisconsin, Wis. Stat. Ann., §111.326.

18. N.J.S.A. 2C:40A-1, *et seq.* A disorderly persons offense is a misdemeanor conviction that generally results in a fine. Contrast this with the Pennsylvania statute which provides a criminal penalty only "for whoever *requires*" a polygraph test as a condition of employment or continued employment, 18 Pa.C.S.A. §7321(a). Under Pennsylvania Law a properly executed waiver may constitute a valid defense. See *Polsky v. Radio Shack,* 666 F.2d 824, 829 (3d Cir. 1981). But see *Berkey Photo,* 150 N.J. Super. 56 (App. Div. 1977) (in which waivers signed by employees after being informed of the statutory ban did not constitute a defense to violation of the New Jersey statute).

19. *State v. Vornado, Inc.,* 155 N.J. Super. 354 (App. Div. 1978).

20. Generally, an employer is free to discharge an employee-at-will for any nondiscriminatory reason or no reason. However, many states have recognized that employment-at-will situations may be modified where termination results from a breach of public policy. See the discussion on the at-will employment relationship in Chapter 11. Legislation is the primary source of public policy.

21. *Citizen State Bank of New Jersey v. Libertelli,* 215 N.J. Super. 190, 195 (App. Div. 1987), *citing State v. Community Distributors, Inc.* Other jurisdictions have recognized liability for wrongful discharge based on violations of statutory ban on polygraph tests. See *Perks v. Firestone Tire & Rubber Co.,* 611 F.2d 1363 (3d Cir. 1979), and *Ambroz v. Cornhusker Square Ltd.,* 2 I.E.R. Cases (BNA) 1185 (Nebraska Sup. Ct. 1987).

22. In *Nothdurft v. Ross,* 429 N.Y.S.2d 844 (Sup. Ct. 1980), *affirmed* 445 N.Y.S.2d 222 (A.D. 1981), the court discussed the differences between polygraph and PSE.

23. States that specifically prohibit use of psychological stress evaluators are California, Cal. Penal Code, §637.3 (must obtain express written consent of subject); Michigan, Mich. Comp. Laws Ann., §37.203; New York, N.Y. Labor Law §§733, 739; Oregon, Or. Rev. Stat., §659.275 (may test if subject consents); and Pennsylvania, 18 Pa. Cons. Stat. Ann., §7507 (may test if subject consents). See also Utah, Utah Stat., §34-37-16, in which surreptitious examinations are prohibited including voice stress tests.

24. See *Scott v. Transkrit Corp.,* 457 N.Y.S.2d 134 (A.D. 1982).

25. N.Y. Labor Law §733(4).

26. Me. Rev. Stat. Ann., Ch.87, §7166.

27. Mich. Comp. Laws. Ann., §37.202(f). Under such a broad definition the term "polygraph examination" includes lie detector test, psychological stress evaluator examination, or other similar tests.

28. See *Nothdurft v. Ross,* 429 N.Y.S.2d 884, 845 (Sup. Ct. 1980) *affirmed,* 445 N.Y.S.2d 222 (1981).

29. California, Cal. Labor Code, §432.2; Connecticut, Con. Gen. Stat. Ann., 31-51g; Hawaii, Haw. Rev. Stat., §378.21; Idaho, Idaho Code, §44-903; Maryland, Md. Ann. Code, Art. 100, §95; Michigan, Mich. Comp. Laws Ann., §338.1726; Montana, Mont.

Rev. Codes Ann., §41-119; Nebraska, Neb. Rev. Stat., §32; Oregon, Or. Rev. Stat., §659.225; Pennsylvania, 18 Pa. Cons. Stat. Ann., §7321; Rhode Island, R.I., §23-5-7(G); Vermont, 21 V.S.A., Ch. 5, §494a; West Virginia, West Va. Code, Ch. 21, §21-5-5a.

30. Mich. Comp. Laws Ann., §338-1726. An employer may not require an employee or applicant to give an express or implied waiver. Pennsylvania permits a voluntary waiver by an informed employee or applicant. See *Polsky v. Radio Shack,* 666 F.2d 824, 829 (3d Cir. 1981), in which a properly executed waiver may constitute a valid defense.

31. *Id.* at §37.203-206.

32. See *New Jersey v. T.L.O.,* 469 U.S. 325, 3734-335 (1985); see also *Capua v. City of Plainfield,* 643 F.Supp. 1507 (D.N.J.) (city testing of firefighters prohibited absent individualized reasonable suspicion).

33. *O'Conner v. Ortega,* 480 U.S. 709 (1987) quoting *United States v. Place,* 462 U.S. 969, 703 (1983).

34. *Id.*

35. *Skinner v. Railway Labor Executives' Association,* 489 U.S. 602 (1989), and *Treasury Employees Union v. Raab,* 489 U.S. 656 (1989).

36. *Local 194A v. Burlington County Bridge Comm'n,* 240 N.J. Super. 9 (App. Div.), *cert. denied* 122 N.J. 183 (1990).

37. *Seelig v. Koehler,* 546 N.Y.S.2d 828 (1st Dept. 1990) (court approved random drug testing for New York City's 10,000 correction officers).

38. See *Burka v. NYC Transit Authority,* 680 F.Supp. 590 (S.D.N.Y. 1990), citing inaccurate laboratory methods and lack of opportunity on part of the employees to challenge the result.

39. P.O. 102-143 (October 28, 1991). The Act modifies Section 202 of the Federal Railroad Safety Act of 1970, 45 U.S.C. §431; the Commercial Motor Vehicle Safety Act of 1986, 49 App. U.S.C. 2701, *et seq;* and Title VI of the Federal Aviation Act of 1958, 49 App. U.S.C. 1421, *et seq.*

40. 49 C.F.R. Part 40 (effective January 2, 1990).

41. See other federal agencies with testing regulations, for example, Federal Railroad Administration, 49 C.F.R. Parts 217, 219, and 225, effective in 1990, with the exception of the application of random drug testing requirements of railroad personnel outside the United States, which is delayed until January 2, 1993; Federal Highway Administration, 49 C.F.R. Part 391, amended April 16, 1991; Urban Mass Transportation Administration, 49 C.F.R. Part 653 (suspended on January 25,1990); and Federal Aviation Administration, 14 C.F.R. Parts 61, 63, 65, 121, and 135, Anti-Drug Program Rules (amended September 15, 1991).

42. See *Treasury Employees (NTEU) v. Yeutter,* 918 F.2d 968 (D.C. Cir. 1990).

43.   Reported in 51 Fed., Reg. 32,889 (1986), E.O. 12564 survived a general constitutional challenge in *National Treasury Employees Union v. Bush*, 891 F.2d 99 (5th Cir. 1989). The court stated that unions and individuals asserting violation of constitutional rights must challenge individual agency plans under E.O. 12564 as such plans are implemented.

44.   Excluded from coverage are the armed forces defined in 5 U.S.C. §2101(2), the U.S. Postal Service, Postal Rate Commission, and units or authorities in the judicial and legislative branches.

45.   Employee assistance program is defined under the Order to be an agency-based counseling programs that offer assessment, short-term counseling, and referral services to employees for a wide range of drug, alcohol, and mental health programs that affect employee job performance. Such programs are responsible for referring drug-using employees for rehabilitation and for monitoring employees' progress while in treatment. E.O. 12564, §7(f).

46.   P.L. 100-690, Title V (D). Our focus is on the contractor; however, the Act imposes similar requirements on entities that receive grants from federal agencies. See Section 5153 of the Act.

47.   Section 5157(1). The term "controlled substances" refers to the controlled substances identified in schedules I through V of Section 202 of the Controlled Substances Act, 21 U.S.C. §812.

48.   The Notice and final rules promulgated by the Office of Management and Budget for the government wide implementation of the Act were issued on May 25, 1990, 55 Fed. Reg. 21,679, and corrected on July 26, 1990, 55 Fed. Reg. 30,465.

49.   *Wilkinson v. Times Mirror Corp.*, 4 I.E.R. Cases (BNA) 1579 (Cal. 1st App. Div. 1989).

50.   *Hennessey v. Coastal Eagle Point Oil Co.*, 247 N.J. Super. 297 (App. Div. 1989), *affirmed*, 129 N.J. 81 (1992).

51.   See *Dimeo v. Griffin*, 6 I.E.R. Cases (BNA) 1288 (7th Cir. 1991); *Shoemaker v. Handel*, 619 F.Supp. 1089 (D.N.J. 1985), *affirmed* 795 F.2d 1136 (3d Cir. 1985), *cert. denied* 107 S.Ct. 577 (1986) (random drug testing of jockeys upheld in light of the State's great concern for racing industry integrity).

52.   See, for example, *Wilkinson v. Times Mirror Corp.*, 4 I.E.R. Cases (BNA) 1579 (Cal. Court of Appeals, 1st App. Div. 1989) (company tested job applicants pursuant to a policy; job was contingent upon results of physical and drug tests; employer did not receive test results only an evaluation of fitness for employment).

53.   See *Hennessey v. Coastal Eagle Point Oil Co.*, 129 N.J. 81 (1992).

54.   See *Johnson-Bateman Company*, 295 NLRB 180 (1989).

55.   See Memorandum on Drug and Alcohol Testing, Office of General Counsel, GC-87-5, NLRB (September 8, 1987); *Taft Broadcasting Co.*, 163 NLRB No. 475 (1967) *enf'd* 395 F.2d 622 (D.C. Cir.), *reh. denied*, 395 F.2d 622 (1968).

56. In 1991, Rep. Pat Williams (D., Montana) introduced HR-1218 and witnesses have testified before the House Education and Labor Subcommittee in Labor-Management Relations on electronic monitoring in the workplace.

57. 18 U.S.C. §2510, *et seq.* (1968), as amended.

58. 18 U.S.C. §2510 (5)(a)(i).

59. See *James v. Newspaper Agency Corp.*, 591 F.2d 579 (10th Cir. 1979), and *Epps v. St. Mary's Hospital of Athens, Inc.*, 802 F.2d 412 (11th Cir. 1986).

60. See *Watkins v. L.M. Berry & Co.*, 704 F.2d 577 (11th Cir. 1983).

61. See Md. Courts & Jud. Proc. Code Ann., §10.402(c)(3) (1989).

62. See Mich. Comp. Laws, §750.539d (1970).

63. See, for example, *Pemberton v. Bethlehem Steel Corp.*, 66 Md. App. 133, 502 A.2d 101, *cert. denied* 306 Md. 289, 508 A.2d 488 (1986), U.S. *cert. denied* 107 S. Ct. 571 (1986) (Maryland Court of Special Appeals found employer had no legitimate reason for affixing a listening device onto a union official's motel room door and found that the employer's actions violated the state's antieavesdropping statutes.

64. See *K-Mart Corp., Store No. 7441 v. Trotti*, 677 S.W.2d 632 (Tex. App. 1984).

65. See the following cases: *Gretoncord v. Ford Motor Co.*, 538 F.Supp. 331 (D.Kan. 1984); State v. Dickerson, 313 N.W.2d 526 (Iowa 1981); *Thomas v. General Electric*, 206 F.Supp. 792 (W.D.Ky. 1962); and *General Paint and Chemical Co.*, 80 Lab. Arb. (BNA) 413 (1983), respectively.

66. *Dupont & Co.*, 301 NLRB No. 14 (1991).

67. *FMC Corp.*, 46 Lab. Arb. (BNA) 335 (1966).

68. *Casting Engineers*, 76 Lab. Arb. (BNA) 939 (1981).

5

COMPLYING WITH TITLE VII OF THE CIVIL RIGHTS ACT OF 1964

Title VII of the Civil Rights Act of 1964, 42 U.S.C. §2000e-2, *et seq.*, covers all terms and conditions of employment and governs decisions relating to hiring, firing, compensation, transfer, and promotion. Employers may not limit, segregate, or classify employees in any way that tends to deprive any individual of employment opportunities or adversely affects his or her employment status because of race, color, religion, sex, or national origin. The scope and effectiveness of Title VII was significantly enhanced by the Civil Rights Act of 1991, which overturned U.S. Supreme Court decisions that had interpreted Title VII in a way less favorable to alleged victims of discrimination.

The anti-discrimination provisions of Title VII impact on every employment-related action. Decisions regarding hiring, termination, promotion, transfer, layoff, job assignment, benefits, and the like all must be made without regard to impermissible factors. This chapter addresses the various theories under which a Title VII claim may be brought, the impact of the Civil Rights Law of 1991, employers' obligations and liability, and enforcement under Title VII. Also included in this chapter are sample EEOC forms and a summary of the provisions of Title VII.

DEFINING THE SCOPE OF TITLE VII

Title VII was enacted in response to the urgent need to remove "artificial, arbitrary, and unnecessary barriers . . . [which] operate individually to discriminate on the basis of racial or other impermissible classification." Today, adverse employment action under various federal laws is unlawful when based upon an individual's race, color, religion, sex, national origin, age, physical or mental handicap, or citizenship status.

Establishing Who Is Covered by Title VII

Employers of 15 employees or more and whose operations affect interstate commerce are prohibited from discriminating against employees or applicants for employment on the basis of race, color, sex, religion, or national origin.[1] Title VII also applies to employment agencies, labor organizations, and apprenticeship programs whose activities affect interstate commerce.

Title VII is unusual in its broad approach of prohibiting discrimination with regard to all terms, conditions, and privileges of employment. Thus every employment-related decision, including hiring, firing, promotion, transfer, pay raises, benefits, and the like, are governed by the constraints of Title VII. Also prohibited are intangible work-related detriments such as harassment that is sufficiently severe or pervasive as to create an "abusive working environment."[2]

Governmental Entities. Federal, state, and local entities also fall within the broad scope of Title VII. Various challenges to the constitutionality of the application of Title VII to these defendants have failed, and it is now an accepted principle of law.[3]

Exemptions and Exceptions.

Religious organizations enjoy special status under Title VII. Although religious institutions are covered under Title VII, these employers are permitted to make certain employment-related decisions on the basis of religion. Two provisions act to insulate religious organizations from liability for religious-based discrimination or require only that a "reasonable accommodation" be attempted for an employee's religious beliefs. The subsection on religious discrimination discusses in detail the limits placed on religious organizations and what other employers may do with regard to employees with differing religious beliefs or practices.

In addition to the limited exemptions, Title VII permits an exception to the no-bias rule in employment where an employer can establish a "bona fide occupational qualification," or a BFOQ. BFOQ is discussed in detail later on in this chapter.

Employees Abroad. The Civil Rights Act of 1991 amends Title VII so that the employment practices of U.S. employers that employ U.S. citizens outside the United States are governed by the prohibitions of Title VII.[4] There is an exemption if compliance with Title VII would cause the employer to violate the law of the foreign country in which it is located.

Title VII still does not apply to aliens employed outside the United States.[5] However, aliens employed within the United States are protected by the provisions of Title VII.[6]

THEORIES OF LIABILITY UNDER TITLE VII

Unlawful discrimination is difficult to prove because there is typically no direct evidence. Since direct proof of discriminatory intent is elusive, the Supreme Court has defined and allocated the burden of proof between employees and employers. Title VII actions may be brought under several theories of discrimination, each with its own standard or allocation of the burden of proof. These theories are:

- – Disparate treatment
- – Adverse (disparate) impact
- – Retaliation
- – Reverse discrimination

Disparate Treatment Theory of Liability

The most frequently used theory of liability under Title VII is known as the "disparate treatment" theory, whereby an employee or applicant alleges that he or she has been treated less favorably than or differently from other employees because of race, color, religion, sex, or national origin. These categories of characteristics make up "protected classes" under Title VII. This theory focuses on the individual treatment of the employee. A complainant under this theory must prove that the employer intentionally discriminated against him or her.

The Supreme Court, in *Texas Department of Community Affairs v. Burdine*, 450 U.S. 248, 253 (1981), clarified the employee's duty to meet the intent requirement. The Supreme Court stated that,

> The ultimate burden of persuading the trier of fact that the defendant intentionally discriminated against the plaintiff remains at all times with the plaintiff.

Elements of a Claim. The intent to discriminate may be inferred from the evidence, direct or circumstantial, produced by the parties. Most frequently, proof of intent is established through circumstantial evidence, whereby the plaintiff makes out a *prima facie* case that the employer is unable to rebut. The term *"prima facie* case" means that the complainant's evidence indicates that the basic elements of a claim exists. However, it only means that there appears to be a valid claim to which the employer must respond and show that there is a legitimate nondiscriminatory reason for the adverse action.

An employee or applicant may make out a *prima facie* case of discrimination by showing by the preponderance of the evidence that

- He or she is a member of a protected class

- He or she applied for a position for which he or she was qualified or that he or she did not apply because it would have been futile to apply (i.e., that such application would have been rejected regardless of applicant's qualifications)

- He or she was rejected or some other adverse employment action was taken against him or her

- The employer continued to seek applicants, or individuals outside of the protected class were treated more favorably or some other evidence of prohibited discrimination exists.[7]

However, it is not necessary that all four factors be present to establish a *prima facie* case of discrimination.[8] There is some flexibility in the application of these factors depending upon the type of adverse employment action taken and the circumstances of the particular case. In cases where an employee presents direct evidence of discrimination, the test is not applied.[9]

The Employer's Rebuttal of a Claim. In the event the employee presents sufficient evidence to establish a *prima facie* case, there is a burden placed on the employer to produce or articulate some legitimate, nondiscriminatory reason for the adverse employment action. The employer may do so by clearly setting forth such reasons through the introduction of admissible evidence. In fact, the employer need raise only a genuine issue of fact, that is, that the pertinent facts are in dispute.[10] However, it is advisable to establish firmly the legitimate reason for the adverse employment action rather than merely articulate such a reason.

The Claim of Pretextual Reason. Once the employer alleges that there is a legitimate, nondiscriminatory reason for the action, the employee has the right to show that the proffered reason is pretextual; that is, it is not the true reason for the employment decision. The employee may establish pretext in the following manner:

- Show evidence that other similarly situated individuals had not been refused employment

- Show evidence of the employer's treatment of the employee during previous employment

- Show the employer's reaction to his or her legitimate civil rights activity

- Show that the employer's general policy and practice with respect to minority employment is biased.[11]

The employee may succeed in establishing pretext either by persuading the court that a discriminatory reason more likely motivated the employer or by showing that the proffered reason is unworthy of credence.[12]

Proving a Claim. The essence of a disparate treatment case is that an individual was subject to treatment different from that received by others. Evidence of intent to discriminate may be established through one or more of the following:

- Direct evidence of a discriminatory motive
- Comparative evidence, for example, comparing treatment of employees in similar circumstances
- Statistical evidence

Direct evidence may be in the form of oral or written statements by supervisors or management. Since direct evidence, such as a written document that clearly reveals that an employment decision was based on impermissible factors, that is, the "smoking gun," is rarely available, employees may utilize circumstantial evidence such as statistics.

Comparative evidence merely refers to comparisons between the individual's situation and how other employees or applicants are treated under similar circumstances. Usually a combination of these types of evidence is used by an individual. Often it is the inconsistent application of work rules, practices, or policies that give rise to discrimination claims.

Keep in mind that the actual presentation of evidence and proofs in a case do not usually occur in the order discussed here. The individual should present all of his or her evidence and the employer should do the same. The fact finder applies the analytical model of

- *Prima facie* case
- Employer's justification
- Pretext rebuttal to all of the evidence and determines whether the individual has proven a case of unlawful discrimination.

Statistical evidence is a mathematical analysis of the percentage of minorities or women at various levels in the work force or in the surrounding community as compared to the number of nonminorities. The Supreme Court has approved the use of statistical evidence in discrimination cases. In *McDonnell Douglas*, the high court stated "Statistics as to petitioner's employment policy and practice may be helpful to a determination of whether [the employer's] refusal to rehire [the employee] in this case conformed to a general pattern of discrimination against blacks."[13]

Statistics have been used to establish a *prima facie* case of discrimination. Statistics showing a racial imbalance between the work force and the composition of the community from which employees are hired may be probative of racial discrimination in hiring practices of an employer.[14] In fact, statistical disparities alone can establish *prima facie* cases of discrimination.[15] However, statistics may also be used to rebut a *prima facie* case established by statistics.[16] Each case should be reviewed to ascertain the appropriate use of statistics, especially in light of the Supreme Court ruling in Atonio v. *Wards Cove Packing Co.* that the showing of a racial imbalance in the work force alone will not establish a *prima facie* case of discrimination.[17] The Supreme Court held that the proper comparison is between the racial composition of the qualified persons in the labor market and the persons holding the jobs in question.

The Adverse Impact Theory of Liability

The **adverse impact theory** of discrimination, also referred to as *disparate impact*, focuses upon an alleged discriminatory effect of an apparently neutral employment practice rather than on the treatment of an individual.

NOTE: Under this theory, employment practices that appear neutral, that is, they seem to apply without regard to race, sex, national origin, or religion, but in fact act to eliminate minorities or women from employment opportunities, may violate Title VII.[18] Unlike the disparate treatment cases, proof of intent to discriminate is not necessary to establish a claim.

Elements of an Adverse Impact Claim.   Generally, an adverse impact claim involves an allegation that a specific employment practice in effect screens out minorities and women through some nonjob-related device or criteria, such as a college degree requirement. Such a requirement may have a substantial disproportionate exclusionary impact on members of a protected class.

As in disparate treatment cases, the individual must show that

– He or she is a member of a protected class
– He or she is qualified for the position
– The challenged employment practice or policy is not job-related or has a disproportionate exclusionary effect

Adverse impact analysis has been applied to tests, educational and skill requirements, and other seemingly neutral or objective criteria. Subjective criteria and evaluation procedures, such as interviews, have also been subjected to the adverse impact analysis.[19]

Case Study

North Valley Services, Inc., a computer consulting firm, seeks a janitor. The company is located in a predominantly white, mid-to upper-middle-class community bordering the city of Newark, New Jersey. One of the requirements for the job is that the individual have a high school diploma. The job involves work around highly sensitive and expensive computer equipment that requires some special maintenance procedures.

Ed Smith, a 48-year-old Afro-American with an eighth grade education, applies for the job. He has 5 years of experience as a janitor in a commercial office building. Ed is rejected because he does not hold a high school diploma. The three other janitors at the company are white and have high school diplomas.

Has North Valley Services discriminated against Ed Smith? Yes. The requirement of a high school diploma may disproportionately exclude certain minorities, that is, a group that has fewer members complete high school, from becoming janitors. There is no evidence that a high school diploma is necessary for the performance of janitorial duties. While it may be necessary for a janitor to be able to read labels on cleaning products, special instructions for cleaning around certain equipment, and the like, it is not shown what reading level is necessary. In addition, Ed had prior experience as a janitor with no apparent problems. Thus the facially neutral requirements of a high school diploma excluded Ed and may have a disparate impact on many other minorities. This requirement should be evaluated, and if it is not necessary to the performance of the job, it should be eliminated.

The Civil Rights Act of 1991. The Civil Rights Act of 1991 (CRA '91)[20] was enacted in part to overrule the Supreme Court's holding in *Wards Cove Packing Co. v. Antonio*, 109 S. Ct. 3151 (1989), which had made it more difficult for protected groups to prove disparate impact.[21] The Court held that the plaintiffs did not make out a *prima facie* case of disparate impact with a simple statistical comparison between white and nonwhite cannery workers. The proper comparison is between the racial composition of the jobs in issue and the racial composition of the qualified population in the relevant labor market.[22]

The Court also held that the plaintiff must show more than a racial imbalance in the work force or identification of a number of allegedly discriminatory practices.[23] The plaintiff must demonstrate that the disparity is the result of one or more of the challenged practices and specifically show that each practice has a significant disparate impact in the employment opportunities for whites and nonwhites.[24] However, the employer, in *Wards Cove* had only to produce evidence of a business justification; it did not have to prove business necessity. Thus *Wards Cove* imposed a significant burden on plaintiffs in establishing a *prima facie* case for a disparate impact claim with the foregoing requirements.

NOTE: CRA '91 amended Title VII and shifted the burden of proof to the employer where a plaintiff has shown that a disparate impact exists.

Title VII now provides that an employment practice or group of practices that results in a disparate impact on minorities or women is unlawful if

– The employer cannot "demonstrate that the challenged practice is job-related for the position in question *and* consistent with business necessity"

– The employer cannot refute the claim that a less discriminatory practice is available and the employer has refused to adopt it.[25]

Under this new requirement, the plaintiff must still show that each particular challenged practice causes a disparate impact, unless it is shown that the individual practices or elements of the decision-making process are not capable of separation for analysis.[26] This provision applies to the situation where a complainant identifies a group or combination of employment practices or policies as having had a disparate impact and these policies or practices are so intertwined that they cannot separately be analyzed. In such cases, the group of practices or policies will be treated and analyzed as a single employment practice.

Case Study

The state has established separate minimum physical requirements for state troopers; they must be at least 5 feet 4 inches tall and weigh at least 145 pounds. It was found that the height requirement would exclude well over one-third of the women in the United States, and the weight requirement would exclude almost an equal amount. Combined, the height and weight requirements would exclude one-half the women in the United States, but only approximately 5 –10 percent of the men.

Under the new law these physical restrictions could be analyzed as if they were one employment practice, and a disparate impact would be clearly established.

The Employer's Burden of Proof. In the event that the employee establishes a *prima facie* case of disparate impact discrimination, the employer must then produce evidence that the practice or policy is job-related and of a *legitimate business necessity* for its use of the challenged practice(s). Since "business necessity" is not defined in the statute, it is left to the courts to decide whether an employment criterion, practice, or policy is supported by business necessity.

The Supreme Court in *Griggs v. Duke Power Co.*, 401 U.S. 424 (1971), ruled that proof of business necessity requires the employer to show that the challenged practice "bears a demonstrable relationship to successful performance of the jobs for which it is was used." In *Griggs*, the employer required a high school diploma and a passing score on standardized intelligence tests for hiring and promotional purposes. These requirements, which had the effect of excluding minorities, violated the law because the employer could not show that they were job-related. Thus general or overly broad requirements that tend to exclude minorities from positions and that cannot be shown to be relevant to the needs and requirements of the job itself are unlawful.

> NOTE: In the face of a disparate impact claim, the employer must be prepared to justify an exclusionary employment practice or policy by proving business necessity for such a practice or policy.

Obviously, if an employer shows that a challenged practice or policy does not have a disparate impact, it does not need to prove business necessity.

A Complainant's Rebuttal of an Employer's Justification. Once the employer succeeds in producing a business justification that overcomes the plaintiff's initial case, the plaintiff must show that there is either

- No legitimate business necessity for using the subjective selection criteria (e.g., it is not related to successful performance of the job) or

- Another method as economically efficient that would achieve the same result with less impact on the protected class

Any alternative proposed must be equally effective in serving the employer's business goals, taking into account such matters as cost and other burdens.[27]

Case Study

> The complainant was unable to demonstrate that the ability to lift consistently 60 or more pounds as a seafood loading dock employee was not related to the job because nearly all the packages unloaded and loaded daily weighed at least 60 pounds. The complainant was able to show an alternative existed that involved a small forklift-type machine that could do 85 percent of the lifting required. However, these machines cost about $20,000 each and required substantial maintenance. Thus the alternative was too costly to the employer in that he would be required to purchase at least ten of these machines and maintain them. Such an alternative would fail to meet second half of the rebuttal standard.

Protection from Retaliation Claims

Title VII prohibits an employer from taking any adverse employment action against an individual exercising his or her rights under the Act.[28] Employees who file charges or who threaten to file charges are protected from adverse retaliatory employment action. An employer may not retaliate against any individual or labor organization because

- The employee opposed an unlawful employment practice or

- Had made a charge, testified, assisted, or participated in any manner in an investigation proceeding or hearing under Title VII.[29]

Also protected are employees' private or internal complaints to management about alleged discriminatory practices.[30]

Establishing a Prima Facie Case. An individual asserting retaliation under Title VII must meet the following criteria which differ slightly from the disparate treatment cases. He or she must be

1. A member of a protected class
2. Qualified for the position
3. Engaged in activity protected by Title VII
4. The adverse employment action must have been based on that activity.

Adverse employment action may be discharge, denial of promotion, fewer benefits, demotion, and generally less favorable treatment.

An employee's complaint or protest of discrimination must be based on a "reasonable belief" that the employer had violated Title VII. Thus, even though no violation of Title VII by the employer is found based upon the complaint, the employee's actions are protected if reasonable.[31]

Other Aspects of a Retaliation Claim. In general, an employer may not be held liable for a retaliation action under Title VII where the employee is allegedly discharged for protesting a discriminatory remark made by a coworker. Title VII prohibits retaliation for opposing discriminatory acts or policies of an employer, but does not apply to acts by individual employees that cannot be attributable to the employer.[32] However, employers should always act to eliminate discriminatory behavior by individual employees because, if the employer is aware of such conduct and permits it to continue, the employer may be liable for a harassment claim.[33]

Retaliatory violations are treated as extremely serious because of the "chilling effect" upon individuals who have brought charges and others who may bring charges, including those who might otherwise actively oppose discrimination in the workplace. Persons who protest against discriminatory employment practices receive broad protection under Title VII.

Examples of Retaliation Claims. Here are some examples where a retaliation claim may be raised:

– An applicant is told by the employer that the application will not be processed until the applicant settles his or her pending EEOC charge against another company.[34]
– A prospective employer declines to hire an applicant based upon a former employer's information that she had once filed a sex discrimination suit.[35]

– A former employee who had filed a discrimination claim is refused a letter of recommendation, and disparaging remarks are made to prospective employers. (Title VII retaliation provision applies to former employees as well as to current employees.)[36]

Injunctive Relief from Retaliation Claims. Temporary injunctive relief is available to the individual, the EEOC, and the Attorney General. An injunction is used to preserve the status quo or to prevent further harm where there is an allegation of unlawful retaliatory action and no other relief is available.[37] However, the availability of injunctive relief does not diminish the right of an employee to go into court to seek relief on his or her own. In any event, injunctive relief is inappropriate where other remedies are available.

Protecting Against Reverse Discrimination

Title VII also protects persons aggrieved because of so-called "reverse discrimination" in which an employer discriminates against a member of an historically favored group.[38] Section 703 prohibits any employment practice based on race or gender, including actions that disadvantage or are directed against majority group members (white and/or male). Title VII specifically provides that employers are not required to grant preferential treatment to any individual or group on account of a work force imbalance that may exist with respect to race, color, religion, sex, or national origin.[39]

> NOTE: Typically, a reverse discrimination claim is made by white males, an historically favored group, whose positions have been taken by minorities pursuant to an affirmative action plan. Since affirmative action plans, mandatory or voluntary, are designed to extend a preference in hiring or promoting to minorities and women, they create a form of reverse discrimination. These plans have been upheld when they are intended to remedy the effects of past discrimination and do not unnecessarily interfere with the rights of white employees.[40]

Prior to 1991, employees could attack an affirmative action plan years after a court-approved plan under a consent decree went into effect, so long as the employees were not parties to the underlying court action or agreement pertaining to the plan. The CRA '91 amended Title VII so as to bar such challenges to consent decrees by persons who had actual notice of the proposed judgment and a reasonable opportunity to present objections and those whose interests were adequately represented by another person who challenged the decree on the same legal grounds and similar facts unless there has been an intervening change in the law or facts. An action not precluded by the amendment is to be brought in the same court and, if possible, before the same judge who entered the original judgment. A complete discussion on the use and validity of affirmative action plans is found in Chapter 10.

How to Establish Reverse Discrimination. The employee may establish a *prima facie* case of reverse discrimination in a disparate treatment case by showing that

1. He or she belongs to a protected group
2. He or she was qualified for the job applied for or discharged from
3. He or she did not get the job or was terminated despite his or her qualifications
4. The job remained available or someone was hired in his or her place.[41]

In an adverse impact case, the *prima facie* elements are adjusted by requiring a showing of background circumstances which support the suspicion that the employer discriminated against the majority. This is an admittedly highly unusual occurrence.[42]

Examples of Reverse Discrimination. The following cases provide some insight into the reverse discrimination analysis:

- A manager stated that women were better workers than men, and she expressed a desire to have an all-female management team; a male employee met *prima facie* requirements, but his termination because of his refusal to work necessary time periods and his refusal to accept his demotion was held to be nondiscriminatory and not a pretext.[43]

- A clause in a collective bargaining agreement between a teacher's union and school district that prohibits layoffs of "minority" teachers was struck down by the court. White teachers with greater seniority were laid off while minority teachers with less seniority were retained. The Court held that the no-minority-layoff provision violated the constitutional rights of the laid-off white teachers. The layoff preference for minority teachers was invalid because it provided that no minority teacher would be laid off until all whites were laid off, thereby effectively increasing, rather than maintaining, the proportion of minority teachers in the district during a reduction in force.[44]

BASIC SUBSTANTIVE PROVISIONS OF TITLE VII

The basic provisions of Title VII are set out in Sections 703 and 704 of the Act. Two basic provisions to be discussed here are unlawful unemployment practices and bona fide occupational qualification.

Defining Unlawful Employment Practices Under Title VII

Section 703(a)(1) declares that it is an *unlawful employment practice* for an employer

(1) to fail or refuse to hire or to discharge any individual with respect to his compensation, terms, conditions, or privileges of employment, because of such individual's race, color, religion, sex, or national origin; or

(2) to limit, segregate, or classify his employees or applicants for employment in any way which would deprive or tend to deprive any individual of employment opportunities or otherwise adversely affect his status as an employee, because of such individual's race, color, religion, sex, or national origin.

Similarly, Section 703(b) states that it is unlawful for an employment agency "to fail or refuse to refer for employment or otherwise discriminate against, any individual" on the same grounds or "to classify or refer for employment any individual on the basis of the protected class of characteristics."

Labor organizations in Section 703(c) are directed not "to exclude or to expel from membership, or otherwise discriminate against any individual" because of his or her race, color, sex, religion, or national origin. A union may not limit, segregate, or classify its membership or applicants for membership or classify or fail or refuse to refer for employment any individual in any way that would deprive or tend to deprive any individual of employment opportunities or would limit such opportunities or otherwise adversely affect his or her status as an employee or as an applicant because of race, color, religion, sex, or national origin. The same prohibitions hold for training or apprenticeship programs conducted by employers, labor organizations, or joint labor-management ventures.

Thus Title VII touches upon all employment matters from the recruitment and hiring process through the course of employment and termination.

Defining Bona Fide Occupational Qualification Under Title VII

Title VII permits a qualified exception to the sweeping prohibitions contained in Sections 703(a), (b), (c), and (d). Section 703(e)(1) recognizes that "certain instances [exist] where religion, sex or national origin is a bona fide occupational qualification reasonably necessary to the normal operation" of a particular business or enterprise.[45] An employer may use religion, sex, or national origin as a basis to hire or train select employees if it meets certain criteria for establishing a BFOQ.

The BFOQ defense to a charge of discrimination is construed narrowly by the EEOC and the courts. For example, unequal treatment based on sex is permitted if the employer can prove that sex is a necessary qualification for a specific job, such as an actress to play a female role. However, it will not apply in the following circumstances:

- – Refusing to hire women based on assumptions of the comparative employment characteristics of women, such as turnover rates or greater absenteeism due to child care

- – Refusing to hire women based on stereotyped characterizations of the sexes, such as the presumption women are passive or weaker

- – Refusing to hire women because of the preferences of coworkers, clients, or customers

However, where the employer can produce evidence that the gender specific requirement really is necessary for the performance of the job in question, discrimination on the basis of sex is permissible.[46] For a BFOQ to exist, there must be "reasonable cause to believe that all or substantially all women would be unable to perform safely and efficiently the duties of the job involved."[47] It is not easy to establish a BFOQ on the basis of sex, religion, or national origin. The basis for using a BFOQ requirement or defense must be carefully established through legitimate concerns for the performance of a specific job.

Case Examples

An employer's fetal protection policy violated Title VII and employer could not establish a BFOQ—fertile women perform in the manufacture of batteries as efficiently as anyone else. Employer's professed concern about the health and welfare of potential fetuses was not sufficient to establish a BFOQ.[48]

A city failed to show necessity for denominational hiring policy for chaplain positions in city prisons, where chaplains run religious programs in section without regard to inmate's religion and city's abandonment of policy has not hindered city's efforts to provide religious assistance to inmates.[49]

Having a Jesuit presence in philosophy department of a Jesuit-run university is reasonable to normal operation of university; thus university's decision to reserve next three openings for Jesuits is based on a BFOQ.[50]

Concern for prison security or for inmate privacy rights does not justify, as a BFOQ, a plan adopted by women's prison to employ only female correctional officers in the inmates' living units.[51]

Gender is a BFOQ for appointment to position in male housing unit in county jail, since it would violate inmates' right to privacy to have female sergeants inasmuch as sergeants are required to conduct announced and unannounced inspections of living areas, including toilet and shower facilities.[52]

NOTE: To establish a BFOQ, the employer must demonstrate that
a factual basis exists for a gender, religious, or national origin-based

employment decision. One way to establish such a basis is to show that any deviation from such a hiring policy would directly undermine the essence of the job or the employer's business.

In cases involving privacy considerations of customers or clients, the employer must also prove that no reasonable alternatives exist to its biased hiring policy.[53]

NOTE: The test for whether a BFOQ exception to Title VII liability is available is whether the requirement that an employee be of a particular religion, gender, or national origin is reasonably necessary to the normal operations of the business or enterprise and *not* whether the sole purpose of the employment decision is promotion of a particular religion or bias in favor or against a sex or ethnic group.

ENFORCEMENT OF TITLE VII

The federal agency responsible for enforcing Title VII is the Equal Employment Opportunity Commission (EEOC). Title VII created the EEOC and provides the basic outline of its powers and authority. This section addresses the procedural aspects of bringing and defending a charge of discrimination under Title VII.

How the EEOC Functions

The EEOC is comprised of five members appointed by the president and approved by the Senate. Each member serves a 5-year term. This body receives, processes, and investigates charges of employment discrimination alleging a violation of Title VII, ADA, Equal Pay Act, and ADEA.

Although the five commissioners are based in Washington, D.C., the EEOC has 23 district offices located throughout the United States. The district office is the first place a discrimination charge is filed and investigated. The EEOC oversees the operation of these offices and is the final arbiter of a discrimination charge.

How Proceedings Are Initiated

An individual initiates a proceeding under Title VII by filing a charge at one of the district offices of the EEOC. The charge should be precise enough to identify the parties and describe the discriminatory action or practice. Charges must be in writing under oath or affirmation. A copy of a "Charge of Discrimination" form that is completed by a complainant and sent to the employer may be found in Exhibit 5.1. The individual filing a charge typically completes an intake questionnaire at the EEOC office where he or she is interviewed by an intake officer. See an example of an intake questionnaire in Exhibit 5.2.

– EXHIBIT 5.1 –
Charge of Discrimination

CHARGE OF DISCRMINATION This form is affected by the Privacy Act of 1974; see Privacy Act Statement on reverse before completing this form.		**ENTER CHARGE NUMBER** ☐ FEPA ☐ EEOC

_____ and EEOC
(State or local Agency, if any)

NAME *(Indicate Mr., Ms., or Mrs.)*		HOME TELEPHONE NO. *(Include Area Code)*
STREET ADDRESS	CITY, STATE AND ZIP CODE	COUNTY

NAMED IS THE EMPLOYER, LABOR ORGANIZATION, EMPLOYMENT AGENCY, APPRENTICESHIP COMMITTEE, STATE OR LOCAL GOVERNMENT AGENCY WHO DISCRIMINATED AGAINST ME *(If more than one list below.)*

NAME	NO. OF EMPLOYEES/MEMBERS	TELEPHONE NUMBER *(Include Area Code)*
STREET ADDRESS	CITY, STATE AND ZIP CODE	
NAME		TELEPHONE NUMBER *(Include Area Code)*
STREET ADDRESS	CITY, STATE AND ZIP CODE	

CAUSE OF DISCRIMINATION BASED ON *(Check appropriate box(es))* ☐ RACE ☐ COLOR ☐ SEX ☐ RELIGION ☐ NATIONAL ORIGIN ☐ AGE ☐ RETALIATION ☐ OTHER *(Specify)*	DATE MOST RECENT OR CONTINUING DISCRIMINATION TOOK PLACE *(Month, day, year)*

THE PARTICULARS ARE *(If additional space is needed, attached extra sheet(s))*:

☐ I also want this charge filed with the EEOC. I will advise the agencies if I change my address or telephone number and I will cooperate fully with them in the processing of my charge in accordance with their procedures.	**NOTARY - (When necessary to meet State and Local Requirements)**
	I swear or affirm that I have read the above charge and that it is true to the best of my knowledge, information and belief.
I declare under penalty of perjury that the foregoing is true and correct.	**SIGNATURE OF COMPLAINANT**
	SUBSCRIBED AND SWORN TO BEFORE ME THIS DATE *(Day, month, and year)*
Date Charging Party *(Signature)*	

EEOC FORM 5 MAR 84   PREVIOUS EDITIONS OF THIS FORM ARE OBSOLETE AND MUST NOT BE USED

FILE COPY

PRIVACY ACT STATEMENT

(This form is covered by the Privacy Act of 1974, Public Law 93-579: Authority for requesting the personal data and the uses are given below.)

1. FORM NUMBER/TITLE/DATE. EEOC Form 5, CHARGE OF DISCRIMINATION, March 1984.

2. AUTHORITY. 42 U.S.C. § 2000e-5(b), 29 U.S.C. § 211, 29 U.S.C. § 626.

3. PRINCIPAL PURPOSE(S). The purpose of the charge, whether recorded initially on this form or in some other way reduced to writing and later recorded on this form, is to invoke the jurisdiction of the Commission.

4. ROUTINE USES. This form is used to determine the existence of facts which fall within the Commission's jurisdiction to investigate, determine, conciliate and litigate charges of unlawful employment practices. Information provided on this form will be used by Commission employees to guide the Commission's investigatory activities. This form may be disclosed to other State, local and federal agencies as may be appropriate or necessary to carrying out the Commission's functions. A copy of this charge will ordinarily be served upon the person against whom the charge is made.

5. WHETHER DISCLOSURE IS MANDATORY OR VOLUNTARY AND EFFECT ON INDIVIDUAL FOR NOT PROVIDING INFORMATION. Charges must be in writing and should identify the parties and action or policy complained of. Failure to have a charge which identifies the parties in writing may result in the Commission not accepting the charge. Charges under Title VII must be sworn to or affirmed. Charges under the ADEA should ordinarily be signed. Charges may be clarified or amplified later by amendment. It is not mandatory that this form be used to provide the requested information.

6. [ ] Under Section 706 of Title VII of the Civil Rights Act of 1964, as amended, this charge will be deferred to and will be processed by the State or local agency indicated. Upon completion of the agency's processing, you will be notified of its final resolution in your case. If you wish EEOC to give Substantial Weight Review to the agency's findings, you must send us a request to do so, in writing, within fifteen (15) days of your receipt of the agency's finding. Otherwise, we will adopt the agency's finding as EEOC's and close your case.

NOTICE OF NON-RETALIATION REQUIREMENTS

Section 704(a) of the Civil Rights Act of 1964, as amended, and Section 4(d) of the Age Discrimination in Employment Act of 1967, as amended, state:

It shall be an unlawful employment practice for an employer to discriminate against any of his employees or applicants for employment, for an employment agency to discriminate against any individual, or for a labor organization to discriminate against any member thereof or applicant for membership, because he has opposed a practice made an unlawful employment practice by this title or because he has made a charge, testified, assisted, or participated in any manner in an investigation, proceeding, or hearing under this title.

The Equal Pay Act of 1963 contains similar provisions. Persons filing charges of discrimination are advised of these Non-Retaliation Requirements and are instructed to notify EEOC if any attempt at retaliation is made.

– EXHIBIT 5.2 –

Intake Questionnaire

	EEOC USE ONLY Name (Intake Officer)

INTAKE QUESTIONNAIRE

This form is affected by the Privacy Act of 1974; see Privacy Act Statement on reverse before completing this form.

Please answer the following questions, telling us briefly why you have been discriminated against in employment. An officer of the EEOC will talk with you after you complete this form.

(Please Print)

NAME _____ DATE _____

(First) (Middle Name or Initial) (Last) DATE OF BIRTH _____

ADDRESS _____ TELEPHONE NO. *(Include area code)* _____

CITY _____ STATE _____ ZIP CODE _____ COUNTY _____

Please provide the name of an individual at a different address who is in the local area and who would know how to reach you.

NAME _____ RELATIONSHIP _____ TELEPHONE _____ *(Include area code)*

ADDRESS _____ CITY _____ STATE _____ ZIP CODE _____

What action was taken against you that you believe to be discriminatory? What harm, if any, was caused to you or others in your work situation as a result of that action? *(If more space is required, use reverse.)*

_____
_____
_____

Do you believe this action was taken against you because of: *(Check the one(s) that apply and specify your race, sex, age, religion or enthnic identity.)*

☐ RACE ☐ SEX ☐ RELIGION ☐ NATIONAL ORIGIN ☐ AGE ☐ RETALIATION ☐ COLOR

☐ OTHER, EXPLAIN BRIEFLY BELOW _____

I WAS DISCRIMINATED AGAINST BY: *(Check the one(s) that apply)*

☐ EMPLOYER ☐ UNION *(Give Local No.)* ☐ EMPLOYMENT AGENCY ☐ OTHER *(Specify)*

NAME _____ NAME _____

ADDRESS _____ ADDRESS _____

CITY, STATE, ZIP CODE _____ CITY, STATE, ZIP CODE _____

APPROXIMATE NUMBER EMPLOYED BY THIS EMPLOYER _____ WHAT WAS THE MOST RECENT DATE THE HARM YOU ALLEGED TOOK PLACE? _____

Are you now employed by the Employer that harmed you? Answer below.

YES: FROM _____ (Date) NO: I APPLIED FOR _____ (Position) OR: I WAS EMPLOYED AS _____ (Position)

CURRENT POSITION _____ ON _____ (Date) UNTIL _____ I WAS _____ (Laid off, fired, etc.)

Normally, your identity will be disclosed to the organization which allegedly discriminated against you.

Do you ☐ consent or ☐ not consent to such disclosure?

Have you sought assistance about the action you think was discriminatory from any Government agency, from your union, an attorney, or from any other source?

☐ No ☐ Yes (if answer is yes, complete below)

NAME OF SOURCE OF ASSISTANCE _____ DATE _____

RESULT, IF ANY: _____

Have you filed an EEOC Charge in the past? ☐ No ☐ Yes (If answer is yes, complete below)

APPROX. DATE FILED _____ ORGANIZATION CHARGED _____ CHARGE NUMBER (IF KNOWN) _____

SIGNATURE _____ SS# _____ DATE _____

EEOC FORM 283

NOTE: A charge must be filed with the EEOC or appropriate state agency before a complainant may file a claim under Title VII in court.

A charge must be filed within *180 days* of the discriminatory act. In a *deferral state*—a state that has its own EEOC-approved civil rights enforcement agency—a charge must be filed within *300 days* of the unlawful act. A state civil rights or human rights agency is independent from the EEOC and enforces the state's anti-discrimination statutes as well as the federal laws. However, the EEOC will not handle claims of discrimination based solely on state law. These state agencies generally work cooperatively with the EEOC and sometimes trade cases.[54]

In a deferral state, a charge is generally filed with the state or local agency. Some municipalities have their own civil rights commissions that enforce city ordinances against discrimination.[55] Often the EEOC district office will refer a charge it has received to the state agency for initial action. The state agency has a minimum of 60 days to investigate and act on the charge before it may be taken by the complainant to the EEOC. Once a charge is filed, notice must be sent to the employer within 10 days.

How a Charge Is Investigated

Upon receipt of a charge, the EEOC begins an investigation that is to be completed, if practicable, within 120 days from the date of filing. The scope of the investigation is generally limited to information necessary to make a determination as to whether reasonable cause exists to believe that unlawful discrimination occurred.

The investigation may include

- – An inspection of the employer's workplace and review of employer's records
- – A request for documentary evidence
- – Summoning witnesses
- – Taking testimony
- – Subpoena power

Holding a Fact-Finding Conference.   Generally, a fact-finding conference is held to allow each party the opportunity to present evidence. Also employers are often asked to submit a written statement in response to the complainant's claims, sometimes referred to as a "position statement."

Conducting On-Site Investigations.   The EEOC may inspect the employer's workplace and examine pertinent documents and records. The visits should be scheduled at such times so as to minimize disruption to business operations. If the employer refuses to permit an on-site investigation or attempts to delay it, the EEOC may seek access through the use of a subpoena.

While touring the worksite, the EEOC representative should be accompanied by a company official. The investigator may view the worksite of the complaining employee and the type of work performed. He or she may also interview witnesses.

If the witnesses interviewed are management employees, the employer has the right to have counsel present during the interview. However, a company representative or counsel may never be present during the interview of non-management employees.

If the investigator notices violations, other than those being investigated during the inspection, the EEOC may broaden the investigation to include the additional potential violations.

Issuing Subpoenas. Only the EEOC has subpoena power in its proceedings. The Commission has the authority to issue subpoenas requiring

- Attendance and testimony of witnesses
- Production of evidence, including books, records, correspondence, or documents in possession or control of the person subpoenaed
- Access to evidence for purposes of examination or copying

Objections to subpoenas must be made within 5 days to revoke or modify them. Grounds for challenging subpoenas include

- Undue burden on the normal operations of the business
- Excessive delay by the EEOC
- Unrecorded information—an employer must interview supervisors and managers, if necessary, to gather the requested information
- Statutory coverage (however, the employer must comply with subpoena so long as the investigation is for a legitimate purpose and there is no evidence of bad faith)
- Confidentiality of the information sought

The EEOC may seek enforcement of a subpoena in a federal district court. However, enforcement will be granted only if the following standards are satisfied:

- Existence of a valid charge
- The materials sought are relevant and description of the materials is sufficiently precise
- The subpoena was issued for a legitimate purpose.[56]

Controlling Access to EEOC Investigative Files. The information the EEOC obtains during the investigation of a charge is confidential and may not be made public by the agency. However, the complainant and the employer are entitled to review the information in their own case files. The EEOC may refuse to disclose information in the case file if premature disclosure would have a "chilling effect" on potential witnesses or dry up other sources of information, hinder the EEOC's ability to shape and control investigations, or make future investigations more difficult.[57]

Determining the Sufficiency of an Investigation.

Parties who are dissatisfied with the length, intensity, or type of investigation are unable to challenge an unfavorable result on that basis. The type of investigation is within the sole discretion of the EEOC. Title VII does not provide a right to challenge the sufficiency of an investigation. Thus the complainant or the employer may not sue the EEOC when a determination is made, even if that determination causes a party hardship in a subsequent court action.

Issuing a Letter of Determination

Once the EEOC has concluded its investigation, it issues a letter of determination of "reasonable cause" or "no probable cause" as to whether unlawful discrimination has occurred. In most cases, the district director of the field office where the charge was filed makes reasonable cause determinations.

Effects of a No-Cause Determination.

In the event that the result of the investigation is a determination that no cause exists to believe that discrimination had occurred, the complainant may seek review of that determination. A review must be requested within 14 days of the issuance of the determination. The review is conducted at the EEOC's headquarters in Washington, D.C. If no review is requested, the determination becomes final on the 15th day. If the determination is made initially by the Commission itself rather than at the field office level, the determination is final when issued.

The fact that the EEOC determined that no cause existed in a particular case does not bar a subsequent lawsuit on the same claim. However, a party may not sue until the EEOC has issued a right to sue letter that is issued after the determination has become final. We discuss the right to sue letter in greater detail after the next section.

Effects of a Reasonable Cause Determination.

A finding that reasonable cause exists to believe that discrimination occurred sets in motion a conciliatory process, and if that fails, the agency may initiate litigation against the employer.

Conciliation Procedure. Once a reasonable cause determination is made, Title VII requires the EEOC to attempt to eliminate the unlawful discrimination through conciliation. Although attempts at conciliation may occur prior to a reasonable cause determination, the EEOC is not required to do so prior to making the determination.

The conciliation process typically includes the following steps:

◆ An EEOC equal opportunity specialist (EOS) meets with the employee to determine what, if anything, has occurred since the investigation that would impact on the prospects of settlement.

◆ If the employer agrees to negotiate, the EOS holds a conciliation conference. The EEOC will attempt to reach an agreement that satisfies the employee, employer, and the Commission.

◆ If an agreement is reached, all parties sign the settlement document whereby they agree to be bound by its provisions. This ends the administrative processing of the charge, except for compliance follow-up pursuant to the terms of the agreement.

◆ If a settlement is not reached, the EEOC notifies the employer that conciliation has failed and will not be resumed unless the employer makes a written request to the Commission to make another attempt at conciliation.

If the parties successfully conclude the conciliation procedure, an executed conciliation agreement prevents the employer from being sued by the EEOC or the employee for any discriminatory acts covered by the agreement. The agreement must be signed by all parties for it to be effective. The consequences of an improperly executed conciliatory agreement are as follows:

◆ Complainants cannot be bound to a settlement unless they sign it—the EEOC's acceptance alone is not sufficient to prevent a suit by the complainant.

◆ An employer can still be sued for the discriminatory acts covered by the agreement if an employee has not signed it.

◆ Where one of two or more parties charged with discrimination does not sign the agreement, the nonsignatory may still be liable.

Failure of Conciliation. In the event that conciliation fails, the file is sent to the regional attorney of the EEOC who decides if the Commission should commence litigation. The EEOC may commence suit after making a good faith effort to conciliate and the employer rejects the attempt at conciliation. In the event that a court finds that the conciliation attempt was not adequate, the appropriate remedy is a stay and not dismissal of the suit. If the EEOC declines to proceed with litigation, it issues the complainant a right to sue letter.

NOTE: A complainant may file a court action even though the EEOC has not attempted conciliation. However, the complainant must first obtain a right to sue letter from the Commission.

Obtaining a Notice of Right to Sue

Before an individual can bring suit under Title VII, it is necessary for him or her to obtain a notice of right to sue from the EEOC. However, failure to obtain the notice prior to instituting an action may not be fatal if the notice is received during the course of the court proceedings. A copy of a typical right to sue notice is shown in Exhibit 5.3.

Issuance of Notice of Right to Sue.   A notice of right to sue may be issued by the EEOC under the following circumstances:

- When the commission finds that it lacks jurisdiction over the claim (e.g., the employer does not have the requisite number of employees or the "employee" is an independent contractor)

- When the administrative proceeding has ended due to the employee's failure to provide necessary information or the employee is otherwise uncooperative

- When, within 180 days of filing the charge, the individual requests a right to sue notice and the EEOC determines that it will be unable to process the charge within the 180-day period[58]

- After 180 days when the EEOC has not yet brought suit or made a determination

- When a finding of no reasonable cause has been made and the process of reviewing the no-cause determination has been made or waived

- When reasonable cause has been found, conciliation has failed, and the EEOC has declined to file a lawsuit

Time for Filing Suit.   The right to sue notice permits the individual to file a civil action under Title VII on the same claims of discrimination brought before the EEOC or state agency. The lawsuit must be filed within *90 days* from the date of receipt of the notice of right to sue.

The 90-day period may be tolled or suspended if circumstances beyond the complainant's control prevent the complainant from timely filing a lawsuit. Generally, the fact that the individual did not receive the notice due to an address change will not suffice in excusing the complainant from acting within the 90 days. The complainant is responsible for providing the EEOC with his or her current address or taking other steps to ensure proper delivery of correspondence. The notice of right to sue may be delivered to the attorney representing a complainant, and such delivery will start the 90 day period. In any event, the complainant should act expeditiously and without unnecessary delay in filing his or her lawsuit.

Remedies

Employers who are found to have violated Title VII may be liable for one or more of the following remedies:

– EXHIBIT 5.3 –
Notice of Right to Sue

EQUAL EMPLOYMENT OPPORTUNITY COMMISSION

NOTICE OF RIGHT TO SUE
(Issued on Request)

TO:	FROM:

☐ On behalf of a person aggrieved whose identity is
CONFIDENTIAL (29 C.F.R. 1601.7(a)).

CHARGE NUMBERS	EEOC REPRESENTATIVE	TELEPHONE NUMBER

(See Section 706(f)(1) and (f)(3) of the Civil Rights Act of 1964 and the other information on the reverse side of this form.)

TO THE PERSON AGGRIEVED:

This is your NOTICE OF RIGHT TO SUE. It is issued at your request. If you intend to sue the respondent(s) named in your charge, YOU MUST DO SO WITHIN NINETY (90) DAYS OF YOUR RECEIPT OF THIS NOTICE: OTHERWISE YOUR RIGHT TO SUE IS LOST.

☒ More than 180 days have expired since the filing of this charge.

☐ Less than 180 days have expired since the filing of this charge, but I have determined that the Commission will be unable to complete its administrative process within 180 days from the filing of the charge.

☒ With the issuance of this Notice of Right to Sue, the Commission is terminating any further processing of this charge.

☐ It has been determined that the Commission will continue to process your charge.

☐ ADEA - While Title VII requires the Commission to issue a Notice of Right to Sue before you can bring suit under that law, you obtained the right to sue under the Age Discrimination in Employment Act (ADEA) when you filed your charge, subject to a 60-day waiting period. ADEA suits must be brought within 2 years (3 years in cases of willful violations) of the alleged discrimination.

☐ EPA - While Title VII requires the Commission to issue a Notice of Right to Sue before you can bring suit under that law, you already have the right to sue under the Equal Pay Act (EPA) (you are not required to complain to any administrative agency before bringing an EPA suit in court). EPA suits must be brought within 2 years (3 years in cases of willful violations) of the alleged EPA underpayment.

An information copy of this Notice of Right to Sue has been sent to the respondent(s) shown below.

cc: (to respondent)   On Behalf of the Commission

☒ Copy of Charge

_____   _____
TYPED NAME AND TITLE OF ISSUING OFFICIAL   DATE

C:

EEOC FORM 161-B
MAR 84   PREVIOUS EDITIONS OF THIS FORM ARE OBSOLETE AND MUST NOT BE USED

CHARGING PARTY

(f) (1) If within thirty days after a charge is filed with the Commission or within thirty days after expiration of any period of reference under subsection (c) or (d), the Commission has been unable to secure from the respondent a conciliation agreement acceptable to the Commission, the Commission may bring a civil action against any respondent not a governmental agency, or political subdividion named in the charge. In the case of a respondent which is a government, governmental agency, or political subdivision, if the Commission has been unable to secure from the respondent a conciliation agreement acceptable to the Commission, the Commission shall take no further action and shall refer the case to the Attorney General who may bring a civil action against such respondent in the appropriate United States district court. The person or persons aggrieved shall have the right to intervene in a civil action brought by the Commission or the Attorney General in a case involving a government, governmental agency, or political subdivision. If a charge filed with the Commission pursuant to subsection(b) is dismissed by the Commission, or if within one hundred and eighty days from the filing of such charge or the expiration of any period of reference under subsection (c) or (d), whichever is later, the Commission has not filed a civil action under this section or the Attorney General has not filed a civil action in a case involving a government, governmental agency, or political subdivision, or the Commission has not entered into a conciliation agreement to which the person aggrieved is a party, the Commission, or the Attorney General in a case involving a government, governmental agency, or political subdivision, shall so notify the person aggrieved and within ninety days after the giving of such notice a civil action may be brought against the respondent named in the charge (A) by the person claiming to be aggrieved, or (B) if such charge was filed by a member of the Commission, by any person whom the charge alleges was aggrieved by the alleged unlawful employment practice. Upon application by the complainant and in such circumstances as the court may deem just, the court may appoint an attorney for such complainant or may authorize the commencement of the action without the payment of fees, costs, or security. Upon timely application, the court may, in its discretion, permit the Commission, or the Attorney General in a case involving a government, governmental agency, or political subdivision, to intervene in such civil action upon certification that the case is of general public importance. Upon request, the court may, in its discretion, stay further proceedings for not more than sixty days pending the termination of State or local proceedings described in subsection (c) or (d) of this section or further efforts of the Commission to obtain voluntary compliance.

(f) (3) Each United States district court and each United States court of a place subject to the jurisdiction of the United States shall have jurisdiction of actions brought under this title. Such an action may be brought in any judicial district in the State in which the unlawful employment practice is alleged to have been committed, in the judicial district in which the employment records relevant to such practice are maintained and administered, or in the judicial district in which the aggrieved person would have worked but for the alleged unlawful practice, but if the respondent is not found within any such district, such an action may be brought within the judicial district in which the respondent has his principal office. For purposes of sections 1404 and 1406 of title 28 of the United States Code, the judicial district in which the respondent has his principal office shall in all cases be considered a district in which the action might have been brought.

An information copy of this Notice of Right to Sue has been sent to the respondent(s) shown.

ATTORNEY REPRESENTATION:

If you cannot afford or have been unable to obtain a lawyer to represent you, you should be aware that the Civil Rights Act of 1964, as amended, 42 U.S.C. 2000e-5(f) (1) provides that the U.S. District Court having jurisdiction in your case may, at its discretion, assist you in obtaining a lawyer to represent you. If you plan to request appointment of a lawyer to represent you, you must make this request of the U.S. District Court in the form and manner it requires. Your request to the U.S. District Court should be made well in advance of the end of the 90-day period mentioned above.

You may contact the EEOC representative named if you have any questions about your legal rights including advice on which U.S. District Court has jurisdiction to hear your case or if you need to inspect and copy information contained in the Commission's case file.

DESTRUCTION OF FILE:

Generally, EEOC's rules call for your charge file to be destroyed after 1 year from the date of this Notice for a determination of no cause (and six months for other types of dismissals listed herein) unless you have notified us that you have filed suit in Federal District Court. If the Commission has been notified that you have filed suit, your file will be preserved for use in your litigation, which could be important to your suit.

If you file suit, you or your attorney should forward a copy of this form and your court complaint to this office within 10 days after you file suit. Receipt of this evidence that you have filed suit will cause your file to be preserved and allow the Commission to consider your suit when taking other actions.

IF YOU FILE SUIT, YOU OR YOUR ATTORNEY SHOULD NOTIFY THIS OFFICE WHEN THE LAWSUIT IS RESOLVED.

- Back pay
- Interest on back pay
- Front pay (where reinstatement is not appropriate)
- Reinstatement
- Declaratory and injunctive relief
- Attorneys' fees and costs
- Compensatory damages
- Punitive damages

The first six remedies identified are the so-called "traditional remedies" that were available under Title VII prior to the enactment of the Civil Rights Act of 1991 (CRA '91). The last two—compensatory and punitive damages—were added under CRA '91 but are available only in disparate treatment cases and are subject to a "cap" discussed next.

Defining Compensatory Damages. Compensatory damages are defined in CRA '91 to include "future pecuniary losses, emotional pain, suffering, inconvenience, mental anguish, loss of enjoyment of life and other nonpecuniary losses." The Act excludes from its definition of compensatory damage items such as back pay, interest on back pay, or any other type of relief authorized under Section 706(g) of Title VII. Other compensatory damages not intended to be limited by CRA '91 include past pecuniary losses, such as medical expenses. Damages excluded from the definition of compensatory damages are not subject to the cap limitations.

Liability for Punitive Damages. Punitive damages may be recovered but only upon proof that the employer acted with "malice or reckless indifference to" the rights of the employee. Punitive damages are to be awarded only in those cases involving extraordinary and/or egregious conduct. Such damages are intended to punish egregious discrimination, reinforce the public policy against discrimination, and act as a deterrent.

> NOTE: Compensatory and punitive damages are not available in disparate impact cases, nor in cases where the employer can demonstrate a good faith effort to find a reasonable accommodation that would not pose an undue hardship.

The Limiting or Cap on Compensatory and Punitive Damages.
Recovery for the compensatory and punitive damages permitted under CRA '91 is not unlimited. The CRA '91 places a cap on the amount a plaintiff may recover for compensatory and punitive damages in Title VII and ADA cases. These limits apply to the combined total of compensatory and punitive damages awarded in

each case and varies with the number of employees. The following schedule is set out in the Act:

Number of Employees	Maximum Award
15–100	$ 50,000
101–200	$100,000
201–500	$200,000
501–or more	$300,000

Moreover, CRA '91 specifically prohibits the court from advising the jury about the cap on compensatory and punitive damages. Undoubtedly, these enhanced remedies, despite the restrictions on recovery, will act as a catalyst for complainants to pursue discrimination claims. It remains to be seen whether Congress will increase these amounts or eliminate them entirely. You should periodically review the pertinent laws for such changes.

SUMMARY OF PROVISIONS OF TITLE VII

1. It prohibits private employers, labor organizations, and employment agencies that supply employees to such employers from discriminating against employees with respect to all terms and conditions of employment because of race, color, sex, religion, or national origin.

2. The employer is responsible for any discrimination that goes on within the employer's organization.

3. It is applicable to employers who have 15 or more employees.

4. It covers U.S. citizens working in foreign countries for American-owned or controlled companies.

5. It is enforced by the Equal Employment Opportunity Commission.

6. Individuals may file charges with the state or federal agency.

7. A claim must be brought within 180 days of discrimination complained of or 300 days where there is a state agency that handles discrimination. The complainant may only institute court action within 90 days of issuance of a "right to sue" letter.

8. A claim for discrimination may be based on intent or effect of an employment decision.

9. There are bona fide occupational qualification exceptions for religion, sex, and national origin only.

10. The elements a complainant must show to establish a basic case of discrimination are:

   a. He or she is a member of a protected class.

      b. He or she applied for and was qualified for a job for which the employer was seeking an applicant.

      c. Complainant was rejected.

      d. After the rejection, the position remained open and the employer continued to seek applicants from persons of comparable qualifications.

11. The employer is entitled to rebut a *prima facie* case by articulating "some legitimate non-discriminatory reason for the employee's rejection in cases of disparate treatment. However, in cases of disparate (adverse) impact, the employer must demonstrate that the challenged practice is job-related for the position in question and consistent with business necessity."

12. In cases of disparate treatment, if the employer comes forth with such a reason, the ultimate burden rests with the complainant to prove unlawful discrimination. The complainant must establish that the employer's legitimate reason was mere pretense and the actual reason for the employment decision was discriminatory. In disparate impact cases, if the employer has met its business necessity burden, the complainant may still prevail if he or she can show that a different practice with less disparate impact is available and the employer unreasonably refuses to adopt such a practice.

13. Remedies available include reinstatement, back pay, front pay, injunctive relief, compensatory and punitive damages, and attorneys' fees (which may include expert fees). But recovery is limited for compensatory and punitive damages depending upon the size of the employer in the range of $50,000 up to $300,000. However, back pay, interest on back pay, and front pay are not included in compensatory damages nor are past pecuniary losses, such as medical expenses.

14. A jury trial is available where compensatory or punitive damages are sought.

ENDNOTES

1. Employers are exempt if they have fewer than 15 employees for each workday in 20 or more calendar weeks in the current or preceding calendar year. Other exempt entities include Indian tribes, members of Congress, employers' foreign operations, and private membership clubs who are exempt from taxation under §501(c) of the Internal Revenue Code.

2. See *Meritor Savings Bank v. Vinson*, 477 U.S. 57 (1986) (sexual harassment that created a hostile working environment was actionable under Title VII).

3. See *Garcia v. San Antonio Metro Authority*, 469 U.S. 528 (1985) (Tenth Amendment does not supersede Congress's Commerce Clause authority to regulate wages and hours of state employees); *Fitzpatrick v. Bitzer*, 427 U.S. 445 (1976) (grounding Title VII in §5 of the Fourteenth Amendment permitted Congress to override the Eleventh Amendment immunity held by states to liability in federal court). The 1972 amendment to Title VII enlarged its scope to include governments, 42 U.S.C. §2000e(a) (governmental agencies and political subdivisions.)

4. See 42 U.S.C. §2000e(f). This amended provision overturns the U.S. Supreme Court ruling in *EEOC v. Arabian American Oil Co.*, 11 S.Ct. 1227 (1991), case below *Boureslan v. Aramco, Arabian American Oil Co.*, 857 F.2d 1014 (5th Cir. 1988), *affirmed* 892 F.2d 1271 (5th Cir. 1990).

5. 42 U.S.C. §2000e-1.

6. *Espinoze v. Farrah Mfg. Co.*, 414 U.S. 86, 95 (1973).

7. The Supreme Court set out the initial foundation for a *prima facie* case in McDonnell Douglas Corp. v. Green, 441 U.S. 792 (1973) (race discrimination against job applicants). These factors were later reiterated in a similar format in *Texas Department of Community Affairs v. Burdine*, 450 U.S. 248 (1981).

8. *King v. New Hampshire Dept. of Resources*, 562 F.2d 870 (1st Cir. 1977).

9. *Trans World Airlines v. Thurston*, 469 U.S. 111 (1985).

10. *Texas Department of Community Affairs v. Burdine*, 450 U.S. 248 (1981).

11. *McDonnell Douglas Corp. v. Green*, 411 U.S. 792 (1973).

12. *Texas Dept. of Community Affairs v. Burdine*, 450 U.S. at 256.

13. *McDonnell Douglas Corp. v. Green*, 411 U.S. at 792.

14. *Teamsters v. United States*, 431 U.S. 324 (1977).

15. *EEOC v. IUOE*, Locals 14 & 15, 553 F.2d 251 (2d Cir. 1977); *Stewart v. General Motors Corp.*, 542 F.2d 445 (7th Cir. 1976); and *Robinson v. Union Carbide Corp.*, 538 F.2d 652 (5th Cir. 1976).

16. See *Hazelwood School District v. United States*, 433 U.S. 299 (1977). A *prima facie* case of racial discrimination was established by showing that the percentage of qualified black teachers in a particular area was at least three or four times the percentage of blacks employed as teachers; the court ruled that the school district could rebut by use of statistics dealing with its hiring practices after it became subject to Title VII in 1972.

17. 109 S.Ct. 3151 (1989). *Wards Cove* dealt with an adverse impact case. The Civil Rights Act of 1991, while overruling the Supreme Court's holding on the burdens of proof (see page 87 in this chapter), does not appear to have altered the Court's analysis of the use of statistical evidence.

18. The Supreme Court first recognized this type of claim in *Griggs v. Duke Power Co.*, 401 U.S. 424 (1971), and further refined its view in *Albermarle Paper Co., v. Moody*, 422 U.S. 405 (1975), and *Dothard v. Robinson*, 433 U.S. 321 (1977).

19. In *Green v. USX Corp.*, 843 F.2d 1511 (3d Cir. 1988), *vacated* and *remanded, sub nom*, *USX Corp. v. Green*, 109 S. Ct. 3151 (1989), on appeal 896 F.2d 801 (3d Cir. 1990), affirming district court's dismissal of disparate treatment claim in 570 F.Supp 254 (E.D.Pa. 1983), the Third Circuit held that disparate impact analysis was applicable to multicomponent hiring systems that included subjective criteria.

20. P.L. 102-166 (November 21, 1991).

21. In *Wards Cove*, plaintiffs challenged a number of employment practices at Alaskan salmon canneries, including nepotism, a rehire preference, a lack of objective hiring criteria, separate hiring channels, and a practice of not hiring from within. The plaintiffs alleged that these practices resulted in unskilled, low-paying jobs being filled predominantly by nonwhites and skilled, higher-paying jobs being filled by whites.

22. 109 S. Ct. at 2121, relying on *Hazelwood School District v. United States*, 433 U.S. 299, 308 (1971), where in a similar case plaintiffs failed to make a *prima facie* case because they did not statistically identify how many blacks as compared to whites were qualified to become supervisors.

23. *Wards Cove*, 109 S. Ct. at 2125.

24. *Id.* at 2125 (emphasis added).

25. 42 U.S.C. §2000e-2(k) added by Civil Rights Act of 1991.

26. See 42 U.S.C. §2000e-2(k)(B)(i).

27. 42 U.S.C. §2000e-2(k)(1)(A)(ii). *Wards Cove*, 109 S.Ct. at 2127. See also *UAW v. Johnson Controls*, 886 F.2d 871 (7th Cir. 1989) *reversed on other grounds*, 111 S. Ct. 1196 (1991) (plaintiff bears the burden of presenting specific economically and technologically feasible alternatives that are equally effective).

28. 24 U.S.C. §2000e-3.

29. *Id.*

30. *Givhan v. Western Line Consol. School Dt.*, 439 U.S. 410 (1978) (private complaints about alleged discriminatory practices are protected by the First Amendment similar to the constitutional protection given protests made in a public forum).

31. *Sias v. City Demonstration Agency*, 588 F.2d 692 (9th Cir. 1978).

32. See *Silver v. KCA, Inc.*, 586 F.2d 138 (9th Cir. 1978).

33. See our extensive discussion on sexual harassment and hostile environment, in Chapter 7.

34. *Barela v. United Nuclear Corp.*, 541 F.2d 1263 (10th Cir. 1972).

35. *Rutherford v. American Bank of Commerce*, 565 F.2d 1162 (10th Cir. 1977).

36. *Pantchenko v. C. B. Dolge Co. Inc.*, 582 F.2d 1052 (2d Cir. 1978).

37. 42 U.S.C. §2000e-5(g), and *Drew v. Liberty Mutual Insurance Co.*, 480 F.2d 69 (5th Cir. 1973), *cert. denied*, 417 U.S. 935 (1974).

38. See *McDonald v. Santa Fe Trail Transp. Co.*, 427 U.S. 273, 280 (1978).

39. 42 U.S.C. §2000e-2(j).

40. The EEOC has adopted guidelines to protect employers from reverse discrimination claims when voluntary affirmative action is taken to correct the effects of past discrimination. The plan should include a self-analysis, a reasonable basis for concluding that the action is appropriate, and a reasonable course of action. 29 C.F.R. §1608.1, *et seq.* See *United Steelworkers of America v. Weber*, 443 U.S. 293 (1979).

41. *E.E.O.C. v. Wendy's of Colorado Springs, Inc.*, 727 F. Supp. 1375, 1384–85 (D.Colo. 1989).

42. *Livingston v. Roadway Express, Inc.*, 802 F.2d 1250, 1252 (10th Cir. 1986) *citing Parker v. Baltimore & O.R. Co.*, 652 F.2d 1012 (D.C. Cir. 1981).

43. *E.E.O.C. v. Wendy's of Colorado Springs, Inc.*, *supra* note 41.

44. See *Britton v. South Bend Community School Corp.*, 819 F.2d 766 (7th Cir. 1987). See the discussion in Chapter 10 regarding affirmative action plans and the criteria they must meet to avoid unlawful reverse discrimination. But see *Kromnick v. School District of Philadelphia*, 739 F.2d 894 (3d Cir. 1984), wherein a policy of requiring the transfer of teachers to maintain a certain faculty ratio was upheld.

45. 42 U.S.C. §2000e-2(e)(1). If your organization is not a religious institution, it will not be permitted to use religion as a BFOQ in any circumstance.

46. See *Gifford v. Atchison, Topeka & Santa Fe Railway Company*, 685 F.2d 1149 (9th Cir. 1982).

47. See *Weeks v. Southern Bell Tel. & Tel. Company*, 408 F.2d 228 (5th Cir. 1972), and *Bowe v. Colgate-Palmolive Co.*, 6 F.E.P. Cases (BNA) 1132 (7the Cir. 1973).

48. *International Union (UAW) v. Johnson Controls, Inc.*, 111 S.Ct. 1196 (1991), wherein the court struck down a fetal protection policy that prohibited fertile women from working in the better paying battery manufacturing jobs due to concerns for the health and safety of unborn children. The court held that the so-called safety exception to the BFOQ is limited to instances where gender or pregnancy actually interferes with the employee's ability to perform and the employer must direct its concerns in this regard to those aspects of a woman's job-related activities that fall within the "essence" of the particular business.

49. *Rasul v. District of Columbia*, 680 F.Supp. 436 (D.D.C. 1988).

50. *Pime v. Loyola University of Chicago*, 803 F.2d 351 (7th Cir. 1986).

51. *Torres v. Wisconsin Dept. of Health & Social Services*, 838 F.2d 944 (7th Cir. 1988), on rehearing in part 859 F.2d 1523 (1989), *cert. denied* 109 S.Ct. 1133 (1989).

52. *State Div. of Human Rights v. Oneida County Sheriff Dept.*, 47 F.E.P. Cases (BNA) 241 (N.Y. App. Div. 1986).

53. See *Norwood v. Dale Maintenance System, Inc.*, 590 F.Supp. 1410 (N.D. Ill. 1984), and *Fesel v. Masonic Home of Delaware, Inc.*, 447 F.Supp. 1346 (D.Del. 1978); *U.S. v. Gregory*, 46 F.E.P. Cases (BNA) 1743 (4th Cir. 1987); *Pime v. Loyola University of Chicago*, 585 F.Supp. 435 (D.Ill. 1984), *affirmed* 803 F.2d 351 (7th Cir. 1986).

54. The following jurisdictions have EEOC approved civil rights enforcement agencies: Alaska, Arizona, California, Colorado, Connecticut, Delaware, District of Columbia, Florida, Georgia, Hawaii, Idaho, Illinois, Indiana, Iowa, Kansas, Kentucky, Maine, Maryland, Massachusetts, Michigan, Minnesota, Missouri, Montana, Nebraska, Nevada, New Hampshire, New Jersey, New Mexico, New York, North Carolina, North Dakota, Ohio, Oklahoma, Oregon, Pennsylvania, Rhode Island, South Carolina, Tennessee, Texas, Utah, Vermont, Virgin Islands, Washington, West Virginia, Wisconsin, Wyoming, and Puerto Rico.

55. For example, New York City, San Francisco, Seattle, and Philadelphia, to name a few, have such agencies.

56. See *E.E.O.C. v. Shell Oil Co.*, 466 U.S. 54 (1984).

57. See *J. P. Stevens & Co. v. Perry*, 710 F.2d 136 (4th Cir. 1983).

58. Not all courts agree with this practice. See *Brown v. Puget Sound Electrical Apprenticeship & Training Trust*, 732 F.2d 726 (9th Cir. 1984).

6

COMPLYING WITH THE AGE DISCRIMINATION IN EMPLOYMENT ACT

Older employees represent a great deal of experience but also represent higher salaries and benefit costs. The dilemma faced by many employers is how to cut costs in the most efficient and fair way without running afoul of the law.

The Age Discrimination in Employment Act of 1967 (ADEA) protects individuals who are at least 40 years of age against arbitrary discrimination in compensation, terms, conditions, or privileges of employment.[1] The anti-discrimination provisions of the ADEA extend to every employment-related action; decisions regarding hiring, promotion, compensation, benefits, job assignments, training opportunities, working hours, transfer, and termination must be made without regard to age. In addition, state laws also proscribe age discrimination in the workplace but vary in their scope and coverage. Employers should recognize the potential resource represented by older workers and find ways to work within the law to balance cost efficiency with the expertise and knowledge their employees have to offer.

DEFINING THE SCOPE OF THE ADEA

The ADEA was enacted to "promote employment of older persons on their ability rather than age, to prohibit arbitrary age discrimination in employment, and to help employers and workers find ways of meeting problems arising from

113

the impact of age on employment."[2] ADEA sought to eliminate the most frequent types of age discrimination such as:

♦ Failure to hire because of age

♦ Failure to promote because of age

♦ Layoff of older employees in general, and specifically as part of a reduction in force

♦ Replacing an older worker with a younger worker

Determining Who Is Covered by the ADEA

Employees. The prohibitions of ADEA are limited to individuals who are at least 40 years of age.[3] While ADEA originally did not extend coverage to employees over age 70, the 1986 amendments eliminated the upper age limit, extending ADEA coverage to all employees of at least 40 years of age.

Employers. Persons engaged in industry affecting commerce who have 20 or more employees are covered.

Labor Organizations. Labor organizations that operate a hiring hall or have 25 or more members if they do not operate a hiring hall are covered.

Government Employees and Entities. Federal employees and applicants for federal employment are covered by the Act.[4] Congress extended ADEA's coverage to state and local government employers in 1974.[5] The Act exempts air traffic controllers, law enforcement officers, firefighters, and Panama Canal and Alaska Railroad employees. Absent the showing of a bona fide occupational qualification, federal, state, and local governments are precluded from setting a maximum hiring age or involuntarily retiring any covered federal employee solely on the basis of age.

Employees Abroad. A foreign employer subject to *in personam* jurisdiction is subject to ADEA coverage.[6] ADEA, as amended, specifies that the term "employee" under the Act includes any individual who is a citizen of the United States employed by a U.S. employer (or a foreign corporation controlled by a U.S. employer) in a workplace in a foreign country. While the U.S. Supreme Court ruled against this provision in *EEOC v. Arabian American Oil Co.,*[7] the Civil Rights Act of 1991[8] amended the ADEA so that the employment practices of U.S. employers that employ U.S. citizens outside the United States are governed by ADEA. However, there is a statutory exception—if compliance with the ADEA would cause the employer to violate the laws of the foreign country in which it is located, then an employer is not bound by ADEA's prohibitions.

BASIC SUBSTANTIVE PROVISIONS OF THE ADEA

ADEA's basic provisions include:

♦ A description of prohibited employment practices by employers, employment agencies, and labor organizations

♦ Prohibition against retaliation

♦ Limitations on recruitment advertisements

♦ Statutory exceptions such as BFOQ and exemptions

These basic provisions are discussed in this section so that you become familiar with this area of the law.

Defining Unlawful Employment Practices

The law prohibits generally any type of adverse employment decision when it is based on an individual's age. We discuss here the unlawful employment practices that an employer, employment agency, and labor organization may be liable for if age discrimination was the basis for such practice or action. Generally, all employment-related actions from hiring, compensation, and discharge may not be based on the individual's age. In addition, an employer may not take an adverse employment action in retaliation for an individual exercising his or her rights under ADEA. The ADEA protections extend to recruitment practices as well.

By the Employer. ADEA provides that the following practices by an employer are unlawful "because of [an] individual's age"[9]:

(1) to fail or refuse to hire or to discharge any individual or otherwise discriminate against any individual with respect to his compensation, terms, conditions, or privileges of employment;

(2) to limit, segregate, or classify his employees in any way which would deprive or tend to deprive any individual of employment opportunities or otherwise adversely affect his status as an employee; or

(3) to reduce the wage rate of any employee in order to comply with this chapter.[10]

By an Employment Agency. It is unlawful for an employment agency to fail or refuse to refer for employment, or otherwise to discriminate against, any individual because of such individual's age, or to classify or refer for employment any individual on the basis of such individual's age.[11]

By a Labor Organization. Labor organizations may not, "because of [an] individual's age,"

(1) exclude or expel from its membership, or otherwise discriminate against any individual;

(2) limit, segregate, or classify its membership, or classify or fail or refuse to refer for employment any individual, in any way which would deprive or tend to deprive any individual of employment opportunities, or would limit such employment opportunities or otherwise adversely affect his status as an employee or as an applicant for employment; or

(3) cause or attempt to cause an employer to discriminate against an individual in violation of this section.[12]

Prohibition Against Retaliation

It is unlawful for an employer, employment agency, or labor organization to discriminate because an individual has opposed any practice made unlawful by ADEA or because such individual has made a charge, testified, assisted, or participated in any manner in an investigation, proceeding, or litigation under this chapter.[13]

Case Study

Mary Jones is a 47-year-old credit analyst with Dollar Bank. Mary filed an age discrimination complaint with the EEOC after she was denied a promotion. Dollar Bank subsequently fired Mary upon receiving notice of Mary's complaint.

Dollar undertook an illegal activity. An employer may not retaliate against an employee who has exercised his or her rights under ADEA.

Limitations on Recruitment Advertisements

It is also unlawful for an employer, labor organization, or employment agency to print or publish any notice or advertisement "indicating any preference, limitation, specification, or discrimination because of age."[14] For example, an employer may not state in a want advertisement that it seeks waiters below the age of 30.

Statutory Exceptions to Prohibited Conduct

Practices that would otherwise be prohibited under ADEA are permissible:

- Where age is a bona fide occupational qualification (BFOQ) reasonably necessary to the normal operation of the particular business

- Where the differentiation is based on reasonable factors other than age

- To observe a bona fide seniority system or bona fide employee benefit plan which is not intended to evade the purposes of the Act

- Where discharge or other discipline is for good cause[15]

Bona Fide Occupational Qualifications. The ADEA permits otherwise prohibited conduct where age is a bona fide occupational qualification reasonably necessary to the normal operation of the particular business.[16] BFOQ is the most difficult statutory defense to prove because it is an admission of exactly what the ADEA seeks to prevent—discrimination based on age.

Two elements must be proven by the defendant to establish a BFOQ defense:

1. The job qualifications used to justify discrimination are reasonably necessary to the essence of the business

2. There is a substantial factual basis for believing that all or substantially all persons over a certain age would be unable to perform the duties of the job safely, or it is highly impractical to deal with older employees on an individualized basis.[17]

The BFOQ defense has traditionally been reserved for employers whose businesses are primarily safety-related or who are engaged in inherently dangerous activities.[18] The BFOQ defense has been allowed in actions involving intra-city bus drivers[19] and airline pilots and copilots.[20] However, the BFOQ defense has not fared well in actions brought by airline flight engineers challenging maximum age limits.[21]

Case Example

Joe Grey, a 45-year-old bus driver, brought suit for age discrimination after he was refused a job at Intra-City (IC) Bus Company because he was too old, according to the company's hiring cap for applicants over 35. IC Bus Co. defended that age is a BFOQ to ensure the safety of the passengers.

Can IC Bus Company use age as a BFOQ for hiring requirements? Yes. Safety is the overriding factor and recurring physical examinations would be unreliable. Under some bus company union seniority systems, low-seniority drivers are assigned the most difficult runs and long hours. Using age as a hiring factor prevents older drivers from having the most difficult assignments.[22]

Reasonable Factors Other than Age. The ADEA permits age discrimination when the differentiation is based on reasonable factors other than age.[23] EEOC interpretations provide that

- The defense that the practice is justified by a reasonable factor other than age is unavailable when an employment practice uses age as a limiting criterion

- An employment practice cannot be justified as a reasonable factor other than age when it is claimed as a basis for different treatment of employees or applicants on the grounds that it is a "factor other than age," and such a practice has an adverse impact on individuals within a protected age group

- A differentiation based on the average cost of employing older employees as a group is unlawful except with respect to employee benefit plans[24]

Physical fitness requirements have usually been considered appropriate in particularly strenuous jobs.[25] Economic savings can be a reasonable factor for discharging older workers when the "necessity for drastic cost reduction is obviously real and forced early retirements are the least detrimental alternative means available to reduce costs."[26]

Case Example

A 54-year-old magazine publisher earning $150,000 a year brought suit under ADEA after his position was downgraded and his salary reduced in a corporate reorganization.

Is the executive's high salary a legal basis for termination? Yes. The district court dismissed the suit, deciding that employers may cut costs by eliminating highly paid positions as long as each decision is handled individually on its merits without any blanket rules that adversely impact older workers. This decision was affirmed.[27]

Bona Fide Seniority System or Benefit Plan. ADEA permits employers to observe the terms of a bona fide seniority system or any bona fide employee benefit plan as long as the plan is not intended to evade the purposes of the ADEA.[28] However, no seniority system shall require the mandatory retirement of any individual because of age.[29]

An employer seeking to invoke the bona fide system/plan defense must establish that

- A system/plan is "bona fide"
- It is not designed to avoid the proscriptions of the Act[30]
- Plaintiff's treatment results from observance of the system's/plan's terms

According to the Older Worker Benefit Protection Act (OWBPA) Amendment to ADEA, an employer can take prohibited action to observe the terms of a bona fide employee benefit plan, but only where the actual amount of payment made or cost incurred on behalf of an older worker is no less than that made or incurred on behalf of a younger worker.[31] A bona fide benefit plan has been defined as a genuine plan that pays substantial benefits.[32] However, the good faith test is not always satisfied if a plan requires retirement too early or pays unduly low benefits.[33] A plan violates ADEA if it denies severance pay to employees eligible for early retirement, but offers both severance pay and retirement pay to persons laid off who are under retirement age.[34]

Discharge or Other Discipline for Good Cause. The ADEA allows discharge or other discipline of individuals for good cause.[35] Good cause can consist of unsatisfactory performance or behavior in violation of work rules. The key to asserting a successful good cause defense is the presence of a complete, objective, and written performance evaluation system.

Other Exemptions.

1. *Compulsory Retirement for Executives.* It is permissible to have *compulsory retirement* for executives at age 65 who for two years prior to retirement were employed in a "bona fide executive or a high policy making position," if such employee is entitled to nonforfeitable retirement benefits of at least $44,000 per annum.[36] Such employees are known as "bona fide executives."

2. *College Professors.* Tenured college professors may be forced to retire at age 70.[37]

3. *Employees Abroad.* An employer in a foreign country is exempt from ADEA provisions where compliance with such subsections would cause such employer to violate the laws of that country.[38]

4. *Securities Industry Employees.* Employees in the securities industry who sign agreements to arbitrate any disputes arising out of employment or termination of employment are bound by that pledge, even though the age claim would be subject to the ADEA.[39]

ANALYSIS OF AN ADEA CLAIM

A claim under ADEA may be asserted under the theories of disparate treatment, disparate impact, or retaliation. A plaintiff may be required before trial to identify those theories of proof on which plaintiff relies. See Chapter 5 for a similar discussion on theories under Title VII.

1. *Disparate Treatment.* Under the disparate treatment theory, an employee or unsuccessful job applicant alleges that he or she was treated less favorably than other employees because of intentional age discrimination.

2. *Disparate Impact.* Discrimination may also be shown on a disparate impact theory, which focuses on the discriminatory consequences of an employment policy that is neutral, and apparently legal, on its face. Employers can defend a disparate impact claim by justifying an exclusionary practice or policy

as a business necessity that "bears a demonstrable relationship to successful performance."[40]

3. *Retaliation.* Retaliation claims allege that an employer, employment agency, or labor organization discriminated against an individual because such individual made a charge, testified, or participated in an ADEA investigation.

The following discussion of the elements of an age claim will focus on disparate treatment since these claims compose the majority of age discrimination claims.

Elements of an Age Discrimination Claim

The plaintiff, in an ADEA lawsuit, has the ultimate burden of persuading the trier of the fact that the defendant intentionally discriminated against the plaintiff.[41] A plaintiff who produces direct evidence of an employer's discriminatory use of age in making an employment decision may be entitled to go to the jury.[42] However, since direct evidence of age discrimination is rare, circumstantial evidence is usually presented in ADEA cases.

Initially, an employee must establish a *prima facie* case which indicates that the basic elements of a claim exist and creates a rebuttable presumption. The burden then shifts to the employer, who must "articulate a legitimate nondiscriminatory reason" for taking the activity in question. The final burden rests with the employee, who has the opportunity to show that the employer's alleged reason for the action was a mere pretext for age discrimination.[43] This method of proof applies only to circumstantial evidence and is not applied in cases where an employee presents direct evidence of discrimination.

The Prima Facie Case.
An employee or candidate for employment may establish a *prima facie* case by showing by a preponderance of the evidence:

- Membership in the protected class (aged 40 or over)

- Adverse personnel action (failure to hire, failure to promote, termination, lower benefits, etc.)

- Proper qualifications for the position or satisfactory job performance

- A younger employee with equal or inferior qualifications was treated better under circumstances giving rise to an inference of age discrimination

It is not always necessary to present all four factors to establish a *prima facie* case, as there is flexibility depending upon the type of adverse employment action taken and the circumstances of the particular case.

A discharged employee can still establish a *prima facie* case of age discrimination if he or she was replaced with a younger person who also falls within the protected class (40 or over).

Case Example

The plaintiff, a 54-year-old manager of a university bookstore, established a *prima facie* case when Hastings College of Law fired him. Hastings replaced him with a 49-year-old employee who was also protected by the Act.

The plaintiff established that he was in the protected age group, was qualified, and was replaced with a younger (yet also protected) member of the class. The court ruled that a *prima facie* case had been established because the evidence was sufficient to support an inference of discrimination. However, Hastings stated that the legitimate reason for the termination was financial mismanagement of the bookstore. Hastings prevailed when the plaintiff was unable to prove that the employer's dissatisfaction was merely a pretext for age discrimination.[44]

Additionally, replacement by even an older employee will not necessarily foreclose *prima facie* proof if other direct or circumstantial evidence supports an inference of discrimination. The rationale for these decisions is that, in some circumstances, it makes no sense to require proof of replacement by a younger employee. For example, in a case of a reduction in force, a discharged employee may not be replaced at all; yet the employee may have been selected for discharge in a discriminatory manner.

Reduction-in-Force Cases. In reduction-in-force cases, the traditional *McDonnell Douglas* four-part disparate treatment analysis has been disregarded because the plaintiff is not being replaced by another employee. The court in *Williams v. General Motors Corp.*[45] allowed a plaintiff to establish a *prima facie* case in a reduction-in-force case by

- Showing that the plaintiff is within the protected age group and that plaintiff has been adversely affected by defendant's employment decision

- Showing that plaintiff was qualified to assume another position at the time of the action

- Producing evidence from which a fact finder might reasonably conclude that the employer intended to discriminate in reaching the decision

To satisfy the third requirement, the evidence must lead the fact finder to reasonably conclude either that defendant consciously refused to consider retaining the plaintiff because of his age or that defendant regarded age as a negative factor in such consideration.[46] (See further discussion of reduction in force cases in this chapter.)

Employer's Rebuttal of Claim. Once an individual has established a *prima facie* case, the burden is placed on the employer to articulate some legitimate, nondiscriminatory reason for the adverse employment action. The employer may do so by clearly setting forth such reasons for the employment action through the introduction of admissible evidence. In fact, the employer need only raise a genuine issue of fact and show that the pertinent facts are in dispute. An employer may even defend an age bias claim with knowledge it gained after the discriminatory firing about the employee's misconduct while on the job.[47] However, an employer has not successfully rebutted a *prima facie* claim if the allegedly legitimate reason is a disguise for age discrimination.

Case Example

Robert Jones, a 53-year-old job applicant, brought suit under ADEA after he failed to get the job. After Robert established a *prima facie* case, the employer asserted that he was "overqualified" and thus unqualified.

An employer may not use "overqualification" as a legitimate reason for rejecting a job applicant. The contention that an applicant was overqualified does not satisfy the employer's burden of articulating a nondiscriminatory reason for the employment action. "Overqualified" may merely be a buzzword for "too old."[48]

Employee's Claim of Pretextual Reason. Once the employer states a legitimate business reason for the adverse action, the employee has the burden to show that the proffered reason was pretextual and not the true reason for the employment decision. The employee may attempt to establish pretext either directly by proving that the employer more likely than not was motivated by a discriminatory reason or indirectly by showing that the employer's rebuttal theory was "unworthy of credence."[49]

A plaintiff may establish pretext in the following manner:

♦ Show evidence that younger workers received different treatment

♦ Show that the employer's policies were selectively applied

♦ Show that discrepancies arose in the employer's explanation

♦ Show that the employer did not follow its own policies with respect to older employees

To prevail in an age discrimination claim, a plaintiff need show only by a preponderance of the evidence that age was a "determining factor" in the employer's decision, although not the sole factor.[50] In a jury case, the plaintiff is entitled to jury instructions that state age need not be the only factor entering into the adverse employment decision; rather the test is that "but for" the age consideration the practice complained of would not have occurred.[51]

How the Plaintiff Can Prove an Age Discrimination Claim

Methods available to the plaintiff to prove an age discrimination claim include direct evidence, circumstantial evidence, and statistical evidence.[52]

Direct evidence may be in the form of oral or written statements by supervisors or management. Direct evidence may consist of a discriminatory advertisement for employment, documentary evidence of age discrimination, or statements clearly revealing that an employment decision was based on impermissible factors, that is, the "smoking gun." Since direct evidence is rarely available, plaintiffs often establish a *prima facie* case and utilize circumstantial evidence to prove that age discrimination was the true reason for the adverse employment action.

Discriminatory impact is frequently evidenced by statistics, from which it may be inferred that the particular plaintiff was affected by an employer's selection methods, employment criteria, or retirement criteria. In *McDonnell Douglas*, the Supreme Court approved the use of statistical evidence in discrimination cases, stating "[s]tatistics as to petitioner's employment policy and practice may be helpful to a determination of whether [the employer's] refusal to rehire [the employee] in this case conformed to a general pattern of discrimination."

Employers' Penalties for ADEA Violations

ADEA incorporates the remedial provisions of the Fair Labor Standards Act (FLSA),[53] which provides that "any employer who violates the provisions of [this Act] shall be liable for such legal or equitable relief as may be appropriate to effectuate the purposes of [the Act]."[54] Available remedies under ADEA include

- Payment of lost wages (back pay)
- Employment, reinstatement, or promotion[55]
- Injunctive relief[56]
- Front pay[57]
- Liquidated damages for "willful violations"[58]
- Reasonable attorney's fees for successful plaintiffs

Back Pay. The general purpose of *back pay* in ADEA cases has been described as serving two primary functions: "First, the prospect of economic penalties more certainly deters illegal employment practice than does exposure to injunctive relief or prospective equitable remedies such as reinstatement. Second, economic exactions recompense individuals for injuries inflicted by employer's discriminatory conduct."[59]

Front Pay. In addition, the court may award *front pay*, which is intended to compensate victims of discrimination for the continuing future effects of discrimination until the victim can be made whole. Front pay is a supplement to back pay, not a substitute for it. Front pay is considered if the employer/employee relationship is damaged beyond repair during litigation or if no position is available at the present for reinstatement. It is often awarded when an individual's age reduces the likelihood of reemployment.

Liquidated Damages. If an employee has not been made whole with back pay and front pay, damages for lost wages can be doubled through liquidated damages if the violation is considered willful and the court determines that reinstatement would not be appropriate. In *Trans World Airlines v. Thurston,* the Supreme Court affirmed the Second Circuit's ruling that an ADEA violation was "willful" when "the employer either knew or showed reckless disregard for the matter of whether its conduct was prohibited by the ADEA."[60] While a liquidated damages award does not require definitive proof showing that the employer intended to violate the ADEA, liquidated damages are not available if the violator knew that the ADEA was "in the picture." The Third Circuit requires a stricter showing of "outrageous conduct" by the employer for the awarding of liquidated damages.[61]

The courts of appeals are unanimous in holding that no punitive damages are recoverable and that a plaintiff is limited to damages measured by lost earnings and an additional amount as liquidated damages. The circuits are also unanimous in denying damages for pain and suffering under ADEA.

Mitigation of Damages. A plaintiff must make reasonable efforts to mitigate damages to be entitled to receive back pay.[62] However, the burden is on the defendant to prove that a plaintiff's failure to exercise reasonable persistence to avoid loss and a reasonable chance the plaintiff would have found comparable work with such persistence.[63] A back pay award is decreased by the amount of severance pay and self-employment earnings but is usually not reduced by pension benefits or unemployment compensation.

HOW AN ADEA CLAIM IS ENFORCED

Now that you have a basic understanding of what an ADEA claim involves, we will discuss the enforcement procedures for such a claim. The EEOC is the enforcement agency, and there are specific procedures and time limitations a complainant must comply with in order to have a claim under ADEA properly addressed.

Describing Procedures and Time Limits

The federal agency responsible for enforcing ADEA is the Equal Employment Opportunity Commission (EEOC).[64] The EEOC receives, processes, and investigates charges of employment discrimination alleging a violation of Title VII, the Americans with Disabilities Act, and the Equal Pay Act in addition to ADEA. The EEOC has 23 district offices located throughout the United States. See Chapter 5 on Title VII for a complete discussion of the EEOC's enforcement role.

How a Claim is Initiated

An individual initiates a proceeding under ADEA by filing a charge at one of the EEOC district offices or in a "deferral state" (a state that has its own EEOC-approved civil rights enforcement agency),[65] at that state's civil rights or human rights agency. The charge should be precise enough to identify the parties and describe the discriminatory action or practice. The charge should additionally provide pertinent surrounding information, names of witnesses, and appropriate information for contacting the complainant.[66] Charges must be in writing and under oath or affirmation.

NOTE: A charge must be filed with the EEOC or appropriate state agency before a complainant may file an ADEA claim in court.

A charge must be filed with an EEOC district office within 180 days of the discriminatory act. In a deferral state, a charge must be filed with the state agency within 300 days of the unlawful act or 30 days after receipt of notice of the termination of proceedings under state law, whichever comes first.[67] The time period begins to run on the date that the employer's intention is clearly communicated to the employee, regardless of actual termination or the continued receipt of severance pay and/or employee benefits.[68]

The 180- and 300-day ADEA time limits are not absolute in that there may be equitable modification when the complainant fails to file within the time period.[69] Equitable modification consists of equitable estoppel and equitable tolling. *Equitable estoppel* means that the employer may not challenge a late EEOC charge when the complainant knows of the existence of a cause of action but the employer's conduct causes the complainant to delay bringing the suit. *Equitable tolling* also acts to prevent the employer from challenging a late EEOC charge and occurs when the complainant is ignorant of his or her cause of action due to the defendant's concealment of pertinent information.[70]

A complainant in a deferral state (1) must utilize the state authorities before instituting suit in federal court, (2) but compliance with state statutes of limitation is unnecessary, and (3) an individual may concurrently exhaust state remedies and file a charge with the EEOC.[71]

How a Claim Is Investigated

Upon receipt of an age discrimination charge, the EEOC begins an investigation that is to be completed, if possible, within 120 days from the filing date. In a deferral state, the EEOC defers jurisdiction for at least the first 60 days, giving the state agency the right to attempt to investigate and resolve the conflict first. The investigation process begins with notice of the charge being sent to the employer within 10 days. The scope of the investigation is generally limited to information necessary to make a determination as to whether reasonable cause exists to believe that unlawful discrimination occurred. The investigation may include a position statement from the employer, a fact-finding conference, an inspection of the employer's workplace, a review of the employer's records, summoning witnesses to take testimony, and the right to subpoena.

Once the EEOC has concluded its investigation, the district director of the appropriate field office issues a letter of determination of "reasonable cause" or "no probable cause" as to whether unlawful age discrimination has occurred.

"No Probable Cause" Determination. If the EEOC determines that "no probable cause" exists to believe the alleged discrimination has occurred, the complainant may file for a review within 14 days. However, a determination made initially by the EEOC in Washington, D.C., is not subject to review. Although a "no-cause" determination in a particular case does not bar a subsequent suit on the same claim, an individual may not sue until after the determination has become final and a "right to sue" notice has been issued by the EEOC.

"Reasonable Cause" Determination. If a "reasonable cause" determination is made, ADEA requires the EEOC to attempt to eliminate the unlawful discrimination through conciliation, conference, and persuasion. If the parties successfully conclude the conciliation procedure, an executed conciliation agreement prevents the employer from being sued by the EEOC or the employee for any discriminatory acts covered by the agreement. The agreement must be signed by all parties for it to be effective.

In the event that conciliation fails after a good faith effort on the EEOC's behalf, the file is sent to the EEOC regional attorney who decides if the Commission should commence litigation against the employer. The EEOC is required to notify complainants when a charge is dismissed or otherwise terminated. These closure notices give the complainant the right to sue. However, private suit is prohibited if the EEOC decides to sue on the complainant's behalf.

Filing a Civil Suit

The Civil Rights Act of 1991 (CRA '91) amends ADEA by providing that a complainant has 90 days in which to file suit after a "right to sue" notice is received.[72] This provision is similar to the "notice of right to sue" issued in Title

VII cases. CRA '91 eliminated the provision for suspending for up to one year the running of the limitation period for filing suit while EEOC attempts to resolve a charge. According to the EEOC's interpretation of the new law, its mandate to issue right to sue notices, effectively, but not expressly, repeals the ADEA two-year (three years for willful violations) time limitations for filing civil suits.[73] However, the ADEA prohibits the filing of civil suit until 60 days after the commencement of federal and/or state administrative action. This provision is intended to screen from the federal courts those discrimination complaints that might be settled to the satisfaction of the grievant in state proceedings.

JURY TRIALS

Private actions by employees for lost wages under the ADEA have consistently been held to include a right to trial by jury.[74] However, because the element of discretion in awards of liquidated damages was adopted from the Portal-to-Portal Act of 1947,[75] such awards remain the province of the court, not the jury.[76] In 1978, the ADEA was amended specifically to authorize trial by jury "of any issue of fact in any such action for recovery of amounts owing as a result of a violation of this chapter, regardless of whether equitable relief is sought by any party in such action."[77] Thus all claims under the ADEA for monetary relief, whether back wages or liquidated damages, may be tried by a jury.[78] However, jury trials are not available in an age claim against the federal government.[79]

FILING SPECIAL TYPES OF ADEA SUITS

ADEA's specialized protection, based solely on age, lends itself to challenges and lawsuits by groups of employees against an employer for real or perceived age discrimination. Typical claims brought by such employees are challenges to a reduction in force, reorganizations, and/or early retirement programs. Often a poorly designed or executed reduction in force or early retirement program may inadvertently or purposefully target older workers who, in turn, feel they are being forced out. These challenges may be brought by a single aggrieved individual or by many similarly situated employees. When a group of employees band together and challenge an employer's practice, it is often in the form of a class action. The discussions in the sections that follow consider these special types of lawsuits.

Suits in Reductions in Force and Early Retirement Programs

Employees protected by ADEA often challenge reductions in force, claiming that age was the reason for the termination. Likewise, protected employees who elect to participate in early retirement incentive programs sometimes file an ADEA suit, claiming that the program was designed to eliminate older workers from the work force or they elected to participate in the program because of perceived "pressure," which amounted to "involuntary" retirement or constructive discharge because of age.

An employer can defend a claim of age discrimination for a reduction in force by showing layoff according to inverse seniority. The employer will doubly attack the discrimination charge because a bona fide seniority system is a statutory defense and the employees hired first are likely to be older. However, productivity concerns usually limit inverse seniority layoffs to the union situation. Instead, most nonunion employers will seek to lay off the poorest performers. Well-documented performance appraisals can show that a reduction in force was designed to retain the most qualified employees and layoff was reserved for the lowest performers.

Employers who are defending an age discrimination charge for a reduction in force should also focus on the skills of the employees. Employees who do not possess skills that match the work to be completed after the reduction in force will obviously be laid off. Employers who undertake reductions in force will run into trouble if a statistical analysis shows that a disproportionate number of older workers was laid off.

ADEA claims challenging early retirement incentive programs as coercive can usually be defended by showing that the offer was given with adequate time and information for consideration and was not accompanied by the threat of individual termination. Such offers must comply with the Older Workers Benefit Protection Act discussed in this chapter.

Class Action Suits

Under ADEA, a person may become a member of a class action suit by giving his or her consent in writing to become such a party and such consent is filed in the court in which such action is brought.[80] This "opt-in" procedure is contrary to the "opt-out" alternative where eligible plaintiffs are included in the class unless they request to be excluded.[81] An administrative charge must claim to represent a class or allege classwide age discrimination in order to support a subsequent class action suit.[82] A proper class charge will permit other plaintiffs to opt into the lawsuit even if their individual claims have been barred for lack of timely filing of individual charges.[83] The circuits are divided over the power of a plaintiff to send notice of the lawsuit to prospective class members.[84]

HOW THE OLDER WORKERS BENEFIT PROTECTION ACT AFFECTS ADEA

The Older Workers Benefit Protection Act[85] (OWBPA) amends ADEA in the areas of employee benefits, disability and severance pay offsets, and releases/waivers of ADEA claims. This legislation is, in part, in response to the

U.S. Supreme Court decision in *Public Employees Retirement System of Ohio v. Betts*, 109 S.Ct. 2954 (1990), which effectively exempted the majority of employee benefit programs from ADEA prohibitions.

Describing the Scope and Coverage of OWBPA

OWBPA makes ADEA applicable to most employee benefit programs and impacts on early retirement and other exit incentive programs. You should become familiar with all aspects of OWBPA.

Dates of Implementation. OWBPA had staggered effective dates to allow the most efficient implementation of these amendments. The waiver and benefits amendments became effective on October 17, 1990, for all waivers and benefits established or modified on or after October 17, 1990, and on April 14, 1991, for all other conduct. Application to employers with a unionized work force began upon the expiration date of present collective bargaining agreement or June 1, 1992, whichever occurred first.

Benefits Covered. *All* employee benefits, including those provided pursuant to a bona fide employee benefit plan, are covered by ADEA. This includes employee benefit plans adopted prior to the enactment of the ADEA.

> NOTE: Employers are required to follow the "equal benefits or equal cost" principle, which mandates that all employees covered by ADEA provide older workers with the benefits at least equal to those provided to younger workers unless the cost of doing so is greater than the cost of providing the benefit to the younger worker. The burden is on the employer to show greater cost.

Case Study

> Jerry Dawson, a 53-year-old accountant, brought suit under ADEA because he received less company-paid life insurance than his coworker, 37-year-old Jennifer James. This action is lawful if the two policies cost the employer the same amount of money.

The Voluntary Early Retirement Incentive Plan. If an exit incentive plan is consistent with purposes of the ADEA, it is exempt from the "equal benefit or equal cost" provision. Thus, certain subsidies and/or supplemental pension are permitted. An employer is permitted to set a minimum age as a condition of eligibility for normal or early retirement benefits. Caution should be exercised in designing such plans because it seems that any program that does not have a non age-related business justification would be suspect.

Severance Payments. Severance pay plans are subject to ADEA and the Employee Retirement Income Security Act (ERISA). Such plans must be thoughtfully implemented as to avoid unforeseen costs.

An employer may deduct from severance payments the value of any retiree health benefits provided to employees eligible for an immediate fully subsidized pension as well as the value of any additional pension benefits. The value of retiree medical benefits may be offset from severance payments to retirees in cases of plant closing, reduction in force, or any other contingent events unrelated to age. The medical benefit offset is prorated, and no pension offset is permitted in the case of a partially subsidized pension.

NOTE: A new direct right of action exists for aggrieved individuals whose severance pay was reduced by the value of retiree health coverage to compel specific performance of the employer's obligations to continue to provide medical benefits.

Disability Benefits. A bona fide employee benefit plan may reduce long-term disability benefits by the amount of any employer-funded pension benefits that an employee voluntarily elects to receive at any age or for which an employee is eligible for after age 62 or the normal retirement age under the plan. This provision overrides EEOC regulations.

Group Exit Incentive Programs. Written notice is required to be given to all eligible individuals. The notice is to include a description of the group or class and time limits for the program, job titles and ages of individuals eligible or selected, and all those not eligible or selected.

In an attempt to insulate themselves from discrimination liability, many employers request employees electing additional severance compensation to release claims under ADEA.

Guidelines for Waiver or Releases. The basic rule to remember here is that a waiver of claims arising under ADEA must be "knowing and voluntary." The basic requirements that must be satisfied are the following:

♦ A waiver must be part of the agreement between employer and employee and must be written in a way that the average eligible employee can understand.

♦ An agreement must refer specifically to waiver of rights or claims arising under ADEA.

♦ An agreement may not extend to rights or claims that may arise *after* the date on which such agreement is executed.

♦ An agreement must be given in exchange for "consideration" (something over and beyond what an employee is already guaranteed).

♦ An agreement (or a separate written notice) must advise the employee to consult with an attorney before signing.

♦ Employees must be given 21 days to review a waiver agreement or, in the case of a group exit incentive program, 45 days.

♦ The agreement must provide that for a period of 7 days following its execution, the individual may revoke the agreement; it does not become effective until after the expiration of the revocation period.

NOTE: Agreements that incorporate waivers which were executed prior to October 17, 1990, are not subject to the previously stated requirements.

When a waiver is part of a settlement of an EEOC charge or court action alleging age discrimination, the waiver requirements just set out must be met and the individual must be given a reasonable period of time within which to consider the waiver.

NOTE: The employer asserting the validity of the waiver has the burden, in case of a dispute, of proving that the waiver was "knowing and voluntary" and complied with OWBPA.

Even if the release and waiver of ADEA claims are valid, the employee may still file an age discrimination charge with the EEOC to alert the agency to a pattern or practice of age discrimination or to challenge the release as not knowing, voluntary, or for lack of valuable consideration. Employees are also protected from retaliation for challenging the validity of an executed release.

COMPARING THE ADEA AND TITLE VII

The substantive portions of the ADEA are almost identical to the anti-discrimination provisions of Title VII,[86] since both prohibit discrimination in compensation and all terms and conditions of employment. The major difference is between the scope of the two acts. Title VII's broad approach prohibits discrimination against employees or applicants for employment on the basis of race, color, religion, sex, or national origin. However, the ADEA prohibits discrimination only on the basis of age. While both acts cover employers, employment agencies, and labor organizations, the ADEA applies to employers with 20 or more employees and nonhiring hall labor organizations with 25 or more members. Title VII applies to employers and nonhiring hall labor organizations with 15 or more employees or members, respectively.

Under both ADEA and Title VII a complainant can bring private causes of action under the respective acts only after he or she has pursued certain administrative remedies. Claims must first be filed with the EEOC district office within 180 days from date of the discriminatory act or, in a deferral state, with the state civil rights agency within 300 days of the alleged act. In both ADEA and Title VII suits, an individual must wait 60 days after filing with the EEOC/state agency to institute a civil action. CRA '91 provided that civil suits brought under ADEA, in addition to Title VII actions, require EEOC-issued "right to sue" notices and mandate the complainant to file suit within 90 days from receipt of such notice.

The similarities in language and policy between Title VII and the ADEA have led most circuits to apply Title VII disparate treatment and disparate impact proof principles to ADEA cases.[87] In *Laugesen v. Anaconda Co.*,[88] however, the court stated that it would be inappropriate to apply Title VII proof guidelines automatically in all ADEA cases because the two acts were separately and independently enacted and had distinctive legislative histories. The two acts are now more similar due to CRA '91's amendments. For example, jury trials are available in both Title VII and ADEA actions.

COMPARING THE EMPLOYEE RETIREMENT INCOME SECURITY ACT (ERISA) PROVISIONS AND ADEA

The Employee Retirement Income Security Act does not preempt ADEA.[89] However, a state age discrimination law may be preempted by ERISA as it applies to "employee benefit plans" to the extent it is inconsistent with ERISA.[90] Thus, personnel professionals should be familiar with the interaction among ADEA, ERISA, and state laws regarding issues of benefits and older workers. All of ADEA's and ERISA's requirements must be complied with by the company. See discussion of ERISA in Chapter 18 on employee benefits.

One point where these laws overlap is in regard to pension benefit plans, where ADEA provides that "it shall be unlawful . . . to establish or maintain an employee pension benefit plan which requires or permits

> . . . In the case of a defined benefit plan, the cessation of an employee's benefit accrual, or the reduction of the rate of an employee's benefit accrual, because of age, or

> . . . In the case of a defined contribution plan, the cessation of allocations to an employee's account, or the reduction of the rate at which amounts are allocated to the employee's account, because of age."[91]

ADEA and ERISA also have similar anti-discrimination and retaliation provisions[92] as well as a provision for bringing a class action based on employer conduct as part of a "pattern or practice" of interference with existing or future rights under a benefit plan.[93]

HOW TO AVOID ADEA VIOLATIONS
AND/OR MINIMIZE LIABILITY

1. Review all pertinent state and federal laws on a regular basis and prior to taking action with regard to an employee over 40 years of age.

2. Be certain that job descriptions, application forms, and interview questions are free of irrelevant criteria that may indicate age.

3. Establish written work rules and indicate that violations can lead to discipline or discharge.

4. Use regular performance reviews and have supervisors review all performance appraisals with their employees. Give employees an opportunity to respond in writing to reviews. Regular reviews put poor performers on notice that termination could result if performance does not improve. Do not praise an employee in a review with the hope of improving future performance. It is more important to document actual shortcomings in an employee's work.

5. Educate supervisors and managers to avoid using phrases like "old dog" or "over the hill" that indicate age bias or refusing employment because an individual is "overqualified."

6. Use progressive discipline that informs an employee that his or her behavior or performance is unacceptable and could lead to discharge if it continues. Be consistent in discipline for all employees.

7. Employee retirement incentive programs must be purely voluntary. Adequate time and information should be given to allow the employee to consult with legal counsel before making a decision about accepting the incentive in exchange for retirement.

8. If you think a soon-to-be-terminated employee may bring a lawsuit, consider getting the employee to release any ADEA claims that might arise after termination in exchange for an enhanced severance package. Such releases must be knowing, voluntary, and for valuable consideration. Provide the employee with sufficient time to consider the release and encourage the employee to review the release with legal counsel.

9. Do not intentionally prevent a terminated employee from obtaining future employment, since an employed worker is less likely to bring suit. An employee with subsequent employment has mitigated his or her damages and offset damage claims under the ADEA.

10. Consider a reference policy of merely confirming dates of employment for references. Avoid, if possible, giving a negative reference that could

be the basis for a defamation suit and good references that could be used as an admission that there was no cause to terminate.

11. Outplacement assistance can be used to avoid litigation and convince a jury of the employer's concern for an employee's subsequent employment and emotional well-being.

SUMMARY OF THE ADEA PROVISIONS

The provision of the ADEA

1. Prohibit discrimination in compensation and terms, conditions, and privileges of employment against individuals aged 40 and over.

2. Prohibit age discrimination against one person in a protected group in favor of another person in the same protected group.

3. Apply to employers with 20 or more employees. They also apply to employment agencies and labor organizations.

4. Cover U.S. citizens working in foreign countries for American-owned or-controlled companies.

5. Include statutory exemptions to compliance

   a. Where age is a bona fide occupational qualification.
   b. Where the differentiation is based on reasonable factors other than age.
   c. To observe the terms of a bona fide seniority system or a bona fide employee benefit plan.
   d. To discharge or otherwise discipline an individual for good cause.

6. Are enforced by the Equal Employment Opportunity Commission.

7. Require a complainant to file a charge with the EEOC within 180 days from date of discriminatory act or, in a deferral state, with a state civil rights/human rights agency within 300 days.

8. Allow a complainant 90 days in which to file civil suit after receipt of the "right to sue" notice, issued at the conclusion of the EEOC investigation.

9. Permit a discrimination claim to be based on intent (disparate treatment), effect of an employment decision or practice (disparate impact), or retaliation.

10. Consist of a shifting burden of proof in civil cases. Once the plaintiff establishes a *prima facie* case, the burden shifts to the employer to articulate a legitimate, nondiscriminatory reason for the adverse employment action. The ultimate burden rests with the plaintiff to prove the unlawful discrimination. The plaintiff accomplishes this goal by

establishing that the employer's legitimate reason was a mere pretense and the employment decision was actually based on discrimination.

11. Elements of *prima facie* case:
    a. Membership in the protected class (aged 40 or over)
    b. Adverse personnel action (failure to hire, failure to promote, termination, lower benefits, etc.)
    c. Proper qualifications for the position or satisfactory job performance
    d. Younger employee with equal or inferior qualifications was treated better under circumstances giving rise to an inference of age discrimination.

12. Include remedies for equitable relief (employment, reinstatement, promotion), injunctive relief, back wages, front pay, liquidated damages, and reasonable attorney's fees.

13. Make jury trial available for all ADEA claims.

14. Permit employers to avoid liability with a release of claims in an exchange for an additional severance payment. Releases must be knowing, voluntary, and for valuable consideration.

ENDNOTES

1. 29 U.S.C. §621, *et seq.*

2. 29 U.S.C. §621(b).

3. 29 U.S.C. §631(a).

4. 29 U.S.C. §633(a).

5. 29 U.S.C. §630(b); see *EEOC v. Wyoming,* 460 U.S. 226 (1983), upholding the extension of ADEA to state and local governments.

6. *Grazder v. Air India,* 574 F.Supp 134 (S.D.N.Y. 1983). *In personam* jurisdiction is the power of a court to issue a judgment against the defendant.

7. 111 S.Ct. 1227 (1991).

8. P.L. 102-166 (1991).

9. 29 U.S.C. §623.

10. 29 U.S.C. §623(a).

11. 29 U.S.C. §623(b).

12. 29 U.S.C. §623(c).

13. 29 U.S.C. §623(d).

14. 29 U.S.C. §623(e).

15. 29 U.S.C. §623(f).

16. 29 U.S.C. §623(f)(1).

17. See *Western Air Lines, Inc. v. Criswell*, 472 U.S. 400 (1985); also see *Usery v. Tamiami Trail Tours, Inc.*, 531 F.2d 224, 236 (5th Cir. 1976).

18. In *Hodgson v. Greyhound Lines*, 499 F.2d 859, 863 (7th Cir. 1974), *cert. denied*, 419 U.S. 1122 (1975), the court held that employers involved in dangerous or safety-related activities need show only "a minimal increase in risk of harm" to establish the BFOQ defense.

19. *Hodgson v. Greyhound Lines*, 499 F.2d 859 (7th Cir. 1974), *cert. denied*, 419 U.S. 1122 (1975), and *Usery v. Tamiami Trail Tours, Inc.*, 531 F.2d 224 (5th Cir. 1976).

20. In *Baker v. Federal Aviation Administration* (CA7 No. 89-2524 10/31/90), the FAA's long-standing "age-60 rule," which bars commercial pilots from flying beyond that age, was reluctantly upheld.

21. The court in *Western Air Lines, Inc., v. Criswell*, 472 U.S. 400 (1985), upheld a jury verdict for plaintiffs in a challenge to an age retirement for flight engineers. Flight engineers are the third-in-command and require less rigorous qualifications. See also *Trans World Airlines v. Thurston*, 469 U.S. 111 (1985) discussed in note 60.

22. See note 18 and *Usery v. Tamiami Trail Tours, Inc.*, 531 F.2d 224 (5th Cir. 1976).

23. 29 U.S.C. §623(f)(1).

24. 29 C.F.R. Part 1625.7(f).

25. C.F.R. §860.103(f)(1)(ii).

26. *EEOC v. Chrysler Corp.*, 733 F.2d 1183 (6th Cir. 1984).

27. *Bay v. Times Mirror Magazine*, 936 F.2d 112 (2d Cir. 1991).

28. 29 U.S.C. §623(f)(2).

29. 29 U.S.C. §623 (f)(2)(A).

30. 29 U.S.C. §623 (f)(2). However, the Older Worker Benefit Protection Act (OWBPA) extended age discrimination protection to almost all employee benefit plans by replacing the term "subterfuge" with "to evade the purposes of this chapter." 29 U.S.C. §623 (f)(2)(A). See pre-OWBPA cases that discuss the meaning of "subterfuge." *United Air Lines, Inc. v. McMann*, 434 U.S. 192, 203 (1977), and *Public Employees Retirement System of Ohio v. Betts*, 492 U.S. 158, 109 S.Ct. 2854 (1989).

31. 29 U.S.C. §623 (f)(2)(B).

32. *Marshall v. Hawaiian Telephone Co.*, 575 F.2d 763, 766 (9th Cir. 1978).

33. *Sikora v. American Can Co.*, 622 F.2d 1116 (3d Cir. 1980).

34. *EEOC v. Borden's, Inc.*, 724 F.2d 1390, 1396 (9th Cir. 1984).

35. 29 U.S.C. §623 (f).

36. 29 U.S.C. §631 (c).

37. 29 U.S.C. §631 (d).

38. 29 U.S.C. §623 (f)(1).

39. *Gilmer v. Interstate/Johnson Lane Corporation*, 111 S.Ct. 1647 (1991).

40. *Griggs v. Duke Power Co.*, 401 U.S. 424 (1971).

41. *Texas Department of Community Affairs v. Burdine*, 450 U.S. 248, 253 (1981).

42. *Rose v. National Cash Register Corp.*, 703 F.2d 255 (6th Cir.).

43. The *Burdine* court affirmed the elements of a *prima facie* case of discrimination and the use of shifting burdens of proof first articulated in *McDonnell Douglas Corp. v. Green*, 411 U.S. 792, 802 (1973). Courts in ADEA cases have liberally accepted the *prima facie* case elements and shifting burden criteria developed in *McDonnell Douglas* and *Burdine* that are used in Title VII discrimination cases. *Geller v. Markham*, 636 F.2d 1027, 1032 (2d Cir. 1980), cert. denied, 451 U.S. 945 (1981).

44. *Douglas v. Anderson*, 656 F.2d 528 (9th Cir. 1981).

45. 656 F.2d 120 (5th Cir. 1981). This test has been adopted by the Second, Fourth, and Eleventh Circuits.

46. *Williams*, 656 F.2d at 129-130.

47. *DeShaw v. Lord and Taylor*, 56 FEP Cases 308 (S.D.N.Y. 1991).

48. *Taggert v. Time, Inc.*, 924 F.2d 43 (1991).

49. *Douglas v. Anderson*, 656 F.2d 528 (9th Cir. 1981).

50. *Cuddy v. Carmen*, 694 F.2d 853 (D.C. Cir. 1982). This standard has been accepted and adopted by each circuit.

51. *Cleverly v. Western Electric Co.*, 594 F.2d 638 (8th Cir. 1979).

52. *Stanojev v. Ebasco Services*, 643 F.2d 914 (2d Cir. 1981).

53. 29 U.S.C. §201, *et seq.*

54. 29 U.S.C. §216 (b).

55. Characterized as equitable relief in 29 U.S.C. §626(b).

56. 29 U.S.C. §626(b). A plaintiff can use a preliminary injunction to obtain reinstatement during the litigation.

57. *Whittlesey v. Union Carbide Corp.*, 742 F.2d 724, 727 (2d Cir. 1984). Front pay has been awarded in all circuits except the Fourth, Seventh, and District of Columbia.

58. The FLSA, 29 U.S.C. §216 (b), which makes the award of liquidated damages mandatory, is qualified in the ADEA by a proviso that a prevailing plaintiff is entitled to double damages "only in cases of willful violations." 29 U.S.C. §626 (b).

59. *Rodriguez v. Taylor*, 569 F.2d 1231 (3d Cir. 1977), *cert. denied*, 436 U.S. 913 (1978).

60. 469 U.S. 111 (1985). The court invalidated a transfer policy that permitted airline captains (copilots) who are disqualified from serving for reasons other than age to transfer automatically to flight engineer positions, but required captains disqualified because of age to resort to bidding procedures. However, the court ruled the violation was not willful, holding that the airline had attempted to bring its retirement policy into ADEA compliance with the help of union and counsel, but had merely failed to focus on the effect of each aspect of the retirement policy for cockpit personnel.

61. *Dreyer v. Arco Chemical Co.*, 801 F.2d 651 (3d Cir. 1986).

62. *Coleman v. City of Omaha*, 714 F.2d 804 (8th Cir. 1984).

63. *Id.*

64. Reorganization Plan No. 1 of 1978 §2, 43 Fed. Reg. 19807, 3 C.F.R. 321 (1978), transferred all ADEA administration and enforcement functions from the Secretary of Labor to the EEOC.

65. 29 U.S.C. §633(b).

66. 29 C.F.R. §1626.8.

67. 29 U.S.C. §626(d)(1)–(2).

68. *Delaware State College v. Ricks*, 449 U.S. 250 (1980); *Chardon v. Fernandez*, 454 U.S. 6 (1981); *Sawchik v. E.I. Dupont de Nemours & Co.*, 783 F.2d 635 (6th Cir. 1986).

69. H.R. Conference Report No. 950, 95th Congress, 2d Session, reprinted in (1978) U.S. Code Cong. & Admin. News 528, at 534.

70. For example, see *McClinton v. Alabama By-Products Corp.*, 743 F.2d 1483 (11th Cir. 1984), wherein the court held that an employer's failure to post the required notice will equitably toll the 180-day notification period, but only until the employee acquires a general knowledge of his right not to be discriminated against on account of age or the means of obtaining such knowledge.

71. *Oscar Mayer & Co. v. Evans*, 441 U.S. 750 (1979).

72. P.L. 102-166 (1991).

73. See January 6, 1992, memorandum issued by the EEOC. The EEOC, until the statute of limitations issue is resolved in the courts, will continue to issue a notice 60 days prior to the expiration of the 2-year period for those cases filed prior to November 21, 1991.

74. *Lorillard v. Pons,* 434 U.S. 575 (1978).

75. 29 U.S.C. §260.

76. *McClanahan v. Matthews,* 440 F.2d 320, 322 (6th Cir. 1971).

77. 29 U.S.C. §626(c)(2).

78. *Criswell v. Western Air Lines, Inc.,* 514 F.Supp. 384, 393 (C.D.Cal. 1981).

79. *Lehman v. Nakshian,* 453 U.S. 156. 101 S.Ct. 2698 (1981).

80. FLSA, 29 U.S.C. §216 (b).

81. "Opt-out" procedures are available to a class action member under Rule 23 of the federal Rules of Civil Procedure.

82. *Kloos v. Carter-Day Co.,* 799 F.2d 397 (8th Cir. 1986).

83. *Mistretta v. Sandia Corp.,* 639 F.2d 588 (10th Cir. 1980).

84. The Second and Seventh Circuits permit notice to prospective class members under the ADEA while the Eighth, Ninth, and Tenth Circuits do not permit such notice.

85. P.L. 101-433 (1990).

86. 42 U.S.C. §2000e-2, *et seq.*

87. See *Kentroti v. Frontier Airlines, Inc.,* 585 F.2d 967 (10th Cir. 1978), and *Stanojev v. Ebasco Services, Inc.,* 643 F.2d 914 (2d Cir. 1981).

88. 510 F.2d 307 (6th Cir. 1975).

89. 29 U.S.C. §621, *et seq.*

90. See *Champion International Corp. v. Brown,* 731 F.2d 1406 (9th Cir. 1984). Montana's age discrimination law is preempted to the extent it conflicts with ERISA-authorized provisions of the pension plan.

91. 29 U.S.C. §623 (i)(1).

92. See 29 U.S.C. §1140.

93. See B. Schlei and P. Grossman, *Employment Discrimination Law,* 2nd ed. (Washington, D.C.: Bureau of National Affairs, 1983) pp.1322–1324.

7

SEX DISCRIMINATION AND SEXUAL HARASSMENT: STRATEGIES FOR HANDLING CLAIMS PROPERLY

All of us are concerned about all aspects of discrimination and equal employment in the workplace. However sex- or gender-based discrimination receives an unusual amount of publicity, perhaps because it is sometimes of an unusual nature.

Most of America watched in shock the Supreme Court nomination hearings for Clarence Thomas. Regardless of which position you found credible, it was significant that a high government official charged with enforcement of the very laws which we are going to discuss was accused of violating them. One of the critical elements in assessing claims of sex-based discrimination is always one of proof. Unfortunately, most of these nefarious activities are done clandestinely so that proof will not be available nor witnesses able to come forward.

HOW TO IDENTIFY PROBLEM AREAS

Your job in human resources and personnel is primarily to be knowledgeable about the law, to be able to assess the validity of claims, to either conduct or direct an internal investigation of the claims, and to administer your department to avoid or minimize claims of sex-based employment discrimination.

There are numerous statutes upon which claims of sex discrimination can be lodged. Primarily, Title VII of the 1964 Civil Rights Act provides a foundation for most claims of sex discrimination.[1] Title VII bars discrimination based upon sex and, as amended, on pregnancy.[2]

Title VII prohibits discrimination in hiring, firing, promotion, and all other terms and conditions of employment. As we learned in Chapter 5, Title VII is enforced through the Equal Employment Opportunity Commission, which has regional offices around the country. For a fuller discussion of EEOC process and procedures, see Chapter 5.

Claims of employment discrimination can either end at the EEOC or find their way into state or federal court. Let's look at an example:

Case Study

Lucy Lane, a typesetter in your plant, believes that her rate of pay and job conditions and promotional opportunities are not the same as those for similarly situated male employees. She earns $5.75 per hour while males in basically the same job earn $9.65. Lucy has five years of seniority with the company, and new male employees in her position still start at $3.00 over her base pay. She has complained to the union without much relief. She has also gone to see a staff member in the HR department who said he would "look into it" but never got back to her. Finally, out of a sense of frustration, and after attending a meeting of "9 to 5," Lucy has filed a complaint of sex discrimination regarding wages and terms and conditions of employment at the EEOC. After you receive a complaint from the agency, what should you do?

At this point, I would hope you have already discussed this matter with or turned it over to your employment law specialist, either an employment attorney on staff or outside counsel whom you regularly consult with regard to these problems.

A thorough investigation should be made of the salaries, job experience, and working conditions for all typesetters in your plant and perhaps in the community, if necessary. On the face of the complaint, it appears that Lucy's claim has merit and should probably be resolved by a review of all salaries and an increase to appropriate levels so that males and females are at the same level for the same job.

NOTE: According to the Equal Pay Act, pay disparities should be corrected by raising salaries, not by reducing them!

When Lucy also complains that she is harassed and sometimes the recipient of vulgar comments at the workplace, that is a different story that may require further investigation and ameliorative efforts on your part.

What happens if you decide to do nothing? It is quite likely that the EEOC will find probable cause that discrimination existed under Title VII as well as under the Equal Pay Act, which requires that men and women receive equal pay for equal work.[3]

In addition, if the matter cannot be resolved through settlement or concil-iation, it is possible that one of two other things might occur:

1. Lucy, on her own, might decide to file a complaint in the U.S. district court charging the company with violations of Title VII and the Equal Pay Act. Based upon the facts we have seen, it is quite possible she might allege class-based discrimination and be successful.

2. Similarly, it is possible if the class were large enough that the agency itself might bring the action in federal court. Assuming that the action is brought and contested, what happens now?

Title VII had not permitted jury trials nor punitive damages prior to 1992. However, under the Civil Rights Act of 1991, jury trials are now permitted for such claims, and punitive damages may be assessed. Damages can be considerable, although the Civil Rights Act of 1991 even places caps so that they are at least not unlimited.[4] Under the Equal Pay Act, however, if claims are found to be "willful," damages can be assessed at twice the level of compensatory pay. In addition, it is possible to award "front pay" under Title VII or a calculation estimated to be equivalent to the amount of pay the individual would have earned if she continued in her employment but for the discrimination.[5]

In this chapter we will go through various specific areas of concern and deal with them separately, although the principles to be applied in personnel management and avoidance of discrimination are the same whether or not you are dealing with pregnancy and maternity concerns, pay concerns, benefit con-cerns, or any other form of discrimination.

HOW TO HANDLE SEXUAL HARASSMENT IN THE WORKPLACE

Sex-based harassment has received much publicity and is sometimes a titillating subject, although for the individuals involved, it is usually unpleasant and difficult. Sex harassment can include a wide range of conduct from unwanted physical contact to "hitting on" a coworker for a date; placing pornographic, vulgar, or otherwise inappropriate photographs in a common area or locker room; or simply creating an atmosphere so hostile and unpleasant in which sexual innuendo and comment make it difficult for an opposite sex-based em-ployee to function.[6]

Generally, sexual harassment is now divided into two categories: (1) quid pro quo discrimination or (2) hostile environment discrimination.

Identifying Quid pro Quo Discrimination

Quid pro quo discrimination (something for something) has been simply defined as conditioning certain workplace conduct, treatment, benefits, promotions, and the like upon the receipt or acquiescence in certain sexual conduct or favors. We are all familiar with the easy-to-spot example of a male boss asking or demanding sexual favors from a secretary or subordinate who is fired if she does not comply. However, that is not the only scenario in which such discrimination may occur; an example might illustrate this area more clearly.

Case Study

Mary Smith, an executive at Tight Automotives, has recently hired a college graduate to be her assistant/secretary. Biff, her new assistant, is a tall, attractive man of 23. Biff is a homosexual who has kept his sexual preference to himself. However, Mary Smith has lately made a habit of walking over to his desk and making suggestive comments while she gives him assignments. Not knowing what to say or how to respond, Biff has said nothing, although he has been telling his lover how uncomfortable he has become at work and that he is feeling extremely pressured on his job. Biff's boss has also lately started to ask him if he could work late on Fridays and then turning the work session into a late dinner. On one recent occasion after several drinks at dinner, she asked Biff if he could take her home because she was unable to drive. Not wanting to offend his boss, Biff gave her a ride. However, when they got to her door, she said she needed help getting in and he carried her in. At that time, she made sexual advances toward him and demanded that he stay if he wanted his job.

The following day at work, Biff decided he had enough. He contacted your office and asked if there was a complaint procedure or if there was someone he could talk to confidentially. You are that person. Biff has also told you that he is a homosexual and he is now concerned that he might lose his job either because he is a homosexual or because he has spurned his superior's advances.

Did Mary Smith commit illegal sexual harassment? Yes. Under the law, federal courts have held that workplace conduct that requires an individual to perform certain conduct or to engage in a sexual liaison because of promised advantage or disadvantage on the job is unlawful sex-based discrimination. Employers are liable in some circuits if such sexual demands are made with their "actual or constructive knowledge," and they do not take "prompt and appropriate remedial action after acquiring such knowledge."[7]

Quid pro quo harassment typically arises, as in the example, when a supervisor conditions the grant of an employment benefit on the performance of a sexual favor.

Employer's Liability in Quid pro Quo Harassment. You should know the following with regard to understanding the employer's position when an employee claims sexual harassment.

- There is usually liability for a supervisor's conduct even if the employer had *no* notice of such conduct.

- There is absolute liability for the conduct of a supervisor who has authority to hire, fire, discipline, or promote and who uses the position of authority to exact sexual favors from a subordinate.[8]

Elements of a Prima Facie Case of Quid pro Quo Sexual Harassment. The following are evidence of a *prima facie* case:

- An employee was subject to unwelcome sexual harassment.

- The harassment complained of was based on sex.

- The employee's reaction to the harassment complained of adversely affected aspects of the employee's compensation or terms, conditions, or privileges of employment.

Under the law, federal courts have held that workplace conduct that requires an individual to perform certain conduct or to engage in a sexual liaison because of promised advantage or disadvantage on the job is unlawful sex-based discrimination.[9]

The *Meritor v. Vinson* Case

The most definitive discussion of sexual harassment by the Supreme Court occurred a few years ago in *Meritor Savings Bank v. Vinson.*[10]

In *Meritor*, the plaintiff was an officer of the bank and she alleged that her long-term relationship with her superior was not consensual. Despite facts which suggested frequent workplace sexual conduct even in bizarre locations like the bank vault, she alleged her participation was coerced due to her position. Ms. Vinson was discharged for excessive use of sick leave despite four years of satisfactory performance and several promotions. She alleged unlawful sexual harassment was the real reason for her termination, primarily because she refused to continue the sexual relationship with the vice president of Meritor. Vinson had progressed from teller/trainee to assistant bank manager.

The lower court rejected Vinson's claim of sex harassment and found that if there was any sexual relationship, it was purely *voluntary* with no impact on her job and, therefore, found no liability on the part of the bank.[11] The record in the *Meritor* case, however, is quite remarkable, particularly with regard to the explicit detail of the facts. The record at the appellate court, for example, noted that

> Taylor caressed her on the job, followed her into the safe depository room when she was there alone, and at times exposed himself to her. Vinson added that Taylor also fondled other women employees. . . .[12]

Significantly, the employer stated as one defense that if its supervisor, Taylor, acted at all, he acted on his own and without the bank's knowledge. The bank also contended that because it had a grievance procedure, Ms. Vinson's failure to use it could have resulted in no liability for the bank.

The *Vinson* case required an 11-day bench trial during which exhaustive testimony was presented regarding Taylor's behavior during Ms. Vinson's employment. She testified that their relationship was almost fatherly at the beginning, but soon thereafter her boss suggested that they go to a motel to have sexual relations. Initially, she refused but eventually agreed out of fear of losing her job. During trial, Vinson estimated that they had intercourse between 40 and 50 times and that his behavior sometimes included fondling her in front of other employees and that he "even forcibly raped her on several occasions."

The U.S. Supreme Court carefully analyzed the history of Title VII in *Meritor* and rejected any contention that Title VII was focused primarily on merely economic discrimination. The Court, in *Meritor*, sanctioned claims for hostile environment sexual discrimination but also cautioned that *a complainant's sexually provocative speech or dress may be considered as factors to determine whether sexual advances were unwelcome.*

Summary of the Supreme Court Ruling.

The highlights of the *Meritor* ruling by the Supreme Court can be summarized as follows:

1. Plaintiff need not prove "economic" damages to sustain a claim of sexual harassment.

2. A claim of hostile environment sexual harassment is a form of sex discrimination actionable under Title VII.

3. Harassment must be severe or pervasive to alter working conditions and create an abusive working environment.

4. Voluntariness of sexual conduct is not dispositive—correct inquiry is whether sexual advances were "unwelcome."[13]

5. "Voluntariness" in the sense of consent is no defense to a sexual harassment claim.

6. Evidence of provocative speech or dress may be introduced at trial since the trier of fact must view "the record as a whole" and examine "the totality of circumstances."

7. Employers are not always liable for the sexual harassment by a supervisor, but absence of notice to employer will not necessarily insulate employer from liability.

8. Mere existence of a grievance procedure and policy against discrimination, coupled with claimant's failure to utilize that procedure, does not necessarily insulate the employer from liability.[14]

Now let's get back to Biff. After *Meritor*, some observations that applied to Biff's dilemma:

1. Mary's harassment of Biff has created an abusive working condition.
2. At least from Biff's point of view, Mary's conduct was unwelcome.
3. There is no evidence in the example of provocative speech or dress by Biff. As a matter of fact, Biff's statement that he is a homosexual would undermine any effort by Mary in this regard to suggest consensual behavior.
4. Biff has specifically advised you that he is troubled by her conduct. You must act!
5. Since there is no evidence of a grievance procedure, Biff has taken the appropriate step by coming to see you. Now what do you do?

How to Identify a Hostile Work Environment

A claim for sexual harassment may arise where an activity, attitude, or conduct creates an intimidating, hostile, or offensive work environment.

Acts that are not overtly sexual can constitute sexual harassment, and incidents of sexual harassment directed at employees other than plaintiff can be used as evidence of a hostile work environment.[15] For sexual harassment to be actionable, it must be sufficiently severe or pervasive "to alter the conditions of [the victim's] employment and create an abusive working environment."[16] A complainant need not show a tangible or economic injury such as a threat of dismissal.

A female employee may be able to sue for a "hostile work environment" alleging sexual harassment after being asked out one time, having her knee patted one time, and being subjected to suggestive remarks. However, these facts are murky and do not necessarily establish that the working environment was "poisoned."

Usually, one incident of sexual harassment is not enough to bring an actionable case, though there are exceptions, specifically where the incident is clear and unambiguous and involves a direct threat to the employee's job (quid pro quo). Most cases that have found the presence of an actionable hostile environment claim have involved situations of marked hostility and abuse of a humiliating nature because of the victim's sex.

For example, in *Meritor*, there were repeated sexual demands and sexual relations (40 to 50 times). In another case, *Egger v. Local 276 Plumbers*,[17] there was physical contact, threats, demeaning pranks, comments on plaintiff's chest size and about her sex life, graphic descriptions of a male employee's sex life in front of her, showing her pornographic books, and asking her to participate in a sexually explicit home video. The conduct in these cases was so offensive that it was readily apparent to be hostile environment sexual harassment.

Some key factors may determine whether a hostile environment has been created, including:

- Whether the conduct was verbal or physical, or both
- How frequently it was repeated
- Whether the conduct was hostile or blatantly offensive
- Whether the alleged harasser was a coworker or a supervisor
- Whether others joined in perpetrating the harassment
- Whether the harassment was directed at more than one individual[18]

Your assessment of these factors should be a primary focus of the investigation and decision to impose discipline.

HOW TO INVESTIGATE HARASSMENT COMPLAINTS

At least to the extent that cases like Biff's present themselves, you must make a serious effort to investigate these complaints once they become known to you. Your company should have a sexual harassment policy and complaint procedure. A sample policy and complaint statement is shown in Exhibit 7.1 on page 160.

Essentially, an employee like Biff should have a person or place to go to present his or her complaints confidentially regarding sexual harassment. Once these complaints are made in confidence, what should you do?

Complaints of sexual harassment should be seriously investigated. If witnesses are involved or other alleged victims of harassment, you should endeavor to meet with those individuals confidentially to ascertain the facts. If no corroborating facts or witnesses are available, you are in a dilemma. Since most cases of overt harassment are discreet instances of behavior between two people, most cases fall into this category. Where there are witnesses or other victims, statements should be secured both to assist and support whatever discipline and termination may result and as evidence. Of course, a dilemma is that you now have perhaps proven a case of harassment which may cause liability to the company.

NOTE: If your investigation reveals actionable harassment, you should take disciplinary measures up to and including termination.

Part of the investigation may require you and/or counsel or both to meet with the alleged harasser to attempt to find out his or her version of the facts. These meetings must be carefully handled since false accusations may result in defamation lawsuits against the company.[19]

If the company fires Mary after investigation, does it still have liability? While the investigation and internal complaint process will not exonerate a company from liability, prompt investigation and discipline are factors to be considered, according to the Supreme Court. It is certainly in your interest to promulgate a sexual harassment policy and to follow it when complaints of sexual harassment are made.

The courts and the EEOC tell us that sexual advances have to be "unwelcome" to be unlawful. Voluntariness is only one factor considered and will not necessarily defeat a claim of harassment.

Following the EEOC Guidelines

The EEOC guidelines on discrimination because of sex[20] provide that unwelcome sexual advances, requests for sexual favors, and other verbal or physical conduct of a sexual nature constitutes sexual harassment in violation of Title VII when the following conditions exist:

1. Submission to such conduct is made a term or condition of employment (quid pro quo).

2. Submission to or rejection of such conduct by an individual is used as the basis for employment decision effecting such individual (quid pro quo).

3. Such conduct has the purpose or effect of unreasonably interfering with an individual's work performance or creating an intimidating, hostile, or offensive working environment (hostile environment).

The guidelines specifically provide as follows:

1. Harassment on the basis of sex is a violation of Section 703 of Title VII. Unwelcome sexual advances, requests for sexual favors, and other verbal or physical conduct of a sexual nature constitute sexual harassment when (a) submission to such conduct is made either explicitly or implicitly a term or condition of an individual's employment, (b) submission to or rejection of such conduct by an individual is used as the basis for employment decisions affecting such individual, or (c) such conduct has the purpose or effect of substantially interfering with an individual's work performance or creating an intimidating, hostile, or offensive working environment.

2. In determining whether alleged conduct constitutes sexual harassment, the Commission will look at the record as a whole and at the totality of the circumstances, such as the nature of the sexual advances and the context in which the alleged incidents occurred. The determination of the legality of a particular action will be made from the facts, on a case-by-case basis.

3. Applying general Title VII principles, an employer, employment agency, joint apprenticeship committee, or labor organization (hereinafter collectively referred to as "employer") is responsible for its acts and those

of its agents and supervisory employees with respect to sexual harassment regardless of whether the specific acts complained of were authorized or even forbidden by the employer and regardless of whether
the employer knew or should have known of their occurrence. The
Commission will examine the circumstances of the particular employment relationship and the job functions performed by the individual
in determining whether an individual acts in either a supervisory or
agency capacity.

4. With respect to conduct between fellow employees, an employer is
   responsible for acts of sexual harassment in the workplace where the
   employer (or its agents or supervisory employees) knows or should
   have known of the conduct unless it can show that it took immediate
   and appropriate corrective action.

5. An employer may also be responsible for the acts of *nonemployees*, with
   respect to sexual harassment of employees in the workplace, where the
   employer (or its agents or supervisory employees) knows or should
   have known of the conduct and fails to take immediate and appropriate
   corrective action. In reviewing these cases, the Commission will consider
   the extent of the employer's control and any other legal responsibility
   which the employer may have with respect to the conduct of such
   nonemployees.

6. Prevention is the best tool for the elimination of sexual harassment. An
   employer should take all steps necessary to prevent sexual harassment
   from occurring, such as affirmatively raising the subject, expressing
   strong disapproval, developing appropriate sanctions, informing employees of their right to raise and how to raise the issue of harassment
   under Title VII, and developing methods to sensitize all concerned.

The guidelines also pertain to other related practices, namely, where employment opportunities or benefits are granted because of an individual's submission to the employer's sexual advances or requests for sexual favors, the
employer may be held liable for unlawful sex discrimination against other persons
who were qualified for but denied that employment opportunity or benefit.[21]

Determining the Scope of Title VII Liability

Liability under Title VII for sexual harassment is limited to the employment
context. It is the "employer" who is legally responsible for acts of sexual harassment not the individual employee. Although the alleged harasser may be liable
for other tort claims such as assault and battery or intentional infliction of emotional distress.

The kinds of relief available are

- Back pay
- Front pay
- Reinstatement
- Compensatory damages
- Injunctive relief (unless there is no reasonable expectation that the discriminatory conduct will recur)
- Punitive damages
- Attorney's fees
- Other equitable relief as the court deems appropriate

You may be wondering about proofs and specific cases you are aware of or may have read about. One concern we hear about frequently is that a certain individual may be overly sensitive: Whose standard should be looked at—a very sensitive employee or an objective person?

Establishing the Reasonable Woman Versus Reasonable Person Standard

Courts have traditionally utilized a "reasonable man" standard to analyze responses to behavior as an appropriate standard. Most courts have utilized an objective gender-neutral reasonable person standard after the *Meritor* decision. But a question has recently emerged with regard to the perspective used to gauge harassment and the appropriate standard of reasonableness.

An emerging line of cases suggest that a "reasonable woman" viewpoint may be relevant when the victim is female in sexual harassment cases.[22] At least three federal courts of appeals (Third, Sixth, and Ninth Circuits) have now adopted a reasonable woman standard. In *Ellison v. Brady*, the court concluded that a reasonable woman standard should be used because a sex-blind reasonable person test tends to be male-biased and ignores the perspective of a woman. By focusing on the perspective of the female victim rather than the stereotypical notions of society, women may be able to participate in the workplace on an equal footing with men.

The "reasonable woman" opinions also require employers to follow a stronger antiharassment policy if they hope to avoid liability. In *Ellison*, for example, the court concluded that the reasonableness of an employer's remedy will depend on its ability to stop harassment by the person who engaged in the harassment.[23] Although the court's language is extremely rigid, it is unmistaken that employers must respond to harassment with heavy sanctions and strong disapproval. The reasonable woman standard protects women who may have a justifiable fear that "even a mild form of harassment may be a prelude to violent sexual assault."[24]

In adopting a reasonable woman standard, courts have concluded that women are far more susceptible to rape and assault than are men and that even mild forms of harassment may be a concern. By attempting to eliminate male bias from the standard, the courts are probably strengthening the sexual harassment claims and lessening proof standards. Thus, rather than relying upon the hypothetical reasonable person to evaluate the conduct, if a reasonable woman would find such conduct sufficiently severe or pervasive to alter the terms or conditions of employment and create an offensive environment, that conduct might constitute unlawful sexual harassment. In *Ellison*, the Ninth Circuit concluded that if the harassment is sufficiently severe to render the work environment hostile or abusive in the eyes of a reasonable woman, a claim of hostile work environment sex discrimination might be made.[25]

Case Example

Take the Ruff-N-Tuff ship repair yard where workers are primarily male. It is not uncommon to have posters of nude and partially nude women from pornographic magazines. Rough conduct and rough talk are commonplace in such an environment. Sally, one of the workers, regularly received comments that were clearly lewd and vulgar.[26] She complained to no avail and eventually filed suit.

But, what if Sally made similar comments to her male coworkers and cursed along with them? Such conduct would probably undermine any claim of harassment.

What if instead it was an office and one of Sally's coworkers told her she was "lovely" and he hoped to get to know her better with no leer. After receiving a dozen roses on Friday, she comes to see you because she feels harassed because of her sex.

A reasonable woman standard does not make this conduct actionable. Using a reasonable woman standard may account for some greater sensitivity, but it does not mean that unusually sensitive responses will convert isolated low-level conduct into actionable sex-based discrimination.

There are some questions that you might focus on when talking to a victim of alleged sexual harassment to get the facts:

- What happened?
- Who was involved?
- Where and when did the incident occur?
- Was the act unwelcome?
- What did you do to discourage it?
- How did it affect your work?
- What is the background to the incident?
- Were there any witnesses?
- Are there any documents to substantiate your position?

   – Are there others who have been sexually harassed by this same person?

   – Whom did you talk with about the incident and when?

   – Is there more information you can add?

Once you have met with and discussed the employee's complaint, you should follow standard reporting and investigation procedures. For example, you should undertake the following:

1. Request employee to make or sign a written statement.

2. Report the complaint and details learned from the complaining employee promptly to the appropriate company officer.

3. Assure employee that the complaint will be kept confidential and discussed only with authorized company officials.

4. Begin an investigation into the complaint by interviewing the alleged harasser and witnesses.

5. Be tactful during these interviews.

6. Once the investigation is completed, prepare a response to complaining employee with your findings.

7. If appropriate, republish sexual harassment policy or re-educate employees in this regard.

8. Keep well-documented records with regard to the complaint, investigation, and any action taken as a result of the investigation.

9. Avoid defamation claims by keeping the matter confidential and avoid focusing attention on an individual matter (i.e., reissuing the sexual harassment policy should be done discreetly with no obvious tie to a particular matter).

10. The appropriate disciplinary steps after investigation including termination.

If you follow these steps, you will minimize the employer's liability for claims of sexual harassment.

Examining Preferential Treatment/Reverse Quid pro Quo Harassment

Employees who have not been sexually harassed may be able to lodge sexual harassment complaints when they have received unfavorable treatment compared to another employee who has submitted to the supervisor's sexual demands, either willingly or under coercion. In most jurisdictions, the courts have declined to find an employer liable under Title VII in a situation where the plaintiff was passed over in favor of a "paramour." In such cases, the "voluntary, romantic relations" cannot form the basis of a sex discrimination claim under Title VII. For example,

♦ Allegedly preferential treatment based on a consensual romantic relationship is not *gender*-based discrimination where supervisor imposed facially neutral job qualifications to his female "paramour."[27]

♦ A paramour claim was rejected by one court holding that favoritism and unfair treatment, unless based on a prohibited classification, does not violate Title VII.[28]

♦ But a different court ruled that an unsuccessful candidate for promotion could recover under Title VII where promotion was awarded to less qualified employee who allegedly engaged willingly in a sexual relationship with the supervisor.[29]

Other Sexual Harassment Considerations

Sexual harassment complaints may generate related claims by those accused of such conduct and by the victims themselves. This area continues to develop as people look for additional grounds for liability stemming from sexual harassment conduct. To illustrate these other considerations, we have provided examples of liability based upon actions related to sexual harassment activity as follows:

♦ An employer violated Title VII when it terminated a male employee because he reported sexual harassment directed toward a female co-employee by a mutual supervisor.[30]

♦ Sexual harassment that rises to the level of intentional discrimination violates the equal protection clause of the Fourteenth Amendment.[31]

♦ An individual alleged to have been sexually harassed may have a claim for defamation.[32]

♦ State law tort claims based on sexual harassment are not preempted by the Railway Labor Act or the Federal Employers' Liability Act.[33]

♦ Extreme or outrageous conduct may form the basis of a claim of intentional infliction of emotional distress (if it is a state tort action).[34]

♦ Sexual harassment may constitute "predicate acts" sufficient to support a Racketeering Influence and Corruption Organization Act (RICO) claim, and "discriminatory sexual animus" sufficient to support a section 1985(3) action.[35]

HOW TO DEFEND SEXUAL HARASSMENT CLAIMS

The cases suggest that the critical element is that a nexus must exist between the employment and the alleged harassment before legal consequences under

Title VII will follow. Conduct based upon personal relationships or "voluntary" conduct will not be imputed to the employer.[36] Employers should, therefore, carefully examine the conduct of the "victim" as well as his or her allegations. Look at workplace relationships, modes of dress, and speech and gossip. If the conduct was welcomed or encouraged, the alleged harassment may not be a violation of Title VII:

◆ Offensive conduct may also not be unlawful where it does not affect the terms and conditions of employment or create a hostile working environment.[37]

◆ Employers may also defend claims of harassment based upon accepted business practices like vulgar language when it is common in the workplace.[38] For example, language and/or conduct which is otherwise inappropriate and impermissible may be acceptable under the guise of a business practice.

◆ Another key factor in defending harassment cases is notice. Post-*Meritor* courts have generally held employers liable for harassing conduct to employees. However, the employer must know or should have known about the conduct.

Employers will not be protected by closing their eyes to what they should have reasonably known.

In general, claims of sexual harassment should be defended like other forms of employment discrimination based upon sex, which means that a thorough investigation, witness interviews, and preparation will assist in defending cases lacking merit.

IDENTIFYING OTHER AREAS OF CONCERN FOR SEX DISCRIMINATION

There have been many questions and concerns raised about partnership decisions, dual or alternate tracks, and the so-called "mommy" track. Many employers have developed interesting ways to deal with some of these issues.

For example, certain large law firms or corporations have established day care centers on site or have made alternate arrangements for child care in an emergency. These child care issues are intrinsically related to partnership and advancement questions which generally affect women primarily.

Handling Questions of Partnership or Advancement

Partnership or related questions deal with the perception of women in senior or executive positions in a law firm or corporation or an accounting firm or myriad other settings. The Supreme Court has looked at this issue in some recent cases, and the new Civil Rights Act of 1991 has also addressed, in part, perceived discrimination based upon sex in promotional decisions regarding women.

In *Price Waterhouse v. Hopkins*,[39] the Supreme Court ruled that employers might avoid liability by showing by a preponderance of the evidence that the same decision would have been made regardless of the gender of the candidate.

> NOTE: The Civil Rights Act of 1991 adds a subsection (m) to Section 703 of Title VII. The amendment specifically declares that if a complainant shows that one of the prohibited factors, that is, race, color, religion, sex, or national origin, motivated an employment action, an unlawful employment practice is established even if other lawful factors also motivated the action.

Thus, Congress has told employers that mixed motive cases will be dealt with strongly and that decisions made based upon gender will not be acceptable. Therefore, traditional notions of sex stereotyping in the workplace should begin to erode and vanish either through voluntary action by employers or by court action.

Handling Employee Benefit Pension Rights

Corporations cannot discriminate either in pension offerings to employees or in the ultimate benefit received by employees. For example, using sex-based mortality tables has been rejected by the courts as unlawful even though women as a group live longer than men. The use of sex-based predictors has been rejected because the courts have suggested that we look at these situations on an individual, not a group, basis.

Case Example

> Due to the obvious longevity of women, Public Gas required its female employees to make larger contributions to its self-administered pension fund than male employees. The benefits upon retirement were the same for similarly situated men and women of the same age, seniority, and salary. The company told employees in writing that the larger contributions were required because mortality tables show that women live longer than men and that the women would therefore receive a greater pension benefit based upon the same contribution.

This practice cannot be justified based upon either the mortality tables or the cost impact on the pension benefit. Use of sex-based mortality tables is unlawful. Title VII does not contain a cost justification defense. However, if the pension reserve proves inadequate to cover reimbursement, retroactive liability will not be applied since it could be devastating to the pension fund.[40]

Implementing Fetal Protection and Reproductive Hazards Policies

Employers, fearing costly liability for injuries to unborn children or the inability to have children, have attempted to implement preventive and/or exclusionary policies that restrict certain groups of employees from performing hazardous jobs.

Certain industries, including chemical, video display, and semiconductor manufacturing, have jobs that may involve significant reproductive health risks. In these areas some employers have implemented policies that limit women's employment opportunities, where such policies are said to protect employees' offspring from reproductive and fetal hazards. The policies have usually not considered impact on male workers.

The U.S. Supreme Court, in *United Auto Workers v. Johnson Controls, Inc.,* ruled that companies may not bar women from jobs that may be hazardous to unborn children.[41]

In *Johnson Controls,* it was found that lead exposure caused harm to male and female reproductive systems; thus the policy was discriminatory. The court also stated that the decisions about the welfare of future children must be left to the parents and not to the employers who hire those parents.

After *Johnson Controls,* it is unlikely that fetal protection policies, unless they are so narrowly drawn as to be almost meaningless, will be lawful as a legitimate way to protect unborn children.

In assessing a reproductive hazards exclusionary policy, you must consider the following:

1. Is there a substantial risk of harm to employees' offspring through the exposure of employees to a reproductive or fetal hazard in the workplace?

2. Does the harm to employees' offspring take place through the exposure of employees of one sex but not employees of the opposite sex?

3. Does the employer's policy effectively eliminate the risk of fetal or reproductive harm?

If your organization has high-risk jobs, you should review the EEOC's policy guide thoroughly before instituting an exclusionary reproductive hazards policy. Also, consult with labor counsel particularly in light of the Supreme Court's ruling in *Johnson Controls.*

Bringing Securities Industry Sex-Based Claims to Arbitration

The Supreme Court recently declared that discrimination claims in the securities industry, when subject to arbitration, must be arbitrated. Before filing a Title VII sex discrimination suit with the EEOC or federal court, an employee in the securities industry *must* first bring a sex bias claim to arbitration under a mandatory clause covering securities firms registered with various national stock securities exchanges.[42]

Handling Pregnancy Discrimination

The Pregnancy Discrimination Act of 1978 (PDA) amended Title VII by specifying that sex discrimination includes discrimination on the basis of pregnancy.[43] The Act declared that all pregnancy- or childbirth-based distinctions constitute discrimination on the basis of sex. Women affected by pregnancy must be treated the same for all employment-related purposes as nonpregnant employees.

Case Example

Female employees of Nice Guys claimed that the company's non-occupational disability plan was in violation of Title VII and the PDA because it did not provide payment for any absences due to pregnancy and required pregnant employees to forfeit their accumulated job seniority upon returning to work after childbirth. However, employees disabled by non-occupational sickness or injury were entitled to sick pay and retention of accumulated seniority.

The female employees were right. Pregnancy must be treated like any other temporary disability for all employment-related purposes. While the company's practice of denying accumulated seniority to employees returning from pregnancy leave was neutral on its face, it nevertheless had a discriminatory effect on women (disparate impact) and thus violated Title VII.[44]

Since employee benefit plans cover spouses, the Pregnancy Discrimination Act extends Title VII discrimination prohibitions to pregnant spouses, not just discrimination in employment, and affects men in addition to women.

A nonoccupational disability plan that covers medical expenses incurred by an employee's spouse must also cover expenses arising from the pregnancy of an employee's spouse.

NOTE: Discrimination because of a women's pregnancy is discrimination because of sex.

Since the sex of the spouse is always the opposite of the sex of the employee, discrimination against female spouses in providing fringe benefits is also discrimination against male employees. A health plan that gives married male employees a benefit plan for their dependents which is less inclusive than the dependency coverage provided to married female employees is unlawful.[45]

The Pregnancy Discrimination Act does not prohibit practices favoring pregnant women. The Act merely sets "a floor beneath which pregnancy disability benefits may not drop—not a ceiling above which they may not rise."[46]

The extent of protection afforded pregnancy classifications may be limited by the availability of the BFOQ defense and the view of the particular court of appeals. In *Harriss v. Pan American World Airways, Inc.,*[47] a policy requiring flight attendants to take mandatory maternity leave immediately upon discovery of pregnancy was justified by the Ninth Circuit as a BFOQ defense. However, in *Burwell v. Eastern Air Lines,*[48] the Fourth Circuit held that a BFOQ justifies mandatory maternity leave only from the commencement of the 28th week of pregnancy.

How to Handle Sexual Preference/Sexual Orientation Discrimination

Federal courts have generally rejected claims by homosexuals or transvestites because Title VII's prohibition of "sex" discrimination applies only to discrimination on the basis of gender (opposite sex) and does not include sexual preference protection.[49]

NOTE: It is significant to note that several states and other jurisdictions have protections for discrimination based upon sexual preference.

For example, Hawaii, Massachusetts, New Jersey, Wisconsin, New York City and San Francisco protect against sexual preference discrimination. These state and local laws bar discrimination against homosexuals, lesbians, and bisexuals.

IMPLEMENTING A SEXUAL HARASSMENT POLICY

All employers are advised to institute or update a policy prohibiting sexual harassment that sets forth a procedure for handling complaints. A comprehensive policy consistently enforced may aid to reduce an employer's liability for sexual harassment claims.

Sexual Harassment Policy Guidelines

1. Establish a formal written policy prohibiting sexual harassment and forbidding retaliation against those making claims for harassment.

2. Include in the policy a definition of sexual harassment sufficiently clear to put all employees on notice of prohibited conduct and the procedures for reporting and investigating claims of sexual harassment. Utilize the definition in the EEOC guidelines at 29 C.F.R. §1604.11.

3. Designate an officer or high-level management individual as the EEO officer to whom complaints of sexual harassment may be made. Advise employees about the confidential nature of the process. Have an alternate complaint mechanism available if complaints are about this EEO officer.

4. Circulate the policy throughout the workplace and include it in the employee manual.

5. Advise all supervisors through management training programs regarding what may be considered to be sexual harassment and the liability for such conduct. Keep them up-to-date on recent changes and developments in the law in your state, as well.

6. Impress supervisors with the importance of recordkeeping. Utilize standard forms to record complaints and witness interview notes.

7. Set up mechanisms for receiving complaints that bypass the alleged harasser.

8. Investigate complaints immediately and thoroughly. Work with counsel regarding witness interviews, statements and affidavits, and discussion of your investigation results within the company or community. If necessary, advise the alleged harasser that he or she should secure individual counsel or the company will provide individual counsel. Let the alleged harasser know what is being said about him (or her).

9. If a complaint is meritorious, take remedial action immediately.

10. As changes are made in your policy restate and redistribute your policy to all employees. Keep your human resources staff current on developments in the law.

Every allegation of sexual harassment should be taken seriously. We cannot advise about any specific instances because the facts are always different. However, by exercising caution and sensitivity, issues of sex harassment can be identified and dealt with in the workplace. Other sex-based forms of discrimination have been reviewed in this chapter. Additional questions may arise regarding various area of law or interpretation. Focused fact questions should be discussed with your labor counsel.

– EXHIBIT 7.1 –
Sample Sexual Harassment Policy

It is the policy of the Company that sexual harassment of employees or applicants for employment in any form is unacceptable conduct which will not be tolerated. Sexual harassment includes unwelcome sexual advances, requests for sexual favors, and other verbal, visual, or physical conduct of a sexual nature.

No supervisor or other employee shall threaten or insinuate, either explicitly or implicitly, that another employee's or applicant's refusal to submit to sexual advances will adversely affect that person's employment, work status, evaluation, wages, advancement, assigned duties, shifts, or any other condition of employment or career development. Similarly, no employee shall promise, imply, or grant any preferential treatment in connection with another employee or applicant engaging in sexual conduct. No supervisor or other employee shall undertake conduct of a sexual nature that unreasonably interferes with an individual's work performance or creates an intimidating, hostile, or offensive working environment.

Any employee who feels that he or she is a victim of sexual harassment, including but not limited to, any of the conduct just listed, by any supervisor, management official, other employee, customer, client, or any other person in connection with employment at the Company should bring the matter to the immediate attention of his or her supervisor or to the designated Administrative Officer of The Company. Any questions about this policy or potential sexual harassment should also be brought to the attention of the same person(s). The Company will promptly investigate all allegations of sexual harassment in as confidential a manner as possible and take appropriate corrective action if warranted.

Any employee who is determined, after an investigation, to have engaged in sexual harassment in violation of this policy will be subject to appropriate discipline up to and including termination.

ENDNOTES

1. 42. U.S.C. §2000e, *et seq.*

2. See 1978 Pregnancy Discrimination Act amendments to 1964 Civil Rights Act.

3. See Chapter 17 for a thorough discussion of the Equal Pay Act.

4. See Chapter 5 for discussion on remedies for Title VII violations and the cap on compensatory and punitive damage awards.

5. See *Thompson v. Sawyer*, 678 F.2d 257 (D.C. Cir. 1982).

6. There have been claims of sex discrimination filed by transvestites. However, the federal courts have generally disfavored these claims, although it is significant to

    note that several states and other jurisdictions have protections for discrimination based upon sexual preference. For example, the city of New York protects against sexual preference discrimination. The state of New Jersey recently enacted legislation barring discrimination against homosexuals and bisexuals, as have many other jurisdictions.

7. *Tompkins v. Public Service Electric & Gas Co.*, 568 F.2d 1044 (3d Cir. 1977).

8. See EEOC Guidelines, 29 C.F.R. §1604.11(c) and (d).

9. See *Meritor Savings Bank v. Vinson*, 477 U.S. 57 (1986).

10. 477 U.S. 57 (1986).

11. *Vinson v. Taylor*, 753 F.2d 141 (D.C. Cir. 1985).

12. 477 U.S. at 60.

13. The challenged conduct must be unwelcome "in the sense that the employee did not solicit or incite it, and in the sense that the employee regarded the conduct as undesirable or offensive." *Henson*, 682 F.2d at 903.

14. Dr. Kenneth C. Cooper, in his book *Stop it Now* (Total Communications Press, 1985), addresses six levels of sexual harassment beginning with aesthetic appreciation and listing active mental groping, social touching, foreplay, harassment, sexual abuse, and ultimate threat. These are concepts that have not yet made their way into court decisions, but are merely techniques of categorizing workplace behavior.

15. See *Hicks v. Gates Rubber Co.*, 928 F.2d 966 (10th Cir. 1991). The court permitted aggregating evidence of racial hostility with evidence of sexual hostility to indicate that a black female security guard was harassed on the basis of her sex *and* race. Separately, the evidence was insufficient to support a claim under Title VII. See also *Hall v. Gus Construction Co., Inc.*, 842 F.2d 1010 (8th Cir. 1988), in which the court held that whenever harassment and unequal treatment occur because plaintiffs were women, nonsexual conduct will constitute sexual harassment.

16. *Henson v. City of Dundee*, 682 F.2d 897, 904 (11th Cir. 1982).

17. 644 F.Supp. 795 (D.Mass. 1986).

18. *Henson, supra*, 682 F.2d at 904.

19. See *Garziano v. Dupont*, 818 F.2d 380 (5th Cir. 1987), in which the harasser was terminated but successfully sued his former employer for defamation. A large jury verdict was ultimately overturned by the court of appeals.

20. 29 C.F.R. §1604.11. On October 17, 1988, the EEOC issued a Policy Guideline on Current Issues of Sexual Harassment [F.E.P. Manual (BNA) at 401:6081], designed to provide guidance on defining sexual harassment and establishing employer liability in light of recent cases.

21. Section 1604.11 reads as amended 45 F.R. 74677, effective November 10, 1980.

22. See *Ellison v. Brady*, 924 F.2d (9th Cir. 1991), and *Robinson v. Jacksonville Shipyards, Inc.*, 760 F.Supp 1486 (M.D.Fla. 1991). See also *Yates v. Avco Corp.*, 819 F.2d 630 (6th Cir. 1987), and *Andrews v. City of Philadelphia*, 895 F.2d 1469 (3d Cir. 1989).

23. *Ellison, supra*, 924 F.2d at 882.

24. See Steven H. Winterbauer "Sexual Harassment—The Reasonable Woman Standard," *The Labor Lawyer*, Vol. 7, No. 4 (Fall 1991).

25. In *Ellison*, the hostile work environment was primarily based upon a coworker's perception of a relationship developing with the plaintiff. He perceived after one lunch date an involvement and began sending her notes that apparently were threatening to her. The text of one of the notes is as follows:

    I know that you are worth knowing with or without sex. . . . Leaving aside the hassles and disasters of recent weeks. [sic] I have enjoyed you so much over these past few months. Watching you. Experiencing you from O so far away. Admiring your style and elan. . . Don't you think it odd that two people who never even talked together, alone, are striking off such intense sparks. . . I will [write] another letter in the near future.

26. *Robinson v. Jacksonville Shipyards, Inc.*, 760 F.Supp. at 1498.

27. *DeCintio v. Westchester County Medical Center*, 821 F.2d 111 (2d Cir. 1987).

28. *Miller v. Aluminum Company of America*, 679 F.Supp. 495 (W.D.Pa. 1988).

29. *King v. Palmer*, 778 F.2d 878 (D.C. Cir. 1985).

30. *Jenkins v. Orkin Exterminating Co., Inc.*, 646 F.Supp. 1274 (E.D.Tex. 1986).

31. *Bohen v. City of East Chicago*, 799 F.2d 1180 (7th Cir. 1986).

32. *Garziano v. E. I. DuPont Co.*, 818 F.2d 380 (5th Cir. 1987). Sexual harassment policy bulletin was subject to a qualified privilege; plaintiff must show bad faith or actual malice.

33. *Pikop v. Burlington Northern Co.*, 390 N.W. 2d 743 (Minn. 1986).

34. *Bowersox v. P.H. Glatfelter Co.*, 677 F.Supp. 307 (M.D.Pa. 1988).

35. *Hunt v. Weatherbee*, 626 F.Supp. 1097 (D.Mass. 1986).

36. See *Gan v. Kepro Circuit Systems*, 28 F.E.P. 639 (BNA) (E.D.Mo. 1982).

37. See *Walter v. KFGO Radio*, 518 F.Supp. 1309 (D.N.D. 1981), and *Clark v. World Airways*, 24 F.E.P. (BNA) 305 (D.C. Cir. 1980).

38. See *Halpert v. Wertheim & Co.*, 81 F.R.D. 734 (S.D.N.Y. 1980).

39. 490 U.S. 228 (1989).

40. *City of Los Angeles, Department of Water and Power v. Manhart*, 435 U.S. 702 (1978); see also Roger B. Jacobs, *Manhart*, "Sex Based Differentials and The Application of Title VII to Pensions," *Labor Law Journal*, Vol. 31 (April 1980), p. 232, and *Norris v. Arizona Governing Committee*, 463 U.S. 1073 (1983).

41. *UAW v. Johnson Controls*, 111 S.Ct. 1196 (1991).

42. *Willis v. Dean Witter Reynolds*, 948 F.2d 305 (6th Cir. 1991), following *Gilmer v. Interstate/Johnson Lane Corp.*, 111 S.Ct. 1647 (1991).

43. 42 U.S.C. §2000e(k).

44. *Nashville Gas Co. v. Satty*, 434 U.S. 136 (1977).

45. *Newport News Shipbuilding & Dry Dock Co. v. EEOC*, 462 U.S. 669 (1983).

46. *California Federal Savings and Loan Association v. Guerra*, 479 U.S. 272 (1987).

47. 649 F.2d 670 (9th Cir. 1980).

48. 633 F.2d 361 (4th Cir. 1980), *cert. denied*, 450 U.S. 965 (1981).

49. *Smith v. Liberty Mutual Insurance Co.*, 569 F.2d 325 (5th Cir. 1978), and *Desantis v. Pacific Telephone & Telegraph Co., Inc.*, 608 F.2d 327 (9th Cir. 1979).

8

COMPLYING
WITH THE AMERICANS
WITH DISABILITIES ACT

Disabled employees and applicants are a class of individuals who are protected from discrimination under a variety of laws. In 1990, major legislation was adopted by Congress enacting the Americans with Disabilities Act, 42 U.S.C. §2101 (ADA). You must also become familiar with the Vocational Rehabilitation Act, 29 U.S.C. Section 791 (discussed in Chapter 9), and the various state anti-discrimination laws that apply. As you will see, dealing with handicapped or disabled persons has become a very important and difficult employment issue.

The employer must deal with a number of issues, including hiring a person capable of performing the job, having realistic and proper prerequisites for hiring, making reasonable accommodation, and avoiding discrimination based on one's disabilities. In other words, the employer must hire and retain people who are capable whether or not they have a disability and to make reasonable accommodations for those with a disability.

HISTORICAL DEVELOPMENT OF THE ADA

Congress declared that the purpose of the ADA was to "provide a clear and comprehensive mandate for the elimination of discrimination against individuals with disabilities." The U.S. Congress found that 43 million Americans had physical or mental disabilities, and they were faced with discrimination in employment, housing, public accommodations, education, transportation, communication, recreation, institutionalization, health services, voting, and access to public services. To remedy the "inferior status" of people with disabilities in our society, Congress adopted the ADA with separate titles dealing primarily with employment (Title I), public services (Title II), public accommodations (Title III), and telecommunications (Title IV).

The ADA is intended to complement the Vocational Rehabilitation Act of 1973, 29 U.S.C. §791 (which is limited to government contractors and recipients of federal financial assistance.)

For the purposes of this discussion our emphasis will be on employment, which primarily appears in Titles I and V of the legislation. We will also focus on the final regulations issued in 1991 and provide guidance for you in everyday employment situations particularly dealing with disabled individuals.

Since this is recent legislation it is likely that some of the interpretation will necessarily happen in the courts and some of our discussion will perhaps be moot in the future. However, we will attempt to provide you with basic information and guidance so that your efforts to understand the act and utilize it on an everyday basis will make sense.

WHAT THE ADA MEANS TO EMPLOYERS

The ADA makes sweeping changes in protecting individuals who have a disability. This chapter will guide you through the law and recommend compliance measures. To begin, we will start with the definitions and who the law covers. There are a number of terms and definitions that you need to understand as well as specific provisions of the law.

Defining Who Is Disabled

The ADA changes the terminology from "handicapped" to "disabled" and introduces other new terminology in contrast to those terms frequently used in the Rehabilitation Act and cases decided thereunder.

A *disability* is defined in the ADA as a physical or mental impairment that substantially limits one or more of the major life activities of an individual, the individual has a record of such impairment, or the individual is regarded as having such an impairment. This definition is similar to the definition in the Rehabilitation Act.[1]

In contrast, certain states have either broader or narrower definitions of the term "disability." For example, under New York law, disability means "(a) a physical, mental or major impairment resulting from anatomical, physiological or neurological conditions which prevents the exercise of a normal bodily function or is demonstrable by medically accepted clinical or laboratory diagnostic techniques, or (b) a record of such an impairment, provided, however, that in all provisions of this article dealing with employment, the term shall be limited to disabilities which do not prevent the complainant from performing in a reasonable manner the activities involved in the job or occupation sought or held."[2]

Major Life Activities. These are defined as those basic activities that the average person in the general population can perform with little or no difficulty. These activities include caring for oneself, performing menial tasks, walking, seeing, breathing, learning, and working.

Determining whether a physical or mental impairment exists is merely the first step to decide whether an individual is disabled. An impairment prevents an individual from performing a major life activity or substantially limits that major life activity.

Several factors are to be considered in assessing substantial limitations:

- Nature and severity of impairment
- Duration of impairment
- Permanent or long-term impact of impairment

Defining a "Major Life Activity of Working"

The ADA has introduced a new concept involving the major life activity of working. Under this concept, an individual who is not substantially limited with respect to any major life activity may, however, be substantially limited with respect to the major life activity of working.

Case Example

An individual who has a back condition that makes heavy lifting impossible would be substantially limited in the major life activity of working because a whole class of jobs are eliminated due to the impairment.

An individual is substantially limited in working if he or she is significantly restricted in the ability to perform a class of job or range of jobs in various classes.

Perceived Disability. The broad definition in the ADA protects individuals who have or had an impairment as well as those *perceived* to be impaired. Thus, if an employee is fired or otherwise adversely treated because someone thinks that he or she has a disease or other impairment, the employer may be liable for handicap discrimination. A frequent example of this is where an employee is thought to have AIDS because of his or her thinness or life-style.

Title I regulations provide certain illustrative conditions as disabling, including HIV infection, AIDS, cerebral palsy, epilepsy, muscular dystrophy, cancers, multiple sclerosis, heart disease, diabetes, mental retardation, emotional or mental illness, or substantial orthopedic, visual, speech, and hearing impairments.

Temporary nonchronic impairments of short duration with little or no long-term or permanent impact are usually not disabilities. For example, broken limbs, concussion, sprained joint, appendicitis, and influenza. The regulations also list obesity, but compare this with the position in New York holding obesity to be a handicap under the New York Human Rights Law.[3]

Pregnancy is specifically excluded under the ADA. However, complications might be covered, depending upon the specific circumstances.

Defining Who Is Covered by the ADA

The ADA targets employers in the private sector and who are not covered under the Rehabilitation Act (which covers only government contractors or recipients of federal financial assistance). The ADA was designed to be phased in over several years covering smaller employers last.[4] The specific employment-related provisions are scheduled to begin as follows:

- In July 1992, employers with 25 or more employees are covered under Title I
- In July 1994, this number is reduced to 15 or more employees

The Act defines *covered entities* as employers, employment agencies, labor organizations, and joint labor management committees. Not all businesses are covered.

Employer is defined as a person engaged in an industry affecting commerce who has 25 or more employees for each working day in each of 20 or more calendar weeks but not (beginning in 1992) for the first two years of the Act's coverage. After two more years, the definition requirement will be reduced to 15 or more employees.

Defining Who Is Not Covered by the ADA

There are exceptions. Various employers are excluded from the Act, including

- The United States or a corporation wholly owned by the government
- Indian tribes
- A bona fide private membership club

Under Title V, certain individuals and conditions are excluded. Homosexuals, bisexuals, and transvestites are not covered (§508,) and homosexuality and bisexuality are not impairments or disabilities according to §511.

Other conditions excluded from coverage under the ADA are:

- Transsexualism
- Pedophilia

- Exhibitionism
- Voyeurism
- Gender identity disorders not resulting from physical impairments or other sexual disorders
- Compulsive gambling
- Kleptomania
- Pyromania
- Psychoactive substance abuse disorders resulting from current illegal use of drugs

How the ADA Applies to Drug and Alcohol Use and Testing

The ADA also clarifies and amends the Rehabilitation Act by stating in §510 that an "individual with a disability" does not include an individual who is *currently* engaging in the illegal use of drugs. Section 512 specifically amends the Rehabilitation Act as follows:

> an "individual with handicap" does not include an individual who is currently engaging in the illegal use of drugs when a covered entity acts on the basis of such use.[5]

The modification of the Rehabilitation Act would not exclude an individual with handicaps who has successfully completed a supervised drug rehabilitation program and is no longer engaging in the illegal use of drugs or has otherwise been successfully rehabilitated or who is participating in a supervised drug rehabilitation program or who is erroneously regarded as engaging in such use.

Sections 503 and 504 of the Rehabilitation Act are also modified to the extent that an "individual with handicap" does not include any individual who is an alcoholic whose current use of alcohol prevents such individual from performing the duties of the job in question or whose employment by such current alcohol abuse would constitute a direct threat to property or the safety of others. See §512(a)(c)(i) of ADA.

Drug and Alcohol Use. Illegal use of drugs is defined as the use of drugs, the possession or the distribution of which is unlawful under the Controlled Substances Act, and a drug is defined as a controlled substance under §202 of the Controlled Substances Act 21, U.S.C. §812.

In other words, individuals who are currently using illegal drugs are not considered to be individuals with a disability under the ADA. Similarly, alcoholics are not included under the ADA's protection if they are impaired due to current use.

Testing. The ADA specifically does not prohibit drug testing of employees. See §104(d). To the extent permitted by law, all employers shall continue to be able to administer drug tests for employees or all job applicants and to make hiring and other employment decisions based, in part, upon their results. The Act specifically states that a test to determine the illegal use of drugs shall not be considered a medical examination.

NOTE: Any drug testing done by the employer must be in compliance with other federal and state laws.[6]

Medical Examinations. The ADA makes clear that preemployment examinations are *not* prohibited. Rather, in §102(c), the new law provides that employers may conduct a medical exam as long as such an examination is required of *all* job applicants and is not restricted only to individuals with a disability. In addition, employers may make preemployment inquiries into the ability of an applicant to perform job-related functions.

The Act's provisions comport completely with the standards normally utilized under the Rehabilitation Act and do not reflect a change at all.

NOTE: Preemployment physical examinations are restricted to the extent that they may be required *only* after an offer of employment has been made to a job applicant and prior to the commencement of the employment duties—if the examination is universally done for all new employees.

The information obtained from a medical examination must be maintained separately and treated as confidential medical records only to be released to supervisors and managers regarding necessary restrictions on their employees, first aid and safety personnel, and government officials regarding affirmative action compliance.[7]

NOTE: Medical examinations may not be limited to disabled individuals nor can they inquire into the nature or the severity of the disability unless such examination or inquiry is shown to be job-related and consistent with business necessity.

There are no restrictions on regular periodic medical exams. Employers may continue to conduct *voluntary* medical examinations as part of their routine health program available to all employees at the work site. In administrating such a program a covered entity may make inquiries into the ability of an employee to perform job-related functions. By properly narrowing the focus of such an inquiry, discrimination should be avoided under the ADA.

NOTE: Physical and mental qualifications for jobs should be reviewed at least once a year. Since federal contractors are required to review their affirmative action plan once a year to comply with Office of Federal Contract and Compliance Programs (OFCCP) requirements, it makes sense to do a complete review at that time. Job specifications should be reviewed so they are job specific. Use job restructuring to make sure you are focusing on ability to do the task in question and not looking for unnecessary physical and mental requirements.

DETERMINING WHAT IS PROHIBITED BY THE ADA

The ADA prohibits covered employers from discriminating against a "qualified individual with a disability" with regard to job applications, hiring, advancement, discharge, compensation, training, or other terms and conditions of employment.

Defining a Qualified Individual with a Disability

A *qualified individual with a disability* is defined in Section 101(8) of the ADA as an individual with a disability who *with or without reasonable accommodation* can perform the essential functions of the employment position that such individual holds or desires. This definition is broader than the "qualified handicapped individual" under the Rehabilitation Act, who is defined as a handicapped person capable of performing a particular job with reasonable accommodation to his or her handicap. Under both laws, individuals who can do the basic aspects of the job with little or some accommodation despite their handicap will be considered qualified and may not be rejected for the position on the basis of their handicap.

Those aspects of the job that a disabled person has difficulty with must be essential to the job in order to make them unqualified. Significantly, for the purposes of the ADA, consideration shall be given to the employer's judgment as to what functions of the job are essential. If an employer has prepared a written description for advertising or interviewing applicants for the job, the description shall be considered as evidence of the essential functions of the job.[8]

Defining Essential Functions

Essential functions means primary job duties that are intrinsic to the employment position the individual holds or desires. It does not include marginal or peripheral duties that are incidental to the performance of primary duties.

NOTE: Job functions may be essential because of the limited number of employees available to perform the task, which may be highly specialized.

However, under the ADA you can demonstrate that tasks are essential by utilizing written job descriptions used for advertising or interviewing job applicants.

All facets of a particular position should be reviewed carefully and an accurate job description drawn. A carefully prepared job description helps an employer defend against subsequent attack regarding the essential functions of a job. Your descriptions should be sufficiently detailed so that all the necessary functions are spelled out. These descriptions should be used in interviewing applicants so only individuals capable of performing these essential tasks are engaged.

In the event that an applicant or employee needs an accommodation to perform one of the essential tasks of a position, the employer should accommodate the employee as much as is reasonable. For example, the employer may redistribute marginal functions as an accommodation by transferring them to another position. However, *an employer is not required to relocate essential functions.*

The essential functions are by definition those that the individual who holds the job would have to perform, with or without reasonable accommodation, in order to be considered qualified for the position. Consideration will be given to the employer's judgment, written job descriptions, the amount of time spent in performing the function, the consequences of not requiring the function, the work experience of past jobholders, and work experience of similar jobholders.

For example, consider the following:

You require a security guard at your premises to monitor personnel flow and bar unauthorized individuals. A legally blind weight lifter applies for the position.

The employer would not be required to provide an assistant for a legally blind applicant or for a physically handicapped individual for that position.

If the applicant were wheelchair bound, he or she might be an acceptable candidate if the primary function of the position were to monitor ingress and egress of people and verify identification cards.

In such a case, if you rejected a candidate because he or she was mobility impaired but did not really need or regularly require a guard to walk the premises, such a position would be discriminatory and unlawful.

Defining Reasonable Accommodation

Employers are required under Section 101(9) of the ADA to make a *reasonable accommodation* to qualified disabled individuals. In the course of determining what, if any, accommodations need to be made to disabled employees, there are many issues you must consider:

◆ What is a reasonable accommodation?

◆ What if we are a small company—are the requirements the same?

♦ How much will it cost?

Accommodations may be necessary regarding the application process; to perform the essential functions of the job; and to utilize such facilities as a lunch room, gymnasium, or transportation.

A reasonable accommodation is any modification or job adjustment that facilitates a qualified individual with a disability in the position. It can be a modification to the work environment or the way the job is performed to better enable a qualified individual with a disability to do the job.

An accommodation may include

- Making existing facilities readily accessible and feasible
- Reassigning nonessential functions
- Adjusting or modifying examinations, training manuals, skill testing, and the like
- Restructuring jobs or modifying work schedules or part-time, acquiring equipment or devices, or providing qualified interpreter or readers

Resonable accommodation may also include reassigning a current employee to a vacant position for which the individual is qualified, if the person becomes disabled and is unable to do the original job.[9] But *there is no obligation to find a position for an applicant who is not qualified for the position sought.*

NOTE: Employers are not required to lower quality or quantity standards in order to make an accommodation, nor are they obligated to provide such items as glasses or hearing aids.

Determining Undue Hardship. All these provisions may require employers to expend additional monies in terms of physical plant or additional personnel. However, the requirement to make reasonable accommodations is *not* an open-ended one. Rather, it is modified specifically in §101(10), which provides that an "undue hardship" is an action requiring significant difficulty or expense by the employer.

However, if you cannot afford a specific accommodation, you may still have an obligation to the disabled applicant or employee. When an employer can show that an accommodation imposes an undue hardship, it will still be required to provide the accommodation if the funding is available from another source. One method is to give the disabled individual requesting the accommodation the option of providing the accommodation or of paying that portion of the cost which constitutes the undue hardship on the operation of business.

To determine the appropriate accommodation, it may be desirable to begin a dialogue with the disabled individual. An accommodation need not be the best one possible as long as it meets the individual's needs. If a suitable accommodation is refused, the individual may not be considered qualified.

Specific factors are designated in the statute to determine whether an accommodation would present an undue hardship on a covered entity. These factors include the following:

- The nature and cost of the accommodation needed under the act
- The overall financial resources of the facility, the numbers of persons employed at such facilities, or the effect on expenses and resources or the impact on the operation of the facility
- The overall financial resources of the covered entity; the overall size of the business of a covered entity with respect to the number of its employees; and the number, type, and location of its facilities
- The type of operation or operations of the covered entity, including the composition, structure, and functions of the workplace of such entity and the geographic separateness, administrative, or fiscal relationship of the facility or facilities in question to the covered entity

For example, if a small business employing 26 people has an opening for a maintenance mechanic, would it be required to hire an individual with a history of back problems? No!

However, the firm must define specifically what the primary tasks are and determine if the applicant can perform them. Thus, in this example, if one of the primary duties required lifting machinery of 50 to 80 pounds on a regular basis, what could be asked?

- Do you have a back problem?
- Due to your back problem, can you lift . . . ?
- This job requires regular lifting of 50–80 pounds. Are you able to do this?
- All of the above.

Probably the wisest course is question 3. You should inquire only as to ability to perform essential tasks.

Suppose you are operating a nightclub and an individual seeks employment as a waiter. However, he has a visual impairment so that he cannot see in dimly lit conditions. Do you have to hire or otherwise accommodate him? No!

While the individual could probably perform the job duties if the lighting were changed, it would completely undermine the ambience of the club and interfere with stage shows. But, if the applicant were also qualified for kitchen work where the conditions were poorly lit, could you still decline to hire him? No; not unless there were other candidates who were more qualified. However, if better lighting was needed so he could see in the kitchen, an accommodation should be worked out.

Thus the question of reasonable accommodation is not significantly different from the same issue under the Rehabilitation Act. The ADA, in large part, appears to codify what cases have routinely held with regard to reasonable accommodation standards as well as defenses for undue hardship.[10]

Accommodation decisions should be made on a case-by-case basis. An employer is only required to accommodate a known disability of a qualified applicant or employee.

NOTE: If the disabled individual does not request an accommodation, the employer is not obligated to provide one.

Defining Discrimination Under the ADA

Discrimination by employers, labor organizations, or joint-management committees against qualified individuals with a disability is prohibited with regard to job application procedures, hiring, advancement, discharge, compensation, job training, and other terms and conditions of employment. The term *discriminate* is defined in the statute as including

1. Limiting, segregating, or classifying a job applicant or employee in a way that adversely affects the opportunities or status of such applicant or employee because of his or her disability.

Covered entities cannot discriminate on the basis of stereotypes and myths about a disability. Each situation must be reviewed on an individual basis. Individuals with disabilities cannot be segregated into separate work areas.

For example, several individuals have identified themselves as HIV positive at your worksite. You have advised them to use *only* the bathroom on the basement level. Is that permissible? No, you may not limit or classify use of facilities due to a disability.

2. Participating in a contractual or other arrangement that has an effect of subjecting such an individual to discrimination.

If you provide training for account representatives through another company, is it permissible for that company to restrict access for mobility-impaired representatives? No, you cannot use a contract to evade your ADA responsibilities. If your employees need access, you must ensure a proper site or make different arrangements so they can attend.

3. Utilizing standards, criteria, or methods of administration that have the effect of discriminating based upon disability or that perpetuate the discrimination of others based upon common administrative control.

The regulations are intended to provide equal access to health insurance coverage as well. However, that does not mean that preexisting conditions are excluded. Thus employers may continue to offer policies that contain such clauses *even* if they adversely affect individuals with disabilities so long as the provisions are not used as a subterfuge.

4. Excluding or otherwise denying equal jobs or benefits to a qualified individual because of a relationship to an individual with a disability.

You may not discriminate against an individual because he or she has a relationship with a disabled person. For example, assuming that an employee will miss work to care for an AIDS-infected lover or will likely come down with the disease as well is unlawful and may not be used as the basis for an employment decision.

The ADA specifically protects individuals, whether or not they have a disability, from discrimination because that person is known to have an association or relationship with an individual who has a disability. The protection would apply whether or not there is a familial relationship.

NOTE: Accommodations are not required for an applicant or employee without a disability. The duty to accommodate reasonably applies only to a qualified applicant or employees with a disability.

5. Not making reasonable accommodations to the known physical or mental limitations of an otherwise qualified individual with a disability who is an applicant or employee unless such covered entity can demonstrate that accommodation would impose an undue hardship on the operation of the business or denying employment opportunities to a job applicant or employee who is otherwise a qualified individual with a disability if such denial is based on the need of such covered entity to make reasonable accommodation to the physical or mental impairments of the employee or applicant.

Are you required to provide a wheelchair to a disabled applicant or eyeglasses so that he or she can properly perform job duties? No, reasonable accommodations do not apply to modifications primarily for the benefit of the individual with a disability but must assist such an individual in performing the duties of a particular job.

The person in a wheelchair may need greater workstation width to perform secretarial duties. Would you be required to modify the workstation, assuming the individual can perform the primary duties? Yes!

NOTE: Employers are obligated to make reasonable accommodations only as to the physical or mental limitations *known* to the employer.

6. Using qualification standards, employment tests, or other selection criteria that tend to screen out individuals with a disability unless the test

utilized is shown to be job-related for the position in question and is consistent with business necessity.

Selection criteria that concern an essential function may not be used to exclude an individual with a disability if that individual could satisfy the criteria with a reasonable accommodation, including the adoption of alternative, less discriminatory criteria.

7. Failing to select and administer tests concerning employment in a nondiscriminatory manner. The test utilized must accurately reflect the skills and aptitude of the applicant or the employee for the job rather than merely reflecting any impaired sensory manual or speaking skills except where such skills are the factor that the test is required to measure.

Individuals with disabilities are not to be excluded from jobs they can actually perform merely because a disability prevents them from taking a test or negatively influences the results of a test that is prerequisite to a job. Applicant preference for a test format is not controlling. Moreover, tests need not be modified if the specific skills being tested are essential functions of the job.

For example, must a typing test be restructured for a secretarial candidate if he or she has dyslexia? No; not if the position requires the individual to regularly read, write, and type written material. The test is not unreasonable. But, can an accommodation be provided?

Reassignment. Reassignment to another vacant position is a possible means of accommodation. However, reassignment is not available to job applicants.

Individuals should be reassigned to equivalent positions in terms of status and pay. An employer may reassign an individual to a lower-grade position if there are no accommodations that would enable the employee to remain in the current position and there are no vacant equivalent positions for which the individual is qualified with or without reasonable accommodation.

NOTE: An employer is *not* required to promote an individual with a disability as an accommodation.

Enforcement. Under Title I, Section 107, complaints and enforcement of the ADA are handled by the Equal Employment Opportunity Commission (EEOC). The ADA adopts all the powers, procedures, and remedies from Title VII, including capped compensatory and punitive damages for intentional discrimination, reinstatement, back pay, front pay, and reasonable attorney's fees and costs. However, under the reasonable accommodation requirements, compensatory and punitive damages cannot be assessed as long as the employer has made a "good faith effort" to accommodate the disabled individual.

Complaints regarding discriminatory employment actions occurring after July 26, 1992, may be filed with the EEOC or designated state human rights agencies. The ADA provides disabled individuals with remedies that include hiring, reinstatement, back pay, and court orders to stop unlawful conduct.

In addition, the ADA requires that an effort be made to develop procedures to ensure that administrative complaints filed under the ADA and under the Rehabilitation Act are dealt with in a manner that avoids "duplication of effort and prevents imposition of inconsistent or conflicting standards for the same requirements." Obviously, the duplication of this statute and the Rehabilitation Act need to be worked out, and that effort may take some time even though the statute requires regulations to be in effect not later than 18 months after the effective date.

Charges must be filed at the EEOC within 180 days of the alleged discriminatory act or 300 days in states with approved enforcement agencies. Usually, the EEOC has 180 days to investigate and begin litigation or issue a right to sue letter. The complainant has 90 days to commence suit upon receipt of the right to sue letter.

States are not immune under the ADA from suit. This provision is in direct contrast to the Supreme Court ruling in *Atascadero State Hospital v. Scanlon*, 105 S.Ct. 3142 (1985), that states are immune from private suits under Section 504 of the Rehabilitation Act by virtue of the Eleventh Amendment doctrine of sovereign immunity.

How Employers may Defend Against Discrimination Charges

Scope of Defenses. Section 103 of the ADA discusses employer defenses to an allegation of discrimination based upon disability. For example, the Act provides that it may be a defense to a charge of discrimination that

- Tests or selection criteria are job-related
- Consistent with business necessity
- Reasonable accommodation cannot be provided

Other defenses that might be asserted to an ADA claim include the following:

- Employer is not covered by the Act
- Accommodation would cause undue hardship
- The employee is not disabled under the Act
- The employee is not qualified to perform essential functions of the job

Qualification Standard. In addition, a new term, *qualification standard*, was introduced in the ADA which provides that a covered entity may include a requirement that an individual shall not pose a direct threat to the health or safety of other individuals in the workplace.

Direct threat is defined in §101 as a significant risk to the health or safety of others that cannot be eliminated by reasonable accommodation.[11] The law permits employers wide latitude in determining whether or not the individual poses a threat to health or safety of others in the workplace.[12]

Case Example

A leading surgeon is working in Good Health Hospital. He becomes ill and enters the same facility for treatment. After some testing, it is learned that PCP is present—a conclusive indicator of AIDS. In addition, the treating physician ordered a blood test to determine if the surgeon was infected with HIV.

The tests for HIV and PCP were positive and the surgeon was advised he had AIDS.

What should be done?

– Should coworkers be notified?

– Should the surgeon's surgical privileges be curtailed?

– Should the surgeon be terminated?

There is no reason to terminate the surgeon as long as he or she can perform his or her duties. A more difficult issue, however, arises around the surgeon's continuing treatment of surgical patients. One court has recently suggested the test to be applied is "whether the continuation of surgical privileges, which necessarily encompasses invasive procedures, poses a reasonable probability of substantial harm to others, including co-employees and, more importantly, patients."[13]

The focus must be on the risk of serious injury. Even though the risk of transmission in the case study is small, it does exist. However, it can be further reduced by enhanced surgical precautions, for example, double gloving and goggles.

In quantifying the risk, consider also the nature of the procedures being performed. When assessing these types of critical issues, consider these options:

– An informed consent of patients could be requested requiring the surgeon to reveal his condition and discuss the very limited risks of transmission.

– Your facility may decide that the risk, albeit small, would be so grave that certain health professionals such as the doctor would not be permitted to continue to do surgery. (Note: This may be a minority position at this time and should be carefully examined prior to its implementation.)

– In general, you should look at the specific nature of the doctor's (or other health professional's) duties to determine if there is a serious risk of transmission. If the employee/health professional has limited patient contact and is able to perform the essential functions of the job, no employment measures should be taken.

How the Act Applies to Religious Entities

Religious entities are given a specific exclusion under the act. Religious organizations may require that all applicants and employees conform to the religious tenets of such an organization. The religious entities may be a religious corporation, association, educational institution, or society, and they may give a preference in employing individuals of a particular religion to perform work connected with the carrying on of the organization. This provision carries forward one of the loopholes in Title VII.

How the Act Applies to Food Handling

The ADA also provides that within 6 months of the enactment of the law, and to be updated annually, the Secretary of Health and Human Services shall review all infectious and communicable diseases which may be transmitted through handling of food and publish a list of infectious and communicable diseases which are transmitted through handling food and publish the methods by which such diseases are transmitted. Any diseases which appear on that list will be a sufficient basis for a covered entity to refuse to assign or continue to assign such an individual to a job involving food handling unless a reasonable accommodation can be made. This provision is a significant inclusion since it appears specifically designed to address the potential problems in the communicable disease area. Employers may require that their workers do not create a direct risk to health or safety of others including customers. Such a determination must be based on a reasonable medical judgment considering the following factors:

- Duration of risk
- Nature and severity of potential harm
- Likelihood that potential harm will occur

To date, there does not appear to be any evidence that AIDS may be transmitted through food handling. It appears likely that this provision may permit the Secretary of Health and Human Services to bar certain individuals from food handling jobs. In this regard the Act speaks of transfer of individuals and not termination.

Identifying Other Subjects Covered by the Act

The questions of posting, retaliation, and attorney's fees are also covered by the Act.

Posting.   All covered entities under Title I are required to post notices in an accessible format to applicants, employees, and others describing the provision of this Act consistent with the 1964 Civil Rights Act. Records must be maintained for 6 months. At the present time, no special reports are required under the ADA.

Retaliation. Title V specifically protects against retaliation where an individual has either opposed an unlawful act or because such an individual has made a charge, testified, or participated in an investigation or hearing under the Act. This provision is consistent with Title VII and other anti-discrimination laws and is codified in §503(a)(b) of the Act.

Attorney's Fees. Attorney's fees are available to the prevailing party other than the United States pursuant to §505 of the Act. The Act provides for "reasonable attorney's fees including litigation expenses and costs."

SUGGESTIONS FOR IMPLEMENTING A PROGRAM TO EMPLOY THE DISABLED

Some general rules summarize this area and provide answers to some key questions that you need to resolve to develop or implement a program to employ disabled individuals in your workplace.

1. Base employment decisions on ability not disability.
2. Place disabled individuals in jobs equal to their training, skills, experience, and ability. Do not attempt to compensate or discriminate because they are disabled. Provide the same career counseling offered to nondisabled employees.
3. Promote qualified disabled individuals.
4. Provide the same supervision for disabled individuals as is provided for nondisabled persons.
5. Make it clear to all employees that disabled workers will have to carry their weight and will not be given "special treatment."
6. Review all job descriptions. Create or modify job descriptions so that essential functions are clearly stated.
7. Discuss with the disabled individual his or her particular needs and attempt to agree on the appropriate level of accommodation.
8. Make a reasonable effort to accommodate a qualified individual with a disability. Prepare documentation when a particular accommodation is an undue hardship.
9. Work with state rehabilitation agencies to promote employment of the disabled.
10. Regularly publicize your efforts to recruit, hire, train and promote disabled workers.

The ADA is *not* an affirmative action statute for the disabled. It is intended to assist qualified disabled individuals to enter and remain in the workplace. Where necessary, employers may be required to make accommodations. This chapter should be read with Chapters 9 and 15, which deal with other disability and workplace health issues.

ENDNOTES

1. Regulations issued under Section 504 of the Rehabilitation Act define physical or mental impairment as "any physiological disorder or condition, cosmetic disfigurement or anatomical loss affecting one or more of the following body systems: neurological; musculoskeletal; special sense organs; respiratory, including speech organs; cardio-vascular; reproductive; digestive; genito-urinary; hemic; and lymphatic; skin and endocrine; or any mental or psychological disorder such as mental retardation, organic brain syndrome, emotional or mental illness and specific learning disabilities."

2. See *SDHR v. Xerox Corp.*, 65 N.Y.2d 213 (1985), in which the New York Court of Appeals said that the term "disability," in contrast to the term "handicap" in the Rehabilitation Act, includes "medical" impairments as well as "physical or mental" impairments. In addition, to qualify as a disability, the condition can manifest itself either by preventing the exercise of normal bodily functions or by being demonstrable by diagnostic techniques, while under the Rehabilitation Act the condition must "substantially limit a major life activity." *Id.* at 218.

3. See note 2 discussing *SDHR v. Xerox Corp.*, wherein New York's highest court held that clinically diagnosed obesity constituted an impairment protected by the state's anti-discrimination law. See also *Gimello v. Agency Rent-A-Car Systems Inc.*, 250 N.J. Super. 338 (App. Div. 1991), wherein the court ruled that obesity may be considered a handicap under New Jersey law whether it is caused by a medical condition or simply by overeating.

4. The following summarizes the various effective dates for different provisions of the ADA.

    Title I: Employment. ADA requirements became effective on July 26, 1992, for employers with 25 or more employees and on July 26, 1994, for employers with 15–24 employees.

    Title II: Public Accommodations. ADA requirements become effective on January 26, 1992, generally and August 26, 1990, for purchase or lease of new vehicles that are required to be accessible; new facilities designed and constructed for first occupancy later than January 26, 1993, must be accessible; generally, lawsuits may not be filed until January 26, 1992. In addition, except with respect to new construction and alterations, no lawsuit may be filed until July 26, 1992, against businesses with 25 or fewer employees and gross receipts of $1 million or less, and January 26, 1993, against businesses with 10 or fewer employees and gross receipts of $500,000 or less.

    Title III: Transportation. Public bus systems: requirements become effective on January 26, 1992, generally and August 26, 1990, for purchase or lease of new buses; public rail systems: light, rapid, commuter, and intercity (Amtrak) rail— ADA requirements became effective on January 26, 1992, generally and August 26, 1990, for purchase or lease of new rail vehicles, by July 26, 1995, one car per train accessibility must be achieved, by July 26, 1993, existing key stations in rapid, light, and commuter rail systems must be made accessible with extensions of up to 20 years (30 years, in some cases, for rapid and light rail); privately operated bus and van companies: ADA requirements become effective on January 26, 1992, generally, July 26, 1996 (July 26, 1997, for small providers), for purchase of new over-the-road buses, and August 26, 1990, for purchase or lease of certain new vehicles (other than over-the-road buses).

Title IV: State and Local Government Operations. ADA requirements become effective on January 26, 1992.

Title V: Telecommunications. ADA requirements become effective on July 26, 1993, for provision of relay services.

5. This might be contrasted, for example, with the position of New York State Division of Human Rights, which has suggested that drug use might qualify an individual as a handicapped person if such use did not interfere with his or her ability to perform the job. See General Counsel memorandum, N.Y. State Division of Human Rights, October 28, 1987, providing, in part, that the Division regards alcohol and drug abuse as disabilities within the meaning of the Act. But compare with Judge Goettel in *Burka v. N.Y.C. Transit Authority,* 680 F. Supp. 590 (S.D.N.Y. 1988), wherein the court declared that "perceived or actual users of illegal narcotics are not similarly situated with those who legally consume alcohol."

6. For example, the New Jersey Supreme Court, in a recent decision, held that the mandatory random urine testing by private employers could be an invasion of privacy sufficient to breach public policy deriving from both common law and the New Jersey Constitution. *Hennessey v. Coastal Eagle Point Oil Co.,* 129 N.J. 81 (1992).

7. Compare this with the Rehabilitation Act under which individuals may voluntarily provide information regarding their handicap. Such information should be kept confidential except that (1) supervisors and managers may be informed regarding restrictions on the work duties of handicapped persons and necessary accommodations, (2) first aid and safety personnel may be informed to the extent appropriate, and (3) government officials investigating compliance with the Rehabilitation Act may be informed. To conform with the Rehabilitation Act, a notice regarding this policy should be posted.

8. Under the Rehabilitation Act the test is whether or not an individual can perform the essential tasks of the job. See *Davis v. Southeastern Community College,* 442 U.S. 397 (1979), and *Strathie v. Department of Transportation,* 716 F.2d 227 (3d Cir 1983). In *Strathie,* a school bus driver with a hearing impairment had been denied employment because he wore a hearing aid. The court of appeals ruled that despite the potential for dislodgement of the hearing aid, or its mechanical failure, or even a diminution of volume by the driver, all the problems could be overcome by minimal adjustment. Such factors, the court held, would not automatically exclude him for employment. The Third Circuit found that under the Rehabilitation Act, a

handicapped individual is not "otherwise qualified" if an accommodation (1) requires modification of the essential nature of the program or (2) imposes an undue burden on the employer. Also provided in that case is an analysis of burdens of proof in §504 cases—to establish a *prima facie* case a plaintiff must establish that (1) he or she is a "handicapped individual," (2) he or she is "otherwise qualified" for the position in question, (3) he or she has been excluded solely due to his or her handicap, and (4) the program is a recipient of federal financial assistance.

The ADA makes no reference to federal financial assistance and has a less restricted scope than does the Rehabilitation Act. There are no such similar requirements under the ADA as long as the covered entity is in an industry affecting commerce and meets the threshold number of employees.

9. See "The Americans with Disabilities Act Questions and Answers," U.S. Department of Justice.

10. See Roger B. Jacobs, "Accommodating the Handicapped," in *Prentice Hall Equal Employment Opportunity Compliance Manual* (Englewood Cliffs, N.J.: Prentice Hall, 1986).

11. This defense is in contrast to cases in many jurisdictions, including New Jersey, that take a very narrow view in this regard. Cf. *Jansen v. Food Circus Supermarkets, Inc.*, 110 N.J. 363 (1988). In *Jansen*, Justice Stewart Pollock, writing for the New Jersey Supreme Court, held that Jansen's epilepsy did not constitute a danger to himself or his coworkers. The New Jersey Law Against Discrimination, N.J.S.A. 10:5-3.1, disapproves employment discrimination against the handicapped "unless the nature and extent of the handicap reasonably precludes the performance of the particular employment." However, the court recognized that an employer "may consider whether the handicapped person can do his or her job without imposing serious threat of injury to the health and safety of himself or other employees." See further discussion in note 12.

12. Cf. *Jansen v. Food Circus Supermarkets, Inc.*, 110 N.J. 363 (1988), discussed in note 11. The test to be utilized is not merely whether the individual has a handicap but whether continued employment in the present position poses a reasonable probability of substantial harm. In *Jansen*, it was not sufficient for Food Circus to conclude from Jansen's seizure at work that he presented a risk of injury. Such a conclusion must be based upon "an individualized assessment of the safety risk posed by the applicant's epilepsy." When asserting the safety defense, the Court ruled, the employer must establish with a reasonable degree of certainty that it reasonably arrived at the opinion that the employee's handicap presented a materially enhanced substantial harm in the workplace. But cf. *Estate of Behringer v. Princeton Medical Center*, 249 N.J. Super. 597 (L. Div. 1991), extending *Jansen* and holding that an AIDS-infected physician may be barred from direct contact with patients due to the extraordinary result of transmission despite a small risk of contagion. Patients have a right to be informed of the physician's contagion and disease. Under the Rehabilitation Act, the courts have taken a dim view of limiting employment rights based on concerns for others rather than a primary focus on the qualified handicapped individual.

13. *Estate of Behringer v. Princeton Medical Center, supra*, note 12.

9

AVOIDING DISABILITY/HANDICAP DISCRIMINATION: A FOCUS ON THE REHABILITATION ACT

Employers have found that it is simply sound business and good economic policy to recruit, hire, and promote disabled individuals into the workplace. You should seriously review your organization's personnel practices to determine if they presently utilize and maximize opportunities for handicapped individuals. If you find that handicapped individuals are simply not being given appropriate employment opportunities, the information in this chapter will be of great help. By modifying your personnel practices to comply with the law, you can fully realize the great potential of disabled workers as a human resource.

ACCOMMODATING THE HANDICAPPED/DISABLED

The principal statutes governing this area are the Vocational Rehabilitation Act of 1973, 29 U.S.C. 701, *et seq.* (Rehabilitation Act), and the Americans with Disabilities Act (ADA), 42 U.S.C. §12101, discussed in detail in Chapter 8, as well as various state fair employment statutes. The focus of this chapter is the Rehabilitation Act, which attempts, through vocational rehabilitative services, affirmative action, administrative enforcement, and litigation, to provide enhanced opportunities for handicapped individuals who are employed in the public sector, by government contractors, or employers receiving federal financial assistance.

The fundamental first step for an employer, as well as an individual, is to determine precisely who is a "handicapped" individual under the Rehabilitation Act.

Provisions of the Rehabilitation Act

The Rehabilitation Act covers federal agencies, federal contractors, and programs and activities of private entities receiving federal funds. In contrast, the ADA will cover all employers with 15 or more employees as of July 26, 1994, including state and local government agencies. Specifically, the federal government is required not to discriminate against and to take affirmative action for the benefit of handicapped persons in employment under Section 501.

Section 503.   Section 503 of the Act obliges federal contractors and subcontractors with contracts over $2,500.00 not to discriminate against handicapped persons and to take affirmative action to provide employment opportunities for them.

Affirmative Action Obligations.   Employers with government contracts over $2,500.00 must include an affirmative action clause in each covered contract. A notice of the employer's affirmative action obligations must be posted in a "conspicuous place" where employees will see it.

Employers with 50 or more employees and federal contracts of at least $50,000.00 must prepare a written affirmative action program within 120 days after getting the contract. The program must be available for inspection to any employee or applicant on request. The program must be reviewed annually and must be prepared at each of the employer's locations. Employers must maintain records regarding complaints, compliance reviews, and all other affirmative action information for one year. Failure to comply with its affirmative action obligations can result in a judicial enforcement by the Department of Labor, debarment from future contracts, contract termination, or withholding of contract payments to correct any violations.

Compliance with affirmative action obligations and information on creating and maintaining affirmative action programs are discussed in Chapter 10.

Section 504.   Section 504 prohibits discrimination on the basis of handicap in any program or activity receiving "federal financial assistance." This term has been broadly defined and includes grants and other forms of federal funds.

The 1987 Civil Rights Restoration Act specifies that even if only one program or activity at an institution, governmental entity, or private employer receives federal funds, the entire institution, entity, or employer is covered by the Rehabilitation Act.

Definitions. The Rehabilitation Act generally defines a handicap as "a physical or mental impairment which substantially limits one or more major life activities." The individual must have a record of such impairment or be regarded as having one. Perception of a handicap is treated as the same as reality in this area of the law.

Section 504 regulations define physical or mental impairment as "[A]ny physiological disorder or condition, cosmetic disfigurement or anatomical loss affecting one or more of the following body systems: neurological, musculoskeletal; special sense organs; respiratory, including speech organs, cardiovascular; reproductive; digestive; genito-urinary, hemic and lymphatic; skin; and endocrine or any mental or psychological disorder such as mental retardation, organic brain syndrome, emotional or mental illness, and specific learning disabilities."

Coverage. Individuals covered under the Rehabilitation Act include those who, due to a physical or mental impairment, are likely to experience difficulty in securing, retaining, or advancing in employment. Also included are those who have recovered from a previous disability but may encounter problems in employment whether or not they are still handicapped. The Act defines a "qualified handicapped individual" as a handicapped person who is capable of performing a particular job with reasonable accommodation to his or her handicap.

Drug Users and Alcoholics. The ADA amended the Rehabilitation Act specifically to exclude drug users and current alcoholics who cannot perform their job duties or whose employment presents a safety risk. Employers may test for the use of illegal drugs. Drug users who have been rehabilitated or who are participating in a supervised rehabilitation program and are not using drugs are protected under both laws.

Cases involving drug users and alcoholics which predate the passage of the ADA, illustrate the variations of "handicapped" employees within the law.

Case Example

In *New York City Transit Authority v. Beazer,*[1] the Transit Authority, which had employed more than 40,000 individuals in the City of New York, automatically excluded present methadone users from employment. However, these individuals had entered methadone programs to treat and/or cure their drug problems. Following its own rule, the Transit Authority refused to employ persons who used narcotic drugs, including those in methadone maintenance programs. Despite the fact that the lower court had found that a major use of methadone was detoxification of drug addicts, the Transit Authority refused to employ such individuals. In *Beazer,* however, the Supreme Court found that the Rehabilitation Act did not necessarily cover alcoholics or drug users whose current use prevented them from performing their job. It ruled that there was no constitutional violation by the Transit Authority's policy of excluding drug users, emphasizing that it was better to have individual employment determinations—especially in light of a legitimate concern for public safety.

Public safety is always an essential consideration in many areas of employment. For example, the FBI was permitted to fire a special agent for repeated drunkenness even though he was in a rehabilitation program.[2]

A case similar to *Beazer* from Pennsylvania, *Davis v. Bucher*,[3] involved rehabilitated drug users instead of present users. However, in that case, Philadelphia had an absolute ban on hiring such individuals. The *Bucher* court held that such conclusive or irrebuttable presumptions were illegal. It said the individuals in that case were fully qualified for city employment and that drug addiction was, in fact, included within the meaning of the Rehabilitation Act.

The *Beazer* and *Bucher* decisions raised serious questions that have been addressed by the ADA. Companies may have to revise their policies to be in compliance with these recent changes.

For example, consider a 30-year employee of a large company who has been a problem drinker during her entire period of employment. After having condoned such conduct for so long, can the employer legally fire such an individual?

Discipline would seem to be appropriate if the employee was drunk on the job, absent from work due to drunkenness, had excessive absenteeism due to drunkenness, or had caused a problem with other employees due to his condition.

However, would your response change if the employee had agreed to go to treatment (Alcoholics Anonymous) and had infrequent, but periodic, problems of which the employer was aware over a long period of time? It would seem that this employee would be protected under the Rehabilitation Act and should be accommodated and tolerated.

NOTE: Be sure to consider the effect, if any, of any applicable collective bargaining agreement and your own rules and regulations. Certainly, if such an individual has successfully filed a grievance over her dismissal, she might then sue under the Rehabilitation Act. Such a case would probably be governed by the Supreme Court's admonition in *Alexander v. Gardner Denver Co.*,[4] entitling individuals to a *trial de novo*[5] in similar Title VII situations. The arbitrator's decision would be considered, but the employee would still be entitled to a full hearing. Note this is not the case where there is a separate, individual arbitration agreement for claims arising out of the employment relationship.[6]

Preexisting Conditions.

An employer may not rely upon the fact that a worker with a preexisting condition may suffer a future injury and deny that person employment.[7] This dilemma frequently emerges with individuals suffering from back problems.

Consider the situation in which an applicant for employment as a lift truck operator presents himself with a preexisting back problem. Yet his physician has certified that he is presently able to handle the job and that there is no present disability of any kind. You are noticeably concerned because there is certainly a possibility or perhaps even a likelihood of difficulty in performing the job and greater likelihood of injury because of the preexisting condition.

An employer may not disqualify an applicant because of his or her preexisting condition, so long as the individual is able to do the job.

The key is present capacity, not future incapacity. There are many cases, in both state and federal court, that clearly suggest that an employer may not disqualify an individual even though the preexisting condition can easily reoccur.[8]

Risk of Future Harm. The threshold issue when looking at applicants or employees with preexisting conditions should be whether or not such an individual is able to perform the job at the time in question. A federal court ruled that "[N]on-imminent risk of future injury may possibly be a reason for rejecting an applicant, but it does not make an otherwise capable person incapable." But the court also suggested that not all presently capable individuals might be entitled to employment under the Act, cautioning that "in some cases, a job requirement that screens out qualified handicapped individuals on the basis of possible future injury, could be both consistent with business necessity and safe performance on the job." However, the court, of course, did not tell us when such a situation would exist.[9]

Determining Who Is "Otherwise Qualified." The key inquiry under the Rehabilitation Act is determining whether an individual is "otherwise qualified." Contrast this with a change under the ADA to "qualified individual with a disability."

The Supreme Court provided some fundamental guidance in determining specifically who is an "otherwise qualified" handicapped individual in *Southeastern Community College v. Davis*, 442 U.S. 397 (1979). The Court said that "an otherwise qualified person is one who is able to meet all of a program's requirements in spite of his handicap."

Consider the facts: Davis was a woman who had sought admission to a nurse training program. She had a hearing problem and was denied admission because the educational institution asserted that she needed eye contact to understand patient needs fully. The school also stated that her participation would have been unsafe and a potential danger to patients.

The Supreme Court ruled that educational institutions may include necessary physical qualifications. Under the Rehabilitation Act, the Court held that individuals must first be qualified for the program before any question of accommodation need be addressed by the institution. Concluding that Davis could participate only if the standards were lowered, the Court said "Section 504 imposes no requirement upon an educational institution to lower or reset substantial modifications of standards to accommodate a handicapped person." The Court did, however, suggest that there may be cases where "a refusal to modify an existing program might become unreasonable and discriminatory. Identification of those instances where a refusal to accommodate the needs of a disabled person amounts to discrimination against the handicapped continues to be an important responsibility of the HEW."

The Court also stated that

> We do not suggest that the line between a lawful refusal to extend affirmative action and illegal discrimination against handicapped persons will always be clear. It is possible to envision situations where an insistence on continuing past requirements and practice might arbitrarily deprive genuinely qualified handicapped persons of the opportunity to participate in a covered program. Technological advances can be expected to enhance opportunities to rehabilitate the handicapped or otherwise to qualify them for some useful employment. Such advances may enable attainment of these goals without imposing undue financial and administrative burdens upon the state.

A more recent case suggests that accommodations and understanding of handicapped individuals has progressed. In *Strathie v. Dept. of Transportation,* 716 F.2d 227 (3d Cir. 1983), a school bus driver with a hearing impairment had been denied employment because he wore a hearing aid. The Court of Appeals in Philadelphia disagreed with the lower court which had ruled against the driver.

The court ruled that, despite the potential for dislodgment of the hearing aid, or its mechanical failure, or even a diminution of volume by the driver, all these problems could be overcome by minimal adjustment. Such factors, the court held, would not automatically exclude him from employment under the Rehabilitation Act.

Thus, a handicapped individual may not be "otherwise qualified" if an accommodation

- Requires modification of the essential nature of the program or
- Imposes an undue burden on the employer

Examples of "otherwise qualified" follow. In a recent case, the Fourth Circuit Court of Appeals found a former civilian employee of the Navy was not otherwise qualified because his security clearance had been revoked based upon failure to disclose addictions. Since he was not otherwise qualified, there was no obligation on the part of the Navy to transfer or reassign him.[10]

Obesity has been found to be protected under New York and New Jersey state laws but not in other jurisdictions.[11]

Contagious diseases are also protected so long as the individual is otherwise qualified and is not a substantial threat to the health of others.[12]

Certain conditions have been found *not* to be a handicap, for example, short stature,[13] chronic lateness,[14] and poor judgment and irresponsible behavior.[15]

In a recent case, *Ward v. Skinner*,[16] the First Circuit Court of Appeals found it was not unlawful for the Department of Transportation to forbid anyone with a history of epilepsy from driving a truck in interstate commerce. This decision stands in contrast to the more typical individualized, case-by-case approach utilized by the courts.

Identifying Factors You Should Consider

In light of these cases, it's clear that the basic employment decision must focus on whether an individual can do the job without changing the essential nature of the program.

Employers should

♦ Determine what is the essential nature of the program involved

♦ Determine whether or not the applicant is able to perform the essential nature of the job without an accommodation or if accommodation imposes an undue burden or is too expensive

In identifying the essential nature of the job, the employer must ascertain the strictly core elements of a position, such as, what is necessary to accomplish the tasks and purpose of a position. Many tasks are incidental to the purpose of a position, so the personnel professional must carefully assess each task assigned to a position.

Once the essential tasks of the position are identified, you must determine whether a person who may have some disability is still able to perform the core duties of the job with or without slight modification to the position and without undue burden to the employer. So long as the individual can get the job done, he or she is "otherwise qualified," even if that means that the job is done in such a way that was not initially envisioned by the employer.

For example, in *Strathie*, getting the children safely to and from school was the essential nature of the job, and operating the bus was the essential task. If the individual with a corrected hearing problem could drive the bus, such an individual would be otherwise qualified, unless in order to drive the bus he required a modification of the essential nature of the program or imposed an undue burden upon the employer.

Determining Burdens of Proof

The *Strathie* court provided a helpful explanation of the burden of proof in Section 504 Rehabilitation Act cases. Essentially, it held that to establish a *prima facie* case, an employee/plaintiff must prove that

- He or she is a "handicapped individual"
- He or she is "otherwise qualified" for the position in question
- He or she has been excluded solely due to his or her handicap
- The program is a recipient of federal financial assistance

Each of these factors must be proved by the complainant in order to maintain a lawsuit. However, the employer may respond by showing that the individual

- Was not handicapped under the law

- Was not otherwise qualified because he or she was incapable of performing the essential functions of the position with or without modifications and/or the employer would be unduly burdened by cost or logistical problems if this person was to be accommodated, and/or

- The program is not within the scope of the Rehabilitation Act because it does not receive any or a sufficient amount of federal funds

In *Strathie*, the school board had already permitted individuals who wore eyeglasses to operate a school bus. But the Board had a different standard for hearing-impaired individuals than for people who wore eyeglasses. However, the evidence showed that a hearing aid could be implanted in eyeglasses and would become no more susceptible to loss or damage than eyeglasses. Therefore, the logic in differentiating between the two policies seemed less plausible to the court. The plaintiff was able to establish successfully all four criteria for a handicap discrimination claim.

POLICY CONSIDERATIONS FOR EMPLOYERS

The key task is to determine who is "otherwise qualified" to handle the job in question.

Eight Ways to Improve Employment Opportunities for Handicapped Personnel

After you and your staff have determined the "essential nature" of each job, serious hiring decisions have to be made. Assuming that your personnel staff has carefully reviewed the law and your specific job requirements, the following steps might be considered in hiring, promoting, and generally enhancing employment opportunities for the handicapped in your facility:

1. Develop a personnel program designed to show employees that there is a strong commitment to the accommodation and hiring of disabled workers.

2. Assign a personnel office specialist to the task of accommodating and placing qualified handicapped workers in your organization.

3. Establish a special procedure for reviewing and tracking handicapped applicants.

4. Include a special budget item to provide for accommodations that may become necessary.

5. Disseminate, formally and informally, information with regard to the opportunities available.

6. Participate in training programs for the handicapped and develop relationships with organizations that train and counsel various handicapped individuals. There are many vocational training centers and organizations available to work with potential employers.

7. Utilize these contacts so that job opportunities will be made available to handicapped individuals on an ongoing basis.

8. The employer should develop a policy statement regarding its affirmative action efforts and commitment to hiring the handicapped. An example is shown in Exhibit 9.1.

– EXHIBIT 9.1 –
Affirmative Action/Hiring the Handicapped Policy Statement

In recognition of the essential right of all employees and applicants for employment to be treated as individuals, our policy is to employ, advance in employment, and otherwise treat qualified handicapped individuals on a nondiscriminatory basis. These objectives are in compliance with our affirmative action program.

The company will make good faith efforts to reasonably accommodate the physical and/or mental limitations of any employee or applicant unless such accommodation imposes an undue hardship on the business.

Maintaining an Affirmative Action Notebook

You might also find it helpful for your hiring and recruiting, as well as Office of Federal Contract and Compliance Programs (OFCCP) compliance reviews, to maintain an "affirmative action handicapped" notebook at each of your facilities. Such a notebook might contain some of the following items:

– A statement of corporate policy regarding employment of the handicapped

– A copy of your notice to handicapped individuals

- A copy of any internal publications that feature the handicapped
- A copy of all physical and mental job requirements (once they have been reviewed to ensure that they do not screen out qualified handicapped individuals)
- Copies of all notifications to recruitment sources
- Copies of all application forms for handicapped individuals who have voluntarily identified themselves to the company
- A copy of a general personnel performance appraisal

A notebook of this sort will aid you in the event that you have a discrimination claim brought against the company. All related information will be there for easy access and review when preparing your response to such a claim. How all handicapped individual applicants and employees are evaluated and treated in the company is important evidence. Keep the notebook up to date.

Determining if Accommodation Is Needed and What Type

Probably the most difficult question for an employer is to determine whether an accommodation is necessary and what it must be. Once the "essential nature" of the job has been identified and the individual's ability to do the job is assessed, the issue of accommodation is presented.

The employer must accommodate the needs of the employee/applicant unless it is unreasonable. Unreasonable can mean that it causes undue hardship to the employer (e.g., excessive cost,) or that making an accommodation is unreasonable due to business necessity. To assess the necessity for and extent of accommodation, many factors need to be considered. For example, collective bargaining agreements may be relevant. A contract may prohibit certain bumping which becomes necessary due to reassignment.

Other relevant factors which must be considered are as follows:

- Size of the employer
- Geography
- Individual preference
- Number of plants
- Type of business
- Composition of the work force
- Costs of the accommodation

Clearly, accommodating the needs of a police officer in Chatsworth, New Jersey, or Corolla, North Carolina, is not the same as accommodating a New York City police officer or one in Los Angeles. A small town with one or two public safety officers is hardly in the same position as a huge metropolitan police force to accommodate the needs or preferences of its employees.

> NOTE: In assessing requests for accommodation of public safety positions, the courts generally have ruled that the critical factor is whether or not rules are uniform, are uniformly applied, and that they relate to the tasks or duties of the job.

For example, if all police officers are required to be fit, able-bodied, and able to make a forcible arrest, then the question of accommodation becomes more difficult. If, however, there are desk officers who are not required to be fit and who are unable to make a forcible arrest, then it would be reasonable and logical to expect the employer to make an accommodation.

Under the Rehabilitation Act, what constitutes a reasonable accommodation must be determined on a case-by-case basis. An undue hardship for a small employer might not be one for a large company. If an employer has a small work force, it might not be able to use job restructuring or reassignment of duties. In addition, the purchase of certain equipment might be prohibitive to a small employer. Redetermining the essential tasks may be a reasonable accommodation and may require assistance like hiring a part-time reader where the impact on an overall agency budget is "minute."[17] Similarly, providing additional supervision for an epileptic nursing assistant was found to be reasonable for a veterans hospital.[18]

Guidelines for Hiring and Accommodating the Handicapped

Certain other considerations should be made in hiring the handicapped. The following policy checklist should provide some guidance:

1. Develop and disseminate a written policy regarding hiring and accommodating handicapped applicants and employees.

2. Disseminate this policy inside and outside the organization. The best steps are to utilize meetings, films and brochures, and other illustrative materials to indicate your serious commitment to hiring and promoting the handicapped.

3. Make sure that your internal managers are well aware of your intention and efforts to recruit, hire, and promote the handicapped. It is just as important to make sure your managers are aware of your policy as to outside sources.

4. Contact outside recruiting sources, that is, vocational rehabilitation agencies, to let them know of your concern in this area. A simple letter outlining your desires is helpful.

– EXHIBIT 9.2 –
Notice to Handicapped Individuals

In conformance with regulations pursuant to Section 503 of the Rehabilitation Act of 1973, as amended, this company has developed an affirmative action program for the employment of the handicapped. The program is available for review by applicants and employees.

Any qualified individual who is handicapped and would like to be considered under the company's affirmative action plan should notify the Personnel Department. Submission of this information is voluntary, and refusal to provide it will not subject any applicant or employee to adverse action. Information on handicapped individuals will be kept confidential, except that (1) supervisors and managers may be informed regarding restrictions on the work or duties of handicapped persons and regarding necessary accommodations, (2) first aid and safety personnel may be informed to the extent appropriate, and (3) government officials investigating compliance with the Rehabilitation Act may be informed.

5. Create a notice to handicapped individuals to be displayed in all buildings on site in employment, applicant testing, and reception areas. A sample notice is shown in Exhibit 9.2.

6. Make clear who is responsible for administering and supervising the effort to hire, train, and promote handicapped individuals in your company in the written program. A corporate executive might be assigned to oversee all handicapped affirmative actions. But an EEO manager should be responsible for more direct implementation. The personnel department should also be directed to develop written job qualifications and review all job requirements. Each facility should have an affirmative action officer in that location.

7. Review all recruiting sources to make sure your message is getting out. Prepare a sample letter to all employees and applicants for employment explaining your company policy with regard to hiring, retaining, and promoting the handicapped.

8. Use only job-related tests. If a test is not job specific, change it. The test should focus on ability to do the specific job in question, that is, the essential task, and not on an individual's handicap or other unnecessary abilities.

– EXHIBIT 9.3 –

Architectural Barrier List

1. There should be at least one building entrance at ground level.

2. Doors should be at least 32 inches wide and open easily.

3. Thresholds should be level.

4. Substitute sloped ramps for stairs, where possible.

5. Safe, close parking for handicapped individuals should be provided.

6. Walks and crosswalks should be level.

7. There should be elevator access.

8. Restrooms should provide wide stalls and grab bars for wheelchair users.

9. All stairs should have hand rails that extend 18 inches beyond the top and bottom steps.

10. Floors should have nonslip surfaces.

11. Lower drinking fountains and public telephones should be provided.

How to Eliminate Barriers

A barrier checklist is shown in Exhibit 9.3. In general, however, you should consider the following problem areas and suggestions:

Getting Tax Benefits by Removing Barriers

Businesses should also note that one of the tax incentives available is the Dole/Mondale amendment (P.L. 94-455) passed in 1976 which allows a deduction of up to $25,000 during a taxable year for the removal of architectural barriers from place of trade or business. For more information, you may wish to contact the Architectural and Transportation Barriers Compliance Board, Washington, D.C. 20201. The Board's telephone number is (202) 245-1591.

ENFORCEMENT ACTIONS UNDER THE FEDERAL REHABILITATION ACT

Employers that have failed to accommodate handicapped individuals properly or that have discriminated against the handicapped may be subject to an enforcement action under the Rehabilitation Act. The principal enforcement mechanism for claimants under Section 503 of the Rehabilitation Act is the administrative procedures within the Office of Federal Contract Compliance Programs (OFCCP).

Administrative Procedures

Handicapped applicants or employees may file written complaints within 180 days from the date of the alleged violation with the OFCCP.

Current regulations provide that, if a contractor has an internal review procedure, the complaint will be referred to the contractor for 60 days.

If the complaint is not resolved through the contractor's procedure, OFCCP will investigate. If no action is contemplated by the OFCCP against the contractor, the complainant may request review by the OFCCP director. If OFCCP finds noncompliance, it will try to conciliate the matter. Conciliating contractors must specifically agree in writing to take corrective action before they can be found to be in compliance. If conciliation is unsuccessful, the contractor may request an administrative hearing before a Labor Department Administrative Law Judge (ALJ). The ALJ makes recommendations and final action is taken by the OFCCP. Final orders are subject to review in federal district court. The director may seek judicial enforcement, withhold payments due on the contract, or disqualify the contractor from future government contracts to obtain compliance.

Administrative responsibility for enforcing Section 504 lies with the federal agency providing financial assistance, under the leadership and coordination of the U.S. Attorney General. Each agency has issued compliance regulations.

Individuals may bring their own enforcement actions under Section 504 of the Rehabilitation Act as long as their employers receive "federal financial assistance." See our earlier discussion on who is covered under the Rehabilitation Act. Also the rights and remedies of Title VII, including reinstatement, back pay, front pay, and attorney's fees, are available to claimants under Section 504 as well as to federal government employees and applicants under Section 501.

Exhausting Administrative Remedies

The Rehabilitation Act establishes a conciliation mechanism which courts may require potential plaintiffs to pursue before instituting a suit. As a general rule, the failure to seek administrative remedies for Title VI and Section 504 claims would require dismissal of a suit brought under these statutes in federal court.[19]

It is apparent that some federal courts will not grant relief, despite meritorious claims, if handicapped plaintiffs have failed to seek an initial administrative remedy. The decisions are not uniform and indicate that handicapped individuals should consider seeking administrative relief unless the process would be futile. Absent such a showing, aggrieved handicapped persons may be denied federal court relief.

State Immunity

By virtue of the Eleventh Amendment doctrine of sovereign immunity, state entities are immune from private suits under Section 504. Resolving a prior conflict among the circuit courts of appeals, the U.S. Supreme Court, in *Atascadero State Hospital v. Scanlon*,[20] rejected the rationale that state agencies, by accepting federal grant money, impliedly waived their sovereign immunity. The court found that, if Congress intended for federal grant money to be conditioned on state and local governments' willingness to subject themselves to Section 504 lawsuits by private parties, the Act would have clearly said so. Thus states may not be sued under Section 504.

Describing Alternative Bases of Relief in Federal Court

Several federal courts have sanctioned relief for handicapped individuals under the due process and equal protection clauses of the Fourteenth Amendment.

Case Example

The Third Circuit Court of Appeals upheld the discrimination claims of Judith Gurmankin, a blind English teacher, based upon a denial of due process, in *Gurmankin v. Constanzo.*[21] The plaintiff had a professional certification from the Pennsylvania Department of Education as a teacher of Comprehensive English. Gurmankin sought employment in the Philadelphia school district. At that time, Philadelphia's medical and personnel policy absolutely excluded blind teachers from teaching sighted students in public schools. Applicants who were certified as having a "chronic or acute physical defect," including blindness, were automatically prevented from taking the teacher's exam in Philadelphia. Consequently, Gurmankin was examined by the director of medical services and was rejected by the school district. Gurmankin persisted in her attempts to take the test, however. In 1974, with the help of a community legal services program, she took and passed the exam. When the school district subsequently reached her name on the eligibility list, Gurmankin was offered positions, but she turned them down because the city refused to grant her full retroactive seniority. The court held that the policy of preventing blind teachers from teaching sighted students created an irrebuttable presumption that blind persons could not be competent teachers and was a violation of due process under the U.S. Constitution. Gurmankin had an expectation, based on state law, of being admitted to the teacher qualifying exam. The only requirement for appointment was certification from the state, which Gurmankin had already obtained.

The court of appeals held the award of retroactive seniority to be appropriate because courts can adjust their remedies to grant the necessary relief when federally protected rights have been invaded. Finally, the court found no difference under the law of equitable remedies among suits brought under Title VII, 42 U.S.C. §1983, and the Fourteenth Amendment.[22]

This type of result illustrates the admonition against the application of conclusive presumptions or irrebuttable presumptions. The Supreme Court firmly rejected the use of such presumptions regarding the employment of pregnant teachers.[23] The Fourteenth Amendment usually requires that an individualized determination before an applicant may be rejected.[24]

The decisions in this area suggest that claims of handicap discrimination may be based solely upon the Rehabilitation Act or a combination of other federal statutes. Many claims will now be brought under the ADA. Constitutional allegations of equal protection and due process violations have also been upheld.

Describing Alternative Bases of Relief in State Court

The majority of the states and the District of Columbia have adopted anti-discrimination statutes that include protection for handicapped or disabled individuals. These laws are of two basic types:

1. Separate legislation affecting only the handicapped (Delaware, Georgia, Idaho, Kentucky, Louisiana, Michigan, Mississippi, North Carolina, Oregon, South Carolina, Tennessee, and Virginia).

2. General civil rights legislation, which includes the handicapped as a protected group (Alaska, Arizona, California, Colorado, Connecticut, District of Columbia, Florida, Hawaii, Illinois, Indiana, Iowa, Kansas, Maine, Maryland, Massachusetts, Minnesota, Missouri, Montana, Nebraska, Nevada, New Hampshire, New Jersey, New Mexico, New York, North Dakota, Ohio, Oklahoma, Pennsylvania, Rhode Island, Texas, Utah, Vermont, Washington, West Virginia, and Wisconsin).

Although state courts have concurrent jurisdiction with the federal courts to enforce the rights of handicapped persons, there is no provision in the Rehabilitation Act of 1973 nor in the 1978 amendments for coordination between the states and the federal government in enforcing their right. As a result, the definitions of "handicapped" and "disabled" have tended to lack uniformity, as have the protections of the rights of the handicapped.

Summary of the Enforcement Provisions of the Rehabilitation Act

The enforcement remedies under the Rehabilitation Act are primarily administrative in nature. The relevant administrative procedures are those provided in Title VI. Handicapped individuals who believe that a federal contractor has discriminated against them are limited to administrative proceedings under Section 503. There is no private right of action to enforce Section 503.

Individuals who believe that recipients of federal funds have discriminated against them should first exhaust their administrative remedies under Section 504 before seeking relief in the courts. A private right of action exists under Section 504, provided that the program the individual has applied to or is employed in receives federal funds.

In addition to the enforcement provisions of the Rehabilitation Act, handicapped discriminatees may have an action based on other federal or state statutes. In addition, the Americans with Disabilities Act opens a far-wider range of relief and enforcement *through* the Equal Employment Opportunity Commission and the courts. For a full discussion of the ADA, see Chapter 8.

A BRIEF REVIEW OF THE VOCATIONAL REHABILITATION ACT

This capsule provides a brief review of the essential provisions of the Rehabilitation Act. You may wish to review this list whenever an issue under this Act arises in the workplace. Each of these points are discussed in detail in the chapter.

1. The Act applies to federal government agencies, government contractors, and recipients of federal financial assistance.

2. It promotes employment of handicapped individuals and prevents discrimination against them.

3. A handicap protected under the Act is defined as "a physical or mental impairment which substantially limits one or more of such person's major life activities." The Act also protects any individual perceived as having such an impairment.

4. Individuals who are handicapped must be "otherwise qualified" to perform the job.

5. An employer must attempt reasonably to accommodate a handicapped employee.

6. The Act requires employment and promotion of handicapped individuals by way of affirmative action under Section 503.

7. Section 503 is enforced by the Office of Federal Contract Compliance Programs of the U.S. Department of Labor.

8. Section 503 requires that any employer with a federal contract which aggregates to $2,500 or more must take affirmative action to hire and promote handicapped persons.

9. Regulations based on Section 503 require federal contractors with a contract of $50,000 or more *and* 50 or more employees to adopt and implement a written affirmative action program for the handicapped.

10. Section 504 provides for a private right of action—this means individuals can file enforcement actions in federal district court.

ENDNOTES

1. *New York City Transit Authority v. Beazer*, 440 U.S. 568 (1979).

2. See *Butler v. Thornburgh*, 900 F.2d 871 (5th Cir. 1990), *cert. denied*, 111 S. Ct 555 (1990). See also, *Rodgers v. Lehman*, 869 F.2d 253 (4th Cir. 1989). But cf. *Railway Labor Executives Assn. v. Burnley*, 839 F.2d 575, *Skinner v. Railway Labor Executives Assn.*, 489 U.S. 602 (1989) (9th Cir. 1988), *rev'd sub. nom.*, holding that substance abusers whose employment would constitute a threat to property or safety are not covered under the Rehabilitation Act. Similarly, a police department was not required to accommodate an officer who was a drug user. *Copeland v. Philadelphia Police Dept.*, 840 F.2d 1139, (3rd Cir. 1988), *cert. denied*, 490 U.S. 1004 (1989).

3. 451 F.Supp. 719 (D.Pa. 1978).

4. 415 U.S. 36 (1974).

5. *Trial de novo* is a legal term of art that is used to indicate that although there may have been earlier proceedings, including a trial or hearing in the case, the reviewing court on appeal may hear the matter as a new trial as if there had been no trial in the court below.

6. The Supreme Court in a recent opinion, *Gilmer v. Interstate/Johnson Lane Corp.*, 111 S. Ct. 1647 (1991), held that an ADEA claim may be subjected to compulsory arbitration pursuant to an arbitration agreement contained in a securities registration application. The Court held that *Alexander v. Gardner-Denver*, 415 U.S. 36 (1974), applies only to statutory claims such as age discrimination in the context of a collective bargaining agreement. Individual statutory rights cannot be waived in a collective bargaining situation.

7. See *Taylor v. Rockwell International, Inc.*, Pa. Human Relations Commission, No. E-16027, June 28, 1985; *Baltimore & Ohio Railroad v. Bowen*, 482 A.2d 121 (Md. Ct. Spec. App. 1984); *Pennsylvania State Police v. Pennsylvania Human Relations Commission*, 457 A.2d 584 (Pa. Comm. W. Ct. 1984).

8. In *E.E. Black, Ltd. v. Marshall*, 497 F.Supp. 1088 (D.Haw. 1980) an individual with a preexisting back condition had been denied employment. However, the court ruled that he was capable and competent for present employment because with

proper exercise he could do the lifting required on the job. The court therein ruled that present capacity rather than future incapacity is the key in such a job determination. See also *Sterling Transit Co. v. FEPC*, 175 Cal. Rptr. 548 (Ct. App. 1981) and *Maine Human Rights Commission v. Canadian Pacific Ltd.*, 458 A.2d 1225 (Me. 1983).

9. *E.E. Black*, see Note 8.

10. *Guildot v. Garrett*, 970 F.2d 1320 (4th Cir. 1992).

11. See *State Division of Human Rights v. Xerox Corp.*, 480 N.E. 2d 695 (N.Y. 1985) and *Gimello v. Agency Rent-A-Car System, Inc.*, 250 N.J. Super. 338 (App. Div. 1991); *but cf. Philadelphia Electric Co. v. Pennsylvania*, 448 A.2d 701 (Pa. Comm. W. Ct. 1982); *Tudyman v. United Airlines*, 608 F. Supp 739 (C.D. Cal. 1984).

12. *School Bd. of Nassau County v. Arline*, 480 U.S. 273, 107 S.Ct. 1123 (1987); *Chalk v. U.S. District Court*, 832 F.2d 1158 (9th Cir. 1987); see also *Doe v. District of Columbia*, 796 F.Supp. 559 (D.D.C. 1992), wherein an applicant for a firefighter's position was found "otherwise qualified" after a job offer was rescinded because he tested positive for the HIV virus.

13. *American Motors Corp. v. Labor and Industry Review Commission*, 338 N.W. 2d 518 (Wis. Ct. App. 1983) *aff'd* 350 N.W.2d 120 (Wis. 1984).

14. *Philadelphia School District v. Friedman*, 507 A.2d 882 (Pa. Commw. Ct. 1986).

15. *Daley v. Koch*, 892 F.2d 212 (2d Cir. 1989).

16. 943 F.2d 157 (1st Cir. 1991), *cert. denied*, sub nom., *Ward v. Secretary of Transportation*, 112 S. Ct. 1558, but contrast with *Duran v. Tampa*, 430 F.Supp. 75 (M.D.Fla. 1977).

17. *Nelson v. Thornburgh*, 567 F.Supp. 369 (E.D.Pa. 1983), *aff'd*, 732 F.2d 146 (3d Cir. 1984), *cert. denied*, 496 U.S. 1188 (1985).

18. *Smith v. Administrator of Veteran's Affairs*, 32 F.E.P. Cases (BNA) 986 (C.D.Cal. 1983).

19. *Green Street Assn. v. Daley*, 373 F.2d 1 (7th Cir. 1967) *cert. denied*, 387 U.S. 932 (1976). In *Drennon v. Philadelphia General Hospital*, 428 F.Supp. 809 (E.D.P.a. 1977), for example, the district court stayed the proceeding pending consideration of Drennon's claims by the Department of Labor. The plaintiff, an epileptic, contended that she was denied employment as a laboratory technician at Philadelphia General Hospital solely because of her handicap. Drennon sought relief based on a denial of due process and equal protection under the Fourteenth Amendment, the Rehabilitation Act of 1973, and 42 U.S.C. §1983.

The court found, preliminarily, that the plaintiff had a claim under the Constitution and Section 1983. In analyzing the Rehabilitation Act claim, the court reasoned that "the legislators anticipated and approved of inclusion of a private right of action to enforce [Section 504]."

After noting that there was overwhelming data in favor of implying a cause of action under both Sections 503 and 504 and that Drennon stated such a cause of action, the court held that she was not entitled to relief because of her failure to exhaust her federal administrative remedies. The district court deferred decision on the merits until the Labor Department considered Drennon's claims.

Similarly, in *N.A.A.C.P. v. Wilmington Medical Center, Inc.*, 426 F.Supp. 919 (D.Del. 1977), the federal district court held that a plaintiff must exhaust administrative remedies unless it can be clearly shown that the Secretary of Labor cannot or will not act on the plaintiff's complaint. In *Wilmington Medical Center*, the plaintiff contended that seeking administrative relief would have been futile. The court, however, was unwilling to conclude that the Secretary was unable or unwilling to perform reviews under Title VI and Section 504. Thus the district court directed the Secretary to make an initial determination of the plaintiff's complaint.

20.   473 U.S. 234 (1985).

21.   556 F.2d 184 (3d Cir. 1977), *cert. denied*, 450 U.S. 923 (1981).

22.   In another case, *Duran v. City of Tampa*, 430 F.Supp. 75 (D.Fla. 1977), a federal district court also struck down the use of an irrebuttable presumption against a handicapped person. Relying principally upon Supreme Court decisions rejecting conclusive presumptions without an individualized determination, the court rejected the Tampa Police Department's automatic medical exclusion for epileptics as a violation of due process. The district court considered these standards to create an irrebuttable presumption to exclude all individuals from employment who have suffered from epilepsy.

23.   *Cleveland Bd. of Educ. v. LaFleur*, 414 U.S. 632 (1974).

24.   In *Davis v. Bucher*, 451 F.Supp. 791 (E.D.Pa. 1978), the plaintiffs, former drug users, brought a class action challenging Philadelphia's hiring practices regarding job applicants with prior histories of drug abuse. Plaintiffs alleged violations of equal protection and due process because they were refused jobs solely based upon their former status regardless of their qualifications. The court declared the city's policy violated both the equal protection and due process clauses of the Fourteenth Amendment. Applying an equal protection analysis, the court said "no rational relationship whatsoever exists" between the city's ban on hiring former drug users and its legitimate interests in hiring qualified individuals. The court suggested that consideration be given to individual factors such as recent employment history, successful maintenance on a methadone treatment program, or evidence of freedom of drug usage. Since the regulations in question failed to consider the merits of each case, the rule was overbroad and irrational.

10

HOW TO COMPLY
WITH AFFIRMATIVE ACTION
REQUIREMENTS

Affirmative action is an attempt by employers to make a conscious effort to hire and promote members of society who have suffered past discrimination. An affirmative action plan may be required by the government, ordered by the court, or instituted voluntarily by the employer. The groups of people aided by affirmative action are blacks, Hispanics, women, Asians, native Americans, and more recently, the disabled and Vietnam veterans. This chapter will address how an employer can develop and maintain an affirmative action program.

HOW AFFIRMATIVE ACTION OBLIGATIONS OCCUR

An affirmative action plan can be implemented in one of three different ways—under Executive Order 11246, under court order, or voluntarily. Executive Order 11246, mandates employers who are federal contractors to develop and enforce an affirmative action plan. These contractors must submit a written affirmative action program to the Office of Federal Contracts and Compliance Programs (OFCCP) for approval. Also an employer may be required by court order to implement an affirmative action program after a court has made a finding of discrimination.[1]

If an employer does not come under one of these categories, an affirmative action program can be implemented voluntarily. There are several reasons why an employer may make this choice. First, adverse effect may have resulted from the already existing employment practices. Second, the effects of past discrimination are evident by comparing the employer's labor force with the labor force at large. Third, there is a limited labor pool. Fewer minorities and women are employed in certain sectors of the economy. The employer should encourage training programs and actively recruit these types of workers.[2]

> NOTE: If an employer is not required to implement an affirmative action program, it may be advisable to create a plan voluntarily. This is good public relations because it shows the employees as well as the community at large that the employer is sensitive to the plight of the disadvantaged. It also provides a defense if discrimination claims arise and may possibly prevent them.

DESIGNING AN AFFIRMATIVE ACTION PLAN

Executive Order 11246 mandates that all federal contractors not discriminate on the basis of race, color, religion, sex, or national origin and must develop an affirmative action program. This program should infiltrate all aspects of recruitment, training, and promotion. Guidelines published by the OFCCP aid the employer in this process.

The contractor must decide if coverage of this order extends to the company. A federal contract is any contract for goods or services that is made between a person or company and an agency or department of the federal government. Included are subcontracts, so if an employer subcontracts with a federal contractor, the subcontractor must also comply with an affirmative action plan. The program extends to all employees of the contractor for the life of the contract. There is an exemption for contracts for less than $10,000. However, an employer cannot get out of its requirement by making a series of $10,000 contracts because the aggregate worth of all contracts with the federal government determines whether the Order applies.

Once an employer comes under the governance of Executive Order 11246, it is required to do the following:

1. Refrain from discriminating against any employee or applicant for employment based on race, color, religion, sex, or national origin.

2. Establish an affirmative action plan to ensure that applicants and employees will not be discriminated against in employment with regard to race, color, religion, sex, or national origin.

3. Send copies of notices supplied by the government to all labor unions or worker representatives describing the contractor's commitments under this Order and also to post notices in conspicuous places.

4. Comply with all provisions of the Order as well as any rules and regulations of the Secretary of Labor.

5. Furnish all information and reports required by the order and permit access to books, records, and accounts by the agency and Secretary of Labor for investigation purposes to decide if the employer is complying with the rules.

6. Agree to cancellation, termination, or suspension of the contract in whole or in part if the procedures are not complied with.

7. Include the clauses in all subcontracts unless exempted and enforce as to subcontractors.[3]

The Executive Order mandates that the contractor exercise good faith in developing and enforcing the affirmative action program. The employer must figure out the areas where affirmative action should be implemented and then set up a plan including goals and timetables to remedy the existing and potential discrimination. The employer must also review the policy periodically to make sure the goals are being met. The affirmative action compliance program developed by the contractor must be submitted in writing to the OFCCP within 120 days of the contract provided the contractor or subcontractor employs 50 people and

1. Has a contract of $50,000 or more

2. Has government bills of lading which, in any 12-month period, total or can reasonably be expected to total $50,000 or more

3. Serves as a depository of government funds in any amount

4. Is a financial institution that is an issuing and paying agent for U.S. savings bonds and savings notes in any amount.[4]

The plan must include a policy statement, utilization analysis, establishment of goals, and a catchall of additional requirements.

Drafting the Policy Statement

The employer should begin by stating the reason for developing and enforcing the affirmative action program. The employer should express its commitment to a plan of affirmative action that will remedy past discrimination and change the composition of its labor force to reflect society. The statement should also include an explanation of the areas where the employer is deficient in recruitment, training, and promotion of minorities and women. Last, the policy should reaffirm that the ultimate goal is to eliminate the deficiencies.[5] A sample policy statement is shown in Exhibit 10.1.

Conducting Utilization Analysis

Utilization analysis is the required method to be used by the contractor to pinpoint where the deficiencies in employment of minorities and women exist.

– EXHIBIT 10.1 –
Affirmative Action Policy Statement

> This Company is committed to equal employment opportunity, which is not only the law of our country but also a basic goal of a free society. The success of this company, as well as the personal development of individuals, results from utilizing and strengthening the abilities of individuals to the fullest extent practical within the framework of the business environment. The policy of employment opportunity will serve the goal of the economic progress of individuals, the Company, and the Nation. To further this goal, we are affirming the following Equal Employment Opportunity Policy and will take Affirmative Action as outlined in Executive Order 11246 as amended:
>
> It has been and will continue to be the policy of this Company to provide employment, training, compensation, promotion, and other terms and conditions of employment without regard to race, color, religion, national origin, sex, age, or handicap (except where sex is a bona fide occupational qualification).

The contractor compiles data on employees and then uses these data to decide the problem areas and then eventually be able to formulate a policy to address and eliminate the problems. Generally, the utilization analysis uses the information from the Employer's Information Reports (EEO-1), which the employer must fill out.

A compilation of these reports will allow the employer to ascertain the number of employees in the following job groups: officers and managers, professionals, technicians, sales workers, office and clerical, and craftsmen. The employer will also be able to calculate easily the number of minorities and women in each of these job groups. The end result is that the employer becomes sensitive to the areas where minorities and women are underutilized and be able to design a program to focus on those areas in particular.

Performing a Work Force Analysis. The utilization analysis begins with the employer doing a work force analysis. All that is involved is simply listing each job in each department by title and pay schedule from entry-level position to manager, including the worker's name and nationality. Any jobs that offer advancement potential should be noted. Then the numbers of incumbent workers should be calculated. An incumbent worker is someone who has been promoted from within the company. The total number of incumbents, the total male incumbents, the total female incumbents, and the total number of those incumbent workers with Spanish surnames, American Indians, and Orientals should also be noted.

Performing a Major Job Group Analysis. Next the employer must include an analysis of major job groups. If minorities and women are being underutilized in those jobs, the reasons why should be given. Underutilization occurs when fewer minorities and women occupy particular job groups than would be reasonably expected. The utilization analysis should compare the use of minority and women workers in the labor force of the company to the labor force as a whole. The contractor must use eight factors contained in the OFCCP guidelines to perform this stage of the utilization analysis. The eight-factor analysis should be done twice, once for minorities and again for women. The eight factors are

1. The minority/women population of the labor area surrounding the facility

2. The size of minority/women unemployment force in that labor area surrounding the facility

3. The percentage of the minority/women work force as compared with the total work force in the immediate labor area

4. The general availability of minorities or women having requisite skills in an area in the immediate labor area

5. The availability of minorities/women having requisite skills in an area in which the contractor can reasonably recruit

6. The availability of promotable and transferable minorities/women within the contractor's organization

7. The existence of training institutions capable of training persons in the requisite skills

8. The degree of training which the contractor is reasonably able to undertake as a means of making all job classes available to minorities/women[6]

This utilization analysis will leave the employer and the federal government with a firm understanding of which groups are not fairly represented in the contractor's labor force as compared to the surrounding area. It will also pinpoint the existing problems allowing specific goals to be created to remedy the situation.

> NOTE: The utilization analysis is important and should be done thoroughly and accurately. It should be updated to reflect changes in the population makeup. Additionally, if an employer is faced with a discrimination claim in the future, the statistics compiled for the utilization analysis could provide relief.

For example, suppose a retail department store in a small town in Kansas does not employ any Asians. This may not be discriminatory because, according to the contractor's utilization analysis statistics, only 1 percent of the surrounding area is made up of Asians.

Establishing Goals

After doing the utilization analysis, the contractor has been able to analyze the data, figure out the problem areas, and begin to formulate solutions. The contractor must now develop a working policy of how to reach those solutions. This is done by mapping out the short-term and long-term goals and establishing a time frame as to when the goals should be met. The contractor must be reasonable in setting these goals and timetables and involve management in the process.

Quotas may be one method of setting goals. The contractor may decide that within a certain period of time a specified number of minorities and women should be hired or promoted. Deficiencies must be addressed and eliminated. The company must keep in mind expansion and turnovers and how they may eventually impact on the affirmative action program. Data from the utilization analysis, applicant flow charts, promotion schedules, and seniority rosters should be used to support goals and timetables. The OFCCP may ask to see the data, so the employer should make sure to keep well-documented records.

If an employer has no goals, the contractor should address the eight factors in the utilization analysis just given together with an explanation of why no goals have been developed. The OFCCP may review and possibly require the contractor to establish goals where the OFCCP deems appropriate.

Meeting Additional Requirements

Employers must provide for implementing, publicizing, and monitoring their equal employment opportunity commitment and programs.

Issuing a Reaffirmation Statement. The employer should reaffirm the company's commitment to equal employment opportunity. It should provide that a reporting and monitoring procedure will be in effect. The chief executive officer can also include in this statement that the company will recruit, train, and promote persons without regard to race, color, religion, sex, or national origin. All personnel actions regarding layoffs and promotions will not be motivated by race, color, religion, sex, or national origin. A sample reaffirmation statement is shown in Exhibit 10.2.

– EXHIBIT 10.2 –
Reaffirmation Statement

---

1. [COMPANY NAME] is an equal opportunity employer. It is our policy to hire, promote, train, and transfer without regard to race, color, sex, age, religion, or national origin.

   We reaffirm this policy in our *Employee Handbook*, which has been issued, and in a statement to all employees from the President of the Company.

2. The Company's personnel practices are administered without regard to race, color, sex, age, religion, physical or mental handicap, or national origin. They relate to benefits, transfer, layoffs, training programs, and recreational programs.

3. The Company's affirmative action plan is available to all employees, upon written request, from the Personnel Department. The plan may be reviewed in the office of the personnel director by appointment.

Disseminating the Policy. The employer should publicize its affirmativeaction policy internally, to the company itself, and externally, to the community at large. Methods for internal dissemination of the policy include

- The employer's policy manual
- Company newspaper, magazine, annual report, and other media
- Special meetings with executives and management to discuss the policy and their responsibility to it
- Special meetings with all other employees to inform them of their responsibilities
- Meetings with union officials to explain the policy
- Posting the policy on billboards in the company
- Feature men and women, minorities and nonminorities in product advertising and handbooks

The company's external dissemination policy should publicize the affirmative action program to the community in ways such as

♦ Informing recruiters about the company policy and asking for active recruitment of minorities and women for positions

- Including the equal opportunity clause in all purchase orders, contracts, and leases that they are covered by Executive Order 11246

- Notifying community minority and women's organizations, community leaders, secondary schools, and colleges of the affirmative action policy in writing

- Including in consumer advertising both minorities and nonminorities

- Notifying all subcontractors, vendors, and suppliers in writing about the policy and requesting their compliance.

A sample letter is shown in Exhibit 10.3.

Appointing an Executive to Implement the Plan. A responsible and qualified official should be appointed to implement the affirmative action program. The person must be a hard worker who has good organizational skills and is able to accomplish goals. The executive would be responsible for the following:

- Developing the policy and communicating it to the employees and community at large

- Collecting, verifying, and compiling data which will enable goal setting

- Setting up a remedial system to identify discriminatory practices and troubleshoot problem areas

- Setting up an internal audit system and a reporting system to monitor the program's effectiveness

- Keeping quarterly reports up to date

- Establishing a foothold in the community to publicize actively recruitment of minorities and women

- Making managers and officers aware of the policy so they can implement it into their departments

- Devising an internal review procedure to handle complaints brought by employees through the OFCCP

The executive should work with management to develop the policy. A large corporation may want the executive to head up a committee to create the affirmative action program.

NOTE: It is a good idea to consider appointing qualified minority or female executives to this position. This position carries much responsibility. As such, a qualified minority or woman would serve as an excellent role model for other employees of the company as well as outside recruitment sources.

– EXHIBIT 10.3 –
Sample of Letter Sent to Suppliers

Dear Supplier:

Under Title VII of the Civil Rights Act of 1964, it is unlawful for any employer to fail or refuse to hire, to discharge, or to otherwise discriminate against any individual with respect to compensation, terms, or conditions of employment because of such individual's race, color, religion, sex, age, or national origin.

In addition, the federal government requires its suppliers to comply with an affirmative action program as outlined in Executive Order 11426. Under this Order we are obligated not to discriminate against any employee, or applicant for employment, and, in addition, we are to take affirmative action to assure that applicants are employed without regard to race, color, religion, sex, age, or national origin.

This Company is an equal opportunity employer, and we are in compliance with the government requirements under Executive Order 11246. We are requesting that our suppliers and vendors also comply with this Order.

Please inform us that you are in compliance with the federal requirements under Title VII of the Civil Rights Act of 1964 by signing and returning this letter.

Thank you for your cooperation.

Yours truly,

Date Approved:_____
Signature:_____
Title:_____

Executing the Program. The program should tackle the areas of recruiting, training, and promotion. In recruitment, the employer should address the areas of position descriptions which should be objectively written, evaluating the selection process to weed out discrimination, and training interviewers to avoid bias. The employer should also consult organizations such as the Urban League and the National Organization for Women as recruiting sources. Referrals from minority and female workers should be encouraged.

The employer may recruit young people at career days and job fairs at secondary schools and develop summer job and work study programs with predominantly minority and female colleges. Additionally, the employer should identify itself as an equal opportunity employer in advertisements, especially in help wanted advertisements.

The employer may address the training issues by devising tuition reimbursement programs or offer career development and counseling services. In the promotion area, the employer should devise a system to announce the opportunities and develop evaluation programs. The employer should make sure it does not require higher qualifications for minorities and women, even on the subconscious level. The employer should write up when a minority or woman or any employee is passed up for a promotion giving reasons why. This policy may avoid a costly discrimination suit in the future.

Finally, the employer should keep social and recreational activities desegregated and actively encourage all employees to attend. Set up a child care program and transportation schedule to increase access to the company to minorities and women.

Conducting an Internal Audit. The contractor should also keep detailed records of referrals, placements, transfers, promotions, and terminations. By monitoring these areas the employer is able to avoid discrimination and fine tune the program if it becomes a problem. Require regular formal reports from managers to see if goals and timetables are being adhered to and if the program needs any adjustments. Top management should be advised of the progress of the affirmative action policy.

Reporting Requirements. The program must be written and a summary made. The summary must be submitted to the OFCCP and published in the *Federal Register* as a notice before it becomes effective.

> NOTE: Compliance is not judged by goals alone. Therefore, it is important to implement a timetable and stick to it. Time periods give teeth to the goals. Do not fall behind in this area, and make sure records are kept up to date so any possible problem can be dispensed with quickly.

SETTING UP A VOLUNTARY AFFIRMATIVE ACTION PROGRAM

Designing a voluntary affirmative action plan involves three elements: self-analysis, reasonable basis for affirmative action, and reasonable action.

How to Perform a Self-Analysis

A self-analysis simply asks the employer to take stock of its company's hiring, training, and promotion activities to see if an affirmative action plan is warranted. The employer must evaluate its current employment practices to see if any protected groups are being excluded which may result in an adverse impact or disparate treatment. If any such problem exists in any aspect, the employer should figure out why and devise a procedure to change the current problems. The self-analysis should be reasonable and honest in the areas of recruitment, training, and promotion.

Determining Reasonable Basis for an Affirmative Action Program

After pinpointing the problem areas, the next step is to decide if there is a reasonable basis for implementing an affirmative action plan. The employer should ask the following:

◆ Have those problem areas affected employment opportunities of previously excluded groups, or have certain groups been limited in certain areas of employment?

◆ Has past discrimination not been corrected resulting in disparate treatment?

◆ Does the composition of the labor force reflect the labor force of the geographic area?

There does not have to be a violation of any civil rights laws for possible discrimination problems to exist.

Taking Reasonable Action

Reasonable action should be taken by the employer by formulating an affirmative action plan that will target the problems within the company. The plan should eliminate the problems while avoiding reverse discrimination. (This is discussed in the next section.) Goals and timetables should be developed to map out a strategy. The goal is to eliminate the problems, but how long it will take depends upon the availability of qualified applicants, what employment opportunities are currently available in the company, and how long it will take to train unqualified present workers for promotions. By having a timetable, the affirmative action plan can be evaluated to see if it is working and if adjustments should be made.

> NOTE: The employer should put the self-analysis and the affirmative action plan in writing and date them. This not only gives notice to employees and prospective employees about the program, but also affords protection to the employer under Title VII. This means that if the employer is charged with a violation, when the commission investigates the charge, it may not require a written statement from the employer. Additionally, it becomes easier to defend against a claim of discrimination because the written policy is credible evidence that the company was interested in helping to eradicate discrimination.

The program should include a statement of the goals and the company's commitment to equal employment opportunity. The program should also tackle the areas of recruitment, training, and promotion.

Including Recruitment Issues.   This section addresses all aspects of the hiring process. The following is a checklist of possible issues to be tackled by the affirmative action plan.

- ♦ If the employer requires an entrance exam, it should be reviewed to reflect different culture or backgrounds of applicants and test only job-related skills. Perhaps the employer may dispense with the exam or change the weight it is given in the hiring process.

- ♦ An employer should encourage qualified women and minorities to apply for positions possibly by implementing a set aside system.

- ♦ Interviewers should be trained in objective interviewing techniques so that the selection of employees will be on the basis of qualifications and individual ability and not bias.

- ♦ Ask questions on job applications that are employment-related only.

- ♦ Evaluate job descriptions and make sure they are written objectively. Inform the sources where prospective employees are recruited of the changes. Keep records of the number of minority applicants and how many are hired, and if not hired why a minority applicant was rejected.

- ♦ Evaluate departments and which ones have underrepresentation of minority members. Keep names of minority applicants on file to use if a vacancy opens up in one of these targeted departments.

- ♦ Hold an open house and travel to neighboring colleges to recruit applicants.

Providing a Training Program. The employer may choose to provide the employee with a system to gain the skills and qualifications necessary to advance in the company. This way, an employer can create a qualified pool of minority and women applicants for promotion within the company. Minorities and women are therefore afforded the opportunity for advancement. Some suggestions to the employer in setting up a training program are

♦ If there are any jobs where training is required, set aside a number of them specifically for minorities.

♦ Set up programs to reimburse tuition for those who choose to return to school for training.

♦ Provide relocation expenses, transportation, child care facilities, and career counseling services.

Making Promotion Decisions. The employer should be careful when making promotion decisions by making sure the person chosen is qualified. The employer should document each step of the promotion process by keeping records of who applied for the position, the person's qualifications, the interviewer, and the reasons why that person was or was not chosen. This system will help the employer to dispense with possible discrimination claims quickly and have the documentation as a backup. Additional suggestions are

♦ Look for minorities and women who are overqualified in their entry-level position and consider them for promotions.

♦ Set up a file of qualified minorities and women. If a position opens up in their department or another, use that list first in hiring before seeking others.

♦ Restructure jobs to create advancement potential.

The voluntary affirmative action program should also include statistical data.

Additional Information You Need

The statistical data that an employer uses can be in the form of a utilization analysis. The plan should be kept current and updated on a quarterly basis.

The affirmative action policy adopted voluntarily by the employer should be communicated to all employees at all levels. In addition, all unions, subcontractors, and suppliers should be notified. The community at large should also be informed of the company's commitment to equal employment opportunity through such things as press releases and publications.

HOW TO COMPLY WITH A GOVERNMENT INVESTIGATION

A government investigation commences when a complaint is filed by an employee against his or her employer. If the employee is claiming a violation of Executive Order 11246, the person would go to the Office of Federal Contract Compliance Procedures to file a complaint. A person challenging a voluntary plan must go to the Equal Employment Opportunity Commission.

Investigating the Complaint

The investigation of the complaint must be completed within 60 days after the office receives the complaint. The employer would receive a copy of the complaint and an internal review notice. The employer can conduct its own investigation of the matter internally and report the results to the OFCCP. The employer must reply within 10 days of receiving the notice whether an internal review will be undertaken.

NOTE: Devise a detailed internal review procedure for complaints so complaints can be investigated and cleared up quickly and efficiently.

The employer has 60 days to complete the internal investigation. If the issue is settled, the employer should notify the office in writing. If it is not resolved, then the office will conduct its own investigation.[7]

The OFCCP will investigate discrimination claims based on the theories of disparate treatment and disparate impact. Disparate treatment occurs when the employer treats minorities and women differently from other workers, and disparate impact is the resulting discrimination. Both can be proven by direct evidence and inferences.[8]

Employer Defenses to OFCCP Charges

After the OFCCP identifies the discrimination, the contractor can respond. The contractor can claim one or all of the following:

♦ The complaint was not filed in a timely fashion.

♦ The facts are incorrect. They do not show differences between group members. The two were not equally qualified.

♦ The decision was made on a facially neutral basis and not on a discriminatory basis.

♦ The statistical evidence proves no intent to discriminate on the part of the employer.

NOTE: The OFCCP is familiar with the usual defenses the employer uses. It is essential to be able to back yourself up with well-documented evidence.

The OFCCP is looking for inconsistencies in the contractor's argument. For example, it will look to the past promotional and recruitment history of the contractor to show a pattern of discrimination. By admitting that the minority or woman was qualified, an employer may lead the OFCCP to an inference that the decision was discriminatorily based. Be very careful when answering the complaint. Be concise and straightforward, and avoid double entendres.

Claiming a "Business Necessity." A contractor can justify its hiring or promotional procedure that is the subject of an adverse complaint by proving a *business necessity*. This means that the discrimination was job-related for the safe and efficient operation of business.

Case Study

The Four Mile Island Nuclear Power Plant employs no minorities in the main control lab. The reason is that although the plant actively recruits minorities, those with Ph.D.s in nuclear physics are not interested in working at Four Mile Island. Management will not hire an unqualified minority because the job is important and if an emergency arises, a qualified nuclear physicist is indispensable. Therefore, out of business necessity for the safety of the community, Four Mile Island does not have to hire an unqualified person in the lab.

The contractor can also defend its choice in a hiring or promotional decision by proving it was validated by the guidelines for employee selection procedures. The contractor must simply show that its selection and job performance procedures comply with the guidelines. Beware, however, because the government may counterargue that there were other less restrictive or discriminatory alternatives available to the contractor.[9]

If discrimination is found, there are remedies that can be imposed. If a violation is found, the contractor has the burden to prove nondiscrimination. The contractor could use evidence such as the person complaining was not as qualified, the better person was chosen, or there was no vacancy at the company. The company must show that it would have treated the situation the same way in the absence of discrimination. The victim could receive back pay and seniority and even the promotion. Keeping good records is essential in this area. The employer does not want to be faced with a situation in which it has to defend itself because a decision it made looks discriminatory on its face.

How to Handle On-Site Reviews

If compliance standards have not been met or the periodical desk audit has indicated the company is not making a good faith effort to implement an affirmative action plan, the OFCCP may investigate potential problems and verify the implementation of an affirmative action program. A desk audit is a periodic check of a contractor's program. The on-site reviews occur in Executive Order 11246 cases. Since a voluntary plan need not be filed with the government, they are not subject to on-site reviews.[10]

The employer will be given notice that the on-site review will be performed and informed of what items to have ready. Again, keep up-to-date detailed records. The OFCCP may formally or informally interview the employees. The contractor does not have the right to have a representative present during these interviews. The contractor should not sign any interview notes until they are examined and he or she believes them to be true.

The government is also able to inspect the facility to make sure a good faith effort is being made to implement the affirmative action policy. The OFCCP will review the goals and information to make sure the contractor is complying correctly with the guidelines. This includes the utilization analysis and internal audit systems. Prevention and good recordkeeping are essential.

HOW TO PREVENT AFFIRMATIVE ACTION COMPLAINTS

The name of the game is *prevention*. The employer should follow this checklist:

♦ Make sure to get involved in the community to actively recruit minorities.

♦ Comply with quarterly reports.

♦ Disseminate information by posting job openings to the employees and also keep information on where, when, and how long the jobs in each class are open.

♦ Provide training opportunities such as apprenticeship programs, on-the-job training, and tuition reimbursement for minorities and women.

♦ Keep updated selection criteria and make sure managers are familiar with EEO policies. Make sure the policies are not discriminatory or have a discriminatory impact.

♦ Make sure recruitment sources are utilized for minorities and women externally.

♦ Use publications that target minorities and women when available. Keep records of how employment openings are filled within the company.

♦ Keep records up to date with applicant flow records, audits of employment activity, and the like.

Describing the Role of the Affirmative Action Officer

The job of the affirmative action officer is very important. If the job is done right and the records are kept and updated, there should be no problem in proving to the government that there are no problems with compliance. It is likely that the government would not choose a contractor in compliance to do a desk check. It is also important to maintain good relations with the community because the government may interview community groups with regard to the contractor's interest in minorities and women. If the contractor faces problems with discrimination, make sure to remedy them and document the situation. If an on-site review is requested, good records will aid in a quick and efficient review.

Exit Conference and Subsequent Action

The OFCCP will conduct a complete examination of the contractor and then set up an exit conference. During the conference it will explain deficiencies and, if they exist, suggest corrections. If the contractor does not comply with these preliminary findings, it can receive a notice for a pattern or practice violation. This will state the problem and the response of the contractor required in fashioning a remedy. There will be a report. When the affirmative action problem has been solved, a notice of review completion will be given to the contractor. Prevention is the best way to avoid these types of claims, and if a review cannot be avoided, then be honest and accommodating with the government during an on-site investigation.

> NOTE: Resolve any conflicts early and avoid any problems; especially avoid receiving any notices of violation. These on-site audits should be taken very seriously, and the employees should be willing to comply with the government so the problem can be solved quickly. If any violations are found, remedy them immediately; do not wait and risk the chance of a notice of violation.

HOW TO AVOID REVERSE DISCRIMINATION CLAIMS

Affirmative action by its very nature is discriminatory. It is a system that confers preferential treatment on members of disadvantaged groups that have suffered past discrimination in employment. These preferences occur in hiring, training, and promotion of employees. By preferring some groups means that other groups will be discriminated against. Affirmative action is essential to achieve equality in the workplace. It is endorsed as a valid system and protected by society to help those who are disadvantaged.

Increasingly, however, there have been cries of *reverse discrimination*. This occurs when members of the majority claim they have been discriminated against in hiring or promotion. Most often the discrimination occurs because a less qualified woman or member of a minority group was chosen for a position or promotion over a more qualified nonminority. It is important for the employer to be sensitive to the issue of reverse discrimination and avoid situations where it may occur. The employer must strike a balance between enthusiastically creating and enforcing an affirmative action program and avoiding infringement on the rights of the majority.

A nonminority can bring a claim of reverse discrimination under Title VII of the Civil Rights Act.[11] All three types of affirmative action programs can be challenged: those in accordance with Executive Order 11246, those mandated by court order, and especially, voluntary programs.

Recommendations for Avoiding Reverse Discrimination

Two most important things for an employer to keep in mind when creating an affirmative action program are

1. The affirmative action program should not deny opportunities for advancement or promotion to white males. This can be done by making sure the person receiving the preferential treatment is qualified for the position, and
2. The program should be updated to evaluate if temporary goals have been achieved. This can be done with statistics.

Case Example

Taxico is a private transportation company in California which adopted an affirmative action program voluntarily. The program does not impose a quota, but it does endorse an expansion of hiring and promotion of minorities to reflect better the composition of the labor force in the area. Taxico plans on using race, color, sex, and national origin in hiring and promotion decisions of qualified applicants. This plan is designed to be flexible and adaptable to change.

A promotional position opened up for a road dispatcher. Taxico employs no women as road dispatchers. Bill Jackson and Susan Smith apply for the position. They both are currently employed by Taxico and take the required test. Bill receives a 75 and Susan a 73. There was also an interview conducted of each applicant for the position. Susan was offered the job. Taxico decided that both were equally qualified, but since there were no women in the road dispatcher positions preference will be afforded Susan. Bill became angry and sued Taxico for reverse discrimination under the Civil Rights Act.

Can Taxico be held liable for reverse discrimination in hiring Susan Smith over Bill Jackson? No, for several reasons. To find reverse discrimination, a court will analyze the following factors in light of the facts of the particular case to decide if an employer's affirmative action policy encourages reverse discrimination deliberately.

♦ Did the employer intend to break down old patterns of segregation in hiring?

♦ Was the policy structured to open employment opportunities to those minorities that were traditionally kept out?

♦ Does the policy trammel the interests of nonminorities in favor of minorities, thereby creating an absolute bar to white employee's advancement?

♦ Has the employer developed a timetable to implement the plan that is temporary in nature?[12]

In this case, the goal of Taxico's affirmative action program was to increase the numbers of minorities and women in its labor force consistent with the makeup of the local labor force. Also the program was created to be flexible and consider the race, sex, color, or national origin of an applicant only after that applicant is deemed qualified. The test served as a qualification in this case, but it was not the sole determination. Susan did not score as high as Bill, but taking her interview and experience in addition to the fact that she was a woman into account, the employer decided she was deserving of the position.

This does not trammel the interests of Bill Jackson, specifically because Susan was equally qualified for the job. Taxico created a flexible system to eliminate the imbalance in its work force. It does not intrude greatly on the rights of other nonminority employees as to be an absolute bar to their promotional ability. If Susan were not equally qualified, Bill would have gotten the job. Finally, this flexibility of the program had room for revision, and the goals were temporary in nature. If the road dispatchers' department were made up of 50 percent women, Susan would not have needed preferential treatment and may not have been hired.[13]

How to Avoid Reverse Discrimination Claims

As the workplace increases the levels of minorities and women, the risk of a nonminority getting a job decreases. Do not make the temporary goals permanent. This is where careful wording and formulation of the goals of the affirmative action program come into focus.

♦ Make sure the program is narrowly written so as to avoid reverse discrimination at all costs.

♦ Update the policy statement to reflect when temporary goals have been met and how.

♦ Rethink the goals of the plan after some have been met.

♦ Make sure each job has been described objectively, listing the qualifications necessary.

♦ Do not promote minorities and women as tokens. Make sure they are qualified to perform the job required.

♦ Avoid preferential layoffs; they are unconstitutional.

COMPLYING WITH STATE AFFIRMATIVE ACTION PLANS

It is important to check state statutes to make sure that your organization complies with any state-mandated affirmative action requirements. Some states have mandatory affirmative action for employers who are state contractors. State contractors are analogous to federal contractors in that a private employer does business with a state department or agency. Other states require only state employees be subject to affirmative action programs. States with both types of affirmative action plans are:

California	Maine	Ohio
Connecticut	Maryland	Oklahoma
Hawaii	Massachusetts	Pennsylvania
Illinois	Michigan	Rhode Island
Indiana	Minnesota	Utah
Iowa	Nebraska	Wisconsin
Kansas	New Jersey	
Kentucky	New York	

States having only an affirmative action program for state contractors are Vermont, Virginia and Wyoming.

States having only an affirmative action program for state employees are:

Alaska	Louisiana	New Mexico
Arizona	Mississippi	North Carolina
Arkansas	Missouri	Oregon
Colorado	Montana	South Carolina
Delaware	Nevada	South Dakota
Florida	New Hampshire	Washington

Both Georgia and Massachusetts have quota systems in place.

The following states have not mandated state affirmative action programs:

Alabama	North Dakota	Texas
Idaho	Tennessee	West Virginia

This does not mean, however, that a voluntary program cannot be developed by an employer. These states also have to comply with Executive Order 11246 nevertheless.

The most progressive place with regard to affirmative action in the United States is the District of Columbia. There discrimination is forbidden on the grounds of race, color, religion, sex, and national origin. It also prohibits discrimination based on sexual preference, physical appearance, age, and family responsibilities to name a few. The affirmative action policy in the District of Columbia is extended to those groups through the human rights law enacted there.[14]

An employer should be on the alert that some states include other categories than the familiar federally mandated categories in their affirmative action programs and that such programs are designed to include those groups. In some states AIDS discrimination has become a very big issue, and some employers may want to develop a program with that in mind or perhaps amend their existing program to include AIDS victims or other disabled individuals. Some state programs require the employment of at least 15 employees to trigger the affirmative action requirement; others have no such limitation.

NOTE: Carefully review your state's requirements with regard to affirmative action plans and who is covered by the law.

TEN GUIDELINES FOR COMPLYING WITH AFFIRMATIVE ACTION REQUIREMENTS

Careful preparation and execution of an affirmative action policy greatly reduces the frequency and severity of discrimination claims. We have developed the following guidelines to aid you in complying with affirmative action requirements, whether imposed by the government, the court or voluntarily by the employer itself.

1. Check to see if the company is a federal or state contractor and thereby comes under the governance of Executive Order 11246 or state law.

2. Even if the company is not mandated to develop an affirmative action plan, decide if one is necessary by doing a reasonable self-analysis.

3. Appoint a qualified and capable company official to develop and enforce the program. Perhaps have the official set up a committee to develop the program.

4. Establish specific temporary and long-term goals.

5. Do a utilization analysis even if it is a voluntary program, this will give the policy teeth and provide statistics in case of any possible discrimination claims.

6. Make sure to publish the policy and distribute it within the company itself and to the world at large. Doing so will communicate to all em-

ployees, potential employees, officers, executives, and all others that this employer will not tolerate discrimination and is doing its part to remedy past discrimination.

7. Keep in contact with minority and women organizations. Develop summer job programs and visit neighboring schools for recruitment.

8. It cannot be stressed enough to keep up-to-date records. This is essential because it is a message to the community that the company is serious about affirmative action.

9. Make sure the program is not implemented in such a way as to prompt reverse discrimination claims. All those hired and promoted should be qualified. If a minority or woman is not qualified, make sure he or she receives the necessary training before any promotion is made.

10. If the government institutes an investigation, comply in a timely manner. Again, if the program is kept up-to-date, the problem can be dispensed with in an efficient and quick way.

ENDNOTES

1. Title VII, of the Civil Rights Act of 1964, 42 U.S.C. §2000e-5(a).

2. EEOC Guidelines, §1608.3.

3. Executive Order 11246, §202.

4. OFCCP Affirmative Action Guidelines §§60-2.1(a)(1)–(4).

5. In the case *Woodbury v. New York City Transit Authority*, 832 F.2d 764 (2d Cir. 1987), the judge commended the transit authority for its comprehensive affirmative action plan. If an employer does have to defend itself against an affirmative action claim, it is important to note that courts will look at the employer's program.

6. OFCCP Affirmative Action Guidelines, §§60-2.11(b)(1)(i)–(viii).

7. Adopted from the OFCCP regulations regarding investigations, 41 C.F.R. §60-1.24(b)(1980).

8. The recent case, *Wards Cove Packing Co., Inc. v. Atonio*, 490 U.S. 642, 109 S.Ct. 2115, 104 L.Ed.2d 733 (1989), addressed the issue of disparate impact. The case involved two salmon canneries which employed both skilled and unskilled workers. The unskilled workers were minorities and constituted a higher number of employees than did skilled workers. The skilled workers were hired mostly from a hiring hall. The employer was sued because minority employees claimed that there was a disparate effect at the plant because a higher proportion of minorities were employed at unskilled jobs and a higher proportion of nonminorities were employed at skilled jobs. The court stated that a disparate impact must be shown by comparing the

employer's labor force to the local labor force, not by comparing employees in each sector of the company.

9. See *Wards Cove Packing Co., Inc. v. Atonio*, at note 8. If plaintiff proves case for discrimination on the part of the employer, the burden of proof shifts to the employer to prove business necessity.

10. See OFCCP regulations on review process, 41 C.F.R. §60-1.20 (1980).

11. Title VII of the Civil Rights Act of 1964, 42 U.S.C. §2000e-2(j).

12. *United Steelworkers of America v. Weber*, 443 U.S. 193, 99 S.Ct. 2721, 61 L.Ed.2d 480 (1979). A white employee brought action against employer and union challenging legality of plan for on-the-job training which mandated a one-for-one quota for minority workers. The Supreme Court held that Title VII's prohibitions against racial discrimination does not condemn all, private, voluntary, race-conscious affirmative action plans. The plan in *Weber* was collectively bargained and reserved for black employees 50 percent of the openings in a training program until the percentage of black craft workers was commensurate with the percentage of blacks in the local labor force. The plan, which was temporary, was found to be valid in its intent to eliminate a manifest racial imbalance.

13. The case example was adopted from *Johnson v. Transportation Agency, Santa Clara County, California*, 480 U.S. 616, 94 L.Ed.2d 615, 107 S.Ct. 1442 (1987). The Supreme Court also took a stand against arbitrary quota systems in *City of Richmond v. J. A. Croson, Co.*, 488 U.S. 469, 109 S.Ct. 706, 102 L.Ed.2d 854 (1989). The city of Richmond adopted a remedial Minority Business Utilization Plan which required all contractors to award city contracts to subcontract 30 percent or more with one or more minority businesses. Minority businesses must be 51 percent black, Spanish-speaking, Oriental, Indian, Eskimo, or Aleut. Croson, a bidder, brought suit challenging the city's plan. The Supreme Court declared the plan unconstitutional because there was no evidence that the city had discriminated before in awarding contracts to those black, Spanish-speaking, Indian, Eskimo, Oriental, or Aleut businesses. The plan also allowed any company in the country that is operated by minorities to have an absolute preference over nonminorities simply because of race.

14. See Title I, Ch. 25, of the D.C. Code (1981).

11

HOW TO MAINTAIN THE AT-WILL EMPLOYMENT RELATIONSHIP

A frequently asked question by employers is

If this is my business; why can't I fire anyone for any reason or no reason?

Actually, in most circumstances the employer may discharge an employee for any reason or no reason, but not for an unlawful reason. This form of employment relationship is referred to as *employment-at-will*. However, this traditional form can be modified by the employer through employment contracts, collective bargaining agreements, and certain employment practices. It has also been modified by statute and the courts, so that there are several exceptions to the traditional rule with which personnel managers must become familiar. The at-will doctrine and its exceptions are discussed in this chapter.

HOW TO INTERPRET THE AT-WILL DOCTRINE

The predominant form of employment in the United States is governed by the *doctrine of employment-at-will;* that is, employment for an indefinite term may be terminated at the will of either party, for good reason, bad reason, or no reason. This doctrine literally permits an employee to be discharged in an arbitrary and capricious manner.

The traditional rule is:

Absent a written employment contract or a collective bargaining agreement, employer and employees are free to terminate employment relationships for *any reason* and at *any time*. However, such termination may not violate federal or state statutory restrictions.

The rationale for the "at-will" doctrine is that both the employer and employee should be free to terminate the relationship at any time so that each can take advantage of new economic opportunities or end an unsatisfactory work situation.

The traditional rule has been modified in various ways that we will explore in this chapter. However, absent these modifications, all employees who do not have an employment contract and/or are not subject to personnel policies or practices that provide for termination only for cause are employees-at-will.

Employees who have been terminated for a discriminatory reason or in violation of an exception to the at-will doctrine may have a claim for wrongful discharge.

Establishing the "For Cause" Standard

Employers may intentionally or unintentionally modify the "at-will" employment relationship by stating in writing or by practice that its employees will be terminated only "for cause" or "just cause." This means that the employer must have a reason for the termination, such as poor performance, misconduct, or cutbacks. Usually, it is necessary to have a legitimate or "good" reason to dismiss an employee under this requirement. Employees subject to a union contract have traditionally had this type of provision, where it is clearly defined and all parties are familiar with what is or is not "cause." However, most employers who are not in a unionized setting may not be familiar with the restrictions that this type of condition places on the employer's freedom to terminate employees.

Employees who have been terminated in violation of a "for cause" standard may pursue a claim for breach of an express or implied contract and/or wrongful termination.

Case Example

Sweets, Inc., a candy manufacturer, has employed Irving Carmel for almost 19 years. He is the quality control manager. Recently, there have been numerous customer complaints that the candy does not seem fresh or as good as it had been in the past. Nothing has been changed in the manufacturing process other than the cleaning procedures. Irving is responsible for instituting and supervising the cleaning procedures for the entire plant. In fact, when assisting a worker with cleaning the taffy vat he was injured and put in a claim for workers' compensation.

Max, the plant manager, has been unhappy with Irving's performance for the past several years. However, he had not really made an issue of it because Irving had been with the company for so many years and he cannot point to anything in particular regarding Irving's performance. Max is upset because Irving filed a claim against the company regarding his injury. Max felt that filing such a claim was disloyal of Irving. Max has decided that Irving has to go and dismisses him without notice or a reason.

The company has an informal policy that it will not discharge anyone unless he or she has done something wrong. There is no evidence that Irving has done anything wrong. Irving has also been told on occasion that he would always have a job with Sweets, Inc., that he should not worry because the company takes care of its own, that he would have to do something very wrong to be terminated, and similar assurances of job security. However, Irving was hired 19 years ago as an assistant taffy puller at an hourly wage, for no set period of time, and with no assurance of a future with the company.

Irving files a claim for wrongful discharge. He states that the company promised him that he would always have a job; that he was fired because he filed a workers' compensation claim; that the company did not treat him fairly, especially since he has devoted 19 years to the success of the company; and that the company failed to give any reason for his summary dismissal.

Consider the following questions:

♦ What type of employment relationship does Sweets, Inc., have with Irving?

♦ If Irving is an employee-at-will, why can't the company simply fire him as it did?

♦ What bases, if any, does Irving have for a wrongful discharge claim?

♦ What other claims may Irving make?

♦ Was the company required to give Irving notice and a reason for his termination?

Irving was an employee-at-will; he was hired for no set term. Under those circumstances the company was not required to give him notice or a reason for his discharge. However, we must examine all the circumstances to see if he was wrongfully discharged based on exceptions to the employment-at-will doctrine.

The company may have modified the employment-at-will relationship by making assurances of job security. If Irving reasonably relied upon such representations to his detriment, he may have a valid claim for wrongful discharge. Also, the company has a policy of not discharging anyone unless he or she has done something wrong. If the company has not followed that policy in this matter, in some jurisdictions, it may have breached an implied contract of employment that dismissal would be only for cause.

Irving also has a claim for wrongful discharge based on the theory that his discharge was in violation of a public policy. If he was terminated because he filed a workers' compensation claim, the company has violated a public policy protecting employees who act on their statutory rights. In such cases, the employer has wrongfully discharged the employee.

Irving may also file a claim for breach of a covenant of good faith and fair dealing; however, this claim is recognized only in a few states though it is gaining recognition.

This situation highlights only a few of the issues that arise in the at-will employment relationship. Exceptions to this doctrine and claims for wrongful discharge are discussed in detail in this chapter.

IDENTIFYING EXCEPTIONS TO THE "AT-WILL" DOCTRINE

In recent years the "at-will" doctrine has been challenged on a variety of grounds and modified in many states in an attempt to provide greater job security to employees.[1] The courts and legislatures have created exceptions or limitations on the employment-at-will relationship, and new theories are continuously tested in the courts.

Federal and State Statutory Restrictions

Several federal laws restrict the employer's freedom to discharge employees. The most frequently used laws to protect employees include

Title VII	Prohibits employment practices/decisions based on race, creed, sex, national origin, religion
ADEA	Prohibits employment decisions based on age
Americans with Disabilities Act	Prohibits employment decisions on basis of physical or mental handicap and requires reasonable accommodation

Most states have a counterpart to the federal restrictions on employment-related decisions, and some provide a broader scope of protection that may include marital status, sexual preferences, or greater age protection.

For example, ADEA generally prohibits age-based discharges of employees over the age of 40, but see New York Executive Law §296 3-a(a) (*McKinney Supp.* 1987), which prohibits age discrimination of individuals 18 years or older.

Several states have recently passed legislation or have proposed legislation that creates a statutory cause of action for wrongful discharge or governs more stringently the at-will relationship. For example, Montana's Wrongful Discharge Act, *inter alia*, provides that a discharge is wrongful if it was not for good cause and the employee has completed the employer's probationary period.[2]

There is also currently being proposed a Uniform Employment Termination Act that would impose a "good cause" standard on most employers, essentially eliminating the at-will employment relationship altogether.[3] We suggest that employers watch the progress of this proposed legislation very carefully.

Applying Contract Theories

A written contract that establishes a fixed term of employment or provides a just cause standard for dismissal removes the employee from at-will status. In addition, several courts have applied a variety of contract law theories to imply that an employment contract exists. The bases for an implied contract may include personnel manuals and/or employment practices, oral representations, and other written documents such as an offer of employment.

Employee Handbooks and Personnel Policies. Written personnel policies and employee handbooks or manuals are sometimes construed to be implied employment contracts in limited circumstances. Employers are being held to promises and representations made in their employment manuals and personnel policy handbooks.[4] See the discussion in Chapter 12 with regard to the advantages and disadvantages of employment manuals.

Written and unwritten personnel policies and practices may be found to indicate an intent by the employer that an employee will not be terminated without cause. In other words, an employee will not be discharged unless there is a good reason for the discharge, for example, poor performance or misconduct.

> NOTE: Employers who give assurances of job security may be held to such representations when it wants to discharge an employee for no reason or a reason that does not rise to the level of a "just cause" standard.

Thus the employer needs to decide if it wants to abide by a just cause standard or retain its discretion to dismiss an employee at will. If the employment relationship is to remain at-will, the employer must be careful in the drafting and implementation of any personnel policies and practices.

> NOTE: Courts will carefully scrutinize all factors concerning employment of an individual. This exception to at-will employment is context sensitive and is analyzed on the basis of the actions of the employer *and* employee in relation to any written employment-related document.

Verbal Representations or Oral Promises. Until recently, most oral assurances or promises of job security were not enforceable because:

◆ Such promises violate the Statute of Frauds, which requires any contract that cannot or is not to be performed within one year to be in writing.

♦ Oral promises could not form the basis of an exception to at-will employment.

However, this traditional rule has been challenged, and several jurisdictions have begun to recognize that certain verbal representations, if relied upon, may constitute an implied contract of employment.

Case Example

The New Jersey Supreme Court has expanded the rights of at-will employees in *Shebar v. Sanyo Business Systems Corp.*, 111 N.J. 276 (1988). The court held that employers are bound to oral representation they give to an at-will employee. In *Shebar*, Mr. Shebar offered his resignation to take another position. Sanyo told him it did not want him to leave, that the company didn't fire its managers, and that he had a job for the rest of his life. Shebar turned down a lucrative job offer and remained with Sanyo—four months later he was fired. Shebar alleged that the oral assurances made by Sanyo were a promise to fire him only for cause. The company's oral assurances may have transformed the plaintiff's at-will employment into employment with termination for cause only. Therefore, the state supreme court denied summary judgment for the company on this issue.

Understanding the Public Policy Exception

Most jurisdictions have adopted some form of a "public policy" exception to the at-will doctrine. Such an exception bans employee discharges that offend a clearly established public policy. Identifying the "public policy" violated by the discharge of an employee is the obligation of the individual asserting such a cause of action. The individual must identify a clear mandate of the public policy that has been violated to establish a basis for his or her claim for wrongful discharge.

The public policy exception is increasingly recognized in most state jurisdictions; however, there is one notable exception: New York has expressly declined to recognize causes of action in tort with regard to abusive discharges. New York's highest court, in *Murphy, supra*, held that such a dramatic change in New York's at-will doctrine should be made by the New York state legislature rather than the courts.

The scope of the public policy exception varies from state to state. However, the courts generally hold that the *termination must be contrary to a clear mandate of public policy*.

Sources of public policy include

– Statutes

– Administrative rules and regulations

– Professional codes of ethics

– Judicial decisions

In the absence of legislation, the courts must determine if a public policy exists that was violated through case-by-case determinations. Examples of several cases illustrating what does or does not constitute public policy that protects an at-will employee from summary termination follow.

Statutory Rights. Employees who have been discharged because they have pursued or asserted rights provided by statute, known as retaliatory discharge, may claim that their discharge violated public policy.

Case Example

ABC Alarm Company (ABC), located in New Jersey, has narrowed its investigation into burglaries of clients' businesses to a group of four employees. These employees are asked to take a lie detector test. Manuel refuses and is terminated for not taking the test. New Jersey has a statute that prohibits an employer from requesting or influencing any employee to take a polygraph test of any kind. ABC does not fall within the one narrow exception under the statute.

The statute is a clear expression of public policy against the use of polygraphs in the workplace. Thus, Manuel has the basis for a wrongful discharge action.

However, if the statutory right that the employee seeks to assert already provides remedies for such retaliation, some jurisdictions will not permit recovery for the tort of wrongful discharge.[6]

For example, if the employee was discharged because of his religious practices, he would be barred from alleging that the public policy violated was the prohibition against discrimination on the basis of religion, since the anti-discrimination statute specifically prohibits such retaliatory action.[7] The statutory prohibitions against retaliating against someone asserting his or her rights under the anti-discrimination law specifically provide remedies for retaliatory discrimination. On the other hand, if the employee is discharged for requesting to see her personnel file in order to determine if she had been discriminated against on the basis of her gender, then that is a violation of the general public policy against discrimination. The employee may succeed on such a claim, since there is no specific statutory remedy for that action and it was related to alleged discriminatory conduct.[8]

Generally, the pursuit of a statutory right, where there is no specific remedy or prohibition against adverse employment actions because of the employee's action, is sufficient to establish a violation of public policy. Otherwise, few statutory rights would have any meaning or value.

Common statutory rights where the statute may not specifically protect the individual seeking to assert them include:

♦ *Workers' compensation benefits:* retaliatory discharge because of employee's pursuit of statutory workers' compensation benefits is contrary to the public policy.[9]

♦ *Safety claims:* retaliatory discharge or adverse employment action for complaints of safety problems or violations of safety or health laws where no "whistle-blower" protection exists.

♦ *Wage and hour claims:* Recognition in some jurisdictions that termination of an employee because of wages or benefits due them, such as commissions, is a violation of public policy. However, in some cases, employees are not protected from a retaliatory discharge where they have filed a civil action against their employer for salary or other claims.[10]

Judicial Decisions and Administrative Regulations.

Public policy is often stated through judicial decisions and administrative rules and regulations. Since judicial decisions are actually interpretations of statutory and common law (unwritten or traditional law), they are sensitive to particular factual context of the decision itself and are subject to modification.

Similarly, administrative decisions, rules, and regulations may be evidence of a public policy. However, these bases for public policy are less compelling than statutory law or judicial decisions.

The courts closely examine any proposed basis for a public policy. They will distinguish similar conduct because the individual acted in his or her own benefit or relied upon a policy that had an individual benefit rather than a public good benefit.

Case Example

A court found that there was no violation of public policy for the retaliatory termination of at-will employees for allegedly *not* covering up corporate misconduct. The court held that private investigation of possible criminal activities of fellow employees did not implicate the same public policy consideration as if plaintiffs had been fired as the result of cooperating with a public law enforcement investigation.[11]

Code of Ethics/Professional Rules of Conduct.

Several occupations are governed by a code of ethics or professional rules of conduct. These rules are generally enforced by a nonjudicial panel of practitioners from that particular profession who are authorized to impose sanctions for violations. Some courts have found that these widely accepted professional rules represent an expression of public policy, especially where the public safety and welfare are the basis for such rules.

Two leading cases from New Jersey clearly illustrate the difference between professional rules of conduct that will or will not constitute a clear mandate of public policy.

In *Pierce v. Ortho Pharmaceutical Co.*, 84 N.J. 58 (1980), the leading case that established the public policy exception in New Jersey, the New Jersey Supreme Court held that in some circumstances, professional employees may refuse work assignments that violate a code of ethics where the public safety and welfare are the basis for the code. In *Pierce*, a doctor refused to continue research on a controversial drug because it contained saccharin. The court noted that the doctor had not argued that the drug itself was unsafe and could not point to a statutory or ethical violation in continuing the research pending Food and Drug Administration (FDA) investigation.

However, in *Warthen v. Toms River Community Memorial Hospital*, 199 N.J. Super 18 (App. Div. 1985), 5 years later, a New Jersey appellate court found that the "Code of Nurses" did not establish a clear mandate of public policy because its provisions defined a standard of conduct beneficial *only* to the individual nurse and *not* to the public at large. A nurse relied on the "Code" in refusing to administer kidney dialysis to a terminally ill patient when the physician and family wanted the treatment. The nurse's claim for wrongful discharge based on violation of public policy was dismissed.

Whistle-blowers. A "whistle-blower" is someone who reports violations of law or misconduct either internally to company superiors or to outside agencies. Whether the reporting individual is protected under statute or by public policy varies from state to state. Therefore, it is important for the personnel manager to check state laws regarding whistle-blowers.

A retaliatory discharge claim by an at-will employee who reports a statutory or regulatory violation is not recognized by the courts. However, such recognized claims are generally where the employee has reported criminal or unlawful conduct to the appropriate government agency. Where there is a specific whistle-blower protection statute, the employee is protected from discharge if his or her activity falls within the scope of the statute.

NOTE: You must refer to the appropriate state laws since there is no uniformity among the state laws protecting whistle-blowers.

Here is a representative sampling of state whistle-blower protection statutes.

California: prohibits employers from preventing employees from disclosing information, where the employee has cause to believe that the information discloses a violation.

Illinois: prohibits disciplinary or retaliatory action against an employee, including reprimand, suspension, discharge, demotion, or denial of promotion (Ch. 127, §19c.1).

Michigan: employer may not discriminate against or discharge an employee who reports or is about to report "a violation or a suspected violation" of any law or regulation to a public body, unless the employee knows such a report is false (Mich. Comp. Law §17.428, *et seq.* (1980)).

Missouri: prohibits disciplinary action against an employee of the disclosure of any alleged prohibited activity under investigation or any related activity or disclosure of information which the employee reasonably believes shows a violation of law, mismanagement of funds, or danger to public health or safety.

Minnesota: prohibits discrimination and retaliation against any employee or person acting in good faith in reporting a violation or suspected violation of law. If identity is necessary for prosecution, the employee shall be informed prior to the disclosure.

New Jersey: prohibits the discharge, suspension, or demotion of any employee who reports or threatens to disclose to a supervisor *or* public body, any practice, policy, or activity of an employer that he or she reasonably believes is unlawful, or who objects to or refuses to participate in any activity, policy, or practice that he or she reasonably believes is unlawful, fraudulent, or incompatible with a clear mandate of public policy concerning public health, safety, or welfare. The employee must notify the employer in writing of the unlawful conduct and afford employer a reasonable opportunity to correct it (except if an emergency situation) (N.J.S.A. 34:12-1, *et seq*).

New York: prohibits discrimination and/or retaliation against any employee who reports a statutory or regulatory violation *and* imminent hazard to the public safety (N.Y. Labor Law §740 (*McKinney Supp.* 1984)).

Ohio: prohibits disciplinary or retaliatory action against an employee who becomes aware of what he or she believes is a criminal offense that could cause an imminent risk of physical harm to persons or hazard to public health. The employee must orally notify his or her supervisor and subsequently file a written report describing the violation. The employer must make a good faith effort to correct the violation within 24 hours.

Texas: prohibits disciplinary action against an employee who reports a violation to an enforcement authority if the report is made in good faith.

Applying Promissory Estoppel/Independent Consideration Given by Employee

An exception to at-will employment has been found where an employee is found to have provided substantial consideration to an employer in the form of detrimental reliance. Examples of detrimental reliance are moving a substantial distance, leaving a previously favorable position, or rejecting a favorable employment position in reliance upon an employer's express or implied promise of job security.[12]

A related theory supporting an exception to at-will employment is the equitable doctrine of promissory estoppel. Promissory estoppel is a legal term that means that an employer may not avoid performance of a promise on which an employee has reasonably relied to his or her detriment. Under this theory, the employer must perform any oral or written promise made to employees who have detrimentally relied upon such a promise. It is applicable in a situation where employees have resigned their prior employment to take a new job or have declined an offer of employment elsewhere to stay in their present position.[13]

Considering Implied Covenants of Good Faith and Fair Dealing

To date there has been a strong reluctance to adopt the theory of implied covenant of good faith and fair dealing as an exception to the at-will doctrine. This theory maintains that in every employment contract there is an implied duty on the employer's part to act in "good faith" and thus not to discharge an employee without fair and substantial reason. The endnote gives several cases wherein California and other jurisdictions have accepted this theory.[14] However, most jurisdictions, including New York and New Jersey, have not adopted this exception to at-will employment.[15]

Interpreting Intentional Infliction of Emotional Distress

To state a cause of action for intentional infliction of emotional distress arising from a discharge, the plaintiff must specifically allege that defendants' conduct was *extreme* and *outrageous* or that it exceeded all bounds usually tolerated by decent society. The type of conduct that reaches the level of "extreme and outrageous" is not easy to predict, especially in the employment context. The conduct must have been intended to inflict emotional distress or was a reckless disregard of the fact that severe emotional distress was a probable result.[16]

Case Study

Sharon, a midlevel manager at a large financial institution, is suddenly required to do her own typing, copying, and the like. She formerly had had research and secretarial support as did all other managers. The other managers at her level have not had to do this. She is 1 of 2 female managers and there are 18 male managers. Sharon has also received an extremely negative performance review, although there had been no marked change in her performance. All prior reviews had been very good to excellent. Six months ago, Bob became her supervisor, and he has been critical of her ever since she spurned his advances. He has stopped his overtures but has removed her research and secretarial support and assigned undesirable projects to her although she is not the most junior person in the department. Her subordinates question her instructions and go over her head to Bob. They no longer seek her advice or assistance. Sharon feels that these actions are deliberate attempts to drive her from her job. Her requests for transfer have been refused.

She is experiencing signs of stress such as nausea, headaches, and irritability. There has been no response to her complaints from upper management, except for an obvious show of support for Bob.

This example demonstrates the outrageous behavior on the part of Bob and the company. Bob has subjected Sharon to humiliation and has attacked her integrity as a fine manager. He has rendered her ineffective in her position. The company has failed to investigate her complaints and has rewarded rather than disciplined Bob for his conduct. This behavior is outrageous in the sense that it was designed to drive Sharon from her job in a cruel manner and is so severe that she is experiencing medical problems as a result.

However, physical symptoms are not always necessary to a successful claim of intentional infliction of emotional harm. The conduct may be outrageous because it is cruel and unjustified, has a malicious intent, or is extremely insensitive to a particular person's situation, especially when such harm could have been avoided. The plaintiff will generally have to show some injury as a result of the outrageous conduct.

Interpreting Negligent Performance on Contractual Obligation

The theory of negligent supervision or performance of contractual obligations holds the employer liable for negligence in performance appraisals, that is, by failing to give an employee the warnings required by a personnel policy manual. In other words, the employer must have breached some duty to the employee with regard to the employee's performance.

To date, this type of cause of action has seen little success. However, the courts—especially in California, Michigan, Minnesota and New Jersey—have continued to expand protections for at-will employees. Therefore, employers must be aware of possible claims arising from poor or negligent supervision of their employees.

NOTE: Employers should conduct periodic evaluation reviews of employees' job performances. The reviews should occur at regular intervals, be consistently done, and be fair. Employers may be vulnerable with regard to a termination of a long-term employee especially where mediocre or poor performance was tolerated for a substantial period of time.

HOW TO DISCIPLINE AND TERMINATE
AT-WILL EMPLOYEES

As we have previously discussed, at-will employees may be dismissed for any reason or no reason as long as it is not an unlawful reason. That does not mean that an employer should not have a structured disciplinary policy. However, the employer wants to ensure that its disciplinary policy does not inadvertently alter the at-will relationship so that it must have "just cause" to dismiss an employee.

The key to disciplining at-will employees is consistency and compliance with the employer's policies and practices that govern the employment relationship and workplace. If the employer varies from its policies or has inconsistent enforcement, it provides a basis for several types of claims when an employee is disciplined or discharged, ranging from discrimination to wrongful termination. Therefore, personnel managers must educate supervisors and others when they are administering discipline to follow the company's policies and procedures as closely as possible.

The employer may elect a flexible progressive discipline philosophy or a rigid approach of mandatory discipline for violations of policy or rules. Whatever is the method of discipline selected, it must be complied with and enforced on a consistent basis.

How to Use Progressive Discipline

The more popular and highly recommended approach is one of progressive discipline. This approach involves a step or graduated method to discipline that progresses from verbal warnings, to written warnings, to probation or suspension, and ultimately to termination. Progressive discipline permits flexibility and allows for the discipline to fit the violation or infraction. It also permits the employer to terminate an employee without going through any prior disciplinary steps in cases of serious violations or extreme misconduct. This policy can be structured to accommodate an employer's particular style; that is, some employers desire to have an amnesty type of policy that permits an employee's infraction to expire after a certain period of time if the employee does not repeat that or other violations.

The progressive discipline concept permits minor infractions such as absenteeism or tardiness to be dealt with in such a way as to provide the employee with an opportunity to correct such behavior. A typical program may consist of one or more verbal warnings for an initial or minor infraction; if the behavior persists, written warnings that go into the employee's personnel file; then the stiffer penalties of probation or suspension; and finally if no improvement is made within a reasonable time, the employee is discharged.

If the objectionable conduct is more serious such as poor performance or disruptive behavior, then the employer may begin with written warnings that indicate that if the behavior or performance is not corrected the employee may be terminated. Such a program permits the employee an opportunity to improve and the employer to retain a productive employer if there is improvement. However, it is not so harsh as to give no one a second chance who may have been experiencing temporary problems in his or her personal life.

Obviously, the type and extent of the discipline varies with the importance of the job or position of the individual employee. There are also occasions where only one instance of misconduct, such as violation of the drug or alcohol policy, theft, or a serious safety violation, will be sufficient to warrant immediate dismissal or suspension. A correctly drafted disciplinary policy will permit the employer latitude to make case-by-case disciplinary decisions while not violating the consistency or compliance rule of enforcement.

> NOTE: The employer should enforce its policies and regulations fairly and be able to base its disciplinary decisions on sound reasons, especially when employees are not treated the same.

Using Mandatory Discipline

Some employers may have a mandatory discipline policy, either by design or through practice, that requires that employees be penalized for every violation in the same manner. There is no step-by-step method of discipline. If the employee violates a rule, there is a set discipline, usually harsh, and not always appropriate to the infraction. Such mandatory policies leave almost no room for an employee to improve or correct his or her errors, and it is demoralizing to employees. This type of policy may be unreasonably applied and invite actions from employees who feel that they have not been treated fairly.

For example, Mary, a midlevel manager, has recently begun to arrive late, appearing tired and withdrawn; her performance has begun to deteriorate, and she has alienated her subordinates. She has been with the company for 14 years, and up to the past 6 months has had an excellent work record. You have begun to receive complaints from her coworkers and clients. You have warned Mary that there seems to be a problem and that she needs to improve her performance and attendance.

Unfortunately, she only temporarily improved her tardiness but not much else. The company has decided that it cannot risk Mary alienating clients and causing a morale problem. You are instructed to have her improve in the next three months or terminate her.

If the company has no counseling program for troubled employees, you may wish to suggest that the company develop one. However, in the case of Mary, where prior informal or verbal warnings have not had an impact on her performance or attitude, stronger measures are required. Meet with Mary and her supervisor, and give her a written warning stating that she has a tardiness problem, that her performance is lacking, and that there have been complaints about her attitude. Advise Mary that since the prior warnings have not been effective, she has been placed on a three-month probation and her performance will be reviewed periodically throughout this period. If at the end of that period her performance has not improved at a satisfactory rate, she may be terminated. Allow yourself the option to extend the probationary period if she has begun to improve but needs additional time.

If she requires help, she should request it in confidence. Do not ask her if she has a drinking or drug problem. You may invite her to request help if there is some problem, since her problems at work only recently developed. If she requests a leave, it should be seriously considered and granted pursuant to your leave policies.

Since she has been a valuable and productive member of your company, you should make the effort to assist her. There is always the option of termination if she fails to improve. If you handle this situation with sensitivity and allow her an opportunity to improve, you will greatly reduce the risk of a claim for wrongful discharge.

Implementing a Grievance Procedure

A grievance procedure may be formal or informal. However, if it is not consistently applied, you risk claims by your at-will employees. Most employers do not have any formal grievance procedure for employees who feel that they have been disciplined unfairly. Grievance procedures are commonly found in the collective bargaining setting where employers are bound by a union contract to follow certain procedures before they may discipline or terminate an employee.

Grievance procedures vary in their formats. Typically, the employee with a complaint regarding working conditions or disciplinary actions must first report his complaint to the supervisor who refers it to a higher level. At each level, the decision is either affirmed or modified, generally within a fixed time frame. There may be only one or three or four reviews of the complaint. The ultimate decision rests with senior management or the board of directors. In the collective bargaining situation the matter may go to arbitration if the grievance is not resolved to the employee's satisfaction. This rarely occurs in the nonunionized setting.

Many nonunion employers have begun grievance procedures to reduce litigation. However, in the at-will employment setting, such a procedure almost assuredly alters the relationship so that the employer will have to have a legitimate reason or good cause to discipline or terminate an employee. So long as the employer realizes the implications of such procedures, there is nothing wrong with instituting a grievance procedure.

One positive effect of such a procedure would be to reduce the number of potential claims against an employer. The grievance procedure permits the employer to explain the reason(s) for the disciplinary action, and the employee has an opportunity to "vent steam" with regard to his treatment. Both parties usually come away with a better understanding of the situation. The down side is that the employer will have to invest additional time and personnel to administer the grievance procedure and is committed to the procedure for all employees.

IMPLEMENTING AN EFFECTIVE PERSONNEL POLICY FOR AT-WILL EMPLOYEES

This checklist is offered as a guide for preventive measures for employees with at-will employees. It is not intended to be exhaustive, nor is it intended to be advice for any particular situation. However, this checklist is designed to provide guidance in creating and reviewing policies:

1. As a matter of good employee relations practice, assure that employees are treated *fairly* and *equally. Discipline or discharge only* for *legitimate, job-related reasons.*

2. Educate interviewers to the fact that oral promises and/or commitments may be enforced as contracts.

3. Consider the addition of a pre-employment acknowledgment form or provision that employment is at-will. Such a statement could be added to employment applications or other documents signed by the employee at the time of hire.

4. Periodically, review written personnel policies (handbooks, manuals, etc.). Delete any language that may expressly or impliedly create a "just cause" standard, unless the employer has adopted such a standard. Consider using such terms as "full-time" or "regular" rather than "permanent" employee.

5. Consider adding a statement to employee handbooks to the effect that the handbook is not an employment contract and that no contractual obligation or liability on the part of the company is intended.

6. Inform employees that the company retains the right to change any and all the stated policies and procedures at any time.

7. Conduct regular performance reviews. Train performance raters to give accurate and frank appraisals. Document incidents of poor performance or misconduct. Establish and use progressive discipline and performance improvement plan procedures, but make it clear that such procedures

are only guidelines, are not mandated, and do not constitute a contract with employees. Specify that the company will have discretion to implement these or other procedures based on the particular facts and circumstances. Oral warnings to employees should be followed, if necessary, by written warnings, submitted to the employee.

8. Avoid statements in brochures, in offer letters, in handbooks, or in memoranda or verbally that indicate employees are entitled to certain training or promotions. Place the burden of an individual employee's advancement on the employee, not on the supervisor or manager.

9. Make sure that discharges are conducted in a humane manner, by instructing and training supervisors and managers. List reasons for discharge in the employee handbook *and* indicate that such a listing is not all inclusive.

10. Give special consideration to the termination of a long-term employee. These employees are more likely to institute lawsuits based upon a variety of claims, including age discrimination.

11. Consider having terminated employees sign a covenant that supported by valid consideration and that what is granted is above what he or she would otherwise receive and is accepted knowingly, voluntarily, and without coercion.

12. Document every termination action. Keep precise records of conferences, warnings, probationary notices, remedial efforts, and other steps that precede termination.

13. Provide advance warning that an employee has taken a course possibly leading to termination unless changes occur in his or her performance. Put these notices in writing or have witnesses present at oral admonitions.

14. Watch for signs of an employee's work problems. Job-related stress or discontent of a worker's position may turn a once satisfactory performer into a termination possibility. Try to reclaim such an employee before termination becomes necessary.

ENDNOTES

1. *Murphy v. American Home Products Corp.,* 58 N.Y.2d 293, 300, 461 N.Y.S.2d 232, 235 (1983). (N.Y. Court of Appeals, in rejecting the notion of a cause of action for abusive or wrongful discharge, reaffirmed the traditional at-will rule in New York.)

2. Ch. 641, L. 1987, §39-2-904(2). Montana also presumes that an employee hired for such length of time as the parties adopt for the estimation of wages. A hiring at a yearly rate is therefore presumed to be for one year. In essence, all employees are hired for a specified time, whether one day, one month, or one year, taking them

out of the at-will relationship. The relationship may be terminated by either party but with notice; §§39-2-503, -601, and -602.

3. The National Conference of Commissioners on Uniform State Laws have been drafting a Uniform Termination Act that has undergone many drafts and is still not fully formulated. However, significant areas that will be covered include "good cause" standard for discharge, all employers would be covered, all full-time employees including high-level executives and those with employment contracts would be covered, but part-time employees would not be covered. Employers may layoff or terminate based on economic conditions or honest business judgment; waivers will be permitted, as will remedies and the dispute resolution process. Once complete, the states will have to elect whether to adopt the uniform law in whole or in part.

4. Cases that illustrate this point and provide useful background are *Woolley v. Hoffman-La Roche, Inc.*, 99 N.J. 284 (1985) (employment manual contained promise not to terminate except for just cause and an employment contract was implied on that basis), but see *Murphy v. American Home Products, Inc., supra*, at note 1.

5. In New Jersey, a contract for lifetime employment is not enforceable. *Savarese v. Pyrene Mfg. Co.*, 9 N.J. 595, 599 (1952).

6. For example, *Kramer v. St. Louis Regional Corp.*, 6 I.E.R. Cases (BNA) 703 (E.D.Mo. 1991) (claim for wrongful termination is not available to handicapped former employee where she also sued under Missouri Human Rights Act and the Rehabilitation Act of 1973; these statutes provide for direct recovery; claim for violation of public policy evinced by these statutes is duplicative and unwarranted).

7. Title VII specifically protects employees who bring a complaint or participate in proceedings against an employer regarding discriminatory practices.

8. See *Velantzas v. Colgate-Palmolive Co.*, 109 N.J. 189 (1988), wherein the New Jersey Supreme Court ruled that the retaliatory discharge of an employee who requested to see personnel records in order to establish a claim of discrimination violated the state's strong public policy against discrimination. The court stated that the public policy of the state should protect those who in good faith pursue information relevant to a discriminatory discharge. The particular action for which the employee was dismissed was not clearly protected by the state's anti-discrimination statute; therefore, that statute did not preclude her tort claim for wrongful discharge.

9. See *Lally v. Copygraphics*, 173 N.J. Super. 162 (App. Div. 1980), *affirmed* 85 N.J. 668 (1981).

10. See *Alexander v. Kay Finlay Jewelers, Inc.*, 208 N.J. Super. 503 (App. Div. 1986) (no violation of public policy where at-will employee was fired in retaliation for filing a civil salary claim against the employer).

11. *Guidice v. Drew Chemical Corp.*, 210 N.J. Super. 32 (App. Div. 1986).

12. See *Shebar* discussed earlier in this chapter (refusing a job offer), and *Sides v. Duke University*, 74 N.C.App. 331, 328 S.E.2d 818 (Ct. App. 1985) (nurse was induced to move from Michigan to North Carolina in reliance upon employer's representation that she could only be terminated for cause).

13. See, for example, *Grouse v. Group Health Plan, Inc.*, 306 N.W.2d 114 (Minn. 1981) (employee who resigned job and refused another offer of employment only to have new employer revoke job offer held to have cause of action against employer on theory of promissory estoppel), but compare with *Carlton v. Interfaith Medical Center*, 612 F.Supp. 118, 125 (E.D.N.Y. 1985) (employee failed to establish detrimental reliance necessary to state promissory estoppel claim because she continued to work and did not look for work elsewhere).

14. This theory has had some success in California. See *Cleary v. American Airlines, Inc.*, 111 Cal.App.3d 443, 168 Cal. Rptr. 722 (1980)(court held that there is an implied covenant of good faith and fair dealing in every contract including the employment relationship in case involving discharge of a long-term employee with 18 years of satisfactory service); *Pugh v. See's Candies, Inc.*, 116 Cal.App.3d 311, 171 Cal. Rptr. 917 (1981), *modified on other grounds*, 117 Cal.App.3d 520 (1981) (discharge of corporate vice president after 32 years was held to violate implied covenant not to discharge absent good cause).

    Other jurisdictions: *Fortune v. National Cash Register Corp.*, 373 Mass. 96, 364 N.E.2d 1251 (1977) (former salesman was discharged in order to deprive him of commissions for work substantially performed in violation of an implied covenant of good faith and fair dealing). But *Fortune* is significantly different from the typical at-will discharge cases because it involved a separate contractual liability for commissions and recovery was not premised on "bad faith" or "wrongful discharge"), and *Monge v. Beebe Rubber Co.*, 114 N.H. 130, 316 A.2d 549 (1947) (a termination by the employer of a contract of employment-at-will which is motivated by bad faith or malice or is based on retaliation is not in the best interest of the economic system in the public good and constitutes a breach of the employment contract).

15. See *Citizens State Bank of New Jersey v. Libertelli*, 215 N.J. Super 190 (App. Div. 1987). (New Jersey has not adopted the theory of implied covenant of good faith and fair dealing. In *Libertelli* bank officer's employment contract was invalid and he was an at-will employee. The court held that the covenant could not be applied to revive a contractual term of employment invalidated by law.)

16. *Agis v. Howard Johnson Co.*, 371 Mass. 140, 355 N.E.2d 315 (1976) (the Massachusetts high court ruled that an employer could not deal with an employee theft problem by discharging his waitresses in alphabetical order); *Cautilli v. GAF Corp.*, 531 F.Supp. 71 (E.D. Pa. 1982) (court rejected claim of disgruntled employee who alleged that he was intentionally induced into continuing his employment while employer knew that employee might be required to relocate to his detriment; held that employer's conduct was not sufficiently extreme or outrageous to support such a claim); *Hume v. Bayer*, 178 N.J. Super. 310 (L. Div. 1981) (New Jersey recognized intentional infliction of emotional distress as an independent

cause of action); *compare Brunner v. Abex Corp.*, 661 F.Supp. 1351 (D.N.J. 1986) (court held that an employee discharged after relocating to follow employer failed to establish sufficiently outrageous conduct to state a claim); *O'Donnell v. Westchester Community Service Council, Inc.*, 96 A.D.2d 885, 466 N.Y.S.2d 41 (2d Dept 1983) (New York again rejects a tort-based claim that would have circumvented the limitations of the "at-will" doctrine).

12

How to Use
a Personnel Handbook
to Prevent Liability

Employers often ask if they should have a personnel manual or handbook. There are many considerations to be looked at in answering this question.

♦ What is the law in your state?

♦ How many employees do you have?

♦ Do you have a collective bargaining agreement?

♦ Do you have a formal personnel office?

♦ Do you have written personnel policies?

WHAT A PERSONNEL HANDBOOK WILL DO FOR YOU

Let's look at the role and utility of a handbook or manual based upon your circumstances, and you will see how a manual will help you.

For some smaller employers—usually those with fewer than 15 employees—it is not practical to draft and develop a manual. In addition, it may be too costly, the personnel function is often handled on an informal or episodic basis.

A personnel handbook or manual, absent a collective bargaining agreement, sets forth the policies and rules and regulations of the workplace. Generally, an employer can establish its own policies and even modify them when it chooses.

247

How a Personnel Handbook Can Be Viewed as a Legal Contract

If we set up a policy manual, have we created a legal contract of any kind that can be enforced in court? The answer to this question depends primarily on two factors:

1. The jurisdiction or state in which you are operating in
2. The scope and contents of the manual

Case Example

A manufacturing company called Green, Inc., employs about 60 people in a plant in New York. Green has a manual that provides that progressive discipline will be followed and that employees have a right to file internal grievances if they disagree with personnel actions up to and including termination. Jay Brown has been a difficult worker for 16 months and has protested every attempt to modify or improve his workplace conduct. Finally, out of exasperation, Mr. Green has fired Brown and told him to leave the premises. As expected, Green hears from Brown's attorney, and a lawsuit in state court in New York is commenced alleging breach of contract based upon the manual.

Here are a few basic questions to consider:

1. Does Brown have any contractual rights?
2. Are there statutory protections?
3. What effect, if any, does Green's manual have on the situation?

Let's examine this example and understand implied contract rights, if they exist.

How New York Courts Handle Employment At-Will

In New York, the Court of Appeals (the highest court) has clearly ruled over the last decade that it will not sanction a cause of action for wrongful or abusive discharge.[1] The court of appeals said in *Murphy* that it would not "alter our long settled rule that where an employment is for an indefinite term, it is presumed to be a hiring at will which may be freely terminated by either party at any time for any reason or even for no reason." The court explained its position at great length as follows:

> Those jurisdictions that have modified the traditional at-will rule appear to have been motivated by conclusions that the freedom of contracts underpinnings of the rule have become outdated, that individual employees in the modern work force do not have the bargaining power to negotiate security for the jobs on which they have grown to rely, and that the rule yields harsh results for those employees who do not enjoy the benefits of express contractual limitations

on the power of dismissal. Whether these conclusions are supportable or whether for other compelling reasons employers should, as a matter of policy, be held liable to at-will employees discharged under circumstances for which no liability has existed at common law are issues better left to resolution at the hands of the legislature. In addition to the fundamental question of whether such liability should be recognized in New York, of no less practical importance is the definition of its configuration if it is to be recognized.[2]

Weiner v. McGraw-Hill. However, in *Weiner v. McGraw-Hill*, the court held that on an appropriate evidentiary showing, a limitation on the employer's right to terminate an employment of indefinite duration might be implied from an express provision in the employer's handbook on personnel policies and procedures. The *Weiner* opinion, written by then Judge Jacob Fuchsberg, was clearly limited to the specific facts in *Weiner*.

The employee (Walton Weiner) had discussions with a McGraw-Hill representative prior to joining the staff in which he was assured that a position with McGraw-Hill would have job security because the company did not terminate employees without just cause.[3] At the time of his application, Weiner signed a printed McGraw-Hill form that specified that his employment would be subject to the provisions of the company's handbook on personnel policies and procedures. The handbook further stated that

> [t]he company will resort to dismissal for just and sufficient cause only, and only after all practical steps toward rehabilitation or salvage of the employee have been taken and failed. However, if the welfare of the company indicates that dismissal is necessary, then that decision is arrived at and is carried out forthrightly.[4]

In February 1977, Weiner was discharged "for lack of application" and sued his employer under the manual. The court of appeals held that plaintiff Weiner had spelled out a cause of action in contract. The court ruled that the agreement between Weiner and McGraw-Hill, whether terminable at will or for just cause, was not one which could be performed within one year and is not barred by the Statute of Frauds.[5] The court also ruled that there was sufficient evidence in that case to establish an implied contract and a breach of contract to sustain a cause of action by Weiner.

The *Weiner* court essentially held that the handbook and policy manual given to the plaintiff during his initial employment application process and relied upon thereafter formed the basis of a contract between the parties. However, it is significant to note that in a series of later cases, the court of appeals and other New York courts have *not* found much room in *Weiner* to expand the rights of employees at will and have continued to wait for the legislature to lead the way.[6]

Understanding the Case Example Based Upon Court Rulings.
Now, having said all this, what does Green do with Mr. Brown?

In understanding this problem, you must pay careful attention to the jurisdiction. At the present time in New York, Green would probably prevail on a contract claim by Brown. New York has been relatively unyielding in its adherence to employment at will and has rejected nearly every post-*Weiner* handbook claim.[7]

New York courts also look for nearly identical *Weiner* facts to be actionable. The key factors that New York courts look for in order for a claim like Brown's to proceed can be summarized as follows:

1. The plaintiff was induced to leave with assurance defendant would not discharge him without cause.

2. This assurance was incorporated into the employment application.

3. Plaintiff rejected other offers of employment in reliance on the assurance.

4. Plaintiff was told to follow handbook procedures to discipline subordinates.

Unless Brown can fit squarely within the *Weiner* four-factor analysis, he probably will not be able to sustain a claim under the handbook in New York.

An interesting variation of that occurred recently in New York concerning a bonus entitlement based upon provisions in an employment manual.[8] A long-term employee of a life insurance company, engaged under a written agreement, sought certain benefits under the employer's handbook which were supplemental to his employment. After termination, the plaintiff sought certain additional incentive compensation provided for in the manual. However, the employee handbook stated that to be eligible for these benefits, he had to continue as a soliciting agent. Since his employment as a soliciting agent had been terminated, the court found he had no entitlement to the incentive benefits according to the manual.

Similarly, in another recent decision, a physician sued a hospital after termination, alleging, in part, that his termination violated the hospital bylaws and personnel manual. With regard to the manual, the court held that the plaintiff could not rely upon the manual or its restrictions on termination because he was unaware of the existence of the manual at the time of his contract. Since he knew nothing about the manual at the time of executing the employment contract, at least in New York, there is no legal basis to the claim of wrongful discharge based upon the violation of manual procedures.[9]

Handling Handbook Claims in Other Jurisdictions

More and more jurisdictions permit handbook claims like Brown's. An early case in New Jersey, for example, held that a personnel handbook created an implied contract at least requiring notice and a hearing *prior* to termination.[10] The Supreme Court of New Jersey later held that "absent a clear and prominent disclaimer, an implied promise contained in an employment manual that an employee will be fired only for cause may be enforceable against an employer even when the employment is for an indefinite term and would otherwise be terminable at will."[11]

Employment handbooks may be construed as employment contracts in limited circumstances, although the answer will vary from state to state. The trend is clearly toward enforcing an implied contract from statements and policy manuals and handbooks. Thus, to the extent the manual clearly stated that termination would be based upon a just cause standard, Brown would probably have a right to litigate his termination in some jurisdictions.

Likewise, if there were internal grievance procedures that could be utilized providing for a hearing prior to termination and Brown was summarily dismissed, he might have those grievance rights implied from the manual as well.

At present, there are no federal statutory protections that would prohibit the termination of Mr. Brown. However, the facts do not define his age, race, origin, religion, sexual preference, handicap, or disability status or other important questions. Prior to answering the question of statutory protections definitively, you must be sure that you have thoroughly investigated the facts and have determined if the employee is a member of any protected groups which might invest him or her with certain additional protections and might cause you to think through your actions more carefully or cautiously prior to termination. For example, if instead of a private facility, Brown worked in a quasi-public or public facility, he might have additional due process rights prior to termination.

Certain states also require the employer to provide a written statement of reasons for an individual's termination upon request.[12]

The effect or impact of Green's manual on the Brown termination has been explored already. In sum, where you have adopted an employment manual, you must pay close attention to the jurisdiction in which you are operating. Interestingly, just the division of a river between places like New York and New Jersey, at least in this area of the law, can be a distance of many miles.

Making the Handbook a Helpful Tool

If you have multiple sites, you should be clear on the prevailing law in each jurisdiction. However, even assuming a jurisdiction that enforces manual provisions as an implied contract, the employment manual can be a beneficial tool for the company in managing the workplace. The simple fact that a contract may be implied should not deter employers from utilizing an opportunity, particularly in a union-free environment, to establish the rules and regulations of the workplace. Some employers even invite participation in the process by employees to gain acceptability and a greater degree of employee cooperation.

In any event, the handbook must be carefully thought through and developed with counsel to present the appropriate corporate philosophy and terms of employment so that you and your employees know exactly where they stand.

Despite the fact that a majority of states have adopted the position that manuals may constitute an implied contract, if the provisions are drawn imprecisely or are lacking in specific contractual terms, the manual may not establish contractual rights. The same will apply if the language is of a non-promissory nature, which merely amounts to declarations of general policy.

Assurances to employees that they would all be treated fairly may not bind an employer and certainly would not impose a just cause standard.[13] Assurances can be tricky, especially if they are connected to specific assurances or oral promises.[14]

HOW TO AVOID A JUST CAUSE STANDARD FOR TERMINATION

The simplest way to avoid a "just cause" standard for termination is to say so. A simple mistake that many employers make is to attempt to be too fair.

Many employers do not adequately define standards for termination or assume that a "cause" standard automatically exists. To the contrary, unless an employer provides a certain level of conduct necessary for termination, none will be automatically implied. Absent a collective bargaining agreement, the only restrictions on management's right to discharge and discipline employees not hired for a specific period of time are state and federal laws dealing with discrimination and labor relations. "Just cause" as a standard for termination implies that the employee has violated acceptable performance or behavior standards.

An arbitrator, Joseph D. McGoldrick, described the essential qualities of just cause as follows:

> It is common to include the right to suspend and discharge for "just cause," "justifiable cause," or "proper cause." There is no significant difference between these various phrases. These exclude discharge for mere whim or caprice. They are, obviously, intended to include those things for which employees have traditionally been fired. They include the traditional causes of discharge in the particular trade or industry, the practices which develop in the day-to-day relations of management and labor, and most recently the decisions of courts and arbitrators. They represent a growing body of "common law" that may be regarded either as the latest development of the law of "master and servant" or, perhaps, more properly as part of a new body of common law of "Management and labor under collective bargaining agreements." They constitute the duties owed by employees to management and, in their correlative aspect, as part of the rights of management. They include such duties as honesty, punctuality, sobriety, or, conversely, the right to discharge for theft, repeated absence or lateness, destruction of company property, brawling, and the like.

Where they are not expressed in posted rules, they may very well be implied, provided they are applied in a uniform nondiscriminatory manner.[15]

Employers, particularly as they grow and get larger, need to understand the dynamics of the workplace. Once rules and regulations are established, they need to be followed.

Rules may be abrogated by practice, but once adopted, rules should be followed.

There is no obligation to adopt a just cause standard for termination or any other standard. Many employment manuals provide that discipline will be progressive but reserve the right to the employer to terminate summarily in its own judgment. Certain other employers use illustrative disciplinary clauses so that employees have an idea of the kinds of conduct and penalties they will receive. I always caution against such provisions because there may be a suggestion of locking in specific penalties.

Including a Disclaimer Clause

One way to avoid most of these problems is to adopt a disclaimer and display it prominently both at the beginning and at the end of the manual.

The purpose of a disclaimer is to avoid formation of a contract and to reduce liability for wrongful termination. Disclaimer clauses also limit employee's expectations regarding the manual.

A disclaimer should include employment-at-will language. Failure to disclaim contractual liability adequately may alter the status of at-will employees. Such a clause should be prominently displayed.

A sample clause is shown in Exhibit 12.1.

– EXHIBIT 12.1 –

Disclaimer Clause

The provisions of this manual apply to all full-time employees of the company. Nothing in this manual is intended to create a contract of any kind between the company and the employee. All employees of the company are employees-at-will. Both the employee and the company have the right to terminate employment at any time for any reason.

In general, companies can protect the right to discharge at will by specifically placing such a disclaimer on the application for employment as well as in the employment manual. The disclaimer should state that termination may be with or without cause or notice and may occur at any time. In addition, representations to the contrary made by anyone other than a specific individual (to be designated by the company) are invalid. This same disclaimer should be repeated and displayed in the manual in various locations, preferably front and back. Language should also be inserted to the effect that the handbook does not constitute a contract either express or implied and that the employer reserves the right to modify unilaterally any and all provisions in the policy manual.

The following states have already accepted or recognized claims for an implied contract under the handbook: Alabama, Alaska, Arizona, Arkansas, California, Colorado, Connecticut, Georgia, Hawaii, Idaho, Illinois, Kansas, Maine, Maryland, Michigan, Minnesota, Montana, New Hampshire, New Jersey, New Mexico, New York, Ohio, Oklahoma, Oregon, South Carolina, South Dakota, Texas, Utah, Vermont, Washington, West Virginia, Wisconsin, and Wyoming; so has the District of Columbia. But note several of the states have specific modifications on the acceptance of contract handbook claims.

In some states, for example, a single sentence in a manual stating that it is informational only and not an employment contract has been found to be too ambiguous and too inconspicuous to be an effective disclaimer.[16] But where a conspicuous and clear disclaimer is added to a handbook even after a long period of employment, the employee's continued employment may be found to be an acceptance of the terms.[17] However, an appellate court in California found that despite at-will provisions in a bank employee handbook and service manual, actual practice was to the contrary—to terminate only for good cause. In such a case, the court ruled that the at-will provisions would not apply.[18]

Employers should not feel that establishment or maintenance of a personnel manual will necessarily constitute a just cause employment contract assuming the disclaimers are prominent, conspicuous, and consistent with practice. Such disclaimers should preserve management's right to terminate employees at will.[19]

> NOTE: In certain circumstances where the employer has a manual that contains a progressive discipline process but also reserves the right to change policies unilaterally and states that the manual is not a contract, courts have found the just cause issue is one for a jury due to the confusion between the for cause and at-will language in the manual.[20]

Disclaimers must be executed nearly contemporaneous with either the issuance or distribution of the handbook so that there is valid consideration for the "waiver" of the implied contractual rights.[21] Obviously, there are many examples of disclaimers as well as implied contract theories.

The simple answer for every employer is to know the law in your jurisdiction since nearly all the 50 states as well as Guam and Puerto Rico and the Virgin

Islands have different holdings in this area. If clear, simple language is used and communicated, you should avoid most problems.

How the Courts Have Interpreted Implied Contract Claims

In addition to claims specifically brought under the employment manual, many individuals have also sought to construct quasi-manual implied contract claims based upon memoranda, letters or other documents supplied by the employer.[22] Generally, where discrete pieces of information have been provided, courts are reluctant to cobble together a contract claim equivalent to an employment manual.

In the absence of clear contract provisions, individuals may attempt to show that they have the equivalent of a manual or its provisions and bring a claim based upon an implied contract.

One court rejected a claim that an individual could not be fired absent poor performance reviews. Despite a provision in an employment contract calling for periodic reviews based upon performance, a federal appellate court rejected the employee's claim that he could not be dismissed absent such a bad review. The court of appeals noted that "as a matter of common sense, every employment contemplates periodic reviews of performance as an aspect of normal employment practices. . . . Such reviews, without more, do not convert an at-will contract into one that can be terminated only on a showing of good cause or honest dissatisfaction."[23]

SUMMARY OF PROS AND CONS OF A PERSONNEL HANDBOOK

The advantages and disadvantages of an employment manual can be summarized as follows:

Advantages

- Sets the parameters of the employment relationship
- Limits the company's liability
- Limits the company's responsibility to its employees
- Can promote morale because employees know what to expect

Disadvantages

- May create certain employee expectations
- Creates a basis for company liability (when the manual is not adhered to)
- May create a contract with employees

SPECIFIC PERSONNEL POLICIES TO INCLUDE IN THE HANDBOOK

An employment manual should generally encompass certain regulations, policies, procedures, and benefits in order to inform your employees adequately. Key provisions that could be in every type of manual are as follows:

The Disclaimer Clause

We have just discussed various concerns regarding disclaimers. The disclaimer clause avoids formation of a contract and reduces liability for wrongful termination. It also limits employee expectations regarding the manual. *All disclaimer clauses should include employment at-will language.* Failure to disclaim contractual liability adequately may alter the status of at-will employees. The disclaimer should appear prominently and boldly at the beginning of the manual and should also appear at the bottom of the employment application. A sample disclaimer was shown in Exhibit 12.1.

The Management Rights Clause

It is important for the employer to establish up front that it may determine the policies and procedures of the company. Such a clause clarifies the rights for employees and preserves employer authority. However, extreme caution should be used if there is a collective bargaining agreement.

A sample management rights clause is shown in Exhibit 12.2.

– EXHIBIT 12.2 –
A Management Rights Clause

> The Company reserves the right to direct and control the operation of its business including, but not limited to, the management, assignment, scheduling, and direction of the work force as well as the right to discipline or discharge employees pursuant to the provisions of this manual. The policies, procedures, benefits, and other information referred to in this manual may be changed without notice at any time by the Board of Directors.

EEO Policy Statements

The employer should always include a statement to the effect that it is an equal employment opportunity employer (unless it is not); that it abides by EEO principles; and that it does not discriminate on the basis of age, sex, creed, religion, color, national origin, marital status, and the like. There may be other protected groups or classes, for example, handicap or disability or sexual preference, which should be included depending upon your jurisdiction. In addition, there may be local laws which also apply and must be reviewed in drafting the particular language of the EEO provision.

NOTE: Check individual state laws before drafting this policy statement.

You may also wish to have a separate portion devoted to sexual harassment in which a specific policy statement is outlined as well as efforts to enforce such a policy. For a full discussion of this subject, see Chapter 7, dealing primarily with sex discrimination issues, including sexual harassment.

References

When framing a company policy with regard to job references, the employer must consider its aim, that is, reward good employees, penalize bad employees, avoid liability, or pass the problem on to someone else. The policy should limit the nature of information for *all* employees, thereby limiting the liability and potential exposure of the company. Consistency in application of this policy is crucial to limiting liability.

The sample shown in Exhibit 12.3 highlights the fact that the employer should release only the individual's description of position or job title and dates of employment. Anything more should be released *only* when the individual (1) makes such a request in writing and (2) signs a release or waiver of all claims against the company that may arise from the release of such information.

– EXHIBIT 12.3 –
Reference Policy

All requests for references for persons who have worked or who are leaving the employment of the Company are referred to the Assistant Director of Human Resources of the Company.

All letters of reference will indicate only

- Date(s) of service and
- Title or description of position(s) held

A reference with regard to one's performance and abilities may be requested, in writing, if the employee signs a release or waiver of all claims against the Company that may arise from the issuance of such a letter of reference.

The Discipline/Termination Clause

The company's policies or practices with regard to discipline should be codified and well-publicized to the employees. Avoid specific language that may be interpreted as a "just cause" standard (such as "fair and equitable treatment" or "will fire for just cause") unless the employer means it and will abide by it. There are several forms of disciplinary policy.

Progressive discipline is a step-by-step procedure generally consisting of a verbal warning, written warning, probation or suspension, and finally termination. Termination occurs after several warnings have been given depending on the seriousness of the violation. Some violations may justify immediate dismissal.

Also, it is common to allow minor infractions that have resulted in a warning to "expire" after a set period of time, thus allowing the employee to start over. On the other hand, more serious violations may accumulate throughout the course of employment.

If the employer does not use a form of progressive discipline, it may simply discipline or discharge any employee-at-will for any or no reason. However, the employer must be aware that inconsistent disciplinary or termination practices may be a basis for liability.

The company should institute some set disciplinary policy, at a minimum, loosely based on the principle of progressive discipline. A set policy enforced consistently will reduce liability and inform employees of the consequences of violating the company's rules. An employer need not adopt an in-depth progressive disciplinary policy, but some form of one is helpful to the employer and its employees. Any disciplinary policy adopted must be consistently followed at all times.

Standard for Dismissal.

1. An employee-at-will may be dismissed for any or no reason, so long as the dismissal is not based on unlawful discrimination.

2. A "just cause" standard can arise in two situations:

   a. *Union contract:* This will almost always contain a provision that permits dismissal only where "just cause" exists, that is, where the employer reasonably believes that the employee violated a company policy and such violation warrants dismissal.

   b. *Voluntary:* An employer may adopt a "just cause" standard through a detailed progressive disciplinary policy or otherwise. If the employer discharges an employee only when it reasonably believes that the situation warrants it, the company may have implicitly adopted a just cause standard.

NOTE: It is important for the company manual and elsewhere to state clearly that the company reserves the right to discharge an employee for any or no reason.

Duty to Warn. If the employer institutes a policy that includes warnings, the failure to warn before discharging an employee may result in liability for *negligent supervision.* An employee in a wrongful discharge case may allege that the employer failed to supervise or warn the employee properly that his or her performance was unsatisfactory.

Prohibited Conduct. Generally, employment manuals or written company rules list prohibited conduct that may result in discipline or termination. A list of prohibited conduct should always include a statement that the list is *not exclusive nor complete.* Such a statement provides management with the flexibility to respond to unforeseen situations that may warrant discipline or termination.

Requiring Employee Acknowledgment

It is recommended that the company require each and every employee to acknowledge receipt of a copy of the employment manual and sign a separate acknowledgment. The acknowledgment has two purposes: it confirms the at-will nature of the employment relationship, and it informs the employee of his or her right to resign at any time. The acknowledgment also preserves the employer's option of discharge for any or no reason unless it is an unlawful reason.

Permitting Access to Personnel Files

Although an employer is generally not obligated to permit access to an employee's personnel file, it is a common practice. If access is permitted, then a standard control policy should be in effect. First, the employer should assure that the records are maintained in a confidential manner. All requests for access should be in writing. Access should be limited to the individual employee and appropriate management personnel. Also have a log sheet for signing by whoever views the file. Some states permit employee access to personnel files by statute — check the local law before you decide the policy.

Establishing a Probationary Period

Employers who use probationary periods should establish a consistent and well-defined policy. Such a policy should identify who is on probation and for what period of time. Any employee on probation after initial hire may be discharged without regard to cause (so long as it is not discriminatory). A consistently applied policy limits liability for wrongful discharge. Note that whenever a union contract exists, its terms and conditions for probation will govern.

Handling Promotion/Internal Transfer

Many employers fill vacancies from within the company. A policy of preferring employees over outside applicants should be consistent and explicit as to the procedure for applying for promotion or transfer.

Implementing Leave Policies

Many employers have formal or informal sick or disability leave policies. Leave is also often granted for the following reasons:

– Bereavement—generally three days for the death of an immediate family member

– Military

– Jury duty

– Personal (generally without pay)

Sick Leave. Sick leave can range from a set number of paid sick days per year to an extended period of time for a serious illness. The employer is not obligated to maintain any type of sick or disability leave policy. However, where one does exist, the employer must consistently adhere to it.

Maternity/Parental Leave. In general, the employer may not differentiate between standards for granting disability and maternity leave to the disadvantage of a pregnant employee. The maternity leave must be treated on an equal basis with disability leave.

Congress is currently considering a national family leave bill. One form of the bill provides that employers must give employees up to 10 weeks of unpaid leave over a 2-year period after the birth, adoption, or serious illness of a child and 13 weeks a year for an employee's own serious illness. Employees of 20 or fewer per site would be exempt. Employee would have to be in the job at least a year before receiving the benefit. Employees would be guaranteed their job or its equivalent upon returning to work.

In *California Federal Savings & Loan Association v. Guerra*, 107 S.Ct. 683 (1987), the U.S. Supreme Court upheld a California law granting mothers up to four months of unpaid leave with reinstatement rights for pregnancy-related disability. The Supreme Court ruled that the Pregnancy Discrimination Act does not prohibit employment practices favoring pregnant women.

NOTE: Employers must check the state and local laws with regard to parental or maternity leave before adopting a policy.

GUIDELINES FOR CREATING A PERSONNEL HANDBOOK

1. Determine the prevailing law in your state regarding handbook and potential contract claims.

2. Determine the effort and investment the company is prepared to make on developing a manual.

3. What is the corporate philosophy regarding employment at-will status, discipline and termination, evaluations, references?

4. The corporate philosophy will help determine the disclaimer that appears in the manual.

5. Disclaimers must be conspicuous, understandable, and clearly communicated to applicants and employees.

6. If you have a collective bargaining agreement, many of the terms and conditions of employment will already be decided.

7. If you do not have a collective bargaining agreement, the company philosophy will determine how most issues are resolved, that is, through an internal grievance procedure. Do you want to permit some form of internal review of discipline or terminations?[24]

8. Have you discussed the manual with employees or groups of employees?

9. What kind of standard for termination do you plan to adopt? If the company does not want to be held to a "just cause" standard, do not include that kind of language either directly or by implication.[25]

10. Say what you mean and mean what you say.[26]

ENDNOTES

1. *Murphy v. American Home Products Corp.*, 58 N.Y.2d 298 (1983); see also *Weiner v. McGraw-Hill, Inc.*, 57 N.Y.2d 548 (1983).

2. 57 N.Y.2d 548 (1983).

3. 57 N.Y.2d at 460.

4. See Handbook Sections 8.2, para. 8 cited at 57 N.Y.2d at 461; Roger B. Jacobs, "Wrongful Discharge in New York: Confusing Signals from the Courts," *New York State Bar Journal*, February 1984, and "Signals Mixed in Rulings on Wrongful Discharge," *New York Law Journal*, August 30, 1983.

5. The Statute of Frauds provides that a contract that cannot be performed within one year must be reduced to writing and the writing must be subscribed to by the party against whom enforcement is sought.

6. See, for example, *O'Donnell v. Westchester Community Service Counsel, Inc.*, 96 A.D.2d 885, 466 N.Y.S.2d 41 (2d Dept. 1983), and *Sabetay v. Sterling Drug, Inc.*, 69 N.Y.2d 329 (1987).

7. In *Sabetay, supra,* the court of appeals again denied a handbook claim because the handbook had only limited distribution. Also, the court found reliance on the "Accounting Code" as a code of ethics and a statement on the employment application taken together did not rise to an express agreement. The court said "significant alteration of employment . . . is best left to the legislature." 69 N.Y.2d at 331.

8. See *Zolotar v. New York Life Ins. Co.*, 576 N.Y.S.2d. 850 (A.D. 1st Dept. 1991).

9. See *Lockwood v. Long Island Jewish Medical Center*, Supreme Court, Suffolk, Index No. 88-15824.

10. *Valdov v. Albanese*, (unpublished, D.N.J. No. 84-1946 (1984)).

11. *Woolley v. Hoffman-LaRoche, Inc.*, 99 N.J. 284, *modified* 101 N.J. 10 (1985).

12. In Missouri, employees have a statutory right to a service letter within one year or discharge requiring the employer to set forth the reasons for discharge, job duties, and dates of service. Damages may be awarded. Many other states provide in varying forms for a service letter: Indiana, Kansas, Montana, Nebraska, North Carolina, Texas, Washington, and Wisconsin.

13. *Knox v. American Sterilizer Co.*, 117 LRRM (BNA) 2341 (D.Ala. 1984).

14. In *Shebar v. Sanyo Business Systems Corp.*, 111 N.J. 276 (1988), the Supreme Court of New Jersey found an implied contract to oral representations given to an at-will employee. The plaintiff had offered to resign and take another position but was induced to stay with promises of longevity. After turning down another position, the plaintiff was terminated a few months later. Note: The Supreme Court of New Jersey cautioned in that case that "not every relinquishment of a prior job or job offer constitutes additional consideration to support the modification of an at-will employment into employment for termination with cause only." The enforceability of each contract will depend on the intent of the parties as established under ordinary principles of contract law. 111 N.J. at 289–290. See also *Shiddell v. Electro-Rustproofing Corp.*, 34 N.J. Super. 278 (App. Div. 1954) *cert. denied,* 17 N.J. 408 (1955).

15. *Worthington Corp. v. UAW, Local 259*, 24 L.A. (BNA) 1, 6-7 (McGoldrick 1955).

16. *Jones v. Central Peninsula General Hospital*, 4 I.E.R. Cases (BNA) 1204 (Ala. Sup. Ct. 1989). See also *Wagonseller v. Scottsdale Memorial Hospital*, 710 P.2d 1025 (Ariz. Sup. Ct. 1985).

17. *Chambers v. Valley National Bank*, 721 F. Supp. 1128 (D.Ariz. 1988).

18. *Wilkerson v. Wells Fargo Bank*, 4 I.E.R. Cases (BNA) 1057, *amended* at 4 I.E.R. cases (BNA) 1217 (Calif. Ct. of App. 1989) *rev. denied,* 5 I.E.R. cases (BNA) 672 (Calif. Sup. Ct. 1989).

19. *Lavery v. South Lake Center for Mental Health,* 5 I.E.R. Cases (BNA) 335 (Ind. Ct. of App. 1991). But see *Badgett v. Visiting Nurses Association of Council Bluffs,* 6 I.E.R. Cases (BNA) 322 (Iowa Ct. of App. 1991), in which the disclaimer stated that an annual employment agreement was no "guarantee of employment." However, the court found the disclaimer insufficient to prevent the manual from forming a one year just cause contract since the reasonable expectation of the employee was that she had a conditional contract and could only be discharged for insubordination, misconduct, or unsatisfactory performance as specified in the manual.

20. *Dalton v. Herbruck Egg Sales Corp.,* 417 N.W. 2d 496 (Mich. Ct. App. 1987). Michigan, for example, has had many cases interpreting disclaimers and contract provisions through handbooks. Interestingly, in a recent case, the Michigan Supreme Court held that it was not necessary for an employee to sign off or assent to disclaimers because she did not have a prior express for cause contract and she had reasonable notice of the at-will provisions of the manual prior to her discharge. *Rowe v. Montgomery Ward & Co., Inc.,* 6 I.E.R. Cases (BNA) 1185 (Mich. Sup. Ct. 1991).

21. *Towns v. Emery Air Freight, Inc.,* 3 I.E.R. Cases (BNA) 911 (S.D.Ohio, 1988).

22. However, where sufficient documents and letters deal particularly with the terms and conditions of employment as well as the termination provisions, reliance on those materials may be the basis for a contract claim. See John Furfaro and Maury Josephson, "Informal Employment Agreements," *New York Law Journal,* June 7, 1991.

23. *Arledge v. Stratmar Systems, Inc.,* 948 F.2d 845, 849 (2d Cir. 1991).

24. In *Montgomery v. Association of American Railroads,* 5 I.E.R. Cases (BNA) 1118 (D.Ill. 1990), an Illinois court, for example, found that discipline procedures were laid out where the policy manual provided for termination for a third offense in one year that warrants probation and the manual's terms constituted a contract. See also *Schumacher v. Frito Lay, Inc.,* 6 I.E.R. Cases (BNA) 156 (D.N.D. 1991).

25. In a recent case, the Minnesota Supreme Court held that an in-house attorney was permitted to bring suit for breach of contract based upon the company handbook that provided that progressive discipline should precede discharge. The handbook, in *Nordling v. Northern States Power Company,* 7 I.E.R. Cases (BNA) 10 (Minn. Sup. Ct. 1991), provided that "positive discipline" in the form of an oral reminder, a written reminder, and a decision-making leave (or a day off with pay) should precede discharge. In other words, the attorney was permitted to proceed with his claim because the manual provided that a specific form of discipline would precede his termination, and he was not barred by any form of attorney/client privilege.

26. A jury recently awarded $26,000 in damages against an employer who breached a commitment in its handbook to gender equality in employment and to a fair system of determining compensation. *Tuttle v. ANR Freight Systems,* 5 I.E.R. Cases (BNA) 1103 (Colo. Ct. App. 1990).

13

AVOIDING CLAIMS OF DEFAMATION—KNOWING WHAT YOU CAN SAY

Defamation is becoming a significant problem in the workplace. Defamation issues can arise in a variety of everyday occurrences, such as a reference request. For example,

> You are asked for a reference regarding a former employee. His prospective employer calls, and you state that this individual was not trustworthy or you simply do not give any information although you know the individual to be not trustworthy.

Is there a potential problem? Yes. If you state that the former employee was not trustworthy and you lack support for such a charge, you may face a claim of defamation. However, if you fail to provide such information, depending upon the job being sought, you may be sued for negligence because you *failed* to notify a prospective employer of a problem that you were aware of and that could affect him. This is a difficult choice to make.

DEFINING DEFAMATION

Defamation is the communication of a falsehood that injures the reputation of another. It can either be written or oral. When defamation occurs in a writing, it is libel. Oral defamation is slander. Harm is presumed from a libelous statement, but slander requires proof of special harm, except that harm is presumed from slanderous statements imputing disease, sexual misconduct, or commission of a crime.

Comments about reputation have long been the subject of commentators. In *Othello*, Shakespeare wrote that, "He that filches from me my good name robs me of that which not enriches him and makes me poor indeed."

The main concern for employers is that communications to and about employees occur everyday in a variety of circumstances. For example, a request for a reference about a former employee may result in the dissemination of information about that individual. Many companies seek to limit and control the source and content of such information in an effort to minimize potential claims of defamation.

In this chapter we will discuss the elements of defamation and how workplace communications may be privileged. We will also discuss "self-publication" and other recent developments.

Identifying Elements of Defamation

For a communication to be defamation, four elements must be present:

1. The communication is not privileged.
2. The communication is false.
3. The communication is injurious to one's reputation.
4. The information is communicated to a third person.

The fourth element is called "publication." Publication can occur by words, by conduct, or even by silence. For defamation to take place, all four of the elements must be present.

In the workplace, the following are areas of concern:

- Performance evaluations of employees, where inappropriate comments may be uttered or written and communicated to other individuals.

- Reference requests, which are probably the single most dangerous area for employers today. A failure to provide information may impute liability under a negligence theory while the disclosure of candid information often results in claims of defamation. Due to these concerns most employers offer only basic "name, rank, and serial number" information about employees. This is a topic that will be discussed at length in this chapter.

- Internal bulletins concerning employee conduct, which may inappropriately characterize or disseminate information.

- Press releases.

- Internal investigations regarding alleged employee misconduct.

- Requests for information from governmental agencies.
- Preparation for litigation.

All these workplace concerns will be addressed in this chapter with suggestions of how to handle each situation. Many of these employment-related activities receive limited or conditional immunity from a charge of defamation. This immunity is referred to as "privileged" and is discussed in the next section.

Determining When a Communication Is Privileged

Basically, there are two kinds of privileges that attach to certain communications and protect against liability for defamation. A privilege may be *absolute* or *qualified* (also referred to as conditional). Communications that are privileged are generally protected from defamation claims.[1]

Absolute Privilege. An *absolute privilege* means that there is complete immunity for the statement. An absolute privilege attaches to the following:

♦ Statements made during judicial or administrative proceedings: the statements must relate to the proceeding and not be published outside of the forum. Statements may be made in writing or in the form of live testimony. The privilege applies to the statements of a witness or a party. Several states have expressly recognized that a witness' testimony before a legislative committee is absolutely privileged.[2]

♦ Statements of legislators: these are absolutely privileged as long as they are made while the body is in session.

♦ Statements by judges during a judicial proceeding.

♦ Statements made during a grievance procedure: these are privileged because they are part of the collective bargaining process. The written comments about an employee which form the basis of a grievance enjoy an absolute privilege as long as the publication is limited to persons with direct interest in the subject matter. This privilege also attaches to statements in notices and during conferences.[3]

♦ Publication of matters arising under the collective bargaining agreement to individuals other than those directly involved, for example, labor relations personnel or supervisors. A communication to the newspaper, however, would likely eliminate the privilege.

Qualified Privilege. A *qualified* or *conditional privilege* will protect certain conduct unless the privilege is abused. When a qualified privilege applies, liability is avoided unless there is excessive publication or malice. A qualified privilege may be lost where

- ◆ A known falsity has been communicated with reckless disregard for the truth

- ◆ The action was motivated by ill will or spite

- ◆ The employer did not reasonably believe the communication was necessary to accomplish any purpose for which the privilege was designed to protect

In the workplace, a qualified privilege applies to administrative proceedings such as unemployment, a performance evaluation, references, a termination discussion, or even a company news release. In this context, a qualified privilege attaches to any statement which is made in good faith if it is based upon a public or private duty to someone who has a corresponding interest.

For example, a conditional privilege would attach to statements made about a former employee, such as a reference, to a prospective employer. Such comments enjoy this limited privilege because of society's interest in encouraging communication, but this privilege is not absolute. Statements regarding termination enjoy a conditional privilege because of a common interest in the free exchange of information for the operation of a business. However, this privilege may be lost through a reckless or unreasonable failure to verify the facts.[4]

Statements Made About Public Officials and Public Figures. If the plaintiff in a defamation action is a public official or a public figure, he or she must prove "actual malice" in order to prevail. See *New York Times Co. v. Sullivan*, 376 U.S. 254, 279 (1964), and *Curtis Publishing Co. v. Butts*, 388 U.S. 130, 164 (1967).

Actual malice exists when the defendant makes a false and defamatory statement with knowledge that it is false or with reckless disregard for its truth or falsity.[5] Whenever actual malice must be proved, the applicable standard of proof is clear and convincing evidence rather than a mere preponderance of the evidence.[6]

The typical plaintiff in the employment discharge–related defamation case will not be considered a public official since it is likely he or she will lack the "pervasive fame or notoriety" necessary to make him or her a general-purpose public figure based upon the Supreme Court's holdings. Most discharged employee plaintiffs will be considered private figures. The Supreme Court held that a private figure plaintiff need not prove actual malice in order to prevail, but must prove some degree of fault as defined by the individual states.[7]

The private figure plaintiff must prove at least negligence on the part of the defendant in failing to ascertain the truth. If actual malice is established, a plaintiff is entitled to recover punitive damages.

NOTE: The dissemination of information to the public must be accurate, and efforts to verify facts must be made.

In a recent case in New York, a newspaper was sued because its employee, a reporter, incorrectly identified an individual as a defendant in a lawsuit.[8] The reporter admitted that he should have recognized the error because the defendant in the story was a pediatrician and the individual he identified was a dentist. The court found such a reporting error to be "grossly irresponsible." However, due to a pleading defect, the claim was dismissed.

Assuring Accurate News Reporting

News reporting by a company, particularly about one of its employees either through internal media or in a press release must be carefully monitored and checked for accuracy. False information about an employee may subject the company to defamation claims.

Press Releases. Press releases should be factual and accurate. They should be limited to the geographic area that has a legitimate interest. Employers should consider their size, location, the importance of the information to the general public, and the veracity of the statements. Do not report any information until all the facts are known.

The following example recounts one company's experience with a claim for defamation based upon a press release.

Case Example

National Steel Company (National) conducted an internal investigation of improper practices by certain employees favoring suppliers. As a result of the investigation, two employees were terminated. A third employee, the plaintiff, had been interviewed during the investigation and suspended by the company. The company issued a press release about the alleged kickback scheme and subsequent employee terminations.

One week after the press announcement the plaintiff was also terminated. The employee sued the company for defamation because of the contents of the press release, and a jury returned a verdict of $225,000 against the steel company.

An appellate court found that the press release was not defamatory, but it was a close call. The court found that there had not been excessive publication by National Steel even though the community at large was practically synonymous with the employees. The community had an interest in the plant particularly since the employees had purchased the company through an employee stock ownership plan. Thus the company narrowly escaped liability for defamation based on a press release.[9]

Internal Bulletins. Internal bulletins can be dangerous, as shown by the following example.

Case Example

In an effort to call attention to a corporate policy on sexual harassment, one large company issued a bulletin to its employees as follows:

The recent sexual harassment incident which resulted in an employee's termination has raised supervisory and employee questions about the subject. This particular incident was determined to be a serious act of employee misconduct, but in deference to employees involved cannot be discussed in detail. However, deliberate, repeated, and unsolicited physical contact as well as significant verbal abuse was involved in this case.[10]

In this bulletin, the employee was not identified. However, most of the other employees knew who it was and that he had been fired.

Did the company have a right to publish this bulletin? Companies have a qualified privilege to disseminate such information because "coworkers have a legitimate interest in the reasons a fellow employee is discharged." However, the bulletin in the above example resulted in a lawsuit in federal court and a jury verdict in favor of the discharged employee for nearly $100,000.[11] The company decided to use an incident of sexual harassment to republicize its policy by pointing to the specific incident. Perhaps a more general review of the policy *without* a pointed reference would have avoided such litigation. Thus employers must be cautious in what they say regarding their employees and to whom it is said.

NOTE: Companies should avoid personalizing internal bulletins or referring to individuals regarding such conduct unless there is a specific need to make public that kind of charge.

Compelled Self-publication

In an increasing number of jurisdictions, employers may be liable for defamation under a doctrine called *compelled self-publication*. Under this doctrine, an employer may be liable even if it says nothing to anyone about a former employee but the employee is required or feels compelled to communicate the reasons for his or her dismissal which are false. Usually, the former employee feels it is necessary to advise a prospective employer of the reasons he or she left or was terminated from a previous position, even if these reasons are without basis and are false. In other words, the reasons used by the former employer to dismiss them are false, and they are forced to repeat those reasons to others.

There is a basic two-part test for compelled self-publication:

1. Was the former employee *compelled* to communicate a false statement?
2. Was it foreseeable that the employee would be so compelled?[12]

In light of compelled self-publication, employers should rethink neutral references as well as place greater care on their pretermination investigation.

In general, employers are not liable for defamation damages if only true statements are made regarding the terminated employee *even* if these statements are injurious to reputation. Sometimes, however, the "truth" or characterization of employees' conduct/misconduct becomes a fact issue to be decided by a jury.[13] In some circumstances, a former employee may seek to use a defamation suit to litigate a "wrongful discharge" where such a suit would not be otherwise available.

Opinions. Opinions about employees are absolutely protected under the First Amendment.[14] Comments by fellow employees are usually not attributable to the employer. Statements regarding an employee's social life or personal characteristics are considered opinion. For example, calling an individual a "bitch" or flirtatious is too imprecise to be defamatory. Often there is a thin line between opinion and what is stated as fact.

In determining whether a statement is fact or opinion, the following factors are considered:

- The precision or specificity of the disputed statement (the more imprecise, the more likely opinion)

- The statement's verifiability (the less verifiable, the more likely opinion)

- The literary and societal context in which the statement is made (including tone of the communication, use of cautionary language, style of writing, and intended audience)

- The statement's public context (the public or political arena in which the statement is made)[15]

Case Example

Mark Slag is an assistant manager who has a reputation of being "difficult" to work with. He is being considered for a promotion. However, many employees do not care for his authoritarian and highly critical style of management. Some employees who had disagreements with Slag have received harassing and threatening phone calls. One such message was recorded, but several employees had received similar calls.

The next day there was a regularly scheduled plant meeting that all employees attended; however, Slag was out on vacation and was not present. The general manager advised the employees that he intended to promote Slag. Several employees objected and referred to Slag as a fascist and that he runs his department like the "Gestapo." During the meeting, the tape of this call was played for the general manager, but no one suggested beforehand that the caller was Slag. The general manager felt that it was likely that the caller was

Slag. He was also very concerned by the statements made by the employees which he initially thought to be simply sour grapes.

The general manager decided not to promote Slag and advised him of the reasons in a memorandum that it also sent to the officers of the company. He refers to the harassing calls and complaints of the employees. Slag returns from vacation and learns of the comments made by the employees at the meeting. He denies that he made the calls. Slag claims that he has been defamed by the general manager who repeated the statements of the employees and by the employees for the comments that they made at the meeting and repeated at work.

Consider the following:

♦ Is there a conditional or qualified privilege attached to the general manager's memorandum and the employee's statements?

♦ Are the employees' statements defamatory facts or simply opinions?

The internal communications by the other employees and the general manager regarding the threatening and harassing phone calls allegedly made by Slag are not actionable defamation since they are qualifiedly privileged statements made without malice. Also the regularly scheduled employee meeting was the proper occasion to discuss these calls. In this case, a supervisor properly may be informed that an employee named for promotion may have made threatening phone calls and the tape was played without mentioning the suspected caller.

With regard to the employees' comments that Slag was a "fascist" and the references to the "Gestapo"—such statements in this context are so indefinite as to be opinion and thus are not defamatory.[16] The social context of these statements would not lead a listener to believe them to be statements of fact.

In cases where the coworker is said to be flirtatious, is making sexually explicit remarks, is someone who "slept her way to the top," or comments of similar ilk, such statements are generally considered to be opinion. Office gossip and banter which occur in a social context are opinion and not defamatory where the listener would not take such statements to be factual.[17]

However, statements made as if they are fact, depending on their specificity and context, may be considered defamatory. Thus, supervisors are well advised to avoid repeating rumors and unsubstantiated statements made about employees.

Silence.   If your policy is to provide favorable references, ones that go beyond a neutral or "bare bones" type of reference may be inviting a defamation claim from a former employee who does not receive the typical favorable reference your company is known to provide. Under such circumstances, providing no reference or only a neutral reference may be defamatory, because those individuals who did not receive a favorable reference would soon realize that a favorable reference is usually given unless there were only negative things that would be said. Thus, a person who is not given a reference or only a neutral "bare bones" type of reference could be injured by the insinuation and inference of wrongdoing or other negative inferences that may be drawn from the lack of a favorable reference.[18]

Defamation may be communicated through silence. A neutral reference or the absence of any reference, where it is known that your company will give positive references unless there is a problem, may be an implicit form of defamation. Silence where there is usually comment lead a third party to believe that the former employee has problems or was not a good employee. In a situation where silence implies a negative reference, there may lie an action of defamation.

HOW TO IDENTIFY, UNDERSTAND, AND DEAL WITH DEFAMATION PROBLEMS

Here are several suggestions that may be helpful in identifying, understanding, and dealing with defamation problems in the workplace:

Providing References

How to handle reference information is probably one of the most difficult questions facing an employer today. On one hand, you appear to be potentially constrained if you provide too much information. On the other hand, if you do not provide information and you are aware of a problem, you may be susceptible to a claim of negligent referral. Employers are clearly on the horns of a dilemma in this regard and should come to a position with which they are comfortable, philosophically as well as businesswise.

My suggestion is to rethink the routine "name, rank, and serial number" type response to a reference request and provide accurate, limited information, but on a uniform basis.

Suppose that Mary Smith, who has been a loyal and dedicated employee, asks for a reference and you really would like to help her. What should you do? If you uniformly provide only name, position, and salary information, then only that kind of information should be provided for her. However, if you regularly provide other information for other employees, provide the same for her.

The problem emerges when you distinguish or discriminate among employees. If you have one policy for those whom you like or do not like and decide that you will give glowing references for those employees that you like but will be very limited in your comments, if any, for those employees that you do not care for, you have a problem. Such a position is easy to see through and is more likely to be a problem than not.

Releases for References. One solution to this problem is to seek cooperation from your employee by way of a written agreement regarding references. You should obtain a release from your employees *prior* to any discussion about reference information. You may wish to make this part of your information kit when an employee joins the company. For example, along with other forms that the individual signs, include a reference release form clearly written and attached to these materials. Exhibit 13.1 is a sample of such a form. However, you should note as a caution that some states have found these kinds of releases against public policy.[19]

– EXHIBIT 13.1 –

Letter of Reference Request
and Waiver and Release of Claims

     I, _____, request that the _____ Inc., submit a Letter of Reference containing information regarding my job performance and qualifications to _____ _____ .

     I hereby release the _____ Inc., and all of its officers, directors, employees, agents, successors and assigns, from any and all claims, demands, causes of action and liabilities of any kind whatsoever, whether known or unknown, arising out of

     's issuance of aforesaid Letter of Reference. This waiver and release is binding on me, my heirs and assigns.

     I hereby affirm that I have entered into this agreement voluntarily and knowingly.

Dated:_____   _____
                                      Signature

     Information to prospective employers should only be submitted based upon a signed written request from the prospective employer and former employee. Information should be released to that prospective employer only when you have a release from your former employee in the file. If you do not have one, ask the prospective employer to obtain one for you prior to releasing the information. Do not permit a verbal discussion of employee performance, particularly with regard to the reasons for termination. These kinds of discussions can lead to potentially serious trouble.

You should provide only undisputed facts. Make sure to the extent possible that characterizations or impressions are not provided about a former employee.

Case Example

The Gun Company has recently been experiencing losses of merchandise from the warehouse. Frank James, a new employee, has been terminated for his involvement in an incident involving possible theft of company materials in violation of company rules. An investigation was conducted and all circumstantial evidence pointed at James. You have heard that he has lied on other occasions regarding his time records and past job experience. He says he did not take anything from the company and his performance has always been very good. However, you have never liked him and thought he was a "no-good" character from the start. James has asked that you contact a prospective employer and provide a reference.

Should you say that Frank James is a dishonest, untrustworthy individual and a thief? No. It would be better either to provide name, job duty or title, and dates of employment, or to state simply that Frank James was terminated for violation of company rules, without providing specific details. Assuming the foregoing facts to be true, this type of response makes sense. Obviously, if you have any hesitation about the veracity of these facts, do not provide them and do not characterize the employee in any way other than what can be supported by the facts. Try to keep your personal feelings out of a reference.

However, if the prospective employer desires additional information regarding his job skills or the like, then you should obtain a release from James before giving any additional information.

There are really two simple solutions to reference request situations:

1. Provide uniform neutral references for all employees and run the potential risk of negligent referrals, if you are aware of information and fail to disclose it.

2. Disclose relevant information of undisputed facts regarding all former employees once you have obtained a written release from them.

NOTE: Obtain consent prior to giving a reference that includes information beyond name, title, duties, and dates of employment. Where the employee has consented to the release of information, this information, if factual, will be absolutely privileged.

Handling Employee Evaluations

Employee evaluations should be limited in their distribution to human resources personnel and supervisors who have an interest in such information. The affected employee should acknowledge the comments in writing and should also be permitted to comment or respond on his or her own. However, the evaluation itself enjoys a qualified privilege unless it is malicious and is excessively published. For that reason, there should be no "publication" of this information whatsoever, and its distribution should be strictly limited on an internal basis.

> NOTE: This information should never leave the company. The kind of information contained in an evaluation should not be released to any outside sources except in litigation and only pursuant to a discovery process or where a specific release has been obtained from the employee or former employee.

Evaluation information should be based upon specific facts and not generalizations.

Case Study

> Employee Walter has been terminated due to a disagreement with the company president about operating procedures. Somehow, this information is reduced to writing by a low-level personnel employee to reflect that Walter was insubordinate and abusive to his colleagues as well as to the company president. That information was included in his final evaluation and was distributed to other individuals inside the company.

Is there a problem? Perhaps. The information, as communicated to others, is both factually incorrect and beyond the amount and kind of information that should be contained in an evaluation. Evaluations should be limited to specific categories and fact responsive information. If a suggestion is made that an employee has been abusive in his or her behavior, the underlying conduct should be detailed rather than merely presented in a conclusive manner.

Initiating Internal Investigations

There are basically two kinds of internal investigations in which defamation is a concern:

1. Those in an effort to determine discipline
2. Those in contemplation of litigation

In both situations you should attempt to gather information from management and exempt personnel as well as neutral fact witnesses. You should encourage the neutral witnesses to participate in a non-threatening manner.

Conducting Internal Investigations to Determine Discipline. In a disciplinary situation there are several factors to consider. If you have an employee manual or handbook, the manual may provide certain rights for your employees. If so, you should follow that procedure carefully since most states will imply contractual rights from the handbook, and you will be expected to adhere to that procedure.[20] Similarly, if you have a collective bargaining agreement with a union, it will be necessary to permit union representatives to be present during investigatory meetings in which discipline may be imposed as a result.

Generally, interview all parties to a dispute. You may also consider having a witness from your department present to verify the statements made especially in a particularly contentious situation or a sensitive one.

Case Example

Alexander accuses Barbara, his supervisor, of sexual harassment. Alexander states that Barbara has been "hitting on him" during work and has told him that if he does not go out with her, he'll never see another raise and she'll make his life miserable. In fact, she has already given him less desirable tasks. Alexander is married and does not want to be involved in such a relationship and has come to you, the personnel director, for advice. However, he is reluctant to file a formal complaint under the company policy at this time.

How do you investigate such a situation? What can you say to Alexander? Follow company guidelines. If there is no policy, you should adopt one regarding sexual harassment. In this regard see Chapter 7, which provides sexual harassment information, an update on the law, as well as sample policy information. Some companies will not investigate a complaint of harassment unless it is formally made. Urge Alexander to make a formal complaint against Barbara. However, if he refuses, you still should investigate the complaint, since you now have notice of the problem.

Interview Alexander and Barbara separately. Advise Barbara of the accusations against her. Watch her reaction or her demeanor, and determine her veracity for yourself. Be careful in presenting the facts because she might file a claim of defamation against the company and some juries may find a claim like this to be meritorious.[21]

Sexual harassment allegations are very difficult to prove and are usually based upon conflicting information; in other words, it is one person's word against the other's. In a case such as this, see if either party has a corroborating witness. If there are no witnesses, you must proceed with your investigation and make credibility determinations yourself.

After you have concluded your investigation, advise the parties of the results. If A's accusations appear to be valid, follow your policy. In other words, if B has committed harassment and discipline appears to be appropriate, proceed. Discipline in a circumstance like this can be anything from a warning to immediate termination. It is important that the company investigate and act in these circumstances since it will probably mitigate your liability, although it may not eliminate it entirely.

Document all steps taken during your investigation and all individuals to whom you have spoken. If, after your investigation, you wish to republish or restate your company policy to send a message to the employees, do so. However, do not name the employee or be so fact specific in this statement that you run the potential risk of a defamation suit from the harasser.[22]

Internal investigations are extremely important both for discipline and prior to and during litigation. These investigations should be handled carefully and sensitively and with the full cooperation of in-house or outside counsel.

Conducting Internal Investigations Prior to or During Litigation.
In the litigation setting, an internal investigation is necessary. The importance of a properly conducted investigation cannot be stressed enough. Here are a few simple rules when conducting an internal investigation in preparation for litigation:

◆ Determine the facts from management or exempt personnel as well as neutral fact witnesses.

◆ Select from your fact analysis those witnesses whom you wish to see.

◆ Interview all fact witnesses carefully.

◆ Do not accuse or be confrontational even though some witnesses may not be cooperative and may even support the plaintiff who is a present or former employee.

◆ Do not confront potentially adverse witnesses or the plaintiff in litigation unless you have carefully checked with outside counsel.

◆ Under no circumstances in litigation should you speak to the adverse party since he or she is already represented by counsel and it would be inappropriate to interview the person informally in the company.

Adverse or potentially adverse witnesses present a more difficult situation because you do not necessarily know that an individual may have adverse information until you begin to speak to them. If, for example, during your investigation you are speaking to someone and you then decide the person may be adverse to your position, stop the interview and advise the individual that he or she may face employment consequences in this regard and conclude your interview at that time.

For example, Company X is defending a sexual discrimination suit. A neutral fact witness, Bill White, is currently involved with another employee in an extramarital relationship. However, Bill may be helpful to your investigation in the present case.

How do you elicit facts and information from Bill? CAREFULLY!

Bill is obviously vulnerable and sensitive and will not respond positively if threatened. You should have another individual present when you question

Bill to verify the information. It is important to avoid accusations or confrontations with potential witnesses. Do not accuse Bill or anyone else of immoral conduct. Such accusations may cause you a defamation suit and stop him from assisting your investigation. Instead, try to put him at ease and invite him to be cooperative.

It is always a dilemma trying to decide whether or not to see potentially adverse internal witnesses. Question them carefully. Do not threaten them, and if they are represented by a union be aware of *Weingarten* rights.[23]

> NOTE: Do not accuse any employee of immoral or unethical conduct or illegal conduct during your internal investigation. If you do, you may invite a defamation suit.

Case Example

> The company president saw Jack, an employee, loading a box, with the company logo on it, into his car in the company parking lot at the lunch break. The president told the plant manager that he saw the employee stealing company merchandise and told him to deal with it. The manager, based upon the president's report, believed the employee was stealing and terminated Jack that same day for theft. Neither the manager nor the president ever saw the contents of the box or asked Jack about it. Only a few necessary people within the company were told that the reason for discharge was theft. However, Jack sued for defamation, claiming that false statements were made about him with reckless disregard for the truth.

Was the manager's action reasonable or did he act in a reckless manner?

In this case, the manager acted unreasonably. The employee was terminated without any inquiry as to the circumstances of why Jack had the box or as to what the box contained. In a similar case, it was found that the employee was improperly terminated and a jury awarded damages for defamation.[24] The manager should have questioned the employee and attempted to inspect the box. He also should have conducted a thorough investigation of the facts, including witness interviews, confronted the employee, and examined his personnel file. The manager's conduct was reckless since verification could easily have been done by examining the contents of the box.

> NOTE: Verify your facts before discharge. Make sure you are thorough.

Handling Recordkeeping

Keep detailed records of all correspondence regarding employees. You should retain the following items in your permanent employee records:

- Job application
- Resumé
- Customer correspondence

- Telephone memos from references
- Evaluations
- Disciplinary records
- Court records

Additional records regarding an employee handicap or disability should be retained but kept confidential. Such information should be made available only to managers (on a need-to-know basis) or medical personnel or for affirmative action reporting.

Determining Termination or Discipline

Employees should be advised of the reasons for discipline or termination. Often unexplained discipline may lead to a confused employee and/or lead to litigation. Where explanations are provided, employees at least understand the basis for your actions. If discipline is properly structured, it should be corrective and not viewed merely as punitive.

Handling Rumors

Do not repeat rumors, particularly those regarding personal health or habits. If an employer hears that coworker Oscar has AIDS, what do you do? Should you confront the employee and ask him or her about this condition? No. Unless the employee comes forward to request leave time or an accommodation, do nothing. As long as employees are doing their jobs at acceptable levels, there is no reason to discuss a possible health condition. In this situation, information or group education is recommended, but it should be done in a manner that does not identify the employee who may have a particular illness.

Monitoring Internal Media

You must monitor your internal media, such as bulletins, newsletters, newspapers, and computer bulletin boards.

Even items of parody may be actionable. In a recent college newspaper the students did a parody issue, and under the title "whoreline," it listed the name of a key faculty person with a phone number—call SEX-Y-ANYTIME. This individual was not amused and filed a lawsuit against the college for defamation and negligent supervision by the faculty. A state court held that parody was not actionable as defamation as long as no reasonable person would read such an account as a factual statement. There still is a strong and firm foundation for the First Amendment and absolute privilege under the U.S. Constitution. The court found that since there was no liability, there could be no negligent supervision.[25]

However, items in a company newsletter could be actionable if they are false and defamatory. While it is unlikely that many of your companies will have items as provocative as the "whoreline," you must maintain vigilance over what goes into your internal media and how they are disseminated. Items must be factual and accurate, or if they are placed in jest, it must be clear that no reasonable person would read them as factual to avoid defamation.

Defamation claims will continue to increase as employees seek other remedies for wrongful discharge, when relief is not otherwise available. The actions that you take to avoid or limit your liability for defamation must also be concerned with measures regarding hiring, supervision, and your overall reference policy. In addition, it is necessary to consider the emerging negligence theories, which are dealt with in Chapter 14.

GUIDELINES FOR MINIMIZING POTENTIAL DEFAMATION CLAIMS

Briefly, here are some steps that may be taken to avoid or minimize potential defamation claims:

1. Establish a company policy with regard to all written communications, with specific guidelines for statements that relate to employee discipline, performance, or conduct.

2. Establish a review procedure before any item is released to the public or to the general work force.

3. Ensure that such policies are complied with, and educate all supervisors and managers of the potential for defamation and other claims. Stress the verification of facts prior to making statements; a reasonable inquiry into the facts should suffice.

4. Restrict the dissemination of information about employees to those who have a direct or identifiable interest in the particular matter.

5. References should be handled in a consistent manner, providing only information that is accurate. Obtain a release from the employee if more detailed information is requested. Keep in mind the risk of negligent referral as well as defamation.

6. Performance evaluations should be undertaken on a regular basis and include only information relevant to performance—a standard format is strongly advised.

7. Confidentiality of personnel records and information should be strictly adhered to and enforced.

8. Internal investigations should be thorough and handled with sensitivity. All witnesses should be encouraged to be forthcoming - threatening behavior should be avoided.

9. Keep accurate records and retain all copies of memoranda and correspondence regarding employees.

10. Advise employee of the reasons for termination or discipline and have a reasonable basis for the employment action.

ENDNOTES

1. See *Walko v. Kean College*, 235 N.J. Super. 139, (Law Div. 1988), in which the court ruled that comments in the spoof issue of the college newspaper were not actionable for defamation. The court declared that "a parody or spoof that no reasonable person would read as a factual statement, or as anything other than a joke—albeit a bad joke—cannot be actionable as a defamation." The plaintiff had also raised claims of negligent supervision as well as claims for intentional infliction of emotional distress, which were dismissed.

2. See *Yip v. Pagano* 606 F.Supp. 1566 (D.N.J. 1985) *affirmed* 782 F.2d 1033 (3d Cir. 1986), *cert. denied* 476 U.S. 1141 (1986). In a recent case, a New Jersey court ruled that "as long as the allegedly defamatory matter would not have been published except to inform the legislative body, and the material is relevant to the legislative proceeding, the privilege attaches regardless of whether the material is solicited or subpoenaed and regardless of whether it is given under oath." *DeSantis v. Employees of Passaic County Welfare Association*, 237 N.J. Super. 550 (App. Div. 1990), *cert. denied*, 584 A.2d 231 (N.J. 1990). The Appellate Division in *DeSantis* extended the absolute privilege to witnesses in a legislative proceeding "where the legislative tribunal is exercising colorable jurisdiction even if it lacks actual jurisdiction."

3. See, for example, *Thompson v. Public Service Co. of Colorado*, 773 P.2d 1103 (Colo. Ct. App. 1988), *rev'd*, 800 P.2d 1299 (Colo. 1990).

4. See *Mendez v. M. S. Walker Inc.*, 528 N.E. 2d 891 (Mass. App. Ct. 1988), wherein the plant manager lost the conditional privilege to disseminate a defamatory charge of theft. The facts were that the company president saw a janitor putting company boxes into his car, and the janitor was fired for theft. However, the manager who undertook the firing failed to inspect the car or question the employee. He was found to have acted recklessly in failing to verify the inference that the janitor was stealing merchandise. The janitor had offered his car and home for inspection that same day. The defamation claim was upheld despite the fact only the foreman and the shop steward were made aware of the reason for the discharge. The company was held to a standard of making reasonable efforts to verify the truth of defamatory statements, where verification is possible.

5. The *New York Times v. Sullivan*, 376 U.S. 254, 279-80 (1964).

6. *Gertz v. Robert Welch, Inc.*, 418 U.S. 323, 342 (1974).

7. *Gertz*, 418 U.S. at 346-7.

8. See *D'Agrosa v. Newsday, Inc.*, 558 N.Y.S.2d 981 (App. Div. 1990), in which plaintiff sought compensation for being falsely identified by *Newsday* in its story about a "miracle baby" being born in 1974. *Newsday* asserted as a defense that its error was merely "a single instance." The single instance rule charges a party with a single dedication in connection with his or her trade occupation or profession. Because such a statement does not accuse a party of general ignorance or lack of skill, it is not deemed actionable in New York unless special damages are pleaded and proven. Since D'Agrosa failed to plead special damages enumerating his actual pecuniary losses, his complaint was dismissed with leave to file an amended complaint.

9. *Straitwell v. National Steel Corp.*, 869 F.2d 248 (4th Cir. 1989).

10. *Garziano v. Dupont*, 818 F.2d 380 (5th Cir. 1987).

11. *Garziano v. Dupont*, 818 F.2d 380 (5th Cir. 1987). However, the court of appeals reversed the jury award for damages but remanded the case for further consideration regarding the possibility of excessive publication to nonemployees at the workplace.

12. See *Lewis v. Equitable Life Assurance Society*, 389 N.W.2d 876 (Minn. 1986). As a reaction to *Lewis*, the Minnesota legislature adopted a statute that permits employees to request the "truthful" reasons for involuntary termination: these reasons cannot be the basis for a defamation action unless false reasons are provided.

13. In *Churchey v. Adolph Coors Co.*, 759 P.2d 1336 (Colo. 1988), Colorado adopted self-publication following *Lewis*. An employee's termination for "dishonesty" became an issue of fact over the use or abuse of sick leave.

14. See *Janklow v. Newsweek, Inc.*, 788 F.2d 1300, 1302 (8th Cir. 1986), *cert. denied* 107 S.Ct. 272 (1986).

15. *Lee v. Metropolitan Airport Commission*, 3 I.E.R. Cases (BNA) 1152, 1155 (Minn. Ct. Appeals 1988) *citing Janklow v. Newsweek, Inc.*, 788 F.2d 1300 (8th Cir. 1986).

16. See *Buckley v. Littell*, 539 F.2d 882 (2d Cir. 1976) *cert. denied* 429 U.S. 1062 (1977).

17. See *Lee v. Metropolitan Airport Commission* at note 15.

18. See, generally, *Tyler v. Macks Stores of South Carolina, Inc.*, 275 S.c 456, 272 S.E.3d 633 (S.C. 1980). (Management's silence after discharging an employee could provide a basis for a finding of defamation. The employee took a lie detector test; then his manager was discharged, and he was discharged thereafter. The employee claimed that this sequence of events gave others the impression that he had been discharged for unlawful activity.)

19. See *Kellums v. Freight Sales Centers*, 467 So. 816 (Fla. 1985).

20. Recently Federal Judge Politan ruled that a terminated employee would also be expected to follow the internal procedures delineated in an employee handbook. See *Fregara v. Aviation Business Jets, Inc.*, 764 F.Supp. 940 (D.N.J. 1991).

21. See *Garziano v. DuPont*, discussed in note 11, in which the harasser brought suit against the company and was successful.

22. See *Garziano v. DuPont*, note 11.

23. In *NLRB v. J. Weingarten, Inc.*, 420 U.S. 251 (1975), the Supreme Court ruled that an employee who was represented by a union has a right to union representation during disciplinary meetings. There may have been many rulings interpreting this right, and the penalties have been significantly reduced by the National Labor Relations Board. However, the principle of *Weingarten* remains intact and should be followed in a unionized setting.

24. See *Mendez v. M. S. Walker Inc.*, discussed in note 4.

25. *Walko v. Kean College*, see note 1.

14

PREVENTING NEGLIGENT HIRING, SUPERVISION, AND REFERRAL

Besides defamation, which we have dealt with at some length in Chapter 13, employers today need to be mindful of other emerging tort theories in the workplace regarding negligent hiring or retention, negligent supervision, and negligent referral. Simply stated, these torts embody the idea that the employer has a duty or obligation to provide information or supervision or simply to do something that may cause it liability if it fails to do so.

Case Study

You have adopted a "name, rank, and serial number" approach as a corporate policy on giving references. Your company receives a request from the XYZ Company, a competitor, for a reference. Following your corporate policy, the information released on employee Mary Jones is simply the dates of her employment and her position. You may or may not confirm her terminal salary. You have been asked for the reasons why she left or was terminated and have stated that no reasons are given as a matter of company policy.

What your records reveal, but you did not state, is that Mary was terminated for masterminding a pilfering ring in which she assisted others in stealing company property which went out at night on delivery trucks. This could have included dishes, ashtrays, furniture, and miscellaneous items which would be hard to check with your multifacility and multimillion-dollar inventory plant. Since your evidence was not airtight and you did not prosecute, you felt it best to say nothing.

Mary has applied for a job as director of security at your competitor's furniture warehouse. You were told during the reference inquiry her job would be to supervise and monitor all inventories and employee integrity.

By saying nothing, will you have a problem? After you have read this chapter, you will be able to answer this question.

HOW TO HANDLE NEGLIGENT HIRING CLAIMS

Negligent hiring or retention of an employee has generally been held to apply where an individual who is incompetent or unfit for a job causes injury to a third person and this injury was proximately caused by the employer's negligence.[1]

Defining the Doctrine of Negligent Hiring

The doctrine of negligent hiring is an extension of tort theory from personal injury cases. The standard is as follows:

Persons must use reasonable care in the employment of *all instrumentalities— including people as well as machinery*—where members of the public may be expected to come into contact with such instrumentalities. An employer whose employees are brought into contact with members of the public, in the normal course of their employment, is responsible for exercising reasonable care in the selection and/or retention of such employees.

The claim of negligent hiring is derived in part from the well-established *respondeat superior* cases. In such cases, the employer may be responsible for injuries to third parties caused by an employee acting *within* the scope of his or her authority or employment. For example, Employee A, driving the company truck, while making deliveries hits a car with passengers. The employer is generally liable for the injuries to the other car's driver and passengers, assuming the employee is at fault.

Negligent hiring is similar to that rule but differs with regard to the scope of the nature and extent of the employer's duty to third parties. In a negligence context, the employee need not necessarily be acting within the scope of his employment; it may be sufficient if his employment status permits him access or places him in a position where he does harm. The next section sets out the factors a plaintiff needs to establish to bring a claim for negligent hiring.

Often a claim of negligent hiring is used in combination with other causes of action like defamation or wrongful discharge. There are numerous strategic reasons why plaintiff's attorney adds these other causes of action which may vary in different jurisdictions.

Identifying the Elements of a Negligent Hire Lawsuit

A plaintiff claiming negligent hire must establish the following factors:

- Existence of an employer-employee relationship
- A duty of the employer to third party
- Foreseeability of harm to third persons
- Proximate cause or failure by the employer to do something which was the cause of injury
- Injury

NOTE: The doctrine of negligent hire significantly expands liability for employers beyond the scope of employment.

Proving the Existence of an Employer-Employee Relationship. An employer-employee relationship is ordinarily easy to prove. The degree of control and direction of an individual is the most significant factor.

However, where the employer has retained an independent contractor, it may be liable in the following situations:

- ♦ When hiring party retains control over some or all of the work
- ♦ When the injury to an employee of an independent contractor was caused or contributed to by an act or omission of the contractor pursuant to negligent orders given by the hiring party
- ♦ When hiring party does not exercise reasonable care to hire a competent contractor or in circumstances involving risk of physical injury

Accepting Duty and Foreseeability. The employer owes a duty to all persons who may foreseeably be harmed to hire and retain competent and safe employees. The test to determine whether an employer owes a plaintiff a duty to exercise reasonable care in the selection of employees is

whether a reasonably prudent and careful person, under the same or similar circumstances, could have anticipated that an injury to the plaintiff or those in a like situation would probably result from his conduct.[2]

Among those typically included as foreseeable are business invitees, clients, or customers. Furthermore, the extent of the duty increases as frequency or likelihood of employee contact with the public increases.[3] Often the determination of whether or not the third party or injury was foreseeable is made in hindsight.

Defining Breach of Duty. The doctrine is limited to the extent that an employer may be liable only where the employer knew or had reason to know of a particular unfitness, incompetence, or dangerous attributes (or propensities) of an employee and could reasonably have foreseen such qualities creating a risk of harm to others.

Such knowledge can be shown through actual or constructive knowledge of the employee's proclivities. *Actual knowledge* exists where the employer has personally witnessed the dangerous propensities of the employee or possesses evidence of same. *Constructive knowledge* can be demonstrated by providing that a reasonable investigation would have alerted the employer.

For instance, in the example of Mary, if a new employer became aware of her employment history, a prudent employer would have known that the risk of injury was great.

A more graphic example, unfortunately, demonstrates the point:

Case Example

In a recent case, a company was found liable for negligent hire where the sexual assault and murder of a 12-year-old boy was committed by one of its employees. The employee had been employed on a work release program. He completed government sponsored training and had been originally hired for carpentry work at an apartment complex. Later, he was also given some security duties because there had been a problem with vandalism in the complex. The security duties included having keys and access to various apartments.

However, the employer should have been concerned about this particular individual because he had been sentenced to serve 30 years for homicide prior to his participation in the work release program and on other occasions had made violent and/or homosexual remarks about certain tenants in the complex.[4]

In that case, the employer should have foreseen a potential problem. The employee had served his time and had demonstrated through the work release program his carpentry skills and ability to be brought back into society. Nonetheless, he had been convicted of a serious and violent crime and had made comments which were known to the employer and which should have tipped off the employer to a potential problem.

Based upon these violent threats, the employer had notice of and should have foreseen a problem. Simply put, the employer knew of the defendant's threats and did nothing. Unfortunately, as a result, a 12-year-old boy was murdered.

In that sad case, the court held that the employer had a duty to select employees who were competent and fit for the work assigned to them. Thus, the difficulty did not arise when the individual was hired to perform carpentry work. The problem arose only when there was a change or addition to the duties of that individual and he was given security tasks and access to third persons which a prudent employer, based upon its knowledge of the individual, should have precluded.

The following are some legal tips which emerge from cases:

♦ To establish a negligent hire situation there must be found a *nexus* between the job duties and the resulting harm.

♦ Where the employer has notice of an individual's past problems or dangerous propensities, it obviously acts at its peril if it places that individual where harm can result to third persons.

♦ Claims for negligent hire have resulted where injuries like rape, assault, or bodily harm have been caused by employees to other individuals.

In many other circumstances, apartment complex owners have been found liable where tenants have been raped by employees for whom the employer has failed to make an adequate background check. Such failure on the part of the employer where information is known or should have been known, and danger or harm results to an innocent third person can result in a claim of negligent hire.

Consider the case where an individual had been incarcerated for armed robbery and then gained employment in a low-level custodial position in an apartment complex. Only a cursory background check of his driving record was made. However, such a position is one of trust and usually provides the custodian with pass keys and access to all apartments. He gets into several abusive arguments with residents. One resident is seriously injured when the custodian, after an argument, enters the apartment and shoots the resident in the leg.

Did the employer fail to investigate adequately the custodian's background, and was there a duty to investigate beyond his driving record?

The employer acted negligently in failing to inquire at least into his past work record and find out if or why there were any gaps in his employment history. In addition, a cursory check of a driving record would not reveal much about an employee nor was it related to his duties. A relatively simple routine background check should have revealed the armed robbery conviction. The negligence by the employer has a nexus to the resident's injury and was foreseeable when a person with a violent background is hired. The employer's failure to check the employee's history properly renders him liable for the damage and injury suffered by the resident. In cases where the individual has violent propensities as evidenced by having served prison time for serious and/or potentially relevant crimes, great care should be exercised.

In the situation just described, it is foreseeable and plausible that the caretaker might cause injury to others and he had unchecked access to apartments. Some additional lessons emerge from this example:

♦ Background checks are extremely important and should not be neglected either for lack of personnel or resources. An inadequate background check may result in negligence and liability against the employer.

◆ If your company adopts the socially conscious policy of hiring ex-con-victs (and it certainly should in most positions), great care should be taken in considering which positions they will be assigned to. Additionally, the job duties for each position should be carefully examined to attempt to eliminate inappropriate duties so that access to third persons and/or the possessions of third persons are not given to individuals who have exhibited violent conduct in the past.

Establishing Causation. The injured party must show that his or her injuries were caused by the employee and that the characteristics of the employee that were responsible for the injury were known or should have been known by the employer and that such characteristics were likely to cause harm. In other words, that employee was capable of or inclined to cause injury and the employer knew or should have known that. However, it is not enough for the plaintiff to show only that the employee was incompetent, had a criminal record, or was dishonest.

> NOTE: An employee's prior conviction should not automatically make him or her ineligible to be employed. In fact, many states prohibit the use of arrest records and limit the use of conviction records in employment decisions. Thus, if an employee has an arrest or conviction, the nature of the offense and length of elapsed time since the offense, are important factors in evaluating whether an employee could be a risk to the public.[5]

Defining Harm. The employee's actions must result in some quantifiable injury, be it physical or psychological. In the absence of injury, the employer is not liable for negligent hiring. However, if an incident occurs where a third party is threatened, the employer is on notice of a problem if such an incident should recur with more serious consequences.

ESTABLISHING A NEGLIGENT RETENTION CLAIM

A claim of negligent retention requires the same factors and analysis as a negligent hiring claim. However, a negligent retention claim arises where an employee has injured a person or property, or where the employer owes a duty to the third party to discharge a dangerous or incompetent employee after becoming aware of the dangerous or incompetent nature of that employee. This usually occurs where a background investigation would not have or did not reveal the potential danger posed by the employee, but the employer had knowledge of same due to the employee's conduct after hire.

Case Study

Bob, employed six years as a line supervisor, came to the job with good references. A routine check showed no criminal record or history of violence. He is divorced and has dated several women in the plant. He also has gotten into shoving matches with male coworkers. Management has received numerous complaints alleging that Bob uses vulgar language, is constantly referring to various parts of the female body, and engages in inappropriate touching. At least 5 female employees have complained of sexual harassment by Bob. He supervises 50 people, 20 of whom are female.

Recently, Bob who had been pursuing Anne for a date, struck her across the face, knocked her down, and broke her arm. Her case will likely be covered by workers' compensation unless gross negligence by the employer is found.

Anne, who had repeatedly complained of Bob's conduct, alleges the company was well aware of Bob's sexual misconduct and his propensity to shove employees who did not agree with him. She intends to sue the company for her injuries and mental anguish.

What liability does the company face, (it had adequately investigated Bob at time of hire and he had a good record for four years)?

There are a number of claims Anne may bring, including sexual harassment under Title VII, workers' compensation, and negligent retention. Her negligent retention claim, if not preempted by the other claims, is based on the company's failure to discipline or discharge Bob for his gross misconduct involving female employees. The company had knowledge of his causing harm, yet it retained him in a position of authority. It was clear from the complaints received and Bob's behavior that sooner or later he could physically injure a female employee. The fact that he had not done so in the past is overshadowed by the overall pattern of his behavior. It was foreseeable that Bob would harm female employees. He had already inflicted psychological harm even if he had not physically caused Anne's injury. Several female employees suffered psychological damage that would be actionable under a negligent retention action.

How Your Company Can Avoid Negligent Retention Claims

The single most important thing you must do is make an appropriate inquiry into the background and references of each and every employee.

You may feel that it is difficult to do; you have to make quick decisions on many positions and do not want or have the time or money to invest for low-level positions.

Unfortunately, in this increasingly litigious society, employers and personnel professionals have to be cautious and ever mindful of litigation at all levels by employees and former employees when they lose a job, are disciplined, or feel that they have been slighted. With regard to negligent hiring, employers must be particularly careful because serious injury and/or harm may result to a tenant, a customer, or innocent third person entering a corporate facility. Thus, unchecked hiring and placement of individuals in all levels of positions should be avoided.

If you are using an employment agency, your company still has a duty to examine a potential employee's past employment record and check references of all employees and new hires. You are not insulated by hiring through an employment agency, although there probably would be joint and several liability. Under the law, the most prudent approach is to exercise care and your duty to inquire.

To inquire, you should make some minimum investigation into the background of a potential employee. The standards of inquiry increase as the level of exposure to third parties increases. For example, a data entry operator who has no interaction with the public and only minimal interaction with co-workers probably requires almost no investigation.

On the other hand, a bus driver or security guard is in a job that has frequent contact with the public or people being served and requires a more substantial investigation that may include a criminal record check. Where conduct with the public is incidental, an independent investigation may not be required. In such cases, the employer may rely on past employment information and personal data supplied by the employee. However, the employer at a minimum should make an effort to confirm the information supplied and check references where possible.

The type of inquiry and background check conducted should be based upon the job and prudence. Not every job requires the same level of intrusion and checking. If a security position is involved, whether it involves access to customers or apartments, common sense should dictate that your inquiry and examination be thorough, careful and cautious.

Hiring an Employee With a Criminal Record. Where you are considering hiring someone with a serious criminal record, extreme caution should be used. You may ask if it is impermissible to deny employment to somebody simply because they have a criminal record. The answer depends upon where your facility is located. Different states have adopted different laws in this regard. Merely making an inquiry into a criminal record may be impermissible depending upon the circumstances.

For example, consider New York. Under the New York Corrections Law, Section 752, an employer cannot deny employment simply because of a prior conviction unless

♦ There is a direct relationship between the offense and job sought

♦ Hiring the individual would involve unreasonable risk to property or the safety or welfare of specific individuals or the general public

So far, even in a state like New York, employers would not be precluded from making an inquiry and denying employment where individuals would be placed in security positions where their criminal pasts and propensities should set off lights and sirens of alarm.

The New York law is even more specific. It provides specific factors which the employer may consider in making such a decision:

- ♦ The public policy of the state is to encourage the hiring of ex-convicts.

- ♦ Employers should consider the specific duties and the responsibilities of the position in question.

- ♦ The employer should consider the relationship between the offenses and the individual's fitness for the job.[6]

- ♦ The seriousness of the offenses should be considered.

- ♦ Consideration must be given to the legitimate interests of the private employer in protecting private property and the safety and welfare of individuals and the general public.[7]

Alas employers in New York are still not out of the woods because the New York Human Rights Law prohibits questions about arrests and discriminating against individuals simply because of prior incarceration.[8] Obviously, employers in New York and all jurisdictions should be mindful of the relevance of their inquiry to the position in question. Where prudence and common sense have been used, problems rarely arise.

Employers should make adequate inquiry particularly for positions which involve protection of private property, safety, and/or the welfare of the general public.

Is greater scrutiny or inquiry required in filling public safety positions? One answer to this question is illustrated in the following example.

Case Example

A woman was raped by a police officer; she sued the town, its mayor, the police chief, and individual defendants.

A thorough background check of prior employment would have revealed that the defendant had been detained in California for indecent exposure prior to his employment and that he had resigned from a police department after refusing to take a polygraph test. The suit against municipal officials was based upon negligent hiring under federal law. Despite a judgment of $4 million against the individual defendant, summary judgment was granted on the plaintiff's case in favor of all other defendants because the court found that there was no gross negligence in its hiring practices.

The town had complied with Texas police standards on background checks except it went back 5 years instead of to the age of 16. The defendant had been examined for psychological fitness, and all references were checked within that time frame, including his ex-wife. A fingerprint check was done, and no negatives were turned up within the parameters of the Texas police standards.[9]

Municipal employers and officials are generally protected from liability under the negligent hire doctrine as long as routine standard procedures for the hiring of individuals are followed. Thus, liability of municipal employers can be avoided even where more detailed scrutiny would have revealed a problem if appropriate procedures have been followed.

Where a Victim is a Co-worker. If you have a case of a co-worker being injured by an employee, the workers' compensation law in your state may bar the co-worker's claim for negligent hiring or retention.[10] Some exceptions may occur such as in cases of gross negligence of the employer that may allow a direct civil suit against the employer outside of the workers' compensation scheme. For further discussion see Chapter 23 which deals directly with workers' compensation and its exceptions.

How to Conduct Background Checks of Applicants

To conduct a thorough background check, you should examine references, review certification, and, if applicable, check criminal records.

Examining References. *Always* check the references an applicant provides. Although many employers are reluctant to give negative information about a former employee, many may say enough for you to get a sense of the type of employee the applicant was. Just checking employment dates, position, and duties is helpful if it conflicts with the information provided by the applicant. If necessary, due to the sensitivity or importance of the position, obtain permission or a release from the applicant which permits you to obtain more detailed information from his or her former employers.

With regard to your own employees who are discharged, you should discuss references with them. It is generally a safe course to agree on a statement and enter into a written agreement before employees move on. Such a procedure might be incorporated into your exit interview process to avoid future confusion and litigation. Releases should be provided and signed off on by former employees before you give out any information. A copy of a proposed form of release is shown in Exhibit 13.1.

Reviewing Certifications. Where licenses, certifications, and/or degrees are required for the position, you should routinely require certified copies of each license, certification, and degree.[11] Confirm authenticity of same with the awarding university, agency, or entity.

Examining a Criminal Record. The nature of the position should dictate the level of appropriate investigation. For example, child care, security, or financial-related positions may warrant or require by law, a criminal record check of the applicant. If an applicant presents a prior criminal record, do not automatically exclude that applicant.[12] Instead, review each and every offense as compared to the job duties and responsibilities. Also, examine the potential risk to the public and co-workers. Be wary of long periods of unemployment or gaps between jobs.

A company is not liable every time an injury results from the conduct of its employees. The injured party must establish that the injury was caused in some way by the breach of a duty owed by the employer to that party. In other words, the plaintiff must show that the employer had a duty to investigate an employee's background and knew of the employee's disposition that related to the injury inflicted. The injury and/or victim must have been reasonably foreseeable. This type of claim is still uncommon and difficult to prove.

HOW TO HANDLE NEGLIGENT SUPERVISION CLAIMS

"Negligent supervision" is the term used for two distinct types of claims. Since negligence is involved, this theory is analyzed in the same way as the negligent hiring claim. The personnel professional must be able to recognize such claims and be able to advise how to avoid them or respond to them should they occur. Negligent supervision is a recently created tort action, but it is anticipated that it will gain ground in jurisdictions favorable to employee rights.

Defining Negligent Supervision

There are generally two kinds of claims for negligent supervision:

1. Present or former employees protesting a discharge or discipline
2. Suits by third persons who are injured or harmed by your employee

In general, the employer may be found liable for failure to supervise and/or warn its employees prior to imposing discipline. Similarly, an employer may be liable under the doctrine of negligent supervision on a claim by a third person or for an injury caused by an employer's lack of supervision. The following case examples illustrate the two types of claims.

Case Example

A patient in therapy sued her treating therapist and her therapist's employer. The plaintiff had been under the care of a therapist for several years. After about four years of therapy and upon his advice she had sex with the therapist to relax her when she began to develop suicidal tendencies. The defendant's position at trial was that the sex was for therapeutic reasons only and that he never looked forward to it. He took the position that sexual intercourse was a bona fide part of her therapy.[13]

The court did not agree with the plaintiff that the mental health center was vicariously liable under the respondent superior doctrine because the therapist acted outside the scope of his authority. However, the court allowed the claims to continue for negligent hiring and supervision of the therapist.

Case Example

A discharged employee brought a wrongful termination action against a hospital employer. Among other claims, the employee asserts that the employer's willful failure to evaluate plaintiff breached an implied contract between the parties. The court found that the plaintiff was an employee-at-will and no duty was owed plaintiff that was breached by the employer's failure to conduct an evaluation and dismissed that claim.[14]

In the second Case Example, there was no finding of a duty owed to the plaintiff employee that evaluations be conducted by the employer. The employee was at-will and had no employment contract. In cases where an employment contract exists and provides that an employer will conduct performance evaluations and/or warnings will be issued prior to disciplinary action, a contract action is created, not a tort claim.[15]

The doctrine of negligent supervision does not mean that every employee has a right to some form of warning prior to every instance of discipline. The employer's policies, procedures, manual, or contract will determine that right. If there is a collective bargaining agreement or an employment manual, employees may have specific contractual rights in most jurisdictions to expect warnings and that certain conduct will be followed. There are still some exceptions to the rule.[16] Such contracts or employment manuals may require termination for just cause only. Similarly, employees may be entitled to an annual performance review. In such a case, employees must be advised of problems prior to termination or employers may face a lawsuit in this regard.[17]

NOTE: Review all employment applications, handbooks, personnel policies, and employment contracts for language that requires termination for just cause only, annual performance review, and/or policy to warn before discipline or termination occurs. As with all personnel policies, say only what you mean or intend to do—if your company follows an annual review policy, ensure that it is followed fully and fairly. Know the consequences of a warning policy—be sure to indicate what discipline, including termination, an employee may expect in the future. If you follow your policies consistently, you will avoid many claims such as negligent supervision.

Identifying Elements of a Negligent Supervision Claim

For an employer to be found liable for negligent supervision, the following elements must be established:

♦ There must be a duty owed to the plaintiff

♦ There must be a breach of that duty

♦ The breach must be the proximate cause

♦ There must be an injury

An employer may have liability if it discharges employees after receiving complaints from customers. The test and analysis are the same. You must determine whether a duty to warn or reprimand or suspend the employee was owed. To find such a duty or obligation, you must look to your corporate policy, your employment manual, or individual employment contracts or collective bargaining agreements. Also, certain states have imposed public policy exceptions to at-will terminations. Most plaintiffs will attempt to attack discipline and/or termination by a combination of theories, including defamation, negligent supervision, and wrongful discharge.

Where there have been customer complaints and they have been noted, if you generally take action based upon them, continue to do so. If, however, you have a collective bargaining agreement and certain rules and regulations apply prior to taking such measures, you must follow them. Likewise, if your manual provides for progressive discipline to be imposed in most circumstances, again, progressive discipline should be followed unless circumstances permit otherwise.

> NOTE: There is generally no duty to warn or initially reprimand an otherwise at-will employee unless some of the policy constraints which have been previously discussed apply.

Companies should be mindful that where a long-term employee is involved, the courts are more likely to find or impose a duty to warn or discipline prior to termination.[18]

HOW TO HANDLE A NEGLIGENT REFERRAL CLAIM

The doctrine of negligent referral was alluded to in the very first case study in this chapter involving Mary Jones. The key question that must be focused on by employers to understand this doctrine is what duty, if any, an employer has regarding references for former employees.

The difficulty in walking the fine line regarding references is that giving too much information may result in defamation suits or other claims. Too little information, especially where there is knowledge, may result in tort suits for negligent referral.

Defining and developing your corporate philosophy in this particular area is a difficult one and one in which great care and thought must be given. More employers still adhere to a name, rank, and serial number approach and would rather suffer the potential consequences from negligent referral suits. Such a position is certainly a plausible one, although the more cautious approach may be to provide pertinent information, especially where it is known and reasonably supported by evidence.

NOTE: If the employer fails to disclose the reasons for termination, and it is aware of deleterious and potentially dangerous information about the discharged employee, a prospective employer and/or third person may have a claim for negligent referral against the former employer if it is not revealed.

Identifying the Nature of the Claim

Negligent referral would be found only if a reason for termination created a foreseeable risk of harm in a subsequent job and failing to disclose the facts created that risk. Under such a scenario, the employer might be liable for a subsequent foreseeable injury under the doctrine of negligent referral. In sum, if you merely provide limited information and you know that a former employee is likely to be unfit for employment by a prospective employer in a particular position, you may be liable.

Case Study

An employment agency referred an individual for a position working with women even though it had been told by this candidate that he was incarcerated in the military in Germany because his German girlfriend charged him with rape and a military court sought to appease foreign women. Neither the agency or the prospective employer checked into his background carefully. Such a background check would have revealed that the employee/defendant had really been jailed for the rape of a fellow employee in the Army. The agency referred this individual for a position working with women but said that he was really not a rapist based upon its knowledge.

In this example, an employment agency may be liable for damages under the theory of negligent referral because it has a duty to check into an employee's background prior to recommending that employee as a candidate for a position with your company. Once the agency had breached its duty and referred the employee, a foreseeable injury occurred.

Such negligence will cause liability for employment agencies and employers. The employer also has a duty to follow up on reference checks.

NOTE: To limit claims, employers should investigate all claims of harassment and/or misconduct, especially when they have prior notice about individual conduct. Once a company is on notice, it acts at its peril and should act carefully.

SUGGESTIONS AND CHECKLIST TO AVOID EMPLOYMENT NEGLIGENCE

This is a complex and troublesome area. Employers are asked to walk a fine line between incurring liability for defamation, discrimination, breach of other employee's rights, and liability for harm to third parties, including co-workers, customers, and subsequent employers. This area of law is constantly evolving; however, the following suggestions are intended to aid the personnel professional in creating and maintaining measures to protect against negligent employment claims.

Negligent Hiring

1. Screen all employees.
2. Do a thorough background investigation, keeping in mind the degree of potential risk of harm. Beware of long gaps in employment history, ask applicant for an explanation.
3. Check all references.
4. Obtain a copy of all required licenses, certifications, and degrees; authenticate all degrees.
5. Inquire into criminal record only where necessary and to extent permitted by law. Where prior criminal records are involved, make a reasonable inquiry; if an individual has been convicted and incarcerated, get the facts.
6. Compare job duties with the offense(s) involved. Are the offenses relevant to the position? Focus your investigation on the position sought by the applicant.
7. If a prior criminal record suggests a risk to persons or safety, do not employ that individual. But do not automatically exclude individuals because of a criminal record. Follow state or local laws in this regard.[19]
8. In promotion, transfer, or change of duties situations,
   a. Review individual employee backgrounds before you make such a decision.
   b. Determine fitness for a particular job before making a reassignment. Caution will pay dividends.
   c. If you are making a change to a different position, check to see if additional contact with the public or safety will result; a background check may be required.

d. Document all aspects of your pre-hire investigation.

Negligent Supervision

1. In at-will employment situations, there may be an obligation to third persons to monitor employee conduct and behavior.

2. There is no obligation to warn in at-will situations prior to terminating an employee unless the following apply:

   a. There is an express or implied contract between your company and the employee.

   b. There are applicable personnel policies including manuals and/or employee handbooks.

   c. There is a relevant collective bargaining agreement covering the individual.

3. If there is a contract or a manual, follow its provisions.

4. If you fail to warn or provide an improper evaluation, your company may be liable for the summary dismissal of an employee.

5. Employer liability can be limited by providing regular or annual evaluations, which should be objective and written.

6. If the evaluations determine that performance has been unsatisfactory, be specific and have employee sign off on the report.

7. When dealing with a long-term employee who has had no negative evaluations or warnings, be cautious; ADEA or lack of supervision lawsuits could be brought.

8. Once you are aware of the negatives or the unfitness of a particular employee, discharge or discipline as appropriate.

9. Once you are on notice and have knowledge of the employee's deficiencies, but fail to act, you may be liable for negligent retention.

Negligent Referral

1. Develop a clear written reference policy to be followed in every case.

2. Keep accurate and detailed records of employee conduct.

3. When information is requested about a former employee, protect the company. One method is to have a written and signed agreement between the employee and the employer releasing the company from any liability if a request for information is presented. To avoid potential liability and difficulty, the safest course is to discuss a proposed reference and enter into a written agreement with former employees. Such a step might be incorporated into an exit interview.

4. Use facts only; do not describe a person's character or permit human resources personnel to give unauthorized information.

5. When providing references, focus on the reason for separation. You may limit the reference information to name, position, and dates of employment, but bear in mind the liability for negligent referral discussed earlier.

6. Balance the information provided against the possibility of a defamation claim or negligent referral suit.

NOTE: A mixed policy where you provide either a neutral or positive reference may in itself be defamatory.

7. In general, avoid oral discussions regarding reference checks. Respond in writing only to written requests. Make sure this policy is known and adopted throughout the company and disseminated. For managers and supervisors who violate this policy, take action and discipline them.

8. Provide information only when a release has been provided to you by a former employee. See the sample release agreement provided in Exhibit 13.1.

In general, the trend will be to continue to impose greater liability on employers for violation of ever more tort standards in the workplace. Employees will continue to seek relief in ever-increasing numbers for termination and possibly discipline especially in light of the diminished role of trade unions in the United States.

ENDNOTES

1. Some of the states that have adopted this doctrine are Alabama, Colorado, Florida, Georgia, Maryland, Missouri, New Jersey, New York, Oklahoma, Tennessee, Texas, and Utah.

2. See *DiCosala v. Kay*, 91 N.J. 159, 450 A.2d 508 (1982), *quoting Hill v. Laskin*, 75 N.J. 139, 380 A.2d 1107, 1109 (1977). See also, *Simmons v. Baltimore Orioles, Inc.*, 712 F.Supp. 79 (W.D.Va. 1989) for example of an incident that was not reasonably foreseeable.

3. *Williams v. Feather Sound, Inc.*, 386 So.2d 1238 (Fla. 1980).

4. See *Henley v. Prince George's County*, 305 Md. 320 (1986).

5. See Chapter 4, which discusses use of arrest and conviction records of applicants and employees.

6. Applying these criteria, for example, should have tipped off the employer that it was imprudent to place a dangerous felon in a position with security clearance and access to the private possessions and persons living in an apartment complex.

7. N.Y. Corrections Law, Art. 23-A, §753.

8. N.Y. Human Rights Law, §296(16).

9. See *Wassum v. Bellaire, Texas*, 861 F.2d 453 (5th Cir. 1988).

10. See *Chinnery v. Government of Virgin Islands*, 865 F.2d 68 (3d Cir. 1989) (co-worker harmed by conduct of employee—workers' compensation is exclusive remedy and bars suit for negligent hiring).

11. Imagine the embarrassment recently when some very prestigious national law firms found that attorneys who had progressed within their ranks had never passed the bar. A simple check of credentials would have remedied such a problem.

12. See *Island City Flying Service v. General Electric Credit Corp.*, 6 I.E.R. Cases (BNA) 1313, 1315 (Fla. S.Ct. 1991) (the type of criminal offense that applicant/employee had committed should be related to the type of injury incurred—there needs to be a connection and foreseeability between the offense and the conduct). See also note 5.

13. See *Cosgrove v. Lawrence*, 214 N.J. Super. 670 (Law Div. 1986).

14. *Murray v. Bridgeport Hospital*, 40 Conn. Sup. 56, 480 A.2d 610 (1984).

15. See *Murray*, note 14; *Pratt v. Delta Air Lines, Inc.*, 675 F.Supp 991 (D.Md. 1987) (employer is bound in contract by terms of employee's employment application, but contract reserved right of employer to terminate employee at any time without notice and employee had received reports on previous misconduct).

16. The state of New York has held fast to its refusal to grant any rights to employees-at-will. See *Murphy v. American Home Products Corporation*, 58 N.Y.2d 293, 461 N.Y.S.2d 232 (1983).

17. See *Chamberlain v. Bissell, Inc.*, 547 F.Supp 1067 (W.D. Mich. 1982), wherein a 51-year-old employee terminated for just cause still prevailed on his negligence claim that employer was negligent with regard to his job evaluation in failing to inform employee that discharge was being considered or was possible without a rapid or drastic change in his job performance. The court ruled that while a complete failure to perform a contractual obligation is actionable only as a breach of contract, the negligent performance of the obligation is actionable as a tort. Also, see *Valdov v. Albanese*, unpublished opinion (D.N.J. 1985), in which the Court held that a public employer has constitutional duties to provide due process to its employees when they have been terminated and comments and knowledge about that termination have been made public.

18. See *Pratt v. Delta Airlines*, note 15.

19. See discussion *infra* on New York State Labor Law and Executive Law, which provides that you cannot refuse to hire individuals with criminal records merely for that reason.

15

A GUIDE TO SAFETY AND HEALTH LAWS

Safety and health issues are ever-present concerns of employers and employees in the workplace. Dangers to health and safety are not always visible, and all threats to safety and health should be treated as a serious matter and handled promptly. The costs of on-the-job injuries are staggering in terms of health care costs and loss of production. Thus, it behooves every employer to ensure a safe and healthy workplace. The government thinks so too and has enacted federal and state laws that define the employer's obligations in maintaining a safe and healthy work environment.

This chapter will address the federal and state laws that regulate safety and health issues in the workplace as well employee right to know laws. Specific health and safety issues such as smoking in the workplace, AIDS, fetal protection policies, and other relevant issues are discussed in this chapter.

A GUIDE TO THE OCCUPATIONAL SAFETY AND HEALTH ACT

The federal law that dominates the area of safety and health in the workplace is the Occupational Safety and Health Act of 1970, known as OSHA, 29 U.S.C. §651, *et seq*. It is a comprehensive regulatory scheme that provides remedial as well as preventive measures to protect the health and safety of the worker.

OSHA has recently increased its enforcement and the amount of fines for violations. Thus, when an incident occurs involving safety or health, you should think about the following questions:

- ◆ What or who is OSHA?
- ◆ What are my obligations as an employer?
- ◆ Who and what do I report to OSHA?
- ◆ Can my premises be searched/inspected?
- ◆ Does the OSHA inspector need a warrant?
- ◆ What happens if I refuse to let the inspector in?
- ◆ Are there fines and penalties for OSHA violations?

Determining Who Is Covered

The Occupational Safety and Health Act of 1970 (the Act) requires *all* private employers whose business affects interstate commerce to provide their employees with safe working conditions. The Act's provisions mandate compliance with specific standards as well as a broad duty to provide employees a place of employment free from recognized hazards that are causing, or are likely to cause, death or serious harm to employees. Most other federal safety and health standards other than those relating to workers' compensation and disability rights and liabilities are superseded by the provisions set forth in OSHA.

Exemptions from OSHA Coverage. OSHA generally applies to private employers with at least one employee. However, certain employers with no more than ten employees are exempt from certain OSHA requirements and penalties (for example, from the requirement of maintaining a log and summary and supplementary records regarding employee illness and injury). OSHA also exempts from coverage federal, state, and local government employers; by its terms, the Act does not apply to working conditions regulated by federal agencies other than the Occupational Safety and Health Administration, such as the federal Mine Safety and Health Administration (mining conditions) and the U.S. Coast Guard (for seamen). OSHA requirements are applicable, however, in the absence of other statutorily intended safety and/or health protection. OSHA regulations exempt homeowners employing domestic employees (who do tasks such as house-cleaning or child care.)

How the Act Is Administered. The provisions of OSHA are promulgated and enforced by the Secretary of the Occupational Safety and Health Administration (the Administration), a branch of the U.S. Department of Labor. The Administration is empowered to investigate and inspect facilities to ensure compliance with the Act's regulations, and citations, pursuant to which a violator may request a hearing before an administrative law judge, are issued where noncompliance is determined to exist.

The Occupational Safety and Health Review Commission (OSHRC, or the Commission), also established by the Act, serves as a quasi-judicial system that adjudicates cases arising from the issuance of such citations. The Commission is independent, and is comprised of three presidential appointees; it can issue orders; uphold, vacate, or modify OSHA citations; and direct other relief and penalties. Moreover, each state has the right to adopt (pursuant to Department of Labor approval) its own safety and health standards which replace the corresponding federal standards.

How the Act is Enforced

The country is divided into regions or areas, each headed by a director who decides whether to issue a citation, determines the penalties to be assessed, and establishes a date for abatement of each violation. Citations must be served on the employer no later than 6 months after the date of the alleged violation.

Assessing Penalties. There are several levels or categories of violations that depend on the seriousness of the nature of the violation. Penalties for violations are various:

- De minimis notice with no monetary fine
- Serious and nonserious—up to $1,000 fines
- Repeated or willful violations—up to $10,000
- Failure to abate notice—up to $1,000 per day

The factors that are considered in assessing the penalty include good faith of the employer, the gravity of the violation, and the employer's past history and size. There are also criminal sanctions for willful violations that resulted in the death of an employee.

Contesting a Citation. The employer or employee (or his or her authorized representative, for example, a union) have 15 working days in which to contest a citation as a whole or any part of it. If no notice of contest is received, the citation becomes final and is not subject to review. Upon filing a notice of contest in good faith, the abatement order is tolled and a hearing is scheduled. The Occupational Safety and Health Review Commission, (OSHRC) a quasi-judicial independent administrative agency, adjudicates violations and reviews periods of abatement ordered for such violations and proposed penalties, if contested by the employer, employee, or an authorized representative of the employee.

If the employer is unable to comply with an abatement requirement after it has become a final order, it may file a petition for modification of abatement

(PMA). If the PMA is contested by the Secretary of Labor or an employee, a hearing is held to determine whether the abatement requirement should be modified.

Applying for a Variance. Employers may also petition the Secretary of Labor for a variance from any standard promulgated under the Act. A temporary variance may be issued if the employer is unable to comply because of unavailability of workers, facilities, or equipment; is making every effort to protect its employees from hazards covered by the standard; and has an effective program to bring the workplace into compliance as soon as possible. A permanent variance will issue only if the Secretary determines that the workplace is as safe as it would be by compliance with the established standard.

From time to time, Congress will enact limited exemptions for small employers (generally with ten employees or fewer) or limits assessing penalties for first-time nonserious violations unless numerous violations are found during the inspection.

Enumerating Employee Rights. Under the Act, employees have numerous rights, including

- ♦ Filing a complaint with OSHA
- ♦ Bringing an action in federal court to compel the Secretary to conduct an inspection where imminent danger exists
- ♦ Participating in an inspection tour
- ♦ Requesting an informal closing conference
- ♦ Having the employer post all citations
- ♦ Filing a notice of contest to the abatement period
- ♦ Opposing settlements and withdrawals
- ♦ Seeking judicial review of an OSHRC decision
- ♦ Being notified of variance applications, notices of contests, and PMAs
- ♦ Participating in the standards-setting process
- ♦ Having an employer's annual summary of injuries and illnesses posted

Additional rights exist where there is a monitoring requirement for exposure to toxic materials. Employees must

- ♦ Be allowed to participate in the monitoring
- ♦ Have access to information obtained
- ♦ Be informed whenever they are being exposed to dangerous levels of toxins

Furthermore, employees or their authorized representatives may request a determination by the Department of Health whether there are toxic substances in the workplace.

Prohibiting Retaliation. The Act prohibits employers from retaliating or subjecting employees to adverse treatment for exercising their statutory rights. An employer may not be discriminated against for filing a complaint, testifying, participating in an agency proceeding, or exercising any other right. Complaints for such discrimination may be filed with the OSHA area director.[1] The remedies available for an employee discriminated against include rehiring, reinstatement, backpay, and injunctive relief.

How to Handle an Employee's Refusal to Work. In conjunction with the statutory protection against retaliation, employees may refuse to work in certain circumstances. Under an OSHA regulation, an employee may not be disciplined for refusing to work if

◆ The employee has a reasonable belief, in good faith, that performing the assigned work would involve a real danger of death or serious injury

◆ The employee was unable to obtain correction of the condition by the employer

◆ There is insufficient time to eliminate the danger through resort to regular statutory enforcement channels[2]

Case Study

Joe is a janitor at an appliance manufacturing plant. From time to time he is required to go up on permanent scaffolding and retrieve objects that have fallen from an overhead conveyor belt into a net suspended 20 feet above the plant floor. He usually does this task with a partner—one holds the other as he leans over the net with a pole designed to retrieve the objects.

Joe has complained several times that this practice is unsafe. One day his partner slips and almost falls from the scaffolding. The next week, Joe is directed to retrieve objects from the net, but his regular partner is out that day. He is to be assisted by a new janitor who does not have experience with this type of work. Joe refuses to go up the scaffolding for this task and complains that it is unsafe. He says that he should have specifically designed safety equipment. His supervisor instructs him to clock out and go home. The next day Joe reports for work and is advised that he has been terminated for insubordination.

Is Joe's refusal to work protected under the guidelines set out earlier? What is the appropriate response by the supervisor in this situation?

Under the guidelines promulgated under OSHA, Joe's refusal to work would be considered reasonable. Joe was asked to work with an inexperienced partner;

his partner had almost fallen the week before; Joe has complained previously that this practice was unsafe; there is no evidence that the task could not wait while alternative safety measures considered, but, he was unable to get the employer to correct the problem; and finally there was risk of serious bodily injury.

The supervisor should have reported Joe's concerns to the company's health and safety director to review the complaint and make alternative safety arrangements, if possible. It is generally best to try to resolve a conflict rather than simply to dismiss an employee's safety concerns.

However, the enforceability of this regulation is not clear.[3] In any event, workers may have other sources of protection for a refusal to work, including Labor Management Relations Act, Section 502 (employees who quit work in good faith because abnormally dangerous conditions are protected); National Labor Relations Act, Section 8(a)(1) (a discharge based on a refusal to continue working under hazardous conditions is a violation); or a union contract, which may provide a right to refuse hazardous work.

> NOTE: Employers who refuse to comply with OSHA standards or valid safety rules implemented by the employer may be disciplined for such conduct under the Act.

Explaining Preemption. The OSHA law preempts any state agency or court from asserting jurisdiction over any occupational safety and health issue with respect to which a federal standard has been issued pursuant to the Act. However, states are permitted under the Act to assume responsibility for development and enforcement of occupational safety and health standards and issues which are at least as effective as standards promulgated under the Act. (See the discussion later in this chapter.)

How to Comply with Procedural and Recordkeeping Requirements

There are several procedural requirements, like conducting hearings and review; hearing appeals; determining the right to settlement; and fulfilling recordkeeping requirements with which the employer must comply.

Conducting Hearings. An employer who has received an OSHA citation is entitled to contest, within 15 days, whether a violation occurred, the date set for abatement of the allegedly harmful condition, and the proposed penalty. The employer must notify the Administration's area director, who in turn notifies the Review Commission of the intent to contest the citation. Once the case is docketed by the Commission, the employer must post a notice to its employees of both the citation and the intent to contest so that affected workers are able to participate if they so choose.

The Secretary must file a written complaint, setting forth detailed allegations of violation, with the Commission within 30 days after the employer indicates its intent to contest. The employer then has 30 days in which to file a written answer containing denials, admissions, and affirmative defenses with the Commission or the administrative law judge to which the case has been assigned. The employer may withdraw its notice of contest at any time, terminating any proceedings before the Commission. (Copies of all complaints, answers, and related notices must be sent to all parties interested in the action).

At the administrative hearing, the Secretary has the burden of proving by a preponderance of the evidence the following:

- Applicability of the cited standard
- Employer's failure to comply with that standard
- Access of employees to the condition regarding which a citation has been issued
- Employer's actual or constructive knowledge of the existence of the allegedly violative workplace condition

Review, Appeal, and Precedential Value of Determinations.

Once a decision has been rendered by the presiding administrative law judge, either party may petition for, or the Commission may independently direct, a review. If the Commission does not accept review, the administrative determination becomes a final order 30 days after its filing.

OSHRC, however, does not accord unreviewed administrative determinations any precedential value. If, however, the Commission does grant review and thereafter arrives at a determination of the case, that decision is accorded precedential value with respect to similar cases *nationwide* notwithstanding a decision by the U.S. Supreme Court overturning it.

A final order by the Commission can be appealed to the appropriate U.S. court of appeals within 60 days. If an administrative determination is overturned by a federal circuit court, it still retains its precedential value in other circuits.

Reaching a Settlement.

The employer and the Secretary have the right to settle pending cases at any time. Employees affected by the alleged violation are not entitled to participate in settlement negotiations or agreements, but may contest only the reasonableness of the agreed-upon date of abatement of the violative condition.

Recordkeeping Requirements.

OSHA regulations mandate that employers maintain accurate records of work-related deaths, injuries, and illnesses other than minor injuries and that they periodically report to the Administration summaries of those records. Furthermore, employers must retain all monitoring, exposure, and medical records relating to some 40,000 allegedly toxic or hazardous substances for periods of 30 years and longer and must make such records available to employees or their representatives.

> NOTE: If you have a question relating to the employer's obligations under OSHA, you should consult with the company's designated health and safety officer or an attorney.

Pursuant to the Act, employers with 11 or more employees must "maintain a log and summary of all recordable occupational injuries and illnesses."[4] The following terms are defined in the statute or regulations and are stated here for your convenience.[5]

"Recordable" occupational illnesses and injuries are defined by the regulations as those which result in

♦ Fatalities, regardless of the time between illness/injury death.

♦ Lost workdays.

♦ Transfer to another job, termination of employment, required medical treatment (other than first aid), or some loss of consciousness or restriction of work or motion.

♦ Diagnosed occupational illnesses reported to an employer but not classified as "fatalities" or "lost workday cases" are also recordable under the regulations.[6]

♦ "Medical treatment" is defined by the regulations as that administered by a physician or a registered professional under a physician's orders, other than first aid.[7]

♦ "First aid," even that administered by a physician or registered professional, is defined as one-time treatment and follow-up observation of scratches, cuts, burns, splinters, and the like which do not ordinarily require medical care. Although employers are granted reasonable discretion in determining whether injuries or illnesses are recordable, they are generally encouraged to resolve doubts in favor of reporting.

♦ The required "Log and Summary of Occupational Injuries and Illnesses" must be kept on a calendar year basis and must include data regarding the particular employee's job and illness/injury, as well as information concerning the total number of cases of each type of injury or illness. These numerical totals must be posted in each establishment from February 1 through March 1 of each year.

Furthermore, supplementary records must be kept for all other injuries or illnesses and must be available within six working days after the employer is notified that a recordable case has occurred.[8] Required information includes data regarding the employer, employee, or accident; specific details about the injury or illness, diagnosis, and treating physician; and the like. All annual and supplementary records must be maintained at each establishment for 5 years, available for Administration inspection. Failure to maintain these records properly may subject an employer to citations and/or penalties.

Moreover, within 48 hours after an employment-related fatality or accident resulting in the hospitalization of five or more employees, the employer must report the occurrence to the nearest OSHA office, describing the circumstances of the accident, the number of fatalities, and the number and extent of any injuries.[9] Falsification of or failure to maintain records may subject an employer to penalties, fines (of not more than $10,000), and/or imprisonment (not more than 6 months).

How to Handle OSHA Inspections and Warrants

When the OSHA inspector comes to your door and demands to be permitted to conduct an inspection of the premises but doesn't say why he or she is there, the employer needs to know when it is prudent to allow entry and when it may bar entry.

Case Study

The Molded Metal Company is a medium-sized sheet metal manufacturer that employs anywhere from 75 to 200 employees. Several of its processes can be dangerous, involving extreme heat, cutting metal, sparks, dust, and at times cramped conditions. There is no union at this plant. The employees have frequently complained of faulty ventilation, lack of masks to filter the dust, a shortage of protective gear, poor housekeeping, and not enough room to cut the metal safely. In the last 6 months alone there have been four injuries involving burns and cuts, two employees were overcome with dust and heat, and one employee reported metal shards in his eye. No one required hospitalization and all are back at work. However, a small group of employees are concerned that a serious accident may occur due to these conditions. Their requests for additional protective gear and a new ventilation system have not been answered.

One night an OSHA inspector comes to the plant's entrance, shows his identification, and says he is there to conduct an inspection. One shift is running and the supervisor refuses to permit the inspector in. The inspector returns the next day and is again turned away. He does not have a warrant. However, he observes dark gray smoke issuing from ventilator shafts. The company is sure that some of the employees called OSHA.

Consider the following questions:

♦ May the company refuse entrance to the inspector if he does not have a warrant?

♦ Do circumstances exist that give the inspector grounds to enter and inspect the premises?

♦ Has the company violated the law by refusing to allow the inspector to tour the facility?

This company should have instructed its supervisor to contact a company officer when the OSHA inspector came and either asked him to return when there was an officer present and/or to return with a warrant. Note that upon presentation of the proper credentials, an OSHA representative may enter without delay and at reasonable times any place where work is being performed.

The refusal to admit an OSHA inspector will not prevent an inspection; it will merely postpone it since a warrant is not difficult to obtain. In addition, the dark smoke may be sufficient to establish grounds for a warrantless inspection, especially if the complaint being acted upon involves smoke and/or ventilation. Under no circumstances is the company permitted to take any adverse action against an employee who makes a complaint to OSHA or otherwise exercises his or her rights under the law.

How OSHA Conducts Inspections. OSHA employs compliance safety and health officers who are authorized, upon presentation of proper credentials, to enter without delay and at reasonable times any workplace or environment where work is performed by an employee. These officers may inspect and investigate during regular working hours and at other reasonable times and in a reasonable manner any place of employment. They may also question privately any employer, representatives of an employer, or employees and review records required to be kept by the Act or which are directly related to the purpose of the inspection. The employer and an employee representative have a right to participate in the inspection tour.

How OSHA Issues Warrants and Notice. The provision authorizing inspections and entry by compliance officers has been limited by the constitutional right to be free from warrantless administrative searches. Moreover, the Act does not contemplate that advance notice of inspections be given. In fact, it is OSHA's view that unannounced inspections are crucial to promoting safe and healthful working conditions. However, advance notice may be provided in the following circumstances:

- In case of imminent danger, to allow immediate abatement
- For inspections *after* normal business hours
- Where special arrangements are needed
- Where notice is needed to ensure the presence of employer and employee representatives

The courts have established that unannounced or surprise inspections, which the majority are, require a warrant prior to any search of a workplace.[10]

A warrant may be based upon

- An employee complaint
- The Secretary's policy of "worst-first" inspections and lack of prior inspections
- The purpose of the Act and the nature of the business to be inspected

Exceptions to the warrant requirement include emergency, consent, and the open view doctrine.

Emergency. The prerequisite for an emergency-based inspection, which is invoked only in extreme cases, is a legitimate life-saving purpose. Thus, the emergency exception is limited to imminent dangers and other life-threatening exigencies *and* where it is impossible to obtain consent.

Consent. Most inspections are conducted with the consent of the employer. Valid consent constitutes a waiver to the Fourth Amendment prohibition against unreasonable search and seizure. Consent is so broadly interpreted that the failure to object to an inspection may constitute consent. Consent may be given by any competent management official, senior employee, foreman, or even a general contractor with regard to subcontractors' work areas. Although an employer may refuse to permit a warrantless search, there is doubt in the wisdom of withholding consent if there is some basis in believing the validity of the inspection.

Open view doctrine. The open view doctrine, under which an inspection may be conducted, turns on whether a business has a reasonable expectation of privacy. An official may lawfully note all evidence that is in plain view if the official has a right to be in that location. Outdoor property may be subject to warrantless inspections because it is in the open.

HOW TO COMPLY WITH STATE REGULATIONS OF SAFETY AND HEALTH

States are entitled to enact and administer occupational health and safety plans that are approved by the Administration and are at least as effective in providing protection to employees as comparable OSHA standards. States may also choose to enforce such approved plans in certain areas within their jurisdiction while retaining OSHA jurisdiction in the remaining areas. State occupational health and safety plans are entitled to receive up to 50 percent of their funding from federal grants and must adopt recordkeeping requirements that are almost identical to those of OSHA.

How States Get Their Plans Approved

State plans may not satisfy the stringent OSHA criteria immediately; those plans designated as "developmental" must establish that the appropriate steps will be taken to make the state plan qualify for OSHA approval within 3 years. During this period, the Administration, also acting as a "monitor," and the state agency administering the developmental plan have concurrent jurisdiction over the applicable activities within the state. Once a state plan is approved by the Administration, it must remain consistent with changes in the federal standards. The state requirements are periodically evaluated to ensure that its protections are at least as effective as those set forth in OSHA.

The statutory scheme requires states that desire to assume such responsibility to submit a plan to the Secretary. If a state's plan is approved, the state has jurisdiction with all the powers granted in OSHA over safety and health issues in the workplace, including the anti-discrimination provision.[11]

There are approximately 24 jurisdictions that have OSHA-approved plans covering both private and public employment: Alaska, Arizona, California, Hawaii, Indiana, Iowa, Kentucky, Maryland, Michigan, Minnesota, Nevada, New Mexico, North Carolina, Oregon, Puerto Rico, South Carolina, Tennessee, Utah, Vermont, Virginia, the Virgin Islands, Washington, and Wyoming. In addition, New York and Connecticut have approved plans that cover only state and local government employees.

> NOTE: Whenever an issue of health and safety arises, the personnel
> professional must consult the appropriate state and local laws, as well
> as the federal OSHA law and regulations. Your state may have more
> stringent compliance requirements.

Although OSHA governs almost every aspect of safety and health on the job, there remain a few areas where a state has chosen to regulate that OSHA has not yet reached or the state has imposed substantially greater protections. The state may have a plan that exceeds the requirements of OSHA, or it may regulate areas that are not covered under OSHA. See the next chapter for a discussion on specific health and safety issues in the workplace.

HOW TO COMPLY WITH EMPLOYEE
RIGHT-TO-KNOW LAWS

OSHA, as well as many states, provide stringent labeling and notice requirements in workplaces where "hazardous" chemicals or materials are used or stored. These types of statutes and regulations are referred to as "employee right to know" laws. The liability from failing to advise your employees of the presence of a dangerous or hazardous material can be staggering; therefore, the personnel professional must ensure that all federal, state, and local labeling and notice requirements are complied with and that all appropriate emergency measures are in place.

Compliance will range from posting all notices in places where employees will see them, actively labeling certain substances, issuing protective gear where needed, training employees and supervisors in the proper use and care of dangerous materials, and the like. However, right to know laws are generally notice requirements.

Case Study

Marvin, a plumber, works in a plastics manufacturing plant where he installs and replaces pipes and valves. The various pipes and holding bins contain anything from water to highly toxic chlorine-related substances. He is ordered to work in the oldest part of the plant where he has never been before. He is unsure of what the pipes there carry. There is a distinct odor, but he does not recognize it. No labels or information is provided regarding the liquids he may encounter.

Marvin is concerned that he may be splashed or may inhale dangerous fumes when he opens up the pipes. He requests information regarding the type of chemicals and what hazards they may pose. His supervisor is in a hurry to replace the pipes because the company is losing valuable production time. He orders Marvin to get to work and refuses to provide any information regarding the presence of hazardous substances. Marvin refuses to work until he is informed of the possible dangers of working in that particular area.

May the employer discharge Marvin for his refusal to work? What are the employer's obligations in keeping the employees advised of potentially dangerous substances in the workplace?

The supervisor acted hastily in refusing Marvin's request for information on potentially dangerous substances in the area he was assigned to work. Many jurisdictions as well as OSHA regulations require the employer to post information regarding the presence of hazardous substances in the various work areas. In fact, workers may refuse to work in certain jurisdictions until their request for information has been answered. If hazardous materials are present, then they must be labeled clearly, and the employee must be permitted to review information regarding safety precautions and dangers of such substances. Thus it is important for supervisors to be aware of employees' right to know of hazardous substances where they are working. In this example Marvin was right and the supervisor acted imprudently. This section addresses the obligations of the employer when employees must work in areas where hazardous materials are present.

How to Meet the Requirements of the Hazard Communication Standard

The Occupational Health and Safety Administration's wide-ranging Hazard Communications Standard (the Standard) is applicable to workplaces of both manufacturing plants and nonmanufacturing places of employment where "hazardous chemicals" are utilized.[12]

The Standard requires chemical manufacturers to label containers of hazardous chemicals with appropriate warnings. Commercial purchasers who used these chemicals in their workplace are obliged to keep the original labels intact or else transfer the information onto any substitute containers.

Material Safety Data Sheets.   Material Safety Data Sheets, (often referred to as MSDSs) must be provided by the manufacturer and be made available to employees wherever the chemical is in use. MSDSs list physical characteristics and hazards of each chemical, the symptoms caused by overexposure, and any preexisting medical conditions aggravated by exposure. They must also contain recommended safety precautions and first aid and emergency procedures in case of overexposure and provide a source of additional information. Employers must provide training on the dangers of the particular hazardous chemicals found at each workplace.

Defining "Hazardous Chemical" and "Health Hazards."   The term "hazardous chemical" is defined broadly in the regulations as any chemical which is a physical hazard or a health hazard. The term "health hazard" includes chemicals which are carcinogens, toxic or highly toxic agents, reproductive toxins, irritants, corrosives, sensitizers, hepatoxins, nephrotoxins, neurotoxins, agents which act on the hematopoietic system, and agents which damage lung, skin, eyes, or mucous membranes.[13]

The range of "hazardous chemicals" covered by the regulations include specialized, industry-specific materials as well as seemingly simple office supplies such as cleaners, inks, and copy machine solutions. In general, the Hazard Communication Standard protects against exposure to any chemical that is

- Listed in the regulations as a carcinogen
- Determined by its manufacturer or importer to be hazardous[14]

Identifying the Employer's Obligations.   An employer must

♦ Identify to employees all hazardous materials to which they may be exposed and all related actual hazards

♦ Legibly and prominently label each container of hazardous material with substance name, warnings, and name and address of manufacturer

♦ Obtain from each chemical manufacturer and make available to employees Material Safety Data Sheets and labels containing the following information

   ♦ Identity and common name of substance and manufacturer

   ♦ Physical and chemical characteristics

   ♦ All known health effects and related information

   ♦ Known carcinogenic effects

   ♦ Appropriate precautionary measures and first aid procedures

♦ Establish a written hazard communication standard and employee training program to educate workers about detecting the presence of the hazardous materials, establish procedures to minimize exposure, develop a labeling system, and make other information available.

NOTE: The specific chemical identity may, under certain circumstances set forth in the regulations, be withheld to protect *trade secrets*, but must be disclosed in the event of a medical emergency.

Exemptions to the OSHA Hazard Communication Standard.
The OSHA Communication Standard does not apply to all hazardous materials found in the workplace. Hazardous substances that are regulated by other federal statutes are not subject to this particular OSHA standard. For example,

- Pesticides subject to the Federal Pesticide, Fungicide, and Rodenticide Act (7 U.S.C. §136 *et seq.*)
- Food, drugs, cosmetics, and the like covered by the Food, Drug, and Cosmetic Act (21 U.S.C. §301, *et. seq.*)
- Alcoholic beverages (Federal Alcohol Administration Act (27 U.S.C. §201, *et. seq.*)
- Consumer products or hazardous substances covered by the Consumer Product Safety Act (15 U.S.C. §2051, *et. seq.*)
- Hazardous waste covered by the Solid Waste Disposal Act as amended by Resource Conservation and Recovery Act of 1976 (42 U.S.C. §6901, *et seq.*)
- Tobacco products
- Wood or wood products[15]

Penalties for Violating the OSHA Hazard Communication Standard.
Violations of the OSHA Hazard Communication Standard that have the potential to result in serious injury or death may subject employers to civil and criminal penalties. In addition, up to $10,000 and/or 6 months' imprisonment may be sought against employers providing false information with respect to any of the requirements.

Identifying State Regulations for Employee Protection Against Hazardous Materials

The OSHA Hazard Communication Standard expressly preempts non-approved comparable state plans; a federal court has, indeed preempted such plans with respect to manufacturing employees and will likely reach the same conclusion regarding nonmanufacturing employees. States may impose additional standards for employee protection against hazardous materials in the workplace.

New York, for example, subjects its employers to additional state "right to know" requirements that impose disclosure and training requirements on nonmanufacturing employers whose employees are exposed to toxic substances.[16] The New York definition of "toxic" substances is even broader than the federal definition of hazardous chemicals and prohibits the discipline or discharge of any employees who have exercised their statutory rights (which may not be waived). An employee must respond to an employee's request for toxic substance information within 72 hours and must maintain both medical records and records of the names and addresses of every employee who handles toxic substances for 30 to 40 years.

New Jersey has had a right to know law since 1984 which provides that an employer file a workplace survey and have on file a hazardous substance fact sheet. The workplace survey reports all hazardous substances present in the workplace to the state Department of Environmental Protection. An employee may request a copy of such survey, hazardous substance fact sheet, or environmental survey. The employer must respond to the request within 5 workdays; the employee has the right to refuse work until the request has been honored without loss of pay. The employer may not discharge or otherwise discipline, penalize, or discriminate against any employee because the employee has exercised his or her rights under the law. An employer may face a $2,500 fine for each violation.[17]

Other states that have some type of right to know statute include Alabama, Alaska, California, Delaware, Florida, Illinois, Iowa, Maine, Maryland, Massachusetts, Minnesota, Missouri, Montana, New Hampshire, New Mexico, North Carolina, Pennsylvania, Rhode Island, Tennessee, Texas, Vermont, Washington, West Virginia, and Wisconsin.

Remember, it is always important to check your local laws periodically with regard to any changes in the law.

GUIDELINES TO USE FOR A SAFE
AND HEALTHY WORKPLACE

The old saying "an ounce of prevention is worth a pound of cure" is no truer than in the employment context. A responsive and thorough safety and health program will result in a safer and healthy workplace that will benefit all parties. Employers will see benefits such as increased productivity, lower health costs, reduced liability, fewer lost workdays, and high morale. Employees will enjoy a job that does not unnecessarily risk their safety or health. The following tips will aid in constructing an effective safety and health program:

1. Review federal, state, and local laws *and* regulations on a regular basis.

2. Establish a written policy clearly stating compliance procedures.

3. Develop specific safety rules for particular jobs and instruct employees in those rules.

4. Appoint one or more health and safety officers who are responsible for recordkeeping, staying current with changes in the law and regulations, and implementing safety and health policies.

5. Conduct safety training programs for employees on a regular basis. Always provide appropriate protective gear and insist employees use such gear.

6. Strictly enforce all safety rules.

7. Act promptly on all health- and safety-related complaints.

8. Investigate working conditions and procedures if there appears to be a pattern of similar or related complaints—find the source of the problem and correct it.

9. Keep work areas well equipped with first aid supplies. Have several employees trained in first aid procedures.

10. Institute and enforce policies for maintaining a clean and orderly workplace.

11. Instruct managers on what to do when an OSHA inspection occurs. For example, identify whom to contact, accompany the inspector on the tour, and know when to demand a warrant and proper credentials. Employees or their representative may also participate on the tour.

12. Comply with all labeling, reporting, and notice requirements regarding hazardous substances present in the workplace.

13. Conduct a safety and health workplace audit annually.

ENDNOTES

1. 29 U.S.C. §660(c)(1).

2. 29 C.F.R. §1977.12(b)(2) (1977).

3. In *Marshall v. Daniel Construction Co.*, 563 F.2d 707 (5th Cir. 1977), the Fifth Circuit Court of Appeals held that the regulation was invalid, based on the legislative history of the Act, including Congress's rejection of a "strike with pay" provision and that employees were not given the right to determine in fact that an employment practice creates an imminent danger.

4. 29 C.F.R. §1904.2 (1988).

5.   The Code of Federal Regulations contains all the rules promulgated by the Secretary of Labor regarding OSHA standards and procedures. Refer to 29 C.F.R. §1904 for recordkeeping, and §1910 for the various industry standards.

6.   29 C.F.R. §1904.12(c) (1988).

7.   29 C.F.R. §1904.12(d) (1988).

8.   29 C.F.R. §1904.4 (1988). OSHA Form No. 101 or any workers' compensation, insurance claim, or other report containing the relevant information may be used as a supplementary record.

9.   29 C.F.R. §1904.8 (1988).

10. See *Camara v. Municipal Court*, 387 U.S. 523 (1967); *See v. Seattle*, 387 U.S. 541 (1967); and *Brennan v. Gibson's Products, Inc.*, 407 F.Supp. 154 (E.D.Tex. 1976).

11. Where OSHA and states have concurrent jurisdiction, the Secretary of Labor may refer discrimination complaints to the appropriate state agency.

12. 29 C.F.R. §1910.1200 (1984 and 1988). This Standard imposes various requirements on manufacturers aimed at ensuring that their employees were informed of the potential hazards posed by chemicals found at their workplace. The personnel professional should consult the regulations cited herein for specific details of an employer's responsibilities in this area.

13. 29 C.F.R. §1910.1200(c) (1990). Additional information on the scope of health hazards covered by these regulations and the criteria used to determine whether or not a chemical is to be considered hazardous are contained in Appendices A and B to §1910.1220.

14. See 29 C.F.R. §1910.1200, Appendices B and C.

15. 29 C.F.R. §1910.1200(a)(5) and (6).

16. New York Labor Law §875 (McKinney 1990) and New York Public Health Law §4800 (McKinney 1990).

17. N.J.S.A. 34:5A-1, *et seq.*, known as the "Worker and Community Right to Know Act," effective date August 29, 1984.

16

CURRENT ISSUES
IN HEALTH AND SAFETY
ON THE JOB

Recently we have witnessed a sharp increase in employees' concerns for their health and safety. Issues that must be dealt with by personnel professionals include when a coworker is suspected of having a communicable disease, such as AIDS, and other employees refuse to work with him or her; the smoker versus nonsmoker; protective policies that may discriminate against a particular group of employees; and other issues. Being prepared to deal with these issues in a responsive manner not only benefits the entire work force and therefore productivity, but it will significantly reduce the likelihood of injury or discrimination claims.

The issues discussed in this chapter are generally regulated on a state or local basis. In some cases, regulation is by statute; in other cases, it is determined by the courts. Areas where states or local governments have taken the lead in regulating health and safety that OSHA may not yet cover include

- Smoking in the workplace
- AIDS and other communicable diseases
- Use of Video Display Terminals (VDTs)
- Fetal protection policies
- Repetitive motion disorders
- Environment-related problems

320

As our understanding of the impact of new technology and the environment on our health increases, more and more regulation in the workplace will occur. This chapter addresses some of these new areas, including fetal protection policies, hazards to reproductive health, VDT screens, repetitive movement injuries, and medical monitoring. Since some of these health concerns appear to affect one segment of the population (e.g., women) more than others, these issues are often intertwined with discrimination issues, as we shall see in the section on fetal protection and reproductive health hazards policies.

NOTE: Personnel professionals should consult state and local laws and comply with health and safety regulations that relate to their circumstances. Check these laws periodically and update your policies accordingly.

HOW TO HANDLE SMOKING IN THE WORKPLACE

The dangers of smoking to the smoker and those around him or her have become well publicized. An employer must face concerns involving workers' health and safety, productivity, costs to business and industry, and legal actions by those affected by smoking and those who smoke.

Case Study

Sue, a nonsmoker, who is highly allergic to tobacco smoke, sits next to Ellen, a chain smoker. Ellen has tried numerous times to quit smoking but has been unable to. However, she has substantially reduced her smoking at work. Sue, however, demands that all smoking in her work area stop because it makes her physically ill. Recently their bickering has worsened.

If you are faced with such a problem, what should you do?

Review all state and local laws to determine if any smoking prohibitions apply to your workplace. If you are not in compliance, institute appropriate policies at once. A restrictive policy required by law may resolve the problem by requiring Ellen to smoke only in designated, enclosed smoking areas. If no such policy is required by law, you may wish to develop a restrictive policy that may help ease the problem. Currently, nonsmokers generally will prevail in a contest between nonsmokers and smokers. If possible, place Ellen with other smokers or Sue with other nonsmokers in a well-ventilated area. Be aware that if you institute an overly restrictive policy, such as a total ban on smoking in the building, Ellen, who is addicted to nicotine, may raise a handicap claim that then might require accommodation. Generally, a thoughtful and properly instituted smoking policy should remedy most problem situations.

As states institute restrictive smoking regulations for the workplace, employers must develop a smoking policy that protects nonsmokers while accommodating smokers. However, employers are not required to permit smoking in their places of business. In fact, some employers have gone so far as to not hire smokers. The practice of not hiring a person who smokes is coming under increasing attack as an invasion of personal privacy and entangles an employer in a possible action involving its right to be concerned with off-duty conduct.[1] In any event, the reality is that a significant number of employees smoke, and you must be prepared with a smoking policy.

How State and Local Regulations Affect Smoking in the Workplace

The federal government has not yet regulated private employers' premises with regard to smoking except where it creates an obvious safety hazard such as smoking near flammable materials. Most states, on the other hand, have instituted restrictive smoking policies that apply to government and/or private workplaces. Typically, a state or local smoking restriction requires that no smoking take place in any public area or open work area. Such areas include reception areas, corridors, secretarial workstations, plant floors, other nonenclosed workstations, and cafeterias or lunch areas. Smoking would be permitted only in a closed individual office or a designated smoking area. In meeting or conference rooms, a smoker must obtain the permission of others at the meeting before lighting up. The policy must be written and posted for employees.

Actual restrictions and penalties vary from jurisdiction to jurisdiction. It is a necessity to consult local and state laws to determine the employer's obligation with regard to establishing and enforcing a smoking policy. The following states and local municipalities have restrictive smoking regulations: Alabama, Alaska, Arizona, California, Connecticut, District of Columbia, Florida, Hawaii, Illinois, Indiana, Iowa, Kansas, Maine, Maryland, Massachusetts, Michigan, Minnesota, Nebraska, Nevada, New Hampshire, New Jersey, New Mexico, New York City, New York State, North Carolina, North Dakota, Ohio, Oregon, Pennsylvania, Rhode Island, South Carolina, South Dakota, Utah, Vermont, Virginia, Washington, and Wisconsin.

How to Clear the Air and Be Fair

The formulation of a smoking policy requires making some hard choices. However, it is clear that the employer, in most cases, should attempt to accommodate the competing interests of smoking and nonsmoking employees. A comprehensive, balanced smoking policy will result in a reduction or elimination of conflict among smokers and nonsmokers by accommodating both sides as fully as possible.

Establishing a Total Smoking Ban. More and more employers are instituting blanket no-smoking policies that absolutely prohibit smoking anywhere in the building and does not set aside any areas for smokers. Such a policy may provide the incentive for smokers to quit smoking and thereby benefit them, but it is not without risks. For example, smokers may assert handicapped status due to a disabling addiction to nicotine. A total ban may fail to accommodate such a handicap reasonably. Even if an absolute ban on smoking is lawful, it may be difficult to enforce, creating a disciplinary nightmare. An employer should be prepared to answer the "Smokers have rights, too" argument.

Also another drawback to this type of policy is that employees who smoke will attempt to find ways around this restriction. They take longer breaks because they have to go outside to smoke, and/or they will be unavailable while they are outside the building.

Establishing a Partial Smoking Ban. The more common and suggested approach is a partial ban on smoking whether as a prelude to a total ban or as the set policy. This policy should try to accommodate the concerns of both smokers and nonsmokers in as equitable way as possible. A partial ban would limit where and when smoking may occur. Designated smoking areas should be enclosed, clearly marked, and conveniently located, if possible. This should be accompanied by improvements in ventilation and grouping of employees as much as possible. The following tips should aid you in establishing an appropriate policy for your organization.

Guidelines for Creating a Smoking Policy

1. Establish a written policy restricting smoking in open work areas and public places, including reception areas, workstations that are open, restrooms, corridors, stairwells, elevators, lobbies, lunch rooms (larger cafeterias may have a small smoking section), and conference rooms. Smoking may be permitted in private offices and in enclosed areas where all employees smoke.

2. Provide separate work areas for smokers and nonsmokers where possible.

3. Designate enclosed smoking areas near employees who smoke. Determine the appropriate number of such smoking areas within the limits of the physical plant.

4. Consider conducting an informal poll of who smokes in the workplace and plan accordingly. Do not make an issue of who smokes.

5. Use existing ventilation systems and physical barriers to minimize smoke in adjacent smoking and nonsmoking areas. Improve the ventilation system and install air cleaning devices to remove smoke and other air impurities more efficiently from the work environment.

6. Remove cigarette vending machines from the cafeteria and lounges.

7. Post "no-smoking" signs in designated areas and instruct employees in the appropriate time and place for smoking. Advise employees that the policy will be strictly enforced.

8. Offer "stop smoking" programs to employees and their families on or off the employer's premises. Sponsor a company "smoke out" day.

9. Post the smoking policy throughout the workplace and incorporate it in any employee handbook or work rule manual.

10. Review all state and local laws and conform the company's policy to the law. Also review collective bargaining contracts to determine if any change in the smoking policy must be bargained.

11. Establish a procedure for resolving disputes arising under the smoking policy in which health concerns are given due consideration.

The success of the smoking policy depends a great deal in its presentation to the employees and its enforcement. Thus the employer should consider presenting the policy through any number of communication tools, including small-group meetings, posters, internal bulletins, brochures, and the like. The policy should be presented with a positive and pro-health approach.

HOW TO HANDLE AIDS AND OTHER COMMUNICABLE DISEASES IN THE WORKPLACE

Today, employers are faced with an unprecedented concern regarding the presence of communicable disease in the workplace and how to protect their employees. This concern is multifaceted:

- Whether the employee with the communicable disease is handicapped

- How to accommodate such an employee

- How to deal with coworkers' fear or refusal to work beside someone with a contagious disease (such as AIDS) without violating handicap discrimination laws

These issues pose a delicate problem that requires sensitivity and a well-planned policy.

This section addresses issues involving the individual handicapped employee, accommodation, and coworkers' fears, including discrimination, defamation, privacy, unlawful search and seizure (with respect to AIDS testing), contract, and negligence. Screening job applicants and employees for the presence of human immunodeficiency virus (HIV) has become the focus of much controversy, as the number of individuals afflicted with the deadly disease has escalated into the hundreds of thousands. To address these rapidly growing concerns, federal, state, and local agencies have promulgated regulations and guidelines to deal with the multitude of questions and lawsuits that have arisen in the wake of AIDS. This is, however, a rapidly and constantly changing area of the law and must be closely monitored.

The communicable diseases that may present problems in the workplace include acquired immune deficiency syndrome (AIDS) and other more common diseases such as tuberculosis and hepatitis. Since the analysis for an employee with any type of communicable disease is basically the same, we will focus on AIDS for purposes of our discussion.

Complying with the Laws Pertaining to Contagious Diseases

Generally, individuals who have contagious diseases, including AIDS or AIDS-related complex, or are perceived to have AIDS, will be covered under the various federal, state, and local handicap discrimination laws.

Federal Laws. Contagious diseases are covered under the Vocational Rehabilitation Act (Section 504) and Americans with Disabilities Act.[2] The U.S. Supreme Court, in *School Board of Nassau County, Fla. v. Arline*, 107 S.Ct. 1123 (1987), ruled that individuals suffering from tuberculosis, a contagious disease, are "handicapped" within the meaning of Section 504 of the Rehabilitation Act of 1973.[3]

Individualized inquiry based upon reasonable medical judgments must determine whether a person poses a significant workplace risk, that cannot easily and reasonably be eliminated, of communicating an infectious disease to others.

There have been several attempts to institute a federal policy regarding AIDS. The proposed federal legislation, "AIDS Federal Policy Act of 1987," illustrates what such a law may provide.[4]

- ◆ It would expand availability of AIDS testing and counseling by authorizing $1 billion in grant programs.

- ◆ It contains antibias provisions (§2341). No "person" may discriminate against an otherwise qualified individual in employment solely by reason of the fact that such individual is, "or is regarded as being," infected with AIDS.

- ◆ It establishes a penalty, namely, a $2,000 civil penalty, for each violation after an administrative hearing.

- ◆ It allows the Secretary of Labor to seek injunctive relief on behalf of an aggrieved individual.

- ◆ It permits an aggrieved individual to file a civil action for actual and punitive damages; prevailing party is entitled to counsel fees and costs.

- ◆ It includes nondisclosure provisions. A "person" who learns of the protected individual's condition is barred from disclosing that information absent a court order.

State Laws Pertaining to AIDS. Many states are considering or have passed some type of antibias AIDS legislation. State laws specifically addressing AIDS typically prohibit involuntary testing of employees, use of test results to determine job qualification, disclosure of test results, use of such tests for insurance purposes, and other types of discrimination based on the presence of HIV. However, agency guidelines and policies rather than actual legislation generally dictate state treatment of AIDS as a handicap. Where AIDS is considered a protected handicap and afflicted workers are otherwise qualified for work, employers must maintain confidentially of test results and provide reasonable accommodations, except isolation, for the afflicted employees just as they would for any other victim of handicap.

NOTE: Specific provisions for medical facilities may exist under state law.

Some examples of state and local antibias laws and regulations follow.

California: AIDS is a handicap within the definition of the California Fair Employment and Housing Law.[5] Also prohibited is the use of HIV test results in the determination of an individual's job qualifications. Certain cities and counties, including Los Angeles, San Francisco, West Hollywood, Berkeley, and Santa Clara County, have passed ordinances banning employment discrimination based on AIDS and either prohibiting or restricting the use of AIDS testing.

Florida: This state prohibits employment discrimination against an employee who has tested positive for the AIDS virus or who suffers from AIDS or AIDS-related complex. An employer may not require an HIV antibody test "as a condition of hiring, promotion, or continued employment" unless absence of the HIV infection is a bona fide occupational qualification for the job at issue. Legislation enacted in 1985 authorizes state testing of individuals suspected of having infectious diseases but prohibits the discriminatory use of such results.

Georgia: The Georgia Task Force on AIDS has cautioned against both exclusion of infected individuals from the workplace and unqualified mandatory testing. However, a 1987 Board of Education policy mandates AIDS testing of teachers suspected of having AIDS and permits discharge of those refusing such testing.

Iowa: This state has enacted four laws that protect persons infected with the AIDS virus from employment discrimination, guarantees confidentiality of test results, establishes a state prevention and intervention plan, and bans the sale of home AIDS testing kits.

Maryland: Maryland's Human Relations Commission has deemed AIDS a protected handicap.

Massachusetts: In Massachusetts AIDS is a handicap under state law.[6] The Massachusetts Commission for Discrimination has construed relevant state employment discrimination statutes as protecting both AIDS-infected workers and those perceived to have AIDS. The state policy also prohibits mandatory testing of state employees and requires the maintenance of confidentiality with respect to those diagnosed with the disease. In addition, a 1987 executive order from the mayor of Boston banned AIDS discrimination with respect to city employees and job applicants.

Michigan: The Michigan Civil Rights Commission has issued a policy statement construing AIDS as a protected handicap under state law. A 1987 policy adopted by the Ann Arbor City Council prohibits both AIDS discrimination and testing of current and prospective city employees.

Minnesota: The state Department of Employee Relations has prohibited AIDS discrimination against state employees where those workers continue to meet acceptable performance and attendance requirements. The policy statement further deems it inappropriate for coworkers who feel threatened by an infected employee to refuse to work where it has been determined that there is no health or safety risk. A 1987 governor's executive order bans AIDS discrimination and employee testing, and the city of St. Paul prohibits mandatory testing of applicants and city workers.

Missouri: Department of Health guidelines group AIDS with other conditions affecting job performance for purposes of all state and personnel laws.

Texas: The Communicable Disease Act prohibits mandatory AIDS testing of employees unless it is a bona fide occupational qualification, and even then only where it is an absolute necessity and the only means of determining the job qualification. Confidentiality of test results is generally required. The city of Austin has also enacted a local ordinance prohibiting AIDS discrimination by employers of 16 or more, employment agencies, and labor unions.

Wisconsin: State law prohibits AIDS testing except where state health officials determine that there exists potential risk of transmission of the disease through employment.

> NOTE: The area of antibias AIDS legislation is rapidly changing on a day-to-day basis. Therefore you should frequently refer to relevant state law or policies prior to making an employment decision regarding an employee who has AIDS or is perceived to have AIDS.

Other Potential State Law Claims.   Claims of discrimination are not the only issues arising from the AIDS epidemic. The following issues also must be considered.

Breach of contract.   Breach of oral contract is often alleged where an employee is promised continued employment despite the disease but is thereafter dismissed. Where written employment manuals provide for leaves of absence for medical or personal reasons, employers frequently object to AIDS victims taking such time off and try to discharge them.

Intentional infliction of emotional distress. This tort claim (possibly arising from the employer's treatment of the afflicted worker in the presence of other employees) and pretextual firing to avoid the costly health care obligations associated with insurance coverage can lead to substantial employer liability.

Privacy and defamation issues. These claims concern the unwarranted disclosure of an employee's private facts and may give rise to causes of action in most states; employers must be aware that the other employees in the workplace generally do not have the right to know that they are working with an individual who has AIDS (although supervisors who must monitor applicable health problems or accommodations may sometimes be informed).

How to Determine the Handicap Status of Employees with AIDS or Other Contagious Diseases

The following step-by-step analysis will assist the personnel professional in assessing whether an individual who has a contagious disease such as AIDS or is HIV positive or is thought to have AIDS is handicapped.

In analyzing, determine if

- The handicap/disability is protected
- The employee is "otherwise qualified" to perform the job

In a contagious disease context, examine

- Nature of the risk or how the disease is transmitted
- Duration of the risk (how long is the employee infectious)
- Severity of the risk (potential harm to third parties)
- Probability that the disease will be transmitted

The key is to determine whether the person can perform the job despite his or her illness. If accommodation is necessary, it should be provided until it is no longer possible.

Identifying the Types of Claims Filed

The list that follows identifies types of claims filed.

- Handicapped discrimination under federal American with Disabilities Act or Rehabilitation Act and/or state laws
- Breach of implied contract (reliance on handbook or employer's policies)
- Invasion of privacy (disclosure of employee's condition to others)
- Tort actions such as defamation, negligence, and intentional infliction of emotional distress

Describing Recent Developments in AIDS Cases

The list that follows describes some recent events pertaining to AIDs cases.

♦ New York's restriction forbidding insurance companies from testing health insurance applicants for AIDS was struck down. However, this may change as the state is appealing.[7]

♦ The discharge of an employee with AIDS was converted to unpaid medical leave. The employee's first doctor note indicated only that he could not lift or stand for prolonged periods of time. The employer discharged him immediately. The third doctor note indicated he had AIDS. Arbitration ruled that discharge on day of receiving the first note was untimely and improper since the possibility existed that he could recover. Arbitrator declined to order reinstatement but indicated that if employee was fully capable of doing his job, he should be allowed to return to work.[8]

♦ A laboratory technician's refusal to perform chemical examinations on bodily fluids from AIDS patients was just cause for her discharge. The technician failed to prove that the laboratory's precautions were ineffective in preventing the spread of AIDS.[9]

♦ A claim of damages resulting from a needle prick incurred while a janitorial employee emptied a waste container survived a motion to dismiss. The defendant company regularly took blood samples from prospective life insurance applicants at its offices. The court ruled that a person claiming mental anguish and "AIDS-phobia" must be able to tie her fear to a distinct event which would cause a reasonable person to develop a fear of contracting the disease. Plaintiff had developed a fear that she would die from AIDS that was so massive and overwhelming that she could not return to work. The court found there was a reasonable basis for her fear that being stuck with a used hypodermic needle from which blood was drawn may lead to contracting AIDS.[10]

Handling AIDS as a Collective Bargaining Issue

The spread of AIDS has recently given rise to new concerns in the context of negotiating collective bargaining agreements. For example, the New York Public Employment Relations Board found that a school board policy temporarily suspending individuals diagnosed as having AIDS represented a unilateral change in conditions of employment where the board has not negotiated the policy with the union in good faith.[11]

In 1986, an arbitrator ruled that the employer was bound by a collective bargaining agreement which contained a provision that corrections officers were entitled to notification of prison inmates diagnosed or medically suspected of having communicable diseases.[12]

A Minnesota prison guard who had refused to conduct pat searches of prisoners for fear of contracting AIDS was found to be unjustly terminated where only a memo had been distributed to inmates expressing the prison's uncertainty regarding AIDS transmission.[13]

Another arbitrator determined that an AIDS-stricken nursing home employee had been improperly dismissed where the home's policy, promulgated pursuant to a state law requiring written policies ensuring that employees with communicable disease not to be permitted to work, stated only that afflicted employees be "suspended until a negative report is received."[14]

Guidelines Regarding Employees/Applicants with AIDS

Employers who are concerned about health conditions in the workplace may consider taking the following steps:

1. In certain fields, for example, public health or safety positions, employers should provide for *medical examinations* of all employees and all new hires to determine their state of health. (Employers cannot test specifically for AIDS or the HIV virus in most cases.)

2. An attempt must be made to identify handicapped individuals voluntarily under the relevant law, including those individuals with AIDS and other contagious diseases. (Employers must provide accommodation.)

3. All medical documentation must be reviewed with regard to an individual's *ability* to perform the job applied for to make sure that there are no health impediments to performance.

4. If an individual is able to perform the *essential tasks* of the job regardless of disability, that individual should be hired and/or permitted to continue in employment. (Employee must be able to do job.)

5. If an individual becomes disabled with a contagious disease, for example, AIDS, he or she should be permitted to work *as long as he or she is able to perform the job*. (Special treatment is not required.)

6. When an individual suffering from AIDS becomes unable to continue work, the individual should be requested to go on disability until he or she is able to return to the workplace. Such handicapped individuals should be treated in the same manner as all other disabled employees and provided with the same benefits. (AIDS is a disability.)

7. Employers should review their workplace procedures, including employee handbooks and benefit regulations to make sure that they have provided for coverage, continuity, and employee concern. (Employers

cannot exclude some employees from coverage; COBRA obligations—if employee leaves—offer continuation coverage.)

8. Employers cannot refuse to hire an individual with AIDS or an AIDS-related condition because of the disease or fear. The only exception is where absence of AIDS or the AIDS virus is a bona fide occupational qualification.

9. Educate your people regarding AIDS. You may distribute literature, discuss the disease in your newsletter, dispense information in your lobby (as Levi Strauss did), and hold group meetings with a medical authority present to answer questions.

Employers and personnel directors should become aware of the need for education, sensitivity, and understanding of the law in dealing with their employees. As the spread of AIDS becomes epidemic, companies must be ready to respond to their needs as well as those of their employees—all their employees.

IMPLEMENTING FETAL PROTECTION AND REPRODUCTIVE HAZARDS POLICIES

Policies regarding fetal protection and reproductive hazards have been of great concern to many employers. Employers, fearing costly liability for injuries to unborn children or the inability to have children, have attempted to implement preventive and/or exclusionary policies that restrict certain groups of employees from performing hazardous jobs, which generally are well-paying jobs. Also certain industries, including chemical, video display, and semiconductor manufacturing, in which a significant number of women are employed, have jobs that may involve significant reproductive health risks. In these areas some employers have implemented policies that limit women's employment opportunities, but not of men, where such policies are said to protect employees' offspring from reproductive and fetal hazards.

Case Example

A national battery manufacturing company implemented a fetal protection policy designed to prevent unborn children and their mothers from suffering the adverse effects of lead exposure. It provides that women of childbearing capacity will neither be hired for nor allowed to transfer into those jobs in which lead levels are defined as excessive. Under the policy all women except those whose inability to bear children is medically documented are excluded from such jobs. There is no dispute that exposure to lead creates a substantial risk of harm to unborn children.

The union and several women groups filed a class action suit against the company alleging sex discrimination that barred women from higher-pay jobs.

The U.S. Supreme Court, in *United Auto Workers v. Johnson Controls, Inc.*, ruled that companies may not bar women from jobs that may be hazardous to unborn children.[15] The bias in this policy was obvious and the court stated, "fertile men, but not fertile women, are given the choice as to whether they wish to risk their reproductive health for a particular job." This type of policy violates Title VII. The company failed to sustain a bona fide occupational qualification exception to the discrimination charge. The BFOQ defense is extremely narrow as the court pointed out: "the safety exception is limited to instances in which sex or pregnancy actually interferes with the employee's ability to perform the job." In *Johnson Controls* it was found that lead exposure also caused harm to male and female reproductive systems; thus the policy was discriminatory. The court also stated that the decisions about the welfare of future children must be left to the parents and not to the employers who hire those parents.

Thus, after *Johnson Controls*, it is unlikely that fetal protection policies, unless they are so narrowly drawn as to be almost meaningless, will be lawful as a legitimate way to protect unborn children. It is the parents who must ultimately decide between their job and the health of their children. Thus, employers are left in the unenviable position of risking liability when things go wrong.

The Court's decision in *Johnson Controls* affirmed the long-standing position of the EEOC, which issued a "Policy Statement on Reproductive and Fetal Hazards Under Title VII" in 1988. The EEOC's position is that employers may not exclude members of one sex from job opportunities because of reproductive hazards unless the policy can be justified by objective, scientific evidence and there is no less discriminatory means of protecting fetal health.

The basic issues in assessing a reproductive hazards exclusionary policy include

- Whether there exists a substantial risk of harm to employees' offspring through the exposure of employees to a reproductive or fetal hazard in the workplace

- Whether the harm to employees' offspring takes place through the exposure of employees of one sex but not employees of the opposite sex

- Whether the employer's policy effectively eliminates the risk of fetal or reproductive harm

However, even if the policy satisfies these elements, it may be found unlawful if it is shown that there exists a reasonable alternative policy that will protect employees' offspring from fetal or reproductive harm and that has a less discriminatory impact on employees of the restricted sex. If your organization has high-risk jobs, you should review the EEOC's policy guide thoroughly (see Chapter 3) before instituting an exclusionary reproductive hazards policy.

How State Laws Regulate Reproductive Hazards

Several states have instituted varying regulations regarding reproductive hazards in the workplace. These regulations range from notice of such dangers to employees to anti-discrimination and accommodation provisions.

For example, in California, if working conditions pose a greater danger to the health, safety, or reproductive functions of applicants or employees of one sex than to individuals of the other sex, the employer shall make reasonable accommodation for the affected employees or alter the working conditions to eliminate the greater danger. The existence of the greater risk to employees of one sex than the other shall not justify a BFOQ defense. Also an employer may not discriminate against members of one sex because of the duties imposed upon it by this statute.[16]

Connecticut requires preemployment notification of workplace reproductive hazards and prohibits sterilization as a condition of employment.[17]

HOW TO HANDLE OTHER HEALTH-RELATED ISSUES IN THE WORKPLACE

This section addresses certain health problems that are the result of changes in the workplace due to technology or the workplace environment. There may or may not exist regulations regarding these problems but that should not prevent the employer from correcting these problems to avoid liability under other causes of action. Employees have experienced problems due to the repetitive motions required in their jobs, use of video display terminals, lack of circulation of fresh or "clean" air, and exposure to hazardous materials such as asbestos, which may require medical monitoring of your employees.

Avoiding Liability for Repetitive Motion Disorders

With the advances in technology and increased automation, office and assembly-line workers are experiencing a new form of occupational injury referred to as repetitive motion injuries officially known as "cumulative trauma disorders," or CTD. These injuries are creating new causes of actions under OSHA, tort, and labor laws.[18] Employee groups most at risk include computer keyboard operators, meat cutters, supermarket cashiers, assembly-line workers, pneumatic hammer operators, and truck drivers. However, any employee who performs thousands of repeated motions during a normal workday is at risk.

As injuries such as tendonitis, carpal tunnel syndrome, epicondylitis (tennis elbow), and other similar ailments become more common, the success of claims against the employer has increased. While workers' compensation may cover the medical expenses and lost income, it does not allow for pain and suffering. Many employees are turning to products liability law as one source of recovery for these painful ailments.[19]

OSHA has introduced guidelines to reduce repetitive motion injuries in the meat cutting industry. However, it is clear that similar guidelines will apply to other industries as well, especially where the use of VDTs is prevalent. Repetitive motion injuries can be minimized through proper workplace engineering and effective employee training.

Regulating the Use of Video Display Terminals

A now common office tool, the video display terminal, has become a bane to many of its users. Many repetitive motion disorders are associated with the use of VDTs. In response to studies that indicate that there are several different types of health problems associated with the use of VDTs, either through poor working conditions or overuse, certain jurisdictions have imposed regulations governing the use of VDTs.[20]

Case Study

Maryann is a word processing clerk in a large insurance agency. She works on a computer with a display terminal for 8 hours a day. She is permitted to take two 10-minute breaks and a half-hour lunch break. However, she rarely takes the morning break.

Maryann has begun to complain of dizziness, headaches, back pain, and pain in her wrists. Her supervisor, Agnes Cole, has ignored her complaints as well as those of other employees. Cole only says to take an aspirin and stop being a whiner. Maryann has missed 10 days of work, half of which she believes is related to her working conditions. She has been placed on probation for excessive absenteeism. Maryann has also visited the eye doctor three times in the past 12 months and has had her prescription changed twice, all at her own expense.

Was the supervisor's response to these complaints appropriate? What should the supervisor do when several employees report similar complaints?

Supervisor Cole may have exposed the company to liability for violations of local regulations that set forth specific guidelines for the safe use of VDTs. She failed to consult with the safety and health officer of the company and the local health and safety regulations. Cole should have contacted the health and safety officer when she became aware of the many similar complaints of the employees. These complaints indicated that something was wrong in the word processing area.

As it happens, the area where the office is located has a local law that sets specific guidelines in the use of VDTs that are designed to eliminate most of the symptoms Maryann and the others have been experiencing. The remedy may be as simple as changing the color of the monitors or the overhead lighting.

NOTE: Employers should pay close attention when a pattern of complaints develops.

OSHA is contemplating issuing guidelines specifically covering use of VDTs in the workplace. Consult with an employment law specialist periodically with regard to developments in this area.

Implementing Medical Monitoring

Employers who require employees to work in conditions that may expose them to hazardous materials may be required to provide future medical monitoring of these employees. If the employees are exposed to substances that may induce a serious disease such as asbestosis some time in the future, they may be entitled to be monitored for early detection and treatment.

Case Example

In a recent case, employees exposed to high levels of asbestos won the right to seek continuous medical monitoring to allow early detection of and treatment for an asbestos-related disease.[21] In that case the employees were required to clean up an area damaged when an asbestos-covered steam pipe exploded. They worked for four days without protective clothing or equipment and alleged that they had been exposed to toxic levels of asbestos.

This case illustrates the growing willingness of the courts to allow novel claims in the area of employees' health. Employers in the future may be required to provide medical monitoring of employees who have been exposed to hazardous substances or even communicable diseases in the workplace. This type of potential liability is intended, in part, to encourage employers to take all necessary and reasonable precautions to protect their employees while engaged in their duties before something happens. The cost to employers, employees, and society is too great not to take appropriate preventive measures.

Personnel professionals should work closely with the health officers to develop reasonable guidelines for foreseeable risks to health and safety.

What to Do About Poor Air Circulation

In enclosed office environments many employees have begun to complain of headaches, nausea, dizziness, poor concentration, frequent sore throats, and similar ailments. Many of these problems have been traced to poor ventilation systems. In those cases it is not fresh air that is being circulated but rather stale or contaminated air. Your supervisors must listen to employees' complaints—if a number of similar complaints are registered, then you should begin an investigation as to the cause. One of the first places to start is with the quality of air in the work area. Inspect the ventilation system; sometimes many problems are alleviated by simple routine maintenance such as replacing or cleaning the air filters, keeping the ducts clean and free of dust, or other simple procedures. A well-ventilated workplace will result in more efficient and productive employees.

ENDNOTES

1. Bias against smokers is prohibited in some states under an employee privacy act or human rights law. For example, the New Mexico Employee Privacy Act, explicitly prohibits a refusal to hire or to discharge any individual because that individual is a smoker or a nonsmoker or require as a condition of employment that any employee or applicant abstain from smoking during nonworking hours. New Mexico Statutes Annotated, Labor Law, §50-11-1 (1991). The New Jersey version of a so-called smokers' rights law provides that employers may not make hiring, firing, compensation, or other personnel decisions based on whether an employee or applicant smokes away from the job "unless the employer has a rational basis for doing so which is reasonably related to the employment, including the responsibilities of the employee or prospective employee." New Jersey's law does not bar employers from establishing policies regulating or banning smoking in the workplace or making distinctions between smokers and nonsmokers with regard to life and health insurance benefits (see Bill A-4699, effective July 15, 1991.) See also the North Dakota Human Rights Act, which prohibits discrimination based on an individual's "participation in any lawful activity off the employer's premises during nonworking hours"; North Dakota Century Code, §§14-02.4-01, *et seq.*, (1991). Other states with similar laws pertaining to the hiring of smokers or nonsmokers are Kentucky, South Dakota, and Mississippi. These recent statutes and amendments represent a trend of protecting an individual's right of privacy regarding his or her lawful off-duty conduct.

2. See *Chalk v. U.S. District Court for the Central District of California*, 840 F.2d 701 (9th Cir. 1988), wherein the court held that an otherwise qualified employee with AIDS is protected.

3. However, the court refused to consider the question of whether AIDS would be viewed in the same way. The Court noted that it was not ruling on whether an AIDS victim could be considered, solely on the basis of contagiousness, "handicapped" under the law. See Roger B. Jacobs, *"Arline,* AIDS, and Employment," *New Jersey Law Journal*, April 16, 1987.

4. Senate Bill 1575 and House of Representatives Bill 3071 (1987).

5. In *Raytheon Co. v. Fair Employment & Housing Commission*, 2 L.R.W. (BNA) 468 (1988), employer was held liable under state's handicap bias law for refusal to reinstate an employee who had AIDS. Court awarded $40,000 in attorneys' fees.

6. *Cronan v. New England Telephone*, 1 I.E.R. Cases (BNA) 658 (D.Mass. 1986).

7. *Health Insurance Association of America v. Corcoran*, 531 N.Y.S. 2d 456 (Sup. Ct. 1988) affirmed as modified 551 N.Y.S. 2d 615, (app Div. 1990) affirmed 564 N.Y.S. 2d 713 (Ct. App. 1990).

8. *Buckler's Inc.*, 90 L.A. (BNA) 937 (1988).

9. *Stepp v. Indiana Employment Security Division*, 3 I.E.R. Cases (BNA) 133 (Indiana Ct. of App. 1988).

10. See *Castro v. New York Life Insurance Co.*, reported in *New York Law Journal*, August 5, 1991.

11. *Jamesville-DeWitt Central School District*, PERB Case No. V-8657 (1986).

12. *Delaware Dept. of Corrections*, 86 L.A. (BNA) 849 (1986).

13. *AFSCME, Council 6 v. State of Minnesota, Department of Corrections*, 85 L.A. (BNA) 1185 (1986).

14. *In re Nursing Home and Union*, 88 L.A. (BNA) 681 (1987).

15. 111 S.Ct. 1196 (1991).

16. California: Fair Employment and Housing Commission Rules and Regulations, §7291.1(d).

17. Connecticut General Statutes, §§31-40(g), (h), and (i) (1981).

18. The following cases are a representatives sample of CTD claims: *Downes v. IBP, Inc.*, 691 P.2d 42 (Kan. Ct. App. 1984) (beef processor experienced severe pain in her hands and arms, diagnosed as carpal tunnel syndrome; the injury was held to be the result of an "accident" and was compensable); *Winn-Dixie Stores v. Morgan*, 533 So.2d 783 (Fla. Dist. Ct. App. 1988) (grocery store clerk suffered collapse of a small bone in his wrist); and *Darling v. Industrial Commission of Illinois*, 530 N.E.2d 1135 (Ill. App. Ct. 1988) (machine operator with a shoulder problem was awarded workers' compensation benefits because he had established a causal connection between work duties and the injury).

19. Lawsuit filed on behalf of nine newspaper journalists against ATEX, Inc., a supplier of computer keyboards and monitors, alleges that ATEX, the designer, manufacturer, and seller of computer equipment, knew or should have known that the repetitive use of its computer systems would expose plaintiffs to risk of developing cumulative trauma disorder. Complaint was filed June 15, 1990, in the U.S. District Court for the Southern District of New York.

20. For example, San Francisco instituted the strictest regulation of VDTs in the nation in December 1990. It attempts to protects employees from vision problems and disabling hand and wrist injuries caused by inadequate workstations and prolonged repetitive motion. Businesses of 15 or more employees must provide adjustable chairs, proper lighting, antiglare screens, training, and 15-minute alternative work breaks every 2 hours. There is also an anti-discrimination provision, and fines may range up to $500 per day for violations. Another local jurisdiction, Suffolk County, New York, had instituted strict VDT regulations, but it was struck down in *ILC Data Device Corp. et al. v. County of Suffolk*, see *New York Law Journal*, January 10, 1990.

21. *Acevedo v. Consolidated Edison, Inc.*, 572 N.Y.S. 2d 1015 (Sup. Ct. 1991). Although the court dismissed claims such as emotional distress and battery, it ruled that the request for medical monitoring was not barred by workers' compensation law since there was no present injury.

17

EMPLOYEE COMPENSATION: WAGES, SALARIES, AND OTHER PAYMENTS FOR WORK PERFORMED

One of the employer's primary obligations is to compensate employees for work performed. However, as you will see, compensation is not always a straight forward cash transaction.

The employer is obligated to compensate employees at least at the federally mandated minimum wage rate. Federal law sets the minimum wage and overtime pay standards. States may set higher levels or greater restrictions on compensation matters. This chapter explores the employer's obligations with regard to rates of pay, overtime pay, child labor, and related issues under federal and state laws.

Compensation is more than the cash paid for "straight wages"; it may include bonuses, travel pay, payments of certain benefits, board, lodging, or meals. The employer is well advised to be familiar with the federal Fair Labor Standards Act, which includes the Equal Pay Act and child labor laws and comparable state laws that govern wages, hours, and other conditions of employment.

Employers are advised to review their compensation practices periodically to ensure that they are in compliance with state and federal law. It may be helpful to consult with your labor/employment counsel, tax specialist, or a compensation management consultant if you have any questions regarding the intricacies of compensation or if you are about to institute new compensation policies.

A GUIDE TO THE FAIR LABOR STANDARDS ACT

The Fair Labor Standards Act (FLSA), enacted in 1938 and amended several times thereafter, is a comprehensive federal wage and hour statute intended to regulate interstate commerce activity.[1] The subsequent amendments to the FLSA have extended its protections to state and local government employees and have set wage and hour standards for large government contractors, public construction projects, service contracts for government agencies, and other types of employment. Like other federal employment statutes, FLSA establishes minimum standards regarding minimum wage, equal pay, overtime, and child labor with which state laws must comply.

Identifying Which Employers and Employees are Covered

Employers subject to the FLSA include

any person acting directly or indirectly in the interest of an employer in relation to an employee and includes a public agency, but does not include any labor organization or anyone acting in the capacity of officer or agent of such labor organization.[2]

Employers covered by the provisions of the FLSA are determined by the "enterprise" test, under which coverage is extended to fellow employers of any employer determined to be covered by FLSA. An "enterprise" is generally considered the related activities performed through operation of or for a common business purpose.

The FLSA also requires that certain businesses meet a minimum dollar volume test. The 1989 amendment to the Act raised from $362,000 to $500,000 the total sales volume threshold for exempting small retail and service establishments from the FLSA.

Certain business activities fall within the "enterprise" coverage regardless of dollar volume:

- Clothing/fabric laundry, cleaning, or repair
- Construction and reconstruction
- The operation of a hospital, nursing home, or school
- Public agency activities

Employers newly exempt from FLSA enterprise coverage because of the higher threshold, however, are required to continue to pay employees at least $4.45 an hour and must comply with FLSA overtime and child labor provisions.

For the purposes of FLSA there are basically two types of employees: exempt and nonexempt. The wage and hour provisions of FLSA apply to the nonexempt employee, that is, employees who are

- ♦ Engaged in interstate commerce
- ♦ Engaged in the production of goods for commerce
- ♦ Employed in "an enterprise engaged in commerce or the production of goods for commerce"

Private household domestic service workers, homeworkers, trainees, and student workers are now also considered to be within the purview of FLSA requirements. (Exempt employees are discussed in the section on exemptions from overtime and minimum wage requirements.)

Handling Enforcement and Liability

The provisions of the FLSA enable the Secretary of Labor to collect unpaid minimum and overtime wages due to aggrieved employees as well as an equal amount in liquidated damages. The Secretary may further move to enjoin employers from violating the Act; federal district courts entertaining such injunction suits are authorized to order payment of back wages and, in addition, may enjoin the interstate shipping of goods produced by employees not correctly paid.

The Justice Department is empowered to bring criminal actions for "willful" violations, punishable by a fine of up to $10,000, imprisonment up to six months, or both. Aggrieved individuals themselves may sue employers for back wages, liquidated damages, attorneys' fees, and costs. The 1989 amendments in addition provide civil penalties of up to $1000 per violation for full or repeated violations of the Act's minimum wage, overtime, or child labor provisions.

Identifying Related Statutes

Several related statutes that amend the Fair Labor Standards Act are discussed in the paragraphs that follow.

Provisions of the Portal to Portal Act. The Portal to Portal Act of 1947 amended the FLSA with respect to time spent by employees doing "unproductive" as opposed to "principal" activities. The amendment was intended to address the spate of "portal to portal" lawsuits flooding the courts resulting from the U.S. Supreme Court's ruling that time spent by employees prior or subsequent to their "principal activity" constituted compensable working time, regardless of contract, custom, or practice.[3] The Act overrules the Court's decision and specifically excludes such activities from the FLSA definition of "working time" unless it was so established by contract, custom, or practice. What constitutes compensable working time is discussed later on in this section.

The Act established a two-year statute of limitations for related back pay civil suits; however, 1966 amendments to the FLSA extended the time period to three years for causes of action arising out of "willful" violations. In addition, the Act provided employers with a "good faith" defense whereby proof of compliance with a written or otherwise approved administrative regulation or policy provides a complete defense to wage-hour actions. The Act contained additional provisions relating to the awarding of liquidated damages and representative actions brought by other groups or individuals.

Provisions of the Davis-Bacon Act. The Davis-Bacon Act of 1931[4] amended the FLSA to require the payment of minimum wages established by the Secretary of Labor to laborers and mechanics employed on federal public works and construction contracts exceeding $2,000. These wages are referred to as prevailing wage rates. In addition to monetary liability for back pay owed employees and potential criminal liability, contractors violating Davis-Bacon requirements risk having their names placed on a "blacklist" distributed to all government departments for three years and losing future public works projects.

Provisions of Other Related Federal Statutes. The Walsh-Healy Public Contracts Act prescribes wages and hour standards for contractors supplying the government with goods exceeding $10,000.[5] The Contract Work Hours and Safety Standards Act,[6] and the Anti-Kickback Act,[7] along with the Davis-Bacon Act, cover public works and construction projects. The Service Contract Act establishes wage standards for employees involved in the performance of government agency service contracts valued at more than $2,500.[8] The National Foundation on the Arts and Humanities Act requires payment of prevailing wages for professionals, laborers, and mechanics retained under programs receiving federal assistance from the National Foundation on the Arts and Humanities.[9] Title III of the Consumer Credit Protection Act restricts the amount of an employee's weekly wages that may be subject to garnishment.[10]

Defining Wages

The term **wages** is defined broadly under the FLSA. Section 203(m) of the FLSA sets forth a general definition of "wages" for purposes of the Act. As you will see, "wages" include more than the cash paid for hours worked or services performed.

Including Board and Lodging. In addition to monetary compensation, "wages" are deemed to include the reasonable cost, as determined by the administrator, of board, lodging, or other facilities furnished to any employees if such facilities are customarily furnished by the employer. Although such "board" compensation may, under certain circumstances, be credited toward the minimum wage requirement, it cannot be included as wages if it is excluded therefrom by the terms of an applicable collective bargaining agreement.

Including Tips. Actual wages paid by an employer are deemed to be increased by any tips received by the employee. The increase is an amount determined by the employer. However, the determined increases may not exceed 50 percent of the minimum wage rate or equal more than the value of the tips actually received by the employee.

> NOTE: The portion of the minimum wage that employers must pay tipped employees was reduced from 60 percent to 50 percent on April 1, 1991, effectively permitting employers to count tips as covering a greater portion of the required federal minimum wage. The employer determining such a wage increase because of tips received must inform all affected employees, and all tips received by the employees must be retained by them individually or in a pool.[11]

Handling Meal Credits. The employee is given the option of whether he or she wants meals to count toward wages. The employer would set up a system whereby employees are aware of when and how they can opt in and out of the plan. Additionally, if the employer decides to implement a meal credit plan, the employer must keep records of each employee and the dedications from wages for meals if the employee is earning less than minimum wage or works in excess of the maximum.

How to Establish Working Time

Activities undertaken for the benefit of the employer, or with the knowledge and consent of the employer, constitute "working time" for purposes of the FLSA. In addition to traditional types of work activity, the following activities are examples of what generally constitutes *compensable working time:*

- Rest or meal periods of 20 minutes or less
- On-duty waiting time
- On-call waiting time[12]
- Reporting time
- Training time
- Civic/charitable work done at the employer's request or direction
- Fire drills
- Travel time between worksites connected with the employer's business

Noncompensable work activities include

- Preemployment tests
- Medical attention

- Bona fide rest or meal periods exceeding 20 minutes in length during which the employee is completely relieved of his or her duties
- Unrelated and voluntarily attended training programs
- Traveling between home and the place of employment

Also leaves of absence, illnesses resulting in absence from work, vacations, and holidays may or may not be considered compensable working time.

ESTABLISHING MINIMUM WAGE STANDARDS

The minimum wage is established by Congress and applies to all employees engaged in commerce or in the production of goods for commerce.

Determining the Minimum Wage Rate

In 1989, in the first increases to the federal minimum pay rates since 1981, the minimum wage was increased in two steps from the then current rate of $3.35 per hour to $4.25 per hour, effective April 1, 1991. The minimum wage rate is adjusted periodically by Congress, and the employer's payroll department should be kept updated with the latest changes.

There are numerous exemptions from the minimum wage requirements of the FLSA (see discussion under "Overtime Exemptions").

Offering a Training Wage. The 1989 legislation also provided for a "training wage" permitting employers to pay workers age 16 to 19 a subminimum rate of $3.61 per hour (also effective April 1, 1991) for a cumulative period of 90 days, after which the individual is entitled to the full minimum wage. The subminimum rate may be extended an additional 90 days for certain employees participating in on-the-job training programs meeting specified requirements. Employers may neither pay the subminimum to more than 25 percent of their employees nor terminate, lay off, or reduce the hours of regular employees to hire individuals at the training wage. Authority for the subminimum wage rate, however, expires on April 1, 1993.

Identifying Factors That Affect Minimum Wage. Certain types of employment are specifically exempt from the minimum wage regulations. Certain disabled workers and employees who are learners, apprentices, messengers, and full-time students (outside school hours) in agriculture, retail, or service positions not ordinarily given to full-time workers may be employable at rates below the minimum where authorized by special certificate. See also the discussion on the 1989 "training wage" earlier.

How to Compute the Minimum Wage. As noted previously in the general discussion of wages under the FLSA, monetary compensation is not necessarily the only form of payment acceptable under the Act. For purposes of the minimum wage, the reasonable cost of certain noncash items may be included in the computation of minimum wage where they are primarily for the benefit of and approved by the employees and certain other conditions are met:

- Meals
- Lodging
- Merchandise (price agreed to by the employee)
- Transportation between work and home
- Tuition (for student employees of a university)
- Authorized savings bond
- Insurance premiums
- Union dues
- Tips

These items may be calculated as part of the wages paid to an employee; therefore, they count toward the minimum wage requirement.

New Jersey Restaurant Occupations Example. The following information is from the Office of Wage and Hour Compliance, New Jersey Department of Labor, and applies to restaurant occupations. This information helps illustrate how tips, food, and lodging are used in the calculation of minimum and overtime pay.

Wages

♦ *Basic minimum wage.*
$5.05 beginning April 1, 1992

♦ *Food service and other occupations in which gratuities are customary.* Cash wages shall not fall below the following after allowances are made for gratuities, food, and lodging:
$3.03 an hour beginning April 1, 1992

♦ *Overtime rates.* Overtime at one and one-half times the regular hourly wage rate shall be paid for all hours worked in excess of 40 in any week starting with the effective dates of this regulation.

Definitions

♦ *Restaurant occupation.* The term "restaurant occupation" as used in this regulation shall mean any activity of an employee in the restaurant industry. The term "restaurant industry" as used here shall include any eating or drinking place which prepares and offers food or beverages for human consumption either in any of its premises or by such service as catering, banquets, box lunch, or curb service.

♦ *Regular hourly wage.* The term "regular hourly wage," shall mean the amount that an employee is regularly paid for each hour of work as determined by dividing the total hours of work during the week into the employee's total earnings for the week, exclusive of overtime premium pay.

Administrative Regulations

♦ Employer substantiation of gratuities received by an employee and the cost of food and lodging shall be as provided in these regulations.

♦ Food and lodging supplied to employees shall not be included in wages for those hours worked in excess of 40 hours per week.

♦ Where cash wages have been established as a condition of employment through agreement between the employer and employee or the employees' collective bargaining agent, gratuities, food, and lodging shall not be included as part of such cash wages.

♦ Meals and lodging shall be considered applicable toward the minimum wage unless the employee elects not to receive such meals and lodging.

♦ The cash wage rates established in this order shall be acceptable in those occupations where gratuities or food and/or lodging are actually received. In no event shall this paragraph be construed to deny to an employee the right to claim additional compensation or to an employer to claim a credit in excess of that so established where it is proven to the satisfaction of the Department that the actual amount of the gratuities received is either more or less than the amount of credit herein established.

ESTABLISHING REQUIREMENTS FOR OVERTIME PROVISIONS

The FLSA and most state laws require employers to pay overtime wages after an employee has worked 40 hours in a single workweek. The overtime rate—by law—is one and one-half times an employee's regular hourly pay.

NOTE: Employees who work a regular 35-hour week are not entitled to the overtime rate until after they have worked 40 hours. The 5 hours over their regular time is paid at their regular rate of pay. However, the employer is free to pay the higher rate for any time worked over the employees' regularly scheduled hours, at its discretion.

Determining the "Regular Rate of Pay"

Section 207 of the FLSA mandates that, in general, an employer may not employ workers for more than 40 hours per week unless that employee receives compensation for the excess hours of at least one and one-half times their regular rate of pay. For purposes of determining an employee's "regular rate of pay," the FLSA specifically *excludes* remuneration to employees including those in the form of the following:

- Gifts intended solely as a reward for service (e.g., at holidays)
- Vacation pay
- Holiday pay
- Sick pay
- Payments for periods where no work is performed because of the employer's failure to provide sufficient work
- Properly reimbursable traveling expenses incurred in furtherance of the employer's business
- Bonuses (timing and amount determined solely by the employer and not made pursuant to any contract or other employment agreement)
- Payments made pursuant to profit-sharing, trust, or savings plans
- Talent fees paid to performers on radio or television programs
- Contributions to retirement, life, accident, or health insurance plans

NOTE: The common thread running through all types of remuneration excludable from an employee's "regular rate of pay" is that these payments are not measured by or dependent upon the hours worked by the employee or his production or efficiency.

In addition, extra compensation at "premium" rates for work beyond applicable daily and/or weekly standards, for work performed on weekends, holidays, or regular days of rest, or for work arranged pursuant to some type of employment agreement need not be included in earnings for determination of "regular" rate. Thus the overtime rate paid to an employee is not part of the employee's "regular rate of pay."

Identifying Exemptions from Overtime and Minimum Wage Requirements

Federal law defines two categories of employees for purposes of minimum wage and overtime provisions: exempt and nonexempt. As discussed, nonexempt employees must be paid overtime for hours worked in excess of 40 hours in a workweek. Generally, exempt employees are not eligible for overtime pay. However, the employer may elect to pay certain exempt employees overtime subject to its policies.

An employee's status is determined by his or her responsibilities, duties, educational qualifications, and salary. Classification of employees, with regard to eligibility for overtime pay, is done in accordance with the criteria set forth in the FLSA. An employee's classification may change as a result of a promotion or salary increase.

General Categories of Exempt Employees. Certain types of employees are exempt from *both* the overtime and minimum wage requirements of the FLSA, including

- Outside salesperson, professional, executive, and administrative personnel, including any employee employed in the capacity of academic administrative personnel or teacher in elementary or secondary schools

- Employees of certain retail or service establishments which do not qualify as or are not in an enterprise engaged in commerce or in the production of goods for commerce

- Employees of certain seasonal amusements or recreational establishments

- Employees of retail establishments which customarily manufacture goods they sell if such establishment would otherwise qualify as an exempt retail establishment

- Domestic service employees neither covered by the Social Security Act nor employed for more than 8 hours per week in the aggregate, from minimum wage, and live-in domestics, from overtime

- Fishing and first processing at sea employees

- Agriculture employees employed by farms utilizing fewer than 500 person-days of agricultural labor, individuals employed by a member of their immediate family, certain local seasonal harvest laborers and seasonal hand harvest laborers 16 years of age or under, and employees principally engaged in the range production of livestock

- Certain learners, apprentices, students, and handicapped workers

- Employees of certain small newspapers

- Switchboard operators of certain independently owned small telephone companies

- Seamen on foreign vessels

- Babysitters employed on a casual basis and persons employed to provide companion services

How Exempt Employees Are Classified. Exempt employees are identified by their level of responsibility, duties, salary, educational background, and the like. The Department of Labor looks at these factors and not simply at a title or whether the employee is on a salary.

NOTE: A salaried employee is not automatically exempt from the overtime provisions; it is the substance of what an employee does that determines his or her status.

Questions regarding application of the so-called "white-collar," exemptions frequently arise. Typically, high-level executives, administrators, and professional employees are exempt. Where the employee does some executive or administrative work but also does other less skilled or more routine work is when many employers fail to comply with the overtime standards. Where a salaried employee is exempt, but may be borderline, such an employee may not be docked pay for fractions of days of work missed.

"Executive" employees. Exempt "executive" employees are those in primarily managerial positions, paid not less than $250 per week (not counting board), and who regularly direct the work of at least two other employees. An "executive" employee earning between $155 and $250 per week may also be exempt under certain circumstances.[13]

"Administrative" employees. "Administrative" employees, who in general make at least $250 per week (or $155 under certain circumstances), exercise discretion and independent judgment, and primarily perform work relating to management policies and general business operations, are also exempt from FLSA minimum wage and overtime requirements.[14]

"Professional" employees. Generally, exempt "professional" employees are paid at least $250 (or $170 under certain circumstances) per week on a salary or fee basis; consistently exercise discretion and independent judgment regarding scientific, specialized, or academic work; and primarily perform work requiring those special skills. However, the salary or fee requirement for professionals is not applicable to attorneys, medical doctors, and teachers actually engaged in practice.[15]

Employees Who Are Exempt from Overtime Only. The following categories of employees are exempt only from the *overtime* provisions of the FLSA:

- Certain employees under collectively bargained guaranteed annual wage plans and wholesale or bulk petroleum distribution employees
- Certain commission salespersons in retail or service establishments
- Motor carrier employees
- Railroad employees
- Airline employees
- Outside buyers of poultry, eggs, cream, milk
- Seamen
- Announcers and news editors of certain small radio and television stations

- Certain sales representatives, parts distributors, and mechanics
- Drivers and their helpers paid on a trip basis
- Agricultural employees
- Farm workers engaged in livestock auction operations
- Employees of certain country elevators
- Maple sap employees
- Employees engaged in transportation farm products
- Taxicab drivers
- Domestic service employees residing on employers' premises
- Substitute parents for institutionalized children
- Motion picture theater employees
- Employees of small logging operations (crews with fewer than nine employees)
- Employees of amusement or recreational establishments located in a national park or forest

Determining the Status of Independent Contractors. Often employers will utilize independent contractors, outside consultants, or casual labor, depending on its needs and the nature of the work. However, where the employer treats the "independent contractor" more like an employee, the individual may be eligible for certain employee rights such as overtime pay. Employers need to become familiar with how to utilize independent contractors and the like properly to avoid giving them employee status.

Case Study

MAXCO, Inc., recently retained two people: Simon, who is a computer software consultant designing and setting up new computer programs, and Scott, who is working on a temporary job inputting data into the new computer programs. Both are only temporary workers who are free-lancers, going from job to job, and are considered by MAXCO to be independent contractors. They are paid an agreed lump sum based on the work to be performed. They are not paid any benefits, specifically no overtime but are expected to accomplish a set amount of work within a specified time. Simon sets his own hours and Scott is on a schedule. Scott is given specific instruction and requires some supervision. Simon is given a great deal of discretion in developing the programs within the parameters of the specifications provided by MAXCO. They regularly work over 40 hours a week.

The state department of labor—wage and hour division—conducts a surprise audit of MAXCO's payroll records. They see Scott and Simon working, but their names do not appear on the employee payroll list. They charge that Scott and Simon are employees and must be paid benefits including overtime.

Are these workers "employees" or "independent contractors" and must they be paid overtime? Several factors must be analyzed in determining whether the two workers are employees owed overtime or independent contractors who are not eligible for overtime. These factors are discussed in the paragraphs that follow. After reviewing these factors, do you agree that Scott will be considered an employee who must receive overtime for hours worked over 40 hours in a week and Simon an independent contractor who is exempt from the overtime requirements?

As indicated, several factors are relevant in determining whether individuals are "employees" or "independent contractors" for purposes of the FLSA. The following factors, known as the "economic reality test," are examined when there is a question as to the status of an individual who does work for an employer:

- The degree of control exercised by the employer over the worker(s)
- The workers' opportunity for profit or loss and their investment in the business
- The degree of skill and independent initiative required to perform the work
- The permanence or duration of the working relationship
- The extent to which the work is an integral part of the employer's business[16]

No single factor is dispositive of the issue; rather it is the totality of the circumstances that is weighed. Also, other relevant factors may be considered in addition to or in lieu of the stated factors.

NOTE: The bottom line is whether the temporary worker actually renders independent services to the employer *or* simply does the employer's bidding.

How to Calculate Overtime Rates

The following examples demonstrate how to calculate overtime rates.

General Requirements for Overtime Eligibility. Employees may work over 40 hours a week but must be compensated at a higher rate. The overtime provisions of the FLSA generally require payment of time and one-half the eligible employee's regular hourly rate of pay for all hours worked in excess of 40 in a week.

If an employee is paid on an hourly basis plus incentives and bonuses or is not paid on an hourly basis, the regular hourly rate is computed by dividing the total hours of work during the week into the total earnings for the week, exclusive of overtime premium pay. Total earnings would include tips, travel, food, and lodging allowances, and incentive pay. If an employee performs different duties during the overtime period, then overtime can be based on time and one-half the minimum wage rather than time and one-half of the regular hourly wage.

Case Study

Employer A needs to calculate the regular hourly rate for employees who receive food and lodging and less than minimum wage in cash wages. The employer needs to determine the fair value of the food and lodging. This example illustrates one approach and then applies it to calculations for overtime pay.

Employer A has three employees who are furnished food and lodging in addition to gross cash wages of $2.50 per hour. The cost of food purchased for the employees is $72.00 total a week. The building housing the employees cost $36,000 in 1978, and subsequent improvements amounted to $4,000. Maintenance costs for the year were $2,480. The estimated life of the building when constructed was 50 years. The building can adequately house six persons.

The "fair value" of food for the week is determined as follows:

Total cost	$ 72.00
"Fair value" per employee ($72.00 divided by 3)	24.00

The "fair value" of lodging for year 1979 is determined as follows:

Cost of building in 1978	$36,000.00
Add: Subsequent improvements	4,000.00
Total costs	$40,000.00
Depreciation for year (1/50 times $40,000.00)	$ 800.00
Maintenance costs for year	$ 2,480.00

Interest on employer's net investment:

Total investment	$40,000.00
Depreciation to date	800.00
Net investment	$39,200.00
Six percent of net investment	2,352.00
Total for year	$ 5,632.00
Total for week ($5,632.00 divided by 52)	$ 108.31
"Fair value" per employee ($108.31 divided by 6 persons)	$ 18.05

Assume that Employee B worked 40 hours in a particular week. His wages would be as follows:

Gross cash wages (40 times $2.50)	$100.00
Fair value of food	24.00
Fair value of lodging	18.05
Gross weekly wage	$142.05

Hourly wage ($142.05 divided by 40) $ 3.55[17]

Assume that Employee B worked 48 hours in a particular week. His wage entitlement would be as follows:

Total earnings exclusive of overtime premium pay:

Gross cash wages (48 times $2.50)	$120.00
Fair value of food	24.00
Fair value of lodging	18.05
Gross weekly wage	$162.05

Overtime wages:

Regular hourly wage ($162.05 divided by 48 hours)	$ 3.38
Overtime pay (8 × $3.38 divided by 2)	$ 13.52
Employee B wage entitlement for 48 hours	$175.57[18]

Calculating Compensatory Time. Generally, compensatory time or time off given in lieu of overtime pay is not permitted for time worked over the 40-hour limit. Many employers traditionally gave employees time off when they had worked overtime instead of paying them for the overtime hours. This was a common practice in not-for-profit organizations. However, that practice is no longer permitted with few exceptions.

The 1985 amendments to the FLSA, however, permit state and local government employers to pay "compensatory time" in lieu of cash for overtime for certain police, fire, emergency, and seasonal personnel. The federal regulations provide a detailed formula for calculating the proper rate of compensatory time for employees in such jobs who are typically on rotating shift schedules.[19] Compensatory time off from work, nonetheless, must be computed on the basis of time and one-half for each overtime hour worked.

Many public employees may accrue up to 240 "comp time" hours (160 overtime hours actually worked) before becoming eligible for cash overtime payment. Public safety, emergency, and seasonal employees, however, may earn up to 480 hours of "comp" time (320 overtime hours actually worked) before cash overtime payments are required.

Calculating Compensation for Piece Work. For employees paid on other than an hourly basis, their compensation must be converted to hourly or "piece" rates for determination of overtime computations. Generally, the piece rate is determined by dividing the total earnings of the employee during a work-week by the total number of hours worked during that period; overtime compensation is thus one-half the "regular rate" so determined multiplied by the number of overtime hours worked.

Determining Compensation for Remedial Work. Under the 1989 amendments to the FLSA, employers are now allowed to pay straight time, rather than time and a half, for up to 10 hours per week beyond the 40-hour workweek to employees attending remedial education, defined as training or activity designed to provide reading and other basic skills. However, job-specific training is *excluded*.

ESTABLISHING CHILD LABOR RESTRICTIONS

Federal law regulates the employment of minors under the age of 18 where the employment involves interstate or foreign commerce, the production of goods related to such commerce, or the furnishing of goods under certain government contracts.[20] The FLSA specifically prohibits producers, manufacturers, and dealers from shipping or delivering any goods where any oppressive child labor has been employed. All workers are covered, male and female, in factory and in office, without regard to the number of employees.

States also regulate child labor to varying degrees, and the prohibited employment may vary from state to state. Federal and state laws duplicate much of the same coverage and complement each other. Where they differ, whichever is stricter applies. Any prohibition in either statute must be observed. For purposes of this discussion, however, we will focus on federal law upon which many states laws are based. Of course, the personnel manager must be familiar with both the federal and appropriate state laws with regard to the employment of minors.

Defining the Scope of Child Labor Laws

There are a number of laws regulating and controlling employment of minors. A discussion of these follows.

Applying Pertinent Age Limitations. In the Fair Labor Standards Act of 1938, the federal government set a minimum age of 16 for general employment, but for those occupations that the Secretary of Labor determines to be hazardous, the minimum age is 18. Employed minors must be above 14 or 16 years of age, depending upon the type of employment and employee involved. Individuals involved in hazardous occupations, however, must be above 18 years of age.

Employment Permissible for Minors. The list of permitted occupations or employment for minors is much shorter than that which is prohibited. Included are the following types of employment exempted from child labor restrictions:

- Newspaper delivery
- Employment as actors or performers in film, theater, radio, or television productions
- Employment by children under 16 by their parents in occupations other than mining, manufacturing, or those found to be hazardous
- Making evergreen wreaths at home
- Employment in areas outside of the United States, District of Columbia, Puerto Rico, Virgin Islands, and other specified territories[21]

Furthermore, children between the ages of 14 and 16 may work in occupations that do not require a minimum age of 16 or are not considered hazardous so long as the employment

- Remains outside school hours
- Does not exceed 3 hours on any school day and 8 on any nonschool day
- Does not exceed 18 hours during a school week and 40 hours otherwise

There are also specific exemptions regarding certain types of agricultural employment.

Employment Prohibited for Minors. Although 16- and 17-year-old minors are permitted to do most types of work, the following common *exceptions apply:*

- Work involving the manufacture, transportation, storage, or use of explosives or highly inflammable substances
- Driving or acting as outside helper on a motor vehicle
- Coal mining
- Logging and sawmilling
- Construction work of any kind
- Operation of certain power-driven woodworking machines, except in a bona fide apprenticeship
- Work involving exposure to radioactivity or benzol or benzol compound which is volatile or can penetrate the skin
- Operation of power-driven hoisting apparatus, including elevators
- Operation of certain power-driven metal working machines
- Mining other than coal mining

- Work in slaughtering, meat packing, and rendering establishments
- Operation of certain power-driven bakery machines
- Operation of certain power-driven paper products machines, including paper lace machines, corrugating, crimping, or embossing machines
- Work in the manufacture of brick, tile, and kindred products
- Operation of power-driven circular saws, band saws, and other machines with a guillotine action
- Wrecking, demolition, and shipbreaking or fabrication or assembly of ships
- Centrifugal extractors or mangles in laundries or dry cleaning establishments
- Work in certain roofing operations
- Work in excavation operations, mines, or quarries
- Work in or about blast furnaces, ore reduction, smelters, foundries, or other places in which heating, melting, or heat treatment of metals is carried on
- Oiling, wiping, or cleaning machinery in motion
- Operation of buffing, polishing, grinding, or abrasive machines (except under a bona fide apprenticeship)
- Work on railroads, including switch tending, gate tending, or track repairing, or as brakeman, fireman, engineer, motorman, or conductor
- Work as fireman or engineer on a boat or vessel
- Work in the manufacture of white or yellow phosphorous or phosphorous matches
- Work in the manufacture or packing of paints, colors, or white or red lead
- Work in places where alcoholic beverages are manufactured, packaged, or sold (except in bowling alleys, restaurants, and retail food stores)
- Any work over 30 feet above floor, ground, or water level

Regulating Work Programs for Apprentices and Students. Sixteen- and 17-year-old minors who are in apprentice training programs or approved cooperative vocational training programs may obtain waivers from some, but not all, of the employment prohibitions. Minors who have completed such training programs may work in the fields in which they are trained regardless of their ages.

Limiting Work for Employees Under Age 16. Permissible work for minors under age 16 is further limited. In addition to the prohibitions just mentioned, minors under age 16 are forbidden to work in a number of settings and in a number of occupations. The broadest prohibition under federal law provides that minors under age 16 may not work in manufacturing, mining, or processing or in workrooms or workplaces where manufacturing, mining, or processing takes place.

Fourteen- and 15-year-old minors are permitted to work in retail, food service, and gasoline service establishments. However, any gas service station with a significant repair facility would be considered a mechanical establishment and therefore prohibited.

The following work is permitted:

- Office and clerical work

- Cashiering, selling, modeling, artwork, work in advertising departments, window trimming, and comparative shopping

- Price marking, tagging by hand or by machine, assembling orders, packing, and shelving

- Bagging and carrying out customers' orders

- Errand and delivery work by foot, bicycle, and public transportation

- Cleanup work, including the use of vacuum cleaners and noncommercial floor waxers, and maintenance of grounds, so long as such maintenance does not require the use of power-driven mowers or cutters

- Kitchen work and other work involved in preparing and serving food and beverages, including the use of some kitchen machines

- The following work in connection with car and truck service: dispensing gasoline and oil, courtesy service, cleaning, washing or polishing by hand, and other duties listed as permitted in this section

- Cleaning vegetables and fruits and wrapping, sealing, labeling, weighing, pricing, and stocking goods

Special provisions apply to minors under age 16 working in agriculture. Such provisions chiefly concern prohibitions on proximity to dangerous animals, chemicals, and conditions and working in dangerous storage areas.

Minors under age 14 generally may not work in commercial employment.

Regulating Hours for Minors.   Federal and state laws limit the hours when minors may work. Under federal law, minors under age 16 may not work during school hours, with extremely limited exceptions for vocational students. They may work between only 7:00 A.M. and 7:00 P.M. and may work only 3 hours per day on school days and 8 hours per day on nonschool days. They may work 18 hours per week in school weeks and 40 hours in nonschool weeks. They may not work more than 6 days per week.

State laws generally provide similar restrictions on hours of employment of minors. Exceptions are made for school vacations and the summer months. Refer to your state's statute for specific rules.[22]

Filing Employment Forms for Minors. Employers of minors are required to obtain appropriate forms for their employment. Possession of the proper forms protects employers from the dangers of hiring minors who may have lied about their ages. An employer of a minor under age 18 must keep on file a certificate stating the age of the minor.

> NOTE: Employers should protect themselves by obtaining proof of age if there is any possibility that prospective employees may be minors being hired for forbidden occupations.

The employer may not rely solely on a statement by the employee of his or her age. You may rely upon an official birth certificate. An employer is protected if it has on file during the period of employment an unexpired certificate of age issued pursuant to regulations showing that the minor meets the minimum age requirements. Generally, states may issue a valid certificate of age. However, there are four states—Idaho, Mississippi, South Carolina, and Texas—where the employer must obtain a certificate of age from the federal government.

Assessing Penalties for Child Labor Law Violations. The Secretary of Labor is responsible for the enforcement of the child labor law. The Labor Department has taken an active interest in prosecuting violators of the child labor law. Employers should be aware that personal liability may be imposed in egregious circumstances. Violators are also subject to criminal prosecution.

The various remedies and penalties provided under the statute include

- Injunction restraining employer from employing minors under the legal minimum age
- Injunction restraining the employer from shipping or delivering goods produced at a facility where oppressive child labor has been employed (these are known as "hot goods")[23]
- Civil penalties (fines)
- Criminal penalties for willful violations (fines up to $10,000 or imprisonment up to six months)
- Personal liability of the individuals responsible for the unlawful conduct (contempt and fines) in cases of extreme intransigence and contempt for the law

A purchaser of "hot goods" who had no knowledge of a violation of the child labor laws is protected; that is, the statute has a proviso that protects the innocent purchaser of goods produced in violation of the law. A shipment of goods acquired by a purchaser in good faith reliance on written assurances from the producer, manufacturer, or dealer that the goods were produced in compliance with the law, but were in fact produced in violation of the law, is excluded from the ban on "hot goods." The purchaser must have acquired the goods for value and have had no notice of any violation. The assurance must be given to the purchaser after the goods had been produced and not simply be a continuing or "standing" assurance that no violations have been committed in the production of goods.

COMPLYING WITH THE EQUAL PAY ACT

The Equal Pay Act and the comparable worth theory appear on their face to be similar ways of attacking pay inequity based on gender. However, they are very different as the following discussion demonstrates. The Equal Pay Act is a federal statute specifically prohibiting discrimination on the basis of sex in paying wages for equal work. The comparable worth theory seeks to gain pay equity among categories of jobs that are different yet may be the equivalent in terms of skill and responsibility and thus of equal worth to the employer. This theory has not yet gained acceptance in the courts, yet it raises interesting issues, for example, why female-dominated professions are the poorest paid. Each of these principles is discussed in the paragraphs that follow and give employers much to contemplate.

How the Equal Pay Act and Title VII Differ

The federal Equal Pay Act of 1963 (EPA) amended the FLSA by adding a new dimension, requiring that male and female workers receive

equal pay for work requiring equal skill, effort and responsibility and performed under similar working conditions.[24]

The EPA and Title VII may apply to the same claim of discrimination. However, given the differences in the statutes, not all conduct that violates Title VII will violate the EPA. The coverage and remedies under the EPA are quite different from those found under Title VII. While the Equal Pay Act is enforced by the Equal Employment Opportunity Commission rather than the Department of Labor—Wage and Hour Division, the same penalties and remedies apply as are found in other provisions of the FLSA.

All employers whose employees are subject to the provisions of the FLSA are covered by the Equal Pay Act. In general, the EPA applies to wages paid to employees who are

- Engaged in commerce
- Engaged in the production of goods for commerce
- Employed in an enterprise engaged in commerce or in the production of goods for commerce.[25]

Under the interpretations given these three categories virtually all employees are covered.

Identifying Exemptions from the EPA. Some employees who are exempt from the minimum wage requirements of FLSA are also exempt under the EPA. Such exemptions are narrowly construed and include

- Certain retail and service establishments
- Agricultural industries
- Auto dealerships
- Food service establishments
- Laundries and dry cleaners
- Local transit
- Newspapers
- Telephone exchanges
- Employment in a foreign country

Identifying Exceptions to the EPA. Pay differentials may be permitted in certain circumstances. There is a general exception for a wage differential based on "factors other than sex." In addition to this general exception, the equal pay provisions contain specific exceptions, including

- Wage differentials paid pursuant to a bona fide seniority system
- Wage differentials paid pursuant to a merit system
- Wage differentials paid pursuant to a system which measures earnings by quantity or quality of production

These exceptions are an affirmative defense to a claim under the EPA. That means that the employer asserting such a defense has the burden of proof in establishing that the wage differential did not violate the act.

The policy or practice of paying wage differentials based on a seniority system or merit system does not have to be a formal written policy in order to constitute a valid defense. Informal or unwritten practices may qualify for an exception under the EPA provided that the employer can demonstrate that the standards have been applied according to an established plan whose essential terms have been communicated to the employees.

NOTE: Consistent application of a permissible basis for granting wage differentials is key where the practice of granting increases or setting wages is based on an unwritten seniority system, merit system, or one's quantity and/or quality of production.

Note that prior salary alone cannot support a pay disparity.[26]

Also, where shift differentials, incentive payments, production bonuses, longevity and performance raises, and the like are applied equally to male and female employees, there is no violation of the EPA. Part-time employees may receive a lower rate of pay than full-time employees so long as the rate is evenly applied to men and women.

Case Example

Marilyn Moss and Rocco Russo were both employed by the Universal Bank Corporation and working as tellers. Marilyn was hired pursuant to a standard bank policy for tellers. Rocco, on the other hand, was categorized as a management trainee, under a new program. Rocco received a higher wage, although he and Marilyn performed the same work and had similar backgrounds. All tellers worked at various positions within the bank. Rocco was the only male performing teller duties and the only employee in the "new program." Marilyn filed a sex-discrimination suit under the EPA.

The bank's defense that the differential was based on factors other than sex was rejected by the court. Any seniority, merit, incentive, or other basis that establishes separate and different rates for men and women without regard to job content is closely scrutinized. The bank, in the example, failed to establish a legitimate basis for differentiating between Rocco, who was essentially a teller, and the other female tellers.[27]

Defining the Standard for an Equal Pay Violation. A complainant must prove the following elements to establish an equal pay violation:

– Employer paid different wages to employees of the opposite sex

– In the same establishment

– For equal work on jobs that required equal skill, effort, and responsibility which are performed under similar working conditions

The "same establishment" requirement is limited to a "distinct physical place of business" rather than to an entire business or enterprise that may include several separate places of business. Thus, what an employer does in a single location is examined and those employees' wage scales will be compared. However, caution should be applied where there are multiple facilities operated by the same employer in close geographical proximity to one another.

NOTE: Employers should institute reasonable pay policies based on the content of the specific job, taking into account such factors as seniority, experience, productivity, and area rates for the same work and skill. These policies should be consistent for all facilities of the employer with adjustments for area rates and other reasonable factors.

Defining Equal Work. The elements assessed in determining what work or jobs are equal include skill, effort, responsibility, and working conditions. The job title or classification means little as to whether the EPA applies to a particular situation. It is the content of the job that is examined with an emphasis on the job requirements and performance.

Skill. The performance requirements of the jobs under scrutiny indicate whether they require equal skill. If the two jobs require essentially the same skill, even though that skill is not exercised to the same degree by the employee in one of the jobs, the jobs are considered equal. Efficiency of an employee's performance is not by itself an appropriate factor in assessing a skill. Note that having a skill not necessary to perform the job is also an inappropriate factor.

Case Example

In a job requiring clerical skills, a male employee's experience will not justify paying him more than female employees, where speed and accuracy were the central skills needed for the job and the female employees were faster and more accurate than the male employee.[28]

Effort. Effort may be difficult to assess. Jobs may require equal effort, but it can be exerted in different ways. However, jobs that appear to involve most of the same routine tasks do not necessarily meet the equal effort requirement. The equal effort factor is lacking in such cases where the more highly paid job involves additional tasks that

- Require extra effort
- Consume a significant amount of time of all higher-paid personnel
- Are of economic value commensurate with the pay differential.[29]

Thus males employed in "heavy" cleaner positions are required to exert a different level of effort in their work than do females working in "light" cleaner positions. But female stewardesses expend the same level of effort as do male pursers, where both groups perform essentially the same duties.

Responsibility. The degree of accountability is the focus of this factor as well as the importance of the job obligation. An employer may justify a wage differential for one member of a group of employees who becomes the acting supervisor in the absence of the regular supervisor. However, minor differences in the level of responsibility will not support a differential.

In a case where an employer assigned a female employee additional supervisory duties without paying her a commensurate salary, a court held that the EPA applied to a female supervisor who was paid less than the workers she supervised where the only difference between her and the workers were her supervisory duties.[30]

Similar working conditions. This factor requires an assessment as to whether the differences in working conditions are the type customarily considered when setting rates of pay. The fact that the jobs in issue are in different departments or are performed at different times of the day (day versus night shift) do not automatically justify a wage differential. An example of dissimilar working conditions is found where some employees work almost exclusively outside the employer's facility and others work exclusively on the premises.

Identifying Remedies Available to the Employee.

An aggrieved employee has two years from the date of the initial violation to bring a civil action against the employer. He or she has three years to bring the action if it is a willful violation. The action may be brought in any federal or state court in the appropriate jurisdiction against any employer, including a public agency.

The remedies available to an employee who successfully prosecutes a claim under the EPA include

- Back pay from date of violation
- Liquidated damages (in cases of willful violations)
- Prejudgment interest
- Reasonable attorneys' fees and costs
- Equitable relief, such as an injunction

The employer may avoid liquidated or double damages if the court finds that the employer had acted in good faith or had reasonable grounds to believe it was not in violation of the law.

NOTE: The statute specifically provides that employers may not reduce the wage rates of any employees in an attempt to comply with the Act's requirements; rather the employer should raise the wages of lower-rated employees to eliminate prohibited differentials.

For quick reference, the pertinent provisions of the Equal Pay Act are summarized in Exhibit 17.1.

– EXHIBIT 17.1 –
Summary of the Provisions of the Equal Pay Act of 1963
(Fair Labor Standards Act)

1. Requires that men and women receive equal pay for equal work on jobs which

    a. Require equal skill and effort
    b. Are performed under similar working conditions

2. Permits exceptions where unequal payment is made according to

    a. Bona fide seniority system
    b. Merit system
    c. System which measures earnings by quantity or quality of production
    d. Differential based on any factor other than sex

3. Is enforced and administered by the EEOC

4. Covers all employees who are covered by the Fair Labor Standards Act

5. Applies to all employees to whom the Fair Labor Standards Act applies, plus executives, administrators, professional employees, and outside salespeople

6. Involves a two-year statute of limitations for filing a claim

7. Involves a three-year statute of limitations for a willful violation

8. An employer who violates the Act is liable for wages owed as a result of a violation; the employer may have to pay an additional sum equal to the amount of money owed ("doubled damages") and other penalties if a *willful* violation is found.

What is the Comparable Worth Theory?

Women and minorities have traditionally held jobs that are less desirable and lower paying yet are as valuable or as necessary to the employer as higher-paying positions historically held by men, even though such jobs do not require greater skills or education.

NOTE: The term "comparable worth" means that employees seek to be compensated on the basis of comparison of the intrinsic worth or difficulty of their job with that of other jobs in the same organization or community.

In other words, women and minorities want to be paid for their work on the same basis as different but comparable positions that generally are paid more and have been traditionally held by white males.

The theory is grounded on the underlying concept that is apparent when you focus on certain female-dominated professions or occupations which have traditionally received lower-pay status, for example, nursing, teaching, and secretarial or clerical work. Workers engaged in these professions receive less than do men working in occupations traditionally male-dominated, such as sanitation or administration. Yet the services provided by nurses and teachers are as vital, if not more so, to our community than are sanitation or administration. The reason for the female-dominated occupations being lower paid is in large part due to the fact that these jobs are held by women. As a result, women have turned to the comparable worth theory to establish pay equity based on the intrinsic value of the work performed rather than on the basis of historical stereotypes or traditional notions of male and female work. Comparable worth appeared to be a theory by which women and minorities would be able to attain more equal footing with regard to compensation and the terms and conditions of their employment.[31]

How Comparable Worth Differs from the Equal Pay Act. Although the theory of comparable worth was developed as a way to remedy past wage discrimination, it differs significantly from the Equal Pay Act. Under the Equal Pay Act, employees performing the same job must be paid the same wage. Under the comparable worth theory, employees performing work that has the same value or worth to the employer should be paid on the same basis.

Case Study

Sheila, Doug, and Jane all work at First Cannery. Sheila works in the office as a secretary, and both Doug and Jane work the same job in the cannery on the assembly line, which is comprised of mostly male workers. Assembly-line workers are paid on the average $30 to $50 a week more than the secretaries who are all females. Since Doug and Jane perform the same work, they must be paid the same scale under the Equal Pay Act.

Sheila performs in a different job from Doug, but the worth of the job to the employer is essentially the same. The employer needs a polite and efficient secretary to have the administrative offices run smoothly. The employer also needs efficient assembly-line workers to have the orders filled promptly. Therefore Sheila and Doug should also be paid on the same scale.

How to Assess the Comparable Worth of Different Jobs. The way to decide if two different jobs are essentially worth the same to the employer is to evaluate the jobs under a set of objective and subjective criteria, such as

– Knowledge and skills necessary for the job
– Mental demands
– Working conditions
– Accountability

An executive and janitor would obviously not be of comparable worth because the knowledge, skills, and mental demands to perform the jobs are quite different. Jobs can be evaluated by the employer according to these or other objective criteria which have had numerical values assigned to each criterion. The employer then totals the values—jobs with similar totals would be considered comparable.

Establishing a Comparable Worth Claim. Comparable worth is a theory that is from time to time asserted in an effort to prove sex discrimination under Title VII and the Civil Rights Act. A cause of action based on this theory has not yet been successful. However, personnel professionals and legal practitioners should be aware of the implications of such a claim.

For example, in *American Federation of State, County, and Municipal Employees v. Washington State,*[32] *(AFSCME v. Washington)*, the federal district court had ruled that comparable worth means the provision of similar salaries for positions that require or impose similar responsibilities, judgments, knowledge, skills, and working conditions. In *AFSCME v. Washington*, two unions representing 15,500 state, county, and municipal employees in mostly female-dominated positions sought implementation of a system of compensation based on comparable worth in response to the state's discriminatory system of compensation wherein employees in male-dominated positions are paid more than are those holding jobs in female-dominated categories. The court found, based on statistical proof, that disparate impact and treatment had intentionally occurred. Thus the plaintiffs were entitled to relief under Title VII.[33]

However, this victory on comparable worth was short-lived, because on appeal the Ninth Circuit Court of Appeals reversed the lower court.[34] The Ninth Circuit held that even where a state-commissioned study has concluded that the male-dominated and female-dominated classifications were comparable in worth, Title VII did not obligate the state to eliminate an economic inequality which it did not create. The Appellate Court held that there was no showing of a discriminatory motive on the part of the state of Washington. The compensation was based on a competitive market, and this does not establish disparate impact discrimination.

General Guidelines for Avoiding Pay Inequity Claims

Although the comparable worth theory is out of favor for the moment, it has certain ramifications that employers should heed. A claim of pay inequity indicates employee unrest that should be addressed. Thus, an employer should make attempts to create pay equity among those jobs that are different yet comparable. The following guidelines are rules of thumb designed to assist an employer in creating an equitable and productive workplace:

1. Review all compensation policies and practices. Compare how they are applied to the various job classifications. Be alert as to whether the compensation system may be viewed as discriminatory.

2. Do not assume that some jobs are better suited for women while others (generally better paying jobs) are more appropriate for men. If a person is qualified, that is all that should be necessary. Regardless of sex or color, the job should go to those who are qualified.

3. Do a job evaluation study. As an employer, make sure the jobs are evaluated on the basis of their value to *you* as the employer, not as they would be to any employer in your situation.

4. Ascertain whether certain job classifications are dominated by men or women and how their compensation compares on that basis. Then examine if the jobs are so different they can support a basis for the pay differential.

5. Design the system with litigation in mind. In the event of a claim of pay inequity, whether or not comparable worth is identified, contact your employment relations attorney.

HOW TO COMPLY WITH FLSA REQUIREMENTS

Employers are responsible for complying with the numerous rules and regulations imposed by the Fair Labor Standards Act, including minimum wage, equal pay, overtime, and child labor laws. We have developed the following guidelines to aid the employer in satisfying these requirements. We have grouped these suggestions under specific headings for ease of use and convenience.

Minimum Wage Compliance

1. Be aware of minimum wage standards.

2. Notify an employee exempted from minimum wage requirements of any change in his or her status.

Child Labor Law Compliance

1. Verify the age and eligibility of each minor employed.

2. Ensure that the minor is properly supervised and not working with or near any dangerous machinery or substances.

3. Periodically review child labor law restrictions and audit your practices to avoid violations.

Compliance With Overtime Provisions

1. Review each job classification and ascertain whether the employee is exempt or nonexempt. Audit scope of duties of each job, salary, and changes in the law on a regular basis.

2. Maintain an overtime recordkeeping policy that provides guidelines as to who is eligible for overtime, when overtime may be accrued, and procedures for recording overtime.

3. Enforce any overtime control policy you may have, for example, "no employee may work overtime without obtaining the prior permission of his or her supervisor."

4. Notify a nonexempt employee whenever there is a change in his or her status to exempt.

5. Award "comp time" for a 35-hour employee up to 40 hours worked in one week. *All* time worked after 40 hours in a single week must be compensated at a rate of one and one-half times the employee's regular hourly rate.

Compliance With the Equal Pay Act

1. Audit all positions and employees who occupy them; ensure that male and female employees who perform essentially the same work and have similar qualifications and training receive the same pay.

2. Correct any differential not exempted under the Act upward only; you cannot reduce another's salary to comply with the Act.

ENDNOTES

1. 29 U.S.C. §201, *et seq.*

2. 29 U.S.C. §203(d). See *Bonnette v. California Health & Welfare Agency*, 704 F.2d 1465 (9th Cir. 1983).

3. *Anderson v. Mt. Clemens Pottery Co.*, 328 U.S. 680 (1946).

4. 40 U.S.C. §276a, *et seq.*

5. 41 U.S.C. §35, *et seq.*

6. 40 U.S.C. §327, *et seq.*

7. 41 U.S.C. §51, *et seq.*

8. 41 U.S.C. §351, *et seq.*

9. 20 U.S.C. §95(m).

10. 15 U.S.C. §1673(a). However, certain exceptions are permitted such as an order for support or debt due for state or federal tax.

11. 29 U.S.C. §203(m), *et seq.*

12. Not all on-call time is compensable. For example, New Jersey specifically excludes on-call time where employees are free to engage in own pursuits, subject only to the understanding that the employee leave word where they may be reached; only when an employee does go out on an on-call assignment is the time actually spent in making the call counted as hours worked. N.J.A.C. 12:56-5.6(a). However, if the calls are so frequent or the "on-call" conditions so restrictive that employees are not really free to use the time for their own benefit, they may be considered as "engaged to wait" rather than "waiting to be engaged." In that event, the on-call time is counted as hours worked. N.J.A.C. 12:56-5.6.(b).

13. 29 C.F.R. Part 541.1.

14. 29 C.F.R. Part 541.2.

15. 29 C.F.R. Part 541.3.

16. See *United States v. Silk*, 331 U.S. 704, 716 (1947); *Rutherford Food Corp. v. McComb*, 331 U.S. 722, 730 (1947); and *Brock v. Superior Care, Inc.*, et al., 840 F.2d 1054 (2d Cir. 1988).

17. Note that $3.55 per hour is below minimum wage. The employer, in this situation, will have to make up the shortfall in cash wages.

18. N.J.A.C. 12: 56-8.8.

19. 29 C.F.R. Part 553.200, *et seq.*

20. Pertinent federal statutes include the primary governing statute FLSA, 29 U.S.C. §212, *et seq.*; Walsh-Healy Act Public Contracts, 4 U.S.C. §35 (under the Walsh-Healy Act, any employer with a government contract of $10,000 or more must certify that no employee is under the age of 16); and the Mineral Lands Act of 1920, 30 U.S.C. §181, *et seq.*

21. 29 U.S.C. §§213 (c) and (d).

22. For example, see New Jersey law, N.J.S.A. 34:2-21.3.

23. The prohibition of removing goods from a violator's establishment applies only to goods produced, manufactured, shipped, or delivered within 30 days of when the oppressive child labor was employed.

24. 29 U.S.C. §206(d)(1).

25. 29 U.S.C. §206(a). The term "commerce" is broadly defined as "trade, commerce, transportation, transmission, or communication among the several States or between

any State and any place outside thereof," 29 U.S.C. §203(b). The term is not limited to simply transportation across state lines or to an activity of a commercial character.

26. See *Hodgson v. Corning Glass Works*, 474 F.2d 226 (2d Cir. 1988).

27. See *EEOC v. First Citizens Bank*, 758 F.2d 397 (9th Cir. 1985).

28. See *EEOC v. First Citizens Bank*, 758 F.2d 397 (9th Cir. 1985).

29. See *Hodgson v. Brookhaven General Hospital*, 436 F.2d 719 (5th Cir. 1970).

30. See *Riordan v. Kempiners*, 831 F.2d 690 (7th Cir. 1987).

31. Roger B. Jacobs, "Comparable Worth," *Case and Controversy*, March/April 1985, p. 12.

32. 578 F.Supp. 846 (W.D. Wash. 1983).

33. The district court in reaching this conclusion had examined a comparable worth study commissioned by the state government. The study showed that based on the content of 121 job classifications that were evaluated, women's jobs tended to be paid less than men's with 20 percent disparity. The court stated "the State of Washington has failed to rectify an acknowledged discriminatory disparity in compensation . . . and is continuing to treat some employees less favorably than others because of their sex, and this treatment is intentional." 578 F.Supp. at 867.

34. 770 F.2d 1401 (9th Cir. 1985).

18

EMPLOYEE BENEFITS: A BASIC GUIDE TO ERISA AND COBRA

Benefits, particularly health, welfare and pension benefits, are probably the most frequently asked about issues by employees. Much of the statutory and regulation material is complicated and can be confusing. In this chapter, we have tried to simplify the rules regarding health, medical, and pension benefits. This discussion is intended only as an introduction to this area; we recommend that the personnel professional consult employee benefit specialists when faced with a complex issue. We have already discussed compensation in Chapter 17, and we will cover unemployment compensation in Chapter 23 and workers' compensation in Chapter 22; this chapter will focus on the requirement to continue health and medical benefits after employment has ended, pension, severance and the Employee Retirement Income Security Act (ERISA).

NOTE: If your company has an employee welfare benefit plan or pension plan, then you must become familiar with ERISA.

Many employee benefits, such as vacation; holidays; personal leave; sick leave; maternity leave; personal days; and medical, dental, and other health benefits; severance pay; pension; and other similar or related benefits, are given by the employer without requirement of law. The decision to initiate such benefits is the employer's alone. Granting these benefits may be a strategy to attract and retain a skilled work force. However, once these benefits are instituted, the employer may be subject to statutory requirements in the administration of such benefits. The key to the administration of these benefits once the employer has granted them is fair and equal dispensation.

Title VII and other anti-discrimination laws may be used to find liability if the benefits are not administered in a nondiscriminatory manner. However, in the past decade, legislation has been enacted that governs the administration of many benefits, including medical and health, severance, maternity leave, pension, and other retirement programs. The focus of this chapter will be on the Employee Retirement Income Security Act of 1974 (ERISA) and the Consolidated Omnibus Budget Reconciliation Act of 1985 ("COBRA"), as amended.

HOW THE EMPLOYEE RETIREMENT INCOME SECURITY ACT (ERISA) GOVERNS EMPLOYEE BENEFITS

Certain employee benefits provided by the employer are exclusively governed by the Employee Retirement Income Security Act of 1974.[1] ERISA, when enacted, was a comprehensive legislative reform of employee benefit law. ERISA was enacted after Congress determined that the growth in size, scope, and number of employee benefit plans had been rapid and substantial.

Employee benefit plans directly affect the well-being and security of millions of employees and their dependents and are an important factor affecting the stability of employment and successful development of industrial relations. ERISA is intended to provide minimum standards for assuring the equitable character of such plans as well as their financial soundness.

The subject of employee welfare and pension plans requires a working knowledge of the provisions of ERISA and the Internal Revenue Code as well as other areas such as civil rights, corporate and individual taxation, securities, and trusts and estates. We will discuss the provisions of ERISA and also provide the personnel professional with basic information so that they are aware of certain issues which should be addressed by the benefits specialist that the company may have in-house or available as a consultant.

Describing the Structure of ERISA

ERISA is comprised of four titles that cover a wide range of topics and requirements.

Title I contains the so-called "labor" provisions of the Act. Title I covers disclosure, minimum participation standards, accruing benefits, vesting, minimum funding standards, fiduciary duties, enforcement, as well as a continuation of benefits requirement. The Department of Labor (DOL) is responsible for administering the provisions of Title I.

Title II covers the tax qualification provisions instituted by way of amendments to the Internal Revenue Code (Code). These are referred to as the Code provisions and parallel the participation, vesting and funding provisions of Title I. Title II also covers programs such as individual retirement accounts (IRAs) and so-called "Keogh plans" (a type of pension plan for self-employed persons) and contribution and benefit limits. Title II is enforced by the Treasury Department.

Title III addresses the division of enforcement jurisdiction between the Treasury Department and the DOL, two of the federal agencies that administer ERISA. There is also a board established to certify pension actuaries.

Title IV contains the provisions governing the termination of certain pension plans and the guarantee of certain benefits by the Pension Benefits Guaranty Corporation (PBGC).

ERISA is primarily remedial in nature, meaning that it is employee oriented and is intended to ensure a fair and equitable administration of benefits.

Employee Benefit Plans that Are Covered by ERISA

Under ERISA, there are two different classifications of employee benefit plans: "pension plans" and "welfare plans."

Pension Plans. Pension plans include any plan, fund, or program established or maintained by an employer or employer organization or both that either provides retirement income to employees or defers the receipt of income until the employee terminates employment or beyond.[2] Under this broad definition, *all* retirement plans are pension plans.

The statute divides pension plans into two categories: "defined contribution plans" and "defined benefit plans."

Defined contribution plans are pension plans that provide a separate account for each employee participating (participant) in the plan and pay benefits based solely on the amount contributed to the participant's account, adjusted for expenses, and investment gains and losses.[3] Examples of defined contribution plans include profit-sharing plans, employee stock ownership plans, 401(k) plans, savings plans, and stock bonus plans. Thus the value of the benefit is not known until the date of retirement. The resulting benefit is dependent upon the decisions made with regard to the level of contributions made during the employee's participation.

On the other hand, a *defined benefit plan* is a pension plan that pays a promised or fixed benefit upon retirement. The benefit is usually determined through a formula based primarily on the participant's compensation and the number of years the participant has worked for the employer.

Under a defined benefit plan, the pension benefit may be calculated in a number of ways, but three basic formulas are used.

♦ *Final or highest average pay formula.* The defined benefit plan promises that the retirement benefit will be 1 percent of a final, or highest, three years' average of salary multiplied by number of years of participation in the plan.

♦ *Career average formula.* A plan states that it will pay a percentage (1.5 percent) of each year's compensation for each year of participation in the plan.

♦ *Flat dollar amount.* The plan has been collectively bargained and offers a stated dollar amount (such as $25.00 per month), which is multiplied by the number of years of participation.

Whichever method of calculation is used, a defined benefit plan defines at the beginning what the benefit will be at the time of retirement.

Welfare Benefit Plans. Welfare benefit plans are employee benefit plans that are not pension plans. These include plans that provide medical, surgical, or hospital care; benefits in the event of sickness, accident, disability, death, or unemployment (such as severance pay); vacation benefits; apprenticeship or other training programs; day care centers; scholarship funds; and prepaid legal services.[4]

Certain employer policies, practices, or programs that are expressly excluded from the definition of employee benefit plans include the following:

– Payment for overtime or premiums for shift, holidays, or weekends

– Wages paid out of employer's general assets during periods of absence for medical reasons

– Wages paid out of general assets during vacation or holidays; while on active military duty, jury duty, or testifying in an official proceeding; or while absent for training, sabbatical leave, or other educational absence.

– Maintenance on or near an employer's premises, of recreation, dining, or other facilities (other than day care centers) or of first aid facilities for work-related injuries or illnesses

– Distribution of holiday gifts such as a turkey

– Sale to employees, whether or not discounted, of articles offered for sale in the course of employer's business

– Maintenance of a hiring hall

– Remembrance funds providing flowers or small gifts during sickness or hospitalization and at death or termination

– Maintenance of a strike fund

– Participation in certain industry advancement programs

- A group or group-type insurance program offered to employees if no employer contributions are made and participation is voluntary for employees; the employer does not endorse the program, though the employer may collect premiums through payroll deductions, and the employer receives no consideration other than reasonable compensation in connection with the payroll deductions[5]

- Maintenance of a scholarship program (including tuition reimbursement) under which payments are made solely from the employer's general assets[6]

Identifying ERISA Title I Requirements

Generally, all employee benefit plans must comply with Title I of ERISA. Title I addresses the following issues: reporting and disclosure, participation standards, vesting, funding standards, fiduciary duties, and continuation of group health benefits.

Reporting and Disclosure. All pension and welfare plans, unless exempted, must comply with the ERISA reporting and disclosure requirements.

Title I requires the person in charge of administering the plan (the plan administrator) to distribute various reports to plan participants, "beneficiaries" (persons designated by a participant or by the terms of a plan who are entitled to plan benefits), and the Department of Labor.[7] The reporting requirements fall into the three major plan phases: plan establishment, plan operation, and plan termination.

Plan Establishment. When a plan is established, the plan administrator must give participants a *summary plan description,* or SPD.[8] The SPD must accurately describe the plan, including, among other things, the plan's benefits, how an employee becomes eligible for benefits, and how the benefits can be forfeited.[9] The SPD requirement furthers ERISA's goals by informing participants and beneficiaries of their rights under the plan.

> NOTE: The SPD is a very important document. It summarizes the employees' rights, entitlements, and procedures regarding claims and termination that must be followed under the Plan. It must be written in a way that the average plan participant will understand his or her rights and obligations under the plan. Great care should be taken in the development and distribution of the SPD.

A newly established plan may also have to file reports with the DOL and the Securities and Exchange Commission (SEC). (Generally, the plan administrator has to file with the SEC if securities are offered under the plan.)

Plan Operation. While the plan is in operation, the plan administrator must annually file a Form 5500 with the Internal Revenue Service (IRS). The IRS forwards copies of the form to the DOL, and if the plan is a defined benefit plan, to the PBGC. ERISA's reporting and disclosure provisions also require the plan administrator to furnish participants and beneficiaries with a summary annual report, which indicates the financial health of the plan, and to periodically update the SPD.[10]

Plan Termination. If a plan terminates, an employer generally need not do more than notify participants of the fact. If the plan is a defined benefit pension plan, however, the plan must comply with the specific reporting and disclosure requirements of ERISA Title IV.

Covered plans must file with the DOL the following:

- Summary plan description
- Annual summary of material modifications, if any
- An annual report
- Termination report

Provisions of ERISA's Participation Rule

ERISA's minimum participation rule, which applies only to pension plans, provides that an employer may not adopt a plan that excludes employees from participating in the plan later than the time the employees both attain age 21 and complete one year of service with the employer. However, the employer can require two years of service if the plan provides for immediate vesting of the employees' entire benefit at the time the benefit accrues.[11] The participating requirements also prohibit plans from having a maximum age cutoff for determining when an employee may participate in the plan. For example, a plan may not exclude employees hired after age 65.[12]

Note that although the participation requirements set a minimum reasonableness standard for establishing plan eligibility requirements, they do not curb the pre-ERISA problem of discrimination against certain classes of employees. Employers may still impose additional requirements for participating, and eligibility may be limited to employees of a particular division of the company or to particular types or classes of employees.

Implementing ERISA's Vesting Standards

A major goal of ERISA is to guarantee to workers that once a plan covers them and they work a specified number of years, they will have earned the right to a pension benefit upon retirement. This is accomplished through ERISA's vesting standards. Like the minimum participation rule, ERISA's vesting rules apply only to pension plans. The vesting rules determine how long an employee must be employed before his or her benefit under a plan becomes non-forfeitable.[13]

Vesting Schedules. ERISA allows employers to choose one of two alternative vesting schedules. The vesting schedule shows the percentage of a benefit an employee is entitled to after completing a certain number of years of service. The alternative vesting schedules are

- *Graded vesting,* under which a certain percentage of a participant's "accrued benefit," (benefit earned) becomes increasingly nonforfeitable with each year of service with the employer.

- *Cliff vesting,* or 5-year vesting, under which a participant becomes fully vested after working five years, without partial vesting during the five years.[14] Collectively bargained and state and local government plans may have 10-year vesting.

Plans with a graded vesting schedule must permit a participant to vest fully after 7 years of service and under §29 U.S.C. 1053(a)(2)(B) and Code §411(a)(2)(B) must provide a vesting schedule no less favorable than the following:

Years of Service	Nonforfeitable Percentage
3	20%
4	40
5	60
6	80
7 or more	100

A participant's vesting percentage is important because it tells the employee what percentage of her accrued benefit she would be entitled to if her employment were terminated on a particular day. This information furthers the goals of ERISA by enabling participants to make educated decisions about terminating employment.

For example, an employee participating in a plan with 5-year cliff vesting who has been employed for 4 years might decide to remain employed with her current employer for 1 more year before changing jobs so she could receive a benefit for the years worked.

Vesting Is Entitlement. A person fully vested in an employee benefit plan may not necessarily be entitled to be paid the benefit immediately. Vesting means only that once the employee has a vested right to a pension, the employee cannot lose the benefit and the employer may not amend or terminate the plan to either reduce or eliminate the nonforfeitable benefit. It does not mean a right to an immediate payout.

The terms of the plan govern when benefits are paid out. Vesting is also distinguishable from "benefit accrual." Vesting determines whether an employee is entitled to a benefit; benefit accrual reflects the amount of the benefit earned to date. Generally, depending on the benefit formula used in a plan, the longer an employee works, the greater the benefit he or she accrues. Thus, even though an employee may be vested in a benefit after 5 or 7 years, the amount of the benefit will generally increase the more years the employee works. Benefit accrual rules require that accruals be relatively proportionate. That is, the benefit must accrue ratably rather than in increasing percentages.[15]

HOW ERISA PROVIDES FOR FUNDING THE PLAN

ERISA provides very complex rules for funding employee pension benefit plans. These rules apply only to defined benefit pension plans and "money purchase pension plans" (defined contribution plans that obligate an employer to make fixed amount contributions).[16] ERISA's funding rules do not cover defined contribution plans other than money purchase pension plans.[17] ERISA's funding requirement ensures that employers contribute enough money to pay benefits when due and prevents employers from promising benefits they cannot deliver.

The funding rules impose a yearly minimum on each employer who establishes a defined benefit plan. The employer must make payments to a funding standard account to fund the costs of benefits accrued during the current year and the amortized costs of benefits that have accrued based on service performed in past years. Actuaries determine the value of benefits needed to fund the plan.

Establishing a Trust. Generally, assets of funded employee benefit plans must be held in a trust maintained by one or more trustees. The trust agreement or the plan document may name the trustee. Alternatively, a "named fiduciary" of the plan can appoint the trustee. The trustee has exclusive authority to manage plan assets held in trust unless the plan document expressly provides otherwise.[18]

Describing ERISA's Fiduciary Provisions

Every employee benefit plan must identify at least one person responsible for making sure that the plan complies with ERISA.[19] The person(s) named in the plan is (are) the "named fiduciary." Typically, named fiduciaries are the trustees of the trust holding the plan's funds and the plan administrators. In addition to the named fiduciary, any person or entity exercising discretionary authority or control over an employee benefit plan or its assets is considered a fiduciary.[20] For example, a claims administrator hired by the plan to administer employees' claims to medical benefits is a fiduciary with respect to claims administration only. The plan document details the extent of a fiduciary's affirmative duties.

Fiduciaries' Duties. ERISA imposes duties and prohibitions on all fiduciaries. The duties include affirmative steps the fiduciary must take to maintain the plan and the restrictions prohibiting the fiduciary from entering into certain transactions. Under the affirmative duties, a fiduciary must act

- Solely in the interest of the participants and beneficiaries
- For the exclusive purpose of providing benefits to participants and beneficiaries and defraying reasonable expenses of administering the plan
- With the care, skill, prudence, and diligence a prudent person in a like capacity and familiar with like matters would use to conduct a like enterprise with like aims under like circumstances
- By diversifying the plan's investments to minimize the risk of large losses, unless under the circumstances it is clearly imprudent to do so
- In accordance with the documents and instruments governing the plan, to the extent that the documents and instruments are consistent with the provisions of ERISA Titles I and IV[21]

Affirmative duties also include selecting proper plan investments, paying plan expenses, properly diversifying plan assets, monitoring investment performance, ensuring that the plan has sufficient assets to pay plan benefits, and managing and making administrative decisions.

Prohibited Transactions. ERISA prohibits a fiduciary from engaging in transactions the fiduciary knows or should know are prohibited.[22] For example, transactions between the plan and a "party in interest" are prohibited under ERISA.[23]

A *party in interest* is defined as any employer or employee organization sponsoring the plan, employees, any fiduciary of the plan, any person providing services to the plan, and persons who have certain specified relationships to any of the foregoing individuals or entities.[24]

Another type of prohibited transaction is one in which the fiduciary has a conflict of interest with the plan.[25] Both types of transactions are prohibited because of the high likelihood of plan losses or insider abuse.

The DOL may grant a *prohibited transaction exemption* if a plan fiduciary or party in interest can demonstrate an ordinarily prohibited transaction poses minimal danger of insider abuse or asset loss.[26] There are also exemptions found in 29 U.S.C. §§1107 and 1108 and the accompanying regulations. In some cases, large numbers of people have sought similar prohibited transaction exemptions, and the DOL has granted a "class exemption."

Fiduciaries' Liabilities. If the fiduciary fails to perform the affirmative duties or engages in a prohibited transaction, the fiduciary can be sued in a civil action and required to restore plan losses or to pay the plan any profits earned through the transaction.[27] A breach of a fiduciary responsibility also subjects a fiduciary or any knowing participant in the breach to a penalty equal to 20 percent of the amount the plan or the participants and beneficiaries recover from the fiduciary.[28] In addition to the risk of liability for a breach of a fiduciary's own duties, fiduciaries can, in certain circumstances, be held liable for cofiduciaries' breaches. Case law has recently extended the fiduciary liability doctrine to persons who are not fiduciaries but who knowingly aid fiduciaries in a breach of fiduciary duty under ERISA.[29]

Requirements of Joint and Survivor Annuity Rules

The joint and survivor annuity rules require a qualified plan to pay the pension of a married participant in the form of "joint and survivor annuity." This is an annuity for the life of the employee with a benefit equal to at least half of the annuity amount payable to the spouse for the spouse's life.[30] The spouse must be the participant's beneficiary unless the employee elects otherwise and the spouse consents in writing.[31]

Enumerating Title IV Requirements

Title IV is administered by the PBGC and applies only to defined benefit plans. The PBGC acts as a guarantor of a certain amount of benefits. The PBGC guarantees payment of a participant's nonforfeitable benefits if an employer terminates a defined benefit plan without sufficient funds to pay its benefit liabilities. The PBGC's guarantee does not ensure that a participant will receive the full level of benefits promised under the defined benefit plan. The PBGC limits the amount of benefits it will pay to a certain dollar amount ($2,250 annuity payment per month per participant for 1991). The PBGC also guarantees vested benefits only under a plan that has been in effect for a least 5 years, as of the date of plan termination.[32]

Reporting and Disclosure. Title IV imposes special reporting and disclosure requirements on defined benefit plans.[33] Under Title IV, the plan administrator of a defined benefit plan must report "reportable events" to the PBGC.[34] Reportable events are events indicating that a plan might be experiencing financial difficulties or is about to terminate.

Examples of reportable events include

- Amendments reducing the amount of benefits

- A significant decrease in the number of participants in an underfunded plan

- Failure to meet the minimum funding requirements

- Inability to make benefit payments when due

- A significant decrease in the number of participants in an underfunded plan

If the PBGC believes that there is a strong likelihood that a plan will terminate without sufficient funds to pay benefits, the PBGC may terminate a plan involuntarily.[35] If the PBGC later determines that a plan can get back on its feet, it may reinstate the plan.[36]

Single versus Multiemployer Plans.

Title IV distinguishes between two kinds of defined benefit plans: single employer plans and multiemployer plans. A *single employer plan* is maintained by one employer; a *multiemployer plan* is maintained by more than one employer or one controlled group.[37] Unions representing employees who work for more than one employer usually establish multiemployer plans (for example, multiemployer plans are common in the construction trades). Benefits in a multiemployer plan are funded through contributions from the various employers in proportion to the number of union employees working for that employer.

Termination of Multiemployer Plan.

If one employer stops contributing to a multiemployer plan (either because it no longer has union employees or because it wants to provide another benefit), the multiemployer plan does not terminate. Upon cessation of contributions, however, Title IV requires the withdrawing employer to pay, in accordance with a specified schedule, its share of the plan's unfunded vested benefits.[38] The amount of this potential liability is called **withdrawal liability.** A multiemployer plan terminates when all employers withdraw from the plan, all benefit accruals cease, or the plan is converted into a defined contribution plan.[39]

> NOTE: Withdrawal liability can be costly and should be carefully considered prior to any decision to closing down.

Voluntary Termination.

There are only two ways that a single-employer plan can voluntarily terminate: with enough money to pay benefits or without it.[40] Terminating a defined benefit plan with assets sufficient to pay benefit liabilities is called a *standard termination.* Terminating the plan without enough money to pay benefits is called a *distress termination.*

When a pension plan is terminated and future benefits are payable, the plan administrator purchases annuities for the participants that will pay the benefit when it becomes due. If an employer is going to terminate a plan, it must notify participants of its intention and file with the PBGC.[41]

Reversion.

An employer that terminates an overfunded plan (having more than enough assets to pay currently promised benefits) can revert the surplus benefits to the company if the plan expressly permits and there is no statutory prohibition. A recent amendment discourages employers from terminating plans to get surplus plan assets. Since 1990, employers have had to pay an excise tax equal to 50 percent of the amount of the reversion, plus income tax, unless the employer rolls over the surplus into a comparable employee benefit plan, reducing the excise tax to 20 percent.[42]

HOW THE INTERNAL REVENUE CODE AFFECTS BENEFITS

The Internal Revenue Code provides certain minimum requirements if the employer elects to adopt a plan that has favorable tax consequences. The election by the employer to adopt such a plan is optional. If an employer wants to adopt a "qualified plan," the plan must then meet the requirements of specific Code provisions. The Code qualification rules constitute Title II of ERISA and apply only to pension plans.

How Qualified Plans Provide Tax Advantages

Qualified plans provide desirable tax advantages to both employees and employers. The primary benefit of a qualified plan is that the employer can deduct its contributions which are not taxed as income to the employee until the employee actually receives the benefit. In addition, any money a funded plan holds is held in a tax-exempt trust and thereby accumulates income tax free.

Qualified plans are subject to extensive requirements with regard to participation, coverage, and nondiscrimination rules. These rules were adopted to encourage employers to provide retirement benefits to those who earn the least and therefore would have the greatest need for these benefits. The tax incentive created under Title IV encouraged employers to provide income to employees who have stopped working. This income lessens the former worker's reliance on social security and, in the case of those who become disabled before retirement, lessens the burden on other welfare plans. The qualified plan rules discussed shortly are designed to further these goals. (Many of these rules duplicate the rules in Title I of ERISA and will therefore not be discussed in detail in this section. The following rules apply only to qualified plans.)

Participation Rules. Many of the Code's participation rules parallel the ERISA participation rules. However, the *50/40* rule is exclusively applicable to qualified plans. Under this rule a qualified plan must benefit the lesser of 50 employees or 40 percent of the employer's work force.[43]

Coverage Rules. The Code's coverage rules require a qualified plan to pay benefits to a significant portion of an employer's "nonhighly compensated employees" (non-HCEs). The rule generally requires a qualified plan to benefit 70 percent of the employer's non-HCEs or that the percentage of non-HCEs benefiting must be 70 percent of the percentage of highly compensated employees benefiting.[44]

Non-discrimination Rules. The Code's nondiscrimination rules prohibit qualified plans from discriminating in favor of highly compensated employees in benefit or contribution amounts. This rule does not limit HCEs to the same amount of retirement income as non-HCEs; rather it requires that retirement income formulas not unfairly favor HCEs.

For example, a benefit formula that pays a percentage of compensation for all participants does not violate the nondiscrimination rules, but a formula that pays an increased percentage of compensation to those earning over $60,000, for example, would not comply with the nondiscrimination rules.[45]

Controlled Group Rules. The participating, coverage, and nondiscrimination rules apply on a "controlled group" basis. This means that organizations within the same controlled group are treated as one organization for determining if a plan complies with these rules. Generally, organizations having at least 80 percent common ownership are deemed to be part of the same controlled group.[46]

Section 415 Rules. Code Section 415 limits the amount of tax-favored contributions that can be paid to a defined benefit or defined contribution plan on behalf of an HCE. This rule presumes that HCEs are in a better position to save for retirement without the tax incentive.

Defining the Maximum Benefit. According to Code Section 415(b)(1)(A), the maximum annual benefit that a plan participant may receive from a defined benefit plan is the lesser of $108,963 or 100 percent of the participant's annual compensation. The limit for a defined contribution plan is the lesser of $30,000 or 25 percent of the participant's annual compensation.[47] Both limits are indexed and increased with the cost of living each year and apply in the aggregate to all similar plans sponsored by the same employer.

In determining who is the "same employer," for Section 415 purposes, the controlled group rules apply, but the 80 percent common ownership test is replaced by a "more than 50 percent" control test which is more inclusive.[48] Thus, if an employee participates in two defined benefit plans sponsored by one or more employers in the same controlled group, the employee can receive no more than the $108,963—the *415 limit*—from both plans. The Code does not aggregate benefits when an employee participates in two defined benefit plans sponsored by two employers who are not in the same controlled group. If the employer participates in both a defined contribution and a defined benefit plan, a special "combined plan limit" applies. Plan benefits payable to an employee in excess of the 415 limits are forfeited to the plan.

Compensation Limits and Mandatory Distribution Rules

If a retirement benefit is based on a percentage of compensation, the amount of compensation taken into account may not exceed $222,220 (indexed and increased each year).[49]

A qualified plan generally may not start paying a pension benefit until the earlier of the date the employee separates from service or turns age 59 and ½.[50] Any payments before age 59 and ½ will subject the employee to a 10 percent excise tax unless the employee rolls over the distribution to an IRA or other qualified plan.[51] An employer must begin paying a pension benefit on April 1 of the year after the employee turns age 70 and ½.[52]

Adopting a Qualified Plan

For a plan to be a qualified plan, it must be established as a qualified plan (the plan document must comply with the foregoing rules) and be operated in accordance with the qualified plan rules. To ensure that they are adopting qualified plans, employers will typically ask the IRS for a "determination letter" that the plan documents comply with the qualified plan rules. If the IRS discovers that a plan is not in compliance with the qualification rules, it can disqualify the plan.

The Effect of Plan Disqualification.
Plan disqualification produces undesirable tax effects: the employee will have taxable income equal to his or her nonforfeitable right to employer contributions, the employer will lose the deduction for amounts contributed but not currently recognized as taxable income by participants, and the trust will be taxed on any trust earnings.

REVIEWING TYPES OF PLANS SUBJECT TO ERISA

The following is a brief description of some popular plans that are subject to the provisions of ERISA and the Code.

Health Plans.
ERISA requires employers with more than 20 employees who maintain a group health plan to permit employees or their dependents to continue their health coverage if the employee or dependent would lose health coverage as a result of certain events.[53] This coverage is often referred to as *COBRA coverage*. See our extensive discussion on COBRA obligations that follows in this chapter.

Cost-Containment Health Plans.
We are regularly asked how to attempt to reduce insurance costs.

Due to the rapid rise in health care costs, employers have sought to limit the cost of providing health care benefits through "cost-containment" measures. Examples of some cost reduction ideas follow:

Managed Care. Two common cost-containment methods include requiring participants to get second opinions before surgery and/or requiring participants to call the insurance company for approval before receiving treatments. If the participant doesn't get the second opinion or the procedure is not approved, the insurance company reduces the amount of medical coverage. The purpose of the second opinion and prior approval schemes, typically called *utilization review,* is to guarantee that participants are not getting (and the insurance company is not paying for) unnecessary treatment. A plan with one or both of these features is known as a system of "managed care."

HMOs and PPOs. Another cost-containment device is the use of a preferred provider organization (PPO) or a health maintenance organization (HMO). HMOs and PPOs provide participants with a schedule of health coverage at fixed prices that are typically lower than those that private providers charge. In an HMO, the participant generally must receive treatment at the HMO facilities. A participant in a PPO must visit one of a list of "participating doctors" to receive the PPO price.

Copayment System. Employers have also reduced the cost of medical coverage by requiring employees to share the coverage costs. Employees share the cost in two ways; by paying a deductible amount and by paying a "copayment amount." For example, if a medical plan covers 80 percent of all covered procedures, the participants must pay a 20 percent copayment amount after the deductible amount has been met.

Cafeteria-Style Welfare Benefit Plans.

A "cafeteria plan" permits employees to use a combination of pre- and post-tax dollars to make selections from a cafeterialike assortment of benefits.[54] For example, a cafeteria plan might permit an employee to purchase medical coverage with employer-provided pre-tax dollars, permit employees to supplement coverage by using pre-tax or after-tax dollars, and permit the employee to use employer-provided dollars to purchase a different benefit such as life insurance. These types of plans may be funded both through employer contributions and employee deferrals. A cafeteria plan may also permit employees to set aside pre-tax dollars in a "flexible spending account."

Flexible Spending Account.

Employers may elect to offer employees either a dependent care or health care flexible spending account, or both. If an employer offers a dependent care flexible spending account, an employee can set aside up to $5,000 ($2,500 if married and filing separately) of pre-tax income to pay for child care.[55] If an employer offers a health care flexible spending account, there is no statutory limit on how much the employee can set aside. The employee can use the amount elected under a health care flexible spending account to pay deductibles and other expenses not otherwise covered under an existing insurance policy. One advantage of a health care flexible spending account is that an employee can use the full amount elected even if it has not yet been deducted from the employee's paycheck.

> NOTE: Flexible spending accounts must provide that employees lose the amount set aside if it is not used in the year it is set aside. This is typically called the "use it or lose it" rule.[56]

Describing Special Qualified Retirement Plans

Certain types of qualified retirement or pension plans, including profit sharing, stock bonus, and employee stock ownership plans, must meet the requirements of Code Section 401(s).

Profit-Sharing Plans.   A *profit-sharing plan* is a defined contribution plan that links plan benefits to an employer's annual profit.[57] A profit-sharing plan must provide a definite, pre-determined formula for allocating contributions made to the plan but may provide that an employer has discretion to contribute to the plan, even in a profitable year. Typically, employer contributions are allocated to a participant's individual account in proportion to the participant's compensation. An employer can also allocate contributions by using a formula based on age, past service with the employer or a predecessor employer, or any other definite formula. A profit-sharing plan is exempt from the minimum funding requirement of ERISA, but an employer must make substantial and recurring contributions to retain the plan's qualified status.[58]

Stock Bonus Plans.   A *stock bonus plan* provides benefits using methods similar to those used in a profit-sharing plan.[59] However, under a stock bonus plan, contributions are not necessarily dependent upon the employer's profit, and distributions are made in employer stock.[60] A stock bonus plan must invest primarily in the employer's securities.

Employee Stock Ownership Plan.   An *employee stock ownership plan* (ESOP) is a defined contribution plan which is either a stock bonus plan or a combination of a stock bonus plan and a money purchase pension plan designed to invest primarily in employer securities.[61] ESOPs were originally devised to give employees an opportunity to build an ownership interest in the employer. ESOPs must give participants certain voting rights and the right to demand distributions of their account balance.[62] In certain circumstances, ESOPs must also require an employer to repurchase the employee's shares when the employee receives a distribution, so that the employee can receive a cash benefit.[63] Unlike any other employee benefit plan, ESOPs may be leveraged (the ESOP may borrow money) to purchase employer securities. This fact has enabled employees to participate in the takeover of their companies from management.

Cash or Deferred Arrangement Plans. A *cash or deferred arrangement*, commonly referred to as "CODA" or a "401(k)" *plan*, is part of either a profit-sharing or stock bonus plan. Under a CODA, an employee may choose between having the employer make payments to a profit-sharing or stock bonus plan on behalf of the employee or to the employee directly in cash.[64] The contributions are usually withheld from an employee's salary before taxes have been deducted. An employer may also contribute an amount to the 401(k) plan as a means of enhancing employee's savings. The employer contributions are usually related to the amount of money the employee contributes, up to a maximum percentage. This contribution by the employer is called a "matching contribution." Employees in a 401(k) plan may save several thousands of dollars in a single tax year by not having to include this amount in gross income.[65]

"Qualified" Annuities. A "qualified" annuity plan is an annuity contract that meets some of the qualified plan requirements of Code Section 401(a), including minimum coverage, nondiscrimination, mandatory distribution, qualified joint and survivor, and annual benefit limitation rules, which are also applicable to qualified plans.[66] Under a qualified annuity plan, the employee pays tax when he or she receives the funds.[67]

Nonqualified Deferred Compensation. This section reviews some commonly established unfunded *deferred compensation arrangements* (DCAs or nonqualified deferred compensation plans) and discusses how the benefits provided are secured. A deferred compensation arrangement is a contract that defers compensation earned in one year for future payment, normally upon retirement, death, or disability of the covered employee. Compared to qualified arrangements, nonqualified deferred compensation is subject to much less regulation. As a result, DCAs are often adapted to a variety of uses. For example, DCAs can provide retirement benefits in excess of the benefits payable under a "qualified plan," as severance package sweeteners and as a means to retain management. Examples of nonqualified deferred compensation plans include top-hat plans, bonus stock plans, golden parachute arrangements, and stock option plans.

A *top-hat plan* is a plan that the employer maintains primarily for providing deferred compensation to select management or highly compensated employees. Top-hat plans are exempt from all provisions of ERISA, except the reporting and disclosure requirement.

A *bonus stock plan* grants employer stock to a designated employee or employees either on a one-time basis or pursuant to an ongoing plan. The criteria used to determine the number of shares granted are usually a percentage of annual salary or a target goal for the employee or the company.

Under a *golden parachute arrangement* an employer makes substantial severance payments to corporate executives triggered by a change in corporate control. If a "parachute payment" is excessive (for example, in the excess of three times an employee's annual salary), the employee must pay a nondeductible 20 percent excise tax on the excess, and the employer is denied a deduction for the excess payment.[68]

A *stock option plan* typically involves an employee option to purchase stock from the company at a specified price. The options are usually nontransferable and are awarded as a bonus. Stock option plans are categorized as either incentive stock option (ISO) plans or nonqualified stock option (NQSO) plans.

An *incentive stock option plan* is an option grant plan that gives an employee the right or privilege to purchase employer stock for any employment-connected reason.[69] An employee participating in an ISO plan receives preferential tax treatment because the employee does not recognize income when receiving or exercising the options and any gain on subsequent sale is taxed as a capital gain.[70] A *nonqualified stock option plan* differs from an ISO in the option exercise price and the tax treatment on exercise. In the case of a NQSO, the options may have an exercise price that is below market.

How Other Laws Affect Employee Benefits Law

Employee benefits law may be dominated by ERISA and the Code, but other laws also impose certain limitations and prohibitions. The most important areas of overlap are civil rights law, securities law, and federal preemption of state laws.

Civil Rights Laws. The civil rights law most likely to come up in the employee benefits area is the Age Discrimination in Employment Act (ADEA).[71] ADEA prohibits employee benefit plans from providing lesser benefits to older persons. A safe harbor in the ADEA permits an employer to provide lesser coverage for certain welfare benefits if the rationale for providing fewer benefits is cost justified.[72] The ADEA also generally prohibits employers from refusing to offer older employees benefits solely because of age.[73]

Securities Laws. Some plans permit investment in the employer's securities. To the extent the plan permits such investment, these plans must comply with the securities laws. Benefits lawyers also work with the securities laws in drafting nonqualified plans for executives. Executives are often given a chance to participate in bonus stock plans which must comply with securities laws.

State Law. ERISA preempts every state law that "relates to" an employee benefit plan except state laws that regulate insurance, banking, and securities.[74] In general, this has been interpreted to mean that a person bringing a claim for benefits or challenging a fiduciary's actions may not also bring breach of contract or tort claims against the plan. ERISA does not preempt laws relating to state disability funds and unemployment insurance, nor does it preempt other federal laws, including federal bankruptcy law.[75]

ENTITLEMENT TO CONTINUATION OF BENEFITS THROUGH COBRA

Once benefits such as health and medical care are instituted in the workplace, the employer becomes subject to certain requirements regarding the continuation of such benefits upon the termination of an individual's employment.

The Consolidated Omnibus Budget Reconciliation Act of 1985 and its amendments (hereinafter referred to collectively as COBRA)[76] imposes a requirement upon employers to offer former employees and their dependents the opportunity to continue their coverage under an employer's group health plan for a specified period of time. COBRA was enacted in response to a growing concern that many people were being cut off from affordable medical insurance when they are most in need of it, particularly upon the loss of employment or loss of the provider of such benefits.

COBRA applies to *all* employers unless there are fewer than 20 employees employed on a typical business day during the preceding calendar year.[77] For purposes of this exception, all members of a controlled group (businesses under the common control of an entity) or an affiliated service group are treated as a single employer. Similarly, leased employees and part-time employees are counted in the total of employees.

Interestingly, COBRA does not, in the first instance, require an employee to provide any health and medical benefits to its employees or former employees. However, once such benefits are provided, the employer is obligated to continue the benefits. COBRA also does not require the employer to provide former employees or other qualified beneficiaries with more favorable coverage than its current employees, only with the same level of coverage.

Identifying Employees and Plans Subject to COBRA

The following plans and employees are included in COBRA coverage.

Covered Health Plans. Group health plans covered by COBRA include any employee welfare benefit plan providing medical care to participants or beneficiaries directly or through insurance, reimbursement, or otherwise.[78] Employers with 20 or more employees that offer a group health benefits plan are required to continue coverage for terminated workers, their spouses and former spouses, and their dependent children.[79] The continuation of benefits requirements began with plan years starting in July 1986 or thereafter for noncollectively bargained plans (nonunion). Application of COBRA to collectively bargained (under a union contract) group health plans began as of January 1, 1987.

The plan may consist of one or more individual insurance policies in an arrangement that involves the provision of medical care to two or more employees, as well as a single group insurance policy. However, COBRA does not apply to disability benefits or to wellness programs that do not provide medical care coverage.

Covered Employees and Qualified Beneficiaries. Any individual who is or was provided coverage under a group health plan by virtue of the individual's employment or previous employment with the employer is a *covered employee* under COBRA.[80] Remember only employers of over 20 employees are subject to COBRA.

The law defines *qualified beneficiaries* generally as any individual other than the covered employee, who on the day before the occurrence of the qualifying event, is a beneficiary under the plan:

- As the spouse of the covered employee
- As the dependent child of the covered employee

If the *qualifying event* is termination or reduced hours of employment, the covered employee is the "qualified beneficiary."[81]

Qualifying Events. COBRA requires certain *qualifying events* to trigger the continued coverage requirements. The term "qualifying events" means with respect to any covered employee, any of the following events, which, absent the COBRA provisions, would result in the loss of benefit coverage:

- Death of the employee
- Termination of employee for any reason other than gross misconduct
- A reduction in hours of employment so coverage would not be available under the employer's plan
- Divorce or legal separation of an employee's spouse
- The entitlement of an employee to Medicare benefits
- A dependent child attaining the maximum age for coverage under the plan
- A proceeding in a case under Title 11, United States Code, commencing on or after July 1, 1986, with respect to the employer from whose employment the covered employer retired at any time[82]

Gross Misconduct Exception. A termination that is the result of gross misconduct of the covered employee is not a qualifying event, and the employee is not entitled to request continuation of his or her group health plan coverage. The term "gross misconduct" is not defined in the law. Thus, gross misconduct will have to be determined by the courts on a case-by-case basis. At least one court has indicated that gross misconduct is a "substantial deviation from the high standards and obligations of a managerial employee that would indicate that said employee cannot be entrusted with his management duties without danger to the employer."[83]

Case Example

Files, Inc., a document storage company, did not offer Frank Folder continuation coverage because Files believed that he disclosed confidential information regarding Files' unique record retrieval system, client list, and rates. Files' position is that this disclosure of confidential information constituted gross misconduct.

Is Files correct in stating that Frank's conduct is gross misconduct under COBRA, thereby disqualifying Frank from continuation of coverage? Perhaps. Under some interpretations of the standard Frank's behavior may not be considered gross misconduct.[84] If the court requires proof of an evil intent to do the employer harm or that the employee's conduct was willful or in such negligent disregard of the employer's interest, then we need more information. For example, was the information disclosed by Frank maintained as confidential by the employer or was all or most of it ascertainable from other sources? As indicated in the discussion, such assessments are made by the courts on the facts of each particular case.

It may be helpful to analyze the following questions when trying to ascertain whether gross misconduct exists:

♦ Was the conduct unlawful?

♦ Was the conduct directly harmful to the employer's interest?

♦ Was the conduct initiated by the employee?

♦ Was similar or previous conduct tolerated by the employer?

The answers to these questions should provide a reasonable basis for determining gross misconduct.

Fulfilling the Obligation to Offer Continuation of Benefits Coverage

Employers and plan sponsors are required to offer eligible employees and their qualified beneficiaries continuation of coverage for a stated period of time unless certain intervening events occur. The continuation coverage must be identical to the coverage provided to active workers, spouses, and dependent children under the regular plan provisions.[85] The specific notice obligations and who is a plan sponsor are addressed in our discussion under complying with notice requirements.

The maximum time periods that coverage must be continued, if no intervening events occur to end such coverage, vary according to certain circumstances. These periods of extended coverage may begin either on the date of the qualifying event or on the subsequent date on which coverage would otherwise be lost under the employer's plan as a result of the qualifying event.[86]

Determining the Length of Extended Coverage. The offer of continuation of coverage should advise the covered employee or qualified beneficiaries of the maximum length of time the coverage may continue. The law provides varying time periods dependent on the circumstances. These periods are

– Eighteen months in a case of termination or reduction in hours of employment

– Twenty-nine months for certain disabled employees. The 11-month extension enables certain qualified individuals to continue coverage until they become eligible for Medicare. A disabled individual is required to complete a 5-month waiting period plus a 24-month period of receiving cash benefits before being entitled to Medicare. These employees must be disabled at the time of the termination or reduction in hours of employment. This determination of disability may be made at anytime during the initial 18-month period of continuation coverage. The qualified beneficiary must give notice of such disability within 60 days of such determination.[87]

– Three years (36 months) when all other types of "qualifying events" occur, including death of the employee, divorce or legal separation, entitlement to Medicare, dependent child ceases to be a dependent under the plan, and bankruptcy (Chapter 11) of the employer.

The Rule for Multiple Qualifying Events. The original 18-month period of continuation coverage may be extended to 36 months from the date of the initial qualifying event in the situation where a second qualifying event occurs during the initial period. This extension applies to qualified beneficiaries under the plan at the time of the initial qualifying event and to those who are also covered by the plan at the time of the second event.

Case Study

The covered employee who has a dependent child but is not married is laid off his job, and he begins continued coverage for 18 months. Ten months after his layoff, the employee dies. However, during that time he has remarried. Under the rule, his new wife would not be eligible for continuation coverage due to his death, but his dependent child would be eligible to receive continued coverage for a total of 36 months from the date of his father's layoff.

The End of Extended Coverage. In our discussion of the periods for extended coverage we referred to the fact that coverage could end prior to the expiration of the statutory period upon the occurrence of certain events. The obligation to continue extended coverage ceases upon

- End of the statutory period
- Termination of a plan
- Employee's failure to pay premium
- Coverage by another group health plan or eligibility for Medicare.[88]

Termination of a plan. The period of coverage ceases when an employer terminates the group health plan for all employees and no successor plan is instituted. However, if the employer is a member of a controlled group and any member of that group has a group health plan in operation, the qualified beneficiary may be entitled to continued coverage.

Qualified beneficiary's failure to pay premium. The obligation to offer continued benefits does not require the employer also to pay the costs of that coverage. The qualified beneficiary who has elected to continue coverage is obligated to timely pay the premiums. However, a minimum of a 30-day grace period must be provided for payment of the premium (or longer if the plan permits), without regard to a shorter period in which active employees may be required to pay their premiums. Coverage ceases upon expiration of the 30-day period or the period specified under the plan, if longer, after the premium is due but not paid.

Qualified beneficiary becomes eligible for Medicare. Coverage will cease on the date the qualified beneficiary becomes entitled to benefits under Medicare. However, COBRA continuation coverage does not end if the qualifying event was the employer's bankruptcy.

Qualified beneficiary becomes covered under another group health plan. Extended coverage ceases on the date the qualified beneficiary becomes covered under any other group health plan as an employee or otherwise, such as a spouse remarrying and becoming covered under the new spouse's plan. However, there may be an exception in the case where the new plan excludes or limits a preexisting condition of the beneficiary. The qualified beneficiary may be entitled to continue coverage with respect to the preexisting coverage under the old plan.

Complying With Notice Requirements

Compliance with COBRA consists mainly of understanding and following the notice requirements. The central obligation imposed by COBRA is that the employee and/or qualified beneficiary receive timely notice of their right to elect continuation of health plan coverage. If the employee or qualified beneficiary does not receive timely notice and his or her window of opportunity is closed, the employer or plan sponsor may be liable for out-of-pocket expenses incurred in obtaining health coverage or in not having such coverage.

Describing the Responsibilities of a Plan Sponsor. An employer that maintains its own insurance plan for its employees is designated the plan sponsor for that plan. In cases where there is a multiemployer plan, that is, a plan established or maintained by two or more employers, the plan sponsor is the association, committee, joint board of trustees, or other similar group of representatives of the parties who establish or maintain the plan.

Initial Notice. The plan sponsor of a group health plan must notify both participating employees *and* their spouses of the continuation coverage option when the employee is first covered by the plan.[89]

Generally, these notices may be sent by first-class mail. If the employee and the spouse or other qualified beneficiary live at separate addresses, each party should be mailed a notice.

Another way of conveying the initial notice to the employee is to include it in the summary plan description for the group health plan. Each employee would have to receive a copy of the summary description in order to satisfy this COBRA requirement. The employee's spouse would still have to receive the initial notice.

Notice Upon Occurrence of a Qualifying Event. There are additional notification requirements upon the occurrence of a qualifying event. The plan sponsor must provide notice to the employee and each qualified beneficiary, who would lose coverage as a result of qualifying event, that they are entitled to elect within a specified period continuation coverage under the plan. Such notices are handled by the plan administrator who is responsible for the daily administration of the plan. Notice of right to continue coverage under the plan to the covered employee or qualified beneficiary must be sent within 14 days of the plan administrator receiving notice of the qualifying event from either the employer or the employee. Notification to an employee's spouse is treated as notice to all qualified beneficiaries living with spouse. A sample of the notice of right to continue coverage and request for continuation of group health coverage is shown in Exhibit 18.1 and is generally a two-sided form.

Describing the Responsibilities of the Employer. Employers must notify the plan administrator of certain qualifying events, including an employee's termination or reduction in hours of employment (such as a shift to part-time status), death, covered individual's eligibility for Medicare, and the employer's bankruptcy filing within 30 days after the occurrence of such event or the date on which coverage would be lost as a result of such event.[90]

– EXHIBIT 18.1 –

Notice of Right to Continue Health Benefits Coverage

IMPORTANT NOTICE

NOTICE OF RIGHT TO CONTINUE COVERAGE

Your group health coverage under the Plan identified on the election form on the back of this notice terminates on the date shown in the upper right corner of that election form. If you or any of your eligible dependents are not covered under Medicare or any other group health plan, you may continue your group health coverage without interruption under the Plan for up to 18, 29, or 36 months, as shown on the election form. If you are entitled to 18 months of continuation coverage, and if you are determined to be disabled under the terms of the Social Security Act as of the date your employment terminated (or the date your hours were reduced), you are eligible for an additional 11 months of continuation coverage after the expiration of the 18-month period. To qualify for this additional period of coverage, you must notify Metropolitan Life--COBRA Unit at the address shown on the back of this notice or on any future bill you may receive within 60 days after you receive a determination of disability from the Social Security Administration, provided notice is given before the end of the initial 18 months of continuation coverage. During the additional 11 months of continuation coverage, your premium for that coverage will be approximately 50% higher than it was during the preceding 18 months.

COST OF CONTINUED COVERAGE

If you elect to continue coverage under the Plan, you must pay the monthly contribution required for the coverages you elect to continue, retroactive from the date Group Coverage ends. The current monthly cost for these coverages is set forth on the election form on the back of this notice. This cost is subject to change. *Failure to pay this amount in a timely manner will result in the loss of coverage.*

WHEN CONTINUED COVERAGE CEASES

The continued coverage will cease for any person either at the end of the 18, 29, or 36 month period shown, or earlier when:
  (a) the cost of continued coverage is not paid on time; or
  (b) that person becomes entitled to Medicare; or
  (c) that person becomes covered under another group health plan, unless that other plan contains an exclusion or limitation with respect to any preexisting condition affecting you or a covered dependent; or
  (d) the Plan terminates for all employees.
  (e) a disabled person is no longer disabled during the 11 month extension period.

CONVERSION RIGHTS

At the end of the 18, 29, or 36 month period a person may be eligible for a personal medical expense policy without evidence of insurability, as provided under the terms of the Plan. If you are eligible timely notice will be provided. (Conversion rights are not available for dental coverage.)

HOW TO ELECT CONTINUED COVERAGE

Complete the REQUEST FOR CONTINUATION OF COVERAGE on the back of this notice. Return it to the address shown on the back of this notice, together with your check or money order for one month's contribution payable to "   -COBRA Unit." If this amount is not received within 45 days after the date you send the REQUEST, your continuation of coverage will lapse. One month's contribution can be determined from the amounts set forth on the back of this notice based on the coverages you elect to continue and the members of your family who will be covered. You will be retroactively billed for any additional amount due for the period prior to the time we receive your REQUEST FOR CONTINUATION OF COVERAGE or for any amount not included when you enroll. To assure coverage, your REQUEST must reach   by the Last Day to Elect, as shown in the box outlined with dark lines in the upper right corner of the REQUEST form, and payment for at least one month's contribution must reach   within 45 days after you submit your REQUEST.

REQUEST FOR CONTINUATION OF GROUP COVERAGE

Please answer all questions. If you omit anything, this form will be returned to you and processing will be delayed.

PART 1 - EMPLOYER INFORMATION (TO BE COMPLETED BY EMPLOYER)

Employer's Name		Group Master No.	Date of Qualifying Event	Date Group Coverage Ends *
Employee's Name		Employee Soc. Sec. No.	Date of Notice	Last Date to Elect

INSTRUCTIONS: Check All Appropriate Boxes	Eligible	Yes	No	Qualifying Event		
	Employee			18 Month Maximum	29 Month Maximum	36 Month Maximum for Dependents Only
	Spouse			☐ Termination of Employment	☐ Totally & Permanently Disabled	☐ Divorce or Separation ☐ Child Ceasing to be a Dependent
	Child(ren)			☐ Reduction in Hours ☐ Retirement		☐ Death of Employee ☐ Employee Eligible for Medicare

PART 2 - COVERAGE AVAILABLE FOR SELECTION AND COSTS TO ELECTOR (TO BE COMPLETED BY EMPLOYER)

INSTRUCTIONS:

(1) Enter group, sub and branch identification for each coverage provided.
(2) If **Medical** coverage involves multiple carriers, show combined rate.
(3) If Non-Met Coverage is checked, indicate HMO or Non-Met Carrier, Name, Address and Coverage
(4) Place XXX's in **EVERY BOX** where coverage is not available.

If coverage is not provided by Metropolitan, identify:

HMO or Carrier _____ HMO or Carrier _____
Address _____ Address _____
City ___ State ___ Zip Code ___ Coverage ___ City ___ State ___ Zip Code ___ Coverage ___

Coverages	Group	Sub	Branch	Check if Non-Met Coverage	Monthly Costs For:			
					One Individual Only	Employee and One Dependent	Family	FSA Reporting (if applicable)
Medical					$	$	$	FSA will be continued Yes ☐ No ☐
Dental					$	$	$	If yes, the monthly FSA contribution $
*FSA Health Care					$			Start date of FSA continuation
*FSA Dep. Care					$			Stop date of FSA continuation*
								*(this is the end of the FSA plan year)

* Participation in these accounts is on an after-tax basis, and therefore does not offer any tax advantage.

Signature of Authorized Employer Representative ___ Ph # ___ Date ___

PART 3 - ELECTOR INFORMATION (TO BE COMPLETED BY ELECTOR)

INSTRUCTIONS: Complete the following information for each person (including yourself) for whom continuation of coverage is elected.

Last Name	First Name	MI	Relationship To Employee	Birth Date (MM/DD/YY)	Social Security Number

INSTRUCTIONS:

Check boxes for coverage(s) elected, and enter appropriate costs from Part 2. Select costs from the column which indicates the type of coverage you want.

Questions about the coverages for which you are eligible and their associated costs should be directed to your employer representative.

Rates are subject to change each year.

COVERAGE	Monthly Cost*
☐ Medical	$
☐ Dental	$
☐ FSA HealthCare	$
☐ FSA Dep. Care	$
TOTAL	$

(send to address shown below)

Send Bills and Correspondence to:

Name _____
Street _____
City _____
State _____ Zip _____
Phone Number ( ) _____

PART 4 - FAMILY EMPLOYMENT (TO BE COMPLETED BY ELECTOR)

Is anyone listed above employed? ☐ No ☐ Yes   If Yes: Person's Name _____

Employer's Name	Employer's Address Street	City	State	Zip Code

Is the person covered by another Group Health Care Plan? ☐ Yes ☐ No
Does the other plan contain an exclusion or limitation with respect to any preexisting condition affecting you or a covered dependent? ☐ Yes ☐ No

Plan Name _____   Group Number _____

PART 5 - I CERTIFY THAT THE INFORMATION FURNISHED IS TRUE AND COMPLETE

Signature _____ Date _____

Check whichever is applicable.

☐ Employee (for self or self and dependents) ☐ Child
☐ Spouse - ☐ Present ☐ Former   ☐ Legal Guardian for _____

* You are responsible for payment for COBRA continuation of coverage from the Date Group Coverage Ends. You will be billed for any additional amount due. Return completed application with check for TOTAL MONTHLY COST shown in Part 3 to:

Metropolitan Life - COBRA Unit
2929 Express Drive North
Hauppauge, NY 11787

The Employee's Responsibilities. Employees or other qualified beneficiaries must notify plan administrators with regard to other types of qualifying
events such as divorce, legal separation, or termination of a child's dependent
status within 60 days of such an event. If this notice is not given, the group
health plan is not required to offer continuation coverage to the qualified beneficiary.

Election of Coverage. Once the covered employee or qualified beneficiary
received notice of his or her right to elect to continue benefits, he or she must
respond within 60 days. The right to elect continuation coverage must be offered
to a qualified beneficiary for a period of at least 60 days, starting with the date
on which plan coverage would otherwise expire and ending no earlier than 60
days from the date notice of the election option is sent by the plan administrator.
Notices and elections made under COBRA are deemed to be made on the date
such notices and elections are mailed.

> NOTE: Generally, an election made by an employee or an employee's
> spouse is binding upon all other qualified beneficiaries.

For example, if a former employee elects continuation coverage on behalf
of himself and his spouse, the election is binding on the spouse. The spouse in
that case cannot independently decline COBRA coverage. However, if the former
employee declines COBRA coverage on the spouse's behalf, the spouse must be
permitted an opportunity to elect COBRA continuation coverage independently
on his or her own behalf.

The covered employee or qualified beneficiary may waive his or her right
to continuation coverage by declining such coverage in writing. The covered
employee may also waive these rights simply by not responding within the
60-day election period. However, a qualified beneficiary who has waived continuation of coverage may revoke the waiver if it is done within the original
60-day election period. Although such a revocation will constitute a valid election
of COBRA continuation coverage, the coverage need not be provided on a retroactive basis.

Determining the Nature and Cost of Coverage

Generally, the qualified beneficiary must be offered the opportunity to elect
the same coverage as was received by him or her just prior to the qualifying
event. The employer is obligated to provide covered employees and qualified
beneficiaries coverage equal to what current employees receive under the plan.

> NOTE: The employer is not required to provide better coverage than
> that received by current employees. Thus, if the plan is modified and
> provides a reduced level of benefits, that is all that an individual
> receiving continuation coverage is entitled to.

However, if a plan offers both "core" coverage (medical) and "noncore" coverage (vision and/or dental), a qualified beneficiary must generally be offered the opportunity to elect either the continuation of the coverage in effect immediately prior to the qualifying event (including noncore coverage) or the core coverage only. Be aware that if the applicable premium for core coverage is at least 95 percent of the premium for core coverage and noncore coverage, the plan need not offer solely core coverage as an option.

The Cost of Continuation Coverage. Under COBRA, continuation coverage may be provided at the expense of the electing employee or qualified beneficiary.

This means that the employer is not required or expected to pay the expense of continuing coverage for former employees or their qualified beneficiaries. The employer is permitted to charge the electing beneficiaries the applicable premium not to exceed 102 percent of such premium. The extra percentage charged is for administrative costs.

The term "applicable premium" means, with respect to any period of continuation coverage of qualified beneficiaries, the cost to the plan for such period of coverage for similarly situated beneficiaries with respect to whom a qualifying event has not occurred (without regard to whether such cost is paid by the employer or employee).[91]

In the event that continuation coverage is extended to 29 months, during the 19th through the 29th month of the continuation period, the beneficiary may be charged up to 150 percent of the applicable premium.

SUMMARY OF COBRA PROVISIONS

1. COBRA covers plan years starting July 1, 1986, and collectively bargained plans ratified after April 7, 1986. For a group health plan maintained under a collective bargaining agreement ratified prior to April 7, 1986, these provisions apply as of January 1, 1987, or the date on which the contract expires.

2. COBRA applies to employers with 20 or more employees that offer group health benefit plans. Employers are required to continue coverage for terminated workers, their spouses (including former spouses), and their dependent children.

3. Qualifying events are:
   a. Termination for any reason other than gross misconduct
   b. A reduction in hours so that employee is no longer eligible for coverage under the plan
   c. Death of employee

    d. Divorce or legal separation of employee's spouse

    e. Entitlement of employee for Medicare benefits

    f. Dependent child's attaining maximum age for coverage

    g. Bankruptcy filing by employer

These events are qualifying if they result in loss of coverage for the qualified beneficiary.

4. Qualified beneficiaries who may elect continuation coverage include the employee covered under the plan, his or her spouse, and dependent children.

5. The continuation coverage must be identical to the coverage provided to workers, spouses, and children under regular plan provisions. However, employer may charge up to 102 percent of the applicable premium for the period of the extended coverage.

6. Continuation coverage must be made available to eligible individuals for 18 months in cases of termination or reduction in force. Disabled individuals may receive up to 29 months of extended coverage. Coverage for all other types of qualifying events must continue for 3 years.

7. The continuation of coverage obligation is reduced by the employee's failure to pay the premiums, coverage of individual under another plan, termination of plan by the employer, qualified beneficiary becoming covered by Medicare, or the widowed or divorced spouse remarrying.

8. Notice and election requirements are as follows:

    a. The health plan must notify both the participating employees and their spouses of the continuation coverage option when the employee is first covered by the plan.

    b. Upon occurrence of a qualifying event, employer must notify the plan administrator of the employee's change in status within 30 days. Employees must notify the plan administrators of a divorce, separation, or termination of a child's dependent status within 60 days.

    c. The plan administrator must notify qualified beneficiaries of their right to elect continuation coverage within 14 days of receipt of notice of a qualifying event.

    d. The right to elect must be offered for 60 days, beginning with date that coverage would otherwise expire and ending no earlier than 60 days from the date notice of election is sent.

ENDNOTES

1. 29 U.S.C. §1001, *et seq.*

2. 29 U.S.C. §1002(2)(A).

3. 29 U.S.C. §1002(34).

4. 29 U.S.C. §1002(1).

5. Section 501 (c)(9) of the Code permits the establishment of a tax-exempt organization known as a voluntary employees' beneficiary association (VEBA) to provide for the payment of life, sickness, accident, or other benefits to the VEBA's members or beneficiaries. Other benefits which may be provided include paying vacation benefits and providing vacation facilities, providing child care facilities, severance benefits, and personal legal service benefits. See 26 C.F.R. §1.501(c)(9)-3(e). To qualify for tax exemption, the VEBA must additionally satisfy the non-discrimination requirements under Section 505 of the Code.

6. See 29 C.F.R. §2510.3-1 and I.R.S. Code §§501(c)(9) and 4980B.

7. 29 U.S.C. §§1021-1025.

8. 29 U.S.C. §1022.

9. 29 U.S.C. §1022(b).

10. 29 U.S.C. §§1022, 1023, 1024(b).

11. 29 U.S.C. §1052(a)(1); Code §410(a).

12. 29 U.S.C. §1052(a)(2); Code §410(a)(2).

13. 29 U.S.C. §1053; Code §411(a).

14. 29 U.S.C. §1053(a)(2); Code §411(a)(2).

15. 29 U.S.C. §1054; Code §411(b).

16. 29 U.S.C. §1082; Code §412.

17. 29 U.S.C. §1081(a)(8).

18. 29 U.S.C. §1103(a).

19. 29 U.S.C. §1102.

20. 29 U.S.C. §1002(21).

21. 29 U.S.C. §1104(a).

22. 29 U.S.C. §1106(a).

23. *Id.*

24. 29 U.S.C. §1002(14).

25. 29 U.S.C. §1106(b).

26. 29 U.S.C. §1108.

27. 29 U.S.C. §§1109, 1132.

28. 29 U.S.C. §1132(a).

29. See, for example, *Brock v. Hendershott*, 840 F.2d 339 (6th Cir. 1988); *Diduck v. Kaszycki & Sons Contractors, Inc.*, 737 F.Supp. 792 (S.D.N.Y. 1990); and *Pension Benefit Guaranty Corp. v. Ross*, 733 F.Supp. 1005 (M.D.N.C. 1990). Compare *Call v. Sumitomo Bank*, 11 Emp. Ben. Cas. 1273 (9th Cir. 1989), and *Nieto v. Ecker*, 845 F.2d 868 (9th Cir. 1988) (both rejecting non-fiduciary liability).

30. 29 U.S.C. §1055; Code §§410(a)(11) and 417(b).

31. 29 U.S.C. §1055(c); Code §417(a)(2).

32. 29 U.S.C. §1322(b)(1).

33. 29 U.S.C. §1343.

34. *Id.*

35. 29 U.S.C. §1342.

36. *Pension Benefit Guaranty Corp. v. LTV Corp.*, 110 S.Ct. 2668 (1990).

37. 29 U.S.C. §1301(d).

38. 29 U.S.C. §1391.

39. 29 U.S.C. §1341a.

40. 29 U.S.C. §1341.

41. 29 U.S.C. §1341(b).

42. Code §4980.

43. Code §410(a)(26).

44. Code §410(b).

45. Code §410(a)(4) and regulations.

46. Code §§414, 1563(a).

47. Code §415(c)(1)(A).

48. Code §415(h).

49. Code §401(a)(17).

50. Code §72(t)(2)(A)(i).

51. *Id.*

52. Code §401(a)(9).

53. Code §4980B; 29 U.S.C. §1161; Treas. Reg. §1.162-26.

54. Section 125 of the Code provides for the establishment of a cafeteria plan pursuant to which a participant can choose between cash and qualified benefits. Qualified benefits include group term life insurance up to $50,000, coverage under a group legal services plan, a dependent care assistance plan, and accident or health plans. See 26 C.F.R. §1.125-1, Q&A 5 (proposed June 15, 1987).

55. Code §129.

56. See Prop. Treas. Reg §1.125-2, Q&A 7.

57. Treas. Reg. §1.401-1(b)(1)(ii).

58. Treas. Reg. §1.401-1(b)(2).

59. Treas. Reg. §1.401-1(b)(1)(iii).

60. *Id*.

61. 29 U.S.C. §1107(d)(6); Code §4975(e)(7).

62. Code §409(e).

63. Code 409.

64. Code §401(k)(4)(B); Treas. Reg. §1.401(k)-1(a)(1).

65. Code §402(8)(1).

66. Code §§403(a), 404(a)(2).

67. Code §§403(a), 72.

68. Code §§4999, 280G(a).

69. Code §§421, 422(b).

70. Code §422(a).

71. 29 U.S.C. §621, *et seq*.

72. 29 U.S.C. §623(f)(2).

73. 29 U.S.C. §623(a).

74. 29 U.S.C. §1144.

75. See *Michigan United Food & Commercial Workers Unions v. Baerwaldt*, 767 F.2d 308 (6th Cir. 1985) (state statute requiring all health insurance policies issued in state provide certain levels of coverage for substance abuse not preempted); see, generally, *Blakeman v. Mead Containers*, 779 F.2d 1146 (6th Cir. 1985).

76. COBRA's initial provisions are codified in the Internal Revenue Code of 1986, the Employment Retirement Income Security Act, and the Public Health Service Act. Amendments to COBRA are contained in the Omnibus Budget Reconciliation Act of 1986, the Tax Reform Act of 1986, the Technical and Miscellaneous Revenue Act

of 1988, the Federal Health Benefits Amendments Act of 1989, and the Omnibus Budget Reconciliation Act of 1989.

77. ERISA, 29 U.S.C. §1161(b).

78. ERISA, 29 U.S.C. §1167(1).

79. ERISA, 29 U.S.C. §§1161(1) and 1167(3).

80. ERISA, 29 U.S.C. §1167(2).

81. ERISA, 29 U.S.C. §1167(3)(A–B).

82. ERISA, 29 U.S.C. §1163(1–6). In the case of the event described in this instance, a loss of coverage includes a substantial elimination of coverage with respect to retirees and their spouses or surviving spouses or dependent child.

83. See *Avina v. Texas Pig Stands, Inc.*, (Docket No. SA-88-CA-13) (W.D. Tex. 1991). But see a more narrow definition in *Paris v. F. Korbel & Brothers, Inc.*, 751 F.Supp. 834 (N.D.Cal. 1990), wherein the court adopted the definition of that term under the state's unemployment insurance law (i.e., an employee's evil design to injure the employer or willful or negligent disregard of the employer's interest) is needed for an employee to be guilty of gross misconduct.

84. See *Paris v. Korbel & Brothers, Inc.*, 751 F.Supp. 834 (N.D.Cal. 1990), cited in note 83. The court in *Paris* applied the definition of gross misconduct found in California's unemployment insurance law and did not find an evil design to injure the employer or willful or negligent disregard of the employer's interest. The employer was found to be in breach of COBRA and penalties were assessed against it.

85. ERISA, 29 U.S.C. §1162.

86. ERISA, 29 U.S.C. §1162(1).

87. See *Poole v. Monmouth College*, 254 N.J.Super. 154, (Ch. Div. 1991), for a discussion of the obligations of the employer and disabled employee under this provision. Employers should note that notices of amendments to COBRA should be promptly sent to those individuals whose rights may be affected by the Amendment.

88. ERISA, 29 U.S.C. §1162(2).

89. ERISA, 29 U.S.C. §§1161(a) and 1166(1).

90. ERISA, 29 U.S.C. §1166(2).

91. ERISA, 29 U.S.C. §1164(1).

19

A GUIDE TO
THE NATIONAL LABOR
RELATIONS ACT

A significant portion of the nation's work force, especially in highly indus-trialized areas such as the Northeast, is represented by a union. Where employees are represented by a union, the employment relationship is usually governed by a collective bargaining agreement, otherwise known as a union contract. The whole area of employer-employee relations is subject to the sweeping provisions of the National Labor Relations Act (NLRA or the Act), 29 U.S.C. §151, *et seq.*, which has been amended over the years. For the purposes of this chapter and related chapters, all references to the federal law is to the NLRA as amended unless otherwise stated. The next three chapters will address the various aspects of the NLRA that directly impact on the employer whether or not it has union employees. Familiarity with the basic provisions of the NLRA will aid the per-sonnel professional in avoiding inadvertent violations of the law and aid in the avoidance of unintentional unionization.

In this chapter we address the basic provisions of the NLRA with regard to its scope, the basic rights it provides, the general enforcement scheme, certain violations (known as unfair labor practices or ULPs), and suggestions in how to avoid violations. We begin with the basic purpose of the Act.

DEFINING THE SCOPE OF THE NLRA

The National Labor Relations Act is legislation designed to minimize disruption of industry by labor-management disputes. The NLRA's stated purpose is to

> eliminate the causes of certain substantial obstructions to the free flow of commerce and to mitigate and eliminate these obstructions when they have occurred by encouraging the practice and procedure of collective bargaining and by protecting the exercise by workers of full freedom of association, self-organization, and designation of representatives of their own choosing, for the purpose of negotiating the terms and conditions of their employment or other mutual aid or protection.

Although an employer may pay fair wages, provide competitive fringe benefits, and practice good employee relations, it may still face a union-organizing campaign if employees do not belong to a union. A union organizational campaign is specifically addressed in the following chapter.

DETERMINING RIGHTS UNDER THE ACT

The National Labor Relations Act guarantees certain fundamental rights to employees. The core of the Act is Section 7, provides that

> Employees shall have the right to self-organization, to form, join, or assist labor organizations, to bargain collectively through representatives of their own choosing, and to engage in other concerted activities for the purpose of collective bargaining or other mutual aid or protection, and shall also have the right to refrain from any or all such activities except to the extent that such right may be affected by an agreement requiring membership in a labor organization as a condition of employment as authorized in Section 8(a)(3).

Section 7 provides the basis for achieving the goal of the Act. Employees have the right to form or join a labor organization (union) or to refrain from such activity. These rights are guaranteed by the Act and vigorously enforced by the National Labor Relations Board.

Defining Concerted Activity

The protection of Section 7 is not limited to the right to join or assist labor activities or to refrain from such activities. Section 7 also protects activity engaged in for "other mutual aid or protection" and may be used to protect activity by employees that is unrelated to union organization.

Employee activity to be protected must be of a "concerted" nature. Concerted activity means that it has some relation to a group action taken in the interests of or on behalf of a group of employees. Such conduct may be deemed "concerted activity" by the NLRB as long as the individual's efforts are directed at goals shared by other employees. However, several factors affect this determination: whether there is a union contract, whether an employee's activity is of a collective nature, whether it was discussed with other employees, or whether it is an action solely on behalf of the employee himself or herself.

The key to a finding of protected concerted activity, where no right contained in a collective bargaining agreement is involved, is whether such activity is "engaged in, with or on authority of other workers and not solely on behalf of the employee himself."[1]

Case Example

Company A has a collective bargaining agreement with a local Teamsters union. Company B has nonunion employees. Both are trucking companies. Al Albert worked for A. One day he refused to drive a truck he believed to have faulty brakes and was unsafe. He was discharged.

Barry Bell works for B and, after complaining about safety defects in his truck, filed a complaint with the state transportation agency and refused to drive the truck in defiance of company orders. Barry was also discharged.

Did Company A violate Section 7 by discharging Al? Did Company B violate Section 7 by discharging Barry?

Company A violated Al's Section 7 rights by discharging him for refusing to drive an unsafe vehicle. The Board concluded that Al had engaged in protected concerted activity where the collective bargaining agreement contained a provision that the employer could not require employees to take out any vehicle not in safe operating condition.[2]

In contrast, Company B did not violate Barry's rights. The NLRB held that the employee had not engaged in protected concerted activity. In Barry's case, there was no evidence that his action was other than individual.

In other words, Barry was not found to have acted with or on the authority of his coworkers. Here the link between group activity and the individual employee asserting his rights under a state safety law was so attenuated that his individual action could not be considered concerted for purposes of Section 7.[3]

However, if the employee's individual action is a "logical outgrowth" of the original protest or complaints by other employees, protected concerted activity has been found. For example, a social worker who is discharged after calling the government's wage and hour division to question an employer's holiday pay practices was found to have engaged in concerted protected activity since it was linked to group activity.[4] In that case, other employees had raised similar questions to the employer, and the telephone call was a logical outgrowth of the original protest.

Protected concerted activity may be conduct by one person. It is not dispositive simply to look at the number of individuals involved. Consideration must be given to the subject and nature of the conduct.

HOW THE NLRA IS ENFORCED

Enforcement of the NLRA is delegated by statute to the National Labor Relations Board (NLRB, or the Board). The Secretary of Labor and the Board have established extensive rules, regulations, and practices designed to enforce the Act and protect individual employee's rights with regard to both employers and unions. Since the Act was enacted in response to employer abuses and initially to aid unionization efforts, it seems that most rules and regulations tend to favor unions. However, the Board is a neutral party in these matters charged with enforcing the Act and protecting workers' rights.

The National Labor Relations Board was established by the NLRA. The five members of the NLRB are nominated by the president of the United States and ratified by the Senate. Members are appointed to a five-year term. The headquarters of the Board is in Washington, D.C. There are also regional offices throughout the United States.

The NLRB is really divided into two main parts: the Board and the Office of the General Counsel. The Board has a quasi-judicial function, operating essentially as a court and making decisions on the basis of a formal record. The General Counsel, on the other hand, performs the preliminary functions of investigation and presentation of unfair labor practice cases.

How the Board Functions

Contrary to many lay perceptions, the Board does not have any investigatory authority over the issuance of formal complaints. It rules only on those unfair labor practice cases which the General Counsel decides to prosecute.

The Board has complete authority over representation questions, that is, questions involving unions as the exclusive bargaining representative of a group of employees. This authority has been delegated to some extent to the various regional directors.[5] The Board is authorized to delegate its authority to any three members.[6] Each Board member has a large staff of legal assistants.

The Board is also assisted by the Executive Secretary who is the chief administrative officer of the Board. He plans and directs the Board regarding case handling, scheduling, and issuing decisions. There is also a Solicitor who advises the Board on questions of law and policy.

Defining the Role of the General Counsel

The Office of the General Counsel supervises the investigation and prosecution of unfair labor practice charges. The General Counsel has the exclusive authority to prosecute complaints. His or her authority not to issue a complaint is *not* reviewable by the Board or courts.[7]

The General Counsel is also responsible for supervising all employees in the regional offices and all attorneys except administrative law judges (ALJs) or those serving on Board member staffs.[8]

The General Counsel's duties may be summarized as follows:

♦ To seek injunctions in court

♦ To handle all representation cases

♦ To prosecute unfair labor practice cases

♦ To seek compliance with Board orders

♦ To apply to appropriate courts for enforcement of Board orders

The NLRA provisions apply to certain employers, employees, and labor organizations. Employers are defined in Section 2(2) of the Act. Generally, any person or company involved in the stream of commerce with a gross volume of $50,000 per year, or more, in interstate commerce will be included. However, the Board does not always exercise jurisdiction.

ESTABLISHING NLRB JURISDICTION

The Board has broad authority over all labor disputes "affecting commerce." However, despite its broad grant of statutory authority, the Board has never exercised its full authority. In practice, the Board considers only cases with a substantial effect on commerce.[9]

Standards Based on Minimum Dollar Volume

To limit the number of cases that it considers, the Board has established general jurisdictional standards based on minimum annual dollar volume:

♦ For general nonretail concerns, sales of goods to consumers in other states, directly or indirectly (called "outflow"), or purchases of goods from suppliers in other states, directly or indirectly (called "inflow"); must be at least $50,000 per year.[10]

♦ For retail concerns, an annual volume of business must be at least $500,000.[11]

♦ For retail and manufacturing combined, the NLRB will use either the retail or the nonretail standard when a single, integrated enterprise manufactures a product as well as sells it directly to the public.[12]

♦ For retail and wholesale combined, if a company is involved in both retail and wholesale operations, the nonretail standard will apply.[13]

♦ The standard of instrumentalities, links, and channels of interstate commerce applies to all passenger and freight transportation enterprises that engage in interstate transportation services and all transportation and other enterprises which conduct the transportation of passengers or commodities in interstate commerce. Annual income must be at least $50,000 from furnishing interstate transportation services or from services performed for employers in commerce valued at $50,000 or more for enterprises that meet any of the standards except indirect outflow or indirect inflow.[14]

♦ For national defense, the enterprise has a substantial impact on national defense.[15]

♦ For territories and the District of Columbia, the same standards applied in the states are applicable to territories. Plenary jurisdiction is exercised in the District of Columbia.[16]

♦ For multiemployer bargaining associations, these associations are regarded as a single employer. The annual business of all members is totaled to determine whether any of the standards apply.[17] A trade association such as the General Contractors Association, whose members include general contractors in construction, negotiates contracts as a single entity and is an example of a multiemployer bargaining association.

♦ For multistate establishments, the jurisdictional standards are the same for single-state and multistate enterprises. Annual business of all establishments is totaled to determine whether the standard applies.[18] If the standard is met, the Board will take jurisdiction.

♦ For nonprofit organizations, nonprofit status does not exempt an enterprise from NLRB jurisdiction standards. Most of the time, the same standards are applied as to those organizations operated for profit.[19] However, purely charitable or religious institutions are outside of NLRB jurisdiction.[20]

♦ For union employers, when unions act as employers, the NLRB cannot decline jurisdiction.[21]

Standards Applied to Specific Industries

The Board's current jurisdictional standards applied to specific industries are as follows:

♦ For apartment projects, NLRB jurisdiction is taken when at least $500,000 in gross annual revenue is received.[22]

♦ For automobile dealers, the same jurisdictional standards hold that are applied to retail operations, even if the dealer has a franchise from a national manufacturer.[23]

- ◆ For building and construction, the appropriate jurisdictional standard is applied in cases involving a single building trades employer. The multiemployer standard is applied if the employer is part of a multi-employer bargaining association.[24]

- ◆ For colleges, universities, and secondary schools, the NLRB will assert jurisdiction if the schools' total annual revenue from all sources except those designated by the grantor as not available for operating costs equals at least $1 million. This applies to both profit and nonprofit institutions.[25]

- ◆ For communications, television, radio, telephone, or telegraph companies must have at least $100,000 annual gross volume of business.[26]

- ◆ For country clubs, the jurisdictional standards for retail concerns are applied.[27]

- ◆ For entertainment and amusement, the same jurisdictional standards are applied as those to retail operations. The Board will not assert jurisdiction over horse and dog racing tracks, but regularly takes jurisdiction in motion picture and broadcasting cases.[28]

- ◆ For federal credit unions, gross income from loans, deposits, and investment or such related areas must total at least $500,000 annually.[29]

- ◆ For gambling casinos, the Board will take jurisdiction over gambling casinos.[30]

- ◆ For guard services, companies furnishing plant guards to employers involved in interstate commerce the value of which meets basic jurisdictional standards are subject to NLRB jurisdiction.[31]

- ◆ For hospitals and health care institutions, federal, state, and municipal hospitals and administrative employers in the health field are exempt. The Board may assert jurisdiction over nursing homes, visiting nurse associations, and related facilities with gross revenues over $100,000 per year and over proprietary and nonprofit hospitals with gross revenues over $250,000 per year.[32]

- ◆ For day care centers, if gross revenue equals at least $250,000, the NLRB will assert jurisdiction.[33]

- ◆ For hotels and motels, jurisdiction is granted to a residential or non-residential establishment if the total annual volume of business is at least $500,000.[34]

- ◆ For office buildings, shopping centers, and parking lots, the NLRB has jurisdiction if at least $100,000 total annual income is earned where $25,000 or more is paid by other organizations which meet any of the standards, except the nonretail standard; then jurisdiction will be granted.[35]

◆ For the postal service, full jurisdiction is provided in the Postal Reorganization Act of 1970.[36]

◆ For printing, publishing and newspapers, jurisdiction is granted if the establishment generates at least $200,000 total annual volume of business and the employer holds membership in or subscribes to interstate news services, publishes nationally syndicated features, or advertises nationally sold products.[37]

◆ For public utilities, NLRB jurisdiction is found if there is at least $250,000 total annual volume of business or $50,000 outflow or inflow, direct or indirect. This standard applies to retail gas, power, and water companies as well as to electric cooperatives. General nonretail standards are applied to wholesale utilities.[38]

◆ For restaurants, the same jurisdictional standards are applied as those to retail operations.[39]

◆ For service establishments, the same jurisdictional standards are applied as those to retail operations.[40]

◆ For sports, professional, they are regarded as industries affecting interstate commerce and therefore are subject to NLRB jurisdiction.[41]

◆ For symphony orchestras, the NLRB will assert jurisdiction if the total annual income is at least $1 million compiled from all sources except those designated by the donor as not available for use as operating costs.[42]

◆ For taxicab companies, the same jurisdictional standards are applied as those to retail operations.[43]

◆ For transit companies, NLRB jurisdiction will be granted if the company shows at least $250,000 total annual volume of business.[44] Local public transit companies are included.

Declining Jurisdiction

The Board will decline jurisdiction in certain circumstances; especially with regard to the following:

◆ Political Subdivisions. An "employer" as defined in Section 2(2) of the Act excludes "any state or political subdivision thereof." Where a state agency or public body exercises control over an employer, the Board will decline jurisdiction.[45] For example, in *Economic Security Corp.*, 299 NLRB No. 68 (1990), and *Woodbury County Community Action Agency*, 299 NLRB No. 65 (1990), the Board considered the status of private nonprofit community service corporations, which were established for the purpose of administering an array of federally subsidized antipoverty programs at the local level. In each case, the Board held that the corporation qualified as a "political subdivision" of a state under Section 2(2) of the Act.

♦ Church-operated schools.[46]

♦ Foreign-owned shipping vessels.

♦ Horse and dog racing.[47]

♦ Real estate brokerage business.[48]

IDENTIFYING EXEMPTED EMPLOYERS

The Act specifically exempts certain employers, generally employees of governmental entities or employees covered under a competing federal statute. Exempt employers under the Act include

– Federal, state, and local governments[49]

– Federal Reserve banks

– Any employer subject to the Railway Labor Act

– "Labor organizations" except when acting as employers

Defining Labor Organizations

A "labor organization" is defined in Section 2(5) of the Act as "any organization of any kind, or any agency or employee representation committee or plan, in which employees participate and which exists for the purpose, in whole or in part, of dealing with employers concerning premises, labor disputes, wages, rates of pay, hours of employment, or conditions of work."

Labor organizations may be formal organized unions with national and local representatives. The AFL-CIO, for example, is a national labor organization with many diverse affiliated union locals. There are also independent union locals that are regional or active only in a limited geographic area. A labor organization may also be a loosely organized group of employees at one plant.

Determining the Status of Quality Circles or Other Employee Committees

A recent area of interest is the employee committee or quality circle that is organized by the employer. Employee committees are often instituted to discuss ways of improving production and/or open an avenue of communication with the employee. However, where an employer has instituted an employee committee and that committee has an active say in policy, wages, or terms and conditions of employment, it may be an "unlawful" labor organization that is dominated by the employer.

Many factors are examined with respect to determining the status of an employee committee; for example, the authority of the committee to act, the topics discussed, the impact of the committee's input in employer decisions with regard to terms and conditions of employment, how the members are selected, their terms of service, whether grievances or complaints are adjusted, and timing of the introduction of a committee. An employer invites trouble if it suddenly introduces an employee committee when the union is knocking on the door.

Recently, the NLRB has decided to reconsider its position regarding employee committees. In *Electromation, Inc.*, the NLRB heard oral argument in September 1991 in a case involving the scope of employer "domination" and the meaning of a labor organization. The leading authority in this area is *NLRB v. Cabot Carbon*, 360 U.S. 203 (1959), in which the Supreme Court ruled that "dealing with" in the statute did *not* necessarily mean "bargaining with" and is subject to a broad interpretation. A significant factor in determining whether an employee committee is unlawful is the motivation of the employer in forming it. If it is determined that the employee committee exists for the purpose of undermining an existing union or an organizing effort, it will be found to be unlawful.

The NLRB has taken a very narrow view of permissible employer conduct when dealing with formalized groups of employees. Certain conduct may become unlawful, particularly during an organizational campaign.

Case Example

Ramjet, Inc., manufactures racing cars in three buildings with about 280 production employees. The company president is committed to employee involvement and an "open-door" policy. He regularly met with groups of employees several times a year. Due to continued growth and expansion, he changed these "rap sessions" into a more formalized program with departmental designation of employee representatives meeting with him on a monthly basis. All meetings were held on company premises during work time, and employees were paid regular wages. During the same period of time, a union organizing campaign began. The employee advisory committee continued to meet and address individual and department concerns.

Does Ramjet have a problem? The NLRB and courts have been focusing more and more on this notion of employee committees. In the abstract, unorganized setting, virtually all contacts with employees by the employer are permissible. However, when employee groups become formalized and an organizing effort is also being made by a labor union, the Board has regularly found that the employer's conduct is unlawful because it has improperly assisted in forming a competing labor organization.

However, a recent federal appellate court has suggested that the Board's approach in this area may be outdated. In *Airstream, Inc. v. NLRB*, 877 F.2d 1291 (6th Cir. 1989), the court of appeals in Cincinnati, in a situation similar to Ramjet, declared that it was not impermissible to meet and discuss workplace conditions with structured groups of employees on a regular basis. The court rejected the Board's conclusion that the employee committee was a statutory labor organization, because it was not designed to convince employees it was a vehicle for collective bargaining.[50]

> NOTE: Human resources managers should pay close attention to developments in this area of the law. Many companies are looking into employee involvement programs and quality circles. There are many legal issues to be considered, for example, formation of an unlawful labor organization, intent to undermine the unionizing effort, interference with a free and fair election process, and/or domination of an otherwise legitimate labor organization.

IDENTIFYING EMPLOYEES NOT COVERED BY THE ACT

Most employees are protected by the Act, including an employee on layoff or out on strike or sick leave. However, there are certain exceptions. The following individuals do not fall within the purview of the Act:

1. Agricultural laborers

2. Domestic servants

3. Any individual employed by parent or spouse

4. Any individual employed by an employer subject to the Railway Labor Act

5. Independent contractors

6. Supervisors (management personnel)

7. Government employee

Generally, the Board uses a "right of control" test in analyzing who is an "independent contractor." Independent judgment and authority must be assessed with regard to the means and ends of work assignments.

"Supervisor" is defined in Section 2(11) of the Act as meaning having authority to hire, transfer, suspend, layoff, recall, promote, discharge or discipline other employees or responsibility to direct them or adjust their grievances.

Case Study

> Mary Roe is the executive assistant to the president at Ajax Powpow. She supervises 11 employees, including Jesse Jones, her aide. Mary asks Jesse to meet with other employees from time to time to counsel and occasionally discipline.

Is Jesse a supervisor? No. His exercise of authority is merely routine and is not based upon independent judgment. However, while Jesse may not have been excluded as a supervisor, he might be considered a "confidential" employee. Confidential employees are closely related to managerial and supervisory employees.

NOTE: The exercise of authority is a critical component of the Section 2(11) analysis.

Confidential employees are employees who participate in the determination of general corporate policy. However, *only those employees whose employment involves labor relations are excluded.* Thus, Jesse may be excluded as a confidential employee because he participates in discussions with Mary regarding employee discipline.

DETERMINING UNFAIR LABOR PRACTICES PROHIBITED BY THE ACT

Certain categories of conduct by employers and unions are deemed to be unfair labor practices under the Act. The Act specifically prohibits certain types of conduct which are broadly stated.

Defining Employer ULPs

Section 8(a) broadly defines unlawful conduct of an employer, or its agent, as follows:

1. To interfere with, restrain, or coerce employees in the exercise of the rights guaranteed in Section 7

2. To dominate or interfere with the formation or administration of any labor organization or contribute financial or other support to it

3. To encourage or discourage membership in any labor organization by discrimination in regard to hire or tenure or conditions of employment, with the one exception of the valid union shop

4. To discharge or otherwise discriminate against an employee because he has filed charges or given testimony under the Act

5. To refuse to bargain collectively with the majority representative of his employees

Identifying Union ULPs

Yes, the unions are also prohibited from engaging in certain proscribed conduct.[51] Section 8(b) states that it is an unfair labor practice for a labor organization or its agents

1. To restrain or coerce employees in the exercise of the rights guaranteed in Section 7 or an employer in the selection of his representatives for the purposes of collective bargaining or the adjustment of grievances

2. To cause or attempt to cause an employer to discriminate against an employee on account of his or her membership or nonmembership in a labor organization

3. To refuse to bargain collectively with an employer, provided the union is the majority-designated representative of the employees

4. To encourage or engage in a strike or refusal to handle goods where an object of such activity is

   a. To require an employer to join a labor organization or to enter into a "hot-cargo" agreement[52]

   b. To require any person to cease using, selling, handling, or transporting the products of any other employer or to cease doing business with any other person or to require some other employer to recognize or bargain with a labor organization which has not been certified by the Board as the representative of that other employer's employees

   c. To require any employer to bargain with a labor organization where another labor organization has already been certified by the Board as the representative of his employees. (These complex provisions are usually referred to as the "secondary boycott" provisions. They are set forth in Sections 8(b)(4)(A), (B), and (C) of the NLRA.)

5. To encourage or engage in a strike in order to force an employer to assign work to members of a particular union or craft rather than to members of another union or craft

6. To charge excessive or discriminatory initiation fees where a union shop is in effect

7. To cause or attempt to cause an employer to pay for work which is not to be performed (otherwise known as "featherbedding")

8. To engage in picketing or threats of picketing where an object is either to organize employees or to force an employer to recognize or bargain with a union (see Chapter 21 on picketing organization or recognition.)

9. To enter into a "hot-cargo" agreement with an employer

Unfair labor practices are investigated and prosecuted by the General Counsel's office of the NLRB.

Initiating Administrative Filings Before the NLRB

Charges or petitions may be filed by any person, employer, or labor organization. Generally, unfair labor practice charges, representation, petitions, objections to an election, requests for unit clarification, and other administrative actions are categorized and case types are designated as follows:

1. Representation cases are designated as "R" cases:

    RC—is a petition for an election filed by an individual or union

    RM—is a petition for an election filed by an employer

    RD—is a petition challenging the majority status of a labor organization

Representation cases are discussed more fully in the next chapter involving union representation campaigns and elections.

2. "C" cases are generally unfair labor practice charges:

    CA—is a petition filed for alleged violations of §8(a) by a labor organization

    CC—is a petition filed by an employer against a labor organization alleging violations of Section 8(b)(4)(i)(ii)

    CD—is a petition filed by a labor organization or employer where there is a jurisdictional dispute

3. A "UC," or unit clarification, petition seeks to clarify the scope of an *existing* bargaining unit. It may be filed by either the union or the employer.

4. An "AC," or amendment of certification, petition seeks the amendment of an outstanding certification of a union to reflect changed circumstances like a change in the name or affiliation of the union. This petition may be filed by a union or an employer.

5. A "UD," or unit determination, petition may be filed by an individual, a labor organization, or a group seeking an election to remove the authority of a labor organization to have a union shop agreement.

This chapter has introduced only a few of the many issues faced by an employer with unionized employees or a unionization campaign. The next two chapters address specifics, such as the union representation campaign, collective bargaining, and strikes.

ENDNOTES

1. *Meyers Industries, Inc. (I)*, 268 NLRB 493, 497 (1984).

2. *City Disposal Systems, Inc.*, 465 U.S. 822 (1984) *on remand*, 766 F.2d 969 (6th Cir. 1985), and *Interboro Contractors, Inc.*, 157 NLRB 1295 (1966) *enforced*, 388 F.2d 495 (2d Cir. 1967).

3. See *Meyers Industries, Inc. (II)*, 281 NLRB 882 (1986) *affirmed sub nom*, and *Prill v. NLRB*, 835 F.2d 1481 (D.C. Cir. 1987).

4. See *Every Woman's Place, Inc.*, 282 NLRB 413 (1986).

5. Sections 9(b) and (c).

6. Section 3(b).

7. *Lincourt v. NLRB*, 170 F.2d 306 (1st Cir. 1948).

8. The Division of Judges consists of administrative law judges who conduct the hearings on unfair labor practice complaints around the country. ALJs serve in a purely judicial capacity and are supervised by the Chief ALJ. Their decisions are appealable to and reviewable by the NLRB.

9. *NLRB v. Denver Building Trades Council*, 341 U.S. 675 (1951).

10. *Siemons Mailing Service*, 122 NLRB 81 (1958), and *American Home Systems*, 200 NLRB 1151 (1972).

11. *Carolina Supplies and Cement Co.*, 122 NLRB 88, 43 L.R.R.M. 1060 (1958).

12. *Man Products Inc.*, 128 NLRB 546 (1960).

13. *Pease Oil Co.*, 122 NLRB 344 (1958).

14. *HPO Service, Inc.*, 122 NLRB 394 (1958).

15. *Ready Mix Concrete and Materials, Inc.*, 122 NLRB 318 (1958).

16. *Carribe Lumber and Trading Co.*, 148 NLRB 277 (1946).

17. *Siemons Mailing Service*, 122 NLRB 81 (1958).

18. *T. H. Rodgers Lumber Co.*, 117 NLRB 1732 (1957).

19. *Drexel Home*, 182 NLRB 1045 (1970), and *Visiting Nurses Assn., et al.*, 187 NLRB 731 (1971).

20. *St. Aloysius Home*, 224 NLRB 1344 (1976), and *NLRB v. Catholic Bishop of Chicago*, 440 U.S. 490 (1979).

21. *Chain Service Restaurant*, 132 NLRB 960 (1961).

22. *Parkview Gardens*, 166 NLRB 697 (1967).

23. *Wilson Oldsmobile*, 110 NLRB 534 (1954).

24. *NLRB v. Denver Bldg. Trades Council*, 341 U.S. 675 (1951), and *Charles E. Forrester*, 189 NLRB 519 (1971).

25. *Cornell University*, 183 NLRB 329 (1970), and NLRB Rules and Regulations, §103.1.

26. *Raritan Valley Broadcasting Co.*, 122 NLRB 90 (1958).

27. *Walnut Hills Country Club*, 145 NLRB 81 (1963).

28. *The League of N.Y. Theatres, Inc.*, 129 NLRB 1429 (1961), and *Universal Security Consultants*, 203 NLRB 1195 (1973).

29. *Lansing Federal Credit Union*, 150 NLRB 1122 (1965), and *Federal Credit Union, East Division*, 193 NLRB 682 (1971).

30. *El Dorado, Inc.*, 151 NLRB 579 (1965).

31. *Detective Agency*, 110 NLRB 995 (1954).

32. Section 2(14) as amended, *Butte Medical Properties*, 168 NLRB No. 52 (1967). But, note that the Board has begun to exercise its rule-making authority over bargaining units in the health care industry. See discussion on health care bargaining units in Chapter 20.

33. *Salt and Pepper Nursery School*, 222 NLRB 1295.

34. *Penn-Keystone Realty Corp.*, 191 NLRB 800 (1971).

35. *Mistletoe Operating Co.*, 122 NLRB 1534 (1958); *Carol Management Corp.*, 133 NLRB 1126 (1961); and *Air Lines Parking, Inc.*, 196 NLRB No. 154 (1972).

36. *United States Postal Service*, 208 NLRB 948 (1974).

37. *Belleville Employing Printers*, 122 NLRB 350 (1958), and *George S. Roberts and Sons, Inc.*, 78 LRRM 2874 (2d Cir. 1971), *enf. in part* 188 NLRB 454, 76 LRRM 1337.

38. *Sioux Valley Empire Electrical Assn.*, 122 NLRB 92 (1958).

39. *Bickford's Inc.*, 110 NLRB 190 (1954).

40. *Clafery Beauty Shoppes*, 110 NLRB 620 (1954).

41. *American League*, 180 NLRB 190 (1969).

42. *Jurisdiction rule*, 82 LRRM 1519; NLRB Rules and Regulations §1032 (1973).

43. *Red and White Airway Cab.*, 123 NLRB 83 (1959).

44. *Charleston Transit Company*, 123 NLRB 1296.

45. See *Lima and Allen County Community Action Commission, Inc.*, 304 NLRB No. 114 (1991); *GMN Tri-County Community Action Committee*, 300 NLRB No. 135 (1990); and *Ohio Inns, Inc.*, 205 NLRB 528 (1973).

46. *NLRB v. The Catholic Bishop of Chicago*, 440 U.S. 490 (1979).

47. NLRB Rules and Regulations, §103.3. Note that these are already heavily regulated industries.

48. See *Seattle Real Estate Board*, 130 NLRB 608 (1961), holding that the services performed by brokers are "essentially local and have at best only a remote relationship to interstate commerce."

49. However, government employees are often covered under a Public Employee Labor Relations Act that permits membership in a union but with limits placed on right to strike and narrower negotiation powers.

50. See also *NLRB v. Streamway Division of Scott & Fetzer Co.*, 691 F.2d 288 (6th Cir. 1982); *Lawson Co. v. NLRB*, 753 F.2d 471 (6th Cir 1985); *Texas Bus Lines*, 277 NLRB 626 (1985); and *Hunter Douglas, Inc.*, 277 NLRB 1179 (1985).

51. See NLRA, 29 U.S.C., §158(b).

52. "Hot cargo" generally refers to goods that are subject to a product boycott. A hot-cargo provision in a contract provides that employees will not be required to handle materials from or sent to plants where a union is on strike.

20

UNION ORGANIZING AND STRIKE STRATEGIES UNDER THE NATIONAL LABOR RELATIONS ACT

In Chapter 19, you were introduced to the breadth of the National Labor Relations Act (NLRA). Most employers who do not have an "organized" work force, that is, a work force that is represented by a union, are concerned with staying union free. These employers desire to be able to institute unilaterally and change all aspects of employment, including wages, hours, work assignments, benefits, workplace conditions, discipline, termination, and the like, without having to sit down with a third party to negotiate such terms and conditions of employment. The third party is generally a union.

This chapter addresses what happens and what to do when a union comes knocking on an employer's door. The union will first ask for or demand recognition as the exclusive bargaining representative for a specific group or unit of employees. The employer may consent to the union's representation of its employees or may require that the union demonstrate that it has the support of a majority of the employees through a representation election.

The NLRA is the law that places significant restrictions on the employer's actions with regard to union organizational efforts. This chapter takes you through the union's quest for recognition and certification as the bargaining agent, the requirement of good faith bargaining if they succeed, the unit of employees covered, the election process, and strike strategies.

HOW A UNION OBTAINS RECOGNITION

The employer generally becomes aware of union activity when employees start talking about being approached to sign a "card" that indicates that the employee is interested in union representation. The union must demonstrate that it has significant support among the targeted work force. The following discussion explores how a union obtains the recognition that it represents the employees. Recognition of a union triggers a duty to bargain in good faith.

Recognition can be granted voluntarily by the employer, by a showing of union authorization cards, or by an election. A union can be designated in one of three ways

1. Employer card check
2. Employee poll
3. Representation election

Section 9 of the National Labor Relations Act deals with representation and election. Section 9(a) provides that

> representatives designated or selected for the purposes of collective bargaining by the majority of employees in a unit appropriate for such purposes shall be the exclusive representative of all the employees in such unit for the purposes of collective bargaining and respective rates to pay wages, hours of employment, or other conditions of employment.

Employers and employees should be mindful that a union selected by a majority of employees eligible to vote will represent all employees in that unit as the "exclusive representative" with regard to terms and conditions of employment. Some employers may not wish to deal with their employees through a union or outside group. In that case, if a union presents itself or begins to organize at the work site, there are many steps that can be taken to mount a successful union campaign. Strategies for handling an organizational drive are discussed later in this chapter.

Soliciting Authorization Cards

The most frequent method for establishing that a union has the support of a majority of employees is the solicitation of authorization cards. Such cards are a signed statement from an employee that he or she designates a union to act as his or her representative in collective bargaining with the employer. Any person other than an agent of management may solicit authorization cards.

A card may be one of the following:

- A regular union membership card
- An application for union membership

- A dues check-off authorization
- A card that explicitly designates a named union as the signee's representative

If a union has secured more than 30 percent of the employees signing authorization cards, it may file a petition for an election with the National Labor Relations Board. The union will probably have also submitted a demand for recognition to the employer. (A copy of a demand for recognition letter is shown in Exhibit 20.1).

– EXHIBIT 20.1 –
Sample Union Demand For Recognition

Gentlemen:

This letter is to advise you that this union represents a majority of your employees in a bargaining unit consisting of [   ].

This unit complies with the terms of the National Labor Relations Act as amended. This is a continuing request for recognition as collective bargaining representative for these employees.

We are prepared to provide proof of this representation to you. Therefore, we are requesting immediate recognition as the sole and exclusive collective bargaining representative in all matters pertaining to wages, rates of pay, hours of work and all other terms and conditions of employment.

We are prepared to meet with you at your convenience to discuss our representation and to set a date to begin to negotiate a collective bargaining agreement. Please contact me at your earliest convenience to set up our first meeting.

Very truly yours,

THE UNION

Types of Authorization Cards.   Authorization cards can be single purpose or dual purpose. Single-purpose authorization cards basically provide that the employee who signs the card wishes to become a member of the union.

Dual-purpose authorization cards request membership in the union and ask that dues be checked off by the employer as well as recognition for the union.

What the Card Must Contain. An authorization card must designate the union seeking to represent the employees and it must be dated.

It is sufficient if the designation of the union on the card is only in general terms. For example, "AFL-CIO" designation without identifying the local or international union is valid.

The card must be dated or have proof of when it was signed. An undated card is invalid. The card must also be signed during the *current* organizing campaign.

It is very difficult to contest the validity of an authorization card once a showing of interest has been made. The NLRB's General Counsel bears the burden of proving the authenticity of a card. However, if an employer has legitimate evidence that employees were unduly coerced or did not understand what they were signing, such evidence should be promptly brought to the attention of the NLRB agent handling your case. It is possible to disturb the showing of interest, although rarely done.

> NOTE: Once an employer reviews the authorization cards from a union, it may inadvertently give the union recognition if the union has already signed up more than 50 percent of its employees.

How to Poll Employees

An employer-conducted employee poll to determine whether a union has the support of the majority of employees is fraught with difficulties. If an employer polls its employees prior to a union's demand for recognition, it will not be bound by the result. However, if the poll is taken after a demand for recognition is received, the employer will be bound by the results if majority support is found.

Polling employees is permitted only in the following circumstances:

♦ The purpose of the poll is to determine the truth of a union's claim of majority.

♦ This purpose is communicated to the employees.

♦ Assurances against reprisal are given.

♦ The employees are polled by secret ballot.

♦ The employer has not engaged in unfair labor practices or otherwise created a coercive atmosphere.[1]

NOTE: Polling employees must be done carefully and be free of any coercive atmosphere. The employer will be bound by a result in favor of union support.

The employer may decide that an election conducted by the Board is perhaps the better course of action depending upon circumstances and perceived union support.

Holding Representation Elections

The employer may decline recognition to a union upon demand despite a strong showing of interest by the union. The union may then petition the NLRB to conduct a representation election. The union needs to support this petition with at least a 30 percent showing of interest based on signed authorization cards. The Board, if all necessary requirements are met, will conduct an election, generally at the employer's facility. The employees vote for or against the union in a secret ballot election. If the majority of valid votes cast are in favor of the union, and the results are upheld, the union is certified by the NLRB as the exclusive bargaining representative of the designated unit of employees.

The entire election process is discussed in detail in the next section, together with unit determination and how an employer may respond to an election and the results.

HOW TO CONDUCT THE UNION ELECTION PROCEDURE

If a union cannot establish a majority through cards, it may petition the NLRB to conduct a representation election. An election is the preferred and most widely used method of determining a union's status.

Filing a Petition

A petition for an election may be filed by an individual or group of employees acting on behalf of employees or by a labor organization. A petition may be filed by an employer only when one or more labor organizations claim to be recognized as the exclusive bargaining representative of the employees.

The petition identifies the unit of employees targeted and is accepted by the NLRB if a "showing of interest" has been demonstrated.

A showing of interest is a technical definition in labor law which essentially means that a petition has been accompanied by a showing that at least 30 percent of the employees in an appropriate unit have demonstrated their desire for the union to be their representative and wish to have an election to determine this issue. A showing of interest is generally made by authorization cards as discussed earlier. Also, a showing of interest may generally not be questioned by the parties. Only the NLRB may determine when a valid showing of interest has been made.

Petitions can also be filed by a labor organization when it seeks recognition or where a union is already recognized by the employer but now seeks the benefits of certification by the NLRB. A union might also file a petition where two or more unions file a joint petition as a joint representative for a single group of employees.

Once a union has proven to the NLRB that the majority of employees want the union to be its exclusive bargaining representative through an election and no objections are filed, the Board "certifies" the union as such. Certification entitles the union to the full protection offered by the NLRA. Certification remains in place until the union is decertified because the majority of employees no longer desire the union to be its representative or if the union is found to be committing unlawful acts.

Petitions are filed with the NLRB regional office in whose area the bargaining unit of employees is located. Most states have at least one regional office. Some of the more densely populated states have several. For example, in the New York metropolitan area, there are regional offices in Manhattan, Brooklyn, and Newark, New Jersey. Similarly, Los Angeles has several regional offices, but more sparsely populated areas may share an office across several states.

Submitting an Excelsior List. After the date for an election has been set, the employer will be required to submit a list of names and addresses of its employees. This list is called an **Excelsior list.**[2] The Excelsior list must be submitted within seven days and may be used by the union to contact employees during the election campaign.

There are basically two different kinds of elections:

1. An **agreement for consent election** basically means that the Regional Director will make the final decision.

2. A **stipulation for certification election** means that an appeal can be made from the region to the NLRB in Washington, D.C., for a final decision.

Handling Representation Hearings and Appeals to the NLRB.
If the parties cannot agree on an election, the regional director takes formal action by serving a notice of hearing. Any pending cases may be consolidated. If an unfair labor practice charge is pending, it may "block" the processing of an election petition. Each party may present its position and evidence and call and examine or cross-examine witnesses. Issues such as size or nature of the bargaining unit may be addressed. Posthearing briefs may be submitted. The decision, whether it be that the election be held or dismiss the petition, is reviewable.

The regional director's decision may be appealed by filing a request for review with the NLRB in Washington. The only request the Board cannot refuse to consider is an appeal made as a matter of right prior to the close of the hearing of a regional director's dismissal of a petition.

Requests for review may be based on four grounds:

1. A substantial question of law or policy is raised because of the absence of or the departure from official Board precedent.

2. The regional director's decision in a substantial factual issue is clearly erroneous and such error prejudices the rights of a party.

3. The conduct of the hearing or any ruling made in connection with the proceeding has resulted in prejudicial error.

4. There are compelling reasons for reconsideration of an important Board rule or policy.

Determining the Makeup of a Unit

Section 9 of the National Labor Relations Act requires that the union seek representation for an election in a unit of employees that is "appropriate." The National Labor Relations Board decides the appropriate bargaining unit on a case-by-case basis. A unit may be an employer unit, a craft unit, a plant unit, or a subdivision of that group. The NLRB *cannot* decide whether any craft unit is inappropriate unless a majority of the employees in the proposed unit vote against separate representation.

Determining Who May Not Be Included in a Unit. The Act limits who may be included in any particular unit. For example, security guards may *not* be included in the same unit with other employees.[3] Also, professional employees may *not* be included in the same unit with other employees, unless a majority of the professionals first vote separately to be included in the unit.[4] Supervisors are not covered by the Act.

The National Labor Relations Act defines a "professional employee" as

(a) any employee engaged in work either predominantly intellectual and varied in character as opposed to routine mental, manual, mechanical or physical work; involving the consistent exercise of discretion and judgment in its performance; of such a character that the output produced or the result accomplished cannot be standardized in relation to a given period of time; requiring knowledge of an advanced type in a field of science or learning customarily required by a prolonged course of specialized intellectual instruction and study in an institution of higher learning or a hospital, as distinguished from a general academic education or from an apprenticeship or from training in the performance of routine mental, manual or physical processes; or

(b) any employee who has completed the courses of specialized intellectual instruction and study described in (a) above and is performing related work under the supervision of a professional person to qualify herself to become a professional.[5]

The Act defines a "supervisor" to be any individual having authority, in the interest of the employer, to hire, transfer, suspend, lay off, recall, promote, discharge, assign, reward, or discipline other employees or responsibly to direct them, or to adjust their grievances, or effectively to recommend such action, if in connection with the foregoing the exercise of such authority is not of a merely routine or clerical nature but requires the use of independent judgment.[6] Supervisors are not accorded the protections of the NLRA nor may they use its election procedures.[7] However, it is lawful for supervisors to organize. Thus, supervisors are not included in so-called "rank and file" bargaining units.

How the Appropriate Unit Is Determined. If the parties can agree prior to an election, the Board will be satisfied unless it is a health care unit which must meet the 1989 guidelines (discussed shortly). If the parties cannot agree on an acceptable unit, the Board will hold a hearing and take testimony regarding unit appropriateness.

Case Study

Spider Webs, Inc., a manufacturer of thread, has received a petition for a representative election from the Spider Men Local for a collective bargaining unit of all web weavers. Due to the intricate nature of the job, each employee actually works on his or her own with a minimal level of supervision. However, the senior web weaver is also an hourly employee but has primarily supervisory duties. He is responsible for developing weaving techniques and design and has studied the dexterity and chemical makeup of the product content. A question might arise with regard to his status.

Is the senior web weaver a supervisor? Is he a professional employee? The determination of these issues would require the parties to review the specific job duties of each of the employees in the petitioned-for unit. If a senior web weaver, for example, met the definition of a professional employee as defined in Section 2(12) of the Act, or as a supervisor, he or she would be excluded. Supervisors, as defined in Section 2(11) of the Act, may not be included in a collective bargaining unit.

Establishing Rules for Health Care Bargaining Units. In 1989, exercising its rulemaking authority, the NLRB adopted special rules applicable to acute care hospitals defining appropriate bargaining units—the only appropriate bargaining units—for petitions filed pursuant to Section 9 of the Act:

- All registered nurses

- All physicians
- All professionals except for registered nurses and physicians
- All technical employees
- All skilled maintenance employees
- All business office clerical employees
- All guards
- All nonprofessional employees except for technical employees, skilled clerical employees, and guards

The Board may also consider other appropriate units by adjudication in extraordinary circumstances.

The Rules also provide that where there are existing non-conforming units in acute care hospitals and a petition for additionl units is filed, the Board shall find appropriate only units which comport, insofar as practicable, with the appropriate units set forth above. The Board will also approve consent agreements providing for election in accordance with the above units. However, nothing shall preclude Regional Directors from approving stipulations not in accordance with the units defined above as long as the stipulations are otherwise acceptable. This Rule applies to all cases decided on or after May 22, 1989.

The term "hospital" is defined in the same manner as the Medicare Act, 42 U.S.C. 1395x(e).

An "acute care hospital" is defined as either a short-term care hospital in which the average length of patient stay is less than 30 days or a short-term care hospital in which over 50 percent of all patients are admitted to units where the average length of patient stay is less than 30 days. An acute care hospital may include hospitals providing long-term care, outpatient care, psychiatric care, or rehabilitative care but shall not include facilities that are primarily nursing homes, psychiatric hospitals, or rehabilitation hospitals.

A "psychiatric hospital" is defined in the same manner as in the Medicare Act previously cited at 42 U.S.C. 1395x(f). A "rehabilitation hospital" includes and is limited to all hospitals accredited as such by either the Joint Committee on Accreditation of Healthcare Organizations or by the Commission for the Accreditation of Rehabilitation Facilities. A "non-conforming unit" is defined as a unit other than those described in the eight specific units above or a combination among those eight units.

If there is already a union for certain employees and a new petition is filed, the Board will look to the eight units just listed as appropriate units.

NOTE: The Board has attempted to simplify organizing in health care. Employers should be mindful that appropriate units have now been delineated by the Board. If a petition is received, contact labor counsel immediately before you respond.

Determining Election Eligibility

All employees of the company are not eligible to vote. Eligibility to vote is limited to those employees in the unit who are on the company payroll in the pay period *prior* to the petition being filed. Employees will be included, however, if they were on vacation, in military service, or out due to an economic strike.

Certain employees are not eligible to vote: those employees who quit or were terminated for cause, employees who abandon struck jobs, and replacements for strikers eligible for reinstatement are not entitled to vote. Supervisors or others not included in the unit defined on the petition are also not eligible to vote.

Holding the Election

The NLRB will generally schedule an election no sooner than 10 days after the NLRB regional office has received the Excelsior list. Usually, an election will be scheduled at least 30 days after the petition has been filed.

The election will usually be scheduled at the employer's premises during such hours so that all eligible employees on all shifts will have an opportunity to vote. An employer can refuse to hold an election on its premises. Such a tactic may give the union a significant but unnecessary advantage. If the company refuses to cooperate, the Board can schedule the election at a time and site of its own selection. The location of the polling place is usually determined by convenience and may not be in an area where supervisors can observe the balloting.

The ballot will simply ask employees whether they wish to be represented for purposes of collective bargaining, and they may vote "yes" or "no." Paper ballots are marked in secret in an election booth monitored by an NLRB official and observers designated by the parties. An official notice of the election will be submitted to the employer in advance of the election and must be posted in the plant at least three days before the election.

The Role of Observers. All parties may be represented by observers of their own selection. For the employer, observers must be nonsupervisory personnel, but they cannot be a person "closely identified with the employer."[8] Observers are responsible for challenging voters because they believe them to be ineligible to vote.

Case Study

Ralph Smith had been working for Ajax Box for three years. During the recent organizational campaign, he had been laid off because of his low seniority and, he alleged, his pro-union views. However, once on layoff, he began picketing the premises, became violent with several customers, and got into verbal and physical fighting with supervisory personnel. The union has designated him as its observer.

Can the union have such an employee as an observer at the election? Probably yes. The NLRB has permitted alleged discriminatees to serve as election observers even if they have committed picket line misconduct.

On the date of the election, the NLRB agent will come to the premises with an election booth to supervise the secret ballot election. Each party may designate two observers from the bargaining unit to monitor the proceedings. Any challenges to the voters will be set aside for later discussion. If the union does not receive a majority of the votes cast, representation will generally be rejected. However, if the number of challenged ballots may be dispositive, the NLRB may determine to open them after review.

How to Handle Objections to an Election

Formal, written objections to the election must be filed within 5 days of the election. They are submitted to the NLRB office conducting the election. If the NLRB determines that the objections are meritorious, it may set aside the election. Objections are filed only by the losing party. If the objections are sustained by the regional director, a hearing may be held on the objection. Objections may include improper procedure by the parties or Board or misconduct by the union or employer that interfered with the employees' right to a free and fair election.

For example, if union representatives threatened employees with physical harm prior to voting and attempted to monitor voting, such conduct might be sufficient to set aside an election.

The way for an employer to avoid many pitfalls and, thus, objectionable conduct is detailed in the section that follows. Also, see further discussion on objections in this chapter.

HOW TO AVOID HAVING A UNION

It is critical that management meet with its supervisors, the people on the "front line," to discuss the company's position and procedures when the union first appears on the scene. Review with your supervisors the election procedures of the Board and what they might expect in the way of potential problems and questions from employees. It is best to begin with how an organizing effort begins.

When a union attempts to organize your company, the normal sequence of events is that the union organizer will try, without going through a National Labor Relations Board election, to prove that the union is authorized by a majority of employees to represent them. Usually, a union organizer will send a letter to the company demanding that it be recognized as the bargaining agent and offering, upon request, to show the company union authorization cards signed by a majority of the employees. Or the union organizer may approach a supervisor directly and ask him to check the union authorization cards. If the union organizer fails in these two attempts, he will probably file a petition for an election at the National Labor Relations Board.

If the supervisor does in fact check the authorization cards and subsequently commits unfair labor practices, the company might well be ordered by the Board to bargain with a union without benefit of an election. As the National Labor Relations Board itself once said, "Union authorization cards are 'notoriously unreliable' and, therefore, most companies feel that the best expression of an employee's desires in union matters is through a free election sponsored by the Labor Board."

Guidelines for Supervisors During an Election Campaign

Supervisors are expected to continue exercising full responsibility for doing their regular jobs with a maximum of efficiency and a minimum of upheaval. Each supervisor should also appreciate that there is no law that prohibits him or her from carrying out this responsibility. *Your only restriction is that you cannot run your shift in a manner which favors the nonunion employees over those who favor the union. You cannot punish the union supporter because of union activities.* In other words, the supervisor should run his or her operation without regard to who is for the union or who is against the union.

A union button is not a license to loaf, be insubordinate, or violate established company rules. Nor does an organizing campaign justify a reduction in output caused by those employees who wish to talk union on company time. *In short, employees may still be disciplined for legitimate reasons as long as it is not based on their union sentiments.*

In large part, success in keeping control during a union campaign will depend on how supervisors have acted in the past. For example, if a supervisor has been lax in disciplining an employee for laziness in the past, the NLRB will find it suspicious should he suddenly start "cracking the whip" at an employee who has become active in the union. Another example would be the discharge for incompetence of an employee who has been with the company a number of years. The NLRB will ask, "If this employee was good enough to last, say, five years with the company, why is he suddenly found wanting in the middle of a union campaign?" Moreover, if a supervisor lets an anti-union employee get away with something, he will find it difficult to punish a pro-union employee for the same thing.

> NOTE: Continue to manage the workplace just as you had prior to a petition being filed. Do not be afraid to discipline even union supporters, but do not discipline merely for being union supporters.

Under the law, a supervisor is an agent of the company, and the company is held accountable for everything the supervisor says or does. For example, if a woman is fired for being a union organizer, the NLRB may order the company to reinstate her with full back pay for the time she is off. If this occurs during an election campaign, the NLRB may set aside the election results if the company wins and, among other things, grant automatic certification or hold another election. Thus, the results to the company could be

- A monetary loss from the back pay
- An election victory set aside
- A new election campaign in which the union is given a potential martyr in the person of the discharged employee
- A union certified as the bargaining agent for employees

Supervisors are expected to tell the employees the company's side of the story, a *truthful and factual* story for which they need apologize to no one: "This Company is a good employer with an excellent record. It is important that the employees know this." Modify the message to fit your own circumstances. Do not exaggerate and do not misstate. If things are good, chances are employees will know it. Likewise, where things are not good, be honest in your discussions with employees.

Do's and Don'ts for Company Supervisors.

Immediately following is a list of some of the things a supervisor *may* and *may not* do in a union campaign. They are not all inclusive for the reason that the NLRB is constantly changing its rules. Before going out on a limb, supervisors should touch base with specific management personnel designated to handle the campaign who will provide necessary instructions on the content and emphasis of communications to employees.

Eighteen Do's

1. Supervisors *may* tell employees that if an election occurs, it will be by a secret ballot on which they can express their true preference in complete privacy and that no one is obligated to vote for a union merely because they have joined a union or signed a union card.

2. Supervisors *may* tell employees the facts. The company is best served in election campaigns by fact and truth. Union campaigns may often be somewhat less than truthful. Unions usually don't choose to give all the facts available. Any union "whoppers" should be countered with the true facts. If a supervisor does not have the facts at his or her fingertips, management will provide them.

3. Supervisors *may* tell employees that unionism may mean strikes and, therefore, a big gap in their income. Wages of employees stop when they go out on strike, but wages of the professional union organizer keep rolling in.

4. Supervisors *may* point out that many policies and demands are set by union bosses who do not work for the company, who are unfamiliar with the

company, and who have little, if any, knowledge or concern for the company's operational or employment problems.

5. Supervisors *may* tell employees that many union demands—and supporting strikes—are often for union benefits, not employee benefits, for example, union security clauses (pay union dues or lose your job), rigid work rules (to spread the work over more men and thereby increase the number of dues payers), and decreased overtime (again to spread the work over more employees and, thus, increase the number of dues payers).

6. Supervisors *may* advise employees of those facts about the union and its record which the union would rather forget.

7. Supervisors *may* remind employees that the company—not the union—pays their wages and the cost of their fringe benefits and that the union campaign promises of more and more are just vote-getting propaganda, that all such promises are subject to what can be bargained out with the company, and that no one can guarantee what can come out of such bargaining.

8. Supervisors *may* tell employees that true job security is determined only by the company's customers, not the union.

9. Supervisors *may* make it clear that an almost sure union demand is for a union shop and that a union shop means that employees *must* pay union dues or lose their job.

10. Supervisors *may* point out that it is very difficult for employees to get rid of an unsatisfactory union once the union is voted in, especially where the union has them locked in under a long-term bargaining contract with a union shop clause.

11. Supervisors *may* ask employees how much consideration they expect from these union strangers after the automatic flow of union dues is assured under a long-term union shop clause with a check-off provision. A check-off provision requires the company to deduct the dues from an employee's pay and send it to the union. The employees never see the money. And in many cases they may not thereafter see too much of the union stranger.

12. Supervisors *may* tell employees that a union contract means a third party will be between the company and its employees.

13. Supervisors *may* tell employees that if they vote in a union, the company *must* deal with the union and cannot—under the law—deal directly with employees, even if that union is doing things of which the employees disapprove.

14. Supervisors *may* point out current wage rates and fringe benefits which the employees presently enjoy without union membership and remind employees that these benefits have constantly increased over the years without necessity of their paying dues, fines, initiation fees, and strike assessments to a union.

15. Supervisors *may* point out the fat salaries and expense accounts of union bosses, all paid for by employees' hard-earned wages. Back this up with facts. A handout *may* detail the salaries of union leaders and their perks as well.

16. Supervisors *may* stop distribution of handbills in *work areas* at any time.

17. Supervisors *may* stop solicitation for union membership during *working hours* (however, it may be done on break time or lunch periods).

18. Supervisors *may* refuse admission of nonemployee union organizers to company property, including company parking lots. (Organizers may, however, stand at the entrances to the parking lot.)

Twelve Don'ts

1. Supervisors *may not* threaten or discipline any employees in any way merely because of his or her union sentiments or legitimate union activity.

2. Supervisors *may not* promise any employee anything directly or by inference for abandoning the union or his or her union activities or for voting against the union or to influence how he feels about the union.

3. Supervisors *may not* spy upon meetings or gatherings.

4. Supervisors *may not* interrogate any employee about his or her union sentiments or activities or about the union sentiments or activities of other employees. However, supervisors *may* listen to what any employee volunteers.

5. Supervisors *may not* threaten a shutdown or curtailment of work as retaliation against the union winning an election.

6. Supervisors *may not* increase wages during the union campaign unless such a raise is part of a previously established pattern.

7. Supervisors *may not* ask employees how they or other employees will vote.

8. Supervisors *may not* prohibit union discussion during nonworking hours such as breaks or lunch periods.

9. Supervisors *may not* prohibit, absent special circumstances, the wearing of union buttons to work.

10. Supervisors *may not* make speeches on company time to a "captive audience" of employees within 24 hours of an NLRB election. This is the extent of the so-called "24-hour rule." But it does not prohibit speeches to employees on company property if attendance is truly voluntary. It does not prohibit campaign literature, and it does not prevent casual conversations with an employee at his or her workstation. Nor does it prohibit supervisors from answering questions about the union from employees.

11. Supervisors *may not* visit employees' homes to talk to them about the union.

12. Supervisors *may not* call an employee or employees into supervisory offices to talk to them about the union. The best place for talks is the employee's workstation. The best place for speeches is an area not exclusively associated with management or supervisors.

More Tips for Conducting the Campaign. The mere fact that supervisors *may* say certain things to an employee does *not* mean that they *should* say them. If an employee is worried about job security, it does little good for a supervisor to assure him about the company's liberal vacation plan.

In short, supervisors must be selective. Once the company finds out what is bothering employees, it will almost surely know what union-planted fears and uncertainties must be combatted. Any campaign must be directed to what is worrying employees and to do this requires information. Again, supervisors may not interrogate employees on union matters, but they can listen and they can inquire as to how things are going on the job. If supervisors have the proper relationship with their employees, this information will come freely, and the chance of a union conducting a successful campaign will be greatly decreased. Again, if a supervisor does not have an answer to an employee's question, he should tell the employee that he will get one, and he should do so at the earliest reasonable time.

Further, during the union campaign, supervisors should carry small pocket notebooks with them at all times. They should make notes of all conversations with employees and union officials, if any, which in any way touch upon the union campaign or gripes or working conditions. They should record the date, time, place, contents, and witnesses to the conversation. The notes should not be taken in front of the employee but as soon thereafter as possible while the events are still fresh in the supervisor's mind. The purpose of the notebook is twofold. It will be an accurate record on which to base communications to the employees, and it may serve to refute a charge that an unfair labor practice was committed. It is not unusual for a union adherent to stretch a few facts in telling the union boss or an NLRB agent what a supervisor said to him.

STRATEGIES TO USE IN UNION ELECTION CAMPAIGNS

After the union has filed its petition, the employer must take control of the workplace. What do we mean by that statement?

♦ Take control of all information that flows to your employees, for example, do not wait for the union to advise employees that an election will take place. The company should notify all employees in writing that it has agreed to hold a secret ballot election at a certain time and date. Remind employees that they are free to vote against the union even if they signed an authorization card. Let them know that you will provide them with more specific information during the campaign.

♦ Affirmatively deal with issues in the workplace.

♦ Do not run a campaign by merely responding to charges of the union.

♦ Set the tone and dialogue for communications. Generally, a union attempts to communicate to employees how much better the environment will be if they are successful. Coincidentally, they regularly fail to explain the costs and limitations incurred by bringing in the union. You may provide that information. They fail to explain, for example, that decisions are generally made by union "bosses" who are unrelated to the shop and that most decisions will not be made at the local level. You must explain the facts on a regular basis to your employees. Your main job during the campaign is to provide information about the company to your employees to keep the union "honest."

♦ Plan to meet directly with employees in small and large groups to get your message across.

♦ Be good listeners—employees will tell you how they feel without too much prodding. Be alert for "intelligence" on union strategies and promises.

NOTE: Consult with your labor relations specialist prior to and during the campaign. It is a good idea to have all communications to employees reviewed by counsel prior to use.

Implementing Communications to Get Your Message Across

Once the campaign has begun, you should consider a few quick operational steps:

1. Set up a campaign coordinating committee (CCC) with key in-plant personnel. A human resources representative and other key staff who will deal with supervisors and employees regarding the direction of a campaign should be on this committee. Obviously, the size of the CCC depends upon the overall size and resources of the company. The CCC must have decision-making authority as far as the campaign is concerned and also provide input and information so appropriate campaign decisions can be made.

2. Set up a campaign calendar through to the very end, leaving room for speeches and small-group meetings. Usually, I like to work backward

from the election day. A 24-hour speech is typically planned on the day before the vote. It is suggested that small-group meetings be held at periodic intervals during the campaign to more informally get your message across. It is impermissible to turn these into grievance solicitation sessions, and promises cannot be made.

3. Appoint someone, either the president or plant manager, to act as a company spokesperson who will communicate information on a regular basis either at small-group meetings or in large plant assemblies. Try to select someone who is credible and well liked.

Types of Employee Communications. Communication with your employees can take several avenues:

1. Continue with conversations with individual employees on a regular basis. This is the easiest and most natural method. Be careful not to hold these in management offices.

2. Schedule small-group meetings a few times during the campaign to discuss your concerns about a union and explain your position about the plant. Be careful *not* to convert this into a grievance session. In that case, it may become unlawful conduct.

3. Distribute written communications during the campaign, getting your message across and responding point by point to allegations made by the union. Be creative and interesting. Avoid boring memos from the boss. Depending upon the size of the plant and the number of employees involved, payroll stuffers may be effective on a weekly basis; don't forget to use cartoons, movies, news clippings, posters, and standard "vote no" buttons.[9] You and your human resources staff or labor counsel are in the best position to assess what will work for you.

4. Schedule speeches at various points during the campaign culminating in what is commonly referred to as the 24-hour speech, which will basically be the last formal communication with your employees.

Keep in mind that the campaign will typically run at least four weeks and should peak for the election. Do not do everything in the first week. Pace your campaign by laying out a logical schedule on a calendar and follow it. Be flexible enough to adjust to union propaganda, but stay the course and get your message across.

Important Information Your Employees Must Have

Some topics that regularly arise and should be dealt with include financial obligations to the union, the constraints on personal freedom, the negotiating process, and the possibility of strikes. But if you overplay certain themes such as strikes and bargaining from scratch, you run the risk of interfering with the election process by way of ULP charges.

You should clearly advise employees that union-imposed fines and sanctions can be enforced in court as can obligations to march on the picket line.

Management actions and reactions during this critical period are closely scrutinized by the National Labor Relations Board. You should plan in advance your conduct, communications, and speeches and fine-tune them as the facts dictate. To make sure that you are getting the information correct, top company officials should meet regularly with supervisors and foremen to get a sense for what is happening in the plant. Additionally, these meetings should be used to reinforce the do's and don'ts and guidelines to supervisors on a periodic basis. Remember, your foremen and supervisors are your first line of defense.

Communicate positive information positively. Your company has wage scales and benefit structures that are probably competitive in your industry and geographic location. If so, make sure that such positive information is affirmatively and positively communicated to your employees. Let them know that not every company has that pay scale or level of benefits in your area or your industry. Also do not be afraid to let employees know that some of your competitors, either in the industry or in the area, are on strike or are going out of business. Put up newspaper clippings letting employees know the status of this conduct.

Make sure you have conducted an appropriate inquiry into the local and international union whom you are dealing with. A review of the union constitution and bylaws as well as LM-1 and LM-2 filings with the U.S. Department of Labor may reveal interesting rules and financial arrangements that your employees may find of interest. You can write directly to the Department of Labor. Be intelligent in obtaining this information, and then distribute it carefully so that your employees understand where the money goes when they join this particular union.

NLRB elections can certainly be won. Just ask most unions. Unions generally lose at least 50 percent of all representation elections. The key to winning the election is what you have done up to that point with regard to your employees. If you already treat your employees fairly and pay them competitive wages and benefits, you should be able to overcome the union. Of course, if there is trouble in the workplace, your employees may seek an outside party as their champion. You must run the shop every day to maximize your relationships with your employees. If the alarm first goes off when the union calls, it may be too late.

WHAT HAPPENS AFTER THE UNION ELECTION

Ballots are tallied at the close of the election by an NLRB agent with observers present. Challenged ballots are segregated and not opened. The results of the election are certified, if no objections are filed. If the union has won the election, it will be certified as an exclusive bargaining representative of the employees.

If the union does not receive a majority of ballots cast, it will not be certified. However, if challenged ballots can affect the outcome, they may be opened by the Board after all legal issues are decided.

Filing Objections to an Election

Objections to an election may be filed by either party within 5 days of the election. Objections can relate to the manner in which the election was held or the conduct which allegedly affected the results of the election. Objections generally fall into four categories:

1. Misconduct during the "critical period" or from date of filing of petition to election
2. Misconduct which occurred prior to petition and after election
3. Unfair labor practices
4. Misrepresentations

A party may take exception to the results of an investigation of the objections and/or challenges. Often, the objections, unfair labor practice charges, and exceptions will be consolidated into one proceeding for hearing purposes. If the NLRB determines that the objections have merit, it may set aside the election and schedule a hearing on the objections.

Objections are filed only by the losing party.

The Hearing on Objections. If objections and unfair labor practice charges are consolidated, a hearing will be scheduled before an administrative law judge from the NLRB. The hearing will be conducted similar to a court proceeding. A record will be made, and the parties will each have the opportunity to present witnesses and to cross-examine witnesses. At the administrative hearing, the General Counsel of the NLRB acts as a prosecutor. Generally, a pretrial conference is held to clarify the issues. The parties make opening statements and present evidence and witnesses. The ALJ will review the evidence and issue a decision and recommended order.

How Rulings Are Reviewed and Appealed

All rulings by the ALJ are subject to review by the full National Labor Relations Board in Washington, D.C. Review may be sought during the hearing, after the close of the hearing, before issuance of the decision, and after issuance of the decision. A party may file exceptions to the ALJ decision with the Board within 20 days.

The NLRB is not bound by the ALJ's conclusions of fact or law, but they will be given great weight. Board decisions may be appealed to the U.S. Court of Appeals either in the geographic area in which the respondent is located or at the U.S. Court of Appeals for the District of Columbia. A Petition for Review of a Board decision is used to initiate the appeal process.

Parties should note that election orders are generally not reviewable or appealable. Courts of appeals lack the authority to interfere with the congressionally mandated jurisdiction of the NLRB to order elections. However, the underlying unfair labor practice charges are reviewable. Most employers tend to accept a Board decision to hold a rerun election and, if necessary, refuse to bargain. Usually, in the context of these charges, the parties can litigate the election issues.

Filing Charges. ULP charges must be filed within 6 months of alleged misconduct. In addition, supporting documentation must be submitted within 72 hours of the charge being filed. Unfair labor practice charges can be submitted by any person, employer, or labor organization.

All charges, whether regarding representation elections or ULPs in general, are processed the same way. The NLRB will conduct an investigation to determine whether or not the charge has merit. If the Board believes that sufficient facts have been presented to the Board, a formal complaint will be issued by the NLRB. The hearing process on such a charge will be nearly identical to the administrative hearing and review discussed earlier for consolidated objection/ULP hearings.

A bargaining obligation falls upon the parties under the NLRA once a union has been certified.

The employer has a legal obligation to bargain with a union, unless it can rebut the presumption that the union has retained majority status. The employer bears the burden of establishing a lack of majority status on the date it attempts to withdraw recognition. The employer must also show that its conduct was taken in good faith. Bargaining obligations and the legal parameters as well as job actions are discussed in the next chapter.

ENDNOTES

1. *Struksnes Construction Co.,* 164 NLRB 1062 (1967).

2. See NLRA, 29 U.S.C. §158(b).

3. 29 U.S.C. §152(11).

4. 29 U.S.C. §164(a).

5. 29 U.S.C. §152(12).

6. 29 U.S.C. §152(11).

7. 29 U.S.C. §164(a).

8. See *BCW, Inc., d/b/a Sunward Materials*, 304 NLRB No. 103 (1991); *Mid-Continent Spring Co.*, 273 NLRB 884 (1985); and *B. P. Custom Building Products*, 251 NLRB 1337 (1980).

9. For more specific information, we suggest you contact labor counsel to review a full-scale campaign.

21

LABOR RELATIONS: COLLECTIVE BARGAINING AND DEALING WITH STRIKES AND OTHER RELATED ISSUES

After the union has won a representation election and has been certified, there are many questions that you must deal with. Probably the first concern is to get ready for collective bargaining and to determine the issues that you wish to focus on. In this chapter, we will explore the parameters of collective bargaining and try to provide an organized framework for your company.

If this is your first contract with this union, it is likely that there may be posturing by both sides prior to and during negotiations. To prepare for negotiations, the company should fully review its wage and benefit levels to assess them in comparison to the marketplace.

Depending on the size of the company, different levels of involvement and sophistication are required. The individuals responsible for budgeting must be consulted so that you have an idea of what has been anticipated, at least for salaries. A negotiating committee should be assembled. There are no hard and fast rules about its size or composition. A senior executive should be involved to ensure decision making and to communicate to the union that serious discussions are about to take place.

Depending upon the size and scope of the negotiations, we suggest that financial input should be available to the committee at all times.

Now you must define your own agenda. Part of the strategy is to attempt to control the issues and agenda on the table: the union must understand that bargaining is a two-way street and the company has issues on its mind as well. The process rarely takes the same course.

In general, bargaining strategies are individualized and can be complex.[1]

GETTING READY TO BARGAIN WITH THE UNION

Generally, each side will prepare a proposal which can be exchanged in advance or at the first session. The union will probably insist that meetings be held on work time and may seek to involve many employees, particularly on the first contract.

NOTE: Keep in mind that a union is basically a political organization—there may be several constituencies within the group. Various proposals may be offered to satisfy those diverse concerns. Your primary task is to discern the primary concerns of your employees and to know your limitations before you sit down.

Labor law has evolved from the Wagner Act, which gave employees the right to organize and bargain collectively and to strike, to the Taft-Hartley Act of 1947, which attempted to place certain limits on unions.[2] The Taft-Hartley Act added Section 7, which provided that employees had a right to *refrain* from participating in labor organizations as well as to join them and also added a free speech provision. Union unfair labor practices (which were discussed in Chapter 19) were codified in Section 8(b) of the Taft-Hartley Act.

One leading commentator has said that a major consequence of collective bargaining is "to change the format from an absolute monarchy to a constitutional monarchy, who must operate within the framework of a union agreement and whose decisions can be appealed to a higher authority."[3] The same commentator said that "unionism increases the worker's sense of participating in economic and political affairs. He is no longer an isolated individual, subject to forces that he can neither understand nor control."[4] All of this is true.

How Other Laws Affect Bargaining

To understand the bargaining process, you must also be aware of the various laws that impact on collective bargaining. For example, Title VII (discussed in Chapter 5) provides for certain statutory rights preventing discrimination in the workplace. Once a collective bargaining agreement is in place, it is likely that a grievance/arbitration machinery will be set up that may dovetail with Title VII rights.[5] Similarly, the Fair Labor Standards Act (discussed in Chapter 17) sets minimum wage rates and regulates overtime. The Fair Labor Standards Act works as a floor for union collective bargaining purposes.[6]

Other legislation that we have discussed throughout the book, including the Americans with Disabilities Act and the Rehabilitation Act, also will impact on the collective bargaining process. Rights that are now protected for the disabled and handicapped may affect dollars that the company would have otherwise utilized in the workplace.

Essentially, collective bargaining is about the allocation of resources. If legislation and regulations require the employer to spend its resources in certain ways, there will be more limited resources to share with other constituencies, including the employees, through collective bargaining. Similarly, the Occupational Safety and Health Act (discussed in Chapter 15) regulates workplace safety and sets minimum standards which, again, require the employer to spend real dollars and limits the available pool for negotiations.

Understanding the Obligation to Bargain

Once a union has been certified as the exclusive representative of the employees, the parties have an obligation under Section 9 of the National Labor Relations Act to meet and confer in good faith and to bargain about terms and conditions of employment. The employer is obligated to meet with and bargain with the union. However, the employer is never required to come to agreement or accept a proposal as long as they are bargaining in good faith. The bargaining obligation may include such things as requests for information by a union in order to prepare for bargaining or requests for specific information in order to determine whether or not a grievance should be filed or pursued on behalf of a member.

Meeting and Conferring in Good Faith. Section 8(d) of the Act requires the parties to meet and confer in good faith. However, as stated, there is no obligation to agree. Interestingly, one of the most difficult questions for both sides is to determine if they are at "impasse" in their negotiations. We will discuss impasse later on in this chapter, but it is essential that companies understand that what may appear to them to be a standstill in negotiations may not necessarily be an "impasse" under the law.

Bargaining with the Exclusive Representative of the Employees. Employers and employees must also understand that under our labor law, the labor organization certified by the NLRB is the "exclusive" representative of the employees.

The union represents *all* the employees in the unit, whether or not they are members of the union.[7]

The employer must deal with the certified or exclusive representative and may *not* bargain with minority or splinter groups of employees. To protect employee rights, the Supreme Court noted in the case of *Emporium Capwell v. WACO*, 420 U.S. 50 (1975), that Congress did not authorize a tyranny of the majority over the minority. For that reason, unit appropriateness issues apply as do limits under the law and the fair representation obligations.

The Duty of Fair Representation Claim. Likewise, the Supreme Court has said that the exclusive representative can be held accountable for its actions under Section 301 of the Labor Management Relations Act if it fails to properly represent all its members or constituents. Such a claim is called breach of the duty of fair representation (DFR). Employees may pursue fair representation claims either in federal court or at the NLRB.[8] In addition, DFR claims may also involve breach of contract suits against the employer.

Identifying "Good Faith" and Refusal to Bargain Issues

Good faith bargaining or refusal to bargain issues can take many forms. For example, in one famous case—*NLRB v. General Electric*, 418 F.2d 736 (2d Cir. 1969)—the Court of Appeals in New York found that GE had engaged in bad faith bargaining simply because it made its best offer and went directly to the employees and the public and told its employees that this was a "firm, fair offer." The court found that the company position was designed to show the futility of the union and that the company's position would not change. In addition, GE refused to provide information regarding costs and benefits which the union had requested. Both the Board and the court found that such a refusal was an unfair labor practice (a violation of Section 8(a)(5)).

The GE approach has been called "Boulwarism" named after Lemuel Boulware, the vice president for labor relations at GE. His approach, the Board found, was unlawful because it was a take-it-or-leave-it approach which included union disparagement and direct communications to the employees.

NOTE: It is unlawful to deal with the union through the employees instead of dealing with the employees through the union.

To engage in collective bargaining, once a union has been certified, the union must be respected and treated as an equal at the table. Efforts to go around, behind, or through the union may result in refusal to bargain charges. Likewise, merely meeting or conducting "surface bargaining" may result in similar unfair labor practice charges.[9]

NOTE: No person or agency can force the parties to agree to anything.

Identifying Subjects for Bargaining

There are certain parameters under the law regarding what may be discussed and bargained about and how those issues may be resolved. Basically, there are three categories of subjects for bargaining. They are classified as follows:

1. Illegal subjects

2. Mandatory subjects

3. Voluntary subjects

Illegal Subjects. Topics that would be illegal or are expressly forbidden under the NLRA are "illegal subjects" of bargaining. Bargaining on these subjects may *not* be required and may *not* be included in the contract even if the other party agrees. Examples of illegal bargaining subjects include "hot-cargo" agreements; a closed shop; a preferential hiring hall; or discriminatory contract provisions based upon race, sex, age, and other unlawful categories.

> NOTE: An illegal subject cannot properly be included in a collective bargaining agreement.[10]

Mandatory Subjects. Section 8(b) of the Labor Management Relations Act requires that both employers and unions bargain in good faith about wages and hours and other terms and conditions of employment.[11] These mandatory subjects must be bargained about by either party and may be insisted upon to the point of impasse. "Other terms and conditions of employment" has been broadly interpreted. This phrase may cover such things as hours of work (including time and length of breaks), policies such as number of sick days or personal days, smoking or drug testing, company housing, discontinuance of a regular holiday bonus, union security arrangements, agency shop provisions, seniority rules, and many others.

> NOTE: Recently, many employers have chosen to impose drug testing or workplace standards on smoking. The Board ruled that these are mandatory subjects of bargaining and must be discussed with the union *prior* to imposing these policies.

Case Study

The Spider Web Company has decided to ban smoking in the workplace due to the highly combustible nature of the webs as well as the chemical testing instruments and the possible effect of smoke on the testing procedures. The company also decided to implement drug testing requirements for all employees because the work required great concentration. Despite a collective bargaining agreement with Spider Men Local 1, the company established "no smoking" rules and drug testing procedures in the workplace on its own and distributed the policies to all its employees without consulting with Spider Men.

It was not permissible for the company to promulgate and distribute the no-smoking and drug testing policies without consulting with the union. The NLRB has found that where the subject is germane to the working environment and it is a substantial and/or material change from past practice, it must be bargained over. A smoking ban was held to be germane to the working environment.[12]

A major change in the smoking policy of the company, whether it is to eliminate smoking entirely or merely to limit it, must be bargained for between the parties. Similarly, the NLRB opined in *Johnson-Bateman Company*, 295 NLRB No. 26 (1989), that subjects like drug testing are mandatory subjects of bargaining which constitute a substantial change in working conditions and require that the company bargain with the union over such a change.

> NOTE: It is mandatory to bargain about these issues. Refusal to negotiate over these items is an unfair labor practice.

Voluntary Subjects. Other subjects that fall outside of the categories of mandatory or illegal are termed "voluntary subjects." They may be placed on the bargaining table by either party. Neither party is required to bargain on them or to agree to their inclusion in the contract. It would be an unfair labor practice to insist upon them as a condition of reaching an agreement.

Determining Who May Bargain

An interesting question also arises over who is at the table.

The Board has ruled that the union has nearly complete discretion with regard to the composition of its negotiating committee at the bargaining table.

A more difficult question arises if the employer deals with, meets with, or bargains with groups of employees who have not been certified by the Board. Since the definition of a labor organization under the Act (discussed in Chapter 19) is a loose and broad one, any such discussion may constitute "dealing with" under the law. Thus the discussion regarding the concept of a "labor organization" from Chapter 19 must be reviewed by the company, especially if a union organizing campaign is under way or if you have an existing union and have decided to impose and/or develop "quality circles" to improve, enhance, and monitor workplace performance. While these issues are somewhat in flux at the NLRB, employers should be prudent before engaging in organized discussions with groups of employees that may impact upon labor relations.

Employers may form a group or association for bargaining purposes and negotiate a generally uniform contract subject to individual adjustments. The result is referred to as a multiemployer contract.

Usually, all of the employers are bound by such an agreement unless they opt out of the group according to the rules and regulations of the association. Most agreements have a provision to let members of an association resign *prior* to the conclusion or termination of the existing collective bargaining agreement.

Changing Conditions of the Job

Employers may *not* unilaterally change the terms and conditions of employment prior to reaching an impasse. Employers also may not change or alter mandatory subjects of bargaining without negotiating with the union. For example, as noted previously, the NLRB held that smoking rules in the workplace and drug testing are mandatory subjects of bargaining. While the Board recognized that these are significant issues, nonetheless, it held that the employer had an obligation to discuss them with the union *before* it imposed its own rules in this regard.

HOW TO RECOGNIZE AND DEAL
WITH A COLLECTIVE BARGAINING IMPASSE

Probably one of the most difficult issues in collective bargaining is recognizing and dealing with impasse. An impasse exists when the parties are unable or unwilling to make any progress through bargaining. While one party may assume that impasse has been reached, the Board does not necessarily conclude the parties are at impasse merely because negotiations are at a standstill.[13]

Impasse is the same as being at a deadlock. It occurs when the parties have discussed the matter and are unable to achieve an agreement despite genuine bargaining. The Board has said that impasse cannot occur if there appears to be any realistic possibility that a continuation of bargaining would be fruitful.[14]

Factors Considered in Defining an Impasse

The Board looks at a range of factors to determine if the parties are actually at impasse. Some of the factors are as follows:

- Whether a strike vote has been taken or the employees are out on strike. However, it should be noted that a strike does not necessarily create an impasse and may break a preexisting one
- Continuation of bargaining[15]
- Fluidity of position by the parties[16]
- Statements of understandings of the parties
- Union evidence of other acts
- The kinds of issues remaining and parties' positions on those issues
- Bargaining history of the parties
- Willingness of the parties to discuss issues further
- Duration of hiatus between bargaining sessions
- Number and duration of bargaining sessions
- Other actions inconsistent with impasse[17]

When the parties are at impasse, the employer can implement some or all of its proposals. However, an impasse does not end the bargaining obligation. It merely halts certain aspects of it temporarily. Interestingly, an impasse can be broken if the possibility of a meaningful discussion is renewed. Likewise, recognition cannot be withdrawn merely because the parties are at impasse. An employer making unilateral changes in working conditions at impasse may not impose just any conditions that come to mind.

Case Study

Automan, Inc., has been meeting with its union, Carworkers Local 1, for several months. The company has proposed red, white, and blue uniforms for its members to maintain uniformity of dress in the workplace and also make a dramatic patriotic statement. The union has insisted that they either be blue or all white and has objected to the company's proposal as unnecessary and as infringing upon individual members' rights to wear union tee shirts and other paraphernalia. The parties have bargained over this uniform issue at every session, and neither side is now willing to change its position because there appears to be a more serious power struggle going on—the uniform question is merely a surface test of strength. In a letter to the president of the local, the employer advises that as far as he is concerned, the parties are deadlocked on this issue (which, for the purposes of this example, is a mandatory issue). No response is received from the union.

In this case, the employer can lawfully make the uniform change. The parties appear to be at impasse on this issue. The employer can adopt his proposal and provide the workers with red, white, and blue uniforms despite the union's intransigence on the subject.

NOTE: At impasse, unilateral changes by the employer must be consistent with the last offer rejected by the union.

How to Fulfill the Duty to Bargain on Other Subjects

Impasse on one issue does not suspend the bargaining obligation on other unsettled issues. The parties have a continuing obligation to bargain. However, as a result of impasse, a strike or other concerted job action may result. Many tactics can be used by both sides to place pressure on the other party to agree to terms. Strikes or picketing can occur in a representation mode or can occur in an effort to make the other side modify or change its position at the negotiating table.

Impasse is generally reviewed on a case-by-case basis and requires that there be no point in future discussions because both sides have ceased bargaining. The key for the company is to avoid declaring impasse prematurely. If an employer acts precipitously in this regard, it may convert economic activity (where employees are protesting the salary or other benefits) into an unfair labor practice strike which will trigger different reemployment rights for employees.

Mediators from federal and state agencies are available to assist the parties in reaching agreement or to break a deadlock in negotiations. Sometimes while bargaining has stalled, the union may decide to place pressure on the company. If the contract has expired, the union may seek a strike vote to force the company to concede on certain issues. If a strike occurs over negotiable subjects (called an economic strike), the employer is allowed to hire permanent replacements for all striking employees. Hiring replacements must be distinguished from discharging strikers. An employer may not discharge strikers.[18]

HANDLING STRIKES AND RELATED ISSUES

The right to strike is one of the major economic weapons of organized labor. The right to strike has been protected by the courts, and it is clearly and fundamentally written into our labor law.[19] Under the National Labor Relations Act, as stated earlier, employees have the right to engage in concerted activity, including the right to strike. The Act also protects workers from termination merely because they have gone on strike.

However, the right to strike is not an unqualified right. Section 8(b)(4) of the NLRA restricts the right of a labor organization or its agents to engage in unlawful strikes designed to induce or encourage "secondary" pressure. Violation of that section may be redressed under Section 303 of the Labor Management Relations Act.

The Act itself attempts to structure a notice and discussion in Section 8(d) prior to permitting strikes. A party seeking to modify or terminate an existing collective bargaining agreement must provide 60 days' advance notice to the other party and continue to work during this period without going on strike. There are also provisions to enjoin strikes that may endanger national health or safety for up to 80 days pursuant to Title II of the Taft-Hartley Act.

For a strike to be protected, there must be a labor dispute between the employees and their employer. Section 2(9) of the Act defines a labor dispute as "any controversy concerning terms, tenure or conditions of employment or concerning the association or representation of the persons in negotiating, fixing, maintaining, changing or seeking to arrange terms of conditions of employment, regardless of whether the disputant's stand in approximate relation of employer and employee."

There are basically two different kinds of primary strikes. A strike can be an **economic strike** or an **unfair labor practice strike.**

Identifying Unfair Labor Practice Strikes

An unfair labor practice strike occurs when an unfair labor practice has been committed by the employer and is a "contributing cause" of the job action.[20] In such a case the strike activity is initiated in whole or in part in response to unfair labor practice conduct committed by the employer.[21] Contrast this with an economic strike discussed in the next section.

If employees go out on strike because of perceived unfair labor practice conduct, they have preferential reinstatement rights to their former jobs. *Employers are not permitted to replace ULP strikers permanently.* However, if employees engage in misconduct during the period they are on strike or have been discharged "for cause" under Section 10(c) of the Act, they may forfeit their right to reinstatement, even if it was a ULP strike. Unfair labor practice strikers are entitled to vote in elections, but their temporary replacements may not.

Strikers who initially went out to protest economic conditions may be converted into ULP strikers depending upon the company's reaction. Thus employees may have initially gone out and been relatively unprotected with regard to recall, but once employer misconduct has occurred, an economic strike can be converted into an unfair labor practice strike, giving such strikers reinstatement rights.[22]

NOTE: The primary distinction with ULP and economic strikes is that ULP strikers have replacement rights while economic strikers do not.

Identifying Economic Strikes

In contrast to a ULP strike, an economic strike is one that is neither caused nor prolonged by an unfair labor practice by the employer. Economic activity, including striking, is simply another method designed to force or pressure the employer to agree to a position.

When an economic strike occurs, the employer is free to hire permanent replacements for the strikers and may refuse to reinstate them if they have been permanently replaced during the strike.[23] However, an economic strike is protected activity under Section 7 of the Act. Therefore, it would be an unfair labor practice for an employer to discharge an employee for engaging in an economic strike, and firing economic strikers would convert that activity into ULP strike activity.

If an economic striker's position has not been filled by a permanent replacement, he or she may apply for reemployment when the strike ends.

Upon receipt of an unconditional request for reemployment, the employer is generally under an obligation to reinstate the striker if a vacancy exists. If positions have been abolished during the strike, the employer is obligated to reinstate strikers when their jobs are reestablished, unless the employer can show "legitimate and substantial business justifications" for failing to do so.[24]

An economic striker who has not been permanently replaced is entitled to be reinstated in a job that is "substantially equivalent" to the one he or she had prior to going out on strike. However, if economic strikers crossed picket lines to return to work, the employer is not obligated to reinstate them if permanent replacements were hired.[25]

Strikers are not automatically entitled to reinstatement; strike misconduct can eliminate the reinstatement rights of economic strikers.

The standard for replacement of strikers was best summarized in *Laidlaw Corp.*, 171 NLRB No. 175 (1968) *enf.* 414 F.2d 99 (7th Cir. 1969) *cert. den'd* 397 U.S. 920 (1970), wherein the Board laid down the basic principals regarding an employer's obligation and the status of replaced economic strikers:

> Economic strikers who unconditionally apply for reinstatement at a time when their positions were filled by permanent replacements: (1) remain employees; (2) are entitled to full reinstatement upon departure of the replacements unless they have in the meantime acquired regular and substantially equivalent employment, or the employer can sustain his burden of proof that the failure to offer full reinstatement was for legitimate and substantial business reasons.

Defining Strike Misconduct

Serious strike misconduct can include verbal threats or physical violence, if the threats are explicit regarding bodily harm. The Board attempted to delineate some clearer standards in this regard in *Clear Pine Mouldings*, 268 NLRB 1044 (1984), in which it stated:

> actions such as the making of abusive threats against non-striking employees equate to "restraint and coercion" prohibited elsewhere in the Act and are not privileged by Section 8(c) of the Act. Although we agree that the presence of physical gestures accompanying a verbal threat may increase the gravity of verbal conduct, *we reject the per se rule that words alone can never warrant a denial of reinstatement in the absence of physical acts.* Rather, we agree with the United States Court of Appeals for the First Circuit that "a serious threat may draw its creditability from the surrounding circumstances and not from the physical gestures of the speaker." See *Associated Grocers of New England v. NLRB*, 562 F.2d 1333, 1336 (1st Cir. 1977). We also agree with the United States Court of Appeals for the Third Circuit that an employer need not "countenance conduct that amounts to intimidation and threats of bodily harm." See *NLRB v. W.C. McQuaide, Inc.*, 552 F.2d 519 (3rd Cir. 1977). In *McQuaide*, the Third Circuit applied the following objective test for determining whether verbal threats by strikers directed at fellow employees justify an employees refusal to be reinstated: Whether the misconduct is such that, under the circumstances existing, it may reasonably tend to coerce or intimidate employees in the exercise of rights protected under the Act. *We believe this is the correct standard and we adopt it.* (emphasis added)

In *Clear Pine*, the Board moved to a more objective standard dealing with coercion and intimidation regarding protected activity. Certain key factors emerge in attempting to identify picket line misconduct.

- ♦ Did misconduct affect supervisory employees?

- ♦ What effect is there on nonstriking employees?

- ♦ What is the effect, if any, on nonemployees including customers or vendors?[26]

In *Clear Pine*, the Board specifically stated that "it is clear that Congress never intended to afford special protection to all picket line conduct, whatever the circumstances," 268 NLRB at 1046. The Board also gave examples that may provide some guidance for employers. For example, it is unlawful for striking employees

> to threaten those employees who, for whatever reason, have decided to work during a strike, to block access to the employer's premises, and certainly no right to carry or use weapons or objects of intimidation. . . . The only activity the statute privileges in this context, other than peaceful patrolling, is a non-threatening expression of opinion, verbally or through signs and pamphlets similar to that found in Section 8(c).

Strike misconduct will be dealt with by denial of reinstatement and back pay where appropriate.[27]

Under the law, violence of any form will not be tolerated. However, noting that a strike is not "a tea party," the Board has upheld an employer's refusal to reinstate an employee for "rough talk" on a picket line.[28] Also, visits by striking employees to the homes of nonstriking employees have been found to be unlawful as threatening and coercive using the *Clear Pine* doctrine.[29]

NOTE: Assessing specific conduct and misconduct is a very difficult task. You should consult with your labor counsel in evaluating strike conduct and misconduct to avoid unfair labor practice charges.

Before you fire, think and check! Specific conduct which has been found unlawful includes the following:

- – Deliberate violence, such as throwing nails at a truck driven by non-employees

- – Jumping onto vehicles entering the premises of a struck employer

- – Grabbing other employees during a strike

- – Blocking ingress and egress to the employer's premises

- – Holding dangerous or potentially dangerous instruments like a baseball bat

- – Making specific verbal threats especially while accompanied by the presence of a potentially dangerous weapon

Unlawful Strikes

Not all strikes are protected. A sitdown strike, for example, does not protect the strikers, and they are not given reinstatement rights under the law.[30]

Various forms of partial strikes or slowdowns or other concerted economic activity are also not protected under the law. Additionally, strikes intended to achieve an illegal objective are prohibited.

Determining Reinstatement Rights

The issues of permanent replacements, picket line misconduct, and striker reinstatement rights have received much comment and interest. Where an economic striker has been permanently replaced, the striker is placed on a recall list and reinstated into his or her former position or a substantially equivalent position when one becomes available.[31] In a time of work force reductions, a striker may wait years for such an opportunity. This situation differs significantly from that of an ULP striker who may only be temporarily replaced and must be reinstated into his or her former position upon the resolution of the labor dispute.

To determine reinstatement rights, it must be determined whether the available job "is the same as, or substantially equivalent to, the pre-strike job" noting, however, that the striker's qualifications are not irrelevant. The issue of whether the striker is qualified to perform the job may shed light on whether the job is substantially equivalent to the pre-strike job.[32]

But, significantly, "the essential point is that mere qualification to perform the job will not suffice." Former economic strikers are entitled to return to those jobs or substantial equivalents "if such positions become vacant, and they are entitled to nondiscriminatory treatment in their application for other jobs." However, former strikers are not guaranteed preference for nonequivalent jobs. Thus, employers are not obligated to offer just any position to a former economic striker—only substantially equivalent ones.

NOTE: If only lesser positions are available, there is no obligation to offer them to former economic strikers.[33]

Establishing the Rights of Workers During Strikes

In several cases, the Board has clarified and addressed the rights of workers either to work during a strike or return to work after a strike and even to cross picket lines and resign from union membership. In a line of cases following *Laidlaw* (in which the Board held that permanently replaced economic strikers who have made an unconditional offer to return to work are entitled to full reinstatement when positions become available and that they must be placed on a preferential hiring list if positions are not available,) the Board has consistently held that the burden is on the employer when it refuses to take back a striker.

A company may not tell strikers they are fired or have lost their jobs. Comments to the effect that the company does not have to take an individual back have been found unlawful.[34] The Board has more recently summarized its position:

> A strike also does not terminate the employment relationship of a striker. Thus, Section 2(3) of the Act provides that an individual whose work ceases as a result of a labor dispute remains an employee if he has not obtained any other regular or substantially equivalent employment. Clearly, replaced economic strikers who unconditionally offer to return to work are entitled to reinstatement upon the departure of replacement workers unless the former strikers have acquired regular or substantial equivalent employment or the employer can sustain its burden of proving that its failure to offer a reinstatement is for legitimate and substantial reasons.[35]

Reviewing the Right to Resign from the Union. Resigning from the union in order to refrain from concerted activities such as strikes, or crossing the picket line was reviewed by the Supreme Court in *Pattern Makers League of North America v. NLRB*.[36] In *Pattern Makers*, the Supreme Court adopted the Board's position regarding Section 8(b)(1)(a) that unions are prohibited from fining members who have resigned. Union members have an absolutely unrestricted right to resign during a strike.

Many unions had constitutional provisions and bylaws which restricted the member's right to resign. They are now void![37] *Pattern Makers* has been followed, adopted, and expanded in many Board cases to continue to remind members that they have a right to resign despite otherwise restrictive provisions in the union constitution.[38]

> NOTE: Members can resign at any time and resume or continue working for the employer against whom the strike has been called.

For a union member to resign effectively and return to work after strike activity has commenced, and avoid union fines or penalties, the member must tender his or her resignation or at least make some attempt to resign from the union *before* returning to work or must demonstrate that an attempt to resign would have been *futile* and the resignation must be unequivocal.[39]

> NOTE: The mere existence of a restriction on resignations is not sufficient to support a finding that it is futile to resign even where the member has knowledge of the restriction.

Employee resignations are effective upon their receipt by the union. The date of receipt of the resignation by the union serves as the cutoff date for the individual's liability to the union. The resigning member may be fined only for conduct occurring *prior* to the receipt of his or her resignation.[40]

In general, where employees have sought to resign and seek your assistance, you should consult with labor counsel.

Becoming a Financial Core Member. Employees working under a collective bargaining agreement containing a valid union security clause face an additional obstacle to resigning as well. The employee who has resigned but remains employed must change his or her status with the union from a full member to that of a financial core member or be subject to termination of union membership. A "financial core member" is one who meets the financial obligations uniformly required of union members but who does not have the right to participate in union business.[41]

Once an employee becomes a financial core member, he or she satisfies the union security requirement of membership in a labor organization. By making this change, the employee places himself or herself outside of the disciplinary powers of the union.

The intent to change membership status must be communicated to the union. The notice to the union must convey the intent to continue with the relationship but on a different basis. An employer may assist employees in changing their status to that of financial core members.[42] The kind of letter that must be sent has become known as a "Hershey letter" from the *Hershey Food Corp.* case, 207 NLRB No. 897, *enf.* 513 F.2d 1083 (9th Cir. 1975). The Hershey letter informs the union of the member's intent to change his or her status and that he would pay the "amount equal to established dues as may be required by a labor agreement."

A sample of specific language may be appropriate to distribute to those individuals who wish to resign. You must notify your employees that they are changing their membership status to a "dues paying member only." Once they change their relationship with the union, their status becomes one of a *financial core member.* They are not able to attend meetings or vote in union elections. However, in return, they may not be fined, penalized, punished, or expelled for crossing the picket line as long as they continue to tender required dues and initiation fees. A sample letter of change of membership status is shown in Exhibit 21.1.

The sample letter along with an explanation of your position and employee rights should be distributed to your employees while they are picketing if you have been informed that several wish to come back to work but are afraid.

Once such a Hershey letter is submitted, it is unlawful for a union to fine an employee for crossing the picket line. Such conduct is a violation of Section 8(b)(4)(1)(a) of the Act by restraining an employee's exercise of his or her Section 7 right to refrain from union activity.

– EXHIBIT 21.1 –

Sample Letter of Change of Membership Status

Dear _____:

I do hereby change my union membership status to "financial core membership" also known as "dues paying only membership" in accord with federal statutory and administrative law. This change is effective immediately. I shall continue to tender to the union the regular and periodic dues required of me. It is my understanding that effective immediately, I will not be subjected to union fines or assessments if I choose to cross a picket line.

_____

Employee signature

DEFINING SELECTED ISSUES FOR BARGAINING

The employer's obligation to bargain extends to many topics. This section focuses on major issues that affect the number of jobs available to union members such as subcontracting workout and plant closings or relocation. Also discussed are subjects that relate to procedure for contract modification or termination which trigger an obligation to bargain and the mediation of bargaining disputes. Finally, we address the contract bar rule which precludes any other union from filing an election petition or the employer from filing a decertification election, both of which challenge the authority of the union as the exclusive bargaining agent of the employees.

The Role of Bargaining in Subcontracting

Let's suppose the Spider Web Company no longer desires to produce webs. It can now purchase them overseas cheaper than it can manufacture them and resell them here. The company would need to discuss such a business decision with the union.

NOTE: The subcontracting of bargaining unit work is a mandatory subject for bargaining.

The Supreme Court of the United States has held that bargaining is required even if the company is motivated by valid, economic considerations and the subcontract eliminates all the jobs in a bargaining unit.[43] In such a circumstance, the NLRB may order the employer to resume the discontinued operation, reinstate the discharged employees with back pay, bargain with the union, and preserve the existing agreement.

The Role of Bargaining in Plant Closings

What if a company simply decides to close a facility or transfer the work elsewhere to avoid dealing with the union? The company still has to discuss this with the union. The Supreme Court has clearly stated that the employer must bargain about the effects of its decision even though an employer's decision to shut down part of its business for economic reasons is not a mandatory subject of bargaining.[44]

The General Counsel of the Board set forth a test for determining whether an employer's decision to relocate is a mandatory subject of bargaining:

> Initially, the burden is on the General Counsel to establish that the employer's decision involved a relocation of unit work unaccompanied by a basic change in the nature of the employer's operation. If the General Counsel successfully carries his burden in this regard, he will have established *prima facie* that the employer's relocation decision is a mandatory subject of bargaining. At this juncture, the employer may produce evidence rebutting the *prima facie* case by establishing that the work performed at the new location varies significantly from the work performed at the former plant, establishing that the work performed at the former plant is to be discontinued entirely and not moved to the new location, or establishing that the employer's decision involves a change in the scope and direction of the enterprise.[45]

Alternatively, the employer may proffer a defense if it shows by a preponderance of the evidence: (1) that labor costs (direct or indirect) were not a factor in the decision or (2) that even if labor costs were a factor in the decision, the union could not have offered labor cost concessions that could have changed the employer's decision to relocate.[46]

The General Counsel has the initial burden in establishing a *prima facie* case by meeting a two-part test. First, the General Counsel must establish that the employer's decision involved a relocation of unit work. Second, the General Counsel must establish that this relocation of unit work was unaccompanied by "a basic change in the nature of the employer's operation."[47] If the General Counsel satisfies this two-part test, he will have established a *prima facie* case that the employer's decision to relocate was a mandatory subject of bargaining. The burden then shifts to the employer to rebut the *prima facie* case by establishing *any one* of the following:

1. The work performed at the new location varies significantly from the work performed at the former plant.

2. The work performed at the former plant is to be discontinued entirely and not moved to the new location.

3. The employer's decision involves a change in the scope and direction of the enterprise.[48]

Cases decided under *Otis* which made an inquiry into whether there has been a change in the "nature and direction of the business" should be helpful in consideration of Case (3) above.[49]

Even if the employer is unable to rebut the General Counsel's *prima facie* case, it may still show that the decision to relocate was a non-mandatory subject of bargaining by proffering an affirmative defense. The employer can establish an affirmative defense by showing by a preponderance of the evidence *either* of the following:

♦ That labor costs (direct and/or indirect) were not a factor in the decision

♦ That even if labor costs were a factor in the decision, the union could not have offered labor cost concessions that could have changed the employer's decision to relocate[50]

Direct labor costs are normally understood to mean wages and fringe benefits, whereas indirect labor costs involve traditional non-economic items in a contract (e.g., seniority, staffing requirements) that can have an economic impact.

If the employer fails to establish that labor costs were not a factor in the decision to relocate, it may still avoid an unfair labor practice finding if it can show that the union could not have offered labor cost concessions that could have changed the employer's decision to relocate.[51] Under this second affirmative defense, the employer would prevail if it could show that, even if labor costs were a factor, it would have relocated anyway based upon non-labor cost considerations.

For example, if an employer decides to relocate, in part, because of a desire to be closer to its customers, or to be in a different climate, an employer may meet its burden by establishing that it would have relocated even absent the labor cost considerations.

Where a decision to relocate is a mandatory subject of bargaining, "the employer's obligation will be the usual one of negotiating to agreement or a bona fide impasse."[52] However, "there may be circumstances under which a relocation decision must be made or implemented expeditiously."[53] The Board will take this into account when determining "whether a bargaining impasse has been reached on the relocation question."[54]

If the employer's evidence establishes rebuttals or defenses recognized by *Dubuque*, a complaint will not be issued by the Board regarding a bargaining obligation over relocation.

Additional requirements have been placed on all employers, unionized and others, with respect to plant closing or mass layoff decisions. For example, the Worker Adjustment and Restraining Notification Act (WARN), which is discussed in Chapter 25, states that employers are required to provide advance notice of large-scale layoffs.

WARN requires companies to provide 60 days' advance written notice of plant closings and layoffs. There are certain exceptions and exclusions where employers are actively seeking capital to avoid a shutdown or for "unforeseeable business circumstances." WARN also provides that the giving of notice in good faith compliance does not constitute a violation of the NLRA or the Railway Labor Act.

Modifying or Terminating a Contract

A company may not just call the union and terminate its contract. Under Section 8(d) of the Taft-Hartley Act, the company or union desiring to modify or terminate a contract must give the other party 60 days' notice in advance of the date the proposed modification or termination would take place. Neither side, however, has the obligation to bargain over contract changes which would take effect before the contract itself provides for reopening.

The 60-day notice provision requires that parties notify each other to offer to meet and confer for negotiating a new contract, notify appropriate mediation authorities, and continue to observe the conditions of the contract without strike or lockout for 60 days (or 90 days for health care) after giving notice or until expiration of the contract whichever occurs later.

Using Mediation Services

The Federal Mediation and Conciliation Service (FMCS) is an independent federal agency created for the purpose of maintaining industrial peace between employers and employees through mediation and collective bargaining. Issues between the two bargaining parties may be more readily settled by making available government facilities to aid and encourage settlement concerning rates of pay, hours, and working conditions.[55]

The FMCS offers mediation assistance in any labor dispute "affecting commerce" for the purpose of preventing or minimizing disruption of the free flow of commerce caused by labor disputes. This assistance may be offered on its own initiative or on request of either of the parties when the FMCS considers that the dispute could result in the interruption of commerce. When FMCS enters a labor dispute, it is required to communicate with the parties and to use its best efforts to effect an agreement through mediation and conciliation.

The service is also available to assist in the settlement of grievances and disputes over application or interpretation of existing labor agreements. This settlement may be accomplished by conference or other means.

Arbitration Panels. As an aid to the peaceful settlement of grievances, FMCS provides an arbitrator selection service. The parties may request that the

Service provide a panel of arbitrators, usually five or seven, from which they will select the one they desire to hear the grievance. Selection may be by mutual agreement or through successive striking of names, with the one remaining selected as the arbitrator. Federal mediation is not alone in providing this service. Most states also provide a Board of Mediation or some other similar panel that offers arbitration services when requested. A number of private organizations, such as the American Arbitration Association, will for a modest fee provide administrative services in connection with choosing an arbitrator and conducting the hearing.

Prior to the expiration of a labor contract, the parties are required to give notice to the FMCS and any appropriate state agency.[56] The party proposing changes in the contract, normally the union, must give notice to the other party 60 days before the contract expires (90 days in the case of employers in the field of health care).

Mediators have no authority to force a settlement. They must rely on their powers of communication and persuasion. They may evaluate issues and demands, consider positions of the parties, and offer possible compromises. Mediators may have expert knowledge about local economic conditions, unions, or industries; they may offer this knowledge to the parties to achieve a settlement. Federal mediators have the official title of "Commissioner."

How the Contract Bar Rule Functions

Once a valid collective bargaining agreement has been signed, that contract will generally act as a bar against holding any type of a representation election for the duration of the contract.[57] However, the contract, to act as a bar, must be current, in writing, executed by both the union and the employer, contain substantial terms and conditions of employment, and be of a definite and reasonable duration. The current rule is that valid contracts of up to 3 years will bar election petitions for the entire period of the contract. Contracts that extend beyond 3 years operate as a bar to election petitions for only the first 3 years of the contract.

The intent of the contract bar doctrine is to stabilize union-management relations. While it helps to solidify the union's position, it also prevents the employees from being subjected to repeated elections for a reasonable time after a collective bargaining agreement has been signed. If you receive notice of an election petition from a rival union or if the employer seeks a decertification election (i.e., an election in which employees vote to remove the union as their representative) and there is a current and valid collective bargaining agreement in force, contact your labor counsel immediately to determine if either action is barred.

HANDLING SUCCESSORSHIP ISSUES

If a company decides to sell the assets of the business to a completely unrelated company, that company, under most circumstances, may have an obligation to assume the collective bargaining agreement. Successor employers may be required to assume collective bargaining agreements.[58]

In *John Wiley & Sons v. Livingston*, 376 U.S. 543 (1964), the Supreme Court held that an acquiring corporation was obligated to arbitrate the rights or retain predecessor employees under the arbitration provisions of the predecessor's collective bargaining agreement. However, in *Howard Johnson Co. v. Detroit Joint Board*, 417 U.S. 109 (1974), the Supreme Court refused to enforce *Wiley* where the issue with the union was retention of the predecessor's work force.[59]

Successorship issues can be very complex and should be carefully examined, particularly if a sale of the business is contemplated. If union collective bargaining agreements are involved, attorneys will normally scrutinize all facets of the transaction as part of the "due diligence" phase of a transaction.

WHAT YOU NEED TO KNOW ABOUT THE UNION CONTRACT

Obviously, the foregoing pages have demonstrated that there are many intricacies to bargaining, dealing with unions at the table and dealing with a strike situation. One thing that we did not discuss in any detail because of its complexity is the existence of certain legal tools designed to shorten or eliminate strike or picket line conduct. For example, certain injunctive procedures may or may not be possible depending upon the circumstances you are dealing with at a given time. However, these are questions that must be addressed by counsel with your assistance.

Assuming that you have reached an agreement and have gone through the mine field of negotiating dilemmas that we have addressed, there are also some contract provisions that you may wish to include in an agreement. For example, we always suggest that a strong management rights clause be included.

Examining the Management Rights Clause

A management rights clause basically gives the employer the right to control the workplace with as much authority as possible. The exact language of the clause will be a subject of negotiation with the union. Sample clauses are shown in Exhibits 21.2 and 21.3.

Describing Union Security Clauses

There exists a range of possible union security provisions that may be the subject of negotiations. Generally, such clauses are the way the union seeks a

– EXHIBIT 21.2 –
Sample Management Rights Clause

Section 1. The Employer shall have the right to promulgate working rules and procedures relating to employment which are not inconsistent with the provisions of this agreement and to change such rules from time to time. The union shall be consulted and advised prior to the promulgation or change of such rules.

Section 2. The Employer retains the exclusive right to hire, lay off, promote, assign duties to, transfer, discipline, or dismiss employees; to introduce new or improved methods or facilities; and to carry out the ordinary and customary functions of management, except as limited by the terms of this agreement.

Section 3. Except as limited by this agreement, all the rights, powers, discretion, and authority possessed by the Employer, in the absence of this agreement, are retained by the Employer and remain exclusively, and without limitation, within the rights of the Employer.

Section 4. The Employer retains the right to determine the extent and scope of each job and to make and change work assignments. Work assignments shall be based upon the manageable unit of work which the employee can reasonably be expected to perform. The Employer shall, if requested by the employees, meet with the employees to discuss work assignments in light of this criterion. The Union shall have the right to participate in such a meeting. The issue of work assignments, or work loads, shall not, however, be subject to the grievance procedure or to arbitration and the Employer's decision thereon shall be final.

Section 5. Within the limitation of the present existing physical facilities, the Employer agrees to provide safe working conditions for its employees.

– EXHIBIT 21.3 –
Sample Management Rights Clause

It is expressly agreed that all rights which ordinarily vest in and are exercised by the Company, except such as are clearly relinquished herein by Company, are reserved to and shall continue to vest in Company. This enumeration, being merely by way of illustration and not by way of limitation, includes the right to:

(a) Manage the plant and direct the work force, including the right to hire and to suspend, discipline or discharge employees for proper cause.

(b) Transfer employees from one department and/or classification to another.

(c) Lay off or relieve employees from duty because of lack of work or for other legitimate reasons.

(d) Promote and/or transfer employees to positions and classifications not covered by this agreement, it being understood employees in the bargaining unit cannot be forced to take a position outside the bargaining unit.

(e) Make such operating changes as are deemed necessary by it for the efficient and economical operation of the plant, including the right to change the normal workweek, the number of hours normally worked during the workweek, the length of the normal workday, the hours of work, the beginning and ending time of each shift or assignment, and the number of shifts to be operated.

(f) Transfer persons from positions and classifications not covered by this agreement to positions and/or classifications covered hereby.

(g) Maintain discipline and efficiency.

(h) Hire, promote, demote, transfer, discharge, or discipline all levels of supervision or other persons not covered by this agreement.

(i) Determine the type of products to be manufactured, the location of work within the plant; the schedules of production; the schedules of work within work periods; and the methods, processes, and means of manufacture and the conduct of other plant operations.

guarantee that employees will join or support a union. A sample union security clause is shown in Exhibit 21.4. Union security clauses vary and may run the gamut from compulsory union membership to a completely open shop where membership in a labor organization is not required and optional. Most contracts have a provision for a union membership after 30 days or a probationary period. This kind of agreement is called a union shop.

In some states, it is illegal to require employees to obtain membership in or become members of a union to hold a job.[60] These states are considered "right to work" states where it is unlawful to have a closed shop which requires all employees to be members of the union.

The Union Shop Clause.   A typical union shop provision requires that employees become a member of the union within a specified period after hire, usually after 30 days or upon completion of a probationary period. Initial employment may not be conditioned upon union membership (such a clause is an illegal "closed shop" provision). A sample contract provision for a union shop clause is shown in Exhibit 21.5.

The Agency Shop Clause.   An agency shop is a lesser form of union security than that offered by a union shop. Typical agency shop provisions provide that employees, as a condition of employment, must either become members of the union or pay the union a service fee. The service fee is generally equal to the amount paid for union dues.[61] A sample of an agency shop clause is provided in Exhibit 21.6.

Maintenance of Membership.   A "maintenance of membership" requires employees who are union members at the time of execution of the collective bargaining agreement or who later join the union to maintain membership during the term of the agreement. See Section 6 of Exhibit 21.4, Sample Union Security Clause.

Establishing Discipline and Termination Standards

Most negotiated agreements will require a form of "just cause," sometimes referred to as "good cause," for termination. There are many different kinds of discipline provisions. Usually, a collective bargaining agreement provides for graduated or progressive discipline, involving oral and written warnings and/or probation or suspension, which may reach a final stage in termination.

Discipline and termination are usually ultimately reviewed through a grievance and arbitration machinery. Arbitration can be administered by the American Arbitration Association or various state mediation and conciliation services or through the federal mediation conciliation services.

– EXHIBIT 21.4 –
Sample Union Security Clause

Section 1. The Employer recognizes the Union as the sole and exclusive bargaining representative of the employees within the collective bargaining unit, as said unit is defined in Article 1 hereof.

Section 2. The parties recognize the right of employees to make their own decisions as to whether they wish to join the Union, subject to the provisions of this Article. The Employer shall have the right to discuss grievances with any individual employee or group of employees, but the Union shall have the right to participate in any discussion involving the interpretation or application of the language of this Agreement.

Section 3. The Employer shall not discriminate against or favor any employee or prospective employee in the collective bargaining unit on account of membership or nonmembership in the Union or on account of membership or nonmembership in the Union or on account of union activity.

Section 4. The Agency shall deduct initiation fees and monthly dues from the wages and/or salaries of employees who have authorized such deductions in writing and who have not resigned from the Union or revoked such authorizations prior to the effective date of this agreement, or who shall hereafter authorize such deductions in writing.

Section 5. No employees will be asked to make any contract which may conflict with this agreement.

Section 6. All employees in the bargaining unit who now are or who hereafter become members of the Union in good standing shall, as a condition of employment, maintain their membership in the Union in good standing, provided, however, that case work supervisors who now are or hereafter become members of the Union shall have the right to resign from Union membership by written notice of resignation mailed or delivered to the Agency and the Union at any time during the month of January in any year hereafter, and further provided that case work supervisors who, at the time they become such, are members of the Union shall have the right to resign from Union membership by written notice of resignation mailed or delivered to the Agency and the Union at any time during the period of 30 days following the date on which they become case work supervisors and during the month of January in any year thereafter. Such resignation shall also constitute immediately effective revocation of any authorization for deduction of

Union dues then in effect for the employee who is resigning. Payment of Union dues and initiation fee shall constitute membership in the Union in good standing.

Section 7. All permanent employees covered by this agreement, who are hired after the date of execution of this agreement, shall, as a condition of continuing employment, become members of the Union in good standing 60 days after the commencement of their employment or upon completion of their probationary period, whichever first occurs, and shall thereafter remain members of the Union in good standing. An employee shall be considered a member of the Union in good standing if he tenders the initiation fee and periodic dues uniformly required by the Union as a condition of membership.

– EXHIBIT 21.5 –
Sample Union Shop Clause

All present employees who are members of the local Union on the effective date of this subsection or on the date of execution of this Agreement, whichever is the later, shall remain members of the Local Union in good standing as a condition of employment. All present employees who are not members of the Local Union and all employees who are hired hereafter shall become and remain members in good standing of the Local Union as a condition of employment on and after the 31st day following the beginning of their employment or on and after the 31st day following the effective date of this subsection or the date of this Agreement, whichever is the later. An employee who has failed to acquire, or thereafter maintain, membership in the Union as herein provided, shall be terminated seventy-two (72) hours after his Employer has received written notice from an authorized representative of the Local Union, certifying that membership has been, and is continuing to be, offered to such employee on the same basis as all other members and, further, that the employee has had notice and opportunity to make all dues or initiation fee payments. This provision shall be made and become effective as of such time as it may be made and become effective under the provisions of the National Labor Relations Act, but not retroactively.

– EXHIBIT 21.6 –
Sample Agency Shop Clause

Section 1. Membership in the Local Union is not compulsory. Employees have the right to join, not join, maintain, or drop their membership in the Local Union, as they see fit. Neither party shall exert any pressure on, or discriminate against, an employee as regards such matters.

Section 2. Membership in the Local Union is separate, apart and distinct from the assumption by one of his equal obligation to the extent that he receives equal benefits. The Local Union is required under this Agreement to represent all of the employees in the bargaining unit fairly and equally without regard to whether or not an employee is a member of the Local Union. The terms of this Agreement have been made for all employees in the bargaining unit and not only for members in the Local Union, and this Agreement has been executed by the Employer after it has satisfied itself that the Local Union is the choice of a majority of the employees in the bargaining unit. Accordingly, it is fair that each employee in the bargaining unit pay his own way and assume his fair share of the obligations along with the grant of equal benefits contained in this Agreement.

Section 3. In accordance with the policy set forth under subparagraphs (1) and (2) of this Section all employees shall, as a condition of continued employment, pay to the Local Union, the employee's exclusive collective bargaining representative, an amount of money equal to that paid by other employees in the bargaining unit who are members of the Local Union, which shall be limited to an amount of money equal to the Local Union's regular and usual initiation fees, and its regular and usual dues. For present employees, such payments shall commence thirty-one (31) days following the effective date or on the date of execution of this Agreement, whichever is the later, and for new employees, the payment shall start thirty-one (31) days following the date of employment.

Handling Grievance Procedures

Contractually defined grievance procedures generally permit employees to protest discipline and/or termination. In addition, grievances can usually be filed by a union itself regarding contractual interpretation. Grievances usually have several different steps which culminate in an impartial arbitration. The Supreme Court has consistently held that arbitration is the preferred means of resolving employment disputes.[62] A sample grievance procedure is set out in Exhibit 21.7.

Recently, the Supreme Court has spoken in the field of labor arbitration. In *United Paper Workers International Union v. Misco, Inc.,*[63] the Supreme Court made clear that matters of public policy could not intrude on the arbitration process. The Supreme Court ruled that unless dishonesty is alleged, "even silly fact finding" will not be a sufficient basis for disregarding the findings of the arbitrator. Courts should not set aside an arbitrator's award unless it is based on fraud or dishonesty or is contrary to a specific public policy, and not just the court's conception of what public policy should be. Public policy must be based on law or statute.

– EXHIBIT 21.7 –
Sample Grievance Procedure

Section 1. A grievance is a dispute between the parties as to (1) the interpretation or application of any of the terms of this agreement or any supplemental agreement, (2) a claimed breach of this agreement or any supplemental agreement, or (3) the dismissal of any employee.

Section 2. Except as excluded from the grievance machinery or any part thereof by the terms of this agreement or any supplemental agreement, grievances shall be handled in accordance with the following procedure:

Step 1. Grievances shall be filed in writing with the supervisor concerned and shall be signed by the employee involved and by his or her steward. Within 5 working days after receipt of the grievance by the supervisor, a conference shall be held between the supervisor, the employee, and the steward. The supervisor shall give his decision in writing to the steward within not more than 5 working days after the conference.

The grievance must be filed within one month after discovery of the facts by the employees or the Union, whichever first occurs, giving rise to the grievance, except that grievances based on discharges shall be filed within 10 working days after the employee is notified of his discharge.

Step 2. If the grievance is not resolved in step 1, the steward of the employee or area involved may submit the grievance to the supervisor representing the Employer at the second step. There shall be a meeting held at the request of the steward to discuss the grievance within 10 working days from the date of the request for such a meeting. The Employer's representative shall give his decision in writing within 5 working days after the meeting.

Step 3. If the grievance is not satisfactorily adjusted in step 2, the Grievance Committee chairman shall notify the Employer's representative at this step, in writing, not more than 10 working days after the date of the step 2 decision, that the Union desires to place the grievance in step 3. A meeting between the Employer and the Union representative, the Grievance Committee, the steward, and the employee involved shall be called and held within 10 working days after the Union's request for such a meeting. The Employer or his representative shall give its final decision, in writing, within 5 working days after the meeting.

Step 4. If the grievance is not satisfactorily adjusted in step 3, the Union representative may notify the Employer or its representative, in writing, within or not more than 30 calendar days after the date of the step 3 decision that the Union desires to go to arbitration, except in those cases where the matter is not subject to arbitration under the terms of this agreement. Arbitrable grievances shall be submitted for arbitration to an arbitrator agreed upon by the parties pursuant to Section 9 of this Article. The fee and expenses of the arbitrator shall be borne equally by the parties. The decision of the arbitrator shall be final and binding.

Section 3. In the event the Union does not present in step 2 a grievance which the Employer has rejected within 10 working days after the date of the Step 1 decision, or in step 3 within 10 working days after the date of the step 2 decision, or request arbitration within 30 calendar days after the date of the step 3 decision, the grievance shall be deemed to have been settled on the basis of the Employer's decision at the previous step.

Section 4. Grievances filed by or on behalf of an employee involving a ruling or order of the employee's supervisor need not be commenced at the step involving that supervisor but may be commenced at the next step. In all cases, however, the first conference must be requested within one month after the discovery of the facts by the employee or the Union, whichever first occurs, giving rise to the grievance.

Section 5. The Employer shall have the right to file grievances. Grievances asserted by the Employer or the Union, as such, may be initiated at step 2 or step 3, instead of step 1, and shall thereafter be processed in accordance with the procedure set forth in Section 2 hereof, and all limitations of time shall be applicable to any such grievances.

Section 6. Where the Employee or the Union, as the case may be, does not proceed with a grievance in due time, it shall be barred. Where the employer does not comply with a request for a meeting within the respective time limits required to carry out the various steps outlined in the grievance procedure, the grievance may be carried to the next step.

Section 7. In the event a retroactive salary adjustment is involved in the settlement of a grievance in which an employee seeks reclassification, such wage retroactively shall not extend prior to the date on which the cause for the grievance first arose or for more than 30 days prior to the date on which the grievance was first presented in writing, whichever is later.

Section 8. The Union and the Agencies shall mutually agree upon a list of five arbitrators to hear the cases which are to be arbitrated. Arbitrators from the list shall be selected on a rotating basis to hear the various cases, and such selection shall be in alphabetical order. Should the arbitrator whose turn it is to hear a case be unable to hear the case, it shall be assigned to the next arbitrator.

GUIDELINES FOR HANDLING
COLLECTIVE BARGAINING ISSUES

The following guidelines will be helpful in addressing any union issue that may arise.

1. Assemble your negotiating committee when preparing for bargaining.

2. Make sure that you have up-to-date financial information and that there is a budget provision already allocated.

3. Review your proposal with counsel *prior* to submitting it to the union.

4. Cost out the union proposal.

5. Identify the main concerns of the union and your employees.

6. Be sure you are prepared for a strike if bargaining breaks down.

7. Before deciding that you are at an impasse, consult labor counsel.

8. If your employees are on strike, tell them about their right to resign and return to work.

9. Prepare and distribute a "Hershey" letter to striking employees.

10. Don't tell strikers they are fired. Be careful: rights to reinstatement and the law regarding permanent replacement are tricky.

11. Have contingency plans to enjoin strike activity.

12. Implement your contract proposals.

13. If your company is considering a merger or acquisition, consider whether it will be liable as a "successor" to labor contracts.

14. If you have decided to move your plant, you may have bargaining obligations that must be addressed.

15. After you have reached agreement with the union, remember, the union cannot require *all* employees to become members of the union.

16. Make sure you have the kind of union security provision you need.

17. Make sure you know if you are bound by arbitration decisions under the law.

ENDNOTES

1. *Walter M. Yoder & Sons, Inc. v. NLRB,* 754 F.2d 531 (4th Cir. 1985); *S. I. Dupont de Nemours v. NLRB,* 744 F.2d 537 (6th Cir. 1984); *Atlanta Hilton v. Touer,* 271 NLRB 1600 (1984); and *NLRB v. St. Joseph Hospital,* 755 F.2d 260 (2d Cir. 1985) *denied enf.* 269 NLRB 862 (1984).

2. 29 U.S.C. §151, *et seq.*

3. Douglas L. Leslie, (Case Book on) *Labor Law*, (Little Brown & Co., Boston, © 1978) p. 47.

4. *Id.* at p. 49.

5. See also *Alexander v. Gardener Denver Co.*, 415 U.S. 36 (1974).

6. The NLRB cannot compel either side to agree to any substantial contract provision according to the Supreme Court: *H. K. Porter v. NLRB*, 397 U.S. 99 (1970).

7. *Steele v. Louisville National Railroad*, 223 U.S. 192, 200 (1944). See also *Ford Motor Company v. Huffman*, 354 U.S. 331 (1952); *Smith v. Evening News Association*, 371 U.S. 195 (1962); and *Vaca v. Sipes*, 386 U.S. 171 (1967). As early as 1944, in a case under the Railway Labor Act, the U.S. Supreme Court said that "the labor organization chosen to be representative of the craft or class of employees is chosen to represent all of its members, regardless of their union affiliations or want of them."

8. See *Miranda Fuel Co.*, 140 NLRB 181 (1962). In *Miranda Fuel*, the Board held that representation claims under Section 8(b)(2) are unfair labor practices. Section 7 of the Act gives employees the right to be free from unfair or invidious treatment by collective bargaining representatives.

9. See, for example, *NLRB v. Reed and Prince Manufacturing Co.*, 205 F.2d 131 (1st Cir. 1953), in which the parties had about 20 sessions, but nonetheless reached no contract. Despite many meetings, the Board found that the employer did not bargain in good faith.

10. See *Honolulu Star Bulletin, Ltd.*, 123 NLRB 395 (1959), *enf. denied* 254 F.2d 567 (D.C. Cir. 1959). It is not unlawful to propose an illegal subject, but it cannot be pressed since to do so would violate the Act.

11. See *NLRB v. Wooster Div. of Borg-Warner*, 356 U.S. 342 (1958) (parties have an obligation to bargain *only* with respect to wages, hours, and other terms and conditions of employment).

12. See *W-I Forest Products Co.*, 304 NLRB No. 83 (1991), wherein the Board found that smoking bans are mandatory subjects of bargaining. However, in this case the union was found to have waived its right to bargain. Cf. *Albert's, Inc.*, 213 NLRB 686, 692–693 (1974), and *Chemtronics, Inc.*, 236 NLRB 178, 190 (1978), where restrictions on smoking were treated as mandatory subjects of bargaining in which a refusal to bargain would violate Section 8(a)(5).

13. The Board and courts generally adhere to the definition of impasse developed in *Taft Broadcasting Co.*, 163 NLRB 475, *affirmed* 395 F.2d 622 (D.C. Cir. 1968), and *Bell Transit Company*, 271 NLRB 1272 (1984), *enf. denied remand* 788 F.2d 27 (D.C. Cir. 1986).

14. *Marriott In-Flite Services Division of Marriott Corp.*, 258 NLRB No. 755 (1981), *enf.* 759 F.2d 1441 (2d Cir. 1981), *cert. denied* 464 U.S. 829 (1983).

15. See *Colfor, Inc.*, 282 NLRB 1173 (1987).

16. See *Arrow Automotive Industries, Inc.*, 284 NLRB 487 (1987).

17. See *Pertec Computer Corp.*, 284 NLRB No. 87 (1987); *Southern Newspapers, Inc.*, 255 NLRB No. 154 (1981); and *J. D. Lundsford Plumbing, Heating and Air Conditioning*, 254 NLRB No. 1360 (1981).

18. *TransWorld Airlines, Inc. v. Independent Federation of Flight Attendants*, 489 U.S. 406 (1989); *C-Line Express* 292 NLRB 638 (1989); *John W. Galbreath*, 288 NLRB 876 (1988); *Laidlaw Corp.*, 171 NLRB 1366 (1968) *enf.* 414 F.2d 99 (7th Cir. 1969); and *Midland National Life Insurance Co.*, 263 NLRB 127 (1982) *cert. denied* 397 U.S. 920 (1969). See also, Henry Baer, "Assumptions About Striker Replacements," *New York Law Journal*, May 22, 1990.

19. See Charles J. Morris, *Developing Labor Law*, (BNA, Washington, D.C. 1971), Chap. 19, pp. 517–538.

20. See *Dayton Auto Electric Inc.*, 278 NLRB 551 (1986).

21. See *NLRB v. Mackay Radio & Telegraph Company*, 304 U.S. 333 (1938).

22. See *Vulcan Heart Corp. v. NLRB*, 718 F.2d 269 (8th Cir. 1983). Similarly, where employer's unfair labor practices are serious, strike activity to protest them may be protected even if a "no-strike" provision exists in the collective bargaining agreement. *Isla Verde Hotel Corp. v. NLRB*, 702 F.2d 268 (1st Cir. 1982). But cf. *Sun Electric Corp.*, 266 NLRB 37 (1983), 732 F.2d 573 (7th Cir. 1984), where the Board found that the employer's unilateral changes in the pension plan did not convert an economic strike to a ULP strike since the changes were mandated by federal law.

23. See *NLRB v. Mackay Radio & Telegraph*, at note 21.

24. *NLRB v. Fleetwood Trailer Co., Inc.*, 389 U.S. 375 (1967) relying upon *NLRB v. Great Dane Trailers*, 388 U.S. 26 (1967).

25. *NLRB v. Harrison Ready Mix Concrete*, 770 F.2d 78 (6th Cir. 1985).

26. See *Clear Pine Mouldings*, 268 NLRB 1044 (1984).

27. There are many cases following *Clear Pine*. See, for example, *Roure-Bertrand Dupont, Inc.*, 271 NLRB 443 (1984); *Western Pacific Construction Materials Co.*, 272 NLRB 1393 (1984); *PreTerm, Inc.*, 273 NLRB 683 (1984); *Southwest Forest Industries, Inc.*, 273 NLRB 276 (1984); and *Glade Springs, Inc.*, 273 NLRB 944 (1985), in which the Board made clear that it would expect specific findings of fact and credibility to be made by ALJs in assessing *Clear Pine* misconduct.

28. *Auburn Foundry Inc.*, 274 NLRB 1317 (1985).

29. *Georgia Kraft Co.*, 275 NLRB 636 (1985). In that case, the employees appeared to have a liquor smell about them and were repeatedly asked to leave the premises. They engaged a nonstriker in threatening conversation and told him he was "screwing them out of their god damn money"; when the nonstriker asked them not to curse, a striker said they would "take care of him" when he returned to work.

30. See *NLRB v. Fansteel Metallurgical Corp.*, 306 U.S. 240 (1939).

31. See *Rose Printing Co.*, 304 NLRB No. 132 (1991), wherein the Board considered the reinstatement rights of former economic strikers relying principally upon *NLRB v. Fleetwood Trailer Co.*, and *Laidlaw*. The Board interpreted its decision in *Laidlaw* to mean implicitly that economic strikers' reinstatement rights concerned their former jobs or substantially equivalent positions.

32. *Rose Printing, supra.*

33. See also, *Harry Hoffman Printing, Inc. v. Graphic Communications International Union Local 261*, 912 F.2d 608 (2d Cir. 1991), in which the court of appeals rejected an arbitration award which had ruled that a company must warn striking workers that they could be fired before hiring new employees to replace them. Also see, "Ruling on Replacing Strikers Reversed," *The Wall Street Journal*, December 23, 1991.

34. See *Emerson Electric Company*, 287 NLRB 1065 (1988), wherein the plant manager said employees would be required to go out on strike if the union were voted in because they would automatically be part of the union and that permanent replacement workers would be hired. So far so good, but in response to a question about returning to work, the manager said they did not have to take employees back. Such comments are unlawful.

35. See *Aquachem, Inc.*, 288 NLRB 1108 (1988); cf. Roger B. Jacobs, "Labor Law," *National Law Journal*, July 11, 1988, p. 22, and *Hilton North*, 279 NLRB 45 (1986).

36. 473 U.S. 95 (1985).

37. Section 8(b)(1)(a) provides that "It shall be an unfair labor practice for a labor organization or its agents—(1) to restrain or coerce employees in the exercise of the rights guaranteed in Section 7 of this title: Provided, that this paragraph shall not impair the right of a labor organization to prescribe its own rules with respect to the acquisition or retention of membership therein. . . ." 29 U.S.C. §158(b)(1)(A).

38. See, for example, *Mark Cadillac, Inc.*, 276 NLRB 1140 (1985).

39. See *New York Telephone Co.*, 278 NLRB 998 (1986); *Local Union No. 1233 Carpenters*, 231 NLRB 756 (1977); *Ghianni Drywall Construction, Inc.*, 275 NLRB 1180 (1985); and *Columbia Machine*, 274 NLRB 123 (1984). But contrast with *Pacific Northwest Bell*, 275 NLRB 1529 (1985), in which several employees returned to work during a strike and then mailed letters of resignation which were found not to be timely.

40. *St. Louis Newspaper Guild Local 47 Pulitzer Publishing*, 272 NLRB 1195 (1984), and *Pacific Northwest Bell, supra.*

41. *Hershey Food Corp., supra; Carpenters Local 470 (Tacoma Boatbuilding Co.)*, 277 NLRB 513 (1985); and *Carpenters District Council for Seattle, Kings County and Vicinity (Tullus Gordon Construction, Inc.)*, 277 NLRB 1385 (1985). The term "financial core" member is derived from the court's interpretation of Section 8(a)(3) summarized in *NLRB v. Hershey Food Corp.*, 207 NLRB 897 (1973) *enf.* 513 F.2d 1083 (9th Cir. 1975), where the Ninth Circuit Court of Appeals quoting from *NLRB v. General Motor Corp.*, 373

U.S. 734, 742 (1963), stated that the courts have narrowly construed Section 8(a)(3) to read: 'Membership' as a condition of employment is whittled down to its financial core." 513 F.2d at 1085.

42. *Tullus Gordon Contracting, Inc.*, 277 NLRB 530 (1985), and *Telon Electrical Corp.*, 278 NLRB 236 (1986).

43. See *Fiberboard Paper Products Corp. v. NLRB*, 379 U.S. 203 (1964).

44. There is now a significant line of cases dealing with plant closings and sales of business. See *First National Maintenance Corp. v. NLRB*, 452 U.S. 666 (1981), and *Milwaukee Spring Division*, 268 NLRB 601 (1984). See also discussion on WARN in Chapter 25.

45. See General Counsel Memorandum 91-9 dated August 9, 1991, relying upon *Dubuque Packing Company, Inc.*, 303 NLRB No. 66 (1991), and interpreting *First National Maintenance Corp. v. NLRB*, 452 U.S. 666 (1981), and *Fibreboard Corp. v. NLRB*, 379 U.S. 203 (1964).

46. Dubuque, slip op. at pp. 17–18.

47. *Id.*, slip op. p. 17.

48. *Id.*, slip op. p. 18. Neither the *prima facie* case nor the rebuttal call for a consideration of the employer's motive underlying the relocation decision. Motive is relevant only to the employer's affirmative defenses.

49. See *Otis Elevator*, 269 NLRB 891, 893. In the following cases, the Board found the decision turned on a significant change in the direction of the business: *Columbia City Freight Lines*, 271 NLRB 12 (1984) (where the decision to transfer work turned on the need to eliminate duplicative costs and services, to maximize usage of the fuel and equipment, and to become smaller because of the loss of a major customer); *Boston Div. UOP, Inc.*, 272 NLRB 999 (1984) (where the decision to consolidate operations and subcontract certain work turned on the need to eliminate duplication of work, costs, and services and to respond to the deteriorating quality of the produce caused by obsolete equipment; and *Kroger Co., Inc.*, 273 NLRB 462 (1984) (where the decision to close an operation and subcontract turned on the employer's inability to compete because of its outmoded operation). Compare *Plymouth Stamping Division*, 286 NLRB 890 (1987) (where the Board concluded that the decision did not turn on a significant change in the direction of the business).

50. *Dubuque*, slip op. p. 18.

51. *Id.*, slip op. p. 18.

52. *Id.*, slip op. p. 20

53. *Id.* at 20.

54. *Id.*

55. 29 U.S.C. §171.

56. 29 U.S.C. §158(d).

57. This doctrine is discretionary, but it is recognized by implication in Section 8 (b)(7) of the NLRA. The doctrine is administered by the NLRB and is not subject to ordinary judicial review. See *Local 1545, Carpenters v. Vincent*, 286 F.2d 127 (2d Cir. 1960), and Charles J. Morris, *The Developing Labor Law*, 2nd ed., American Bar Association, (BNA, Washington, D.C., 1983), p. 361.

58. See *Burns International Detective Agency*, 182 NLRB 348 (1970), in which the NLRB ruled that it is an unfair labor practice for a successor employer to refuse to recognize and bargain with the union of its predecessor employees and to refuse to abide by the terms of the predecessor's contract. The Board has routinely upheld a successor's obligation to bargain, to arbitrate and assume predecessor collective bargaining agreements as long as its own criteria for successorship have been met. See *NLRB v. Burns International Security Service, Inc.*, 406 U.S. 272 (1972), and *NLRB v. Fall River Dyeing and Finishing Corp.*, 482 U.S. 27 (1987), holding that a successor has an obligation to bargain with the predecessor's union once it begins operation with a "substantial and representative complement" of its total planned work force and at that time a majority of its employees had been with the predecessor.

59. In *Wood v. Teamsters Local 406*, 807 F.2d 493 (6th Cir. 1986), the Sixth Circuit Court of Appeals reaffirmed principles of the *Burns* and *Wiley* as well as *Howard Johnson*. The court denied successorship status because the employer was not "an alter ego" and had not assumed the collective bargaining agreement, and there was not a substantial continuity of the business. Relying upon *Howard Johnson*, the court of appeals reiterated that there must be continuity both in terms of the work force and the operations in order to find successor liability under a collective bargaining agreement. For a related discussion see Roger B. Jacobs, *Unforeseen Obligations of Successor Employers* (New York: NYU Conference on Labor, 1987), Chap. 6.

60. The following states are considered "right to work" states: Alabama, Arizona, Arkansas, Florida, Georgia, Idaho, Iowa, Kansas, Louisiana, Mississippi, Nebraska, Nevada, North Carolina, North Dakota, South Carolina, South Dakota, Tennessee, Texas, Utah, Virginia, and Wyoming.

61. Morris, *Developing Labor Law*, p. 1387.

62. See *Steelworkers Trilogy (United Steel Workers v. American Manufacturing Co.*, 363 U.S. 564 (1960); and *United Steel Workers v. Enterprise Wheel & Car Corp.*, 363 U.S. 593 (1960); *United Steel Workers v. Warrior and Gulf Navigation Co.*, 363 U.S. 574 (1960)).

63. 484 U.S. 299 (1987).

22

PROTECTION FOR WHISTLE-BLOWERS IN THE WORKPLACE

Of increasing concern in the workplace are employees who threaten to report or actually report wrongdoing by the employer to outside entities. These complaints range from health or safety issues and financial transactions to violations of government regulations or other conduct perceived to be unlawful. Such employees are frequently referred to as "whistle-blowers." Federal and state laws vary widely with regard to protecting employees who complain about or report violations of law or government regulations. In particular, the law tends to protect those individuals who report conduct that endangers the health, safety, or welfare of the public. This chapter gives you an overview of federal and state protections that prohibit retaliatory acts against a legitimate whistle-blower.

HOW WHISTLE-BLOWERS ARE PROTECTED

Many employers are caught unprepared when they are confronted with an employee who is threatening to report or has reported real or perceived misconduct or violation of governmental regulations occurring in the workplace. Such employees are often referred to as "whistle-blowers," that is, employees who disclose alleged improper employer practices or policies such as safety or health hazards, improper waste disposal, corruption, defective products, or other unlawful activities. There is a strong public interest in encouraging employees to come forward with information regarding improper practices or conduct by an employer, particularly if such conduct adversely affects the public health or safety or government operations.

There are basically three types of protected activities under the various whistle-blower protection provisions:

1. Disclosure of certain information to employers or public authorities
2. Appearance before public bodies or courts for hearings or inquiries or some other participation in a proceeding under a statute
3. Refusals to obey a directive to commit an unlawful or unsafe act

There are a number of theories under which an employee may pursue a whistle-blower–type claim, such as federal, state or common law. The elements will vary in accordance to the theory utilized. However, some basic elements of any such claim include the following:

1. The parties are covered by a specific statutory provision or common law.
2. The employee or applicant is engaged in protected whistle-blowing activity.
3. The employer took adverse action against the employee or applicant.
4. There is a causal connection between the adverse action and the protected activity.

An increasing number of federal and state authorities have acted to protect whistle-blowing activity from employer reprisals in the workplace. These federal and state laws prohibit retaliation against certain employees who have reported unlawful activity on the part of the employer. However, these laws generally are not comprehensive or uniform in their coverage. Most of these laws may protect only a certain category of employee (such as government workers) and/or protect particular types of disclosures (such as health or safety violations). In some jurisdictions, where no specific anti-retaliation law exists, certain whistle-blowing activities may be protected by the First Amendment or common law tort (nonstatutory law) such as a public policy exception to the doctrine of employment-at-will. A typical whistle-blower claim is illustrated in the following example.

Case Study

Oscar Itoldi works as a janitor in the By-the-Sea Nuclear Reactor plant, which is privately operated by the Shorelite Energy Company. He has complained off and on for the past three years that strange odors are present from time to time in different areas of the basement but usually near an exhaust pipe. He notices that he is sick more often and that others have complained of headaches. He also knows that the management cuts corners with regard to the proper procedures for hazardous waste disposal. He complains again to his supervisor, but this time he also says that he will contact the "proper authorities" if the odors are not eliminated and that he knows "all about their ways of getting around the rules." The next day he is fired for excessive absenteeism.

Does Oscar have a whistle-blower claim? Yes, under a number of theories. First, there is a federal law protecting workers in nuclear power plants who complain or report violations to their employer and/or a government agency. There may also be a state law that protects any employee who reports safety or health violations to his or her employer or government agency. Finally, there may be an exception to the employment-at-will doctrine that prohibits discharges that violate a public policy. The state may recognize a public policy in encouraging employees to report violations involving public safety or health. The employer in the preceding case study could be faced with serious liability triggered by dismissing Oscar. The fact that Oscar did not get as far as reporting the violations to an outside government authority usually does not matter; he threatened to do so and was dismissed because of that threat. Employers faced with an Oscar Itoldi should have a procedure in place to defuse the situation and promptly investigate his claims of violations.

How Federal Employees Are Covered

Protection for federal employees who report violations of laws or regulations occurring in the workplace, internally or to government authorities, depends upon whether a specific statute exists containing such protection. Where such a statute exists, it protects only those federal employees specifically covered by the statute and for only certain types of unlawful conduct, if reported to the proper authorities. These statutes tend to be narrow and must be strictly adhered to in order for the whistle-blower to be protected.

This section will briefly discuss representative examples of federal whistle-blowing protection provisions that appear in various statutes.

The Civil Service Reform Act. The Civil Service Reform Act (CSRA), as amended by the Whistle-blower Protection Act of 1988, protects federal employees from discipline or discharge for making disclosures that serve the public interest where such disclosures assist in the elimination of fraud, corruption, waste, abuse, and unnecessary government expenditures.[1] CSRA also makes a strong statement that public policy is not served by frivolous complaints, meritorious complaints about trivial issues or for improper political motives, or complaints made simply to gain favorable publicity. Under CSRA, employees must be able to show that they are acting with a proper motive and that an important public issue is at stake.

The Scope of the Act. CSRA applies to disclosures by an employee, former employee, or applicant for employment of any information that such person reasonably believes is evidence of

- A violation of any law, rule or regulation
- Gross mismanagement, gross waste of funds, or abuse of authority
- A substantial and specific danger to public health or safety

However, such a disclosure can be otherwise specifically prohibited by law or required by Executive Order to be kept secret in the interest of national defense or the conduct of foreign affairs.

The Office of Special Counsel was created to deal specifically with claims of retaliation against employees, former employees, and applicants who "blow the whistle" on their federal employers.

The Private Right of Action. Aggrieved employees under this whistle-blower protection act may seek corrective action from the Merit Systems Protection Board (MSPB) before seeking such action from the Office of Special Counsel, if that employee has the right to appeal directly to the MSPB under any law, rule, or regulation. The MSPB may order a stay of the personnel action challenged.

NOTE: The MSPB may not order corrective action if the agency-employer demonstrates by clear and convincing evidence that it would have taken the same personnel action in the absence of the whistle-blowing activity.

If the employee prevails before the MSPB, the offending party, individual, or agency may be liable for reasonable attorney's fees and other reasonable costs incurred.

If the employee is adversely affected or aggrieved by the decision of the MSPB, he or she may seek judicial review of the order or decision. A petition for review must be filed within 30 days.

Recent regulations published by the Office of Personnel Management (OPM) provides that the prevailing parties in initial MSPB decisions in whistle-blower cases are to receive the ordered relief pending the outcome of any petition for review.[2] Such interim relief may include interim appointments, promotions after demotions, and interim within-grade increases, among other relief.

Other Federal Laws That Apply. A number of other federal statutes protect employees in specific industries or categories from reprisals for certain whistle-blowing activity. Each of these whistle-blower provisions has its own specific provisions dictating what disclosures are protected—in almost every instance, the employee, to be protected, must follow a prescribed pattern that relates to the nature of the disclosure, to whom it is disclosed, and the adverse employment consequence based on the disclosure.

For example, employees of a federal defense contractor may not be discharged, demoted, or otherwise discriminated against as a reprisal for disclosing information relating to a substantial violation of law related to the defense contract.[3] The disclosure, however, must be made to a member of Congress or an authorized official of the Department of Defense or the Department of Justice.

The following federal statutes are representative examples of statutory forms of whistle-blower protection:

- *False Claims Act.* Employees of federal contractors are protected from retaliation for disclosing fraudulent acts committed against the government.[4]

- *Surface Transportation Assistance Act of 1982.* Employees of interstate trucking enterprises are protected against discharge for refusing to operate an unsafe truck or for alleging in a complaint that the employer has failed to comply with federal or state safety laws.[5]

- *International Safe Containers Act.* Discriminatory retaliation is prohibited against employees who report the existence of an unsafe container to the Secretary of Transportation.[6]

- *Asbestos School Hazard Detection and Control Act.* State and local educational agencies receiving assistance under the Act may not retaliate against any employee who has made public any information concerning a potential asbestos problem in school buildings.[7]

- *Energy Reorganization Act.* Retaliatory discharge or discrimination in employment is prohibited against an employee who commenced or caused to commence a proceeding under this Act or the Atomic Energy Act of 1954 or a proceeding for administration or enforcement of any requirement imposed under these laws or otherwise assisted or participated in such a proceeding.[8]

- *Clean Air Act.* Retaliation against an employee who commences, testifies, assists, or participates in proceedings under the Act is prohibited.[9]

Preemption of State or Common Law Claims. In certain cases, the federal statutory provisions governing a particular area or industry may preempt all other actions based on state or common law. Preemption means that the employee may bring a claim only under the appropriate governing statute and all other related claims must be dismissed. For example, the Occupational Safety and Health Act (OSHA) has been found to have exclusive jurisdiction over claims by employees alleging retaliation for safety- or health-related complaints.[10]

However, preemption is not always the rule where federal statutory protection exists. For example, a tort claim for intentional infliction of emotional distress brought by a discharged employee from a nuclear facility who had complained about perceived nuclear safety standards violations to her employer and the government was not preempted by the Energy Reorganization Act's whistle-blowing provision.[11]

> NOTE: Preemption is a legal defense to a claim of retaliation which often requires complex legal analysis. However, it is important to be aware of this type of defense and whether it may apply to a claim that is filed against your organization. Discuss this issue with your legal counsel.

How State Whistle-Blower Protection Laws Affect Employees

Many states have adopted some form of whistle-blower protection statutes ranging from broad to narrow. These statutes vary in scope and remedies. States with some form of statutory whistle-blower protection for employees (in the public and/or private sector) include Alaska, Arizona, California, Colorado, Connecticut, Delaware, Florida, Hawaii, Illinois, Indiana, Iowa, Kansas, Kentucky, Louisiana, Maine, Maryland, Michigan, Minnesota, Missouri, Montana, Nevada, New Hampshire, New Jersey, New York, North Carolina, Ohio, Oregon, Pennsylvania, Rhode Island, South Carolina, Tennessee, Texas, Utah, Washington, West Virginia, and Wisconsin.[12]

A review of the various state laws shows that the states have very different approaches to protecting the employee whistle-blower. It is therefore extremely important for the personnel professional to refer to the appropriate state and local laws when faced with a whistle-blowing situation. The following is an example of a comprehensive state statute—the Ohio statute—that contains several elements that typify state regulation in this area.

Case Example

> The Ohio statute provides that an employee, in the private or public sector, who becomes aware, in the course of his or her employment, of a violation of any state, federal, or local law or regulation and orally notifies his or her supervisor or other responsible officer of the employer and also files a written report describing the violation may not be retaliated against for making such report. The employee must reasonably believe that the violation is a criminal offense that is likely to cause "imminent risk of physical harm to persons" *or* a hazard to public health or safety *or* is a felony.

> The violation must also be one that the employer has authority to correct. If the employer does not correct the violation or make a reasonable good faith effort to correct within 24 hours of receiving oral notification or receipt of the report, whichever is earlier, then the employee may file a written report with a prosecuting authority, peace officer, inspector general, or other agency with regulatory authority over the employer.

The statute also protects employees who become aware, in the course of their employment, of violations of air and/or water pollution, solid hazardous waste, and safe drinking water statutes which are criminal offenses. In such cases, employees may directly notify appropriate public officials orally or in writing.

Another protected category are employees who become aware of violations by fellow employees of state, federal, or local laws or regulations or any work rule or company policy which is either a criminal violation likely to cause imminent risk of physical harm or a hazard to safety or is a felony. The employee, in this situation, must orally notify a supervisor of the violation and make a subsequent written report.

To be protected, the reporting employee must make a reasonable and good faith effort to determine the accuracy of information reported. Failure to do so may subject the employee to disciplinary action. The statute does not permit disclosures that would diminish or impair rights to continued state or common law protections of confidentiality of communications.

Under the statute the employer may not take disciplinary or retaliatory action for making a report under the statute or for attempting to ensure the accuracy of a report of violations. Prohibited employment actions include

- Removing or suspending the employee from employment
- Withholding salary increases or employee benefits to which the employee is otherwise entitled
- Transferring or reassigning employee
- Denying promotion to which otherwise entitled
- Reducing pay or position[13]

NOTE: The employee's disclosure is usually protected only if the employee took all steps required under state law, for example, reporting the violation in the manner prescribed by law and to the proper authorities.

The range of protected activities varies significantly from state to state. For example, Louisiana has the narrowest scope, protecting only the reporting of environmental violations; Montana limits protected activities to the reporting of actions that are contrary to health, safety, or welfare laws; and New York protects only those violations of law, rule, or regulation that create a "substantial and specific danger to the public health."[14]

New Jersey has one of the broadest statutes protecting three categories of employee conduct:

1. Reasonable belief that the employer's policy, practice or conduct is in violation of a state law, rule or regulation.

2. Participation in some way in a government sanctioned proceeding.

3. Objection to or refusal to participate in any activity, policy, or practice that he or she reasonably believes is unlawful, fraudulent, criminal, or incompatible with a clear mandate of public policy concerning the public health, safety or welfare.[15]

NOTE: Many state statutes require that the employee's belief that the employer is in violation of law, rule, or regulation must be reasonable. Some statutes also require that the employee has reported or actually intends to report such violations to the proper authorities. Thus, it is important that you check your state's law to see what it requires.

In addition, many statutes provide a wide range of remedies to a discharged whistle-blower, such as

- Compensatory damages, including back pay, front pay, lost benefits, out-of-pocket costs, and medical expenses
- Reinstatement (including lost seniority and benefits)
- Injunctive relief
- Attorneys' fees and costs
- Liquidated damages[16]
- Punitive damages
- Civil fines
- Criminal fines or imprisonment

Identifying Other Forms of Protection

Common law protection and constitutional protection are also available for employees who engage in whistle-blowing activity.

Common Law/Public Policy. Employees who allege that they were wrongfully discharged because they refused to commit wrongful acts or engaged in other forms of whistle-blowing–type activity, in some jurisdictions, may base such a claim on a violation of public policy. Common law protection is found in public policy–based prohibitions against retaliatory discharge or discipline. Depending upon the state or nature of the claim, a whistle-blower may be permitted to bring a claim under both statutory and common law bases.

NOTE: The aggrieved employee seeking relief under this theory must first establish that there exists a public policy that was violated by the adverse employment action.

California leads the way in successful claims for wrongful discharge in violation of public policy in whistle-blower type cases. The state courts in California have recognized claims for retaliation in violation of public policy based on disclosure activities protected by many of the state statutes discussed in the previous section. For example, an employee who protested what he believed to be hazardous working conditions based on the smoking of a coworker was protected from discharge,[17] and a union business agent's claim—he had alleged that he was discharged when he refused to testify falsely to a state legislative committee—was recognized.[18]

In California and elsewhere, the guiding principle in these cases is that there must exist a recognized public policy that has been violated by the retaliatory action of the employer. In most jurisdictions only reported violations that affect the public in some way are protected. Disclosure of violations of internal company policies or rules is generally not a protected whistle-blower activity.[19]

> NOTE: Generally, to be protected, the employee's disclosure activity or statements must serve some public interest, not just the interests of the company or the individual.

Constitutional Protection. In some cases, the First Amendment, right to free speech, protects government employees from discharge when they speak out on matters of public concern.[20] In such cases, the court will focus on the content, form, and context of the statements for which protection is sought.

Case Example

> Charlie Bond, a police officer in a major city and member of the police officers union, wrote to the state Attorney General. He alleged matters ranging from interference by the police chief with the constitutionally protected rights of a union membership to the improper use of funds. He requested that an official investigation be conducted into these matters. Officer Bond was terminated as a result of this letter.

Officer Bond prevailed on a claim of violation of his constitutional rights. The court found that the officer had engaged in speech on matters of public concern which was protected by the First Amendment. His letter was submitted through proper channels to the appropriate authorities. His statements did not affect his ability to perform his duties, and his working relationship with the police chief did not require personal loyalty and confidence. There was also no evidence of any disruption of police department activities or morale as a result of the letter. The officer was awarded $242,465 for back pay, $389,806 in front pay, $250,000 for mental anguish, $50,000 in punitive damages against the police chief, as well as reasonable attorneys' fees.[21] Thus employers, particularly public employers, face additional liability under the Constitution when an employee brings forth matters of public concern.

GUIDELINES FOR PREVENTING
WHISTLE-BLOWER CLAIMS

You can help avoid retaliatory whistle-blower discharge claims by implementing policies that dissuade employees from "blowing the whistle." To prevent whistle-blower claims, employers need to establish a basis upon which the employees can rely and trust that their attempts to correct or report violations will not result in adverse employment action. Employees need to feel confident in bringing complaints or concerns about possible violations or wrongdoing internally. The following steps are suggestions for developing a policy that will encourage an employee to keep the complaint within the company.

1. Articulate the company's insistence upon compliance with all applicable laws and regulations in the workplace.

2. Consider implementing a formal policy requiring employees to comply with all relevant statutory rules and regulations. Remember to tailor the policy to your organization's needs. The size and nature of the employer are important factors in developing the proper policies.

3. Identify all areas that are potential sources of improper conduct or for whistle-blower complaints.

4. Establish an open-door policy that encourages employees to bring complaints or concerns to the attention of their supervisors or designated company official at any time.

5. Instruct supervisors and company officials to be receptive to employee's complaints. Supervisors should be advised of such complaints and instructed not to retaliate. Employees should be permitted to take their complaints up through a chain of command.

6. Designate a specific company official to whom complaints or concerns should be directed as an alternative or in addition to going to the supervisor. The individual selected, depending upon the size of the organization, should have sufficient time available to respond adequately to the employees. He or she should be a senior executive with credibility and authority to make changes.

7. Establish an internal procedure mechanism that provides the complaining employee with an opportunity to have his or her complaint reviewed by someone not involved in the dispute.

8. Hold regular departmental meetings to avoid misunderstandings that could lead to whistle-blowing. This can be done on a companywide basis where all departments hold regular meetings or target the departments likely to develop such complaints.

9. Conduct ethical training sessions for management and employees.

10. Use disinterested third parties, from another department internally or from outside the company, to resolve internal disagreements that are likely to lead to whistle-blowing.

11. Limit the type of complaints to be handled by the internal procedure mechanism to significant issues regarding public health and safety. You may require that the employee have a good faith belief that an immediate and significant danger to the public health and safety would result or does exist from a particular course of conduct.

12. Institute an arbitration program, or other form of dispute resolution, when informal efforts to resolve a whistle-blower complaint has failed. This is not the right policy for every situation, but where appropriate, obtain the agreement of the employees to arbitrate any disputes arising out of their employment, including whistle-blowing complaints.

13. Review all pertinent state and federal laws that govern whistle-blowing conduct. These laws vary significantly in application.

14. Seek a restraining order against any employee or outsider who you believe to be reporting untrue statements to outside entities. You should seek such injunctive relief only in cases where it can be established that the harm caused to the company's reputation or interests by such false statements is immediate and irreparable.

ENDNOTES

1. 5 U.S.C. §7701(b)(2)(a) strengthening the provisions found in 5 U.S.C. §2302(b)(8) enacted in 1989.

2. OPM Regulations, 5 C.F.R. §§772.101 and 772.102, effective March 2, 1992. However, interim relief is available only to employees and applicants, not to individuals who are applicants for retirement. Interim relief is to end upon the issuance of a final board order. 5 C.F.R. §831.201.

3. Department of Defense Authorization Act of 1987, 10 U.S.C. §2409(a); See also 10 U.S.C. §1587.

4. 31 U.S.C. §3730(h).

5. 49 U.S.C. §2305.

6. 46 U.S.C. §1506.

7. 20 U.S.C. §4018; see also Asbestos Hazard Emergency Response Act of 1986, 15 U.S.C. §2651.

8. 42 U.S.C. §5851(a), known as the "whistle-blower" provision of the Energy Reorganization Act. See *Norris v. Lumberman's Mutual Casualty Co.,* 881 F.2d 1144 (1st Cir. 1989), involving an inspector auditing a nuclear power plant.

9. 42 U.S.C §7622; see other environmental protection-related statutes for a similar provision, including Comprehensive Environmental Response, Compensation and Liability Act of 1980 (CERCLA), 42 U.S.C. §9601; Federal Water Pollution Control Act of 1972, 33 U.S.C. §1367; Safe Drinking Water Act, 42 U.S.C. §300j-9; Solid Waste Disposal Act, 42 U.S.C. §6971; and Toxic Substances Control Act, 15 U.S.C. §2622.

10. See *Meadows v. Container Research Corp.*, 117 L.R.R.M. (BNA) 3356 (D. Md. 1983), and *Braun v. Kelsey-Hayes Co.*, 635 F.Supp. 75 (E.D. Pa. 1986).

11. See *English v. General Electric Co.*, 496 U.S. 72, 110 S.Ct. 2270 (1980).

12. States without some form of general statutory whistle-blower protection include Alabama, Arkansas, District of Columbia, Georgia, Idaho, Massachusetts, Mississippi, Nebraska, New Mexico, North Dakota, Oklahoma, Vermont, Virginia, and Wyoming.

13. See Ohio Rev. Code Ann. §§4113.51–4113.53 (Baldwin 1990); see also *Haynes v. Zoological Society of Cincinnati*, 567 N.E.2d 1048 (Ohio Ct. Comm. Pleas 1990) (improper for employer to transfer bear keeper to entry-level position in bird house based on her whistle-blowing activity).

14. See *Vella v. United Cerebral Palsy of New York City, Inc.*, 535 N.Y.S.2d 292 (1988).

15. N.J.S.A. 34:19-3.

16. See, for example, Louisiana's statute La. Rev. Stat. Ann., §30:2027(B), which provides for triple damages for injury resulting from actions taken against employees.

17. *Hentzel v. Singer Co.*, 138 Cal. App. 3d 290, 188 Cal. Rptr. 159 (1982).

18. *Peterman v. International Brotherhood of Teamsters*, 174 Cal. App. 2d 184, 344 P.2d 25 (1959).

19. See *Foley v. Interactive Data Corp.*, 47 Cal. 3d 654, 765 P.2d 373 (1988).

20. See *Connick v. Myers*, 461 U.S. 138 (1983).

21. See *Wulf v. Wichita*, 644 F. Supp. 1211 (D.Kan. 1986), *affirmed in part, revised in part*, 883 F.2d 842 (10th Cir. 1989).

23

HANDLING WORKERS' COMPENSATION CLAIMS

Workers' compensation is a system that provides wage benefits and medical care to workers who are victims of work-related injuries.[1] The costs of the injuries are covered by insurance and ultimately are placed on the consumer when premiums are passed on in the cost of products.[2] Most claims for work-related injuries are governed by state law. As you will see, states vary in what type of illness or injury is covered under workers' compensation as well as the procedures under each system. This chapter will explain the legal aspects of workers' compensation that affect the employer.

IDENTIFYING THE GENERAL PROVISIONS OF THE WORKERS' COMPENSATION LAW

With the advent of the industrial revolution, injuries in the workplace became more severe and the employee's only recourse against the employer was a lawsuit. This was a time-consuming and risky venture because the employer had numerous defenses available which could absolve liability. Thus, the system of workers' compensation developed. The states are able to control whether to develop and maintain a workers' compensation scheme by enacting a statute. The federal government provides workers' compensation only to longshore and harbor workers and federal employees.[3] The statutes are generally-liberally construed by the courts. The personnel professional should consult the appropriate state law and periodically review it.

Defining the Scope and Purpose of the Law

Most state workers' compensation statutes provide for a system under which benefits are paid to injured workers in the event of an accidental injury or occupational disease. If the worker dies, death benefits are available to beneficiaries. The injury or occupational disease must either arise out of or in the course of employment. The injured employee usually receives a percentage of his or her weekly wage based on the type and degree of injury. Occupational disease is also covered by most workers' compensation statutes. The diseases covered are listed in the statute itself. For example, the Ohio statute covers diseases that are "peculiar to a particular industrial process, trade, or occupation and to which an employee is not ordinarily subjected or exposed outside or away from his employment."[4]

Employers' Obligations Under State Law. Under most state plans, the employer must obtain insurance through one of three ways: a state plan, a private carrier, or self-insurance. The employee, in return for this protection, gives up the right to sue the employer for injuries sustained during work. In some states compliance with workers' compensation statutes is mandatory, and in others the employer can elect whether to participate in the program.

For example, in New Jersey participation is on a voluntary basis. However, an employer electing not to participate gives up any defenses to a lawsuit by an employee for a work-related injury. This essentially ties the hands of the employer and assures that the employee will win any lawsuit. Thus, the New Jersey plan is practically compulsory,[5] and most employers opt to be included in the workers' compensation plan.

Eight Elements Found in Typical Workers' Compensation Statutes. The typical workers' compensation statute covers injuries and occupational diseases which arise out of and in the course of employment and includes the following characteristics:

1. The injured employee receives automatic entitlement. Some states require that the employee be out a specified number of days before compensation payments begin.

2. Negligence or fault on the part of the employer or employee does not preclude compensation.

3. The coverage is limited to the number of weeks specified in the statute.

4. The benefits that can be received are cash wages and medical care.

5. The employee gives up his or her common law right to sue for negligence claims.

6. The employee retains the right to sue third parties such as a fellow employee or the manufacturer of equipment for negligence.

7. Workers' compensation is handled by an administrative office of the state government. Any cases that find their way to court are heard in administrative court where the rules are more relaxed.

8. The employer must secure its liability through insurance that is state funded, private, or self-imposed.[6]

On the whole, the workers' compensation scheme is beneficial to both the employer and employee. It is for the most part a fair system. The employer secures insurance to cover its employees' workplace injuries and is insulated from liability. The employee in return collects cash wage benefits and gives up the right to sue the employer.

The first thing to do as an employer is familiarize yourself with your state's workers' compensation statute. See if it is elective or compulsory. If it is an elective system, calculate whether the risk for not participating in the statutory scheme would be a feasible alternative.

Most workers' compensation statutes cover employers who are engaged in a business, occupation, trade, or profession that in some states must be for profit.[7] Some states require that the employer have a minimum number of employees before the statute will apply.

Determining Which Employees and Circumstances Are Covered

All employees who are not specifically excluded by a state statute are covered. The circumstances under which an employee may be covered varies greatly from state to state. However, all agree if an employee is engaged in duties of his employment and is injured on the employer's premises, he or she is clearly covered. Similarly, the different states cover varying types of injuries from physical to mental. The personnel professional needs to be familiar with the appropriate state's statute and rules in this area.

Covered employees range from professional athletes to factory workers and include part- and full-time employees. Since so many types of employees are covered, it is more logical to discuss employees that are not covered by the statute.

Employees Not Covered by the Statute. Examples of workers generally excluded from coverage are

– Clergy

- Domestic and farm workers
- Longshore and harbor workers, who are covered by the federal act
- Casual employees whose employment is either incidental or temporary to complete an isolated job
- Independent contractors

Independent contractors are workers hired by the employer to do a specific job. The test as to whether one is an independent contractor is who retains control over the job. If the employer is in control, there exists an employment relationship for the purposes of workers' compensation. If the contractor maintains control, then there is no entitlement to compensation for any worker who is injured.

Case Study

Fine's Department Store asks John Smith to come in periodically to repair the escalators and elevators. He made a deal with Fine's that he would work only after hours, bring his own tools and equipment, and lock up when he finished. John had no supervision. Sometimes his son Tom Smith came along to help. Last week, John fell and broke his leg while fixing an escalator. He wants to collect workers' compensation from Fine's. However, John maintained control over when and how he worked, thus making him an independent contractor. He cannot now collect workers' compensation from the department store.

Also note that an employer who hires minors illegally or without the proper working papers can be subject to possible fines and an increase in the amount of compensation owed if a work-related injury results. The message here is clear: Do not employ minors illegally.

Circumstances Under Which an Employee Is Covered. After deciding that the employment relationship exists, it is necessary to determine when employees are entitled to collect workers' compensation. In general, an injury is compensable if it arises out of or in the course of employment.

This seems simple enough. However, it can become quite convoluted. For example, an employee who slips in the shower at home getting ready for work in the morning obviously cannot collect workers' compensation. However, an employee who after work slips in a shower provided by the employer may be entitled to workers' compensation.[8] Both injuries were due to accidents, but only accidents and occupational diseases that are work related are covered by workers' compensation.

"Arising out of employment" and "in the course of employment" are two distinct areas. The only place where these phrases have been interpreted is in the courts. Therefore the following sections sometimes refer to court cases as examples of when workers' compensation can be collected. This will give the employer a feeling for when workers' compensation has been awarded and how some injuries may be prevented.

> NOTE: Since workers' compensation obligations can rarely be avoided, it is important that the employer try to prevent workplace accidents from occurring. Just because an employer is immune from employee suits does not mean the workplace should not be kept clean and safe. In some states if federal health or safety codes are violated, employer misconduct occurs, and the compensation received by the employee increased.

Six Examples of Injuries Arising Out of Employment. Arising out of employment means there must be a "showing that the injury was caused by an increased risk to which claimant, as distinct from the general public, was subjected by his employment."[9] The following are examples of injuries arising out of employment.

1. *Acts of God.* Employees have recovered workers' compensation for being struck by lightning or caught in a tornado or windstorm while working.[10]

2. *Exposure.* Employees who have been exposed to heat, cold, and sickness due to weather are subject to compensable injuries that arise out of employment. Even exposure to contagious disease has been compensable.[11]

3. *Street risks.* A worker can recover for an injury sustained when venturing onto the street in two situations. First is a worker who occasionally goes on a work-related errand. Second is a worker who is continuously on the road such as a traveling salesperson. Any injury sustained is compensable as long as it was during employment. Street risks have been "broadened far beyond the original idea of traffic perils, and had been applied to almost any mishap whose locale is the street, including simple falls, stray bullets, falling trees, and foul balls."[12]

4. *Positional risks.* If the employer puts an employee in a position for a risk of danger, then the employer can be held compensable for any resulting injury. This includes unexplained falls and even deaths due to heart attacks.

5. *Assaults.* Assaults that occur during work as a result of a fight between two employees or as part of the duties of an employee can be compensable by the workers' compensation statute. Assaults by children, intoxicated persons, and the mentally incapacitated and even assaults that are mistakenly committed or unexplainable are included.

6. *Risks personal to the employee.* Injuries or occupational disease sustained by an employee that exacerbate previous medical problems are com-

pensable. If a person with arthritis gets a job as a cashier that makes the arthritis worse, then the injury can be compensated.

NOTE: As an employer, it may be beneficial to keep a log of employees who are off the premises along with the reasons they have left and when they will return. This will give the employer an idea of how many people are out at once, the areas where they go, and the risks that they may be subject to. Try to keep this under control and carefully supervised.

Five Examples of Injuries Occurring During the Course of Employment. An injury takes place **during the course of employment** when it occurs at a time during regular or assigned employment hours at a place where the employee is working or doing something incidental to work at a place where he or she is reasonably expected to be.

Case Study

Jack Jackson is an auto mechanic at the neighborhood Chrysler dealership. His employer requires him to stay at his station even if he has no work. To occupy his time he writes a novel. An overhead machine hits him on the head while he is engaged in writing. He is still in the course of employment, and the injury is nevertheless compensable.

The following is a list of situations that give rise to compensable injuries as occurring in the course of employment.

1. *The going and coming rule.* When employees work a fixed hour schedule at a specific place, any injury sustained going to or coming from work or during lunchtime is compensable if it occurs on the premises. There are exceptions to this general rule that extend to injuries that occur where the employee is within the risk of danger associated with the job. This is an area filled with nuances. For example, an employee on the job who leaves to go to the dry cleaners and falls while climbing over a fence is covered.[13] However, a woman who goes to get dinner on a business trip after business hours and is hit by a car cannot collect for her injuries.[14]

2. *When a journey going to or coming from work is the service.* An injury occurring off premises is compensable if it occurs during a journey going to or coming from work where the journey is itself a service for the employer. For example, an employee who journeys to a mine every night to turn on the pumps, which takes only a moment and then journeys back, would be covered for any injury occurring during the journey since the journey is itself part of the service.[15]

3. *Using the Employer's Conveyance.* When an employee is going to and from work in a van, truck, bus, car, or other employer-owned vehicle, any injury resulting is considered in the course of employment. A man who falls off a seat

on an employer-owned van that regularly takes employees to and from work can collect workers' compensation.[16]

4. *Dual-Purpose Trip.* When an employee goes on a business and pleasure trip, but the injury sustained happens on pleasure time, the injury is compensable if "the trip involves the performance of a service for the employer which would have caused the trip to be taken by someone even if it had not coincided with the personal injury."[17] An employee who went on a business trip to fix electrical appliances and saw relatives during the trip and was injured on his return was able to collect workers' compensation.[18]

5. *Deviations.* A deviation takes the employee out of the course of employment for a period of time and then the employment continues. An example would be an employee who has to go to New York City on business and takes the train into New York then stops at Lord & Taylor to buy a shirt, falls in the store, and then continues on the trip. Most states do not compensate injuries occurring in this manner.

Describing Specific Types of Injuries Covered

When a worker is physically injured by accident in the course of or arising out of employment, the injury is usually compensable under workers' compensation. Injuries covered by workers' compensation span the spectrum from readily discernible injuries such as broken arms or legs, burns, or severe cuts that clearly were the result of a work-related accident or occupational diseases such as asbestosis or black lung to injuries that are less obviously work-related such as heart disease, stress-related illness, cancer, or mental illness. Even damage to prosthetic devices has been held compensable.[19] The list of covered injuries and illnesses varies from state to state—so check state law.

This section addresses the second category of injuries and illnesses that may or may not be covered under a particular statutory scheme. In cases where the injury does not necessarily, on its face, appear to be linked to the individual's employment, the connection to work must be made before he or she is eligible to collect benefits.

Compensable Heart Cases. When the worker is injured at work from heart attack or heart disease, the injury may be compensable. The biggest problem in this area of injuries is *causation*. The heart attack or heart disease does not have to occur immediately after exertion. The injury could occur at home after work and therefore be compensable if its cause can be traced back to an event at work. Compensability depends upon which rule of causation your state follows.

The usual exertion rule means that a heart attack is compensable even when the exertion is usual to the workers' normal and routine duties.[20] States that subscribe to this rule with respect to heart cases include Alabama, Arizona,

Arkansas, Delaware, Georgia, Idaho, Illinois, Kentucky, Maine, Michigan, Minnesota, Mississippi, Missouri, Nebraska, New Hampshire, New Jersey, New Mexico, Ohio, Oklahoma, Oregon, Texas, Utah, West Virginia, and Wisconsin.

The unusual exertion rule means that the worker must be doing something that is more strenuous than his or her usual duties which brings on a heart problem in order for it to be compensable. The Kansas workers' compensation heart amendment is an example of this rule:

> compensation shall not be paid in case of coronary or coronary artery disease or cerebrovascular injury unless it is shown that the exertion of the work necessary to precipitate the disability was more than the workers' usual work in the course of the workman's regular employment.[21]

About one-third of the other states employ this type of test, including Colorado, Florida, and Louisiana.

The states not in one of these categories have other rules. For example, New York follows the *wear and tear* rule, which examines the issue of whether there is "a question in each case as to whether the regular job activity itself entails greater exertion than the ordinary wear and tear of life."[22] Thus, if the injury can be linked to exertion that exceeds the regular demands of ordinary life, it will be compensable.

Nevada has a rather harsh rule excluding coverage for heart cases, which states that "for the purposes of this chapter, coronary thrombosis, coronary occlusion or any other ailment or disorder of the heart and any death or disability ensuing therefrom, shall not be deemed to be an injury by accident sustained arising out of and in the course of employment."[23]

Case Study

> Bob Giant is a radio talk show host. He frequently gets into heated arguments with callers on various political issues of the day. One day Bob gets into verbal altercations with several callers in a row. He gets worked up as he usually does and begins to loosen his tie. During the next call he gets chest pains and collapses. It is later revealed Bob suffered from a heart attack while on the air.

Is Bob Giant's heart attack compensable under the usual exertion rule? It most likely would be compensable if Bob routinely is excited by callers and reacted in his usual manner.

Is Bob Giant's heart attack compensable under the unusual exertion rule? If the state has a statute making only unusual exertion compensable in heart attack cases, then Bob probably would not be able to recover. However, it could be argued that it is unusual for Bob to get angry for a series of phone calls. The stress and anger from this unusual event was greater. If, instead of taking calls, Bob came to work one day and the manager asked him to move some heavy boxes of fan mail into his office, and Bob exerted himself physically and suffered a heart attack, then the injury would most likely be compensable under the unusual exertion rule.

Would Bob Giant's injury be compensable under a New York–type "wear and tear" rule? If in ordinary life Bob is a calm and quiet man and he gets agitated and angry on the air as a part of an act, then the strain put on his heart is greater than that of ordinary life and his injury would be compensable.

If Bob Giant lived in a state that had a no compensation for heart disease rule, he would not be able to collect for his injury.

> NOTE: Avoid asking employees to do strenuous work especially if they are not used to it and especially if you are aware of any possible heart problems that the employee may suffer. It is best to try and avoid possible workers' compensation claims whenever possible.

Compensable Mental Disorders. There are types of injuries that are not solely physical and yet are compensable just the same. These injuries include those that are mental, nervous, psychological, or stress related. The three basic categories of such illnesses are mental strain causing physical injury, physical strain causing mental injury, and mental strain causing mental injury.[24] In the first two categories, there must be physical actions of some sort involved.

Mental Strain Causing Physical Injury. Mental strains can include such emotions as excitement, fright, and anger. For example, a salesclerk who faints and injures her knee after a heated argument with a customer would be able to collect workers' compensation.[25] Usually, cases where mental strain causes physical injury are like the preceding example and occur right away. The harder cases are when the injury occurs later or the mental strain gradually builds up. The injury resulting is similar to cases involving a heart attack.

Case Study

> Michael Martin is a buyer for a large retail store. He is sent to various places around the country to find and order unique designer clothing. He is told by management that the sale he just made with a jewelry designer in Santa Fe has fallen through and this would mean a half-million-dollar loss for the store. Michael cannot sleep or eat for a week. After repeated contacts with the designer, he travels to Santa Fe to continue negotiations. He has never had any heart problems before. He cannot salvage the deal, and in the cab on the way back to the airport he suffers a heart attack. The mental strain of losing the deal and possibly his job caused the physical injury, and he is able to collect workers' compensation.

A person is not eligible to collect workers' compensation if the mental strain is no greater than that of everyday life or if the evidence will not support the case. *Unusual strain* is one of those phrases that can be interpreted to mean different things depending on the state. There are three different standards of unusual strain that are used by the states:

1. Unusual compared with this employee's normal strains

2. Unusual compared with the stress of employment life generally

3. Unusual compared with the wear and tear of everyday nonemployment life[26]

However, state case law and statutes never explicitly specify a definition. There may be 50 different interpretations that may not fall into these three categories. For example, in Arizona, the statute requires that "a mental injury, illness or condition shall not be considered a personal injury by accident arising out of and in the course of employment and is not compensable pursuant to this chapter unless some unexpected, unusual or extraordinary stress related to the employment or some physical injury related to the employment was a substantial contributing cause of the mental injury, illness or condition."[27] Unusual stress here possibly fits into the first or second category.

Physical Strain Causing Mental Injury. If a physical accident causes prolonged trauma or hysteria, then all types of disabilities resulting are covered by workers' compensation. Included in this category are types of neurotic, psychotic, psychosomatic, and depressive mental ailments.[28]

Case Study

Wendy Jones works as a delivery person at Sam's Diner. While she is delivering lunch to a construction site, she is hit on the head with falling debris. She is knocked unconscious. After her hospital stay, Wendy begins to show signs of paranoid schizophrenia. She is examined by a doctor and is diagnosed as having this illness. The schizophrenia is compensable under workers' compensation because she suffered the physical injury at work and the mental condition resulted from that injury.

The types of injuries compensable under this heading are expansive. A preexisting tendency for the condition is not necessary. Some states argue that these types of injuries are compensable as scheduled injuries. Each state in its workers' compensation statute compensates workers' rendered disabled during work with cash wage benefits. Whether it is permanent or temporary and total or partial, there is a schedule set up that lists the parts of the body and the amount each is worth in percentage of weekly wages ranging from 1 percent disability to total. This is in addition to the medical care and hospitalization available under the statute. Someone like Wendy Jones may be rendered totally disabled by a mental disease or problem, but whether this allows her to collect disability payments as well is another issue because an identifiable part of the body has not been injured.

For example, in Delaware there is a catchall clause in the statute, stating:

the Board shall award proper and equitable compensation for the loss of any member or part of the body up to 300 weeks which shall be paid at the rate of 66 ⅔ percent of his weekly wages, but no compensation shall be awarded when such loss was caused by the loss of or the loss of use of a member of the body for which compensation payments are already provided by the terms of this section.[29]

Some injured workers have tried to argue that a mental illness can qualify as a scheduled disability. However, the courts in Delaware interpreted that an organ or tooth as well as a member is a part of the body but a psychological disorder is not and the legislature should have stated that in the statute. Thus, in Delaware a mental illness is not a scheduled disability.[30]

NOTE: Most of the time workers' compensation will be denied if there is a lack of causation based on the evidence.[31]

Mental Strain Causing Mental Injury. In these cases, there does not have to be any physical event or involvement to make the injury compensable. A majority of states have recognized these types of injuries.

Case Study

Vinnie DeLuca is a truckdriver working for a trucking company. One night while driving an 18-wheeler he blacked out. Luckily it was at night on a long, straight highway. Vinnie was not physically hurt but became very nervous whenever he had to go back on the road. He was afraid he would black out again. As a result of the incident, he developed a panic disorder. The mental disorder was compensable under workers' compensation even though the mental blackout caused the panic disorder and no visible physical injuries resulted to any parts of his body.

There are states that will not recognize these types of injuries. In fact, the Florida statute does not include any neurosis caused only by fright or excitement.[32] The other states that will not recognize mental strain causing mental injuries are Alabama, Arizona, Georgia, Kansas, Louisiana, Minnesota, Montana, Nebraska, Ohio, Oklahoma, Rhode Island, and South Dakota.

Compensable Stress-Related Injuries. Under the category of mental strain causing mental injury is stress. The most rapidly growing area of injuries covered by workers' compensation in the past 15 years are stress-related disorders. California leads the way in this area.[33] California has held workers' compensation coverage extends to injuries suffered by a black employee who was discharged because of discrimination and subsequently suffered emotional distress.[34]

It has been said that many stress claims are characterized by "absence of physical injury, little time off work, low medical treatment costs, insignificant retraining costs, but a lot of litigation."[35] California, Maine, Oregon, and New Mexico have passed amendments to their state statutory schemes to make a stress claim harder to prove and have excluded stress-related events in employment such as discharge or transfer.[36] An injury resulting from stress must also occur by accident in the course of and arise out of employment.

Case Example

A school bus driver with a bus filled with children saw an automobile accident and stopped to offer help. The driver suffered psychic trauma brought on by this event, and this was considered a compensable accident under workers' compensation.[37]

There are four levels to compensability for a stress-related claim.

1. Mental strain causes stress gradually, and the stress is not unusual compared to ordinary life or employment. The states that follow this rule are: Arizona, Arkansas, Colorado, Illinois, Maine, Massachusetts, New York, Oregon, South Carolina, Rhode Island, Washington, Wisconsin, and Wyoming.

2. Stress is compensable in cases where it is gradual and unusual. The states that follow this rule are: Hawaii, Indiana, Kentucky, Michigan, New Jersey, and New Mexico.

3. Mental strain causing mental stress is compensable only if the triggering event is sudden. The states with this type of rule are: Maryland, Mississippi, Tennessee, Texas, and Virginia.

4. The only time stress-related injuries are compensable is when there are physical manifestations.[38]

In the following states, compensation is excluded for stress-related injuries of any kind: Florida, Georgia, Kansas, Louisiana, Minnesota, Montana, Ohio, and Oklahoma.

NOTE: Be aware of mental, emotional, and psychological injuries and how your state views them. Make it a point to check your state statute. It may be a good idea as an employer to offer counseling services to employees to nip possible injuries of this type in the bud and also maintain a mentally healthy work force.

How the Law Prohibits Retaliation by the Employer in Most States

In general, an employer is prohibited from discharging an employee for filing a workers' compensation claim. States that have a statute prohibiting retaliatory conduct are: Arizona, Florida, Hawaii, Maine, Maryland, Minnesota,

Missouri, New York, Ohio, Oklahoma, Texas, and Wisconsin. Other states prohibiting retaliation through case law are: Illinois, Indiana, Kansas, Kentucky, Louisiana, Massachusetts, Michigan, Nevada, and Tennessee. Some states have done both, namely California, New Jersey, and Oregon. However, Alabama, Georgia, Mississippi, and South Carolina have neither a statute nor any case law prohibiting retaliation by an employer.

> NOTE: Discharging an employee for filing a workers' compensation claim is forbidden. Never terminate anyone for filing a workers' compensation claim. It is best to avoid even the appearance of a retaliatory act because defending against such an action is time consuming and costly.

Retaliatory Discharge of Nonunion Employees versus Union Employees.

An employee not covered by a collective bargaining agreement who is discharged in retaliation for filing a workers' compensation claim has certain statutory or common law remedies available. In some states the employer can be subjected to both civil and criminal penalties. An employee can sue in civil court for wrongful termination.[39] Other states have statutes prohibiting retaliatory discharge by the employer.[40] The statutes vary in details, and you should check your state statute and comply with its specific statutory requirements.

An employer with a union shop is presented with another issue. Union employees may have remedies for retaliatory discharge under the collective bargaining agreement. The employer should be aware of such a clause. Whether union employees should be limited to those remedies has sparked a division in the courts. On one side the courts have said that employees have the right to other remedies against the employer. On the other side courts have argued that the employee is limited to remedies in the collective bargaining agreement.[41]

> NOTE: If your workplace is unionized, do not assume that the only redress that employees have is in the collective bargaining agreement. You may even want to consult with labor counsel on this issue to take preventive measures.

How an Employer Can Defend Against Retaliatory Discharge Charges.

The employee has the burden of proving retaliatory discharge for filing a workers' compensation claim. The employer will have to go through the expense of defending against such a charge and should be aware of the defenses it may have available.[42]

The defenses available to the employer may include

- Violation of employer's safety policy
- Unexplained tardiness or absenteeism

- Lying as to previous compensation claims
- Physical inability to do the job
- Employee is no longer qualified to perform duties
- The time period for filing a workers' compensation claim has expired (statute of limitations)
- The collective bargaining agreement has limited remedies

Case Example

Ed and Tony are employed by Pepperidge Farm in Connecticut, and each sustained work-related injuries. Both subsequently filed workers' compensation claims. Neither Ed nor Tony returned to work within 12 months of their injuries, and this violated company policy. Ed and Tony filed wrongful discharge actions claiming Pepperidge Farm discharged them for filing workers' compensation claims, and this was illegal according to Connecticut law. Ed and Tony would have to prove through convincing evidence that their employer had a discriminatory intent in discharging them. If the employer's policy on absenteeism was neutrally applied, then Ed and Tony would not be able to win.[43]

However, some states may specify and limit an employer's affirmative defenses. An example of such a statute is the North Carolina Workers' Compensation Act, which states that

Any employer shall have as an affirmative defense to this section the following: willful or habitual tardiness or absence from work or being disorderly or intoxicated while at work, or destructive of an employer's property; or for failure to meet employer work standards not related to the Workers' Compensation Claim; or in malingering; or embezzlement or larceny of employer's property; or for violating specific written company policy of which the employee has been previously warned and for which the action is a stated remedy of such violation.[44]

The best way for the employer to handle retaliatory discharge suits is to avoid them by following well-planned policies consistently and documenting the reasons for a discharge.

Other Forms of Retaliation. Discharge is not the only form of retaliation: the employer may retaliate in other ways against an employee for filing a workers' compensation claim. Employees may experience recriminations from the employer in the form of verbal comments, less desirable work assignments, denial of a raise or promotion, or a change in work duties. However, all forms of retaliation are prohibited as illustrated by the New Jersey statute that provides the following broad prohibition:

[i]t shall be unlawful for any employer or his duly authorized agent to discharge or in any other manner discriminate against an employee as to his employment

because such employee has claimed or attempted to claim workers' compensation benefits from such employer.[45]

In addition, unlawful discriminatory retaliation occurs where a prospective employer refuses to hire a person because he or she has filed a workers' compensation claim while under the employ of another. It also raises an issue of handicap discrimination. Thus, at the time of hire, questions regarding prior claims of this nature should be avoided.

The Fireman's Rule

The fireman's rule bars fire, police, and emergency workers responding to any emergency from suing owners or occupiers of land for injuries due to negligence.[46] The rule protects owners and occupiers of land and can be applied to employers. Any employer who is an owner or occupier of land is shielded from any lawsuit brought by a public employee for negligence who was injured while working in an emergency capacity. The remedy available to the injured worker is workers' compensation. The rationale for such a rule is that in response to an emergency, a firefighter, police officer, or emergency worker subjects himself or herself to any inherent risks and dangers. However, willful or intentional misconduct on the part of the employer/landowner or occupier may provide for a remedy.

Case Example

A police officer responds to an emergency medical call from a donut shop. He arrives at the shop and runs into the kitchen to help the unconscious employee. As he carries the employee on a stretcher to the ambulance, he slips on flour on the floor. The officer injures his foot. He sues the donut shop for negligence.[47]

Can the officer recover damages? No, the fireman's rule bars any recovery in tort brought by the officer. His exclusive remedy is workers' compensation.

Vicarious Liability

An injured worker is barred from filing a suit for negligence against his or her employer and in return is entitled to collect workers' compensation benefits. However, the injured worker can sue a fellow employee for negligence. Some injured employees have nevertheless tried to hold their employers vicariously liable for the wrongful, negligent acts of a coemployee. An employer should be aware of this type of situation. Remember that, generally, workers' compensation is the exclusive remedy, and the employer cannot be held liable for the negligence of an employee. Check your state law and consult with labor counsel to avoid time-consuming and costly litigation. It may be that the court will find that workers' compensation is the only recovery available to the injured employee.

Case Example

Jean has been seeing the doctor employed by her employer during her pregnancy. She has suffered a miscarriage and subsequently sues both the doctor and her employer for negligence and medical malpractice. She claims that her employer is vicariously liable for the acts of the doctor it employs.[48]

Is the negligence action barred by the workers' compensation statute? Workers' compensation is an exclusive remedy, and the conduct of the employer was not intentional or deliberate and therefore falls within the coverage of the Act.

However, an employer can conceivably be found liable for acts of an employee if those acts are willful, deliberate, and intentional.

NOTE: The employer may prevent liability for intentional and deliberate acts if an employer supervises employees properly and keeps the workplace free of tension and turmoil. Again prevention is the best solution. If the employer becomes aware of bad blood between employees or incompetency on the part of an employee, the problem should be solved before any violent or negligent act occurs.

ADMINISTRATIVE PROCEEDINGS AND DETERMINATIONS OF WORKERS' COMPENSATION CLAIMS

Most workers' compensation schemes operate in a similar manner. The state requires the employer to secure workers' compensation insurance. Generally, an injured employee files a claim with the employer's insurance carrier or the appropriate state agency. Workers' compensation cases may be contested or uncontested. The following discussion covers what happens on an administrative level in each of these cases.

How to Handle Uncontested Cases

Uncontested cases are claims that are not challenged by the employer. This decision is solely in the employer's hands. The employer, supervisor, or foreman should be notified of the accident or injury, immediately. If the employee requests medical treatment, it should be promptly provided. Any medical treatment or hospitalization will be covered by workers' compensation. The employer should commence an investigation to decide if the injury is legitimate. At this point, the employer can choose not to challenge the employee's claims, and the employee would be able to collect benefits.

If the employee loses time from work, then workers' compensation benefits kick in. A mere papercut will not involve workers' compensation. An injury that lasts beyond the statutory period will enable the worker to collect cash wage benefits retroactive to the first day lost. The cash wages are equal to a percentage of weekly wages and are calculated by the state. Benefits can be collected for a period of time which is in the statute.

If an employee is disabled by the injury, he or she can collect for that as part of the cash wage benefits. The parts of the body are valued monetarily and are set up in a schedule. The percentage of disability to the part of the body injured is compensable. The disability may be permanent or temporary, partial or total. A sample of a schedule is shown in Exhibit 23.1. Death benefits are available to dependents of the deceased worker. The rate of dependency benefits varies with the number of dependents. Dependents usually include spouse and children and are defined by statute.

Case Study

Susan Smith is employed by Shoe City. At Shoe City the customers usually help themselves to shoes off the racks labeled by size. One night, a customer asks Susan to get her a size 12 women's shoe off the top shelf. Susan stands on a ladder and as she reaches for the box she loses her balance and falls. Susan suffers a broken leg. Her coworkers immediately notify the supervisor who summons an ambulance. Susan is taken to the hospital. She is out of work for two months.

Can Susan collect workers' compensation? Yes, because she was accidentally injured in the course of employment. The insurance company or employer must pay the medical bills and cash wage benefits, including any temporary partial disability benefits.

How to Handle Contested Cases

If an employer investigates an employee's injury and concludes for whatever reason that the claim is not legitimate, then the employee's right to workers' compensation is contested. The employer, in contested cases, has refused to pay benefits based on its investigation or lack of information. While the lack of notice of the injury makes it harder for the employer to investigate possible causes of the injury and determine its legitimacy, recovery is not barred if the employer is not given notice. When the employer has refused to pay benefits, the employee has to initiate and prevail on a claim before benefits can be received.

Filing a Claim. If the employer refuses to pay for medical care or cash wage benefits for whatever reason, the injured worker can file a claim with the state administrative office that handles workers' compensation. The filing of the complaint should be timely. There is usually a statute of limitations on the time for filing a claim. After the claim is filed, there is an investigation whereby the employee is examined by doctors to determine the nature and extent of injuries. Additional evidence can be gathered by both sides at this time as well.

– EXHIBIT 23.1 –

Schedule of Disabilities and Maximum Benefits Exclusive of Amputation and Enucleation, Effective January 1, 1990

PER-CENT	HAND 245 WEEKS	ARM 330 WEEKS	THUMB 75 WEEKS	FIRST 50 WEEKS	SECOND 40 WEEKS	THIRD 30 WEEKS	FOURTH 20 WEEKS	LEG 315 WEEKS	FOOT 230 WEEKS	GREAT TOE 40 WEEKS	OTHER TOE 15 WEEKS	EYE 200 WEEKS	1 EAR 60 WEEKS	2 EARS 200 WEEKS	PARTIAL TOTAL BASED ON 600 WEEKS	PER-CENT
1	2.45 / 242.55	3.3 / 326.70	0.75 / 74.25	0.5 / 49.50	0.4 / 39.60	0.3 / 29.70	0.2 / 19.80	3.15 / 311.85	2.3 / 227.70	0.4 / 39.60	0.15 / 14.85	2 / 198.00	0.6 / 59.40	2 / 198.00	6 / 594.00	1
1½	3.675 / 363.83	4.95 / 490.05	1.125 / 111.38	0.75 / 74.25	0.6 / 59.40	0.45 / 44.55	0.3 / 29.70	4.725 / 467.78	3.45 / 341.55	0.6 / 59.40	0.225 / 22.28	3 / 297.00	0.9 / 89.10	3 / 297.00	9 / 891.00	1½
2	4.9 / 485.10	6.6 / 653.40	1.5 / 148.50	1 / 99.00	0.8 / 79.20	0.6 / 59.40	0.4 / 39.60	6.3 / 623.70	4.6 / 455.40	0.8 / 79.20	0.3 / 29.70	4 / 396.00	1.2 / 118.80	4 / 396.00	12 / 1,188.00	2
2½	6.125 / 606.38	8.25 / 816.75	1.875 / 185.63	1.25 / 123.75	1 / 99.00	0.75 / 74.25	0.5 / 49.50	7.875 / 779.63	5.75 / 569.25	1 / 99.00	0.375 / 37.13	5 / 495.00	1.5 / 148.50	5 / 495.00	15 / 1,485.00	2½
3	7.35 / 727.65	9.9 / 980.10	2.25 / 222.75	1.5 / 148.50	1.2 / 118.80	0.9 / 89.10	0.6 / 59.40	9.45 / 935.55	6.9 / 683.10	1.2 / 118.80	0.45 / 44.55	6 / 594.00	1.8 / 178.20	6 / 594.00	18 / 1,782.00	3
3½	8.575 / 848.93	11.55 / 1,143.45	2.625 / 259.88	1.75 / 173.25	1.4 / 138.60	1.05 / 103.95	0.7 / 69.30	11.025 / 1,091.48	8.05 / 796.95	1.4 / 138.60	0.525 / 51.98	7 / 693.00	2.1 / 207.90	7 / 693.00	21 / 2,079.00	3½
4	9.8 / 970.20	13.2 / 1,306.80	3 / 297.00	2 / 198.00	1.6 / 158.40	1.2 / 118.80	0.8 / 79.20	12.6 / 1,247.40	9.2 / 910.80	1.6 / 158.40	0.6 / 59.40	8 / 792.00	2.4 / 237.60	8 / 792.00	24 / 2,376.00	4
5	12.25 / 1,212.75	16.5 / 1,633.50	3.75 / 371.25	2.5 / 247.50	2 / 198.00	1.5 / 148.50	1 / 99.00	15.75 / 1,559.25	11.5 / 1,138.50	2 / 198.00	0.75 / 74.25	10 / 990.00	3 / 297.00	10 / 990.00	30 / 2,970.00	5
7½	18.375 / 1,819.13	24.75 / 2,450.25	5.625 / 556.88	3.75 / 371.25	3 / 297.00	2.25 / 222.75	1.5 / 148.50	23.625 / 2,338.88	17.25 / 1,707.75	3 / 297.00	1.125 / 111.38	15 / 1,485.00	4.5 / 445.50	15 / 1,485.00	45 / 4,455.00	7½
10	24.5 / 2,425.50	33 / 3,267.00	7.5 / 742.50	5 / 495.00	4 / 396.00	3 / 297.00	2 / 198.00	31.5 / 3,118.50	23 / 2,277.00	4 / 396.00	1.5 / 148.50	20 / 1,980.00	6 / 594.00	20 / 1,980.00	60 / 5,940.00	10
12½	30.625 / 3,031.88	41.25 / 4,083.75	9.375 / 928.13	6.25 / 618.75	5 / 495.00	3.75 / 371.25	2.5 / 247.50	39.375 / 3,898.13	28.75 / 2,846.25	5 / 495.00	1.875 / 185.63	25 / 2,475.00	7.5 / 742.50	25 / 2,475.00	75 / 7,425.00	12½
15	36.75 / 3,638.25	49.5 / 4,900.50	11.25 / 1,113.75	7.5 / 742.50	6 / 594.00	4.5 / 445.50	3 / 297.00	47.25 / 4,677.75	34.5 / 3,415.50	6 / 594.00	2.25 / 222.75	30 / 2,970.00	9 / 891.00	30 / 2,970.00	90 / 8,910.00	15
20	49 / 4,851.00	66 / 6,534.00	15 / 1,485.00	10 / 990.00	8 / 792.00	6 / 594.00	4 / 396.00	63 / 6,237.00	46 / 4,554.00	8 / 792.00	3 / 297.00	40 / 3,960.00	12 / 1,188.00	40 / 3,960.00	120 / 12,756.00	20
25	61.25 / 6,063.75	82.5 / 8,167.50	18.75 / 1,856.25	12.5 / 1,237.50	10 / 990.00	7.5 / 742.50	5 / 495.00	78.75 / 7,796.25	57.5 / 5,692.50	10 / 990.00	3.75 / 371.25	50 / 4,950.00	15 / 1,485.00	50 / 4,950.00	150 / 16,896.00	25
30	73.5 / 7,276.50	99 / 10,308.00	22.5 / 2,227.50	15 / 1,485.00	12 / 1,188.00	9 / 891.00	6 / 594.00	94.5 / 9,378.00	69 / 6,831.00	12 / 1,188.00	4.5 / 445.50	60 / 5,940.00	18 / 1,782.00	60 / 5,940.00	180 / 21,788.00	30
33⅓	81⅔ / 8,084.99	110 / 11,546.00	25 / 2,475.00	16⅔ / 1,649.99	13⅓ / 1,320.01	10 / 990.00	6⅔ / 659.99	105 / 10,971.00	76⅔ / 7,589.99	13⅓ / 1,320.01	5 / 495.00	66⅔ / 6,599.99	20 / 1,980.00	66⅔ / 6,599.99	200 / 34,600.00	33⅓
35	85.75 / 8,489.25	115.5 / 12,202.50	26.25 / 2,598.75	17.5 / 1,732.50	14 / 1,386.00	10.5 / 1,039.50	7 / 693.00	110.25 / 11,575.50	80.5 / 7,969.50	14 / 1,386.00	5.25 / 519.75	70 / 6,930.00	21 / 2,079.00	70 / 6,930.00	210 / 36,330.00	35
40	98 / 10,200.00	132 / 14,322.00	30 / 2,970.00	20 / 1,980.00	16 / 1,584.00	12 / 1,188.00	8 / 792.00	126 / 13,524.00	92 / 9,118.00	16 / 1,584.00	6 / 594.00	80 / 7,920.00	24 / 2,376.00	80 / 7,920.00	240 / 47,280.00	40
45	110.25 / 11,575.50	148.5 / 16,674.00	33.75 / 3,341.25	22.5 / 2,227.50	18 / 1,782.00	13.5 / 1,336.50	9 / 891.00	141.75 / 15,686.25	103.5 / 10,801.50	18 / 1,782.00	6.75 / 668.25	90 / 8,910.00	27 / 2,673.00	90 / 8,910.00	270 / 59,940.00	45
50	122.5 / 13,076.00	165 / 19,251.00	37.5 / 3,712.50	25 / 2,475.00	20 / 1,980.00	15 / 1,485.00	10 / 990.00	157.5 / 18,051.00	115 / 12,141.00	20 / 1,980.00	7.5 / 742.50	100 / 10,416.00	30 / 2,970.00	100 / 10,416.00	300 / 74,100.00	50
55	134.75 / 14,701.50	181.5 / 31,399.50	41.25 / 4,083.75	27.5 / 2,722.50	22 / 2,178.00	16.5 / 1,633.50	11 / 1,089.00	173.25 / 20,622.00	126.5 / 13,590.50	22 / 2,178.00	8.25 / 816.75	110 / 11,546.00	33 / 3,267.00	110 / 11,546.00	330 / 89,430.00	55
60	147 / 16,452.00	198 / 34,254.00	45 / 4,455.00	30 / 2,970.00	24 / 2,376.00	18 / 1,782.00	12 / 1,188.00	189 / 32,697.00	138 / 15,150.00	24 / 2,376.00	9 / 891.00	120 / 12,756.00	36 / 3,564.00	120 / 12,756.00	360 / 106,560.00	60
65	159.25 / 18,327.50	214.5 / 42,256.50	48.75 / 4,826.25	32.5 / 3,217.50	26 / 2,574.00	19.5 / 1,930.50	13 / 1,287.00	204.75 / 35,421.75	149.5 / 16,822.00	26 / 2,574.00	9.75 / 965.25	130 / 14,056.00	39 / 3,861.00	130 / 14,056.00	390 / 124,800.00	65
66⅔	163⅓ / 18,979.33	220 / 43,340.00	50 / 4,950.00	33⅓ / 3,300.01	26⅔ / 2,639.99	20 / 1,980.00	13⅓ / 1,320.01	210 / 36,330.00	153⅓ / 17,406.00	26⅔ / 2,639.99	10 / 990.00	133⅓ / 14,506.01	40 / 3,960.00	133⅓ / 14,506.01	400 / 138,000.00	66⅔
70	171.5 / 20,328.00	231 / 45,507.00	52.5 / 5,197.50	35 / 3,465.00	28 / 2,772.00	21 / 2,079.00	14 / 1,386.00	220.5 / 43,438.50	161 / 18,604.00	28 / 2,772.00	10.5 / 1,039.50	140 / 15,436.00	42 / 4,158.00	140 / 15,436.00	420 / 144,900.00	70
75	183.75 / 31,788.75	247.5 / 54,945.00	56.25 / 5,568.75	37.5 / 3,712.50	30 / 2,970.00	22.5 / 2,227.50	15 / 1,485.00	236.25 / 46,541.25	172.5 / 20,496.00	30 / 2,970.00	11.25 / 1,113.75	150 / 16,896.00	45 / 4,455.00	150 / 16,896.00	450 / 166,500.00	75
80	196 / 33,908.00	264 / 58,608.00	60 / 5,940.00	40 / 3,960.00	32 / 3,168.00	24 / 2,376.00	16 / 1,584.00	252 / 55,944.00	184 / 31,832.00	32 / 3,168.00	12 / 1,188.00	160 / 18,446.00	48 / 4,752.00	160 / 18,446.00	480 / 177,600.00	·80
85	208.25 / 36,027.25	280.5 / 69,283.50	63.75 / 6,311.25	42.5 / 4,207.50	34 / 3,366.00	25.5 / 2,524.50	17 / 1,683.00	267.75 / 59,440.50	195.5 / 33,821.50	34 / 3,366.00	12.75 / 1,262.25	170 / 20,076.00	51 / 5,049.00	170 / 20,076.00	510 / 188,700.00	85
90	220.5 / 43,438.50	297 / 73,359.00	67.5 / 6,682.50	45 / 4,455.00	36 / 3,564.00	27 / 2,673.00	18 / 1,782.00	283.5 / 70,024.50	207 / 35,811.00	36 / 3,564.00	13.5 / 1,336.50	180 / 21,786.00	54 / 5,346.00	180 / 21,786.00	540 / 199,800.00	90
95	232.75 / 45,851.75	313.5 / 84,958.50	71.25 / 7,053.75	47.5 / 4,702.50	38 / 3,762.00	28.5 / 2,821.50	19 / 1,881.00	299.25 / 73,914.75	218.5 / 43,044.50	38 / 3,762.00	14.25 / 1,410.75	190 / 32,870.00	57 / 5,643.00	190 / 32,870.00	570 / 210,900.00	95
100	245 / 54,390.00	330 / 89,430.00	75 / 7,425.00	50 / 4,950.00	40 / 3,960.00	30 / 2,970.00	20 / 1,980.00	315 / 85,365.00	230 / 45,310.00	40 / 3,960.00	15 / 1,485.00	200 / 34,600.00	60 / 5,940.00	200 / 34,600.00	600 / xxxxx	100

Footnote: Hand, or Thumb and First and Second Fingers (on 1 Hand) or 4 Fingers (on 1 Hand)

EXPLANATION: The percent columns on the outside of the chart represent percentage of disability. The remaining columns show this percentage in terms of weeks and total benefits. The top figure in each box represents weeks; the lower figure, dollar benefits.

NEW JERSEY MANUFACTURERS INSURANCE COMPANY
SULLIVAN WAY, WEST TRENTON, N.J. 08628

The Role of the Administrative Law Court and Enforcement Agency.

Since civil courts may take years to hear a case, to have the already overburdened courts handle workers' compensation would be devastating to the injured employee who may need to pay medical bills and have income. Generally, there is a specific state administrative court that handles only workers' compensation claims. An administrative court offers a swift disposition of the case in an informal setting. "Compensation procedure is generally as summary and informal as is compared with an orderly investigation on the merits."[49] Since workers' compensation is liberally construed, the true adversarial nature of a court would hamper the process. Any decision of the administrative court is subject to judicial appellate review.

The state agency that handles such claims is responsible for receiving claims and assigning them to the administrative law court. The report of the National Commission on State Workmen's Compensation Law has identified six primary obligations of the state administrative agency:

1. To take initiatives in administering the act

2. To provide for continuing review and seek periodic revision of both the workers' compensation and supporting regulations and procedures based on research findings, changing needs, and the evidence of experience

3. To advise employees of their rights and obligations and to assure workers of their benefits under the law

4. To apprise employers, carriers and others involved of their rights, obligations, and privileges

5. To assist in voluntary resolutions of disputes, consistent with the law

6. To adjudicate disputes which do not yield to voluntary negotiation[50]

State agencies vary on how they implement workers' compensation systems because economic and social interests vary from state to state. It cannot be stressed enough for you to familiarize yourself with your state workers' compensation scheme.

Describing the Hearing and the Settlement.

The administrative hearing is presided over by an administrative law judge. The hearing is similar to a trial but less formal. The procedure and rules of evidence are relaxed. Each side has an opportunity to present its evidence and arguments to the administrative law judge. The judge decides the case without a jury and renders an opinion as to whether compensation should be granted and to what extent.

Anytime before the hearing the parties can try to settle the case with the approval of the administrative agency. Some states will not allow a compromise settlement for less than the statutory amount. In New York "compensation or benefits due under this chapter shall not be assigned, released or commuted except as provided by this chapter."[51] Even at trial, a lump-sum settlement can be agreed upon. The worker, instead of receiving cash wages and disability, gets a lump sum in fulfillment of the weekly payments.

> NOTE: Just because administrative proceedings are relaxed does not mean they should not be taken seriously. The best way to avoid such problems is to keep the workplace safe for all employees. If you really feel the case is worth contesting, then do so, but remember that the statute is construed liberally and most of the time you will be able only to get the payment decreased instead of dismissed. It is always a good idea to check the statute and consult with counsel to resolve any problems quickly and efficiently. You may even decide the case is not worth disputing.

Remember, a state appellate court can review the decision of the administrative judge if there is an issue of law involved.

COMPLYING WITH FEDERAL COMPENSATION LAWS

Both the federal Longshoremen's and Harbor Workers' Compensation Act (LHWCA) and the Federal Employee Compensation Act provide for separate federal systems of workers' compensation. Each is discussed briefly.

The Longshoremen's and Harbor Workers' Compensation Act

This Act covers longshore employees who suffer disability or death if it results from an injury "occurring upon the navigable waters of the United States (including any adjoining pier, wharf, dry dock, terminal, building way, marine railway or other adjoining area customarily used by an employer in loading, unloading, repairing, dismantling or building a vessel)."[52] The Act also excludes government workers.[53]

The Act was passed in 1927 and is considered a precursor to the state's workers' compensation schemes. The law explicitly states, however, that any recovery for the same injury under another system will be credited to the liability imposed by the law.[54] This means that an injured worker covered under this Act can recover compensation under both the state workers' compensation and federal Longshoremen's Act. However, any money collected from the state will be credited to the federal amount of the award to prevent double recovery.[55] If the injury occurs on land, the state can apply its workers' compensation system even though the federal system may also apply.[56] The employee cannot after receiving a state award go back and try to get a larger federal award.

Case Example

Mel is a longshoreman who was injured when he slipped on the docks. He filed for workers' compensation under the state system and received an award. He is dissatisfied with the amount he received and subsequently files a federal claim for the same injury under the Longshoremen's and Harbor Workers' Compensation Act to see if he could get more money.

Can Mel recover under the LHWCA? No. After he filed with the state, he effectively lost his chance to collect under the federal act. The state law is not preempted.[57] The federal workers' compensation act is intended to provide compensation and avoid employer liability. Thus, tort awards are not recoverable under LHWCA either.[58]

The Federal Employees' Compensation Act

This Act applies to any employee or civil officer employed in any branch of the U.S. government as well as individuals rendering personal service to the United States as a civil officer, District of Columbia employees including pensioned police and fire workers, employees on Wisconsin reservations, jurors of the U.S. government, and workers appointed by the president.[59] Under the system, the United States pays compensation for disability or death of an employee resulting from personal injury in the performance of his or her duty *unless* the injury or death is

- ♦ Caused by willful misconduct of an employee

- ♦ Caused by an employee's intention to bring about the injury or death of himself or herself or of another

- ♦ Proximately caused by the intoxication of the injured employee[60]

The Act also covers employees who are disabled or die and are employed outside the United States in Alaska, and Panama and suffer war risk hazard as a result of capture, detention, or other restraint by a hostile force or individual.[61]

Unlike the Longshoremen's and Harbor Workers' Compensation Act, the Federal Employee's Compensation Act has been interpreted by courts to be an exclusive remedy to employees and preempts state law. This means state remedies are null and void to an injured federal employee and the filing of a claim or issuance of an award under a state scheme will be invalid.[62]

This chapter is intended only to give the employer an idea as to what is involved in workers' compensation. It is best to consult with counsel to address specific areas of inquiry.

SEVEN GUIDELINES FOR HANDLING
A WORKERS' COMPENSATION CLAIM

The following steps are intended to give the personnel professional a brief summary of what to do when questions arise regarding workers' compensation claims. Remember that these claims should be handled thoughtfully and with caution so as not to cause inadvertently additional liability to the company.

1. Familiarize yourself with your state workers' compensation statute and review it on a regular basis.

2. Decide if you come under the act as an employer and obtain the necessary insurance.

3. Keep abreast of safety codes, and remedy any violations immediately. Prevention of workplace accidents is very important.

4. Set up a system of investigation. If faced with a possible contestable claim, be able to investigate it quickly.

5. When an accident occurs in the workplace, have a written policy in place that instructs employees and managers alike as to the proper procedures. Include instructions to seek prompt medical attention, report any accident to immediate supervisor, file a written report on the incident, and interview witnesses.

6. Assess whether the injured individual is a covered employee under the statutory scheme and whether the injury or illness is also covered.

7. Do not discharge, discipline, or otherwise subject an employee who has filed a claim for workers' compensation to adverse employment conditions.

ENDNOTES

1. Arthur Larson, *The Law of Workmen's Compensation*, §1.00 (Matthew Bender).

2. Larson, *Workmen's Compensation*, §1.10.

3. See discussion on the Longshoremen's and Harbor Workers' Compensation Act, 33 U.S.C. §903, *et seq.*, and the Federal Employees Compensation Act, 5 U.S.C. §8101, *et seq.*, on pages 510 and 511.

4. Ohio Rev. Code Ann. §4123.68 (Page's 1991).

5. See N.J.S.A. 34:15-1 to 34:15-6.

6. Larson, *Workmen's Compensation*, §1.10.

7. Corpus Juris Secundum, Workers' Compensation, §35 (West, St. Paul 1987).

8. See *Delker v. Ohio Edison Company*, 47 Ohio App. 3d 1, 546 N.E.2d 975 (1989).

9. Larson, *Workmen's Compensation*, §6.00.

10. *Merrill v. Penasco Lumber Co.*, 27 N.M. 632, 204 P. 72 (1922).

11. See *Travelers Insurance Co. v. Williams*, 378 S.W.2d 110 (Tex. Civ. Ct. App. 1964).

12. Larson, *Workmen's Compensation*, §9.00.

13. *Voight v. Rochester Products Div.*, 125 A.D.2d 799, 509 N.Y. Supp. 2d 909, (1986).

14. *Mangigian v. Franz Warner Assoc. Inc.*, 205 N.J. Super. 422, 501 A.2d 1239 (App. Div. 1984).

15. *Cymbor v. Binder Coal Co.*, 285 Pa. 440, 132 A. 363 (1926).

16. *Constantine v. Sperry Corp.*, 149 A.D.2d 394, 539 N.Y. 2d 499 (1989).

17. Larson, *Workmen's Compensation*, §18.00.

18. *Jecker v. Western Alliance Insurance Co.*, 369 S.W.2d 776 (Tex. Civ. Ct. App. 1963), 371 S.W.2d 904 (Tex. Civ. Ct. App. 1963), *reversing* 362 S.W.2d 137 (1963).

19. Compensability for prothesis is compensable under the statutes of Alaska, California, Indiana, Kentucky, Louisiana, Mississippi, Missouri, New York, North Dakota, Pennsylvania, South Carolina, Vermont, Wisconsin, and Wyoming.

20. Larson, *Workmen's Compensation*, §38.00.

21. Kansas Statutes Annotated, §44-501.

22. *Lerner v. Terry Cole Company*, 245 N.Y.S.2d 565, 566-7 (1963).

23. Nevada Revised Statutes, §616.110(2).

24. Larson, *Workmen's Compensation*, §42.21.

25. See *Christilles v. H. J. Wilson Co.*, 513 So.2d 208 (Fla. Dist. Ct. App. 1987).

26. Larson, *Workmen's Compensation*, §38.64(d)94.

27. Arizona Revised Statutes, §23-1043.01(B).

28. Larson, *Workmen's Compensation*, §42.22(a).

29. Delaware Code Annotated, §2326.

30. See *Burton Transp. Center v. Willoughby*, 265 A.2d 22 (Del. 1970).

31. Larson, *Workmen's Compensation*, §42.22(f). See also *Industrial Comm'n v. Saffeel*, 150 Colo. 41, 371 P.2d 438 (1962), where a 17-year-old who lost three fingers at work wanted to recover for traumatic nervous disorder because he could not get dates and fights with his family.

32. Florida statute §440.02(18).

33. A California study based on the reports submitted by employers found that nine out of ten cases of workers' compensation involved cumulative stress. The claims

were filed by 30- to 49-year-old mostly women and two-thirds held white-collar jobs.

34. See *Tilford v. Monsanto*, 4 I.E.R. Cases (BNA) 1865 (N.D.Cal. 1989).

35. Larson, *Workmen's Compensation*, §42.25(a).

36. *Id.*

37. See *Matter of Wood v. Laidlaw Transit*, 77 N.Y.2d 79 (1991).

38. Larson, *Workmen's Compensation*, §42.25(b).

39. The wrongful discharge claim could be based on a public policy argument; that is, it is against public policy to terminate an employee exercising his or her statutory right under a statute like workers' compensation. *Herring v. Prince Macaroni of New Jersey, Inc.*, 799 F.2d 120 (3d Cir. 1986).

40. States include California, Hawaii, Maine, Maryland, Minnesota, Missouri, New Jersey, New York, North Carolina, Ohio, Oklahoma, Oregon, South Carolina, and Wisconsin.

41. *Baldracchi v. Pratt & Whitney Aircraft Div., United Technologies Corp.*, 814 F.2d 102 (2d Cir. 1987) (allowing common law remedies), and *Johnson v. Hussmann Corp.*, 805 F.2d 795 (8th Cir. 1986) (limiting recovery to the collective bargaining agreement).

42. Defenses include legitimate nonpretextual discharge. See *Axel v. Duffy-Mott Co., Inc.*, 47 N.Y.2d 1, 416 N.Y.Supp. 2d 544, 389 N.E.2d 1075 (1979).

43. See *Chiaia v. Pepperidge Farm, Inc.*, 24 Conn. App. 362, 588 A.2d 652, *appeal denied* 219 Conn. 717 (1991).

44. N.C. Gen. Stat., §97.6.1(c).

45. *Nash v. Oberman*, 498 N.Y.S. 2d 449 (A.D. 2d Dept. 1986).

46. See *Krauth v. Geller*, 31 N.J. 270 (1960).

47. *Rosa v. Dunkin Donuts of Passaic*, 122 N.J. 66 (1991).

48. *Nash v. Oberman*, 498 N.Y.S. 2d 449 (A.D. 2d Dept. 1986).

49. Larson, *Workmen's Compensation*, §77A; this is referred to as the informality principle.

50. See the National Commission on State Workman's Compensation Law, Washington, D.C., 1972.

51. N.Y. Workmen's Compensation, §33 (McKinney's 1965).

52. 33 U.S.C. §903(a).

53. *Id.*

54. 33 U.S.C. §903(e).

55. See *Hong Duong v. W.C.A.B.*, 215 Cal. Rptr. 609 (Cal. App. 4th Dist. 1985). A worker preparing ships in dry dock sustained injuries. He was covered by federal law and state workers' compensation, the court stated, "when dual federal and state coverage is available, simultaneous applications under each act is permitted because the delay in determining whether both or only one of the acts covers injuries incurred in employment arguably overlapping both the state and federal jurisdictions may allow a statute of limitations to run for claims where the applicant files only with an agency. Concurrent jurisdiction allows coverage under both the state and federal acts but no chance of double recovery because an employer's contributions under one will be credited against the other."

56. See *Sunship, Inc. v. Pennsylvania, Pa.*, 447 U.S. 715, 100 S.Ct. 2432, 65 L.Ed.2d 458, *reh. denied* 101 S.Ct. 37, 448 U.S. 916, 65 L.Ed.2d 1179 (1980).

57. See *R. J. Shea v. Texas Emp. Ins. Ass'n.*, 249 F.Supp. 207 (D.C. Tex. 1966), *affirmed* 383 F.2d 16 (5th Cir. 1967).

58. In *Peter v. Hess Oil Virgin Islands Corp.*, 903 F.2d 935 (3d Cir. 1990). Peter injured his lungs by prolonged inhalation to jet fuel while he worked with fuel hoses at the St. Croix refinery. He sued under tort law for damages and won a $1.5 million award. The district court reversed because the LHWCA covered his injuries and the jury award frustrated the congressional intent of the act. The court held, however, that the LHWCA does not preempt any state workers' compensation statute when there is concurrent federal and state jurisdiction. In this case the LHWCA applied and not common law tort.

59. 5 U.S.C. §8101(1)(A)–(F).

60. 5 U.S.C. §8102(a).

61. 5 U.S.C. §8102(b).

62. See *Black v. Frank*, 730 F.Supp. 1087 (S.D.Ala. 1990), which stated "the federal workers' compensation program is a comprehensive scheme of statutory and regulatory enactments specifically intended to exclusively and preemptively remedy an employee for all work related injuries."

24

STRATEGIES FOR HANDLING UNEMPLOYMENT COMPENSATION CLAIMS

Unemployment insurance claims are a routine occurrence for most employers. Such claims are usually viewed as a nuisance. Many employers choose not to contest an unemployment claim or do not take it seriously at their own risk. Employers may elect not to contest an unemployment claim for a variety of reasons: the time and expense, unpleasantness, and the view that it is a trivial matter and/or a cost of doing business. However, there are potential liability issues that a personnel professional must be cognizant of whenever an unemployment claim is filed. Not only will the employer's contributions increase with every claim, but there are far more serious issues present if the former employee claims wrongful discharge or discrimination. The personnel manager should become fully familiar with the local and state laws governing eligibility for benefits and liability issuing from unemployment claims.

When an employee is discharged, the first place he or she will have an opportunity to complain about mistreatment, discrimination, or wrongful discharge is the unemployment insurance benefit office. The single most important concern for the employer when a disgruntled employee is terminated and files for unemployment is that the matter be handled in a straightforward manner with good records to support the reason for the discharge. If the unemployment claim is improperly or carelessly handled, a relatively simple administrative matter can become a major litigation nightmare. This chapter will start with an

516

overview of the unemployment insurance benefit law and handling a basic claim. The chapter will also focus on the pitfalls for employers who do not treat these claims with attention and anticipation of potential civil claims related to the employee's termination.

What you say, or do not say, or how you say it at the unemployment administrative claim level may create serious problems in a future lawsuit based on a claim of discrimination or wrongful discharge claim. Therefore, it is well worth the employer's time and effort to have an organized and well-thought-out policy with regard to unemployment claims. This chapter is intended to aid the personnel professional in establishing and maintaining such a policy.

EXAMINING FEDERAL UNEMPLOYMENT COMPENSATION

Unemployment compensation is a dual federal/state system that, by providing "emergency income" to individuals during periods of unemployment, promotes some degree of financial security to workers and their dependents. The federal aspect of unemployment compensation is dictated by both the Federal Unemployment Tax Act and the federal Social Security Act.[1]

The Social Security Act component governs both federal grants to states and the operation of a federal unemployment trust fund containing the proceeds of state unemployment funds. The Secretary of the Treasury is responsible for investing these funds in specified securities, maintaining proper records, disbursing payments from the funds in specified securities, and disbursing payments from the funds to each contributing state. The provisions of the Federal Unemployment Tax Act (FUTA), part of the Internal Revenue Code, set forth basic standards with which state laws and administrative agencies must comply to qualify for federal unemployment tax contributions and tax credits.[2]

FUTA regulates unemployment tax rates imposed on employers and specifying certain threshold definitions relating to coverage. This law exercises substantial control over the otherwise broad authority the states have with regard to drafting and administering their individual systems of unemployment compensation. States failing to meet FUTA requirements risk losing federal grants for administrative expenses and credit toward federal unemployment taxes for state contributions; as a result of such failure, employers would be faced with higher tax liabilities.

Determining Who Is Covered Under the Federal Unemployment Tax Act

General Provisions. An employer is subject to FUTA regulation and therefore liable for taxes on wages if, during the current or preceding year, it

◆ Paid wages to employees of $1,500 or more in any calendar quarter.

◆ Employed at least one worker for some portion of at least 1 day during each of 20 different, not necessarily consecutive, calendar weeks.

Domestic and Agricultural Employers. Domestic and agricultural labor is excluded from this general definition. Domestic employers are liable for FUTA taxes if they paid cash wages totaling $1,000 or more in any calendar quarter. Agricultural employers are liable if, during the current or preceding year, they either

◆ Paid cash wages of $20,000 or more in any calendar quarter to persons employed in agricultural labor.

◆ Employed 10 or more individuals for some portion of at least 1 day during each of 20 different, not necessarily consecutive, calendar weeks.

Public and Nonprofit Employers. Furthermore, employees of nonprofit organizations and state and local governments are required to be covered by state unemployment compensation laws; failure results in disallowance of the credit against federal tax for all the employers in the state.

Covered Employees. Employers must also be aware that employees out on sick leave, disability leave, vacation, or any other type of excused absence from work continue to be considered "employees" for purposes of determining FUTA status.

Exclusions. There are a number of exclusions from wages for FUTA purposes, including

- Compensation (over) $7,000 (higher in some states) paid to an employee within one calendar year

- Facilities privileges (e.g., discounts, recreation)

- Payments other than cash for services not in the course of the employer's trade or business

- Tips paid directly to the employee by a customer and for which the employee makes no accounting to the employer

- Employer payments on account of sickness/accidental disability, medical or hospitalization expenses, or death of employees/dependents

- Payments to/from certain tax-exempt trusts/annuity plans

- Payments from trust funds for supplemental unemployment benefits

- Holiday gifts of minor value distributed as goodwill

- Moving expense reimbursement deductible by the employee as a business expense

- Payments made under qualified group legal services plan

- Payments that would be deductible to employee under qualified educational assistance or dependent care assistance program

- Value of meals/lodging furnished to employees for employer's convenience

- Payments made by employer to survivor/estate of former employee after the calendar year in which the employee died[3]

HOW TO MEET STATE REQUIREMENTS
FOR UNEMPLOYMENT COMPENSATION

FUTA provides minimum standards with which state systems of unemployment compensation must comply. Each individual state, however, remains free to establish structures falling within the federal requirements. Each state, therefore, sets its own rules regarding eligibility for benefits.

NOTE: All personnel managers must become familiar with the local and state rules governing unemployment compensation claims. The requirements vary from state to state.

We will briefly review the requirements a state must meet in its unemployment compensation scheme.

Establishing Minimum Requirements for a State Unemployment Compensation Plan

The Secretary of Labor will approve a state law that meets the minimum requirements set out in FUTA. Briefly the requirements of most interest to an employer include the following:

♦ There are certain controls over the money received in and withdrawn from the unemployment fund

♦ Compensation shall not be denied to any otherwise eligible individual for refusing to accept new work under any of the following conditions:

  ♦ If the position offered is vacant due directly to a strike, lockout, or other labor dispute

  ♦ If the wages, hours, or other conditions of employment offered are substantially less favorable to the individual than those prevailing for similar work in the locality

  ♦ If as a condition of employment the individual is required to join a company union or to resign from or refrain from joining any bona fide labor organization

- An individual who has received compensation during his or her benefit year is required to have worked since the beginning of such year in order to qualify in his next benefit year

- Compensation shall not be denied to an individual because he is in training with the approval of the state agency

- Compensation shall not be denied solely because the individual resides in another state or he or she files a claim in another state

- Compensation shall not be denied by reason of cancellation of wage credits or total reduction in his or her benefit rights for any cause other than discharge for misconduct connected with his or her work, fraud in connection with a claim for compensation, or receipt of disqualifying income

- No person shall be disqualified solely on the basis of pregnancy or termination of pregnancy

- Compensation is not payable on the basis of services performed by an alien unless that alien is lawfully admitted for permanent residence at the time services are performed, was lawfully present for performance of such services, or was permanently residing in the United States under color of law

- The amount of compensation shall be reduced (but not below zero) in a period where an individual is receiving a pension, retirement pay, annuity, or other payment which is reasonably attributed to that week; in certain circumstances, the state may set the amount of the reduction[4]

The Secretary of Labor must certify each year that a particular state's plan meets the federal requirements. Institutions of higher education are subject to certain exceptions which may be found in the law. See note 4.

Due to the federal regulation in this area, all state plans will share common provisions. However, how the state may implement these requirements or interpret them can vary significantly from state to state. An example of a comprehensive state plan follows.

New York State Unemployment Insurance Coverage. New York State covers most employment within its boundaries with unemployment insurance. In general, employers paying wages in excess of $300 per calendar quarter, substantially within the $1,500 federal threshold, must provide such coverage to its employees.

Domestic employers paying cash wages of $500 or more, again substantially within the $1,000 federal requirement, in a calendar quarter must protect their employees. New York state coverage of agricultural employees is equivalent to that mandated by FUTA.

Nonprofit organizations paying cash wages in excess of $1,000 per calendar quarter or employing 4 or more individuals in 20 different calendar weeks, local and state government employers, and federal government civilian and military employers are required to protect their workers under New York State law.

Like many other states, New York excludes certain categories of employment from unemployment insurance coverage. Employment excluded includes

◆ Certain nonprofit organization employment, namely, ministerial or other duties of a religious nature performed at a place of worship (although such employment may be covered by agreement with the Department of Labor)

◆ Student (and sometimes the student's spouse) work performed for the educational institution being attended

◆ Work-study programs for students under the age of 22

◆ Work, including that during vacations, performed by daytime elementary or secondary school students

◆ Work as a golf caddy

◆ Work performed by individuals under the age of 14

◆ Babysitting performed by individuals under the age of 18

◆ Work by an individual under age 21 for that person's parent, if the business is a sole proprietorship

◆ Work for one's spouse where the business is a sole proprietorship

◆ Work as a sole proprietor or as a partner in a partnership

◆ Self-employment

◆ Nonprofit or government agency work performed by inmates of a custodial or penal institution

◆ Work performed by elected officials

◆ Certain work performed by freelance shorthand reporters, licensed real estate brokers, and sales associates

New York also has limitations on the payment of benefits to certain employees of educational institutions, professional athletes, and illegal aliens.

Defining Eligibility for Unemployment Compensation

The basic requirements regarding eligibility for unemployment compensation are essentially the same in all states. Generally,

◆ Claimants must have worked at least three months

◆ Either with one or several different employers

◆ During the past year

Although the unemployment compensation system was initially intended to provide out-of-work individuals with approximately one-half their average weekly full-time wage for approximately 16 weeks, the trend among the states has been to increase the duration during which benefits are received and decrease the amount of the weekly payments. From time to time the Congress may also authorize extensions of time for receipt of benefits.

Most states require a one- to two-week waiting period before which unemployment benefits may be received by a claimant. It is also common for state unemployment regulations to establish a minimum with regard to the wages earned by the claimant during the prior period of employment. A claimant eligible for benefits must register with a branch of the state unemployment office and thereafter report as directed, either in person or by mail, be available for and able to work, and continue actively and systematically to seek employment throughout a verifiable effort. Partial claims are generally available to workers who earn less than their benefit amount in a given week (usually the difference between the weekly benefit amount and the wages earned) for the duration of the benefit period. An example of eligibility rules follows.

California Eligibility Rules

An unemployed individual in California is eligible to receive unemployment compensation benefits in a given week provided the Director of Employment Development finds

(a) a claim for benefits for that week has been made according to regulations

(b) the individual has registered for work and has continued to report to a public employment office or place approved by the director

(c) the individual was ready, willing, and able to work that week

(d) the individual has been unemployed for the waiting period of one week in accordance with the statute

(e) the individual has searched for suitable work following the instructions of a public employment office[5]

Generally, an individual, to remain eligible to receive unemployment compensation, must continue actively to seek employment in areas for which he or she is trained during the benefit period and keep detailed records of a job search. Claimants are required to seek and be prepared to accept employment paying the "prevailing wage" in their occupation, even though it may be less than what they were previously earning. In addition, claimants may be required to report for periodic eligibility and employability reviews at the state agency. Their employment prospects, job search activities, and continued eligibility for benefits are subject to review at that time.

Defining Employment. "Employment" for purposes of the unemployment compensation law may include the performance of any service for any amount of time (i.e., may be parttime or freelance and not fulltime).[6] For example, an individual is considered employed if he or she works on a straight commission basis and may not receive any money for time spent, spends time during evening or weekends preparing for or actually operating a business, or performs what appear to be minor "favors" for another's business, regardless of payment. Check your state unemployment compensation statute to see how employment is defined.

What benefits does a claimant typically receive? In Ohio, for example, during a claimant's "benefit year," which is 52 consecutive weeks beginning on the day a valid application for benefits is first filed, he or she may generally receive up to 26 weeks of total unemployment benefits (or the equivalent for weeks of partial unemployment). There is a 1-week waiting period.[7] No benefits are payable during this period. Partial benefits may also be available where the claimant works several days a week. Benefit rates vary extensively and are based on a claimant's average weekly wage during the year prior to which the claim was filed.

Determining Employers' Liability for Payments. Employers subject to FUTA are required to pay an unemployment tax on the first $7,000 of each employee's annual wages at a gross rate of 6.2 percent (although a surtax is imposed from time to time). Employers, however, are entitled to subtract certain credits based on the amounts of their contributions to state unemployment insurance funds.

> NOTE: Liability for unemployment insurance tax is solely that of the employer; deductions from employees' wages for this purpose are not permissible.

State unemployment compensation systems may require employers to furnish specified information regarding claimants. New York, for example, contacts each of claimant's employers in the last 52 weeks to determine the actual number of weeks worked, the wages earned, and whether there is any reason benefits should not be awarded.

Unemployment payments by the employer can become substantial where an employer has a high turnover of employees. For this reason and the potential for other litigation alluded to at the beginning of the chapter, we now turn to disqualification of employees and employer strategies when confronted with an unemployment claim.

HOW TO DISQUALIFY A CLAIMANT FOR COMPENSATION

A personnel manager should be trained to respond properly to an inquiry from the state unemployment compensation agency regarding a claim of a former employee for benefits. Typically, the inquiry consists of completing a form and perhaps answering questions from a field investigator.

> NOTE: The employer should designate only certain company officers to respond to an unemployment inquiry to ensure that it is properly handled. Many problems arise when a payroll clerk answers the inquiry and does not know the full circumstances surrounding that particular discharge. In this section we will discuss first the basis for disqualifying a claimant for unemployment compensation. We will then discuss how an inquiry should be answered and what to do if the matter goes to a hearing or an appeal.

Identifying Federal Disqualification Rules

As we noted at the beginning of the discussion on federal regulation in this area, FUTA provides only the basic guidelines for disqualification standards. For example, FUTA provides in its requirements for a state plan that "compensation shall not be denied by reason of cancellation of wage credits or total reduction in his benefit rights for any cause other than *discharge for misconduct connected with his work, fraud in connection with a claim for compensation, or receipt of disqualifying income*" (emphasis added).

FUTA also mandates that workers not be disqualified from the receipt of unemployment compensation in any state because of refusal to accept employment where

♦ The position in question is currently available directly because of a strike, lockout, or other labor dispute

♦ The wages, conditions, or hours surrounding the position are substantially below those prevailing for similar work in the locality

♦ The employment would require the worker to either join a company union or refrain from joining a bona fide union

These are only bare bones rules on who may not be disqualified from receiving compensation. These rules do not give employers much guidance with regard to determining when it is appropriate to oppose a claim for unemployment. However, some states have explicit criteria for disqualification, and case law helps fill in the gaps.

The next example illustrates the dilemma faced by employers in a case of "is she or isn't she [disqualified]" or "did he or didn't he quit"?

Case Study

Wanda Smythe has just been discharged for insubordination, theft, excessive absenteeism, and a bad attitude. She was caught with company-bought supplies as she was leaving work as a payroll clerk. She had been employed at Cookies, Inc., for over five years.

Wanda was not a model employee. She had a history of tardiness and absenteeism, which had grown progressively worse in the past six months. Whenever her supervisor tried to discipline her or correct her errors, Wanda would become abusive to him and sometimes use foul language. The company tolerated this behavior until she was suspected of taking company supplies, including baking ingredients. The company had been experiencing a sharp rise in missing flour, shortening, and chocolate jimmies. She was the last to leave one day, so she thought, when the company president met her in the parking lot. Wanda had a large carton which the president asked to see. She refused and was abusive to him.

He fired her on the spot. Wanda filed for unemployment compensation the next day. The unemployment field investigator called Cookies, Inc., and asked the reason for her termination. Susie, the other payroll clerk, advised the unemployment office that Wanda was dismissed for "talking back to the boss" and for stealing.

Will Wanda receive unemployment compensation? Possibly. The company had at least four reasons to terminate Wanda's employment. However, the payroll clerk, Susie, only gave two reasons, one vague and the other based on circumstantial evidence. In this instance, all valid reasons for termination should be stated in the initial response to the unemployment agency. The charge of theft is not proved since the contents of the box were never seen by the president. Insubordination, alone, may or may not be sufficient misconduct to disqualify Wanda for benefits. Excessive absenteeism may be sufficient in many cases; however, it was tolerated by the company in Wanda's case for many years and is therefore not enough to disqualify Wanda now. Her bad attitude was also tolerated for a long time, and it will be difficult for the agency to assess, so it is unlikely that it is enough to disqualify Wanda.

> NOTE: All inquiries regarding unemployment claims should be answered by a company officer who has all the facts; all valid reasons relied upon for a discharge should be provided to the unemployment agency.

In this example, an organized response to the agency's inquiry could have resulted in a much stronger case for disqualification of the former employee's claim. A personnel officer who had all the facts should have responded, specifying all the grounds for termination. The company could address the problem of the company's apparent acquiescence to Wanda's bad attitude and excessive absenteeism by explaining that in the past six months, it had increased and become intolerable and her abusive confrontation with the president was the final blow. In addition, the alleged theft incident should have been handled first by the president insisting on seeing the contents of the box, preferably with a witness, and/or having a company policy that require employees to permit inspection of all bags or packages upon leaving the premises. If such a policy were in place, Wanda could have been terminated for violation of a company policy. Either or both of these factors would have strengthened the company's position and may have disqualified Wanda from receiving unemployment compensation benefits.

> NOTE: The failure to provide all valid reasons relied upon for a termination could present problems at a later unemployment proceeding or civil action based upon the discharge. To add new reasons for a discharge may be seen as inconsistent and casts doubt upon the legitimacy of any of the reasons. This is particularly dangerous in a later discrimination claim, where inconsistent or additional reasons for a discharge may give the appearance of pretext designed to mask the true discriminatory reason.

Determining State Disqualification Standards

Using the minimum guidelines set by FUTA, every state has developed its own standards for determining eligibility or noneligibility of a claimant. The following discussion highlights typical disqualification standards. We cannot stress enough that these standards and the type of conduct that constitutes disqualification vary from state to state, and you, as the personnel professional, must be familiar with the applicable rules for your locale.

Six Basic State Rules of Disqualification.

1. "Voluntary quit" without good cause.

2. Discharge for misconduct.

3. Failure to apply for or to accept suitable employment.

4. Participation or interest in a labor dispute that causes a stoppage of work (although benefits are usually suspended or postponed for the duration of the work stoppage, rights to unemployment compensation are neither canceled nor reduced). Generally, the labor dispute disqualification does not include lockouts on the theory that employees should not be penalized by the actions of employers. State regulations concerning this particular topic vary widely and thus should be closely scrutinized where applicable.[8]

5. Receipt of certain other forms of unemployed benefits such as dismissal pay, social security benefits, workers' compensation, or retirement benefits. Severance pay is not always a bar to eligibility for benefits.[9]

6. Various types of fraud.

An example of disqualifying events follows.

Texas Disqualifying Events

A claimant in Texas may be denied benefits for failing to meet the basic qualifying employment standards just described. In accordance with FUTA, Texas may withhold benefits under other specified circumstances, such as:

1. *Voluntary quit.* A claimant who quit his or her employment without good cause is disqualified from receiving benefits.

2. *Misconduct.* Loss of employment due to misconduct in connection with that job is grounds for disqualification. Disqualification continues until the individual returns to work and works for six weeks or earns wages equal to six times the weekly benefit amount.

3. *Job Refusal.* Refusal without good cause to accept a position or apply for available suitable work and which offers the prevailing wage for that kind of work is grounds for denial of benefits.

4. *Labor Disputes.* Job loss due to stoppage of work or other industrial controversy suspends rights to unemployment insurance, unless it is shown to the commission that the individual was not participating, financing, or directly involved in the labor dispute. Failure to cross a picket line is considered participating in a labor dispute.[10]

5. *Remuneration.* The individual is receiving or has received remuneration in the form of wages, workers' compensation benefits under any state or federal law, and social security or similar payments under an act of Congress.

6. *Education.* The individual has left employment to attend an established educational institution.

7. *Pension.* The individual is receiving governmental or other pension or retirement pay.

8. *Communicable disease.* The individual has been discharged for refusal to serve anyone who has a communicable disease even though facilities to preclude infection of claimant with contracting the communicable disease were provided by the employer.

9. An individual who has an involuntary work-related reason of an urgent, compelling, or necessary nature to separate from employment shall not be disqualified from unemployment.[11]

UNDERSTANDING THE IMPORTANCE OF AN ADMINISTRATIVE HEARING AND DETERMINATION IN UNEMPLOYMENT PROCEEDINGS

In general, a claimant determined to be eligible and not disqualified from receiving unemployment compensation will not receive notice of such a favorable determination other than receipt of actual benefits. The claimant's prior employer will usually be notified of such a determination and may request a hearing on the claim. Similarly, a claimant denied benefits (e.g., because of a voluntary quit without good cause or other disqualifying event) will be notified and may request a hearing examining the accuracy of the determination and is entitled to be represented by an attorney or other person.

How to Make Effective Use of the Unemployment Proceedings

The unemployment proceedings in most states allow both the employer and the former employee to appear before an impartial referee with both testimony and documentary proof related to the case. Relevant documentary evidence would include the employee's time records (or sign-in sheets), periodic performance evaluations, written warnings to the employee, written complaints about the employee from others, and the like. Testimony of supervisors, coworkers, or outside individuals who can attest to the claimant's wrongdoing help substantiate an employer's position that an employee was, indeed, discharged for good cause or because of misconduct. Similarly, production at the hearing of documentary or testimonial proof relating to any of the other disqualifying events can facilitate a determination in the employer's favor. An administrative hearing provides a forum for the production of evidence; an employer is well advised to take advantage of this opportunity to prove its case and avoid the need to return with relevant evidence, which can potentially be costly and time consuming.

In Michigan, for example, such hearings take place before impartial referees. The interested parties are afforded the opportunity for a fair hearing. The referee can hear and decide cases of redetermination as to the rights of the claimant or the liabilities of the employer. The referee must make a decision within 60 days setting forth findings and reasons.[12] Both parties are entitled to inspect any documents relative to the particular case prior to the hearing and may present readily available or subpoenaed witnesses and documents to the referee. Parties to a hearing may also cross-examine opposing parties and request adjournments for good reason.

Reviewing Administrative Determination

The procedure following administrative determination of eligibility for benefits varies from state to state. The procedure in Michigan is typical and is as follows. Either the claimant or the employer, if they were present or represented at the hearing and disagree with the decision of the impartial referee, may file an appeal with the Board of Review. The Board can review the determination on previous and additional evidence.

An oral hearing will be conducted by the Board if the interested party makes an application to the Board and it is approved by two or more members. Denial of an oral hearing does not mean the case is over. Under some circumstances, a written argument will be granted. If neither is done, the Board decides the case on the record of the referee. Its decision need not give reasons and must be rendered within 60 days. The Board of Review serves the right to reopen or review a prior decision after the 30 day appeal period has expired.[13]

The decision is otherwise final unless the claimant seeks judicial review. This means the claimant can appeal his or her case to a county circuit court within 30 days of the mailing of the decision. Further appeals to the state appeals courts may follow.

Impact on Related Employment Claims: Res Judicata and Collateral Estoppel

Both employers and employees must keep in mind that the outcome of an unemployment compensation hearing and/or appeal is likely to affect subsequent actions surrounding an employee's termination. Although the determination of whether or not a claimant is entitled to unemployment benefits arising from the administrative proceedings involves relatively little money, it may be binding upon the parties in subsequent lawsuits focusing upon state or federal anti-discrimination provisions, employment-at-will (where applicable), or any other bars or vehicles to actions regarding dismissal.

The doctrines of res judicata (claim preclusion) and collateral estoppel (issue preclusion) set forth the principles upon which subsequent litigation of facts or issues previously determined in administrative unemployment proceedings are likely to be barred. Under the doctrine of res judicata, subsequent actions regarding the same claim between the same parties are absolutely barred where a valid, final judgment has already been rendered on the merits.[14] Similarly, collateral estoppel bars relitigation of previously litigated issues necessary to the outcome of the first action.[15]

Courts have consistently held that the doctrines of res judicata and collateral estoppel are applicable in administrative as well as judicial contexts. Preadjudication issues frequently arise in cases regarding a disability and workers' compensation.[16] The U.S. Supreme Court has specifically stated that where an administrative agency, acting in a "judicial" capacity, has already rendered a decision regarding a disputed question of fact where the parties had an opportunity to litigate, courts deem that decision valid and binding.[17] Similarly, the Supreme Court more recently held that a New York State Division of Human Rights decision upheld by a state court prohibited the claimant from bringing a federal action under Title VII.[18]

NOTE: Unemployment compensation proceedings are administrative and may be subject to the rules of res judicata and collateral estoppel.

Case Example

In an Iowa case, a dismissed employee was denied unemployment benefits when it was determined that she had left her position voluntarily and without good cause.[19] The denial was upheld on appeal, and the employee brought an action in federal court alleging that she had been discriminatorily discharged on the basis of sex. The employer moved to dismiss the action on the grounds that the doctrine of collateral estoppel prohibited an allegation of discharge since the issue had already been litigated and resolved in the administrative proceeding. The court agreed with this analysis, granting summary judgment and expressly stating that "the Supreme Court [had recently] . . . emphatically reaffirmed [that] . . . collateral estoppel and res judicata are directly applicable to actions brought under [a civil rights statute]. In the absence of countervailing considerations or policy arguments peculiar to . . . Title VII, therefore, the Court deems it appropriate to accord collateral estoppel effect to the factual findings of the [unemployment] department hearing officer. Since such findings are from the sole underlying premise of, and are thus dispositive of, plaintiff's civil rights claims," the court ruled in the employer's favor.[20]

Case Example

In another case, a federal court ruled that the doctrine of res judicata barred a claimant from relitigating the reason for his discharge where it had already been disposed of in an administrative proceeding before the Nevada State Personnel Advisory Commission. The court held that under res judicata, the prior administrative order was "conclusive of the rights of the parties in any litigation on the same claim" and collateral estoppel rendered conclusive an agency determination in any subsequent litigation on the same or different issue.[21]

How These Doctrines Affect Employers. The cases just described illustrate how the doctrine of res judicata and collateral estoppel operate with respect to agency determination in favor of employers; the principles serve to bar former employees denied unemployment compensation from relitigating the issue in another forum. However, employers must also realize that they, too, are subject to these legal principles. For example, if an employer unsuccessfully contests an issue of fact in an administrative unemployment forum that may be predisposed toward the claimant, the employer could be barred from relitigating that issue in a later action. Issues of fact that would be relevant to unemployment insurance proceedings include whether (1) there was just cause for termination, (2) warnings had been issued to the employee regarding his or her performance, and (3) the employee had been adequately made aware of company policies.

In general, employees filing for unemployment insurance benefits are favored and are thus likely to receive compensation. Without application of the doctrines of res judicata and collateral estoppel, an employee awarded benefits after being found to have been discharged without "good cause," for example, would then be able to use the unemployment determination to allege other violations, such as age or sex discrimination, relating to unlawful dismissal. One defense an employer may have in such an action might be negotiation of an agreement between the company and the departing employee whereby the employer agrees not to contest an application for unemployment insurance benefits and both parties agree not to use any related administrative determinations for any other purpose in any other forum. However, employers are urged to verify applicable state laws regarding enforceability of such agreements as well as those concerning the conclusiveness of administrative decisions.

TWO RECENT DEVELOPMENTS IN SUPPLYING BENEFITS

Two recent developments—the enactment of the Emergency Unemployment Compensation Act of 1974 and the growth of interstate coverage agreements—have made benefits available under special circumstances.

The Emergency Unemployment Compensation Act of 1974

In 1974, the Emergency Unemployment Compensation Act was passed to provide federal supplemental benefits to individuals who exhaust their rights to regular and extended benefits. Under the Act, state benefit periods are "triggered on" when the unemployment rate in either the nation or the state exceeds certain preset high levels; the periods "trigger off" when the rate of insured unemployment in the state averages less than (5) percent over a consecutive 13-week period.

From time to time there is proposed legislation to extend benefits past the 26-week period. Federal and state laws should be reviewed periodically for any procedural or substantive changes.

Interstate Reciprocal Coverage Agreements

In recent years, many states have entered into reciprocity arrangements to provide for workers who do not fall squarely within the jurisdiction of a single state for unemployment compensation purposes. States involved in such agreements determine jurisdiction by considering the location of an employee's actual service and activities, residence, the base of operations, and the place of employee control or direction. The employer of such an "interstate worker" can elect to have all of that employee's activities covered in any state in which any part of the services are performed, the worker has a residence, or the employer maintains a place of business that has a reasonable relation to the employee's services.

However, employees will not be permitted to collect from two states for the same period of unemployment.[22]

A GUIDE TO RESPONDING
TO UNEMPLOYMENT CLAIMS

This chapter has provided you with a review of the general unemployment compensation scheme and what pitfalls to be wary of when confronted with a claim for unemployment compensation. As noted at the outset of the chapter, these claims are not to be treated as trivial matters. The following guidelines sum up the discussion and serve as a quick refresher for handling unemployment claims.

1. Ensure that all claims for unemployment compensation are handled by an authorized company official who is familiar with the facts of the particular dismissal.

2. Be familiar with all the facts and the company's position with regard to each dismissal prior to responding to inquiry from the unemployment agency.

3. Be consistent with the reasons for the dismissal and provide all valid reasons for the dismissal that were relied upon.

4. Maintain adequate records to support the decision for the dismissal. Provide only the necessary information to the unemployment agency to support the reason(s) for dismissal.

5. If there is a hearing, come prepared with documentary evidence as well as witnesses, if any. Have present the company official who dismissed the employee. Be aware that the hearing officer may take hearsay evidence.

6. While many such claims may be handled by an experienced human resource professional, if there is an issue of discrimination or wrongful discharge, involve the company attorney at an early stage of the unemployment proceeding. What you do at the unemployment agency level may be determinative of the issues in a later employment-related civil action.

7. If the company elects not to oppose an unemployment claim and other potentially serious claims are present, the company should consider a modest settlement that includes a release of *all* employment-related claims. An agreement not to oppose an unemployment claim in exchange for a release of all other claims, without other consideration, may not be enforceable in some jurisdictions.

ENDNOTES

1. See 26 U.S.C. §3301, *et seq.*, and 26 U.S.C. §3101, *et seq.*

2. See 26 U.S.C. §3304.

3. 26 U.S.C. §3306(b).

4. See 26 U.S.C. §3304(a). Note that not all requirements are discussed in the text. For further information, please refer to the section cited.

5. California Labor Code Ann., §1253.

6. New York is one state that uses this definition of employment. N.Y. Labor Law §2(7) (McKinney's 1986)

7. Ohio Rev. Code Ann., §4141.29(B) (Page's 1991).

8. For example, in New York, employees who cease working due to a labor dispute such as a strike are ineligible to receive unemployment compensation for the first seven weeks of the work stoppage. Thereafter, employees may begin to receive the benefits. New York Labor Law, §592, but see New Jersey law that denies benefits to anyone engaged in a labor dispute including strikes and lockouts. N.J.S.A. 43:21-5(d).

9. See *Dingleberry v. Board of Review, Dept. of Labor and Industry,* 154 N.J. Super. 415, 381 A.2d 809 (App. Div. 1977).

10. Contrast this with New York, which has the practice of awarding unemployment compensation to strike participants after an initial delay of 7 weeks. This is unique; the majority of states do not permit participants in labor disputes to draw benefits absent extenuating circumstances. See note 8.

11. Texas Labor Code Ann., §5221b-3 (West 1991).

12. Michigan Comp. Laws Ann., §421.33 (West 1983).

13. Michigan Comp. Laws Ann. §421.35 (West 1983).

14. *Brown v. Felsen,* 442 U.S. 127 (1979).

15. See, for example, *Anthan v. Professional Air Traffic Controllers Organization,* 672 F.2d 706, 709 (8th Cir. 1982). In *Anthan,* the court delineated several standards for the application of collateral estoppel:

    (a) The issue must be identical to the one in a prior adjudication.

    (b) There must have been a final judgment on the merits.

    (c) The estopped party was a party or is in privity with a party to the prior adjudication.

    (d) The estopped party was given a full and fair opportunity to be heard on the adjudicated issue. *Id.* at 709.

16. *Ryan v. New York Telephone,* 478 N.Y.S.2d 823, 62 N.Y.2d 494 (Ct. App. 1984).

17. *U.S. v. Utah Construction & Mining Co.*, 384 U.S. 394 (1966).

18. *Kremer v. Chemical Construction Corp.*, 456 U.S. 461 (1982).

19. *Gear v. City of Des Moines*, 514 F. Supp. 1218 (S.D. Iowa 1981).

20. *Id.* at 1224.

21. *Snow v. Nevada Department of Prisons*, 543 F.Supp. 752, 756-7 (D.Nev. 1982).

22. See, for example, *McLaughlin v. Board of Review, Unemployment Compensation Commission*, 7 N.J. Super. 12, 71 A.2d 650 (1950) *citing* N.J.S.A. 43:21-5(f).

25

A GUIDE TO CLOSING OR RELOCATING A FACILITY

This chapter addresses what the employer must do when it has decided that a plant or facility is no longer a viable operation in its current location. The decision may be simply to close the plant, institute a major layoff, relocate the operations to another location, and/or consolidate the operations with those at another location. All these decisions may result in the loss of employment for a significant number of workers.

The federal government has joined several states in governing the employer's decision to close or relocate a plant or facility. Federal law, the Worker Adjustment and Retraining Notification Act[1] (WARN), creates a uniform law that all employers who meet the basic threshold criteria for coverage must comply with and has few exceptions. However, there are varying state laws which must also be considered as well as the presence of a collective bargaining agreement for unionized employees.[2] This chapter discusses the employer's obligations involved in closing or relocating a facility and suggests steps to avoid liability and ensure compliance with the laws.

HOW THE WORKER ADJUSTMENT AND RETRAINING NOTIFICATION ACT AFFECTS CLOSINGS OR LAYOFFS

Employers have certain obligations owed, under federal law and some states' laws, to their employees when faced with a decision to close a facility or lay off large numbers of employees. For example, WARN requires employers to provide 60 days' advance written notice of plant closings and layoffs. The Act imposes strict notification requirements on employers in an attempt to alert the local community, employees, and labor organizations to a closing or mass layoff.

Upon its enactment, it was thought that WARN would aid in preventing some closings or layoffs by encouraging the employees, union, and communities to work with the employer to find an alternative to the closing or layoff. However, such an effort on the part of the employer or the affected parties is not required under the law. WARN raises many questions and problems while solving little. This chapter reviews the provisions of the Act and what it means to employers contemplating a shutdown or mass layoff.

The Scope of the Act

WARN provides specific requirements that covered employers must follow in the event of a decision to close the facility or layoff significant numbers of employees.

The Notice Requirement. All employers do not have to comply with WARN. The 60-day notice requirement applies to

- Employers of 100 or more full-time employees
- Employers of 100 or more employees (including part-time employees) who in the aggregate work at least 4,000 hours per week (exclusive of overtime hours)

NOTE: Employees laid off more than 90 days prior to the triggering event are not included in the total number of employees for purposes of triggering the employer's responsibility under WARN.[3]

Triggering Events. Events that trigger the notice requirement are

- Plant closings, permanent or temporary
- Layoffs that exceed 6 months
- A reduction in hours of work of more than 50 percent during each month of any 6-month period

NOTE: The triggering event must have been ordered by the employer. Where the closing is ordered by an entity not the employer, no liability incurs to the actual employer.[4] But government-ordered closings are not always exempt from the requirements of WARN.[5]

Notice must be given if *50 or more* employees (excluding part-time employees) at one site of employment are to lose their jobs due to a *permanent or temporary* plant shutdown during any 30-day period.

Notice of a *layoff* must be given if *50 or more* employees (excluding part-time employees) will lose employment *and* if the affected workers constitute at least 33 percent of the employees. Layoffs affecting at least 500 employees (excluding part-time employees) must be accompanied by 60 days' notice.

Who Must Receive Notice. WARN identifies who must receive notice of a plant closing or mass layoff. The affected employee, if not represented by a labor organization, must receive individual notice of the event. In all other cases, written notice must be provided to the designated representative of the affected employee.

Notice must also be given to the state dislocated worker unit, if any, and the chief elected official of the local government where such closing or layoff is to occur. The purpose of notice to community officials and agencies is to encourage a cooperative effort to find a means of avoiding the closing or layoff.

Who Must Provide Notice. In most cases, upon the occurrence of a triggering event, the employer at the time of the event is responsible for providing timely notice to employees, labor organizations, and the community. However, in some cases it may not be quite clear who is responsible, and therefore liable, regarding the proper notice.

For example, in the case of a sale of part or all of an employer's business, the seller is responsible for providing notice for any plant closing or mass layoff up to and including the effective date of the sale. After the date of the sale, the purchaser is responsible for providing such notice. Under WARN, any person who is an employee of the seller shall be considered an employee of the purchaser immediately after the sale.

Also responsible for providing notice under WARN, in appropriate circumstances, is the parent corporation in the event that its subsidiary has failed to provide proper notice of a plant closing or mass layoff. The issue of whether a subsidiary is to be treated as a separate employer or as part of its parent depends upon the subsidiary's "degree of independence." Factors considered in this analysis include the following:

- Common ownership
- Common directors and/or officers
- De facto exercise of control
- Unity of personnel policies emanating from a common source
- Dependency of operations[6]

Case Example

Fasteners, Inc., a division of International Fasteners Corporation, had employed 110 full-time employees until yesterday. The employees are represented by the Buttoners Union, which alleges that Fasteners and its parent, International, failed to provide the requisite 60-day notice of the plant closing. The union believes that Fasteners, alone, will be unable to pay any judgment awarded under WARN, so it brought suit against Fasteners and International for failure to provide proper notice.

International, as the parent corporation of Fastener, is liable for Fastener's failure to give 60 days' notice if it has sufficient control over Fastener as determined by examination of the factors specified in the regulations. In addition, the court utilized the "single-employer" test which considers the same factors set out in the Department of Labor regulations. Here, the companies shared the same president and same secretary-treasurer, and the subsidiary's general manager was the son of the president. Also, labor relations were centrally controlled because the president and secretary-treasurer, as directors of the parent, made the decision to close the subsidiary, which was the "most critical policy decision in terms of control of labor relations." There was evidence that the decision to close the plant was in the best interests of both the parent and subsidiary. It is a question of economic reality. In the example, the court found that the parent corporation exercised de facto control of the operations of the subsidiary and was therefore liable for the subsidiary's alleged violation of WARN.[7]

> NOTE: It is not enough for parent corporations to strictly adhere to corporate formalities to avoid liability for a subsidiary's violation of WARN. WARN is remedial in nature, and a parent is liable if it exercises control in fact over the operations of the subsidiary.

Identifying Events Excluded from WARN

No employment loss has occurred if the closing or layoff is the result of the relocation or consolidation of an employer's business *and*, prior to the closing or layoff,

♦ The employer offers to transfer the employee to a different site within a reasonable commuting distance with no more than a 6-month break in employment,

♦ The employer offers to transfer the employee to any other site regardless of distance with no more than a 6-month break, and the employee accepts within 30 days of the offer or the closing or layoff, whichever is later.

Reduction of Notification Period. An employer may be able to avoid liability for failing to meet, in part or in full, the notice period requirement if it satisfies one of the following exceptions.

"Faltering Business" Exception. An employer may shut down a site of employment before the conclusion of the 60-day notice period if the following conditions are met:

♦ At the time that notice is required the employer is *actively* seeking capital in business, which, if obtained, would enable the employer to avoid or postpone the shutdown, and

♦ The employer, in good faith, reasonably believed that giving notice would have interfered with acquiring the needed capital or business.

The "faltering business" exception is extremely difficult to assess and is expected to generate a significant amount of litigation.

"Unforeseeable Business Circumstances" Exception. Additionally, an employer may shut down its facility or lay off employees before the conclusion of the notice period if the closing or layoff is caused by business circumstances that were not reasonably foreseeable. The "unforeseeable business circumstance" exception includes natural or financial disasters.

Employers relying on the foregoing exceptions are requested, under WARN, to give as much notice as is practicable and to provide a brief statement of the basis for the reduced notice period.

NOTE: It is prudent that notice be given as soon as the employer can without doing harm to the business. The employer should be prepared to support any decision to withhold or delay notification.

Other Exceptions. Furthermore, the Act does not apply to a plant closing or mass layoff if the closing

– Is of a temporary facility
– Is the result of the completion of a particular project and employees were aware that their employment was limited
– Constitutes a strike or lockout not intended to evade the Act's requirements

For example, temporary job sites such as construction sites or limited-purpose projects performed outside of the employer's usual place of business are not subject to the notice requirements under WARN.

NOTE: The Act does not require an employer to serve written notice when permanently replacing an economic striker under the terms of the National Labor Relations Act.

Circumstances Under Which WARN May Apply

The following situations may be subject to the Act.

A Change in Circumstances. A layoff that was initially announced to be one of 6 months or less, so that WARN did not apply, but that extends beyond the 6-month period will be treated as a loss of employment under the Act. However, the Act exempts certain of these layoffs from the 60-day notice requirement. For example, where a layoff is caused to extend beyond 6 months by business circumstances not reasonably foreseeable at the time of the initial layoff, notice must be given at the time it becomes foreseeable that a layoff beyond 6 months will be required. Such business circumstances include unforeseeable changes in price or costs.

Single versus Multiple Facilities. If an employer, who has a single site but several separate departments, lays off 30 employees from Department A and 30 employees from the separate and unrelated Department B, WARN may apply.

Employers with diversified facilities should be aware that liability may be incurred where employment losses for two or more groups at a single site of employment, each of which is less than the threshold number of affected employees, when aggregated exceed the threshold *and* occur within a 90-day period. This provision raises numerous issues involving what constitutes a "single site" and whether the employment losses are the result of separate and distinct actions or causes.

If the employer maintains separate facilities, but they are closely related geographically and in purpose, the job losses at these sites may also be aggregated for the purposes of WARN.

NOTE: An employer will not be held liable if it demonstrates that the employment losses are the result of separate and distinct causes and *not* an attempt to evade the Act's requirements.

Case Example

The Blackstone Mining Co. operates two mines and a preparation plant in Buck County. The company had 110 employees at Mine A and 40 employees at Mine B. It also maintained a companywide seniority list for all employees for purposes of layoff and bumping. The employees are represented by the United Mine Workers Union. The company combined certain mining operations that resulted in the elimination of 57 positions in Mine A. Under the company's bumping policy, 43 Mine A workers and 14 Mine B workers were dismissed. Prior to these layoffs, the company knew that fewer than 50 workers at Mine A would be dismissed and did not send a 60-day notice to these workers or the union.

Did the company's dismissal of a total of 57 employees from these two separate mines constitute a plant closing or mass layoff under WARN, thereby requiring 60 days' notice?

In this case, the court said no.[8] The elimination of 57 positions during a layoff by a single employer did not trigger the 60-day notice requirement under WARN. The threshold requirement that 50 employees suffer loss of employment at a single site was not met. In this example, although 57 positions were eliminated from Mine A, only 43 employees at that site were laid off. The other 14 employees from Mine A "bumped" 14 workers from Mine B. Thus the 14 workers from Mine B who were laid off are not counted toward the threshold requirement. Where such cross-plant bumping rights exist, it is not the total number of employees who lose their jobs, but the number at a particular site that determines whether the employer is subject to the WARN requirements.

HOW WARN IS ENFORCED

WARN is enforceable only through civil actions brought by an aggrieved employee, the affected community, or appropriate labor organization. The Department of Labor has no role in administering or ensuring compliance with the Act.[9] It is up to the individual employee, his or her community, or his or her union to seek remedies for a violation under WARN in a civil action against the employer. Thus it is anticipated that relatively few individual cases will be brought under WARN due to the expense of litigation and the limited recovery. However, the potential for class actions and liability for attorneys' fees should be a sufficient basis for concern on the part of all covered employers.

Incurring Penalties

The employer who fails to provide the requisite notice may be liable to each aggrieved employee for

- Back pay for each day of violation
- Benefits under an employee benefit plan, including cost of medical expenses
- Attorneys' fees to prevailing party
- Punitive damages[10]

Liability for back pay and benefits is based on the period of violation up to 60 days, but for no more than one-half the number of days an employee was employed. Back pay is limited to the number of days of violation; for example, an employee who has received 20 days' notice would be entitled to receive only 40 days' back pay. However, the employer may not subtract what employees are owed in severance pay and vacation benefits from the back pay owed under WARN.

NOTE: Employers should act promptly and provide notice as soon as practicable so as to minimize their liability for back pay and other penalties.

Mitigation of Damages.   The Act delineates only three circumstances where damages may be reduced. Under WARN, the amount of damages are reduced by

- Any wages paid by the employer to the employee for the period of the violation

- Any voluntary and unconditional payment by the employer to the employee that is not a legal obligation

- Any payment by the employer to a third party on behalf of and attributable to the employee for the period of the violation (includes health care premiums if payments are to a defined contribution pension plan)

WARN does not address the effect on the damage award of earnings from other employment during the period of violation. However, the general principle of mitigation of damages indicates that such earnings should be deducted from back pay awards.

Civil Penalty/Injunctive Relief. Noncomplying employers may be liable for a civil penalty of not more than $500 for each day of the violation except where the employer pays each aggrieved employee within three weeks from the date the employer orders the shutdown or layoff. A significant provision of the Act provides that a federal court has no authority to enjoin a plant closing or mass layoff.

The Good Faith Defense. WARN provides a "good faith" defense for employers who demonstrate a reasonable belief that their failure to provide notice was not a violation of the Act. Moreover, the Court may, within its discretion, reduce the amount of liability or penalty.

Other Contractual Rights of Employees. The Act does not preclude employees from bringing actions for violation or breach of other contractual or statutory rights. However, the Act provides that the giving of notice in good faith compliance with the Act does not constitute a violation of the National Labor Relations Act or the Railway Labor Act. A cursory review of these two provisions reveals internal inconsistencies and potential conflict. For example, the Railway Labor Act permits injunctive relief for a layoff or closing, but the plant closing law does not.[11]

State Plant Closing Law versus WARN

Several states have plant closing laws of their own, most of which predate WARN. However, WARN provides a minimum standard of conduct required by employers in the event of a plant closing or mass layoff. States may legislate even stricter standards that could cover a greater number of employers or require a longer notice period. You should also be aware that certain local municipalities have also enacted plant closing ordinances.[12]

States that have some form of statutory notice requirement to employees and/or the community include Connecticut, Hawaii, Kansas, Maine, Maryland,

Massachusetts, Michigan, Minnesota, Montana, Oregon, South Carolina, Tennessee, and Wisconsin. The territory of the U.S. Virgin Islands has restrictions on plant closings or relocations as well.

In addition, New York established voluntary guidelines for employers and labor organizations that are designed to avoid the economic consequences of layoffs, plant closings, and strikes. These guidelines are known as the New York Compact and represent an agreement that employers will voluntarily give notice of plant closings and layoffs and will lay off employees only as a last resort; the labor unions will use strikes only as an "economic weapon of last resort," and the state will temporarily fund a program to pay four months of extended health benefits to workers laid off due to a plant closing. However, this Compact is not legally binding on any particular state or labor union or on the state.

NOTE: Check carefully to see if state regulation exists and whether your business operations are covered by such regulation.

When state regulation exists, it typically covers certain reductions in operations involved in a relocation of all or some portion of an employer's operation from one workplace to another site in or outside of the state and closings that result from a permanent cessation of business. Covered employers may have a minimum of 50 or 100 employees.[13]

The state regulation may specify the level of reduction in operations in terms of the number of affected employees.[14] At least one state's law applies to employers who require their employees to provide notice prior to resigning.[15] The period of notice required under the various state laws ranges from 45 to 60 days. One state's statute recommends 90 days, whenever possible. Keep in mind that these obligations are separate from the WARN requirement of 60 days; complying with a state's notice period of less than 60 days runs afoul of WARN.

NOTE: Where the state's statutory notice period is less than 60 days, always provide at least 60 days' notice so as to comply with WARN.

Where exceptions are provided, they typically include

- Agricultural, construction, or seasonal operations
- Temporary workplaces
- Labor disputes
- Natural disaster
- Employer bankruptcies
- Unforeseen accident/breakdown of machinery

Again, these exceptions vary from state to state, and state law must be consulted to see if your organization or situation falls under an exception.

Similarly, the penalties for failing to comply with state requirements vary significantly and include fines ranging from $50 per terminated employee to $5,000 for failure to post the required notice. Violations may be criminal misdemeanors in some states. In Maine, the employer is also liable to the affected employees for severance pay. In Connecticut, the employer is required to continue existing group health insurance for each affected employee for a specified period. In Hawaii, the employer must provide affected employees a dislocated worker allowance as a supplement to unemployment compensation benefits. Generally, these employer obligations are superseded by an existing collective bargaining agreement.

SUMMARY OF GUIDELINES FOR COMPLIANCE WITH WARN AND STATE AND LOCAL LAWS

WARN imposes significant notification requirements on midsized to large-sized employers. Careful planning and consideration must be given to the Act's requirements whenever a plant closing, reduction in hours, or layoff is contemplated. The following guidelines should aid the employer in complying with WARN and local laws.

1. Review WARN, DOL regulations, and pertinent state and local laws on a regular basis. Adopt a policy that provides for compliance with these laws.

2. Documentation and recordkeeping significantly aid in establishing a good faith defense to an action alleging violations of the Act.

3. Employers should consider consulting with labor unions and/or community leaders, which could result in salary reductions or tax benefits that will postpone or avoid a closing or layoff.

4. All options should be analyzed and documented before acting to close down operations or institute layoffs.

5. The liability for a violation of the notification requirements can be reduced by prompt action when a layoff or closing cannot be avoided even after the 60-day period has started to run.

ENDNOTES

1. 29 U.S.C. §2101, *et seq.* WARN survived a challenge to its constitutionality in *Carpenters District Council of New Orleans and Vicinity v. Dillard Department Stores*, 778 F. Supp. 297 (E.D.La. 1991).

2. The effect of federal regulation on a plant closing, layoff, or relocation decision by an employer who is party to a collective bargaining agreement is discussed in Chapter 21.

3. *Damron v. Rob Fork Min. Corp.*, 739 F. Supp. 341 (E.D. Ky. 1990).

4. See *Office & Professional Employers Local 2 v. FDIC*, 6 I.E.R. Cases (BNA) 1316 (D.D.C. 1991) (bank closed and taken over by the FDIC—no notice required); *Hotel & Restaurant Employees Local 54 v. Elsinore Shore Associates*, 768 F.Supp. 1117 (D.N.J. 1991) (casino shut down by state regulatory agency for economic reasons—no notice required); *Hotel & Restaurant Employees Local 54 v. Elsinore Shore Associates*, 724 F.Supp. 333 (D.N.J. 1989) (government-appointed conservator who continued to operate casino was not required to provide notice before state shut casino down).

5. See *Finkler v. Elsinore Shore Associates, Inc.*, 7 I.E.R. Cases (BNA) 161 (D.N.J. 1992), wherein that court held that, in fact, government-ordered closings are not generally exempted from WARN. Such closings are only entirely exempt when they are "absolute," such as a closing of a bank by a federal agency where "the previous ownership is ousted from control" and the government "assumes control of the enterprise" such that "there is no employer to give notice." In other government-ordered closings, they are to be evaluated under the unforeseeable business exception to the extent that they were not reasonably foreseeable as of the time that notice would have been required. In such cases, notice is required as soon as practicable.

6. See Department of Labor regulations, 20 C.F.R. §693.3(a)(2) (1989).

7. See *Local 397, 16E v. Midwest Fasteners, Inc. d/b/a Erico Fastening Systems et al.*, 7 I.E.R. Cases (BNA) 65 (1992).

8. See *Mine Workers v. Harman Mining Corp.*, 7 I.E.R. Cases (BNA) 75 (W.D. Va. 1991).

9. The Department of Labor is responsible for promulgating interpretive regulations that describe ways for employers to appropriately provide the requisite advance notice. Final regulations can be found at 29 C.F.R. §639.

10. *Finnan v. L. F. Rothschild & Co., Inc.*, 726 F.Supp. 460 (S.D.N.Y. 1989).

11. 45 U.S.C. §152 provides that all carriers and employees must exert every reasonable effort to maintain agreements and to settle all disputes to avoid any interruption to commerce or to the operation of any carrier. See, generally, *Ashley, Drew, Northern Ry. v. United Transportation Union, Local No. 1121*, 625 F.2d 1357, 1368 (8th Cir. 1980), and *Chicago & North Western Ry. v. United Transportation Union*, 402 U.S. 570, 578–81 (1971).

12. For example, Philadelphia and Pittsburgh have such ordinances.

13. Hawaii, Maryland, Massachusetts, Tennessee, and Wisconsin cover employers with 50 or more employees. Connecticut and Maine cover employers with 100 or more employees. In Massachusetts, plant relocation law covers commercial, industrial, and manufacturing establishments with 12 or more persons employed.

14. For example, Maryland's law applies in cases where the shutdown reduces the number of employees by at least 25 percent or 15 employees, whichever is greater, over a 3-month period.

15. South Carolina.

INDEX